Language Classification

How are relationships established among the world's languages? This is one of the most topical and most controversial questions in contemporary linguistics. The central aims of the book are to answer this question, to cut through the controversies, and to contribute to research in distant genetic relationships. In doing this the authors show how the methods have been employed, revealing which methods, techniques, and strategies have proven successful and which ones have proven ineffective. The book seeks to determine how particular language families were established and offers an evaluation of several of the most prominent and more controversial proposals of distant genetic relationship (such as Amerind, Nostratic, Eurasiatic, Proto-World, and others). Finally, the authors make recommendations for practice in future research. This book will contribute significantly to understanding language classification in general.

LYLE CAMPBELL is Professor of Linguistics in the Department of Linguistics at the University of Utah.

WILLIAM J. POSER is Adjunct Professor of Linguistics in the Department of Linguistics at the University of British Columbia.

Language Classification

History and Method

Lyle Campbell and William J. Poser

P
143
.C36
2008

CAMBRIDGE UNIVERSITY PRESS
Cambridge, New York, Melbourne, Madrid, Cape Town, Singapore, São Paulo, Delhi

Cambridge University Press
The Edinburgh Building, Cambridge CB2 8RU, UK

Published in the United States of America by Cambridge University Press, New York

www.cambridge.org
Information on this title: www.cambridge.org/9780521880053

First published 2008

Printed in the United Kingdom at the University Press, Cambridge

A catalogue record for this publication is available from the British Library

Library of Congress Cataloguing in Publication data

Campbell, Lyle.
Language classification: history and method / by Lyle Campbell and William J. Poser.
   p.   cm.
Includes bibliographical references and index.
ISBN 978-0-521-88005-3 (hardback)
1. Comparative linguistics.   2. Language and languages–Classification.   I. Poser,
William John. II. Title.

P143.C36 2007
401'.2–dc22   2007048556

ISBN 978-0-521-88005-3 hardback

Contents

Figures, tables, and charts

Figures

Tables

Charts

Acknowledgments

We would like to thank a number of friends and colleagues for answering specific questions, for providing comments and feedback on particular issues, or for helping us to obtain access to materials. We do not mean, however, to imply that any of them is necessarily in agreement with what we have written, and certainly all mistakes are our own. We sincerely thank:

M. Lionel Bender
Andrew Carstairs-McCarthy
Rodolfo Cerrón-Palomino
Terry Crowley
Alan Dench
Nick Evans
Andrew Garrett
Ives Goddard
Matt Gordon
Verónica Grondona
Alice Harris
Bernd Heine
Jane Hill
Juha Janhunen
Jay Jasanoff
Brian Joseph
Harold Koch
Joe Kruskal
James Matisoff
David Nash
Elisabeth Norcliffe
Andrew Pawley
Robert Rankin
Don Ringe
Aryon Rodrigues
Malcolm Ross

Tapani Salminen
Joe Salmons
Pekka Sammallahti
Larry Trask

We also acknowledge the support of a Marsden grant from the Royal Society of New Zealand, awarded to Lyle Campbell, which aided significantly in the preparation of this book.

Preface

We began talking together and thinking about the subject matter of this book when we prepared a paper for the Spring Workshop in Reconstruction in 1991, held at the University of Pittsburgh. We later decided to write this book, but were not able to do that until now due to other obligations. With respect to the division of labor, William Poser is primarily responsible for the writing of Chapter 5, part of Chapter 3, and parts of Chapter 4 (especially sections 4.8 and 4.11). Lyle Campbell is the principal author of the other chapters and sections of this book.

1 Introduction: how are languages shown to be related to one another?

> I fear great evil from vast opposition in opinion on all subjects of classification.
>
> (Charles Darwin 1838 [Bowlby 1990:225])

1.1 Introduction

How are languages shown to be related to one another? How are language families established? Judging from media attention, it might be thought that this is one of the "hottest" questions in contemporary linguistics. Proposals of distant linguistic kinship such as Amerind, Nostratic, Eurasiatic, and Proto-World have been featured in *Atlantic Monthly, Nature, Science, Scientific American, US News and World Report, The New York Times*, and in BBC and PBS television documentaries. Nevertheless, these same proposals have been rejected by the majority of practicing historical linguists. The difference of opinion is reflected in much debate and considerable confusion about the methods for demonstrating family (phylogenetic) relationships among languages as yet not known to be related, and about the ways that language families have come to be established. Some enthusiasts of long-range linguistic relationships, disappointed that proposed language connections they favor have not been accepted in the profession, have at times responded bitterly. For example, we read charges that these rejections are just "clumsy and dishonest attempts to discredit deep reconstructions [proposed macro-families]" (Shevoroshkin 1989a:7, also 1989b:4). Nor is the strong rhetoric just from fans of distant language relationships; for example, Dixon (2002:23) lambasts the so-called "long-rangers": "at a different level – which transcends scientific worth to such an extent that it is at the fringe of idiocy – there have in recent years been promulgated a number of far-fetched ideas concerning 'long-distance relationships,' such as 'Nostratic,' 'Sino-Caucasian' and 'Amerind.'"

Some proponents of remote relationships have sometimes attempted to give their claims a sense of legitimacy by associating their methods with those of revered founding figures in historical linguistics, in particular those credited with contributions to establishing the Indo-European family of languages. Given

1

these claims and the importance assigned to methods in the debates, one of the purposes of this book is to review and evaluate the methods which have been used throughout the history of linguistics to establish language families, that is, the methods for demonstrating genetic relationships among related languages.[1] The successful methods employed in the past provide important lessons for current practice. The picture which emerges from this historical survey of how major language families came to be established is very different from that which is often claimed. Therefore, one goal of this book is to set the historical record straight. Our aim, however, is not to dwell on past linguistics, but to assess current claims about past methods and in so doing to contribute by refining current practice.[2] The contribution to linguistic historiography is a fortunate by-product of this, but is not our main goal.

The broader and more central aim of this book is to contribute to language classification, to research in distant genetic relationships generally by: (1) showing how the methods have been employed, (2) revealing which methods, techniques, strategies, rules of thumb and the like have proven successful and which ones have proven ineffective, (3) finding out how particular language families were established – that is, what methods were utilized and proved successful, (4) evaluating a number of the most prominent and more controversial proposals of distant genetic relationship in the light of the methods which prove most adequate, and (5) making recommendations for practice in future research. In brief, we hope to contribute significantly to understanding of language classification in general.

Several scholars – outside the mainstream of historical linguistics – have in recent years made pronouncements in favor of very remote language relationships, and several of them (though not all) have urged methodological points of view with which most historical linguists do not agree. Their claims figure in

---

[1] In linguistics, "genetic relationship" among languages means a phylogenetic, genealogical relationship, that is, descent from a common ancestor. While there is potential for confusion with "genetic" in reference to biological species, in this book we continue the common linguistic practice of speaking of languages as being genetically related. In contexts where potential confusion may arise, we speak of "human genetic" to distinguish it from the use of "genetic" for linguistic kinship. Also, in general, we speak of languages being "related," of "related languages," and of "language relationships" in reference to genetic relationships. Of course, languages can be "related" through borrowing and other means, but "relationship" in the context of historical linguistics usually refers to a phylogenetic relationship.

[2] We concur with Hoenigswald (1974:346) and Wilbur (1977:ix) that linguists have been too obsessed with the nineteenth century. The claim of historical antecedents in attempts to justify particular methods used today is an example of this. As Wilbur (1977:ix) says:

Henry M. Hoenigswald's undisguised complaint [is] that we are "obsessed" with the nineteenth century. He suggests to the linguist a therapeutic program by insisting that he face up to this presumably morbid preoccupation. With a certain amount of pathos, Hoenigswald (1974:346) also deplores our "extreme working dependence" upon that century. It would be intellectually more honest and psychologically more salubrious to admit that, as far as historical linguistics is concerned, we are, to a very great degree, still in the nineteenth century.

discussions in this book. While understanding of the methods of the founding figures in historical linguistics does offer object lessons for us today, as will be seen, interpretations of this part of the history of linguistics have often been mistaken.

In Chapters 2, 3, and 4, we examine the methodological pronouncements and practices of these founding figures, and in the process we discover their real outlook on language relationships and how they have contributed to understanding of language classification. Jones', Rask's, Bopp's, and the others' methods owe much to their predecessors, discussed in Chapter 2, and therefore we approach our historical survey by considering events roughly in chronological order, first earlier developments (Chapter 2), then Sir William Jones' much misconstrued role (Chapter 3), followed by a consideration of the work of Rask, Bopp, and others influential in the development of comparative linguistics, including the claims of the Neogrammarians and their contemporaries (Chapter 4). In Chapter 5 we look at how several languages were shown to belong to Indo-European, and discover that the methods used were not as some have claimed, and the methods that were employed provide valuable insights. In Chapter 6 we see how prominent language families were established, and we look at work in linguistic classification in other areas of the world. We inspect the methods that were employed to establish the Finno-Ugric (and Uralic), Semitic, Dravidian, Austronesian, Sino-Tibetan, and several Native American language families, and also those utilized in work on the language families of Africa and Australia. We find that the methods which were utilized to establish the accepted language families have generally been consistent with those of the Indo-Europeanists, and the work on non-Indo-European families frequently further contributed to historical linguistic thinking in general. We survey principles, criteria, and methodology in general in Chapter 7. In Chapter 8, the "other" tradition in historical linguistics is considered, the attempts to get at language history and classification through a combination of psychological, typological, and evolutionary notions. This was a highly influential tradition in the history of linguistics which ultimately was supplanted by the approach now associated with the Neogrammarians and their legacy. In Chapter 9 we employ the methods and criteria surveyed in Chapter 7 to evaluate the better known long-range proposals, Altaic, Ural-Altaic, Nostratic, Eurasiatic, Amerind, and Indo-Pacific – well-known but controversial "macro-family" hypotheses. We show why most historical linguists do not accept these proposals. Chapter 10 deals with various recent attempts to see beyond the comparative method and with proposed frameworks which depart significantly from traditional methods. In particular, Chapter 10 looks critically at proposals argued to be able to recover aspects of linguistic prehistory beyond the limitations of the traditional comparative method. Chapter 11 presents a critique of recent proposals concerning how and why linguistic diversification and language dispersal take place, followed by our recommendations for how these are best approached. Chapter 12 evaluates critically the "Proto-World" hypothesis, the idea that it is possible to show that all the languages of the world are related and descend from a single original language. In Chapter 13, the conclusions, we reiterate the main findings of the book and attempt to point the way to productive future research. Finally, in the Appendix we list, but do not discuss or evaluate, most of the proposals of distant genetic relationship that have been made.

1.2   Evidence and criteria

It will not spoil any surprises to come if we disclose here at the outset that throughout the history of linguistics the criteria employed in both pronouncements about method and in actual practice for establishing language families consistently included evidence from three sources: **basic vocabulary**,[3] **grammatical evidence** (especially morphological), and **sound correspondences**. Hoenigswald's summary of the points upon which seventeenth- and eighteenth-century linguistic scholars agreed is telling. Hoenigswald (1990a:119–20) quotes from Metcalf's (1974:251) similar summary:

First, . . . there was "the concept of a no longer spoken parent language which in turn produced the major linguistic groups of Asia and Europe." Then there was . . . "a concept of the development of languages into dialects and of dialects into new independent languages." Third came "certain minimum standards for determining what words are borrowed and what words are ancestral in a language," and, fourth, "an insistence that not a few random items, but a large number of words from the basic vocabulary should form the basis of comparison" . . . fifth, the doctrine that "grammar" is even more important than words; sixth, the idea that for an etymology to be valid the differences in sound – or in "letters" – must recur, under a principle sometimes referred to as "analogia."[4]

---

[3] For a general discussion of the importance which basic vocabulary as a criterion for comparing languages has had throughout the history of linguistics, see Muller 1984.

[4] That is to say, there was a great deal of individual variation in the criteria used and the kinds of evidence sought in early attempts to establish language families and not every scholar used all three of these sources of evidence, but many did use all three and on the whole, these three were widely recognized and accepted.

We note also, as Hoenigswald shows here, that many have mistakenly claimed Jones was the first to imagine the ancestor language "perhaps no longer" existed (cf. Pedersen 1983[1916]:34–5). The view was quite common, repeated from at least Ludolf in 1692 onward (Waterman 1978:61). Hoenigswald's citation also shows the inaccuracy of Greenberg's belief that "none of these families [Indo-European, Uralic, or Austronesian] was discovered by finding regular sound correspondences" (1996a:133).

Thanks to past scholarship, we have the evidence that demonstrated the family relationships at our disposal. However, today we are confronted not just by the question of how accepted language families were established, but also with the issue of how to tackle possible genetic relationships among languages where the answer is not at all obvious. That is, on all sides we encounter far-flung proposals of very remote relationships among languages not at present known to be related. Janhunen and Kho's (1982:179) characterization of attempts to find distant relatives of Korean applies equally well to many other enthusiastically proposed but poorly supported long-range relationships:

The various hypotheses concerning genetic affinities . . . offer an instructive record of what the use and misuse of well established scientific methods can yield . . . it is a record of unchecked attempts at proving preconceived ideas, which often from the very beginning stand in sharp contradiction with the suggestions of common sense. The characteristic feature of this type of proposals is the axiomatic belief in the existence of discoverable genetic connections, while the possibility that a language might actually not have any living (or historically recorded) relatives is left without due considerations.

We do not mean to say that there is no reliable work that attempts to establish new language relationships – quite the contrary – our purpose in this book is to encourage such work. Nevertheless, many unrestrained and indefensible hypotheses plague the literature at present. We hope to put the more influential ones in perspective in this book, emphasizing methodological implications for all such work.[5]

1.3   Setting the stage

A ubiquitous mistaken belief is that comparative linguistics and the discovery of Indo-European started with Sir William Jones' famous declaration of 1786, often called the "philologer" passage (see Chapter 3). We set the stage for the historical survey of methods for establishing language relationships by considering briefly some precursors and contemporaries of Jones who reveal a very different history. This is seen by contrasting Jones' famous statement with those of some of his predecessors. Jones' philologer passage, so often cited, is:

The *Sanscrit* language, whatever be its antiquity, is of a wonderful structure; more perfect than the Greek, more copious than the Latin, and more exquisitely refined than either; yet bearing to both of them a stronger affinity, both in the roots of verbs and in the forms of grammar, than could possibly have been produced by accident; so strong indeed, that

---

[5] We are, of course, not the only nor first ever to be concerned with methodology for establishing language relationships. See, for example, Aalto 1965; Adam 1881; Allen 1953; Austerlitz 1983, 1991; Bright 1970; Callaghan and Miller 1962; Collinder 1946–8, 1964; Cowan 1962; Doerfer 1967, 1973; Fähnrich 1971; Gatschet 1879–80, 1886; Grolier 1990; Joki 1963, 1973; Kroeber 1913; Lehmann 1994; Pisani 1971; some papers in Shevoroshkin and Sidwell 1999; Starostin 1999a, 1999b; Thomason 1993; Voegelin and Voegelin 1985; and many others.

no philologer could examine them all three without believing them to have sprung from *some common source*, which, perhaps, no longer exists. There is a similar reason, though not quite so forcible, for supposing that both the *Gothic* and *Celtick*, though blended with a very different idiom, had the same origin with the *Sanscrit*; and the old *Persian* might be added to the same family, if this were the place for discussing any question concerning the antiquities of *Persia*. (Jones 1798[1786]:422–3)

Although highly celebrated, this quotation is, nevertheless, remarkably similar to Andreas Jäger's statement of 1686, a hundred years earlier:

An ancient language, once spoken in the distant past in the area of the Caucasus mountains and spreading by waves of migration throughout Europe and Asia, had itself ceased to be spoken and had left no linguistic monuments behind, but had as a "mother" generated a host of "daughter languages," many of which in turn had become "mothers" to further "daughters." (For a language tends to develop dialects, and these dialects in the course of time become independent, mutually unintelligible languages.) Descendants of the ancestral languages include Persian, Greek, Italic (whence Latin and in time the modern Romance tongues), the Slavonic languages, Celtic, and finally Gothic and the other Germanic tongues. (Quoted in Metcalf 1974:233)[6]

Statements such as this one from Jäger and various others (Chapter 2) require adjustments in the traditional thinking about the role of Jones and the origin and development of the comparative method and Indo-European linguistics. For example, before Jones' famous "philologer" passage was published (delivered in 1786, published 1798), Jonathan Edwards, Jr. (1788[1787]) had discovered and reported the family relationship among the Algonquian languages with methods not unusual for his day but superior to Jones' (see Chapter 6):

This language [family] is spoken by all the Indians throughout New England. Every tribe . . . has a different dialect [language]; but the language is radically [genetically] the same [i.e. members of the same family]. Mr. Eliot's [1663] translation of the Bible is in a particular dialect [i.e. the Natick or Massachusett language] of this language. The dialect followed in these observations is that of Stockbridge [i.e. the Mohegan language]. This language [i.e. the Algonquian family] appears to be much more extensive than any other language in North America. The languages of the Delawares in Pennsylvania, of the Penobscots bordering on Nova Scotia, of the Indians of St Francis in Canada [Abnaki?], of the Shawanese [Shawnee] on the Ohio, and of the Chippewaus [Ojibwa] at the westward end of Lake Huron, are all radically the same with the Mohegan [are of the same language family]. The same is said concerning the languages of the Ottowaus [Ottawa], Nanticooks [Nanticoke], Munsees, Menomonees, Messisaugas, Saukies [Sauk], Ottagaumies [Fox], Killistinoes [Cree], Nipegons [Winnebago], Algonkins, . . . &c. That the languages of the several tribes in New England, of the Delawares, and of Mr. Eliot's

---

[6] Note also that Jäger includes Slavic, which Jones thought was connected with non-Indo-European Central Asian languages, and unlike Jones, for whom Celtic and "Gothic" (Germanic) were "mixed" with non-Indo-European languages, Jäger accurately classifies them as members of the same family without the assumed admixture.

Bible, are radically the same [belong to the same family] with the Mohegan, I assert from my own knowledge. (Edwards 1823[1788]:8)

It is not to be supposed, that the like coincidence is extended to all the words of those languages. Very many words are totally different. Still the analogy is such as is sufficient to show, that they are mere dialects [i.e. sisters] of the same original language [family]. (Edwards 1823[1788]:11)

To show the genetic relationship, that is, "to illustrate the analogy between the *Mohegan*, the *Shawanee* [Shawnee], and the *Chippewau* [Ojibwa] languages" (Edwards 1823[1788]:9), Edwards presented a list of "some 60 vocabulary items, phrases, and grammatical features" (Koerner 1986:ii). Jones, in contrast, presented no actual linguistic evidence at all. In Jones' words:

I am sensible that you must give me credit for many assertions which, on this occasion, it is impossible to prove; for I should ill deserve your indulgent attention, if I were to abuse it by repeating a dry list of detached words, and presenting you with a vocabulary instead of a dissertation; but, since I have no system to maintain, and have not suffered imagination to delude my judgement; since I have habituated myself to form opinions of men and things from *evidence* . . . I will assert nothing positively, which I am not able satisfactorily to demonstrate. (Jones 1799a:49)

Edwards concluded from the evidence he presented that these languages are "radically the same" (i.e. related, from the same family), though he was fully aware also of differences among them and of their differences from Iroquoian languages, members of an unrelated family (with which he also had first-hand acquaintance).

Edwards' case is striking; it shows that neither Jones nor Indo-European occupy the privileged position so often attributed to them in the history of linguistics. The discovery of the Algonquian family relationship has a pedigree comparable to Indo-European, but, as we will see later, Edwards' methods were superior to Jones', and Edwards was not alone (see Chapters 3 and 6).

As this shows, and as will be seen in more detail in subsequent chapters of this book, Jones' role in the history of linguistics has been misread; there is much in this history which will prove methodologically interesting for attempts to establish family relationships among languages as yet not known to be related.

1.4   Classification, but of what?

Until relatively recently, many classifications of languages were not intended to be purely linguistic in nature. They were usually seen as classifying nations or "races," as well as languages, and quite often they were not based on linguistic evidence alone. As we shall see (Chapter 3), Sir William Jones was interested in the history of the "human races" rather than in language per se. This was a common theme which persisted in scholarship until the beginning of the twentieth century. Jones' plan was to write a history of peoples of Asia – language ("and letters") was only one source of information which Jones believed could be used towards this end, to be utilized in conjunction with information from philosophy and religion, remains of sculpture and architecture, and documents of sciences and arts (Jones 1798[1786]:421). In this regard, again, Jones was not unusual among early linguistic scholars. The view was shared by Kraus, Leibniz, Hervás y Panduro, Monboddo, Vater, Schlegel, Grimm, Humboldt, Schleicher, and others (see Chapter 2).[7] As Humboldt (1836–9:220) put it, "The relatedness of the nations is very often confused with that of the languages, and the demands of historical and ethnographic research with those of linguistics."[8]

For these scholars, their linguistic comparisons were part of a broader history and anthropology (also philosophy and psychology) of the nations and "races" of the world. Hervás y Panduro (1800:1), in his broad-scaled classification of languages of the world, confirmed how common the use of these non-linguistic sources of evidence was for historical interests:

In the histories of nations, all authors claim to arrive at their primitive state with the telling of their deeds. Taking the various directions which they are presented by hieroglyphic monuments, mythology, tradition, calendars, alphabets or writing, and historical accounts of the nations, they fly through immense stretches of the obscure times of antiquity.[9]

The theme of language in concert with other sources of evidence to establish origins and to determine the classification of nations and "races," as well as of languages, was to persist into the early twentieth century.

An especially clear instance which tells how intertwined the classification of race, nation, and language were, and how various sources of information could serve these ends, comes from David Cargill's response to questions about Fijian and its relatives (see Chapter 6). Cargill was among the first missionaries to Fiji, a scholar well-trained in Latin, Greek, Hebrew, and Bible translation, and he knew Tongan before being sent to Fiji. When asked in 1839 by the Secretaries of the Wesleyan Methodist Society in London to discuss the relationship of Fijian to "the other Polynesian dialects," he responded:

---

[7] For example, Leibniz wrote in 1692, "Languages are the most ancient monuments of the human race, and they serve best for determining the origin of people" (Waterman 1978:59). Court de Gébelin (1773–82), in his search for the primitive or first language of humans, "undertook an impressive etymological analysis of Greek, Latin and French. Nor did he neglect coats of arms, coins, games, the voyages of the Phoenicians around the world, American Indian languages, medallions, and civil and religious history as manifested in calendars and almanacs" (Eco 1995:94).

[8] "Man verwechselt sehr häufig die Verwandtschaft der Nationen mit der Sprachen, und die Forderungen der geschichtlichen und ethnographischen Forschung mit den sprachwissenschaftlichen" (Humboldt 1836–9:220).

[9] "En las historias de las naciones todos sus escritores pretenden llegar al estado primitivo de ellas con la relación de sus hechos. Ellos tomando los varios rumbos que les presentan los monumentos geroglificos, mitología, tradición, calendarios, alfabetos ó escritura, y las noticias de la historia de las naciones vuelan por inmensos espacios de los obscuros tiempos de la antigüedad."

The difference between the Feejeean [Fijian] language, and the other Polynesian dialects forms the second topic which you have suggested. The points of contrast will be more clearly seen, by first mentioning the points of resemblance between that language and the other members of the Polynesian family. If the Feejeean's consanguinity with the other South Sea Islanders were clearly established, the affinity between his language and theirs would be an inference from that fact. But as it is not the design of this statement to attempt to prove that the Feejeean is the offspring of that branch of the human family to which all the other Polynesian tribes belong, I shall merely enumerate some of the arguments which appear to favour that hypothesis. The principal arguments are his physical conformation, – his political and religious customs, – his unequivocally Polynesian vices, and his language. The last argument relates to the present subject. That the language of Feejee and all the dialects of Polynesia with which I have any acquaintance are not different members of different families but members of one and the same family, and of consequence of one common origin appears demonstrable on the following grounds. 1st. There are words which are common to all the dialects; 2ly. There are other words which have evidently sprung from one stock, but have assumed a different appearance in adaptation to the genius of the people; 3ly. All the dialects are characterized by the same peculiarities, and 4ly. the same idiom [overall grammatical structure and typology] prevails among all the languages. (Quoted in Schütz 1972:4)[10]

In our attempts to sort through methods and classifications of languages, it will be important to keep in mind exactly what evidence was presented in each case, for what goals it was utilized, and which methods were employed. It will be necessary to concentrate on linguistic considerations while separating out, so far as possible, non-linguistic evidence and interests.

As is evident already from some of the quotations cited above, the terminology encountered in earlier works both varies much and often does not match that employed today. It is important not to read present-day content that was not in the minds of the original authors into past work, nor to misread seemingly similar terms when they do not in fact refer to the same thing now as then. For example, we have seen in these quotes reference to "analogy" in the sense of sound correspondence (though not precisely equivalent to today's sense of that term), to "radical" for "genetic relationship," and reference to "dialect" where today's sense would be "independent language," and to "language" with today's sense

---

[10] See Chapter 7 for more on Cargill. Debates at around the close of the nineteenth century concerning the basis for classifying the tribes of North America for the Smithsonian Institution's Museum exhibits reflect a more recent instance of the failure to separate language and "race," and of linguistic classification serving as a primary basis for the historical and anthropological understanding of peoples in general. Smithsonian's Otis T. Mason leaned towards basing the Museum's displays on a classification along the unilinear lines assumed in social Darwinism, that is, assumed "progress" in social evolution from "savagery" to "barbarism" to "civilization" (cf. Hinsley 1981:99). However, at that time Major John Wesley Powell, founder of the Bureau of American Ethnology, produced the first comprehensive classification of American Indian languages of North America (Powell 1891), after which Mason was stimulated to adopt for the museum the principle of displaying the peoples of Native America organized along language family lines (Hinsley 1981:110). In fact, the primary value of Powell's linguistic classification was persistently seen to be its utility for ethnological classification.

of "language family." Johann Reinhold Forster (1778), naturalist on Captain Cook's second voyage (writing slightly before Jones' "philologer" statement was published), uses such terminology in a way that makes its different sense clear (see Chapter 6); he also reflects the assumed race–nation–language correlation of the times:

It has always been customary among the more critical and chaste historians, to reckon all such nations as speak the *same general language* [members of the same language family], to be of the same tribe or race . . . By the SAME GENERAL LANGUAGE, I understand all the various subordinate dialects [languages] of one language [family]. No one for instance, acquainted with the subject, will deny, that the Dutch, Low-German, Danish, Swedish, Norwegian, Icelandic, and the English (in respect to such words as owe their origin to the Anglo-Saxon) are dialects [languages] subordinate to the *same general language* [language family], together with the present High-German, and the remains of the Gothic in Ulfila's New Testament. But allowing for this, yet we find that these dialects differ in many respects . . . many words, however, though somewhat modified, always preserve enough of the original type, to satisfy the critical etymologist, that they belong to the *same general language*, as subordinate dialects. This short digression will therefore open a way to prove that the five races [Polynesian groups], which I enumerated as belonging to the first tribe, are really descended from the same original nation; for they all speak a language [individual but related languages] that has in the greatest part of their words, a great and striking affinity. (Forster [1778], in Rensch 1996:184–5)

1.5   Similarity vs. proof of language relationships

In the chapters to follow, we will see that observation of similarities among languages is the logical and most frequent starting point for attempts to demonstrate relationships among languages. Unfortunately, we will also see that some scholars' methods stop at the identification of similarities among compared languages, where they assume this is sufficient to demonstrate that the languages under comparison are related to one another by virtue of descent from a common earlier ancestor. However, assembling similarities among languages is just the beginning. Similarities can be due to several things other than just inheritance from a common ancestor (genetic relationship). The following are the major explanations for similarities among languages (see Chapter 7):
1. Accident (chance, coincidence).
2. Borrowing (language contact).
3. Onomatopoeia, sound symbolism, and nursery forms.
4. Universals and typologically commonplace traits.
5. Genetic relationship – inheritance from a common ancestor.
As will be seen in the chapters of this book, in order to establish a plausible hypothesis of genetic relationship it is necessary to eliminate other possible explanations (1–4), leaving a genetic relationship (5) the most likely. The core of the generally accepted methodology for investigating possible relationships

among languages is aimed precisely at that. It eliminates alternative possible explanations for evidence offered, and it seeks positive evidence of genetic relationship. A plausible demonstration of genetic relationship does not in fact depend precisely on similarities among the languages compared, but rather on systematic correspondences among sounds in compared words, especially basic vocabulary, and on patterned grammatical evidence of the appropriate sort (see Chapter 7). Related languages can undergo so much change that they no longer appear superficially similar, but elements in them can exhibit systematic agreements which nevertheless demonstrate the relationship.

1.6   What drives linguistic diversification?

Why do languages split up and become families of related languages? What accounts for languages spreading to new territory? Throughout the history of linguistics there have been numerous theories about what causes languages to diversify, involving, for example, migration, war and conquest, trade, geographical isolation, cessation of communication, social and economic organization (e.g. mounted warriors with expansionist proclivities, militaristic patriarchalism), linguistically marked group identity entailing rights to resources, technological advantage (food production, herding, navigation, metallurgy, military organization), even divine vengeance for the Tower of Babel caper. A common theme has been a belief that communicative isolation leads to linguistic diversification. Many see in this an analogue to the belief in biology that reproductive isolation leads to speciation. This has led to speculation about the cultural, geographical, demographic, ecological, economic, political, ideological, and other factors that could bring about communicative isolation. Recent claims about why languages diversify and spread are discussed in detail in Chapters 10 and 11. The investigation of how and why language families develop, how and why they diversify and spread requires attention to the following questions:

1. The *linguistic* question: what drives linguistic diversification (the formation of language families)?
2. The *geographical* question: why and how do languages spread over space?
3. The *structural* questions: (a) how and why do related languages come to be structurally distinct from one another?, and (b) how and why do unrelated (and also related) languages sometimes come to be structurally more similar to one another?
4. The question of *language shift and maintenance*: why do some languages wither and die while other languages thrive and spread?
5. The *means of language shift* (replacement) question: in any given case, is it a matter of (a) the language spreads but not the population (new language, old genes), (b) the people spread taking their language with them (new language and new genes), or (c) are both (a) and (b) involved?

6. The *social* question: how do people's choices and social behavior (rather than just, say, physical geography) determine linguistic diversity?

Sleuthing linguistic movements, like solving murders, requires attention to *motive* (were the speakers of these languages pushed or pulled to move?), *means* (did they move by land, water, on foot, horse, boat?), and *opportunity* (were there physical bearers? did neighbors impede movement? did those moving have some technological or other advantage which would facilitate encroachment on neighbors' territories?). And there is also the question of *habeas corpus* – what evidence is there that a migration was actually committed? For example, too often for proposed linguistic migrations there is no clear archaeological or human genetic support.[11] (See Chapter 11.)

1.7   Prospects for future demonstrations of new language families and broader linguistic relationships

By learning from the object lessons of past successful research, we can be optimistic about what would be needed and how we ought to go about the investigation in order to establish new language families or to show broader connections among languages not at present known to be related. Still, we also see in past performances much that is negative, that is, errors and pitfalls to be avoided, and the assessment of prominent proposals of distant genetic relationship (Chapter 9) comes out being largely a long list of problems and what not to do. Nevertheless, even this provides positive contributions. It points the way to proceed with the confidence that by following legitimate procedures and avoiding the pitfalls that so many proposals fall into, it may be possible to present appropriate evidence for future genetic relationships that will not be rejected because the evidence marshalled in their favor could as easily be explained by other factors (see Chapter 13).

1.8   Conclusion

In summary, our intention in this book is to place the methodology for investigating possible cases of distantly related languages on firm footing and to evaluate numerous claims relevant to proposed but as yet undemonstrated remote relationships. The overall result, we hope, will constitute a significant contribution to linguistic classification in general.

---

[11] While linguists have not shied away from referring to migrations (population movements), migration has not been in favor with most archaeologists in recent years – it could be a matter of large or small movements of people (of few or many people) at one time or over an extended period, of one longer movement or several shorter movements in sequence, of purposeful incursions or aimless wandering, and so on.

2 The beginning of comparative linguistics

And the whole earth was of one language, and of one speech . . . And they said, Go to, let us build us a city and a tower . . . And the Lord came down to see the city and the tower . . . And the Lord said, Behold, the people is one, and they have all one language . . . Go to, let us go down, and there confound their language, that they may not understand one another's speech . . . Therefore is the name of it called Babel; because the Lord did there confound the language of all the earth; and from thence did the Lord scatter them abroad upon the face of the earth.

(Genesis 11:1–9)

2.1 Introduction

We begin our investigation of how language relationships are established by considering the earliest attempts at classifying languages into families. This history is revealing with respect to both how the field developed and why later scholars thought as they did. Our focus is on methods and on what we can learn from the procedures employed by the earliest practitioners of comparative linguistics.

2.2 The rise of the comparative method

Through voyages, conquests, trading, and colonization from the sixteenth century onward, Europe became acquainted with a wide variety of languages. Information on languages of Africa, Asia, and the Americas became available in the form of word lists, grammars, dictionaries, and religious texts, and significantly, Hebrew became known, through Johannes Reuchlin's (1506) grammar. Attempts at language classification followed. Historical linguistic interests of the time had as their background the Greek tradition with its nature-vs.-convention debate and its interest in etymology, and the biblically based interpretation of Hebrew as the original language (*Lingua Adamica*, *Lingua Paradisiaca*) before the confounding of tongues at Babel. It was common to attempt to fit the European languages into the biblical tradition. From the catalogue of languages and peoples given in Genesis, the tradition of *Sprachlis-ten* [language lists] grew, "inventories of known languages of the world succes-sively fitted into the Biblical ('Mosaic') framework, usually placing Hebrew at the head, between the third and seventeenth centuries" (Robins 1990:86; see Borst 1957–63). For example, Bibliander (1548) – sometimes called the earliest comparative linguist – held Hebrew to be "timeless" (*zeitlos*), while his influential friend Konrad Gesner (1555:5) asserted that all languages had a close relationship to Hebrew, that there were no languages which contained no Hebrew words (Peters 1974:17). Nevertheless, Gesner (1555) recognized several language families, including Semitic, Hellenic, Italic, Celtic, Slavic, and Germanic.[1] Leibniz grouped such scholars as members of his "Etymologi hebraizantes," those for whom in Stipa's (1990:188) words Hebrew served for "gelehrter Wortakrobatik" [learned word-acrobatics].

What counts as the earliest development of comparative linguistics is sub-ject to interpretation, explaining why each of the following at one time or another has been considered the "father" [founder] of comparative linguistics: Giraldus Cambrensis (1146–1220?) 1194; Dante Alighieri (1265–1321) 1305; J. J. Scaliger (1540–1609) 1610[1599]; Georg Stiernhielm 1671; Andreas Jäger 1686; Ludolf 1702; Relander [Relandus] 1706; Edward Lluyd 1707; Philip Johan Tabbert von Strahlenberg 1730; Johan Ihre 1769; Jo[h]annis [János] Sajnovics 1770; Sir William Jones 1798; Christian Kraus 1787; Sámuel Gyarmathi 1799; Franz Bopp 1816, 1833–52; Ramus Rask 1818; and Jacob Grimm 1818; among others. Hoenigswald's (1990a:119–20) summary of the points upon which seventeenth- and eighteenth-century scholars agreed con-cerning criteria for establishing language families, cited in Chapter 1, is telling; they include "an insistence that not a few random items, but a large number of words from the basic vocabulary should form the basis of comparison," "the doctrine that 'grammar' is even more important than words," and "the idea that for an etymology to be valid the differences in sound – or in 'letters' – must recur."

One of the earliest applications of a comparative method for determining linguistic affiliations is that of Sebastian Münster (1544) in his *Cosmographey*, where he found the genetic relationship between Finnish, Saami (Lapp), and Estonian (Finno-Ugric languages), based on a comparison of words and gram-matical structures in texts of the Lord's Prayer in these languages (Stipa 1990:38). Here we see that almost from the very beginning grammatical evi-dence, along with vocabulary agreements, was utilized as a criterion for estab-lishing language family relationships.

---

[1] Gesner (1555) also held that Ethiopian and Indic were related (Peters 1974). It is possible that this had some influence on Jones, who expressed a similar view (see Chapter 3). Also, as will be seen in Chapter 3, though not commonly recognized, a major intent of Sir William Jones was to fit his conclusions within this Mosaic tradition.

Though not as methodologically sophisticated as Münster, both Sigismundus Gelenius (1537) and Joseph Justus Scaliger (1610[1599]) were early to recognize distinct language families in Europe. Scaliger's work is better known. He opposed the Hebrew-origin hypothesis, positing eleven language families (*matrices linguae*) – four major families (Romance, Greek, Germanic, and Slavic) and seven minor ones (Albanian, Tatarish, Hungarian, Finnish [with Saami], Irish, Old British, and Basque). These families were considered not to have any more remote relationships among themselves, "neither in the words [*verbis*] nor in the inflectional system [*analogia*]" (Metcalf 1974:238; see also Stipa 1990:135–6). Here again, evidence from both grammar and vocabulary was employed. Scaliger's term *matrices linguae*, 'mother tongues,' equivalent roughly to our current understanding of 'language family,' recurs with some frequency in early works involving comparative linguistics. Other early equivalents were *radicales*, *orginales*, *primogeniae seu matriculares*, as well as *matrices linguae*.

Grammatical comparisons, together with lexical agreements, became more or less a standard ingredient of linguistic comparison. For example, Wexionius (1650), in another early demonstration of Finno-Ugric relationships, compared Finnish, Estonian, and Lapp (Saami), dedicating two full chapters to comparing grammar, and another to the case systems. He compared inflectional paradigms (nouns, verbs, pronouns), comparative constructions, passives, and moods, among others (Stipa 1990:146). J. A. Comenius (Komenský) (1657) recognized four "cardinal languages" (language families) of Europe, though he distinguished twenty *matrices minores*. Comenius also required grammatical evidence to show relationship among the languages within each of his cardinal languages (*matres*, 'mother languages'). For example, he grouped Slavic languages together in one family based on the personal endings in verbal paradigms (cf. Stipa 1990:138).

2.3   The Dutch scholars

From the fifteenth century onward, etymology had been shifting away from its sense in classical antiquity of unfolding the true meaning of words, toward a historical search for earlier stages in languages and the origin of words (Robins 1990:86). Etymology thus viewed was to become important in attempts to establish linguistic relationships and in the developing notions about the role of sound correspondences.

The **Dutch Etymologists** played an important role in the development of the historical study of language. They distinguished between primitive and derived terms, and their analysis of words into their component pieces and roots later became a fundamental feature of comparative grammar. Greek and Roman grammarians had not arrived at the notion of "root" or "affix," but rather employed a Word-and-Paradigm model of description (Law 1990:799). It was from grammars of Semitic languages (Reuchlin's 1506 grammar of Hebrew in particular) that the notion of the 'root' as basic and historically prior to derived and structurally complex forms came (see below).

Abraham Vander Mylius (Abraham van der Myl) (1612) recognized four *linguae matrices* (or *primogeniae seu matriculares*, i.e. language families): Greek, Latin, Teutonic, and Hebrew. In anticipation of the understanding of Indo-European to come, the *lingua belgica* (Flemish) was proposed as the mother tongue of Persian, Phrygian, Scythian, Celtic, Cimbric, Flemish, and German (Swiggers 1984:27). Mylius discussed four possible causes of similarities among languages, still recognized today: chance, "natural" congruence of word and thing (i.e. onomatopoeia), common inheritance from an earlier language, and borrowing due to trade and social intercourse (Metcalf 1953b:537–8). He gave weight to genetic relationships among languages, but also emphasized borrowing. He and his contemporaries paid particular attention to the criteria necessary for etymologizing. Among others, an incipient notion of sound correspondences was an important consideration which constrained the wild etymologizing for which some were known. Mylius' (1612) criterion of attested phonetic variations involved a notion of sound correspondences broader than that which came to characterize the comparative method. As Metcalf (1953b:540–1) explains:

The careful etymologist, in comparing words from two different languages, would admit only those specific examples of interchange already attested within dialects of the same language or in successive temporal stages of the same language . . . *s* and *t* were certified as alternates from Attic *glotta*, non-Attic *glossa*, or Belgian *water*, High German *wasser* . . . The exchangeability of sounds was thus limited to those pairs that could be clearly demonstrated within closely related dialects; but once such sound pairs had been established, they could be applied to any potential cognates in any languages at any period. However elastic such a standard was, it did offer a rule by which wilder etymologizing could be avoided.

This notion of sound correspondences, that sound laws were "natural" and "universal" and so could be found attested in dialects or changes elsewhere, not just in the language where they were first identified, was held by a number of scholars (for example, by Kaspar Cruciger as early as 1616). An explicit statement of this more mechanistic general view of *lois phonétiques* comes from Court de Gébelin (1776[1773–83], cited in Auroux and Boes 1981:36): "These principles or laws hold in all languages, whatever they be, in all times and all places: they are at the base of all etymological research and of all language comparison."[2]

---

[2] "Ces principes ou lois ont lieu dans toutes les langues, quelles qu'elles soient, en tout temps et en tout lieu: ils sont a base de toute recherche étymologique et de toute comparaison de langue."

Some scholars, however, maintained views about correspondence of sounds much more akin to modern ones, dealing with changes in individual languages without assuming that the same changes would hold for other languages or for all languages at all times (cf. Droixhe 1984:9–10). This means that in some early instances it is unclear just what was intended when sound correspondences were discussed.

Dutch etymologists utilized both sound and grammar among their criteria for genetic relationship. For example, Adrianus Rodonius Sc(h)ri(e)ckius (Adriaan van Schrieck) (1614) compared articles, prepositions, and prefixes among languages as evidence of relationship (see Swiggers 1984). The importance of grammatical similarities in comparative linguistics was also stressed by Johannes (Jean) de Laet (1643) and by Lambert ten Kate (1723) (cf. Stankiewicz 1974:186; Diderichsen 1974:303; Droixhe 1984:9; Hoenigswald 1990a:120). De Laet argued against the general reliance on *pauca vocabula*; he was for the use of the genius of the language itself, the system of pronunciation, the mode of construction (i.e. grammar), and above all he was for basic vocabulary (Droixhe 1984:9; Hoenigswald 1985:65). Ten Kate, sometimes called the first "comparative grammarian," classified verbs in Germanic and solved problems of ablaut in the strong verbs (Metcalf 1974:244; Arens 1969[1955]:105); he believed that elements of language were interconnected due to the principle of "analogy" (so much discussed by the Greeks and Romans). He had very strict restrictions for correct etymologies; he listed sound correspondences in seven Germanic languages and dialects (Law 1990:817).

We also find **basic vocabulary** utilized widely as a criterion in considerations of linguistic relationship (cf. Muller 1986:17–19), as revealed in a polemical disagreement between Hugo Grotius (1642) and Johannis de Laet (1643). Grotius' etymological methods (by which he intended, among other things, to show that the American Indian languages are the result of immigration from Norway) were very loose, while De Laet insisted that the compared "vocabula" represent "nomina earum rerum quae domesticae et maxime communes illi genti sunt," that is, names of body parts, numbers one to ten, kinship terms, and geographical matters (Muller 1984:36, 1986:17) – basic vocabulary. The notion of basic vocabulary came to play a major role throughout history as one source of evidence for genetic relationship.

In summary, among the Dutch etymologists, we see the three principal criteria that were recognized throughout history and are still utilized today: basic vocabulary, sound correspondences, and grammatical agreements. The methods and assumptions of these Dutch-school linguists were important in the development of comparative linguistics. For example, Franz Bopp (Chapter 4) acknowledged his indebtedness to them (cf. Diderichsen 1974:285; Stankiewicz 1974:170).[3]

---

[3] Justus-Georgius Schottelius (Schottel) (1612–72) (1663[1641]), a German, applied their etymological approach to Germanic. Schottelius believed that the basic structure of a language

2.4   Word collections

Large-scale word collection for language comparisons was a notable feature of the centuries after the Renaissance, and this played an important role in the development of comparative linguistics. Some word-collection landmarks were Adrien Balbi (1826), Konrad Gesner (1555),[4] Gottfried Wilhelm Leibniz (1768[1717]), Philip Johan Tabbert von Strahlenberg (1730), Johan Ihre (1769), August Ludwig von Schlözer (1770), Antoine Court de Gébelin (1773–82), Johan Christoph Adelung (1781, 1806–17), Filippo Salvadore Gilij (1782), Lorenzo Hervás y Panduro (1784, 1800–5), and Peter Simon Pallas (1786–9). While vocabulary was clearly a central concern of these works, most also employed morphological evidence in their comparisons and asserted the importance of grammar for establishing relationships. The notion that the vocabulary compared for genealogical inferences should be basic is shared by most of these writers and is quite explicit in the work of Leibniz, Monboddo, and Adelung. For Nathaniel Brassey Halhed (1778), associate of Sir William Jones who influenced him significantly (see Chapter 3), basic vocabulary included words for numbers, family relationships, body parts, etc., that is, "the appellations of such things as could be first discriminated in the immediate dawn of civilization" (cited by Muller 1986:17–18).

2.5   The Scythian hypothesis and the foundation of Indo-European

Eventually, comparative linguistics came to have Indo-European languages as a central concern. Early recognition of the family relationship among Indo-European languages is connected intimately with the "Scythian hypothesis." The *Scythica* (from Greek *skuthia*) of Classical writers (for example, of Herodotus, Strabo, Dexippeus, Justin, etc.) referred to a nation who inhabited the region to the north of the Black Sea. The Greeks attributed their origin to Scythes, a son of Hercules, the great archer (Torday 1997:1). Edward Gibbon (1737–94) equated the Scythians with Tartars (Williams 1979:175), as did Sir William Jones, at least in part (Jones 1979b[1788]:19–20), though sometimes

---

remained, though the various elements could vary phonetically very much even to the point of complete disappearance. Reliance on the structure of words (root and endings) lay behind Schottelius' basis for etymologizing, including that of relating words to one another in different languages (Metcalf 1953a).

[4] Gesner was a Swiss naturalist, who classified languages much as he did plants and animals; thus he is in a long line of scholars who treated linguistics as a natural science (akin to biology) which includes, among others, Friedrich von Schlegel, Jacob Grimm, Franz Bopp, and August Schleicher (cf. Law 1990:812). The impact of biological classification, and in particular Linnaeus' work, on linguistics is a theme which should be treated in greater depth. Jones, for example, was also highly involved in such classification, and several others profess or exhibit such influence in their linguistic thinking.

Jones appears to equate Scythians with Goths (cf. Jones 1799a[1789]:51).[5] Some attributed to them a great empire, later said to be centered in Persia, with the Persian connection being significant to linguistic hypotheses involving them. Josephus and early Christian writers took the Scythians, who by that time had become mythical, to be the descendants of Japheth, son of Noah and assumed father of Europe (Droixhe 1984:5). These notions were the prelude to later Scythian linguistic proposals. Some other scholars associated "Scythic" with languages grouped in what later would be called the "Ural-Altaic" hypothesis (see Chapter 9). Today, archaeological evidence from the mid first millennium BC and linguistic evidence suggests an Iranian identification for the Scythians (cf. Nichols 1998a:231; Ostler 2005:43, 108; Torday 1997:1).[6]

The Scythian linguistic hypothesis, which saw several Indo-European languages as genetically related, was proposed first by Johannes Goropius Becanus (Jan van Gorp van der Beke) (1518–72) (1569) in his *Origines Antwerpianae*. Goropius emphasized "Scythian" as the source of several languages, a notion which initiated the recognition of Indo-European as a language family (Metcalf 1974:241; Stipa 1990:135).[7] He was influenced by the belief that Gothic held the key to Dutch antiquity, and by the belief that the cradle of Europe was situated near the Caucasus, from which he took the idea of a Crimean axis, the "North" sea around which the West had its ancient history (Droixhe 1984:7). Franciscus Raphelengius (Ravlenghien) (1539–97), Leiden professor of Hebrew working in Goropius' Antwerp environment, reported correspondences between Persian and Germanic languages and that "the similarities could be due to genetic affinity" (van Driem 2001:1042). Bonaventura Vulcanius (de Smet) (1538–1614) (1597) published several cognates among some Indo-European languages (Droixhe 1984:8; Muller 1986:13); for example, he adduced such Persian–Dutch comparisons as <berader>/*broeder* 'brother,' <dandan>/*tand* 'tooth,' <dochtar> /*dochter* 'daughter,' <mus>/*muis* 'mouse,' <nam>/*naam* 'name,' <nau>/*nieuw* 'new,' <ses>/*zes* 'six,' and <lab>/*lip* 'lip,' concluding that "a certain affinity with the Dutch language is evidenced by the fact that many words are common to both languages" (van Driem 2001:1043). Orientalist

---

[5] Priscus, soon after 476, equated Attila's "Huns" with "Scythians," with "Scythian" meaning nomadic nations generally, and "Huns" as one of them (Torday 1997:173).

[6] As will be seen in Chapter 3, Sir William Jones was a defender of such views. A generally accepted idea was that Shem, Ham, and Japheth – Noah's sons – were the forefathers of the three recognized human "races." For example, Japheth's sons included Javan, Gomer and Madai (see Genesis 10:2), sometimes equated with Ionians (Greeks generally), Cimmerians (compare Greek *Gimirrai*, a people of Anatolia, with Georgian *gmiri* 'hero'; see Torday 1997:257), and Medes; Ashkenaz, a son of Gomer, was assumed connected with the Scythians (called *Asguza(i)* in Assyrian tablets, Torday 1997:23, 257; cf. the designation Ashkenazy for Jews of German or eastern European descent).

[7] Goropius, a physician and "linguist," is especially remembered for his wild etymologies and for having claimed that Dutch (Flemish), his native language, was the language of Paradise and even older than Hebrew.

Andreas Müller (1630–94) opined that "every verse written in Persian was understandable by a German [*Germain*]," and a bit later, John Marsham published the well-known formula, "Scythae sunt tam Persae quam Gothi Germanique" [Scythians are as Persian as Goths and Germans are] (Droixhe 1984:8).

In particular, Marcus Boxhorn(ius)'s role in promoting the Scythian hypothesis has received attention:

> The [Scythian] idea was . . . propounded in a never published book of Marcus Zuerius Boxhorn (1602–53), called the Scythian Origins of the Peoples and Languages of Europe. Boxhorn in that book "observed that innumerable words were common to the Germans, the Latins, the Greeks and other nations throughout Europe. He conjectured therefore that the resemblance started from a common source, that is, from the common origins of all those peoples . . . He postulated some sort of common language, which he called Scythian, as the mother of the Greek, the Latin, the German and the Persian, from which these, like dialects, would start" (Bonfante 1953, 691, quoting the testimony of Georg Horn [1620–70]). This has led Fellman (1974) to attribute to Boxhorn the epithet "first historical linguist."

> Boxhorn was skeptical about the success that his ideas might have with the public. In 1647 the publication of an anonymous pamphlet forced him to formulate his theory in the 100-page essay *Antwoord von M. Z. von B. gegeven op de Vraaghen . . .* . Together with Salmasius' (Claude de Saumaise) *De hellenistica . . . commentarius* (1643), this constitutes the classical formulation of the Scythian theory. *Feeling that accumulation of lexical analogies does not suffice for genetic proof, Boxhorn also draws on the testimony of morphology: "the ordinary manner to vary words and nouns as in declensions, conjugations," to prove "that these people all learned their language from one same mother."* (Droixhe 1978:93; quoted in Muller 1986:10; our emphasis, LC/WP)

In his method for establishing language relationships, Boxhorn shunned loanwords and apparently relied on basic vocabulary, "native, inherited words which denote matters of things which are used, borne or encountered on a daily basis" (cited in van Driem 2001:1045). He sought morphological evidence, in "remnants of the oldest manner of speaking amongst the Scythians, which many of the nations of Scythian ancestry, such as the Teutonic, still follow to this very day in their manner of declining and conjugating" (cited in van Driem 2001:1046). Moreover, he made use of the criterion of shared grammatical aberrancies, generally held to be very strong evidence of genetic relationship among languages (see Chapter 7):

> That these peoples too acquired their language from a single mother is also evidenced by the common ways in which words and names are variously treated, viz. by the ways in which they are declined and conjugated, and in other ways as well; *especially by anomalies themselves.* (Cited by van Driem 2001:1046; our emphasis, LC/WP)

Claudius Salmasius (Claude de Saumaise) (1643) further elaborated the Scythian hypothesis in his Indo-Scythian theory, in which "Latin, Greek,

Persian, and the Germanic languages were all descended from a lost common ancestor" (Law 1990:815–16). As Muller (1986:11) says:

In his *De hellenistica* (1643, 366–396), Saumaise (1588–1643) affirms the same underlying linguistic unity [of "Scythian" languages], venturing even to reconstruct lexical items of the Scythian "Ursprache" from the comparison of Greek, Latin, Persian and German words . . . Saumaise introduced the Indians into the picture under the guise of the "Indo-Scythians." (Droixhe 1978:90)[8]

Salmasius' methods matched in large part the comparative method as understood in modern times, including the recognition of sound correspondences:

Salmasius employed techniques familiar to us from nineteenth-century comparative philology: the comparison of cognate forms such as Greek *patér*, German *Vater*, Persian *badar*; phonological correspondences, such as the fact that Germanic languages regularly have initial h- where Latin has a c- as in Old English *heafod*, Danish *hoffuit*, Dutch *hoofft* for Latin *caput*; and reconstruction . . . Salmasius' work gave rise to a generation of careful historical and comparative studies. (Law 1990:816)[9]

Significantly, Salmasius also brought Sanskrit into the emerging picture of Indo-European relationships embodied in the Scythian theory (and Boxhorn agreed with him). Of the Sanskrit words recorded by Ctesias in his fifth-century BC description of India, Salmasius observed:

All the Indian utterances which have come down to us, recorded by Ctesias in his *Indika*, can, with only minor modification, be found in modern Persian. From this it is clear that the Indian of Ctesias is Indoscythian and it follows that either modern Persian is the descendant of the language spoken by the Indoscythians, or that the Indians of Ctesias descended from the Scythians who descended into India, whilst the people who migrated to Parthia trace their origin to the same stock. (Salmasius 1643:379–80, cited in van Driem 2001:1047)

---

[8] Benfey (1869:242) seems to present a contradictory account of Salmasius, saying that Salmasius could see similarities (for example among numerals) only as borrowings into Greek from Scythian languages.

[9] Salmasius' work relates to that of his physician, Johann Elichmann (see Salmasius 1640), who had earlier served as physician to the Persian court and observed both lexical and grammatical similarities between German and Persian. Salmasius wrote in the preface to Elichmann's book, *Tabula Cebetis graece, arabice, latine*:

He has brought to light that the German and Persian languages have sprung forth from the same source, to which conjecture he was led by an infinite amount of words common to both languages, but also by words with similar flexional endings and showing the same morphological composition, and by other arguments. Because, moreover, many words are also found in Persian that are also Greek, but Greek in the sense that they also resemble German, it may not without reason be concluded that the Greeks too have much to thank to their Scythian origin, from which source both the Persian and German languages have come forth. (Elichman 1640:iii, cited and translated by van Driem 2001:1043)

(See Muller 1984:392–3 for Salmasius' detailed comparisons between Greek, German, and Persian.)

With respect to methodology, it should be noticed that these Scythian works, early attempts at establishing genetic relationships among languages, employed (as in the case of Boxhorn) "lexical analogies," but required "the testimony of morphology" for proof, and sound correspondences were also known and utilized, as in the case of Salmasius. (Cf. also Droixhe 1980.)

Georg Stiernhielm (1598–1672) (1671) extended Salmasius' Scythian classification to include in addition to Latin, Greek, German, Gothic, and Persian, also the Romance, Slavic, and Celtic languages (Law 1990:816). Stiernhielm (1671), in his edition of Ulfila's Gothic translation of the Bible, had compared similarities in the paradigms of Latin *habēre* ('have, hold') and Gothic *haban* ('have'), concluding that the two languages were closely related descendants of a single ancestor (Metcalf 1974:233, 236). Thus he also relied on both grammatical and lexical evidence in arguing for language relationships.

Andreas Jäger's (1686) formulation of the Scythian hypothesis is perhaps the best known; it presents a modern-sounding view of Indo-European relationships. As Muller (1986:11–12) explains:

Another distinguished representative of the Scythian tradition was the Swede Andreas Jäger who on February 6, 1686 . . . gave a public defense of his master's thesis at the University of Wittenberg, titled *De Lingua Vetustissima Europae* . . . For Metcalf [1974:234], the fact that Jäger's thesis was reprinted unaltered as late as 1774 . . . shows the favour which the Scythian theory enjoyed until the time of Jones.

It is worth repeating the following passage from Jäger (cited in Chapter 1), because of its particularly modern sound and because of the remarkable similarities that Jones' famous "philologer" passage (Chapter 3) bears to it, though Jones' proclamation came a hundred years later:

An ancient language, once spoken in the distant past in the area of the Caucasus mountains and spreading by waves of migration throughout Europe and Asia, had itself ceased to be spoken and had left no linguistic monuments behind, but had as a "mother" generated a host of "daughter languages," many of which in turn had become "mothers" to further "daughters." (For a language tends to develop dialects, and these dialects in the course of time become independent, mutually unintelligible languages.) Descendants of the ancestral languages include Persian, Greek, Italic (whence Latin and in time the modern Romance tongues), the Slavonic languages, Celtic, and finally Gothic and the other Germanic tongues. (Quoted in Metcalf 1974:233)

Works relying on the Scythian hypothesis, well known in their day, continued to appear, for example in Jones' various discourses (see Chapter 3). Leibniz also wrote of Scythian languages and supported the Celto-Scythian hypothesis, for example:

And going back further for understanding the origins as much of Celtic and Latin as of Greek, which have as many common roots with the Germanic or Celtic languages, one can guess that this comes from the common origin of all these peoples descended from the Scyths, having come from the Black Sea, who crossed the Danube and the Vistula, of which a part could have gone to Greece, and the other may have filled Germany and the Gauls . . . The Sarmatic (supposed to be Slavic) in half at least of an either German origin or one in common with Germanic. (Leibniz 1709:259)[10]

(See Borst 1957–63:3.1:iv, 2; Droixhe 1978.)

Sanskrit's similarities to other Indo-European languages had been noted and the Scythian hypothesis had been called upon to explain these, before Sir William Jones came on the Sanskrit scene. So well known was the Scythian hypothesis that in 1733 Theodor Walter, a missionary in Malabar, "recognized similarities between Sanskrit, Greek, and Persian numerals and explained these with . . . Scythian theory" (Fellman 1975:38; also Muller 1986:16). Sir William Jones, too, was familiar with and influenced by the Scythian hypothesis (see Chapter 3). Rasmus Rask, also, was influenced by it, citing Jamieson's (1814) *Hermes Scythicus or the radical affinities of the Greek and Latin languages to the Gothic* (see Chapter 4). In brief, the Scythian hypothesis as precursor to and precedent for the Indo-European family was highly significant.

2.6   Other luminaries of the eighteenth century

Hiob Ludolf's (1702) importance in the history of linguistics is shown by the number of scholars who, following Benfey (1869:236), cite him as the first comparative linguist (cf. Arens 1955:88; Jankowsky 1972:23, etc.). Ludolf's much cited *Dissertatio de harmonia linguae aethiopicae cum ceteris orientalibus* echoed J. J. Scaliger's (1610) approach and constitutes an important early contribution to the Semitic family. For Ludolf, grammar was an important criterion of relatedness:

In order to say that one language is related to another, it is necessary not only that it have some words in common with the other, but also that the grammatical structure for the greater part be the same, as one finds it in the Oriental languages, the Hebrew, Syrian, Arabic, and Ethiopian. (Cited in Diderichsen 1974:283)[11]

Ludolf also required basic vocabulary, as Benfey (1869:236) points out:

He also shows that the corresponding words denote simple, natural items, for instance parts of the body, things we would say with regard to which it is absolutely improbable

---

[10] "Et en remontant d'advantage pour y comprende les origines tant du Celtique et du Latin que du Grec, qui ont beaucoup de racines communes avec les langues Germaniques ou Celtiques, on peut conjecturer que cela vient de l'origine commune de tous ces peuples descendus des Scythes, venus de la mer Noire, qui ont passé le Danube et la Vistule, dont une partie pourroit estre allée en Grèce, et l'autre aura rempli la Germanie et les Gaules . . . Le Sarmatique (supposé que c'est l'Esclavon) a sa moitié pour le moins d'une origine ou Germanique ou commune avec le Germanique" (Leibniz 1709:259).

[11] "Si linguam alteri dicere affinem velimus, necesse est, non tantum ut ea contineat nonnulla alterius cujusdam linguae vocabula, sed etiam ut Grammaticae ratio, maxima sui parte, eadem sit, qualis convenientia cernitur in Orientalibus, Ebraea, Syriaca, Arabica et Aethiopica" (quoted by Benfey 1869:236).

that one language might have borrowed them from another, which thus provide conclusive evidence of an original family relationship.[12]

The requirement that words compared for family relationships be from basic vocabulary became a common criterion. The reason often given for this was that with basic vocabulary one had some protection against the possibility that the similarity among the lexical items being compared was due to borrowing. (See Chapter 7.)

William Wotton (1713) is another who relied on grammar. Of his criteria and his findings he wrote:

My argument does not depend upon the difference of words, but upon the difference of grammar between any two languages . . . when any words are derived from one language into another, the derived words are then turned and changed according to the particular genius of the language into which they are transplanted. I have shewed, for instance, in what fundamentals the Islandish [Icelandic] and the Greek agree. I can easily afterwards suppose that they might both be derived from one common mother, which is and perhaps has for many ages been entirely lost. (Wotton 1730[1713]:57; quoted in Koerner 1990c:254)

We see in Wotton once again both the emphasis on grammatical criteria and the notion of a perhaps no longer existing parent language, a notion the origin of which is often erroneously attributed to Jones, but which was in fact a common notion in seventeenth- and eighteenth-century linguistics (as seen in Chapters 1 and 3).

Johan Ihre (1707–80) was the only true linguistic genius of the eighteenth century, according to Adolf Noreen (Droixhe 1984:7). He contributed significantly to the methods of comparative linguistics (in his *Glossarium Suiogothicum*, 1769). He extended Stiernhielm's verb correspondences in Gothic and Latin (see above) to nouns, contributing to comparative Germanic linguistics and he employed standard criteria, sound and grammar, for language relationships:

He [Ihre] achieved extraordinary things with the methods of comparative linguistics in particular for Germanic studies (*Glossarium sucogothicum* 1769). Owing to the fact that he made phonology and morphology the basis of comparative philology and recognized the significance of Icelandic for Nordic studies, he had an inspiring effect on the research of the following century (Rask and Grimm). (Stipa 1990:191)[13]

---

[12] "Auch bringt er darauf, daß die übereinstimmenden Wörter einfache natürliche Gegenstände, etwa Theile des Körpers bezeichnen, wir würden sagen solche, bei denen es absolut unwahrscheinlich ist, daß eine Sprache sie von der andern entleht habe, die also ein unwiderlegliches Zeugniß ursprünglicher Stammverwandtschaft ablegen."

[13] "Außerordentliches leistete er [Ihre] mit den Methoden der vergleichenden Sprachwissenschaft ins besondere für Germanistik (*Glossarium Suiogothicum* 1769). Dadurch, daß er Laut- und Wortbildungslehre zum Grundlage der Sprachvergleichungen machte und die Bedeutung des Isländischen für die Nordistik erkannte, wirkte er inspirierend auf die Forschung des folgenden Jahrhunderts (Rask und Grimm)."

In **Gottfried Wilhem Leibniz's** (1646–1716) (1692) work, the various linguistic (and philosophical) currents of the times came together in an integrated focus on language history. Leibniz's interests included etymology, vocabularies of many languages, the German language, and the nature of language itself (Aarsleff 1982:46). He fostered data collection, of both texts (particularly the Lord's Prayer) and vocabularies; he believed that etymology held the key to "wonderfully illustrate the origins of nations," though he linked his collection efforts with his philosophical concerns: "Man's original vocabulary was not arbitrary, but was based on a harmony between words and things" (quoted in Robins 1990:91; cf. Aarsleff 1982:46, 93, 97; Stipa 1990:162). Leibniz wove together the comparative linguistics of his day with notions of the philosophy of language (for Leibniz's more philosophical–psychological thinking in relationship to historical interpretations, see Chapter 8). He believed "those who study the march of the human mind must march at every moment with the torch of etymology in hand" (quoted in Aarsleff 1982:69; see Leibniz 1697, 1710a, 1717; cf. Aarsleff 1982:84, 169).

Leibniz, too, was acquainted with and wrote about the Scythian hypothesis. Sir William Jones (see Chapter 3) had read Leibniz, and hence was acquainted with the Scythian notion from this source as well from others (cf. Cannon 1964:28; Muller 1986:12). Leibniz was also a significant figure in the development of Finno-Ugric linguistics (see Chapter 6).

Anne Robert Jacques Turgot's (1756) article "Etymologie" in the famous *Encyclopédie* was very influential. It laid out the criteria for historical linguistic research and the need for coherent argumentation, presenting the view of close association between universal grammar and the origin of language. His was the most exact and advanced exposition of philosophical etymology in the eighteenth century, and therefore became a point of departure for nineteenth-century comparative linguistics. Rasmus Rask paid particularly close attention to Turgot's methods (Swiggers 1992:158; cf. Rosiello 1987:76; see Chapter 4).

Jo[h]annis [János] Sajnovics (1770), very often called the father of comparative linguistics, demonstrated the relationship between Saami (Lapp) (together with Finnish) and Hungarian with clear methods, which accorded a central role to grammatical comparisons, but he also utilized the other criteria. He made specific and accurate grammatical comparisons between Saami and Hungarian (Diderichsen 1974:284, 303; Hanzeli 1983:xix; Stipa 1990:211–12); in his opinion, such morphosyntactic correspondences were essential for proving relationship among languages (cf. Stipa 1990:211). (See Chapter 6.)

As Hoenigswald (1985:65) points out, scholars both before and after Sajnovics, including Jones, usually did not make clear what they meant by grammatical evidence, whether they intended it to be understood as "(1) particular affixes or particles with a given grammatical meaning (say, a given case ending), (2) processes (like ablaut), or (3) the semantics of grammatical structure (say, the presence of a dual, or ergativity)." For Rask (1818[1993]), for example, it seems clear that all these were intended, i.e. the overall grammatical/morphological structure (sometimes called the "genius" or the "inner structure") of the languages in comparison. The idea of comparisons of the overall "genius" or ground plan of a language was certainly prevalent in a number of early works on "comparative grammar" (see Chapter 4). Sajnovics' grammatical comparisons were more specific than this.

Sound comparisons also played a role in Sajnovics' work:

> Other important criteria that he [Sajnovics 1770] formulated were to base comparisons on pronunciation, since orthography can conceal the identity of words (1770, 13) . . . He also warned against uncritical permutations of "litterae" . . . (Muller 1986:23)

Sajnovics' work was very influential in the subsequent development of comparative linguistics (see Chapter 6).

2.7   The emergence of Sanskrit

As mentioned above, several individuals had observed the similarity and possible relationship between Sanskrit and various other Indo-European languages before Jones, for example, Thomas Stevens (or Stephens) (1549–1619)1583, Fillipo Sassetti (1540–88)1585, Jean François Pons 1743, Benjamin Schultze (1689–1760) 1725, Father Gaston Laurent Cœurdoux 1767, Nathaniel Halhed 1778, and Lord Monboddo (James Burnett) 1773–92, 1779–99. These cases are well known.

In 1583, in a letter to his brother, Thomas Stephens, English Jesuit, noted the similarities in grammatical structure (as well as vocabulary) between languages of India and Greek and Latin (Muller 1984:38–9, 1986:14–15).[14] As another indicator that Sir William Jones' observation about Sanskrit having a connection to Classical European languages was by no means new or unique, we have Joseph de Guignes' (1770:327) report that "an infinity of travellers have already noticed that in the Indian languages and even in Sanskrit, the learned tongue of these peoples, there are many Latin and Greek words" (quoted in Auroux 1990:223). Since Jones (1799b:372, 1979b[1788]:18, 23, and elsewhere) cited de Guignes in other contexts, Jones was probably aware of this statement. Twenty years before Jones' celebrated Third Anniversary Discourse

---

[14] Stephens wrote, "Lingue harum regionum sunt permultae. Pronunciationem habent non invenustam et compositione latinae grecaeque similem; phrases et constructiones plane mirabiles. Literae syllabarum vim habent, quae toties variantur quoties consonantes cum vocalibus, vel mutae com liquidis combinari possunt" [The languages of these regions are very numerous. They have a not unpleasing pronunciation and a structure similar to Latin and Greek; they have sentences and constructions that are simply wonderful. Letters have the force of syllables and are as variable as the possible combinations of consonants with vowels or mutes with liquids] (quoted in Muller 1986:14–15). He appears to draw no conclusions about possible historical explanations for the similarities he noted.

(see Chapter 7), Gaston Laurent Cœurdoux (1784–93[1767]), Jesuit missionary in South India, answered a request for information from Abbé Barthélémy of the French Académie des Inscriptions et Belles-Lettres in which he pointed out Sanskrit's similarity with Latin and Greek. Cœurdoux included word lists (with "essential terms," i.e. basic vocabulary) and grammatical and phonological similarities. He compared, among other things, conjugated forms of Sanskrit *asmi* and Latin *sum* (both 'to be'), and the paradigm of other verbs in Sanskrit, Latin, and Greek in present, indicative and optative, and number (singular, dual, plural) in nouns and verbs (Jankowsky 1972:27; Muller 1986:24; Swiggers 1990:290). His conclusion was that "common origin" explained the similarity (Godrey 1967:58), though Cœurdoux did not mean by "common origin" what Jones meant a few years later. Edgerton (1946:236) showed that the oft-cited quote from Cœurdoux about "common origin" apparently referred more to borrowing, i.e. mixing of vocabularies (see also Arlotto 1969:417):

These seven Japhetic tribes, starting on their wanderings, remained for some time in mutual contact. During this period their languages borrowed from each other; "that is why there is some Greek and Latin in Sanskrit, and some Sanskrit in Latin and Greek" (665)... The only common language he [Cœurdoux] saw was that before Babel, therefore common to all men. (Edgerton 1946:237)[15]

In any case, Cœurdoux's report was not published until 1784–93, after Jones' claim became known, and so it had no direct impact on the development of comparative linguistics, but it and other reports show that ideas similar to Jones' were already around.

Lord Monboddo (James Burnett) not only wrote of Sanskrit's connections with other Indo-European languages, drawing from Jones' predecessors and contemporaries, but also had considerable influence on Jones' thinking (see Chapter 3). Monboddo accepted Jean François Pons' (1743) notion that Sanskrit was derived from a certain number of primitive elements, seeing Greek as similarly so derived. He attributed the resemblance between Sanskrit and Greek to the fact that "both Indians and Greeks got their language, and all their other arts, from the same parent-country, viz., Egypt" (Rocher 1980a:13; cf. Cannon 1990:324) – not unlike views expressed later by Jones (see Chapter 3). Nathaniel Halhed (1778), posted to India before Jones, claimed that Sanskrit was "equally refined with either the Arabic or the Greek," and that it was "the Parent of almost every dialect from the Persian Gulph to the China Seas." He compared Sanskrit with Greek and Latin, pointing out among other similarities,

---

[15] Notice Cœurdoux attributes the similarities among Sanskrit, Greek, and Latin to the son of Japhet (Noah's son), and not of Ham, as Jones did. One recognizes the same sort of biblical interpretation in both Cœurdoux and Jones, in spite of the choice of a different son of Noah in the two accounts from whom to derive the descendants (Trautmann 1998:113–14).

the verbs ending in -*mi* 'first person' in both Sanskrit and Greek. Monboddo was much taken by his correspondence with Halhed (Rocher 1980a:13–14). Rocher (1980a:15) affirms that "Halhed's views were one of the foundations for Sir William Jones' famous statement of the kinship of Sanskrit with Latin, Greek, and other languages later known as Indo-European." Charles Wilkins (1749?–1836), of the East India Company, became Monboddo's primary source of Sanskrit. Wilkins had supplied him with lists of items which showed similarities between Sanskrit and Greek. These were not only of a lexical nature, but were also related to "composition, derivation, and flection." However, Wilkins supplied less information on these grammatical features than on vocabulary, and Monboddo sought them from others. Monboddo held these shared grammatical traits to be "of greater consequence for proving them [Latin, Greek, and Sanskrit] to have been originally the same language" (Rocher 1980a:14–15).[16] Halhed was the most important influence on Monboddo's later view, even though Monboddo's early publications had played a central role in the development of Halhed's linguistic ideas (Rocher 1980a:15). It is interesting in this context to speculate upon the influence that the Indian grammatical tradition may have had on Halhed, since he studied Sanskrit with pundits who taught with this view, and through Halhed in turn on Monboddo, and through both Halhed and Monboddo – and later directly from the pundits with whom he studied – on Jones (see Chapter 3). All three dealt with roots and affixes, which are emphasized in the Indian grammatical tradition.

2.8   Sound correspondences

Sound correspondences, the third criterion or source of evidence for language affinity, also played a role in the evidence for many early proposals of language families, as in the work of Salmasius and others already mentioned above. During the nineteenth century, both before and after the Neogrammarian emphasis on the exceptionlessness of sound change, many scholars employed sound correspondences in arguments for genetic relationship. Today, sound correspondences are generally considered an important source – for many the most important source – of evidence for hypotheses of linguistic relationships (see Chapter 7). The following cases show that this criterion played an important role in the history of how various language families were established.

Georg von der Gabelentz (1891:26) says of **Hadrianus Relandus** (1706–8):

The first comparative linguist in today's sense of the word known to me is the learned Dutchman, Hadr. Relandus, who in his *Dissertationes miscellaneae*, Utrecht 1706–8,

---

[16] As Rocher (1980a:15) explains: "Coming to 'the *third* and greatest art of language,' flection, Monboddo pointed to the present singular of the verb 'to be,' on Wilkins' testimony, and to Halhed's general statement that flection likewise abounded in Sanskrit . . . the similar group of verbs in -*mi*, but erroneously credited Bengali, not Sanskrit, with this feature."

demonstrated the wide spread of the Malay language family, and even *demonstrated laws of sound substitution between Malay and Malagasy.*[17] (Our emphasis, LC/WP)

(See also Benfey 1869:241–2; Davies 1975:617.) Relandus observed the relationship of "Madagascarica" (Malagasy) with some other languages of what came to be known as the Austronesian family. In particular, he compared a list of 23 probable cognates with "Malaíce" (Malay), and observed a *v* : *b* sound correspondence in eight of the sets (see Chapter 6 for details).

Edward Lhuyd's (1660–1709) (1707) use of sound correspondence evidence, however, was clearer. His comparison of several Indo-European languages (including Celtic, Germanic, Slavic, Persian, etc.) is particularly impressive. He collected a rather long list of cognates, listed sound correspondences (including unsystematic ones), noted sound changes, and considered regular sound correspondences as solid evidence against accidental similarity and in favor of family relationship. Anna Morpurgo Davies (1975:629) gives the following account of his work:

Not only do we find in his [Edward Lhuyd's] . . . works a long list of sound correspondences between some Indo-European languages, but it is also said that it is necessary to distinguish between letters and their "potestates" and between "idiomatal" and "accidental" alternations, i.e. between alternations which can be established for one particular language and alternations which recur in an accidental way. *The regularity of sound correspondences is considered to be proof of common origin.* (Our emphasis LC/WP)

Unlike Relandus, Lhuyd (1707:1) had solid understanding of dialect and language diversification and family relationships, and offered many observations about various kinds of language changes, with abundant examples of each. For example, he correctly identified a portion of Grimm's law, before Rask and Grimm: "C or K, in the Greek, Latin, Italian, Spanish, French, British, and Irish, is chang'd into H in the Teutonic languages" (Lhuyd 1707:35). Lhuyd was considerably more sophisticated in his methods and perceptions than Jones some eighty-five years later.

Johann Eberhard Fischer (1697–1771) was a philologist from Württemberg and known for his Siberian expeditions and collection of linguistic materials on languages of that region. He was interested in sound correspondences involving both vowels and consonants; for example, he reported the correspondence of Hungarian *f* and *h* to *p* and *k* respectively in the other Finno-Ugric languages in his *De origine Ungorum* (Fischer 1770[1756]) (Muller 1986:22; Stipa 1990:185; see also Hoenigswald 1990a:124–5). (See Chapter 6.)

Fr. Filippo Salvatore Gilij (1721–89) (1780–4) lived nineteen years in central Venezuela, on the Orinoco river, until the expulsion of the Jesuits in 1767.

---

[17] "Der erste mir bekannte Sprachvergleicher im heutigen Sinne des Wortes ist der gelehrte Holländer Hadr. Relandus, der in seinem Dissertationes miscellaneae, Utrecht 1706–08, die weite Verbreitung des malaischen Sprachstammes, sogar *Lautvertretungsgesetze zwischen Malaisch und Madegassisch nachweist.*"

He traveled widely and became familiar with several of the languages, speaking Tamanaco (Mayapoyo-Yavarana [Cariban], now extinct) well (Del Rey Fajardo 1971.1:178). His linguistic insights were remarkable; he discussed sound change and sound correspondences in several language families, which he was the first to identify (see Campbell 1997a:31–3). For example, he recognized sound correspondences among several Cariban languages:

Letters [sounds] together form syllables. The syllables *sa, se, si*, etc., very frequent in Carib [probably Cariña], are never found in its daughter language Tamanaco, and everything that is expressed in Carib as *sa*, etc., the Tamanacos say with *ča*. For example, the bowl that the Caribs call *saréra* the Tamanacos call *čaréra*. Pareca is also a dialect [sister] of the Carib language. But these Indians, unlike the Tamanacos and Caribs, say softly in the French fashion, *šarera*.[18] (Gilij 1965[1782]:137)

Among three Arawakan languages, Maipure, Güipunave, and Cávere, Gilij reported a large "correspondencia," saying, "in the language of the Maipures and in their dialects [sister languages] I see greater agreement [coherencia]."[19] He cited the following examples:

	Maipure	Güipunave	Cávere
tobacco	yema	dema	shema
hill, bush [monte]	yapa	dapa	shapa[20]

[18] "Las letras juntas forman las sílabas. Las sílabas *sa, se, si*, etc., frecuentísimas en la lengua caribe, en la tamanaca, aunque su hija, no se hallan nunca, y todo lo que el caribe expresa por *sa*, etc., los tamanacos lo dicen con *chá*. Así por ejemplo, la escudilla que los caribes llaman *saréra* los tamanacos la llaman *charéra*. Es también dialecto de la lengua caribe el pareca. Pero estos indios, dejando a los tamanacos, y caribes, dicen suavemente, al modo francés, *sharéra* [<sh> = /š/, spelling changed by Spanish translator]."

[19] "En la lengua de los maipures y en sus dialectos veo una coherencia mayor."

[20] Gilij did not indicate precisely what he meant by *coherencia* and *correspondencia*, but it probably was not the meaning we understand by the technical term "sound correspondence," and may have been intended for matchings of whole words, though his understanding clearly also involved the corresponding sounds. He also compared the pronunciation of the Avanes with that of Maipure, citing forms which exhibit the correspondence of Avane (Maipurean family) *x* with Maipure medial *y*, and of *t* with *k*, as in:

	Maipure	Avane
I	nuya	nuxa
I go	nutacáu	nuxacáu
women	tiniokí	inioxí
axe	yavatí	yavaxí
tiger [jaguar?]	quatikí	quaxixí

Although he did not state it specifically, since he was speaking here of pronunciation, it seems safe to conclude that he recognized these sound correspondences (Gilij 1965[1782]:173).

Gilij was not the only early scholar to use the sound-correspondence criterion to establish language families in the Americas; numerous others are cited in Campbell (1997a:52–4), and these demonstrate that the criterion played an important role in the establishment of several families in American Indian linguistics, particularly during the last third of the nineteenth century and early twentieth century.[21]

It is worth emphasizing the frequent use of sound correspondences in work to establish language families in the past, since, for example Greenberg (1987, 1991, 2005) claimed that sound correspondences are not important for distant genetic relationship, and he asserted further that "none of these families [Indo-European, Uralic, or Austronesian] was discovered by finding regular sound correspondences" (Greenberg 1996a:133). This view is not consistent with what the historical record reveals, as seen here (see also Poser and Campbell 1992). Scholars happily utilized sound correspondences in proposals of family relationship, though they did not rely on them exclusively. (See Chapters 6 and 7.)

2.9   Conclusion

In this chapter we began our investigation of how language families are established by considering the earliest attempts at classifying languages into families. We saw that long before Sir William Jones, comparative linguistics was developing, and understanding of the Indo-European family was emerging. The evidence for claims that languages were related to one another generally included the three criteria, basic vocabulary, patterned grammatical agreements, and sound correspondences. In the following chapter, we turn to the true nature of Sir William Jones' thought and why his contribution is so commonly misconstrued.

---

[21] These cases were discussed in detail in Campbell (1997a) because of Greenberg's (1987, 1990a, 1991, 2000b, 2000c, 2005) claim that sound correspondences as evidence of genetic relatedness played no role in the establishment of language families in the Americas.

3   "Asiatic Jones, Oriental Jones":
     Sir William Jones' role in the raise
     of comparative linguistics

> Others affirm that in the tower [of Babel] there were only nine materials, and
> that these were clay and water, wool and blood, wood and lime, pitch, linen,
> and bitumen . . . These represent noun, pronoun, verb, adverb, participle,
> conjunction, preposition, interjection.
>
> (Auracepit na n-Éces, Irish grammarians; cited in Eco 1995:16)

3.1   Introduction

We come now to Sir William Jones (1746–94), to whom so much credit for
developments in historical linguistics has been given. Jones' (1786[1789])
famous "philologer" passage – that most momentous soundbite of yore –
declared a relationship between Sanskrit and several other Indo-European languages, and is often cited as the beginning of Indo-European and of comparative-
historical linguistics. Nearly all introductory textbooks on historical linguistics
repeat this claim, as do linguistic publications generally. On all sides we see
statements such as Bengtson and Ruhlen's (1997:3) that Sir William Jones
"discovered the method of comparative linguistics – and with it the Indo-
European family," and Michalove *et al.*'s (1998:452) that "it was Sir William
Jones' famous statement in 1786 that not only led to the recognition of Indo-
European . . . but also put linguistic taxonomy on a solid foundation for the
first time." Emeneau (2000:545) called Jones' announcement in the philologer
passage "that prime event in the linguistics of India and the Indo-European
linguistic world." Gray (1999:116–17) speaking of Jones' "earth-shattering
discovery," asserts that "Jones used careful etymological analysis to demonstrate that [here the philologer passage is repeated] . . . The significance of
this statement cannot be overestimated. It rested on an empirical demonstration . . ."; "Jones stimulated a stampede of philologists" (Gray 1999:116–17).
Cannon (1990:246) declares that Jones' "was the first known printed statement
of the fundamental postulate of Indo-European comparative grammar; more
than that, of comparative linguistics as a whole." Murray (1998:3) reports as
general knowledge that Jones "had founded comparative philology, or historical
linguistics," and Trautmann (1998:105), immediately after repeating the famous

philologer passage, remarks that "the modernity of the formulation is remarkable . . . these are exactly the views historical linguists hold today." As seen in the previous chapters, these views of Jones' philologer statement are erroneous. As Koerner (1986:iii) says, "if Jones' fame rested with this often quoted passage concerning the relationship of Sanskrit with the European languages, his claim to fame would be rather weak indeed."

By 1772, Jones had "established himself as the foremost exponent of Oriental studies in England and as a scholar and writer of rare attainments" (Arberry 1946:10). Jones' "reputation was such that intellectuals were literally *expecting* major discoveries in colonial India, since Jones' Persian grammar and his translations from Greek, Persian, and Arabic were well-known" (Cannon 1991:23).

It will pay us to look carefully at Jones' thinking, and his methods. In this chapter, the following well-known facts are considered which gainsay the popular, commonly repeated, but mistaken view of Jones' role in the development of Indo-European and comparative linguistics:

1. Connections among Indo-European languages had been observed long before Jones (cf. Boxhorn 1647; Giraldus Cambrensis 1194;[1] Comenius

---

[1] Giraldus Cambrensis (Gerald of Wales, c.1146–c.1220, of English descent) took holy orders in 1172 and became Archdeacon of Brecknock; he was at the University of Paris, then returned to England in 1184 to be one of the king's chaplains. He is frequently mentioned as a founder of Indo-European and/or the comparative method, and while his observations were highly interesting, their relation to later comparative linguistics is probably optimistically overestimated. He avoided Welsh in his sermons, giving them in Latin and French, and there is doubt concerning whether he knew Welsh at all (Gerald of Wales 1978:29). Giraldus saw the Britons as a remnant people escaped from Asia Minor after the fall of Troy. He says, "of the three peoples left alive after the fall of Troy, the Britons alone kept the vocabulary of their race and the grammatical properties of their original tongue . . . You must know, too, that all the words in Welsh are cognate with either Greek or Latin. The Greeks say 'ύδωρ [hudo:r] for water, the Welsh 'dwfr' [du:fr]; 'άλς [als] for salt, the Welsh 'halem'; μις [mis] and τις [tis] for I and you, the Welsh 'mi' and 'ti'; όνομα [ónoma] for name, the Welsh 'enw' [enu:]; πέντε [pénte] for five, the Welsh 'pump'; and δέκα [déka] for ten, the Welsh 'deg.' The Romans said 'frenum,' 'tripos,' 'gladius' and 'lorica,' and the Welsh say 'ffrwyn,' 'tribedd,' 'cleddyf,' and 'llurig.' The Romans said 'unicus,' 'canis,' and 'belua,' and the Welsh say 'unig,' 'ci,' and 'bela'" (Gerald of Wales 1978:246). And, "he [David II, bishop of St. David's] made himself acquainted with the language of that nation [Welsh], the words of which, in his younger days, he used to recite, which, as the bishop often had informed me, were very conformable to the Greek idiom. When they asked for water, they said Ydor ydorum, which meant bring water, for Ydor in their languages, as well as in Greek, signifies water . . . and Dûr also, in the British language signifies water. When they wanted salt they said Halgein idorum, bring salt: salt is called 'άλ [sic] in Greek, and Halen in British, for that language, from the length of time which the Britons (then called Trojans, and afterwards Britons, for Brito, their leader) remained in Greece after the destruction of Troy, became, in many instances, similar to the Greeks. It is remarkable that so many languages should correspond in one word, 'άλ in Greek, Halen in British, and Halgein in the Irish tongue, the g being inserted; Sal in Latin, because, as Priscian says, 'the s is placed in some words instead of an aspirate,' as 'άλς is called Sal in Latin, έμι [hemi] – semi – έπτα [hepta] – septem – Sel in French – the a being changed to e – Salt in English, by the addition of t to Latin; Sout, in the Teutonic language: there are therefore seven or eight languages agreeing in this one word. If a scrupulous inquirer should ask my opinion of the relation here inserted, I answer with Augustine, 'that the divine miracles are to be admired, not discussed'" (Giraldus 1908:78). Thus Giraldus did observe some true cognates, but offers no clear opinion as to why they bear the similarity he points out.

1657; Dante 1305; Gelenius 1537; Goropius 1569; Ihre 1769; Jäger 1686; Salmasius 1643; J. J. Scaliger 1599[1610]; Stiernhielm 1671; Lhuyd 1707; Wotton 1713; Lomonosov 1755; among others).

2. The relationship of Sanskrit with certain other Indo-European languages, especially with Greek and Latin, had also been perceived prior to Jones, for example, Thomas Stephens (1549–1619) 1583 (see Muller 1986:14–15); Fillipo Sassetti (1540–88) 1585; Salmasius 1643 (see van Driem 2001:1047); Jean François Pons 1743; Benjamin Schultze (1689–1760) 1725; Gaston Laurent Cœurdoux 1767; Nathaniel Halhed 1778; Lord Monboddo 1773–92, 1779–99 (see Zeller 1967). Moreover, there were at least forty-seven published accounts of Sanskrit before Jones' third discourse (Muller 1986:14). Jones was well aware of the views of some of these predecessors.

3. Jones' procedures bear scant resemblance to the comparative method practiced by later linguists and in any case they were not original to him (see below).

4. Jones' interpretation of affinity among Asian peoples and their languages reflects not so much the linguistic facts as the biblical framework with Mosaic chronology in which Jones couched his thinking; this interpretation, based on the descendants of Noah, naturally involved a genealogical orientation, and this both reflected and imposed views of how languages could be related to one another – this was Orientalism directed in defense of Christianity; Hinduism made safe for Anglicans (Trautmann 1998:107, 109).

Moreover, Jones' philologer passage is usually read out of context, with too much of present-day understanding injected into its interpretation (Mukherjee 1968:95), with little real understanding of Jones' own intentions or of the intellectual environment in his day. The purpose of this chapter is to set the record straight with respect to Sir William Jones' contribution, to examine the methods he used and to put them in proper perspective with regard to the investigation of possible language families, and indirectly in this way to set the stage for understanding the successful methods for establishing genetic relationships among languages, the major goal of this book.

3.2   Jones' game plan

Jones (1798:415) declared that his "design" (intent) was to prepare for the annual meetings of the "Asiatick Society of Bengal" (which he founded, later called the Royal Society of Bengal, which held its first meeting in January 1784), "a series of short dissertations" (presidential addresses), the theme and purpose of which he specified as:

The *five* principal nations who have in different ages divided among themselves, as a kind of inheritance, the vast continent of *Asia*, with the many islands depending on it, are the *Indians*, the *Chinese*, the *Tartars*, the *Arabs*, and the *Persians*: *who* they severally were, *whence* and *when* they came, *where* they now are settled, and *what advantage* a more perfect knowledge of them all may bring to our *European* world, will be shown, I trust, in *five* distinct essays; the last of which will demonstrate the connexion or diversity between them, and solve the great problem, whether they had *any* common origin, and whether that origin was *the same* which we generally ascribe to them. (Jones 1798:417–18)

Jones saw his several essays delivered before the Society, eleven in all, as interconnected parts of a whole, and it is only in treating them as a whole that Jones' methods, claims, and conclusions become clear and can be fully apprehended. Jones' grand plan was to write a history of humankind in Asia. These were published in *Asiatick Researches*, the journal of the Asiatic Society, the first four volumes of which Jones edited. His direct interest was not in historical linguistic matters, and language was but one of four sources of information relevant to his goals:

We seem to possess only *four* general media of satisfying our curiosity concerning it [(pre)history]; namely, first, their *Languages* and *Letters*; secondly, their *Philosophy* and *Religion*; thirdly, the actual remains of their old *Sculpture* and *Architecture*; and fourthly, the written memorials of their *Sciences* and *Arts*. (Jones 1798:421)

Jones always maintained that languages were not worth studying for their own sake, but only as means to a higher end: "I have ever considered languages as the mere instruments of real learning, and think them improperly confounded with learning itself" (quoted by Godrey 1967:58; cf. Rocher 1980b:178). As Trautmann (1998:106) points out, "it is ironic that Jones is best remembered for his contributions to linguistics, given that he said more than once that he did not wish to be considered a mere linguist, and always regarded language as a means to other ends. Restored to its own context, the famous [philologer] passage on the Indo-European languages reveals its extra-linguistic ends very clearly." "The Anniversary Discourses taken together form a wide-ranging essay on Asian ethnology" (Trautmann 1998:106). The third through seventh discourses follow a formula; in each discourse, one finds a description of the boundaries of the area in question, followed by sections dedicated to each of the "media," language, religion, monuments, and arts and sciences. In the third discourse, the philologer quote comes in section I, the section on language and letters.

As pointed out in Chapter 1, Jones' more general interest in the history of the human races rather than in language per se was not unusual for eighteenth- and nineteenth-century linguistic scholars. It was shared by Leibniz, Hervás y Panduro, Monboddo, Vater, Schlegel, Grimm, Humboldt, and others (see also Nicols 1996a:42–4). For all of these scholars, linguistic comparisons were seen as part of the means for getting at a broader history of the nations and races of the world. The theme of language in concert with other sources of evidence to determine the classification of nations and races, as well as of languages themselves, was to persist into the twentieth century (see Chapter 8).

3.3   The "philologer" passage

Jones pursued this grand plan in his anniversary discourses, delivered to the Royal Society of Bengal each February from 1784 to 1794 (see Jones 1798, 1979a, 1979b, 1799a–e). The third to the ninth discourses were dedicated to solving the "common origin of the five principal Asiatic nations: India, Arabia, Tartary, Persia, and China," with each nation allotted a distinct essay (Teignmouth 1805[1804]:387; Cannon 1952:44). The "philologer" citation is from the third discourse (*On the Hindus*), given in 1786 (Jones 1798). We quote it here in fuller form, including connected material in the immediately preceding context which is never cited with the philologer passage itself that is so often repeated in linguistic texts:

Five words in six, perhaps, of this language [Hindustani (= Hindi)] were derived from the *Sanscrit* . . . but the basis of the *Hindustáni*, particularly the inflexions and the regimen of verbs, differed as widely from both these tongues [Sanskrit and Hindi–Urdu] as *Arabick* differs from *Persian*, or *German* from *Greek*. Now the general effect of conquest is to leave the current language of the conquered people unchanged, or very little altered, in its ground-work, but to blend with it a considerable number of exotick names both for things and for actions . . . and this analogy might induce us to believe, that the pure *Hindì*, whether of *Tartarian* [Turkic and other central Asian peoples] or *Chaldean* [i.e. Semitic] origin, was primeval in Upper India, into which the *Sanscrit* was introduced into it by conquerors from other kingdoms in some very remote age; for we cannot doubt that the language of the *Véda's* was used in the great extent of country which has before been delineated, as long as the religion of *Brahmá* has prevailed in it.

[Here begins the "philologer" passage as normally cited.] The *Sanscrit* language, whatever be its antiquity, is of a wonderful structure; more perfect than the Greek, more copious than the Latin, and more exquisitely refined than either; yet bearing to both of them a stronger affinity, both in the roots of verbs and in the forms of grammar, than could possibly have been produced by accident; so strong indeed, that no philologer could examine them all three without believing them to have sprung from *some common source*, which, perhaps, no longer exists. There is a similar reason, though not quite so forcible, for supposing that both the *Gothic* and *Celtick*, though blended with a very different idiom, had the same origin with the *Sanscrit*; and the old *Persian* might be added to the same family, if this were the place for discussing any question concerning the antiquities of *Persia*. (Jones 1798[1786]:422–3; cf. Teignmouth 1805[1804]:388; Pachori 1993:175)

This passage is understood accurately only when seen in the context of Jones' overall thought and that of his times, which will emerge as we proceed.[2]

---

[2] Scholars are happy to point out how soon after his arrival in India, in 1783, and how early in his Sanskrit study Jones made his famous third discourse: "On February 2, 1786, only about half a year

3.4   Jones' failings

Jones erroneously included a number of languages and peoples with Indo-European (Egyptians, Chinese, Japanese, ancient Mexicans and Peruvians, see below). Moreover, it seems strangely selective of subsequent historians to extol Jones for seeing Sanskrit's connection with other Indo-European languages, while neglecting his misinterpretation in the immediately preceding paragraph of the Sanskrit–Hindi relationship, which he saw as due to diffusion, to the introduction of Sanskrit into a pre-existing Hindi geographical context. Moreover, even in the famous paragraph, Jones' view of Gothic and Celtic as "blended with a very different idiom" (i.e. mixed with non-Indo-European languages) is passed over without comment, and his leaving open the possibility that the "common source" of these Indo-European languages may still survive is forgotten (cf. Cannon 1990:245). Also, Slavic was misassigned; Jones believed it belonged with non-Indo-European languages of Central Asia. It is also disingenuous of historians not to have given attention to the final paragraph to Jones' famous third discourse, where he presents his conclusions, which is much more revealing of his real thinking – and of his errors – than the isolated philologer passage, from which it differs significantly:

Of these cursory observations on the *Hindus* . . . this is the result; that they had an immemorial affinity with the old *Persians*, *Ethiopians*, and *Egyptians*; the *Phenicians*, *Greeks*, and *Tuscans* [Etruscans]; the *Scythians* or *Goths*, and *Celts*; the *Chinese*, *Japanese*, and *Peruvians*; whence, as no reason appears for believing that they were a colony from any one of those nations, or any of those nations from them, we may fairly conclude that they all proceeded from some *central* country, to investigate which will be the object of my future Discourses. (Jones 1798:431; cf. Pachori 1993:178)

after he [Jones] began to study Sanskrit, he delivered his third 'anniversary discourse'" (Edgerton 1946:231). "He [Jones] had therefore been working on this [Sanskrit], his twenty-eighth language, only a few months [began late summer of 1785] when the time came to prepare the third of his annual presidential addresses to the Asiatic Society, in January of 1786" (Godrey 1967:58). In Jones' own words, written to Dr. Patrick Russell (a scholarly friend from the Royal Society, a naturalist of the East India Company) on September 8, 1785, "I am now at the ancient university of Nadeya, where I hope to learn the rudiments of that venerable and interesting language which was once vernacular in all India, and in both the peninsulas with their islands"; then to Charles Chapman (former Bengal commander in chief, magistrate at Bhagalpur) on September 27, 1785, "I am proceeding slowly, but surely, in this retired place, in the study of Sanscrit"; and written to John Macpherson (senior member of the Supreme Council, later governor-general) upon return to Calcutta in October, "I would rather be a valetudinarian, all my life, than leave unexplored the Sanscrit mine which I have just opened" (cited in Arberry 1946:21). On September 28, 1786, after the famous third discourse of February that year, he wrote Russell, "I am tolerably strong in *Sanscrit*"; in November of that year he wrote Macpherson, "by rising before the sun, I allot an hour every day to Sanscrit, and am charmed with knowing so beautiful a sister of Latin and Greek"; and by September 27, 1787 he could write Thomas Caldicott of longing for the long vacation "close to an ancient university of Brahmans, with whom I converse familiarly in Sanscrit" (Arberry 1946:22).

As this shows, in fact, Jones incorrectly classified many languages as related, based on his four "media" or sources of evidence. In what follows we call attention to several of these errors.

In the third discourse, based on certain similarities between religions, Jones found that "it is very remarkable, that the *Peruvians*, whose *Incas* boasted of the same descent [i.e. the sun] . . . whence we may suppose that South *America* was peopled by the same race [as the Hindus]" (Jones 1798[1986]:426). Jones repeated his assumed Peruvian connection and added Mexico to the picture in his ninth and tenth discourses (for example, Jones 1799d[1792]:491, 1799e[1793]:xv.)

Also in the third discourse, based on the remains of architecture and sculpture, religion, and "letters on many of those monuments," Jones concluded that "all these indubitable facts may induce no ill-grounded opinion, that *Ethiopia* and *Hindustàn* were peopled or colonized by the same extraordinary race" (Jones 1798:427). We scarcely need mention that Ethiopian languages belong primarily to the Semitic and Cushitic language families, and in no way belong to the same Indo-European family as those of "Hindustan" (in the Indian subcontinent) with which Jones dealt.

In the fifth discourse, on the Tartars, Jones (1979b[1788]:25) asserts a genetic affinity between "Indian" (Indo-Aryan) and "Arabian" (Semitic) languages:

I will not offend your ears by a dry catalogue of similar words in those different languages; but a careful investigation has convinced me, that, as the *Indian* and *Arabian* tongues are severally descended from a common parent, so those of *Tartary* [all the other languages of Central Asia] might be traced to one ancient stem essentially differing from the two others.

In Jones' (1799a[1789]) sixth discourse, on the Persians, we find that even his more linguistic methods led him astray in several cases, since he failed to distinguish loans, basing his conclusions on a fairly superficial comparison of the languages involved. For example, Jones misidentified Pahlavi, an Indo-European language of the Iranian branch, as Semitic (cf. Jones 1799a[1979]: 51–3).

In the seventh anniversary discourse, on the Chinese, Jones concluded:

All the circumstances, which have been mentioned under the two heads of *Literature* and *Religion*, seem collectively to prove (as far as such questions admit of proof) that the *Chinese* and *Hindus* were originally the same people. (Jones 1799b:378)

(See also Jones 1799b:380–1.) Jones concludes this discourse with a statement of his belief that he has "now shown in five discourses, that the *Arabs* and *Tartars* were originally distinct races, while the *Hindus*, *Chinese*, and *Japanese* proceeded from another ancient stem" (Jones 1799b:381; cf. also Mukherjee 1968:98; Teignmouth 1805[1804]:395).

In his eighth discourse, on the "borderers, mountaineers, and islanders" of Asia, Jones arrived at several classifications known today to be erroneous. Repeating from his sixth discourse, he "believe[d] on the whole, that the *Ethiops* of *Meroë* were the same people with the first *Egyptians*, and consequently, as it might easily be shown, with the original *Hindus*" (Jones 1799c:5). He also mistakenly classified other Iranian languages as Semitic (Jones 1799c:7–8), in addition to Pahlavi (seen above): "there is very solid ground for believing, that the *Afghans* [identified by Jones as *Patans* (Pashtos?) and *Balójas* (Baluch), i.e. speakers of Iranian languages] descended from the *Jews*; . . . principally, because their language is evidently a dialect of the scriptural *Chaldaick* [Aramaic]" (cf. also Jones 1999c:9). Jones (1799c:10) also mistook Malay as Semitic: "As to the *Moplas* [Tamil-speaking Muslims], in the Western parts of the *Indian* empire, I have seen their books in *Arabick*, and am persuaded, that, like the people called *Malays*, they descended from *Arabian* traders and mariners after the age of Muhammed." Jones (1799c:12) also mistakenly regarded other Austronesian languages, in addition to Malay, as Indo-European, especially connected with Sanskrit (Jones 1799c:12).

Jones (1799c:13) also wrongly regarded Tibetan as Sanskrit, thus Indo-European.

Jones began his ninth discourse with a "short review of the propositions, to which we have gradually been led":

that the first race of *Persians* and *Indians*, to whom we may add the *Romans* and *Greeks*, the *Goths*, and the old *Egyptians* or *Ethiops*, originally spoke the same language and professed the same popular faith, is capable, in my humble opinion, of incontestible proof; that the *Jews* and *Arabs*, the *Assyrians*, or second *Persian* race, the people who spoke *Syriack*, and a numerous tribe of *Abyssinians*, used one primitive dialect, wholly distinct from the idiom just mentioned, is, I believe, undisputed, and, I am sure, indisputable; but that the settlers in *China* and *Japan* had a common origin with the *Hindus*, is no more than highly probable; and, that all the *Tartars*, as they are inaccurately called were primarily of a third separate branch, totally differing from the two others in language, manners, and features, may indeed be plausibly conjectured; but cannot from the reasons alledged in the former essay, be perspicuously shown, and for the present, therefore, must be merely assumed. (Jones 1799d:418–19)

This summary of Jones' conclusions from all his interconnected discourses is strikingly different from the image usually derived from the philologer passage, and his methods were a far cry from those of later comparative grammar and the comparative method (cf. Rocher's 1980b:179–80; Koerner 1990c:255).

Jones' ninth discourse is quite different from the previous ones; it is almost wholly an attempt to accommodate Jones' conclusions about the nations of Asia within a biblical framework, one influenced heavily by the writings of his friend, Jacob Bryant (1774–76), to whom Jones makes occasional reference throughout his discourses and whom Jones praises highly at the beginning of the third, where he begins his treatises on the five principal Asian nations. Jones seems to abandon the better part of the comparative linguistics of the day in favor of a very long-standing biblical account, speculating about descent from the sons of Noah and about Mosaic chronology:

Three sons of the just and virtuous man, whose lineage was preserved from the general inundation, travelled, we are told, as they began to multiply, in *three* large divisions variously subdivided: the children of Ya'fet [Japhet] seem, from the traces of *Sclavonian* names, and the mention of their being *enlarged*, to have spread themselves far and wide, and to have produced the race, which, for want of a correct appellation, we call *Tartarian*: the colonies, formed by the sons of Ham and Shem, appear to have been nearly simultaneous; and, among those of the latter branch, we find so so [sic] many names incontestably preserved at this hour in *Arabia*, that we cannot hesitate in pronouncing them the same people whom hitherto we have denominated *Arabs*; while the former branch, the most powerful and adventurous of whom were the progeny of Cush, Misr, and Rama (names remaining unchanged in *Sanscrit*, and highly revered by the *Hindus*) were, in all probability, the race which I call *Indian*. (Jones 1799d[1792]: 485–6)

From testimonies adduced in the six last annual discourses . . . it seems to follow that, the only human family after the flood established themselves in the northern parts of *Iran*; as they multiplied, they were divided into three distinct branches, each retaining little at first, and losing the whole by degrees, of their common primary language . . . that the branch of YA'FET was *enlarged* in many scattered shoots over the north of *Europe* and *Asia* . . . and had no use of letters, but formed a variety of dialects [languages], as their tribes were variously ramified; that, secondly, the children of HAM, who founded in *Iran* itself the monarchy of the first Chaldeans, invented letters . . . they were dispersed at various intervals, and in various colonies, over land and ocean; that the tribes of MISR, CUSH, and RAMA, settled in *Africk* and *India*; while some of them, having improved the art of sailing, passed from *Egypt*, *Phenice*, and *Phrygia*, into *Italy* and *Greece* . . . whilst a swarm from the same hive moved by a northerly course into *Scandinavia*, and another, by the head of *Oxus*, and through the passes . . . as far as the territories of *Chin* and *Tancut* . . . nor is it unreasonable to believe that some of them found their way from the eastern isles into *Mexico* and *Peru*, where traces were discovered of rude literature and mythology analogous to those of *Egypt* and *India*; that thirdly, the old *Chaldean* empire being overthrown by the *Assyrians* . . . other migrations took place . . . while the rest of Shem's progeny, some of whom before had settled on the Red Sea, peopled the whole *Arabian* peninsula. (Jones 1799d[1792]:490–1)

In the tenth discourse, this is reaffirmed:

We cannot surely deem it an inconsiderable advantage that all our historical researches have confirmed the Mosaic accounts of the primitive world . . . Three families migrate in different courses from one region, and, in about four centuries, establish very distant governments and various modes of society: Egyptians, Indians, Goths, Phenicians, Celts, Greeks, Latians, Chinese, Peruvians, Mexicans, all sprung from the same immediate stem. (Jones 1799e[1793]:xiv)

We can but ask how such a mistaken classification, forced to conform to preconceived biblical interpretations, could have been so misunderstood by generations of scholars as the foundation of comparative linguistics, how it could have had such a monumental impact in the linguistic literature?

3.5   Jones' methods

We turn now to a closer look at Jones' linguistic methods. This is particularly relevant in view of claims some have made to justify their own methodological beliefs by calling upon Jones' authority. It is helpful to recall Max Müller's (1861:162) assessment, that "it was impossible to look, even in the most cursory manner, at the declensions and conjugations, without being struck by the extraordinary similarity, or, in some cases, by the absolute identity, of the grammatical forms in Sanskrit, Greek, and Latin." Because the relationship of Sanskrit to these other Indo-European languages was so unmistakable, it was obvious to Jones (and others) without the application of any specific historical linguistic method. This being the case, Jones' methods (or lack of method) may not be particularly instructive when it comes to more challenging cases of potentially related languages where the relationship may not be so obvious.

In assessing Jones' historical linguistic methods, it is important to bear in mind not only the cases in which he mistakenly grouped unrelated languages together (above), but also the cases of related languages which his methods led him to dismiss (for example Hindi and Sanskrit; Pahlavi and other Iranian languages), and even those he correctly grouped together but for the wrong reasons.

In this context, it is instructive to contrast Jones' view of the role of grammar for showing language relationships with that of his contemporary Nathaniel Brassey Halhed (1778). Halhed had remarked in the preface of his Bengali grammar:

I have been astonished to find this similitude of Sanskrit words with those of Persian and Arabic, and even of Latin and Greek; and these not in technical and metaphorical terms, which the mutation of refined arts and improved manners might have occasionally introduced; but in the main groundwork of language, in monosyllables, in the names of numbers, and the appellations of such things as could be first discriminated on the immediate dawn of civilization. (Cited in Müller 1861:162–3)

Both Halhed and Jones recognized "the same facts about Sanskrit and the modern languages of northern India" (Robins 1990:93), but drew diametrically opposite conclusions from them:

Both saw the etymological links between Sanskrit and the modern vocabularies, and both noted the structural differences exhibited by the verbal inflexions and the verbal phrases. Halhed (1778:ix) declared that on the evidence of the etymologies the Hindustani language(s) were "indubitably derived from the Sanskrit" although "the inflexions by which the words are affected and the modes of grammatical regimen are widely different." But Jones (1799b:25–6), despite his admission that "five words in six" in Hindi are derived from Sanskrit, argued that the typological diversity of the languages in "the inflexions and regimen of verbs" precluded any relation of descent, asserting that Hindi was a surviving original language of India which had been heavily invaded by Sanskrit loanwords. (Robins 1990:92)

There is methodological irony in this: the same structural criteria which allowed Jones to group Sanskrit with the other Indo-European languages – as well as with several unrelated languages – prevented him from accepting the correct genetic relationship between Sanskrit and Hindi, i.e. the relationship between Sanskrit and the Indo-Aryan languages which Halhed had postulated and "conveyed to Europe" (Trautmann 1998:97–8).

This should constitute a strong warning to anyone who would praise the methods Jones used to propose linguistic families too enthusiastically. For example, Joseph Greenberg saw Sir William Jones as a historical precursor to his method of multilateral (or mass) comparison; he claimed, in effect, that Jones actually practiced "multilateral comparison," that is, Greenberg's own method:

With Jones's background knowledge of Arabic and, no doubt, Hebrew, on the one hand, and Latin, Greek, Germanic, and so forth, on the other, the addition of Sanskrit to his repertoire enabled him to see a valid grouping based on differential resemblances. In later work he accurately outlined the Semitic and Finno-Ugric families . . . In other words, even though he did not state it explicitly, he was in effect applying what I called earlier the method of mass comparison and more recently multilateral comparison. (Greenberg 1991:127)

In other words, I am asserting that results, universally viewed as valid, were attained by assessing non-typological resemblances as significant in a number of languages against a tacit background of other languages which were not Indo-European and of whose knowledge in the case of Jones we have valid historical evidence.[3] (Greenberg 2005:155)

Above we saw various of Jones' errors – grouping languages which should not have been combined, and failing to combine languages which should have been grouped. Contrary to Greenberg's claim, it was precisely Jones' notions about typology which led him to misinterpret the Hindi–Sanskrit relationship. Jones did require grammatical evidence when speaking of the "affinity . . . in the roots of verbs and in the forms of grammar." However, the criterion of grammatical evidence for family relationships, as we have seen, was widely employed in historical linguistic studies before Jones and was accepted by almost all practitioners. It is appropriate to recall the influences which oriented Jones to think

---

[3] Works on Jones are fond of reporting the twenty-eight languages he knew.

as he did. As Cannon points out, Jones was influenced by William Robertson's (1769) typology with its view of social evolution from savagery to barbarism to (European ethnocentric) civilization. Presumably Jones had difficulty reconciling contemporary Hindi and its association with Indian society as he then saw it with the beauty of Sanskrit and its association with the glory of Indian classical civilization. As is well known, such views of social evolution later strongly influenced views of language classification and genetic relationship (see Chapter 8). The reason for Jones' reference to verbs is clearly not, as asserted by Greenberg (2005:155), because Jones "and others of this period were particularly struck with the resemblances of the verbal [pronominal] endings." The following are, we believe, some of the real underlying reasons for why Jones spoke of "roots" and "forms of grammar":

1. Jones studied Sanskrit with natives of India and they taught him using the Indian grammatical tradition. This tradition held that the language was composed of amalgamations of lexical roots and derivations.
2. His British associates in India who had studied before him and had influenced his thinking had also obtained this orientation to the structure of Sanskrit from the pundits with whom they studied.
3. There was a well-established tradition in European linguistics (derived from Semitic grammars), with which Jones was familiar (see Chapter 2), which saw roots as older and basic. It is certainly not the case that Jones wrote about "roots" and "grammatical form" in this way because he had somehow discovered this aspect of comparative grammar on his own. (Cf. Hoenigswald 1985:65).

Jones was already familiar with the claims made by his predecessors and contemporaries concerning historical linguistics in general. He corresponded with and associated with David Ruhnkenius, Everardus Scheidius, Hendrik Albert Schultens, Henry Thomas Colebrooke, Anne Robert Jacques Turgot, Sir Charles Wilkins, and others concerning such matters and about Sanskrit's relationship to various Indo-European languages, even before he left England for India in 1783. Lord Monboddo (1773–92), with whom Jones had a well-known association, speculated about Greek and Sanskrit relations (though claiming they both got their language and other arts from Egypt) (Cannon 1991:25; mentioned in Chapter 2). Jones had read the Jesuit missionary sources with their occasional report of similarities between Sanskrit, Greek, and Latin (cf. Pons, Cœurdoux, Sassetti [Marcucci 1855]; Cannon 1990:243, Cannon 1991:25; cf. Chapter 2). Jones also was versed in the Scythian hypothesis from his readings of Leibniz and others (Fellman 1975; see Chapter 2), and he mentioned Scythians several times in his anniversary discourses (e.g. Jones 1798:418, 425, 430; 1799a:64, 65; 1799b:368). What he meant by Scythians is not always clear; he sometimes speaks of "Indoscythians," sometimes seeming to equate Scythians directly with "Goths." However, in a letter answering queries from Prince Adam Czartoryski

(Polish general), dated February 17, 1779 – Jones was not posted to India until 1783 – he gave a more direct report of what he understood by "Scythian," i.e. essentially the Scythian hypothesis of his predecessors (in Chapter 2) which lay behind what is understood today as the Indo-European family:

How so many European words crept into the Persian language, I know not with certainty. Procopius, I think, mentions the great intercourse, both in war and peace, between the Persians and the nations in the north of Europe and Asia, whom the ancients knew by the name of Scythians. *Many learned investigators of antiquity are fully persuaded, that a very old and almost primeval language was in use among these northern nations, from which not only the Celtic dialects, but even the Greek and Latin, are derived* [emphasis ours, LC/WP]; in fact we find pater and mêtêr in Persian, nor is thugatêr so far removed from dockter [daughter], or even onoma and nomen from nam, as to make it ridiculous to suppose, *that they sprang from the same root* [emphasis mine (Muller)]. We must confess that these researches are very obscure and uncertain. (Quoted in Muller 1986:17)

Jones' good friend, Dr. Samuel Johnson – something of a linguistic superstar for his day – also influenced Jones' thinking. Johnson's (1755) famous dictionary of English contained an abbreviated genealogical chart of the Germanic languages on the first page of the prefatory "History of the English language," which gives as one possibility that Saxon and Gothic were "descended from some common parent" (Cannon 1991:27; cf. Cannon 1990:59, 242, 245).

Jones knew Nathaniel Halhed, read his books, quoted from them, and was probably influenced by Halhed's Sanskrit–Latin–Greek comparisons (cf. Rocher 1980b). Halhed's (1778) grammar of Bengali, which he sent to Jones, spoke of Sanskrit as the parent of Greek and Latin, and it contained a list of Sanskrit roots and infinitives which, as already mentioned, may have had some impact on Jones' idea of "affinity in the verb roots" (Cannon 1991:26). Jones accepted the grounds on which Halhed established the kinship of Sanskrit with Greek and Latin; he accepted Halhed's view that Sanskrit was very ancient; but he did not accept Halhed's suggestion that Sanskrit might be the parent language (Rocher 1980b:178; cf. also Teignmouth 1805[1804]:172; Mukherjee 1968:93).

While Jones' methods and proposals were for the most part not original with him, nor were they particularly linguistic, he did, nevertheless, leave us with some direct indications of what he considered important for historical linguistic methods. For example, concerning what he regarded as the wrong way to go about things, he was particularly critical of poorly constrained etymological practices. Jones began his essays with a discussion of some methodological issues, as we read in the second paragraph of the famous third discourse:

Etymology has, no doubt, some use in historical researches; but it is a medium of proof so very fallacious, that, where it elucidates one fact, it obscures a thousand; and the more frequently borders on the ridiculous, than leads to any solid conclusions. It rarely carries with it any *internal* power or conviction from a resemblance of sounds or similarity of letters; yet often, where [it] is wholly unassisted by those advantages, it may be indisputably proved by *extrinsick* evidence. We know *à posteriori*, that both *fitz* and *hijo*, by the nature of two several dialects [sic], are derived from *filius*; that *uncle* comes from *avus* . . . which etymologies, though they could not have been demonstrated *à priori*, might serve to confirm, if any such confirmation were necessary, the proofs of a connection between the members of one great empire; but when we derive our *hanger*, or *short pendant sword*, from the *Persian* because ignorant travellers thus mis-spell the word *khanjar*, which, in truth, means a different weapon, or *sandalwood* from the *Greek*, because we suppose that *Sandals* were sometimes made of it, we gain no ground in proving the affinity of nations, and only weaken arguments which might otherwise be firmly supported. (Jones 1798:416)

(See also in other essays, Jones 1799d[1792/1979e]:431, 488.)

Cannon (1990:244) summarizes the criteria which Jones "specified":

(1) The analyst must be "perfectly acquainted" with the relevant languages; (2) the meaning of possible cognates must be identical or nearly identical; (3) vowels cannot be disregarded; (4) there can be no metathesis or consonantal insertions; and (5) phonetic correspondence cannot be postulated solely on articulatory position.

We must conclude that phonology also played a role, if somewhat indirect, among the criteria Jones advocated, and this involved some notion of more tightly constrained phonological correspondences than some others at the time might have applied in their etymological proposals.

Jones also relied on basic vocabulary: "material elements, parts of the body, natural objects and relations, affections of the mind, and other ideas common to the whole race of man" (Jones 1799a:55; cf. Cannon 1991:39–40). However, Jones' use of vocabulary as evidence of family connections was far from modern. Jones was aware of the possibility of borrowing, and that borrowing is especially likely in cultural and technical vocabulary and unlikely in basic vocabulary. However, as revealed in the following quote, he did not recognize that extensive borrowing was possible nor the extent to which even basic vocabulary can be borrowed (see Chapter 6):

No supposition of a mere political or commercial intercourse between the different nations, will account for the *Sanscrit* and *Chaldaic* words, which we find in the old *Persian* tongues; because they are, in the first place, too numerous to have been introduced by such means; and secondly, are not the names of exotic animals, commodities, or arts, but those of material elements, parts of the body, natural objects and relations, affections of the mind, and other ideas common to the whole race of man. (Jones 1799a:54–5)

Here, Jones misperceived the nature of the lexical similarities he found in "Persian" (i.e. Iranian) languages with Sanskrit (genetically related languages, of the Indo-Iranian branch of Indo-European) and with "Chaldaic" (Semitic), where "Persian" and "Chaldaic" are not genetically related, though several Persian languages have borrowed extensively from Arabic. As Pierce (1965:31) pointed out, approximately 15 percent of the 3,000 most common words in Persian are Arabic in origin. As a result, Jones was ready to postulate a genetic affiliation on the basis of large numbers of similar words (similar to mass or multilateral comparison, see Chapter 7), which would have been wrong in the case of Persian and "Chaldaic" (Semitic). On the other hand, this sort of vocabulary comparison was the basis for his conclusion that Romani is descended from Sanskrit (Jones 1799c:8), which happens to be in the right direction, since Romani is an Indic language, but comparison of large numbers of similar words was not sufficient to keep Jones from erring in other cases, as seen above.

Jones (1799c:4) also addressed the relative weights of grammatical versus lexical evidence, in connection with his discussion of Semitic relationships:

That the written *Abyssinian* language, which we call *Ethiopick*, is a dialect of old *Chaldean* [Aramaic], and sister of *Arabick* and *Hebrew*, we know with certainty, not only from the great multitude of identical words, but (which is a far stronger proof) from the similar grammatical arrangement of the several idioms.

(See also Jones 1799a:51.)

We end this discussion of Jones' methods with a citation which reveals just how very different his views of language relationships were from those of today:

Any small family detached in an early age from the parent stock, without letters, with few ideas beyond objects of the first necessity, and consequently with few words, and fixing their abode on a range of mountains, in an island, or even in a wide region before uninhabited, might, in four or five centuries, people their new country, and would necessarily form a new language, with no perceptible traces, perhaps, of that spoken by their ancestors. (Jones 1799c[1791]:2)

Today it is generally accepted that there are no languages "with few words," and that languages do not change so rapidly as to lose all "perceptible traces" of their ancestry in only 400 or 500 years – typically only dialect differences develop in 500 years, and even with 1,000 years' separation, often the question remains of whether one is dealing with divergent dialects of a single language or with separate but very closely related languages.

3.6   Conclusions

In sum, in spite of Jones' relative lack of linguistic interest and the numerous mistakes among his proposed family groupings and his failure to recognize other relationships, he did, nevertheless, in his discussions of methods, deal in some way with the three primary criteria for linguistic genealogy which were common in his day and later: basic vocabulary, correspondences among sounds (if only tangentially), and grammatical agreements. Jones is justifiedly recognized as "one of the greatest polymaths in history" (Murray 1998:3) and "supremely gifted" (Trautmann 1998:93), who "played a significant role in the formation of English Romanticism" (Trautmann 1998:101). Nevertheless, Jones was far from being the initial discoverer of Indo-European relationships or the founder of the comparative method in linguistics. Rather, Jones' thinking was on the whole consistent with the trends of his day. His several errors make it necessary to be extremely cautious concerning the methods which led him to his conclusions. We explore the origins of the comparative method further in the next two chapters.

4   Consolidation of comparative linguistics

The diversity of languages originated in the building of the tower after the deluge . . . There are . . . three sacred languages: Hebrew, Greek and Latin which are the most excellent in the whole world . . . Five varieties of Greek can be distinguished . . . *Koine* . . . Attic . . . Doric . . . Ionic . . . Aeolic. Some say that the Latin language is four languages, that is Ancient, Latin, Roman and Mixed. Ancient . . . [was] used during the reign of Janus and Saturn . . . Latin is the language which the Etruscans and other peoples in Latium spoke during the reign of Latinus and the kings . . . Roman is the language which the Roman people after the banishment of the kings started to use and which the poets Naevius, Plautus, Ennius and Virgil and the orators Gracchus and Cato and Cicero and others made current. Mixed is the language which, after the empire had been enlarged . . . burst into the Roman state together with customs and nations and corrupted the integrity of the word through barbarisms and solecisms.

(Spanish Bishop Isidorus [*c*.560–636]) (Hovdhaugen 1982:110)

4.1   Introduction

There is nothing in the methods used by scholars for establishing language families which distinguishes the pre-Jones era from post-Jones times, though the methods gradually came to be more refined and their employment led increasingly to the establishment of more language families and to further refinements in the language families already accepted. Our goal in this chapter is to chart these developments. We consider the work of influential scholars in the period just after Sir William Jones, several of them contemporaries of Jones, proceeding chronologically, to show how comparative linguistics developed. Our primary concern is with the methods for determining language relationships and classifying languages.

4.2   Kraus

One year after Sir William Jones read his third discourse before the Asiatick Society, but before it was published, Christian Jakob Kraus (1753–1807) (1787), professor of philosophy and *Cameralwissenschaft* [political economics] at the University of Königsberg, surveyed the historical linguistic methods of the day in his review of Pallas (1787). He discussed the methods in an explicit and refined manner, and had a significant impact – Adelung (1815[1806–17]:111) reported that this review made Kraus known "bei dem ganzen Gelehrten Deutschland" [among all of scholarly Germany] (quoted in Kaltz 1985:235). Kraus, like others of his time, saw the purposes of language comparison as contributing to "the whole process of thinking," "enriching our knowledge about psychology," "increasing knowledge of ethnological history," and getting "knowledge about mankind" (Kraus 1985[1787]:240–1). More specifically, Kraus reiterated the importance of investigating grammatical structure instead of lexical items alone:

A similarity of words alone may or may not be indicative of genetic relationship [*Geschlechtsverwandtschaft*]. If, however, the grammatical structure [*Sprachbau*] of two or more languages contained far-reaching similarities, the only possible conclusion is an underlying genealogical relationship of the languages concerned. (Cited by Jankowsky 1972:31; cf. Arens 1955:118–27; Hoenigswald 1974:348)

Only grammatical information could supply guiding principles for a fruitful and adequate word comparison which otherwise would have to be made haphazardly. (Kraus 1985[1787]:247)

Kraus also distinguished between genetically shared traits and borrowing (*gemischte Sprachen*).

Kraus' review shows that even in Jones' day commonly understood methods for getting at family relationships among languages were much more sophisticated than those applied by Jones, so often taken as the premier path-breaker in comparative linguistics.

4.3   Gyarmathi

Sámuel Gyarmathi (1751–1830) wrote the very influential *Affinitas linguae Hungaricae cum linguis Fennicae originis grammatice demonstrata* (1799), which both reflected and led the intellectual concerns of the day. The work was praised by generations of linguists (cf. for example Schleicher 1850). Like Sajnovics (1770) on whose work Gyarmathi leaned (see Chapter 2), Gyarmathi's work too was in Finno-Ugric (see Chapter 6) and pre-dated better-known developments in Indo-European. It was a major contribution to the establishment of the comparative method, that kingpin of historical linguistics so important for, among other things, research aimed at establishing linguistic relationships. Benfey (1869:278) called it "the first truly scientific comparison of languages." Gyarmathi obeyed the methodological requirement advocated by Kraus (1787) that the grammatical structure of a language must be considered in order to establish genetic relationship among languages (cf. Arens 1969:148; Muller 1986:23). This emphasis on grammatical rather than lexical comparisons is reflected in the words *grammatice demonstrata* of his title. His evidence included comparisons of derivational morphology, noun declensions and comparatives, the meaning and form of pronominals (especially possessive suffixes), suffixes generally, conjugations, adverbs (including postpositions), and syntax. While others had also advocated and used grammatical comparisons, Gyarmathi's procedure was the most thorough and consistent to that date (cf. Stipa 1990:214–15). Pedersen (1962[1931]:105) called Gyarmathi's use of inflectional systems for linguistic comparison "the principle which became the lodestar of incipient Indo-European linguistics," i.e. the key to the "comparative grammar" of many subsequent scholars.

Astutely, Gyarmathi warned against arguing for a genetic relationship based on similarities in the syntactic rules of two languages which are actually rules of universal grammar and, as such, cannot be used to establish a genetic relationship:

I do not propose to list here individual syntactic rules and to offer my readers trivial examples of constructions. For it is beyond dispute that there are universal syntactic rules shared by most nations . . . I believe that it is much more appropriate for my demonstration to bring up the kind of examples which are specifically found in Hungarian, Lapp [Saami] and Finnish and which can hardly be expressed at all in Latin, German and other European languages, or can be rendered periphrastically only. (Gyarmathi 1983[1799]:33)[1]

In short, he avoided typologically commonplace traits as evidence of genetic relationship. Gyarmathi's thought on genetic relationships was significantly more sophisticated than Jones' and had far more impact on subsequent research in Indo-European and on the development of the comparative method. His work was cited as a model by subsequent comparativists for decades to come.

4.4   Hervás y Panduro

Lorenzo Hervás y Panduro's (1784–7, 1800–5) outlook and methods were similar to Jones' and less advanced than those of some of his contemporaries, though he was familiar with and was influenced by Sajnovics (1770) (Stipa 1990:158; cf. Chapter 2).[2] Hervás y Panduro's (1784–7:18.174) methods

---

[1] Gyarmathi's earlier *Okoskodva tanító magyar nyelmester* [Hungarian grammar taught rationally] (1794) was the first *grammaire raisonnée* of a non-major language; it followed the Port-Royal model of "universal grammar."

[2] Lorenzo Hervás y Panduro (1735–1809; born in Horcajo, Spain), entered the Jesuit Order in 1749, and resided as a missionary in Mexico until the Order was expelled in 1767. Returning with the Order to Rome, he prepared a catalogue of the world's languages (Hervás y Panduro 1784, 1800–5), which contained many vocabularies and much information, particularly much original information on indigenous languages of the Americas which he had solicited from his missionary colleagues (Del Rey Fajardo 1971:1.190).

included, among other things, also an emphasis on grammatical evidence: "The similarity in structure among languages is a sure indication of their relatedness, even when their vocabularies are very different" (cf. Stipa 1990:158; also Haarmann 1979:45–9, 56). His methods, nevertheless, also relied on phonology and on basic vocabulary. With these sources of evidence, he established several previously unrecognized language families. He also paid attention to the phonological structure of words and to certain correspondences in the consonantism of basic words (Stipa 1990:235).

Hervás y Panduro spoke at length about the three criteria for showing family relationship among languages:

Practical application of the observation of the languages in order to classify the nations . . . The principal characteristic features of each language, as said before, are three: it is appropriate to know its words, its grammatical devices, and its pronunciation . . . Whereas in the languages of the nations, which are observed to be corrupted with foreign words, those [words] should be sought which are primitive [original] which mean things of greater necessity, or of more frequent use or conversation among men [basic vocabulary]. (Hervás y Panduro 1800–5:15–16)[3]

The method and the means that I have kept in view in order to form the distinction, graduation and classification of the nations which are named in this present work, and these are almost all those known in the world, consist principally of the observation of the words of their respective languages, and principally their grammatical devices. This device has been in my observation the principal means which has proved valid for determining the affinity or difference of the known languages and to reduce them to determined classes. (Hervás y Panduro 1800–5:23)[4]

(See also Hervás y Panduro 1800–5:22.)

In spite of Hervás y Panduro's seeming awareness of appropriate methods, he applied them haphazardly, and his view of language families and linguistic change was imprecise. For example, he never grasped that the *lengua matriz*, the original language akin to a "proto-language" from which others descend, would not still survive alongside its daughters, though many others of his time had come to this conclusion (see Hoenigswald 1990a:119–20). Nevertheless, he did correctly identify several language families using these methods, though

---

[3] "Práctica aplicación de la observación de las lenguas para clasificar las naciones . . . Tres son, como ántes se dixo, los principales distintivos característicos de cada lengua: conviene á saber, las palabras de esta, su artificio gramatical, y su pronunciacion . . . Por tanto en los idiomas de las naciones, que se advierte estar corrompidos con palabras forasteras, se deben buscar como primitivas las que signifiquen cosas de la mayor necesidad, ó del mas freqüente uso ó conversacion de los hombres."

[4] "El método y los medios que he tenido á la vista para formar la distincion, graduacion y clasificacion de las naciones que se nombran en la presente obra, y son casi todas las conocidas en el mundo, consisten principalmente en la observacion de las palabras de sus respectivos lenguages, y principalmente del artificio gramatical de ellas. Este artificio ha sido en mi observacion el principal medio de que me he valido para conocer la afinidad ó diferencia de las lenguas conocidas, y reducirlas á determinadas clases."

he usually presented little evidence for his classifications. Sometimes he relied also on geographical and cultural, i.e. non-linguistic, evidence rather than solely on the three linguistic criteria of which he wrote. (For problems with the use of non-linguistic evidence, see Chapter 7.)

Some examples of Hervás y Panduro's successful classifications follow. He determined that several Mayan languages were genetically related: "*Maya* [Yucatec Maya], *Cakchi* [Q'eqchi'], *Poconchi* [Poqomchi'], *Cakchiquil* [Kaqchikel] and *Pocoman* [Poqomam],"[5] but he added "quizá la *maya* sea la matriz" [perhaps Maya (Yucatec) is the mother tongue] (Hervás y Panduro 1800–5:304). His evidence for this family included number words, many other words, and "not a little of their grammatical structure" (Hervás y Panduro 1800–5:304). He also correctly related Otomí, Mazahua, and "Chichimec" (Otomanguean languages; Hervás y Panduro 1800–5:309), and he identified several other family groups in the Americas (see Campbell 1997a: 33–4).

In short, though inconsistent and sometimes flawed in his applications of the generally recognized criteria for linguistic kinship, Hervás y Panduro, nevertheless, did recognize a number of language families utilizing such methods.

4.5   Adelung

Even before Kraus (1787), and before Sir William Jones, Johann Christoph Adelung (1781) had written directly on the criteria for determining language relationships. In 1781 he wrote his *Über den Ursprung der Sprachen und den Bau der Wörter, besonders der Deutschen* [On the origin of languages and the structure of words, particularly of German], in which he utilized both grammar and phonology as criteria for showing kinship with other languages and recognized distinct levels of relationship:

The relationship and distinctness of various languages must . . . be determined entirely according to the theory of the structure of words previously expounded. If two languages are in complete agreement in their root words, inflectional and derivational syllables, that is, apart from individual exceptions, and the difference lies merely in the vowels . . . and related consonants, then they are merely dialects of each other. But if the deviation also relates to sounds other than related principal sounds, and if notable differences are apparent in the inflectional and derivational syllables, then they are merely related languages. One can easily see that this relationship is capable of very many levels, according to whether the agreement or the difference in the relevant component is greater or lesser. If one had two languages, most of whose root-words were similar with regard to both sound and meaning, but whose inflectional and derivational syllables were different, then from that it could be inferred that the two peoples separated before the development of their languages, then from there each must have gone its own way.

---

[5] "Tienen pues afinidad las lenguas *maya, cakchi, poconchi, cakchiquil,* y *pocoman.*"

Completely different types of derivation and inflection and a notable difference in the roots and their meaning eventually produce more or less different languages. (Quoted in Arens 1955:130–1)[6]

A look at Adelung's actual practice (see Adelung 1806:16, 87–90) reveals that he used verb conjugations and especially pronouns as evidence of relationship for several of the language families he proposed. (See also Chapter 8.)

4.6   Vater

Johann Severin Vater (1771–1826), a theologian, orientalist, and linguist, contributed also to comparative linguistics (see Vater 1810; also Adelung and Vater 1816[Adelung 1806–17]).[7] He was in contact with many of the linguistic intellectuals of his day, including Joseph Dobrovsky, Thomas Jefferson, Jernej Kopitar, Wilhem von Humboldt, and of course Johann Christoph Adelung, with whom he worked, completing and publishing portions of Adelung's work posthumously. Vater criticized others (e.g. Barton 1797) for limiting comparisons to vocabulary; he advocated that the key to linguistic affinity included also structure (cf. Greene 1960:515). Volume 3 of Adelung and Vater (1816[Adelung 1806–17]), written mostly by Vater, recognized the genetic relationship among several Mayan languages, including Huastec for the first time (Adelung and Vater 1816[Adelung 1806–17]:5–6, 14–15, 106; see also Vater 1810; Fox 1978:6). Vater presented a list of seventeen mostly correct cognates shared by Poqomchi', Yucatec Maya, and Huastec, together with some structural comparisons (Adelung and Vater 1816[Adelung 1806–17]:22–3). He also presented a list of thirty cognates (again mostly correct) shared by *Mexikanisch* (Nahuatl), Cora, and Tarahumara, again citing also structural similarities (Adelung and

---

6 "Die Verwandschaft und Verschiedenheit mehrerer Sprachen muß . . . ganz nach der im vorigen vorgetragenen Lehre von dem Baue der Wörter bestimmet werden. Wenn zwei Sprachen in ihren Wurzelwörtern, Biegungs- und Ableitungssilben im ganzen, d.i. bis auf einzelne Ausnahmen, miteinander überstimmen und der Unterschied bloß in den Vokalen (an welchen sich die Abweichung immer am ersten äußert) und verwandten Konsonanten bestehet, so sind sie bloße Mundarten voneinander. Betrifft die Abweichung aber auch andere als verwandte Hauptlaute, und finden sich in den Biegungs- und Ableitungssilben merkliche Unterschiede, so sind es bloß verwandte Sprachen. Man siehet leicht, daß diese Verwandschaft sehr vieler Stufen fähig ist, nachdem die Übereinstimmung oder der Unterschied in den angezeigten Bestandteilen größer oder geringer ist. Hätte man zwei Sprachen, deren meiste Wurzelwörter, sowohl dem Laute als der Bedeutung nach, ähnlich, die Biegungs- und Ableitungssilben aber verschieden wären, so würde daraus geschlossen werden können, daß beide Völker sich vor der Ausbildung ihrer Sprachen getrennet, daher denn jedes in derselben seinen eigenen Weg gehen müssen. Ganz verschiedene Arten der Ableitung und Biegung und ein merklicher Unterschied in den Wurzeln und ihrer Bedeutung geben endlich mehr oder weniger verschiedene Sprachen."

7 Vater studied theology from 1790 to 1792 at the University of Jena (where theology and oriental languages were closely connected) and in 1809 became a professor of theology and oriental languages at the University of Königsberg.

Vater 1816[Adelung 1806–17]:87–8) – these are now recognized as members of the Uto-Aztecan family. Thus, Vater, using standard criteria – basic vocabulary and grammatical agreements – was able to recognize genetic relationships among a number of languages.

4.7   Schlegel

Friedrich von Schlegel (1772–1829) (1808) introduced "comparative grammar" as a continuing focus in Indo-European studies, although the term itself (or very similar ones) had been employed earlier, for example by Vater in 1801, August Ferdinand Bernhardi in 1801 and 1803, and by Schlegel's elder brother, August Wilhelm von Schlegel, among others.[8] Schlegel also drew from biology and comparative anatomy, and employed the notion of a family tree, often associated in histories of linguistics with August Schleicher some half century later, though Grimm, Bopp, and others also employed this biological metaphor. "Grammatical structure" was Schlegel's principal criterion of relatedness, i.e. two languages were to be considered truly related when their morphological systems and "the inner [internal] structure" present distinct resemblances. The notion of "inner structure" and the important role it played in linguistic thinking was not original with Schlegel, but rather was a feature of several other scholars' work (see Chapter 8). Schlegel compared case endings, particles, and pronouns, among other things. His historical inquiry into the internal structure of language was followed and further advocated by Jacob Grimm (1822:xvi) and Wilhelm von Humboldt (see Chapter 10; cf. F. Schlegel 1808:6–7, 28; Hoenigswald 1963:4; Jankowsky 1972:53; and Koerner 1990a:13).

4.8   Rask

Rasmus Rask (1787–1832) wove together in his work the historical linguistic currents leading up to his day, seen especially in Rask (1818). He wrote this essay in response to the competition question put forward by the Royal Danish Society of Sciences and Letters, who awarded him the prize for the best answer:

Investigation with historical criticism and illustrating with appropriate examples, from which source the old Scandinavian language may most safely be derived; stating the character of the language and its relations from ancient times and throughout the Middle Ages both to the Nordic and to the Germanic dialects; and *ascertaining the exact principles upon which all derivation and comparison in these idioms should be based.* (Rask 1993[1818]:8; our emphasis, LC/WP)

---

[8] Aarsleff (1982:303–4) argues that Friedrich von Schlegel's book, *Ueber die Sprache und Weisheit der Indier* (1808), except for the initial chapter, depended heavily on Sir William Jones' anniversary discourse.

As formulated, the question called for a declaration of principles of linguistic comparison, and at the same time reveals assumptions of the day concerning relationships among Germanic languages. In response, Rask laid out explicitly "the principles one considers it most proper to follow" (1993[1818]:9), fortunately providing us an exceptionally clear picture of his criteria and of the state of comparative linguistics at the time, and of how he actually applied these methods. He stressed the importance of comparing grammatical structures of languages according to the methods of Sajnovics and Gyarmathi, applying Turgot's (1756) etymological principles to the genetic classification of languages (Rask 1993[1818]:11; cf. Rask 1820; Diderichsen 1974:301) (see Chapter 2). While Rask explicitly used the criteria that others had employed before him, he apparently viewed the task of comparing languages to see if they might be related as involving the investigation of both the individual pieces and especially the overall system, a sort of all-at-once full-scale comparison of the entire form, content, and structure of the languages in question (Rask 1993[1818]:33), or as he put it, "a thorough study of etymology requires considerable insight into all parts and corners of the language in question, as well as an extensive familiarity with the languages related to it" (Rask 1993[1818]:12).

A significant insight of Rask's, usually not addressed by others, is his reasoning concerning a starting point for attempting to detect linguistic relationships. He explained that principles of comparison do not tell us which languages to compare but only "what properties of a language" should be taken into account. His solution to the question of where to start was "comparison involving all surrounding languages" (Rask 1993[1818]:11). Thus, he presents a comparison of Icelandic with Finnic, Eskimo, Basque, and a number of Indo-European languages (though, as we will see directly, in doing this, he was not applying the method of multilateral comparison, rather something more akin to Boas' "areal-typological" comparison, see Campbell 1997a:63–4).

In Rask's methods, grammatical concerns were in high focus, as for example in his *The endings and forms of the Danish grammar explained by derivation from the Icelandic language* (1820a), where he wrote:

The present dissertation contains an attempt at a Danish grammatical etymology and etymological grammar, viz. an explanation of the origin of the endings and forms which are found in present-day Danish . . . Up to now it has been regarded as sufficient to etymologize, treating only the words, but nobody has bothered to find out about the origin of their inflectional features. (Quoted in Diderichsen 1974:296)

As Rask explained, "grammatical agreement is a much more certain sign of kinship or basic unity," rarely subject to borrowing or the other problems lexical comparisons present (Rask 1993[1818]:34). In spite of the prominence given to grammatical evidence, Rask also presented 400 lexical comparisons as proof of a family relationship between "Tracian" (Greek and Latin) and Icelandic (and other Germanic languages, his "Gothic class") (Rask 1993[1818]:283), and he relied on both basic vocabulary – "the most essential, most concrete, most indispensable and very first words" (Rask 1993[1818]:34) – and sound correspondences as evidence. As is well known, Rask discovered the set of sound correspondences which later became known as Grimm's law (Rask 1993[1818]:161–2).[9] Specifically about the role of sound correspondences in establishing family relationships, he declared:

When correspondences are found between two languages in such words [basic vocabulary], in fact so many of them can be deduced for the shifts of letters [sounds] from one to the other, a basic kinship is found between these languages. (Rask 1993[1818]:35)[10]

Rask (1820b) also recognized the genetic relationship between Aleut and Eskimo – one of the earliest applications of comparative methods to Native American languages. Here he stressed "grammatical proof," but also employed lexical comparisons and some phonetic parallels (see Thalbitzer 1922).[11]

---

[9] It is worth mentioning that the standard histories of linguistics fail to point out that Rask's (1993[1818]:161) formulation was not so refined as Grimm's, where Rask spoke of "innumerable changes" in words and noted "the most frequent of these shifts from Greek and Latin to Icelandic." Specifically, he noted $\pi(p)$ to f; $\tau(t)$ to $p(\theta)$; $\chi(k)$ to h; $\beta(b)$ "is mostly kept" (with two apparently onomatopoetic sets of forms, probably non-cognates, compared) – recall, Grimm's law would also have Greek correspondences to Germanic of b to p; $\delta(d)$ to t; $\gamma(g)$ to k; $\phi(p^h < *bh)$ to b; $\theta(t^h < *dh)$ to d; and $\chi(k^h < *gh)$ to g. These are said to be "frequent, especially at the beginning of words," but Rask (1993[1818]:162) also pointed out other correspondences "in the middle and after a vowel" which later would come to be understood as examples of Verner's law, k to g, and t to d (as in *pater/fadir* 'father' and *frater/bródir* 'brother').

[10] Pedersen (1983[1916]:35–6) also cited this quotation from Rask, summarizing Rask's methods in the following way:

In his [Rask's 1818] *Undersøgelse* . . . he points, on pp. 34–35, quite clearly to the inflectional system as a sign of linguistic kinship. Subsequently, however, on pp. 35–36, he adds a remark which shows that he was completely aware of the fact that also another firm methodological basis exists in addition to the inflectional system: "When, in the most essential, most carnal, most indispensable and original words [basic vocabulary], the foundation of the language, there are similarities between two languages, and then a sufficient number to allow for the formulation of rules for the changes of letters from the one to the other, then there is a basic kinship between these languages."

[11] It should be pointed out that Rask's view of genetic relationship among languages does not seem to correspond fully to that of later comparative linguistics in that Rask seems not to have distinguished between the notion of origin or source of a language and degrees of relationship, some sister languages being more closely related than others. Thus he often seems to speak about distance of relationship and source of language at the same time as related notions, as for example, in speaking of "a true, albeit very distant, kinship between these languages [Armenian and 'Thracian' (Greek and Latin)], although this class certainly is much too remote to be considered as the source of the Tracian or Gothic class" (Rask 1993[1818]:286). He says of his Germanic ("Gothic class") and Slavic comparisons that "what was listed here undoubtedly already fully entitles us to the conclusion that an essential kinship obtains between the Slavic and the Gothic language class . . . However, . . . the agreement between the vocabulary of both also perhaps [is] too small to assume one to have sprung from the other" (Rask 1993[1818]:136).

As Rask's writings show, he adeptly wielded the three principal criteria, grammatical agreements, sound correspondences, and basic vocabulary, in his attempts to show languages were related to one another. He benefited from the methods of his day, but also refined them considerably.

Just after erroneously claiming that Sir William Jones employed multilateral comparison as his principal method (Chapter 3), Greenberg (1991:127), went on to claim:

> Rask is the linguist of the pioneer period of comparative linguistics that followed Jones who seems to have most clearly articulated this point [multilateral comparison]. Diderichsen (1974:297) paraphrases Rask as follows: "The more languages and dialects you take into the comparison, the more gaps you are able to fill by intermediate forms." Diderichsen goes on to quote one of Rask's letters, probably written in 1809 . . ., in which he states, "that I discovered such a fundamental coherence between so distant languages (Greek, Latin, Gothic, Icelandic, German) led me to investigate so many tongues as time would allow."

The quote from Diderichsen, however, is not about multilateral comparison of lexical items, but rather about inflectional endings exhibited in Indo-European languages already known to be related. The fuller passage from Diderichsen begins:

> No doubt, at this early stage of his studies Rask was struck by the *close accordance*, first pointed out by Stiernhielm and Ihre, *between some inflectional endings* of Gothic and Latin; but during his work with Icelandic grammar (1805–9) he was aware that the *congruity between the systems* of Germanic, Greek, Latin, and Romance languages was almost perfect when the apparent differences were explained by the new methods of *etymological grammar*: the more languages and dialects you took into consideration, the more gaps [in the inflectional paradigms!] you were able to fill out by intermediate forms. (Diderichsen 1974:297; our emphasis, LC/WP)

Diderichsen (1974:297) continues in this passage on the topic of inflectional endings and grammatical paradigms, not on multilateral comparison, and it is in this context that the mention of many "tongues" comes up:

> "I resolved to go through as many languages as possible, and make an abridgement of each recast according to my own principles . . . That I discovered such a fundamental coherence [*en sådan Grundsammenhaeng*] between so distant languages (Greek, Latin, Gothic, Icelandic, German) led me to investigate so many European tongues as time would allow," he writes in a letter, probably from 1809.

That is, Rask determined to examine as many Indo-European languages as possible in order to place them within his grammatical abridgements to see correspondences in their inflectional morphology. There is a very important difference between what Greenberg reported and what Rask (and Diderichsen) actually said. Greenberg's reading has Rask intending to "investigate as many tongues as possible," where Rask declared that grammatical coherence among such "distant[ly related] languages" as Greek, Latin, Gothic, Icelandic, and German led him to want to "investigate so many *European* tongues" as he could, i.e. Indo-European languages, which were already seen to be related and could therefore contribute to the task of filling in Indo-European grammar. This is clear in the next line from Diderichsen (1974:127–8):

> The point of departure of this rearrangement of grammars was Rask's observation that the distinction between the 'strong' and the 'weak' conjugations (as Grimm called them) was common to Icelandic (and the younger Scandinavian languages), Gothic, German, English, Dutch; namely, all the Germanic languages . . . By highly acute reinterpretation of the structure of the inflectional forms of Latin and Greek he succeeded in demonstrating that the grammars of these languages also might be rearranged into exactly the same system . . . and that the endings of the paradigms in question matched on all essential points.

In fact, Rask seems to have explicitly opposed the kind of lexical inspection inherent to multilateral comparison (see Chapters 7 and 8):

> Let us, however, bear in mind how very easily, among the innumerable words of one language, not to speak of those of several related languages, two words may happen to be found which look a lot alike without being in the very least related. (Rask 1993[1818]:14)

In short, Rask did not use multilateral comparison to detect genetic relationships, but rather employed fairly standard criteria to work out aspects of Indo-European relationships. Rask's methods represent a sound application of comparative linguistic techniques which depended on the three by-now well-known criteria, about which Rask was extremely well informed and was adept in using.

Rask also exercised an astute resistance to the evolutionary typology preferred by some in his day, as seen in his discussion of similar ideas applied to Indo-European languages. In a context in which Rask is doubting the status of Persian and Sanskrit, he is recommending that the question be left open for further study; he says:

> I know Frank's opinion according to which the more complex languages should be explained from the simpler, and thus Sanskrit derived from Persian; but by this rule Latin should be derived from French, Icelandic from Danish, etc., which is contrary to the usual course of nature in the change of human language. (Rask 1993[1818]:iii)

Already in 1806–7 (before the famous typological statements of Schlegel, Bopp, and others; see Poser and Campbell 1992), Rask had contrasted the Dutch creole of the Danish West Indies, which lacked inflections, with Eskimo (Inuit) of Greenland, which was highly inflected. He observed that although the creole represented (according to this view) the last stage of evolution from Greek through Gothic and beyond to the modern language, it had the character attributed to the most primitive stage of language (according to the evolutionary typology of the day). Conversely, Eskimo had a highly complicated system of derivation and inflection, said to represent an advanced type of language, in spite of the assumed "primitiveness" of Eskimo culture (Diderichsen 1974:295). (The full impact of the evolutionary views against which Rask wrote will become apparent in Chapter 8.)

4.9   Grimm

Jacob Grimm (1785–1863) (1822), of Grimm Brothers' fairytale fame, is well known both for phonological and grammatical comparisons – one of the largest of the linguistic luminaries in the past; Delbrück (1989[1880]:33) called him "the creator of historical grammar." In the second edition of his *Deutsche Grammatik* (1822) Grimm included a section "Von den Buchstaben" [On the letters], inspired by Rask's formulation of Indo-European sound correspondences. Grimm spoke of the regular permutation of "letters" between languages, and stressed the regularity of phonological correspondences between related languages and between successive states of the same language (though this regularity did not exclude some exceptions). His formulation of this for Germanic was later to be called "Grimm's law." He recognized the importance of sound correspondences as evidence of genetic affinity. Thus, he said of his law that it had "important consequences for the history of the language and the validity of etymology", and also *"provided sufficient evidence for the kinship of the languages involved"* (our emphasis, LC/WP; quoted in Davies 1992:161).

4.10   Humboldt

Wilhelm von Humboldt (1767–1835) is somewhat difficult to situate chronologically, since his career spanned the lives (and ideas) of various scholars usually thought of as belonging to different periods. For example, some influential contemporaries with whom Humboldt had contact were: Johan Christoph Adelung (1732–1806), Sir William Jones (1746–94), Peter Stephen Duponceau (1760–1844), Friedrich von Schlegel (1772–1829), John Pickering (1777–1846), Jacob Grimm (1785–1863), Rasmus Rask (1787–1832), and Franz Bopp (1791–1867). Humboldt's life also overlapped in time that of Sajnovics (1733–85), Gyarmathi (1751–1830), and Pott (1802–87), among others. Given such contacts, it is easy to see how ideas about comparative grammar could have come to be widely shared. Humboldt's own outlook appears to have changed also over the span of his life, and the generally recognized opaque nature of his writings does not lend itself to ready understanding of his overall views or the methods he preferred.

Humboldt's methodology concerning language genealogy was complex, but included an emphasis on grammar (morphosyntax):

In an Essay which was read to the Asiatic Society in 1828 (but published in 1830), and in an outstanding explanation of the aims and methods of comparative linguistics, Humboldt (1903–36:VI 76–84) argued that even the *fundamental vocabulary* cannot be guaranteed against the intrusion of foreign elements, *warned against any comparison based exclusively on lexicon*, and finally maintained that "*if two languages . . . exhibit grammatical forms which are identical in arrangement, and have a close analogy [correspondence] in their sounds, we have an incontestable proof that these two languages belong to the same family.*" (Davies 1975:627–8; our emphasis, LC/WP)

Clearly, Humboldt understood and recommended the three principal sources of evidence of relationship, basic vocabulary, sound correspondences, and grammatical agreements. Humboldt (1822, 1836) also emphasized typology and aspects of universal grammar, distinguishing between genetic and typological classification (see Chapter 8). His approach to genetic affinity helps to explain the welding of philosophical/typological/grammatical concerns (treated in Chapter 8) with the more lexically based considerations often found in the literature of the time. As Robins (1990:97) explains this:

Comparison of the semantic content of grammatical classes and categories (e.g. whether the verbs of a language have a passive voice), the means whereby grammatical distinctions are maintained (e.g. affixes, vowel alternations, etc.), and the actual inflectional morphs themselves . . . and it was this last that carried the greatest weight in historical affiliation. This clarifies Friedrich Schlegel's . . . reference to "die innere Struktur der Sprachen oder die vergleichende Grammatik" [the inner structure of languages or comparative grammar](1808:28). But it was still comparative grammar, the comparison of inflectional morphs, rather than general lexical etymologies, that constituted the key, in Humboldt's eyes, to genetic relations.

(Cf. also Hoenigswald 1990a:127.)

Humboldt maintained that the recovery of the "different possibilities of historical connection among languages" involved generalizations concerning the role of grammatical type, words, and affixes (Hoenigswald 1974:350). For him, "the science of languages is the history of progress and evolution of the human mind" (quoted in Aarsleff 1988:lxv); thus, "the *comparative study of languages* . . . loses all higher interest if it does not cleave to the point at which language is connected with the shaping of the *nation's mental power*" (Humboldt 1988[1836–9]:21).

Humboldt's clearest work on genetic relationships, perhaps his only real one, is that published just after his death in his *Kawi-Sprache* (Humboldt 1836–9), where he demonstrated some Austronesian relationships via standard comparative linguistic techniques. This work is very relevant to issues of distinguishing material shared due to contact from that due to common inheritance, since the Kawi language is an old literary and sacred language of Java, Austronesian in structure, but with a high number of Sanskrit loans in its vocabulary. Humboldt emphasized grammatical structure as the criterion of linguistic affinity and determined that Kawi was "Malayan" (Austronesian) in spite of the vocabulary of Sanskrit origin it contains (Aarsleff 1988:xii). Recall, Jones had been misled in this regard, concluding that Sanskrit was the parent of this and many other island languages (Jones 1799c:12; see Chapter 3). (See Chapters 6 and 8.)

4.11   Bopp

Franz Bopp (1791–1867) was arguably the first to study language primarily for its own sake and not just as a tool of literature or history (cf. Davies 1992:161). Bopp's influence in the development of historical linguistics and in Indo-European studies was monumental. Delbrück (1989[1880]:1) calls him "the founder of comparative philology," and Max Müller (1861:170–1) asserted that Bopp's (1833–52) work "will form for ever the safe and solid foundation of comparative philology."[12] Bopp is very often called the father/founder of comparative linguistics (cf. Watkins 1995:58). Given his significance in the history of linguistics, it is important to assess the successes and failures of the language classifications he proposed for the methodological lessons they provide us relevant for today's needs.

While Bopp's contribution to establishing the Indo-European family and to the character of comparative linguistics is not to be underestimated, he, like Jones, committed some serious blunders, and understanding them can help us today to avoid similar mistakes. Perhaps Jones' mistakes could be excused, given that comparative linguistics was in its infancy and since Jones was not really interested in language history for its own sake, and thus relied also on other sources of information beyond mere linguistic ones – though perhaps it is more difficult to absolve him for forcing his conclusions to fit a preconceived Mosaic mold. However, Bopp has no such excuse, given that he is routinely cited as representing a more mature stage of comparative grammar. All this notwithstanding, Bopp is scarcely unanimously recognized as the founder of the comparative method. In fact, that honor has also been credited to several others (listed in Chapter 2). Bopp himself acknowledged the influence of his predecessors' methods on his own work, in particular Gyarmathi and members

---

[12] Greenberg (2000b:164), recognizing earlier comparative work in Finno-Ugric, sees Bopp's 1816 monograph as "the beginning of comparative linguistics in relation to Indo-European."

of the Dutch school (see Chapter 2), and Pedersen (1962[1931]:237) points out Bopp's use of the works of Rask, Grimm, Dobrovský, and other earlier scholars. Greenberg, once again, felt that Bopp's methods were similar to his own:

It is against the background of the common traits of these languages [Sanskrit, Greek, Latin, and Germanic; here Greenberg likening Bopp's procedure to his own multilateral comparison] that he [Bopp] successively added Lithuanian (1833), Celtic and Slavic (1839), Albanian (1855), and Armenian (1857) . . . All this occurred, of course, before linguists recognized the principles of regular sound change and of phonetic correspondences. (Greenberg 1991:127; cf. 1996b:534)

However, as seen in previous chapters, linguists before Bopp did utilize sound correspondences, and Bopp himself recognized the value of sound correspondences in hypotheses of linguistic genealogy, as well as for establishing etymologies in already recognized language families. As Wells (1979:41) affirms, "Grimm, Pott, Diez, and Schleicher all taught the doctrine of the regularity of sound-change; but not until the next stage, the Neogrammarians, was regularity taken to mean exceptionlessness." Delbrück (1989[1880]:17–24) provided an extended discussion of the use of "physical and mechanical laws" in Bopp's (1833–52) "Comparative Grammar." He reported that "Bopp did ascribe infallibility to a phonetic law [=regularity] in single cases, where the facts seemed to prompt it, but by no means as a general rule . . . he granted to language the freedom of occasionally emancipating itself from the existing laws" (Delbrück 1989[1880]:23).

Greenberg repeated his high praise of Bopp's methods in a number of publications and likened them to his multilateral comparison. This raises two questions: (1) Were Bopp's methods in fact similar to Greenberg's, and (2) were Bopp's methods successful?

With respect to the second question, Greenberg should have been sobered by the fact that in 1841, between Bopp's great and highly influential *Vergleichende Grammatik* [Comparative grammar] (1833; cf. also Bopp 1816) and his "Albanian proof" (Bopp 1854) – cited approvingly by Greenberg (1987:32) –, Bopp used the same methods to argue, erroneously, for a relationship between Indo-European and Malayo-Polynesian in *Über die Verwandtschaft der malayisch-polynesichen Sprachen mit den indisch-europäischen* [On the relationship of the Malayo-Polynesian languages with Indo-European] (Bopp 1841; cf. also 1842).[13] Far from representing the Indo-Europeanist norm, Indo-European scholars generally considered this work a disaster, although Bopp's evidence

[13] Bopp was not entirely alone in seeing remoter connections for these languages. Court de Gébelin (1776[1773–82]) joined all of these together, also implicating the Phoenicians, and hypothesizing that peopling of the Americas may have come via the South Seas and southern Asia (Auroux and Boes 1981:45); and, as seen in Chapter 3, Sir William Jones had also grouped Malayo-Polynesian and Indo-European together.

included many look-alikes from basic vocabulary (1841:7–78), some morphological resemblances, and similarities in the pronoun systems (1841:79–111),
assembled as in a kind of multilateral comparison. However, this was not
Bopp's only blunder; he also erroneously argued for a relationship between
Indo-European and Georgian (a member of the Kartvelian family), using such
methods and relying on similar arguments (Bopp 1846).

That is, once again methods praised by Greenberg – because he perceives
them to be similar to his own – failed, as did Jones' methods (Chapter 3),
to distinguish genetically related languages (here Indo-European) from others
(e.g. Malayo-Polynesian, Georgian). One wonders why these lessons of history,
Bopp's and Jones' follies, did not have a more salutary influence.[14]

Bopp's failure in these cases was well known and did not escape censure
from other historical linguists of the time. Sayce (1875:67) attributed Bopp's
error in attempting to "attach the Polynesian idioms to the Aryan family" to "the
enthusiasm of a new discovery." Greenberg quoted Delbrück's (1880:121–2)
report on Bopp's methods approvingly:

It was proved [*erwiesen*] by [Franz] Bopp and others that the so-called Indo-
European languages are related. The proof [*Beweis*] was produced by juxtaposing
[*Nebeneinanderstellung*] words and forms of similar meaning. (Greenberg 1987:30)

Nevertheless, it is instructive to juxtapose this with Delbrück's (1880:20–5,
1989[1880]:23–8) own sharp criticism of the methods which Bopp used in his
comparison of Malayo-Polynesian (Austronesian) with Indo-European:

This want of method in Bopp's investigations . . . became very conspicuous, however,
when Bopp undertook to introduce into his comparison languages whose relationship
to our linguistic branch [Indo-European] was not established – I refer to the Malay-
Polynesian. I think it is now universally acknowledged by philologists that these languages have nothing in common with the Sanskritic languages [Indo-Aryan], but Bopp
was under the impression that they stood in a daughterly relation to the Sanskrit, and
attempted to establish this relationship in the same way as he had that of Indo-European

---

[14] Bopp is not the only early Indo-Europeanist to have erred in linguistic classification with methods
such as Greenberg's. Alexander Murray (1823:143), for example, compared basic vocabulary
(father, mother, brother, man, heart, etc.) in English, Celtic, Welsh, German, Slavic, Finnish,
Persian, and Sanskrit, concluding from the look-alikes that "the coincidence among the words
of the above list is obvious, and cannot be accidental", that these were "originally a common and
single stock" (1823:4). While the issue of whether Uralic (the family to which Finnish belongs)
and Indo-European (to which the other languages in Murray's list belong) are ultimately related
remains controversial, Murray did not intend Finnish as such a distant relative, but rather as a
member on the same level with the other Indo-European languages he cited.

Interestingly, Murray's method is much like Greenberg's (1987:24) of multilateral comparison in which it is suggested that Finnish and its two relatives in the chart stand out immediately
as distinct from the other Indo-European languages. It will be noted that Murray's data have
two spurious forms (a common complaint about Greenberg's data, see Chapter 7) which make
Finnish seem more similar to Indo-European than it really is, i.e. Finnish *atkia* 'father' (actually
isä) and *mori* 'man' (actually *mies*).

languages in his Comparative Grammar – so far, that is, as was permitted by the character of these tongues, which "have undergone a total dissolution of their original structure." Here, also, he formed no table of phonetic correspondences, but compared words which seemed to him identical (e.g. numbers), and tried to account for the phonetic changes in each separate instance. (Delbrück 1989[1880]:24; cf. 1880:23)

Delbrück was very explicit in his explanation of why Bopp's Malayo-Polynesian-Indo-European proposal did not work – for lack of sound correspondence tables (*Lautentsprechungstabellen*). He criticized the carelessness of Bopp's comparisons (1880:24–5), concluding:

Nor is it wholly correct that Bopp, as is often asserted, invented the *method* of linguistic comparison [the comparative method]. Bopp is incomparable in his power of recognizing the former unity of what has been separated, but he has introduced no methodic art which could be learned from him in turn. Indeed, his weak point lies on just this methodic side, as has been shown above. (Delbrück 1989[1880]:26; cf. 1880:25)

Georg von der Gabelentz (1891:164–8) was especially critical of Bopp's work; we cite here just the beginning and the end of his four-page rant on the matter:

It is terribly tempting to wander about in the world of languages comparing vocabulary [words] aimlessly and then to bestow upon science a series of newly discovered relationships. *Terribly many stupidities result from this; for everywhere unmethodical minds are the most pressing discoverers.* He who, endowed with a good memory for words, has gone through a couple of dozen languages from different parts of the earth, – he need not at all to have studied them –, he meets with approval everywhere. And if he records them, investigates them prudently, tests whether the signs prove reliable, then he does only what is right. Logically consistent thought alone belongs here, and where it is not lacking from the outset, then it gladly gets lost in the fever of the joy of discovery. So it was, as we saw, for the great Bopp, when he tried to assign Caucasian and Malaysian languages to the Indo-European language family. Fate worked curiously. It was as though he had doubly to prove the correctness of his principles, first positively through his magnificent major work, which is based on them, then, negatively, by coming to fault as soon as he was unfaithful to them . . .

Languages are different because sound change has taken different paths. But it has gone its way consistently hither and thither; that is why order reigns in the diversity, not arbitrariness. *Language comparison without comparison of sounds is thoughtless nonsense.* (our emphasis, LC/WP)[15]

---

15 "Es ist schrecklich verführisch, in der Sprachenwelt umherzuschwärmen, drauf los Vocabeln zu vergleichen und dann die Wissenschaft mit einer Reihe neu entdeckter Verwandschaften zu beglücken. *Es kommen auch schrecklich viele Dummheiten dabei heraus; denn allerwaert sind unmethodische Köpfe die vordringlichsten Entdecker.* Wer mit einem guten Wortgedächtnisse begabt ein paar Dutzend Sprachen verschiedener Erdtheile durchgenommen hat, – studirt braucht er sie gar nicht zu haben, – der findet überall Anklänge. Und wenn er sie aufzeichnet, ihnen nachgeht, verständig ausprobirt, ob sich die Anzeichen bewähren: so thut er nur was recht ist. Allein dazu gehört folgerich richtiges Denken, und wo das nicht von Hause aus fehlt, da kommt es gern im Taumel der Entdeckungslust abhanden. So ging es, wie wir sahen, dem grossen

Holger Pedersen's (1983[1916]) response to Bopp (1841, 1842) was no less critical:

As it happens, he [Bopp] specializes in and concentrates on Indo-European. His ventures outside this are unfortunate . . . The attempt to establish cognation between Austronesian (Malayo-Polynesian) and Indoeuropean yielded a valuable lesson: The comparative method, or at least Bopp's version of it, could not distinguish between sound and unsound applications. (Pedersen 1983[1916]:32)

Precisely because Bopp had absolutely no other Adriadne-thread in the labyrinth of the linguistic world than the observation of agreement in the inflectional system, precisely for this reason he was bound to commit frightful acts once this Ariadne-thread came to an end; his undertakings in the area of the Malay-Polynesian languages are no chance misfortunes. (Pedersen 1983[1916]:50)

So how do we account for the fact that the methods employed by Jones and Bopp to establish aspects of Indo-European also permitted such erroneous proposals of genetic relationship? Obvious close relationships can often be detected (though not necessarily proven) even with flawed methods, such as those employed by Jones and Bopp for Indo-European or those employed by John Wesley Powell (1891) in his famous classification of American Indian languages, based on sheer visual inspection of short word lists. At issue is not how to get a handle on close and relatively clear relationships, but rather how to be able to frame plausible hypotheses of family relationships and evaluate them for languages which are only distantly related and therefore whose relationship is not obvious, and to distinguish these from languages that cannot be shown to be related. Since Powell (1891) grouped mostly only obviously related languages, his inspection of short lexical lists was sufficient to detect many family groupings which have stood the test of time (though he also erred in several instances; see Campbell 1997a:57–66). However, today no one applauds Powell's methods, which failed for more distant relationships. We must assess the similarities in a potential case of distantly related languages also against the possibility that the shared features may be similar due to non-genetic factors, e.g. to chance, borrowing, onomatopoeia, sound symbolism, universals, etc. That is, success in relating languages depends on the nature of the languages to be compared, i.e. the remoteness of the relationship and the amount of change that may have

Bopp, da er es versuchte, kaukasische und malaische Sprachen dem indogermanischen Verwandtschaftskreise zu zuweisen. Das Schicksal hatte es merkwürdig gefügt. Es war, als hätte er die Richtigkeit seiner Grundsätze doppelt beweisen sollen, erst positiv durch sein grossartiges Hauptwerk, das auf ihnen beruht, – dann negative, indem er zu Schaden kam, sobald er ihnen untreu wurde . . . (von der Gabelentz 1891:164)

Die Sprachen sind verschieden, denn die Lautentwicklung hat verschiedene Wege eingeschlagen. Hüben und drüben aber ist sie ihre Wege folgrichtig gegangen; darum herrscht in den Verschiedenheiten Ordnung, nicht Willkür. *Sprachvergleichung ohne Lautvergleichung ist gedankenlose Spielerei.*" (von der Gabelentz 1891:168)

taken place making detection of cognate material difficult, and on the validity of the methods employed. Detecting a genetic relationship among closely related languages is not difficult. This explains why Jones and Bopp could see certain Indo-European relationships and yet at the same time fail to see others, and even seriously err by including some non-Indo-European languages in their Indo-European groupings.

4.12   Schleicher

We move on now to August Schleicher (1821–68), skipping over several other scholars whose influence was substantial. Sound correspondences played a strong role in Schleicher's work (and in that of other linguists of the time), before the official Neogrammarian declaration that "sound laws suffer no exceptions." Pedersen (1983[1916]:63) affirmed that Schleicher (and Curtius) "announce[d] as their platform 'strengste Beobachtung der Lautgesetze' [strictest observance of the sound laws], 'strenges Festhalten an den Lautgesetzen' [strict adherence to sound laws]." Similarly, Hoenigswald (1963:6) reports that Schleicher "was one of the first in placing phonology at the center of his work" and that "his view of grammar was much more refined than that of Jones, Schlegel, and Bopp."[16]

However, notwithstanding the praise or criticism of Schleicher for his more conventional methods, Schleicher (like Jones and Bopp) was also guilty of some classificatory folly. We quote an example:

Tatar possesses a not insignificant number of elements which are also found in Indo-European, even though Tatar belongs to the agglutinating class of languages, thus it is in principle fully distinct from Indo-European. The known languages of this family are Manchu, Mongolian, Turkish, Hungarian, Finnish, Lappish [Saami] and Estonian with their dialects. *Their relationship to each other is completely obvious.* (Schleicher 1848:108; our emphasis, LC/WP)[17]

Schleicher's assertion that a controversial relationship is "completely obvious" has a familiar ring (cf. Greenberg 1949a:79, 81, 1955:1; Murray 1823:143). However, the languages Schleicher grouped are not all demonstrably related to one another. First, most prominent "Altaicists" have abandoned the Altaic

---

[16] In this case, since Greenberg (2005:157–8) perceived Schleicher's methods as more akin to those used by linguists today, and since Greenberg saw no need for sound correspondences in establishing language relationships, he was more critical, remarking that Schleicher's reconstruction of Indo-European phonology and morphology are now rejected.

[17] "Das Tatarische besitzt ein nicht ganz unbedeutendes Quantum von Elementen, die sich im Indogermanischen wiederfinden, während doch das Tatarisch zur agglutinirenden Sprachclasse gehört, im Principe also völlig verschieden von Indogermanischen ist. Die bekannten Sprachen dieses Stammes sind das Mandschu, Mongolische, Türkische, Magyarische, Finnische, Lappische und Estnische mit ihren Dialecten. *Ihre Verwandtschaft unter einander ist ganz augenfällig . . .*"

hypothesis (which would include the Manchu, Mongolian, and Turkish mentioned here by Schleicher) (see Chapter 9). Second, the broader Ural-Altaic hypothesis (which would group all the languages mentioned here by Schleicher) is also rejected (again, see Chapter 9). For example, Austerlitz (1983:54–5) informs us of the Ural-Altaic hypothesis that:

It has thrived, especially outside the circle of practitioners of Uralic and Altaic studies . . . its main habitat is the domain of encyclopaedias and handbooks, where it has been and still is being kept alive . . . But the main difficulty with Altaic is Altaic itself: it is questionable whether *it* is a family . . . To sum up: The Ural-Altaic hypothesis, historically the first attempt to link Uralic to another language family, has done more harm than good because (1) it is founded more on typological resemblances than on systematic grammatical and lexical correspondences and (2) the Altaic hypothesis itself is questionable.

While it is not possible to prove conclusively that these languages (or any two languages, for that matter) are not related, it is clear that the extant evidence does not adequately support the hypothesis asserted as "obvious" by Schleicher (details in Chapter 9).

Schleicher's error was in relying on typological notions, the assumed genetic relationship among the agglutinating type languages, rather than following the otherwise valid techniques employed within Indo-European studies. Views on typology did play an important part in the methodological considerations many used in arriving at decisions about family relationships, as seen here in the case of Schleicher's erroneous genetic grouping of the agglutinating languages. In fact, debate over this issue became central in the Neogrammarian controversy (below). The impact of such typologies as Schleicher's and others' is treated in depth in Chapter 8.

4.13   Neogrammarians and their contemporaries

Greenberg (2005:158) asserted, "as to how one actually classifies languages, both the Neogrammarians and their opponents say almost nothing," and "the only one of the leading Neogrammarians, to my knowledge, who seriously considered the problem of classification was Anton [*sic*, read "Berthold"] Delbrück, Brugmann's collaborator on the famous *Grundriss*" (Greenberg 1996a:132; see also 2005:159). He asserted further that "statements by Neogrammarians about how to do classification are virtually never found in the literature of this period. The citation from Delbrück (1880:121–2) is the only one I could find" (Greenberg 2005:163). The citation mentioned was:

My starting point is that specific result of comparative linguistics that is not in doubt and cannot be in doubt. It was proved [erwiesen] by Bopp and others that the so-called Indo-European languages were related. The proof [Beweis] was produced by juxtaposing

[Nebeneinanderstellung] words and forms of similar meaning. When one considers that in these languages the formation of the inflectional forms of the verb, noun and pronoun agrees in essentials and likewise that an extraordinary number of inflected words agree in their lexical parts, the assumption of chance agreement must appear absurd. (Quoted in Greenberg 2005:158–9)[18]

In face of the successes and failures of their predecessors, we are led to ask, what did Neogrammarians and others of their time have to say about methods for establishing language families and about the classification of languages? What we find is that they had much to say that is relevant on how to classify languages, and we can learn from their methods and from their statements about their methods.

4.13.1   Anonymous (1866), Müller (1861), and Garnett (1894[1874])

We begin with a telling report from just prior to the Neogrammarian procla-mations. The state-of-the-art review of comparative philology by an unnamed contributor in the October 1866 *Quarterly Review* (119:211–12) is illuminating with respect to what was considered methodologically proper at that moment:

The mass of Sanscrit MSS. brought over to Europe furnished the missing key to the students of comparative philology . . . [Sanskrit and Greek] were members of a great family of languages . . . It was then seen that comparative grammar was a true science, reposing upon sound foundations, and strictly conformed to the inductive method; that the elemental sounds may be classified according to the very organism of our speech and *their variations and interchanges explained by fixed laws; that thus a test is furnished to distinguish between accidental resemblances of words and the real affinities which depend on fixed laws; and above all, that the surest indication of a family connection between languages is furnished by the permanent structure of their grammar.* Such were the leading principles of the new school of comparative philology, taught by A. von Schlegel, by Lassen, by the brothers Grimm, and by Pott, and embodied in the great "Comparative Grammar" of Bopp [120:176]. (Cannon 1991:34–5; our emphasis, LC/WP)

This is by no means an anomaly for its times, as Max Müller's (1861:174) extremely well-known and popular lectures reveal, where he confirms this view of how to establish language relationships:

Whereas, for establishing in a general way the common origin of certain languages, a comparison of numerals, pronouns, prepositions, adverbs, and the most essential nouns and verbs, has been sufficient, it was soon found that a more accurate standard was required for measuring the more minute degrees of relationship. Such a standard was supplied by Comparative Grammar; that is to say, by an intercomparison of the gram-matical forms of languages supposed to be related to each other; such intercomparison being carried out according to certain laws which regulate the phonetic changes of letters [sounds].

---

[18] We could not find this quote on the pages Greenberg cited.

We also have from James Garnett (1894:xxii), citing an 1874 address: "The reign of [sound] law in the philological world has come to be recognized ... and he who would etymologize regardless of it, is no longer entitled to a hearing." (See also Giles 1895.)

4.13.2 Whitney

From William Dwight Whitney (1887[1867]:246), a contemporary of the Neogrammarians and the most famous American linguist of his day, we have rather pointed criticism of methods which compare superficial vocabulary similarities:

Upon how narrow and imperfect a basis those comparative philologists build who are content with a facile setting side by side of words; whose materials are simple vocabularies, longer or shorter, of terms representing common ideas ... *surface collation without genetic analysis, is but a travesty of the methods of comparative philology.* (Quoted in Trumbull 1869:58–9; our emphasis, LC/WP)

4.13.3 Sayce

Archibald H. Sayce (1874) stated explicitly the three by now well-known criteria for establishing family relationships, including a clear statement of the importance of sound correspondences:

Now our facts [sources of evidence], scientifically considered, are, firstly, similarity of general structure in language; secondly, similarity of grammar both in form and meaning; and thirdly, a regular and uniform interchange of phonetic sounds between the languages we are comparing. When once a sufficient number of instances have shown that a certain letter [sound] in one dialect [language] is replaced by a certain other letter [sound] in another dialect [language], we must never admit any violation of the rules unless it can be explained by the action of subordinate laws; and the explanation of these interchanges of sound and their mutual relationship is part of the duties of philology. (Sayce 1874:102–3)

Nothing is more deceptive and dangerous, it is agreed on all hands, than the comparison of words only, unless we are guided by rules like Grimm's law, more especially when the original meaning of the words is vague and obscure. In order that our conclusions shall be sound, we must begin by the comparison of the grammar. (Sayce 1874:107)

4.13.4 Hovelacque

Abel Hovelacque (1877) provided the following revealing discussion of "how to recognise linguistic affinities," with emphasis on grammatical arguments:

Many writers but indifferently acquainted with the science of language, will often unhesitatingly group together linguistic families, that really competent authorities do not venture to bring into the same category, or will at times even declare to be radically distinct [members of distinct families]. It is here above all that we see the danger of etymology, which in truth rides recklessly over all obstacles. (Hovelacque 1877:302)

In comparing idioms [languages], we must, above all, take no heed of the mere likeness of words to each other. Two words of nearly or even absolutely similar meaning in two different languages, may possibly have nothing in common, so that lexical apart from grammatical agreement is nothing to the purpose. The etymologist pounces upon such resemblances, rests satisfied with them, and refuses to look farther afield, while the philologist passes them unheeded . . .

The comparison of hundreds of ready-made words in two languages whatsoever, would never advance by a single step the question of their mutual relationship. What requires to be proved, is not the existence of these casual resemblances, but the identity of the roots when reduced to their simplest form, the identity of the formative elements, the identity of the grammatical functions of these elements; in a word, the grammatic identity of the languages compared.

The so-called comparative studies not based on these inexorable principles, can be no longer taken into account; all such trifling belongs to a bygone day. (Hovelacque 1877:303; our emphasis, LC/WP)

4.13.5   Brugmann

Other statements from Neogrammarians (in addition to the one Greenberg mentioned from Delbrück, above) are readily available, for example, from Karl Brugmann (1884) himself, the most famous founder of Neogrammarianism:

It is not a single or a few phenomena appearing in two or several areas at the same time which furnish proof of closer community, but only a large mass of *agreements in sound, inflectional, syntactic, and lexical innovation* [*Neuerungen*], the large mass of which excludes thought of accident. (Dyen's [1953:580] translation; our emphasis, LC/WP)

4.13.6   Gabelentz

Similarly, Georg von der Gabelentz's (1891) statement is particularly relevant:

Now the question is: how is the proof of relationship supplied? And for this too certain principles may be established . . .

1. If related languages are so dissimilar that their relationship is not immediately apparent, then the relationship is a distant one . . .

2. That not all the word and sound similarities are equal we have just seen . . .

3. In this way one discovers more or less *regular sound representations* and can finally say: if such and such a word recurs in that language, then it must sound like such and such . . . *Where such regularity rules, there the relationship exists without a doubt* . . .

Linguistic comparison without sound comparison is thoughtless foolery. (Gabelentz 1972[1901/1891]:158; our emphasis, LC/WP)[19]

On the efficacy of sound correspondences as evidence of genetic relationship, Gabelentz is very instructive:

A single glance shows us that the wolf belongs to the canine family. But that the slow-worm is not a snake but rather a kind of lizard we learn only when we remove the skin from the animal and examine it anatomically. Both sorts are found in the world of languages as well, only here far more often the signs of relationship are to be sought under the skin. (Gabelentz 1891:151)[20]

4.13.7　Meillet

Antoine Meillet (1914, 1925, 1966[1954/25]) also provided a rich discussion of methods for establishing genetic relationships. His opinions conform with those of the other Neogrammarians and their contemporaries; his emphasis on morphological evidence and on sound correspondences is well known – it is the foundation of modern practice. He said of lexical evidence, "vocabulary can only serve to point the way; the proof is found elsewhere" (Meillet 1948[1921/14]:97).[21] He believed the strongest evidence was to be found in peculiar morphological correspondences (see Chapter 7):

What does constitute proof in establishing continuity between a "proto-language" and some later language, are the individual properties of morphological expression. (Meillet 1966[1954/25]:25)[22]

The more unique the facts seen to agree between two languages, the greater the demonstrative force of that agreement. So exceptional forms are the ones most appropriate for establishing a "proto-language."

---

[19] "Jetzt fragt es sich: wie wird der Beweis der Verwandtschaft geliefert? und auch hierfür lassen sich gewisse Grundsätze aufstellen . . .
　　1. Sind verwandte Sprachen einander so unähnlich, dass ihre Verwandtschaft nicht ohne Weiteres in die Augen fällt, so ist diese Verwandtschaft eine entferntere . . .
　　2. Dass nicht alle Wort- und Lautähnlichkeiten gleichwerthig sind, haben wir vorhin gesehen . . .
　　3. Auf diese Art enddeckt man nun mehr oder minder *regelmässige Lautvertretungen* und kann schliesslich sagen: kehrt das und das Wort in jener Sprache wieder, so muss es so und so lauten. . . . Wo solche Regelmässigkeit herrscht, da steht die Verwandtschaft ausser Zweifel . . . *Sprachvergleichung ohne Lautvergleichung ist gedankenlose Spielerei.*"
[20] "Dass der Wolf zum Hundegeschlechte gehört, lehrt uns ein einziger Blick. Dass aber die Blindschleiche nicht eine Schlange, sondern eine Eidechsenart ist, erfahren wir erst, wenn wir dem Thiere die Haut abstreifen und es anatomisch untersuchen. Beiderlei kommt auch in der Sprachenwelt vor, nur dass noch viel öfter die Wervandtschaftsmerkmale unter den Haut zu suchen sind."
[21] "Le vocabulaire ne peut servir qu'à orienter la recherche; la preuve se trouve ailleurs."
[22] "Ce qui est probant pour établir la continuité entre une 'langue commune' et une langue ultérieure, ce sont les procédés particuliers d'expression de la morphologie."

The more a language includes non-meaningful grammatical categories or anomalous forms, the easier the demonstration of genetic relationship and reconstruction of the original proto-language are for the linguist. (Meillet 1966[1954/25]:27)[23]

(For details, see Chapter 6.)

Meillet was also strong on sound correspondences as evidence; we cite just one representative quote:

If dealing with related languages that have ceased to be very much alike among themselves, a strong superficial resemblance between two words is, for the linguist, reason to doubt that they represent a single proto-language expression. French *feu* ['fire'] has nothing to do with German *feuer* ['fire']; . . . [however] it is easy to show the relationships that exist between French *cinq* . . . and the equivalent English *five*, Russian *piat'* [pjatj], (and) Armenian *hing*; but at first glance these words hardly look alike at all. *But it is not outward resemblances on which linguists rely when they compare words and establish etymologies for them; rather it is on formulae of regular correspondences.* (Meillet 1948[1921]:92–3; our emphasis, LC/WP)[24]

(Cf. also Meillet 1966[1954/1925]:36–7.)

4.14   Conclusions

In spite of individual differences, it is clear that for most of the scholars who played a significant role in the history of comparative linguistics and in the establishment of linguistic families, grammatical correspondences, basic vocabulary, and sound correspondences were the three sources of evidence most commonly felt reliable upon which conclusions concerning language relationships were based. We conclude from the survey here and in earlier chapters that many of the classificatory errors committed by well-known scholars in the past stem from the employment of inadequate methods, particularly from methods that rely on casual inspection of lexical similarities. From the works by Neogrammarians and their contemporaries cited here, it is clear that pronouncements about methods for investigating language relationships are not as rare as has been claimed

---

[23] "Plus sont singuliers les faits dont on constate entre deux langues la concordance, et plus grande est la force probante de la concordance. Les formes anomales sont donc celles qui sont le plus propres à établir une 'langue commune.'

Plus une langue comprend ainsi de catégories grammaticales non significatives ou de formes anomales, et plus la démonstration des parentés et la restitution d'une langue commune initiale sont faciles pour le linguiste."

[24] "S'il s'agit de langues parentes qui ont cessé d'être très semblables entre elles, une forte ressemblance extérieure entre deux mots est, pour le linguiste, une raison de douter qu'ils représentent un même terme de la langue originelle. Le français *feu* ['fire'] n'a rien de commun avec l'allemand *feuer* ['fire']; . . . il est facile de montrer quels rapports il y a entre le français *cinq* . . . et les équivalents *five* de l'anglais, *piat'* du russe, *hing* de l'arménien; mais au premier abord, ces mots ne se ressemblent guère. Ce n'est pas sur la ressemblance extérieure des mots que se fondent les linguistes pour les rapprocher et en faire l'étymologie, mais sur des formules de correspondances régulières."

and that they were quite specific, even insistent, concerning the roles of sound correspondences and grammatical (morphological) agreements. It is revealing to see not just the pronouncements about methods, but also how the methods were employed in actual practice. That is the subject of the next chapter, which deals with how various once controversial languages were shown to belong to the Indo-European family.

5 How some languages were shown to belong to Indo-European

> **Babel, Tower of** (babel, *gate of God*), **Babylon**, the Greek form of the Hebrew word *bavel*, which is closely allied and probably derived from the Akkadian *babilu* or *"gate of God."* The date of its foundation is still disputed.
>
> (Cornwell 1995)

5.1   Introduction

There has been considerable confusion recently about how certain languages came to be established as members of the Indo-European family. In this chapter we take up the cases that have been discussed most, setting the record straight and deriving methodological object lessons from these successes. The methods used to establish these as Indo-European languages are quite instructive. Specifically we examine how Hittite, Armenian, and Venetic were shown to belong to the Indo-European family. (For Indo-European more broadly, see Chapters 2, 3, and 4.)

5.2   Hittite

Hittite was the language of the ancient Hittite empire in central Anatolia (present-day Turkey), and came to be known from the many clay tablets, written in cuneiform (and the earliest of these in Hieroglyphic Hittite), some from Tel el-Amarna in Egypt, but mostly known from the libraries containing Hittite and other clay documents in Boğaz Köy (today called Boğaz Kale), Turkey. Ultimately these were deciphered. Hittite (and the Anatolian branch generally to which Hittite belongs) proved to be Indo-European, against earlier intuitions. The first substantive claims concerning the Indo-European affiliation of Hittite were made by Knudtzon (1902) (cf. also Bugge 1902 and Torp 1902) in a book devoted to two letters between a Hittite ruler and the king of Egypt found at Tel el-Amarna in Egypt. Knudtzon, Bugge, and Torp argued that Hittite was Indo-European based largely on the morphology, as this passage from Torp (1902:108) indicates:

The assumption that an Indo-European language is at issue here seems to me very much suggested by Knudtzon's discovery of *estu*, the third-person-singular imperative of the verb "to be," and of *mi* and *ti*, as enclitic possessives of the first and second persons respectively.[1]

Knudtzon, Bugge, and Torp also pointed to other affixes, such as the accusative singular -*an* and the first person singular preterite active in -*n*, which have analogues in other Indo-European languages. Although they were right (and their evidence was quite reasonable), their proposal that Hittite was Indo-European was generally not embraced at the time and it was not until after the work of Friedrich Hrozný (1915, 1917) that Hittite was acknowledged to be an Indo-European language.

Hrozný had at his disposal the vast number of Hittite tablets discovered at Boğaz Köy, and based on these he prepared a comprehensive grammar of the language, justifying his decipherment and analysis with numerous examples. He announced his results in Hrozný (1915), a paper which concentrated on his evidence for the Indo-European affinity of Hittite, and in Hrozný (1917), a grammar of Hittite. The evidence for Indo-European affiliation that he presented (in Hrozný 1915) was largely morphological; it included the form of the present active participle (23), the case morphology (24), the existence of *r/n*-stems (24–5), the pronouns (25–6), the verbal paradigm (27), and the adverbs (27–8). When he discussed the case morphology, he did not present isolated affixes, but rather comparisons with other Indo-European languages of a full set of six case endings. When he discussed pronouns, he did not present an isolated pronoun or two, but a set of twenty-three, including multiple case forms of the same pronoun, some involving irregular alternations (see below and Chapter 7). When he discussed the verbal paradigm, he did not present isolated forms but rather the complete paradigm of six person/number forms, which are explicitly compared with their Vedic and Greek counterparts.

Indeed, it is clear that Hrozný did not consider isolated morphological resemblances probative. The first example to strike him was the present active participle. Nonetheless, this did not convince him immediately of an Indo-European genetic relationship; as he says: "When I found the first correspondences of Hittite with Indo-European, I also considered the possibility that Hittite had perhaps been merely influenced by Indo-European" (Hrozný 1915:24, fn.1).[2] Only after presenting all this morphological evidence did Hrozný (1915) tack on an addition of thirteen lexical comparisons.

---

[1] "Die Annahme, dass hier eine indogermanische Sprache vorliege, scheint mir durch Knudtzon's Entdeckung von *estu*, Imp. 3. Sing. des Verbs 'sein,' und von *mi* und *ti* als enklitischen Possessiven resp. der 1. und der 2. Pers. sehr nahe gelegt."

[2] "Als ich die ersten Übereinstimmungen des Hethitischen mit dem Indogermanischen fand, erwog ich auch die Möglichkeit dass das Hethitische vom Indogermanischen vielleicht bloss beeinflusst worden sei."

We can see why Knudtzon's argument had little impact while Hrozný's a mere decade later overcame all opposition. Not only was Hrozný's argument based on a much more secure analysis of the language itself while Knudtzon could offer only isolated affixes, Hrozný provided complete paradigms and idiosyncratic alternations. In Hrozný (1915) lexical comparisons played a minor role, and the morphology invoked does not consist of mere isolated affixes.

The evidence offered in Hrozný's (1917) grammar included that presented in the 1915 paper with other things added to it. However, since the book's purpose was to present a grammar of Hittite, the evidence of its Indo-European affiliation is diffused throughout the book. There is no part of the book devoted solely to the argument for Hittite's Indo-European affinity. Therefore Greenberg's claims about Hrozný's argument are not supported. Greenberg (1991:129) quotes Hrozný (1917:vii) as follows:

Everyone who wishes to interpret the Boghazköi texts, from the moment of their publication, will, like the author, come to the same conclusion on the basis of instances like the fact that *wadar* means 'water,' that its genitive is not *wadaras* but, remarkably enough, *wedenas*, that the Hittites have a participle in -*nt*-, that 'what' (masc[uline]) is *kuis* and in the neuter *kuid*, that 'I' is *ug* (cf. Latin *ego*), 'to me' *ammug* (cf. Greek *emoige*), 'thou' *zig* (cf. Greek *suge*), 'to thee' *tug* (Gothic *thuk* etc.), that the Hittite present is inflected *jami, jasi, jazi, jaweni, jatteni, janzi*, etc., etc.

Greenberg (1991:129) said of this:

Hrozný does not present a table of correspondences of the kind that have become *de rigueur* in the pages of *IJAL* [*International Journal of American Linguistics*], nor has anyone since . . . Note also that the resemblances adduced by Hrozný as decisive are with various Indo-European languages or with none in particular as with the verb paradigm he cites.

(See also Greenberg 1990a:12; Greenberg *et al.* 1986:493.) Although Greenberg's English translation lacks specific comparisons with other Indo-European languages for the verbal forms in the quotation, Hrozný did give a Greek comparison for every Hittite form, as seen in the original German text (followed by our translation):

Jeder, der die Boghazköi-Texte, sobald sie veröffentlicht sind, wird deuten wollen, wird gleich dem Verfasser zu dem Ergebnis kommen, dass *wâdar* "Wasser" bedeutet, daß der Genitiv hierzu nicht etwa *wâdaraš*, sondern merkwürdigerweise *wedenaš* lautet, daß die Hethiter ein Partizipium Präs. auf -*nt*- haben, daß "welcher" bei ihnen *kuiš*, "welches" *kuit/d* heißt, das "ich" hethitisch *ug* (vgl. lat. *ego*), "mir" *ammug* (vgl. griech. ἐμοιγε), "du" *zig* (vgl. griech. σύγε), "dir" *tug* (vgl. got. þuk usw.) lautet, daß das hethitische Präsens folgendermaßen flektiert wird: *jami* (vgl. griech. τίθημι), *jaši* (vgl. τίθης), *jazi* (vgl. τίθησι), *jawêni* (vgl. τίθημεν), *jattêni* (vgl. τίθετε), *janzi* (vgl. τίθέασι), usw. usw. (Hrozný 1917:vii)

[Whoever will want to interpret the Boghazköi texts, as soon as they are published, will, like the author, come to the conclusion that *wâdar* means "water," that the genitive of this is not something like **wâdaraš*, but rather, strangely, is pronounced *wedenaš*, that the Hittites have a present participle in *-nt-*, that for them "which" (masc., *welcher*) is called *kuiš*, [and] "which" (neuter, *welches*) [is] *kuit/d*, that "I" is pronounced in Hittite *ug* (cf. Latin *ego*), "me (dative)" *ammug* (cf. Greek ἔμοιγε), "thou" *zig* (cf. Greek σύγε), "thou (dative)" *tug* (Gothic *þuk* etc.), that the Hittite present is inflected as follows: *jami* (cf. Greek τίθημι), *jaši* (cf. τίθης), *jazi* (cf. τίθησι), *jawêni* (cf. τίθημεν), *jattêni* (cf. τίθετε), *janzi* (cf. τίθέασῑ), etc., etc.]

More importantly, in this passage Hrozný is not, as Greenberg suggested, attempting to present evidence for the Indo-European affiliation of Hittite. As the text reveals, the various facts cited are just what Hrozný considered to be firm conclusions about Hittite. Greenberg transformed Hrozný's list of conclusions into a list of evidence for a conclusion. This different interpretation is made clear in the immediately following lines of Hrozný's text:

These and the author's other results stand firm; they cannot be avoided. Each new text which the author has recently obtained suggests this new interpretation, demands it and confirms it. Thus the Hittite present schema referred to here is supported by many hundreds of passages. The same is true, for example, of the Hittite pronouns, which are so important for linguistic comparison, whose meaning is made certain in an immense number of passages. (Hrozný 1917:vii)[3]

In sum, Greenberg's treatment of this passage is inaccurate and misleading. It is not true that the Hittite verb forms were not compared explicitly with forms from other Indo-European languages, and the passage was not even intended as an argument for the Indo-European affinity of Hittite.

A passage in the 1917 grammar in which Hrozný actually does summarize his reasons for believing Hittite to be Indo-European is revealing:

However, a systematic, sober, and careful examination of a large part of the Boghazköi texts kept in the Constantinople Imperial Ottoman Museum brought the author in a few months to the firm conviction that Hittite is essentially an Indo-European language. Words such as *wâdar* 'water' (compare Old Saxon *watar* 'water' etc.), genitive *wedenaš* (compare Greek υδατος from υδη τος), participles such as *dân* 'giving' (compare Latin *dans*), plural *dantes* (compare Latin plural *dantēs*), pronouns such as *kuiš* 'which' (masculine) (compare Latin *quis*), neuter *kuit/d* (compare Latin *quid*), etc., etc., as also, and

---

[3] "Diese und die übrigen Ergebnisse des Verfassers stehen felsenfest da, man wird um sie nicht herumkommen können. Jeder neue Text, den der Verfasser neuerdings erhält, legt wiederum diese Deutungen nahe, fordert und bestätigt sie. So wird das hier angeführte hethitische Präsensschema durch viele Hunderte von Stellen gestützt. Dasselbe gilt z.B. auch von den für die Sprachvergleichung so wichtigen hethitischen Pronomina, deren Bedeutung durch eine unübersehbare Reihe von Stellen gesichert ist."

indeed above all, the entire form of the Hittite language which gradually revealed itself in the course of the investigation leaves no doubt. (Hrozný 1917:v)[4]

Here it is clear that Hrozný's emphasis is on the morphology, both its overall structure and its idiosyncratic alternations, and not on individual lexical items. That is why he cites pairs of related forms, including such distinctive items as an *r/n*-stem. In the chapter on *Formenlehre des Nomens* [nominal morphology] he refers again to the importance of the *r/n* stems for establishing the Indo-European affinity of Hittite (1917:61), and again, after a discussion of the declension of *r/n* stems like *watar* 'water,' he says (64): "We have already noticed . . . [in Hrozný 1915] that this correspondence in such a conspicuous type of declension – alongside many others – is to be regarded as a convincing proof for our thesis that Hittite is an Indo-European language."[5]

Hrozný was not alone in his evaluation of the importance of the morphological evidence. Carl Marstrander (1919:63–7) referred specifically to the argument from the *r/n*-stems: "Mr. Hrozný has succeeded in establishing a series of anomalous Hittite stems in *r/n* and thus in furnishing one of the most positive proofs of the Indo-European character of the Hittite language" (63).[6] Marstrander (1919:7) also emphasized the peculiar pronominal paradigm:

About the Indo-European origin of these forms there can be no doubt. Their inflection shows the same peculiar alternations in the stem that we find in practically all of the Indo-European languages. That *u-ga* and *am-mu-ga* derive from the same source as ἐγώ: ἐμέγε, *ik* : *mik*, *ego* : *me*, leaps to one's eyes.[7]

Roberto Gusmani (1968:7) gave a similar assessment of Hrozný's evidence, saying that it contained:

---

[4] "Eine systematische nüchterne und vorsichtige Prüfung eines großen Teiles der in dem Konstantinopeler Kaiserlich Ottomanischen Museum aufbewahrten Boghazköi-Texte brachte indes den Verfasser bereits in wenigen Monaten zu der festen Überzeugung, daß das Hethitische eine im wesentlichen indogermanische Sprache ist. Wörter wie *wâdar* 'Wasser' (vgl. altsächs. *watar* 'Wasser' usw.), Gen[itiv] *wedenaš* (vgl. griech. υδατος aus ύδη τοος), Partizipien wie *dân* 'gebend' (vgl. lat. *dans*), Pl. *dantes* (vgl. lat. Pl. *dantēs*), Pronomina wie *kuiš* 'welcher' (vgl. lat. *quis*), Neutr. *kuit/d* (vgl. lat. *quid*) usw. usw., wie auch, und zwar vor allem, der ganze im Laufe der Untersuchung sich allmählich ergebende Bau der hethitischen Sprache konnten Zweifel darüber übrig lassen."

[5] "Wir haben schon Mitteilungen d. deutsch. Orient-Ges. Nr. 56, S. 24f. [Hrozný 1915] bemerkt, dass diese Übereinstimmung in einer so auffälligen Deklinationsart – nebst vielen anderen – als ein zwingender Beweis für unsere These zu bewerten ist, dass das Hethitische eine indogermanische Sprache ist."

[6] "M. Hrozna réussi à établir une série de thèmes hitites anomaux en *r/n* et à fournir ainsi une des preuves les plus positives du caractère indo-européen de la langue hitite."

[7] "Sur l'origine indo-européenne de ces formes il ne peut y avoir aucun doute. Leur flexion montre la même alternance particulière de thèmes que nous retrouvons dans presques toutes les langages indo-européennes. Que *u-ga* et *am-mu-ga* proviennent de la même source que 'εγώ: 'εμέγε, *ik* : *mik*, *ego* : *me*, cela saute aux yeux."

nearly a whole series of correspondences which are morphological in character (suffixes, etc.), as well as various lexical coincidences between Hittite and the other Indo-European languages which should corroborate his theory of the Indo-European character of the recently discovered language.[8]

Finally, we find Jaan Puhvel's (1991) reasons for concluding Hittite to be a fully authentic Indo-European language remarkably similar to Hrozný's (in fact, similar to the passage above from Hrozný which Greenberg cited):

> The notion that Hittite is not pure Indo-European . . . is laid to rest merely by reciting some of the most basic root verbs. The paradigms of *es- 'to be,' *ey- 'to go,' and *ed- 'to eat' in Hittite are perfect matches for the best-preserved specimens elsewhere: Hittite ēsmi, ēssi, ēszi cover Old Lithuanian esmi, esi, esti; Luwian and Hittite iti, yanzi, idu, iyandu, iyant- correspond to Vedic éti, yánti, étu, yántu, yánt-; and Hittite edmi, ezsi, adanzi, ezdu, adandu, adant- fit exactly over Vedic ádmi, átsi, adanti, attu, adantu, adánt-. I rest my case right there, for I know of no better definition for an Indo-European language. (Puhvel 1991:54–5)

It is important to stress that in Hrozný's (1917) book the arguments that Hittite is Indo-European are not restricted to any single passage. Hrozný's entire monograph is, in effect, an argument for the Indo-European affinity of Hittite – its full title is *The Language of the Hittites: its Form and its Membership in the Indo-European Language Family*, and thus, in the passage quoted above, Hrozný cited as evidence "the entire form of the Hittite language which gradually reveals itself in the course of the investigation." The evidence is found throughout the book, in the many places in which Hrozný points out the relationship between some aspect of Hittite morphology and that of other Indo-European languages. Among many examples, we may cite the two tables in his chapter 3 (1917:153, 162–3) in which Hittite verb forms are given along with their Vedic Sanskrit counterparts.

Hrozný gave importance to morphological evidence, but did not neglect sound correspondences. Greenberg (2005:161) said that "Hrozný does not cite sound correspondences." Nevertheless, in Hrozný's chapter 5, (1917:186–90), "Der Lautbestand des Hethitischen" [The inventory of Hittite sounds], we find a table of sound correspondences between Hittite and Proto-Indo-European. Hrozný did not offer this table of sound correspondences as his primary evidence for the Indo-European character of Hittite, since he felt that the morphological evidence was the most striking and sufficient for proof, but he did indeed work out and present sound correspondences. Moreover, he used them to determine Hittite's place with respect to the other Indo-European languages (subgrouping it as a "Centrum-Sprache"; cf. for example Hrozný 1915:29–30).

---

[8] "accanto a tutta una serie di concordanze di carattere morfologico (desinenze ecc.), anche diverse coincidenze lessicali tra l'ittito e le altre lingue indoeuropee che dovevano corroborare la sua teoria del carattere indoeuropeo della lingua di recente scoperta."

Nor is it true that subsequent authors have had no concern for sound correspondences involving Hittite. Marstrander (1919:169) presented a table of sound correspondences showing the relationship between Proto-Indo-European and Hittite, and Sturtevant (1933) devoted much of his chapter 3, "Phonology" (1933:87–143), to the sound correspondences involved in his Proto-Indo-Hittite, citing in every instance numerous Hittite comparisons with other Indo-European languages.

We have seen that Hrozný's methods, which Greenberg so praised but apparently misunderstood, are very much in tune with those that have so often been employed in research on relationships among languages in general, and they are not at all related to multilateral comparison as Greenberg thought. Because they resulted in a definitive proof of the genetic relationship of a language whose classification was formerly unknown, they show the efficacy of these standard methods.

5.3   Armenian

Next we turn to Armenian, an example relating more specifically to subgrouping than to its overall affiliation *per se*, but still instructive methodologically. Armenian was recognized as an Indo-European language by Julius Heinrich Petermann (1801–76) in 1837.[9] It was soon classified, erroneously, as belonging with Iranian by Friedrich Heinrick Hugo Windischmann (1811–61) (1846) on the basis of the many Iranian loanwords in its lexicon. This remained the dominant view, accepted by, among others, Franz Bopp – in spite of doubts expressed by August Pott and despite the suggestion from Paul Anton de Lagarde (1827–91) (1877) that the Iranian words represented loans – until Heinrich Hübschmann's (1875) classic paper. Hübschmann demonstrated to the satisfaction of subsequent scholars that Armenian belongs to a distinct subgroup of Indo-European, not to Iranian.

Hübschmann's discovery of the correct position of Armenian within the Indo-European family owes itself to his recognition that words are easily borrowed and may therefore be a poor indicator of genetic affiliation, inferior to morphology:

If we have now become distrustful of the lexicon, we can turn trustingly to the grammar: this is, after all, in all living languages the palladium which foreign influence cannot touch. How messy is the lexicon in Afghan and Modern Persian, or in English, and

---

[9] Rask (1993[1818]:286) had earlier recognized "a true, albeit very distant, kinship between" Armenian and his Thracian class (Greek and Latin), which in turn were seen as the closest branch to his "Gothic class" (Germanic). However, he presented no evidence, no comparisons involving Armenian data, and he added that Armenian "is so little known and inaccessible that it would not be worth our trouble to investigate it in more detail."

how clearly the grammar shows that there we have before us Iranian, here Germanic! (Hübschmann 1875:10)[10]

He concluded that in its morphology Armenian exhibits no specifically Iranian features, differs in important ways from Indo-Iranian, and corresponds most closely to Balto-Slavic (Hübschmann 1875:13).

The remainder of Hübschmann's paper is devoted to a detailed examination of the sound laws and the demonstration, on the basis of the sound laws, that two strata of Iranian loans can and must be distinguished from the truly Armenian vocabulary, which exhibits very different sound correspondences. His ultimate conclusion is that Armenian is an independent subgroup of Indo-European.

The first lesson that we draw from this example is that reliance on the lexicon alone can be dangerous, for we run the risk of being misled by loans (as in the case of some of Jones' errors; see Chapter 3). Second, phonological correspondences play a crucial role in distinguishing loans from native vocabulary and can be vital for correct classification of languages. It should be noted, moreover, that Hübschmann's appeal to sound correspondences preceded the famous pronouncements of the Neogrammarians concerning the exceptionlessness of sound laws. In fact, this paper appeared in the same issue of *Zeitschrift für Vergleichende Sprachforschung* as Karl Verner's (1875) famous paper which laid out what came to be known as Verner's law and contributed to the foundation to Neogrammarian thought.

As with Hittite, Greenberg (2005) also made claims about how Armenian's affiliation was shown and specifically about the role of Hübschmann's (1875) article in this. Greenberg (2005:175) acknowledges that the "existence of a number of unobvious correspondences has indeed made the study of Armenian historical phonology notoriously difficult," but he asserts that "there are a large number of obvious similarities between Armenian and the other Indo-European languages." He listed sixty-five examples of Armenian "look-alikes" with other modern Indo-European languages (Greenberg 2005:165–7) and challenged those "who do not understand that the discovery of widespread similarities is the starting point of classification" to produce a similar list "comparing Armenian to Afroasiatic or some other stock" (Greenberg 2005:165). Three observations seem called for. First, while Greenberg seems to be suggesting that the listing of look-alikes is merely a starting point – with which most would agree – he himself does not take them to be just a beginning, but rather stops here, assuming them to be cognates, what he calls "etymologies" (Greenberg 1987). Second, the very point of Hübschmann's (1875) article was to show

---

[10] "Sind wir nun gegen das lexicon misstrauisch geworden, so dürfen wir uns vertrauensvoller an die grammatik wenden: ist diese doch bei allen lebenden sprachen das palladium, das fremder einfluss nicht berühren kann. Wie wüst ist das lexicon im afghanischen und neupersischen, oder im englischen, und wie klar lehrt die grammatik, dass wir dort iranisch, hier germanisch vor uns haben!"

how mere lexical parallels are insufficient for correct classification, since it was on this basis that Armenian had been misclassified as Indo-Iranian in the first place, and the evidence from regular sound correspondences revealed both the large number of Iranian loans and Armenian's separate status within the family. Third, Greenberg's comparison of Armenian to other Indo-European languages is irrelevant as a demonstration of how lexical similarities may demonstrate remote linguistic relationships, since Armenian is clearly an Indo-European language and was already recognized as such before its subgrouping status within the family was determined.

More specifically about the Armenian case, Greenberg (2005:168) asserted:

In a recent statement (Bateman *et al.* [1990a, 1990b] . . .), after first enumerating common origin, borrowing, accident and sound symbolism as sources of resemblances, without justification and without looking at the facts about languages, the conclusion is drawn that since there are alternative explanations to the genetic, resemblances of these other kinds become so overwhelming in number as soon as one passes from the most obvious low-level groupings, that genetic groupings of a deeper sort are impossible [read "difficult"] to discover. An actual examination of the data, as in the case of Armenian, shows that this is a myth resting on monumentally incautious statements made by linguists who have not bothered to look at the empirical data on a broad scale.

But this simply misses the issue. Armenian is not an appropriate example to test the difficulty of establishing distant genetic relationships, since Armenian's membership within Indo-European has not been in question, its non-obvious phonological correspondences and many Iranian loans notwithstanding. Rather, Armenian is a striking example of the efficacy of the comparative method in determining both genetic relationships and sorting out loanwords:

the resilience and power of the comparative method lies in its sensitivity to similarity due both to genetic affiliation and areal diffusion alike, demonstrated once and for all . . . by Hübschmann (1875), when he proved that Armenian was a separate branch of Indo-European, and not a dialect of Iranian as previously thought. (Watkins 2001:59)

Also, as Meillet (1948[1914]:98) put it, "in the area occupied by the Indo-European languages, the question of knowing whether a language is or is not Indo-European is never asked: the answer is always obvious."[11] A more appropriate example for Greenberg's method would be some hypothesis of genetic affinity involving languages not previously thought to be related or whose suspected relationship is uncertain, where an application of his methods might demonstrate definitively and accurately the relationship.

---

[11] "Dans le domaine occupé par les langues indo-européennes, la question de savoir si une langue est ou non indo-européenne ne se pose jamais: la réponse est toujours evident."

5.4   Venetic

Our final Indo-European case study is Venetic. Venetic was spoken in the vicinity of Venice prior to the spread of Latin and is known only from about 300 short inscriptions, mostly in the Etruscan alphabet. It was recognized as a distinct language by Carl Pauli (1885), who argued that Venetic was Indo-European on the basis of the case morphology. In his monograph on Venetic, Pauli (1891) added an argument based on a weak/strong grade alternation in the same root. The explicit arguments in favor of an Indo-European affiliation were strictly morphological, although he also gave interpretations of words with obvious Indo-European counterparts. The next broad work on Venetic was Madison Beeler's (1949) monograph, in which he gave the following summary of the evidence for the Venetic–Indo-European connection:

Venetic is an Indo-European language. Some of the evidence which proves this point is the following:
(a) The contrast between the inflectional endings of two series of names, one with *-os*, *-oi*, and *-on* (like the nominative, dative, and accusative singulars respectively of I[ndo-]E[uropean] stems), and the other with *-a*, *-as*, and *ai* (like the nominative, genitive, and dative singulars of I[ndo-]E[uropean] stems).
(b) The verbal ending *-to*, presumably that of the third person singular of the secondary indicative middle, Greek *to*, Sanskrit *-ta*.
(c) A large number of derivative suffixes, i.e. *-o-*, *-no-*, *-so-*, *-tor-*, which can be abundantly paralleled in the languages of the I[ndo-]E[uropean] family.
(d) Many striking lexical correspondences, such as *é 'Xo* = Lat. *ego*, *meXo* = Gothic *mik*, *zoto* = Greek *eí!-doto*, *lo·u·zera·i '* = Latin *Libera*.
(e) The characteristic Indo-European nature of the vowel alternation is *vho·u·χo·n·tah* and *vhuχoiia* (Pauli). (Beeler 1949:13)[12]

Of the five pieces of evidence that Beeler cited, four are morphological, including facts about ablaut, not merely correspondences in affixes. Furthermore, the evidence cited in this passage is by no means all that Beeler was aware of, as he explicitly states. In particular, Beeler established phonological correspondences between Venetic and Proto-Indo-European, and discussed them at some length (Beeler 1949:16–42).

In sum, the evidence offered for the Indo-European affinity of Venetic was at first morphological and then was extended to include sound correspondences. Superficial lexical comparisons played a very small role at best.

The evidence adduced for the subgrouping of Venetic is also instructive. Pauli argued for subclassifying it with Messapic as Illyrian, on the grounds

---

[12] The raised dots in the transliteration of Venetic reflect the practice in that language, as well as later Etruscan, of marking syllable-initial vowels and coda consonants and glides with one or two raised dots. The letters corresponding to the Greek aspirates are believed to reflect voiced stops, but the conventional transliteration of Venetic reflects Greek practice.

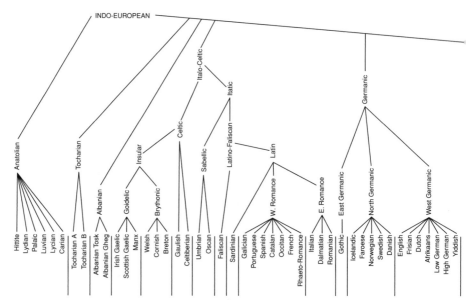

Fig. 5.1 The Indo-European family tree (above and opposite)

that both languages had a genitive singular in -h.[13] Beeler's classification of Venetic as Italic (as opposed to the Illyrian alternative) is based partly on morphology and partly on phonology, e.g. the fact that PIE *bh yields f in Venetic, as it does in Italic, in contrast to the b it yields in Messapic (Beeler 1949:51). Subsequent discussions of the subgrouping of Venetic, such as by Krahe (1950) and Hamp (1959), have concentrated on phonological and morphological isoglosses. The present standard reference on Venetic is Lejeune (1974). Of the 54 traits he discussed relevant to the classification of Venetic within Indo-European, 21 are phonological ("*isoglosses phonétiques*," 165–7), 9 are morphological ("*isoglosses morphologiques*," 167–8), and 25 involve lexical peculiarities ("*isoglosses lexicales*," 168–70). To cite just one example, with respect to sound correspondences he points out that "Italic" as the name of an Indo-European subgroup has meant different things to different scholars, but that if it is intended to include the languages which share the innovation of *bh- > f-, *dh- > f, *gh- > h- (i.e. Oscum–Umbrian and Latin, but excluding Messapic, Celtic, Germanic), then Venetic will also belong to Italic.

This review of Venetic reveals a different state of affairs for the methods which were used to establish its Indo-European affinity (and its subgrouping within Indo-European) from what Greenberg (2005) claimed about it. He cited

---

[13] On this point Pauli turned out to be wrong. As Sommer (1924) demonstrated, Pauli's understanding of the writing system was imperfect, and what he took to be genitives in -h are actually datives in -i.

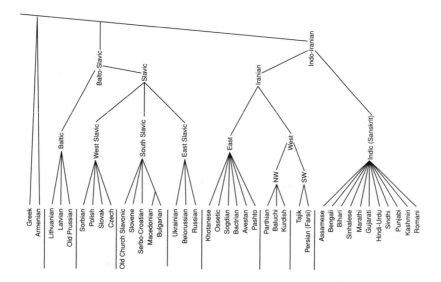

from Beeler (1949), which he called "the standard work on Venetic," only the passage quoted above (Beeler 1949:13, with some differences from the original), concluding:

> Once again, and this could be repeated for every language whose Indo-European affiliation has been recognized in the post-Brugmann era, there is no mention [in Beeler] of sound correspondences, but rather references to concrete sound–meaning resemblances in forms diagnostic of Indo-European as a whole, considered against the general background of knowledge of the family rather than by comparison with some single member to prove relationship. (Greenberg 2005:161–2)

As we saw, it is not the "concrete sound–meaning resemblances" (i.e. lexical material or isolated morphemes) or the "general background of knowledge of the family rather than by comparison with some single member" (i.e. multilateral comparison) which was decisive for Beeler (or for Pauli or Lejeune). Rather, it was extensive morphological agreements, together with such irregular or idiosyncratic features as ablaut, and sound correspondences, which served as the evidence proving the relationship of Venetic with Indo-European.

5.5   Conclusion

In this survey of how the family membership of some of the more challenging Indo-European languages was proven and of how these languages were classified within the family, we see, once again, that the methods for establishing family relationships involved morphology, sound correspondences, and basic vocabulary as the primary sources of evidence for genetic relationships. Many scholars favored morphology, some sound correspondences or vocabulary, but none has favored a method which relies for its principal evidence on the comparison of superficial lexical resemblances or mass comparison of vocabulary alone, except for the few cases where the scholars utilizing such a method arrived at erroneous results, as shown in previous chapters of this book.

This finding about Indo-Europeanist practice contrasts with Greenberg's view. After briefly discussing several cases (those cited here), he gives the following conclusion concerning the methods applied in the past:

in actual practice no Indo-Europeanist used sound correspondences to prove the Indo-European affiliation of newly discovered languages, nor in the extended discussion of sound laws in the 1870–1880's did the notion that sound correspondences were relevant in any way to the establishment of the Indo-European family arise. (Greenberg 2005:162–3)

Greenberg's (1996a:160) view of how Indo-European affinities were demonstrated was:

It was precisely in this way [the comparison of stable and basic morphemes, whether grammatical or lexical, over a wide area that leads to a classification of the languages into families at various levels] that the Indo-European family was discovered before even the term "sound law" existed in linguistics.

As seen in the cases discussed in this chapter, the reality of how the Indo-European kinship of these languages was established was quite different, methodological business as usual, as seen in the other chapters of this book. See Figure 5.1.[14]

Having surveyed the history of linguistics and established which methods and sources of evidence proved useful and which misleading for determining family relationships, we turn in the next chapter to a more detailed examination of the valid methods and principles employed in research on potential distant genetic relationships, together with cautions that need to be exercised.

---

[14] The particular family tree presented here for Indo-European (Figure 5.1) and in Chapter 6 for Uralic (Figure 6.1) are representative, but far from universally agreed upon. In both families, there is general agreement about the major lower-level subgroups (subfamilies), where the evidence is fairly clear. However, there is disagreement about the higher-order branches. In both families, the evidence for the higher branches, those closer to the proto-language, is limited and often unclear. The most common tree given traditionally for Indo-European usually presents some ten separate subgroups branching directly from Proto-Indo-European with little intermediate branching for higher-order subgroups. The Indo-European family tree presented in Figure 5.1 incorporates some recent hypotheses about higher-order branching, but this is still inconclusive. The position of Albanian, in particular, is unclear. Other ancient Indo-European languages should also be represented, for example, Phrygian, Thracian, Illyrian, Messapic, and Venetic, though where they should appear in the tree is less clear. (For discussion of the classification of Indo-European, see Garrett 1999; Jasanoff 2002; Mallory and Adams 1997: 550–6; Ringe, Warnow and Taylor 2002.)

6   Comparative linguistics of other language families and regions

In the distant past, no one could speak, which is one reason that people were destroyed at the end of the First and Second Creations. Then, while the sun deity was still walking on the earth, people finally learned to speak (Spanish), and all people everywhere understood each other. Later the nations and munici-pios [towns] were divided because they had begun to quarrel. Language was changed so that people would learn to live together peacefully in smaller groups.

(Tzotzil oral tradition, Gossen 1984:46–7)

6.1   Introduction

Much of the discussion of how language families are established so far has involved the history of Indo-European research, appropriately so, given its role in the development of comparative linguistics. In this chapter, we survey how several other important language families came to be established. The particular language families discussed are well known, universally accepted, were for the most part established relatively early in the history of linguistics, and so potentially had some impact on the development of the historical linguistics. We examine the methods used to establish these families in order to determine what criteria and principles were involved and what lessons we can take from them. We also consider language classification in Africa, Australia, and the Americas, with an eye towards the methods utilized in language classification in these regions. We discuss some of the well-known but disputed proposals of distant linguistic affiliation involving the languages of these areas, in part because it is methodologically insightful to consider both the established families and the controversial proposals in these areas at the same time. However, the other better-known proposals of distant genetic relationship are evaluated in Chapter 9.

6.2   Finno-Ugric and Uralic

Finno-Ugric is a well-studied and well-documented language family (see family tree in Figure 6.1).[1] Finno-Ugric is also a branch (subgroup) of the more inclusive Uralic family, which has two branches: Finno-Ugric and the Samoyed – also well established. Finno-Ugric and Uralic are typically discussed at the same time in the literature, though they differ in magnitude and age. The Finno-Ugric family was established before Indo-European was; the comparative linguistic work on these languages inspired investigators of Indo-European and was highly influential in the development of comparative linguistics generally (see Chapters 1, 2, and 4). This makes Finno-Ugric a particularly relevant case for our interests. As in the case of most language families, full understanding of the membership of Finno-Ugric (and Uralic) developed over time (see Gyula 1974; Stipa 1990).

One of the earliest applications of a sort of comparative method for determining linguistic affiliations was **Sebastian Münster**'s (1489–1522) *Cosmographey* (1544), mentioned in Chapter 2, where he found the genetic relationship between Finnish, Saami (Lapp), and Estonian, based on a comparison of words and grammatical structures in texts of the Lord's Prayer in these languages (Stipa 1990:38). Nevertheless, the "discovery" of the Finno-Ugric genetic relationship is attributed jointly to three scholars, Wexionius, Skytte, and Comenius (Stipa 1990:141). **Michael Wexionius** (1609–70) (1650) also compared Finnish, Estonian, and Saami (Lapp), dedicating two chapters to comparing grammar, and another to the case systems. He compared inflectional paradigms (in nouns, verbs, and pronouns), comparative constructions, passives, and moods, among others (Stipa 1990:146). This constitutes one of the earliest recognized efforts at comparative grammar. From details of grammatical correspondences, Wexionius analyzed the relationship between Finnish and Estonian as having its roots in an old common language, with Karelian being nearer to Finnish than to Estonian, with Estonian being nearer to Livonian than to Finnish, and with Saami (Lapp) as an offspring of Finnish, but with all these bound together by the same "foundation" (Stipa 1990:147). **Bengt Skytte** (1614–83) is credited with initiating Finno-Ugric linguistic research. His planned but unfinished

---

[1] The Uralic tree given in Figure 6.1 represents a more traditional classification of the family, though recent opinion is divided. Some find little support for the branching classification with its higher-order intermediate subgroups (see Häkkinen 1984, 2001: 169–71; Salminen 2001). Others are sympathetic to the problems pointed out due to the limited evidence for higher-order internal branches, but nevertheless see sufficient evidence to support much of the branching classification (see Sammallahti 1988, 1998:119–22). There is fairly general agreement that the former Volgaic branch (not given here), which would group Mari and Mordvin more closely together, should be abandoned. Salminen (2001) would prefer to drop not just this branch, but most of the others, leaving several groups diverging directly from the proto-language with very little intermediate branching in any of these. (For discussion, see Abondolo 1998; Häkkinen 1984, 2001; Janhunen 2001; Salminen 2001; Sammallahti 1988, 1998:119–22.)

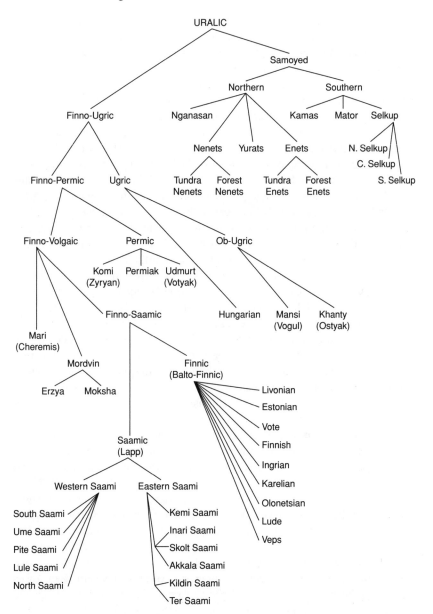

Fig. 6.1 The Uralic family tree

Sol praecipiarum linguarum subsolarium contained abundant word comparisons between Finnish and Estonian, as well as Hungarian. This unpublished work influenced other scholars through Skytte's correspondence with them and through portions of it which they had seen. Leibniz held **J. A. Comenius** (Komenský) (1592–1670) to be the discoverer of Finno-Ugric linguistics (Stipa 1990:139). Together with J. J. Scaliger and Sigismundus Gelenius (Chapter 2), Comenius recognized four "cardinal languages" of Europe, with some twenty additional European languages, among them Saami (Lapp), Finnish, and Hungarian. He required grammatical evidence for the relationship within the cardinal languages. For example, his grouping of the Slavic languages as a family was based on pronominal suffixes of the verb paradigm (Stipa 1990:138). Comenius and Skytte exchanged word comparisons such as Finnish *pää* with Hungarian *fej* 'head,' and as Stipa (1990:141) sees it, through this exchange "the spark of a recognition of the linguistic relationship was ignited." Comenius' recognition of the Finnish–Hungarian cognates had an impact on Leibniz and Fogel, through whom Finno-Ugric interests grew much further.

   Martin Fogel (Martinus Fogelius) (1635–75), considered a founder of Finno-Ugric linguistics, first came to the family relationship apparently for the wrong reasons. He observed the interchange of *f* and *h* in many languages and saw the seeming *f-h* correspondence in the names "Finns" and "Hunns" (i.e. "Hungarians") as suggesting a relationship (though these names are not cognate, in fact, are not even words found natively in these languages, cf. *suomi* 'Finn, Finland' in Finnish, and *magyar* 'Hungarian' in Hungarian). In spite of this inauspicious reasoning, Fogel came to compare words, morphology, and grammar, and on this basis demonstrated the genetic relationship between Finnish and Hungarian (Stipa 1990:142–3).[2]

   Georg Stiernhielm (1598–1672), known for his edition of Ulfila's Gothic Bible and his Scythian–Indo-European writings (Chapter 2), is sometimes mentioned as the discoverer of Finno-Ugric (Stipa 1990:145). Stiernhielm found Hungarian words in common with Finnish, some published in Stiernhielm (1670), but his unpublished manuscripts contain numerous Hungarian words compared with Finnish, as well as with Estonian and Saami. He had good evidence for connecting these languages (Stipa 1990:89, 145). **Johannes Scheffer** (1621–79) (1673), known for his work in Classical philology, clarified the relationship between Saami and Finnish, which others had noted, though he spoke about it in a confused way. Many had come to think that Saami (Lapp) was a mixed language or that the Saami had spoken some other original language which they had given up upon wandering into their present location. In addition to vocabulary, Scheffer compared the morphological structure in these

---

[2] It was recently noted that Fogel also made numerous Turkish–Hungarian comparisons, though it is unclear from his manuscript what conclusion concerning linguistic connections he may have intended to draw from these (Stipa 1990:143).

languages to reach his conclusions. He was also favorably inclined towards a relationship between Saami (Lapp) and Samoyed, and the notion of a closer Lapp–Samoyed connection was much discussed from then on (Stipa 1990:54–5, 148–9).

Olaus Rudbeck, Sr., became recognized through his use of Skytte's Hungarian material, published by his son, **Olaus Rudbeck, Jr.** (1660–1740) in his *Specimen* (1717). Rudbeck junior later did fieldwork in Lappland in a scientific expedition of 1700. Based on his one hundred Finnish–Hungarian word comparisons in the appendix to his *Analogia linguae Finnonicae com Ungarica*, Rudbeck junior declared a "blood relationship" between the languages, and on this basis was often held to be the discoverer of the Finno-Ugric family (Stipa 1990:141–2).

Towards the end of the seventeenth century, Finns who had traveled with Swedish diplomatic missions to Persia discovered in Mordvin as they came along the middle course of the Volga River some basic vocabulary connections between it and their own language, and word spread to Sweden, Finland, and beyond of a Finnish "dialect" spoken in the region. **Nicolaas Witsen** (1641–1717) (1692), mayor of Amsterdam, proclaimed Mordvin and Cheremis were as closely related (based on word similarities), as High German to Low German (Stipa 1990:84, 148–9, 164–5). Others also collected brief word lists and commented on other connections in the region.

Gottfried Wilhelm Leibniz (1646–1716) (see Chapters 2 and 8) knew of the Finnish–Hungarian connection; he had a special interest in the origin of Hungarian. He had heard of the Volga connection which Witsen had made known (Stipa 1990:148); he knew the position of Saami, Finnish, and Estonian through Scheffer (1673); and he collected materials, especially translations of *Pater Noster*, but also word lists, from many of the Uralic languages. Through his wide correspondence and collections of materials, he came to understand Finno-Ugric linguistics well, most of which had already been discovered by his time. He became a significant figure in the history of Uralic linguistics, synthesizing and clarifying the work to that date in a more comprehensive understanding of the whole family. Significantly, Leibniz grouped Finno-Ugric and Samoyed together as belonging to the same family, an early step toward the recognition of Uralic (Finno-Ugric + Samoyed) as a proper linguistic family (cf. Leibniz 1710b) (cf. Stipa 1990:163–4).

Knowledge of Uralic languages was solidified and extensively increased with the contributions of Messerschmidt and Strahlenberg. **D. G. Messerschmidt** (1685–1735) was contracted by Peter I of Russia for research expeditions, which lasted seven years (1720–7), to describe the peoples and languages of Siberia. He was extremely successful and gathered abundant materials, though he was not permitted by the St. Petersburg Academy of Science to publish his own results. His contribution to both sources of material on the languages and to the relationship of many of them can now, nevertheless, be seen in Messerschmidt (1962–77). For example, he was the first scholar personally to collect material on several Samoyed languages and to come to conclusions (based apparently on superficial comparisons of lexical lists) concerning their relative closeness to one another; he also hypothesized that the Finnic languages had split off from Samoyed (Stipa 1990:175, 177). **Philip Johan von Strahlenberg** (Captain Tabbert before he was given a title) (1676–1747) was a Swedish prisoner of war when he attached himself to Messerschmidt and helped with the expedition through Siberia. He utilized his friend Messerschmidt's material heavily without acknowledgment (see Strahlenberg 1730). This work contained a comparative table of the languages of the peoples of the Boreal East and a map of Russia with Siberia. The language table achieved fame. Strahlenberg had three main groups of peoples, based on their languages. To the first belonged Finns and Hungarians together with Voguls, Morvins, Cheremis, Permyaks, Votyaks, and Ostyaks – all Finno-Ugric and all correctly identified. The second joined Turkish groups, Siberian Tatars, Chuvash, and Tungus – all Turkic except Tungus, a member of the Tungusic family (see Chapter 9). In the third were six groups designated as "Samoyed" (Stipa 1990:179). Under the heading for each of these peoples, words from their language were given in a comparative word list. Strahlenberg was influential, but virtually all that he presented on Finno-Ugric and Samoyed was taken directly from Messerschmidt (1962–77), even the hypothesis of the relationship between Finno-Ugric and Samoyed (Stipa 1990:179).

Johann Eberhard Fischer (1697–1771), philologist and Rector of the St. Petersburg Academic Gymnasium, undertook a research expedition for the St. Petersburg Academy of Science through central and eastern Siberia from 1739 to 1747. He realized he would not succeed in publishing his great work *Vocabularium Sibiricum* in St. Petersburg and therefore gave the original to August Ludwig von Schlözer, with a copy made for the Academy in St. Petersburg. Schlözer (1768) published considerable linguistic material from it under Fischer's name, whereby Fischer's *Vocabularium Sibiricum* came to be known as the oldest Finno-Ugric etymological dictionary. In this work, Fischer collected material from numerous languages (several now extinct), and he compared some forty languages in lists of words arranged etymologically in order to determine relationships among the various peoples. Fischer was interested in real sound correspondences in both vowels and consonants, and as a professional philologist his correspondences were not concerned with just the similarity among letters which sometimes impressed lay persons. As mentioned in Chapter 2, in *De origine Ungorum* (Fischer 1770[1756], published in Schlözer 1770), Fischer reported, for example, the correspondence of Hungarian *f* to *p* and *h* to *k* in the other Finno-Ugric languages (Muller 1986:22; Stipa 1990:185; cf. Hoenigswald 1990a:124–5). Fischer's method of determining etymologies in his *Vocabularium Sibiricum* employed sound changes and often regular sound correspondences (see Fischer 1995[1747]:21).

With respect to Uralic, Fischer's completed comparisons are in a *Tabula harmonica linguarum* arranged in three groups, (1) Hungarian with the other Finno-Ugric languages, (2) Hungarian with Finnish, and (3) Vogul and Ostyak with Hungarian. Siberian languages were divided into (1) Turkic and (2) what he called "Scythian," i.e. Finno-Ugric–Samoyed. Schlözer placed Fischer's manuscript at the disposal of Sámuel Gyarmathi, his doctoral student, so that through Gyarmathi's famous work (see below) it came to have a significant impact on the better-known developments in Finno-Ugric linguistics (Stipa 1990:186–7), and this work, in turn, was to be a major influence in early comparative work on Indo-European and in the development of the comparative method.

August Ludwig von Schlözer (1735–1809), the famous Göttingen historian, contributed significantly to Uralic linguistics. He took methodological inspiration from Leibniz, holding languages to be the oldest documents on the history of peoples (Schlözer 1768:3). Schlözer (1768, 1770) synthesized and critically evaluated the results of previous research on the genetic relationship of the various individual languages, and included rich word lists in his 1770 work. He brought the classification of Finno-Ugric peoples based on their languages to a completeness and scientific grounding not yet seen to that point (Stipa 1990:198).

The Hungarian Jesuit mathematician **Jo[h]annis [János] Sajnovics** (1735–85) (1770) demonstrated the relationship between Hungarian and Saami (Lapp), including Finnish. His proof was so compelling and his methods so clear that he had immense influence on subsequent scholarship in comparative linguistics (see Chapter 2). Grammatical comparisons were central to his approach, but he also utilized basic vocabulary and sound correspondences in arguments for relationship.

On an astronomy research trip to the Norwegian arctic, Sajnovics attempted to test the claim that Hungarian, Saami (Lapp), and Finnish were related. He elicited Saami words and transcribed them in an orthography he devised himself. These "field" data demonstrated to him that these languages were related. Nevertheless, he reasoned that to convince skeptics he must rely on previously published data. Thus Sajnovics (1770) selected examples from the only sources available, Leem's Lapp (Saami) textbook (1748) and lexical samples (1768–81), recorded in an inadequate Danish orthography with Danish glosses, both of which were major obstacles to Sajnovics (Stipa 1990:209–11).

Theodor Benfey (1861), in his famous history of historical linguistic work in Germany, declared Sajnovics the first to employ the principle of grammatical comparison in the pursuit of genetic relationship among languages (cf. Stipa 1990:158). Benfey notwithstanding, Sajnovics had a number of forerunners in both comparative Finno-Ugric and in grammatical comparison of languages in general, from whom he took inspiration (and whom he acknowledged; see Sajnovics 1770:2–3, 111–19; see Chapter 2). Sajnovics' grammatical comparisons between Saami and Hungarian presented agreements in suffixes (e.g. plurals, comparatives), declension of nouns, verb aspect, causatives, tense, pronouns and pronominal suffixes, parts of speech, and particles (Diderichsen 1974:284, 303; Hanzeli 1983:xix; Stipa 1990:211–12). In Sajnovics' opinion, morphosyntactic correspondences were essential for proving relationship among languages (cf. Stipa 1990:211).

Sajnovics' work proved to be very influential on the subsequent development of comparative linguistics (cf. Öhrling 1772; Dobrovsky 1794, 1796; Stipa 1990:193). For example, so well known and influential was Sajnovics that Rask (1993[1818]:283) argued that his own evidence of Germanic kinship with Greek and Latin should be considered compelling because it compared favorably with Sajnovics' "proof that the Hungarian and Lappish [Saami] languages are the same," proof which, Rask said, "no one has denied since his day."

Sámuel Gyarmathi's (1751–1830) (1799) work and influence were discussed in Chapter 4. His thought on genetic relationships was advanced for his day and far superior to Jones' at roughly the same time. Both his and Sajnovics' work had a strong impact on subsequent research in Indo-European and on the development of the comparative method. Gyarmathi was cited by most comparativists for decades afterwards as the model which should be followed. As noted in Chapter 4, Gyarmathi held that grammatical structure was important evidence for establishing genetic relationship among languages, and he presented much in his evidence for Finno-Ugric relationships. As mentioned in Chapter 4, Pedersen (1962[1931]:105) called Gyarmathi's use of inflectional systems for linguistic comparison "the principle which became the lodestar of incipient Indo-European linguistics," i.e. the key to the "comparative grammar" of many subsequent scholars.

In short, Finno-Ugric and broader Uralic were established with reliable methods based on solid evidence – morphological agreements and sound correspondences – very early in comparative linguistics and this early work had a major impact on thinking in the field and on the development of Indo-European study.

6.3   Semitic

The term "Semitic" comes from August Ludwig von Schlözer's (1781) division of human groups according to the sons of Noah, with Semitic for descendents of Shem. With this term, he formally named a linguistic affinity between the languages of the Hebrews, Aramaeans, Arabs, and others which had long been recognized (Ullendorff 1970:261). The Hebrew linguistic tradition began with attempts to deal with the problem of establishing the correct Hebrew text of the Old Testament, and between AD 900 and 1200, Hebrew grammarians, influenced by contemporary Arabic linguistics, developed a system of morphological analysis (Percival 1986a:22). Hebrew grammarians from the tenth century onward compared Hebrew, Aramaic, and Arabic, noting grammatical correspondences (Téné 1980; Ullendorff 1970:261; Brockelmann 1908:1). The tradition culminated in David Qimḥi's (c.1200) grammar, *Sepher mikhlol*, whose main features included the analysis of verbal forms in terms of a set of affixes and roots (not words). This sort of analysis came to have a strong impact on Europe (as mentioned in Chapter 1). Johannes Reuchlin's (1506) comprehensive *De rudimentis Hebraicis* "expound[ed] the analysis of words into root and affix," and introduced the Hebrew method of morphological analysis to European linguistics, and Theodor Bibliander (1548) recommended it for the study of all languages. He thought languages described in the Hebrew manner would be "in conformity with nature" and could therefore be meaningfully compared (Percival 1986b:23, 26, 28, 63).

Semitic comparisons not necessarily intended for historical ends were also undertaken in Europe by Petrus Victorius Palma in 1596 (cited by Gregersen 1977:94), who compared grammatical paradigms among Semitic languages, and by Christian Raue (1650) in his *A general grammar for the ready attaining of the Ebrew, Samaritan, Calde, Syriac, Arabic and Ethiopic languages*. With respect to historical connections, Konrad Gesner's (1555) several language families included Semitic, also Hellenic, Italic, Celtic, Slavic, and Germanic.[3] Mylius (1612) recognized four *linguae matrices* (or *primogeniae seu matriculares*), i.e. language families: Greek, Latin, Teutonic, and "Hebrew." The well-known orientalists of the eighteenth century in general had a correct conception of the Semitic linguistic unity and language relationships, before Indo-European was clearly established (Brockelmann 1908:1).

Hiob Ludolf (1624–1704) was a celebrated founding figure in Semitic linguistics. He worked within the Arabic and Hebrew traditions of analysis and wrote grammars of Ge'ez (Ludolf 1661) and Amharic (Ludolf 1698). His much cited *Dissertatio de harmonia linguae aethiopicae cum ceteris orientalibus* (1702) held grammar to be an important criterion of relatedness:

In order to say that one language is related to another, it is necessary not only that it have some words in common with the other, but also that the grammatical structure for the greater part be the same, as one finds it in the Oriental languages, the Hebrew, Syrian, Arabic, and Ethiopian. (Quoted by Benfey 1869:236; cited in Diderichsen 1974:283)[4]

---

[3] Gesner (1555) also held that Ethiopian and Indic were related (Peters 1974). It is possible that this had some influence on Jones, who expressed a similar view (see Chapter 3).

[4] "Si linguam alteri dicere affinem velimus, necesse est, non tantum ut ea contineat nonnulla alterius cujusdam linguae vocabula, sed etiam ut Grammaticae ratio, maxima sui parte, eadem sit, qualis convenientia cernitur in Orientalibus, Ebraea, Syriaca, Arabica et Aethiopica."

In addition to grammatical evidence, Ludolf also required basic vocabulary, words resistant to borrowing (Benfey 1869:236).

Ludolf's significance in the history of linguistics is shown by the number of scholars who, following Benfey (1869:236), cite him as the first comparative linguist (cf. Arens 1955:88; Jankowsky 1972:23, etc.).

The Semitic works of Antoine Isaac, Baron Silvestre de Sacy (1758–1838) (founder of Arabic and Persian studies in Europe), and Ernest Renan (1823–92) (professor of Hebrew, Syriac, and Chaldaic at Paris University; see Renan 1855, 1878) are often cited as important in the history of Semitic linguistics; their works generally agree about the membership of the Semitic family. Semitic languages are so closely and so obviously related that their family affiliation is easily recognized from shared grammatical traits and overall similarity in structure and vocabulary. As Max Müller (1861:131) reported it:

when theologians extended their studies to Arabic, Chaldee, and Syriac, a step, and a very important step, was made towards the establishment of a class or family of languages. No one could help seeing that these languages were most intimately related to each other, and that they differed from Greek and Latin on all points on which they agreed among themselves. (Müller 1861:131)

it is impossible to mistake a Semitic language; and what is most important – it is impossible to imagine an Aryan [Indo-European] language derived from Semitic, or a Semitic from an Aryan language. The grammatical framework is totally distinct in these two families of speech. (Müller 1861:293)

Müller credited Estienne Guichard (1606) as an early example of a European classification which united these Semitic languages.

Ultimately, the establishment of Semitic as a language family and the determination of its members are perhaps not particularly interesting for our pursuits, since these languages are so closely related that their affinity was easily recognized. As Moscati et al. (1964:16–17) point out, Semitic diversity is not comparable to that of Indo-European; it would "be more appropriate to compare . . . Semitic with the Romance, Slavonic, or Germanic languages."[5] Similarly, typological reasoning, which characterizes the work of several nineteenth-century scholars, was often given for joining Semitic tongues together, for example, the shared triconsonantalism and the role of vowels to signal morphological distinctions which in Indo-European are signaled by inflection (cf. Brockelmann 1908:5). These typological traits later came to be seen as insufficient for establishing a family relationship. Nevertheless, standard methods involving regular sound correspondences do support Semitic and were called upon in later work; Gray's (1934) introductory paragraph shows this concerning the nature of Semitic relationships and the methods utilized in Semitic research:

[5] Moscati et al. (1964:17) also point out that conjectures about broader hypotheses such as "Aryo-Semitic" or "Nostratic" are "very highly speculative."

The Semitic group of languages, like all other linguistic divisions, is characterized by certain regular correspondences in sounds, in inflexions, and, in the main, in syntax between its various members, whereas no such regular correspondences exist between the languages of this group and those of other linguistic families. Resemblances, and even identities, in vocabulary are of minor importance in determining linguistic affinities, since chance coincidences are not unknown, and since words are frequently borrowed by one language, or even by a whole language-group, from another, such loan-words often begin so completely assimilated that they share in all subsequent mutations in phonology and morphology which take place in the adopting language or group of languages. None of the "characteristics" commonly alleged for the Semitic group (or for other groups), e.g. triconsonantal bases, fundamental nature of the consonants as contrasted with the flexional role of the vowels, etc., really characterizes it over against all other groups in the world. Its particular regular correspondences, on the other hand, truly delimit it and contrast it with every other linguistic family. (Gray 1934:3)

(See Moscati *et al.* 1964 for more details.)

In short, while the demonstration of Semitic as a language family was not particularly challenging, the methods utilized were consistent with those we encounter in the establishment of other language families. (See Chapter 9 for attempts to link Semitic with other language families; see below for Afroasiatic.)

6.4   Austronesian

As with other language families, the fuller picture of which languages belong to the Austronesian family developed gradually. Sidney Herbert Ray (1926:6) marked Alvaro de Mendaña's discovery of the Solomon Islands in 1568 as the starting point of "Oceanic Philology," although the "discovery" of the language family is usually attributed to Hadrian Relandus (Relander, Reland) (1706–8) (see Chapter 2). He recognized the relationship between Malay, Javanese, Malagasy and some others, through a comparison of words in the languages that were better known in the region at that time (cf. Schütz 1994:322). Gabelentz (1891:26) calls Relandus "the first comparative linguist in today's sense of the word," claiming that he "even demonstrated laws of sound substitution between Malay and Malagasy" (mentioned in Chapter 2; cf. Benfey 1869:241–2, Davies 1975:617). Relandus' "demonstration" of the relationship of "Madagascarica" (Malagasy of Madagascar) with "Malaíce" (Malay) relied on a comparison of 23 probable cognates, and Relandus also observed the sound correspondences of $v : b$ in eight of his 23 lexical comparisons.

In spite of Relandus' clear erudition in his comparison of these languages, the case for Relandus' seeming historical linguistic precociousness appears overstated. Relandus offered only one paragraph on the topic in which he suggests not what we today would understand as a clear family relationship, but rather speaks of language mixture and borrowing:

If with these things we combine the fact that many Malay words are mixed in with the language of the island of Madagascar, we will be even more astonished that a single language, such as Malay is, has left its footprints in such far-removed tracts of land as the island of Madagascar, by the shore of Africa, and the Cocos island, in the sea that lies between Asia and America. I wish here to add a brick to [the edifice of?] Malagasy words, so as to confirm what I have said. (Relandus 1706–8:XI.138)

Note that everything that will begin with V, like *Vourong, voulou* ['avis' ('bird'), 'arundo' ('reed')], etc. is pronounced by the Malagasys with B (*bourong, boulou* ['bird', 'reed']), when the preceding word ends in a consonant. Thus the correspondence of the same words with Malay ones will shine through more clearly.[6] (Relandus 1706–8:XI.139)

Since Relandus speaks here imprecisely of "mixture," of Malay words in Madagascar, and of Malay "footprints" (tracks) in Madagascar, it is unclear how he thought about the language connections he had discovered. Thus, in spite of his recognition of sound correspondence, it is probably not accurate to assert that Relandus was thinking in ways consistent with modern comparative linguistics. Relandus deserves credit for his observation, but the fuller demonstration of a family relationship for these and other Austronesian languages developed over considerable time.

Not all were as accepting of Relandus' "discovery" of the relationship as Gabelentz was. For example, Wilhelm von Humboldt (1836–9:208) noted that since olden times the dominant opinion had been that the Polynesian languages were related to Malay,[7] though he found the evidence too complicated and incomplete for the proposed relationship to be accepted without doubt. Humboldt himself is often credited with establishing the family relationship; however, some give the credit to Lorenzo Hervás y Panduro's work (1784):

Nay, one of the most brilliant discoveries in the history of the science of language, the establishment of the Malay and Polynesian family of speech, extending from the island of Madagascar . . . to Easter island . . . was made by Hervas long before it was announced to the world by Humboldt. (Müller 1861:142; see below)

Van Driem (2001:306) credits Julius Klaproth (1823, 1826) as "the father of the [broader] Austronesian language family" for his conclusion that the Formosan languages and Malayo-Polynesian languages were genetically related.

Today Austronesian is recognized as the largest language family in the world, both in terms of the number of languages – with *c*.1,200 languages (Pawley

---

[6] "Quibus cum si conferamus illud quod linguae insulae Madagascar plurima vocabula Malaica sint permixta, magis adhuc stupebimus linguam unam, qualis Malaïca est, vestigia sua reliquisse in tam dissitis terrarum spatiis qualia sunt insula Madagascar ad litus Africae & insula Cocos in mari inter Asiam & Americam interjecto, Lubet hic laterculum addere vocum Madagascaricarum, ut dicta nostra confirmemus . . . Nota omnia, quae ab V incipient uti *Vourong, voulou*, &c. a Madagascaribus per B. *Bourong, boulou*, pro nuntiari, quum vox praecedens in consonam definit. Ita magis elucescet convenientia earundem vocum cum Malaïcis." We thank Andrew Carstairs-McCarthy for help with the translation.

[7] To cite just one example, Kraus (1985[1787]:247) presumed a relationship between "Otahitisch" (Tahitian) and "Maleyisch" (Malay) (cf. also Kaltz 1985:256).

and Ross 1993:429) –, and in geographical area – from Taiwan to New Zealand and Hawaii, and from Madagascar to Easter Island. There are about 270 million speakers of Austronesian languages (Tryon 1995:6). In spite of early discoveries, the full extent of the family and a relative consensus concerning its subgrouping has emerged only since the 1970s. In earlier work, it was often called "Malayo-Polynesian," though not all the subgroups were yet recognized, in particular not the more distant relatives in Taiwan. Most scholars today see Proto-Austronesian (PAN) as splitting *c*.5,000–6,000 years ago into Formosan and "Malayo-Polynesian." It is not certain whether the Formosan languages (some ten indigenous Austronesian languages spoken mostly in the interior of Taiwan) constitute a single branch or several distinct branches of the Austronesian family tree: "Formosan languages may comprise more than one first-order branch of AN [Austronesian], perhaps dividing Atayalic (northern), Tsouic (central), and Paiwanic (southern) groups" (Pawley and Ross 1993:436; see Ross 1995a:46–7). Taiwan or perhaps the south China coastal mainland is generally thought to be the area of the PAN homeland. "Malayo-Polynesian" (MP) is a clear subgroup; it branches into Western MP and Central/Eastern MP, which then divides into Central MP (including languages of the Lesser Sundas, Maluku, and coastal regions of Irian Jaya), and Eastern MP – these three, Western MP, Central MP, and Eastern MP, are less secure groupings, and Western (which includes all the Philippine languages, and languages of Sumatra, Java, Madura, Bali, Lombok, and parts of Kalimantan [Borneo], plus AN languages of the Malay peninsula, Chamic languages [spoken by ethnic minorities in Vietnam and Cambodia], Malagasy [Madagascar], Chamorro, and Palau) is controversial. Eastern MP split into two branches, South Halmahera–West New Guinea and Oceanic. The very large Oceanic group, some 500 languages, includes Polynesian, Rotuman, Fijian; Northern New Guinea, Papuan Tip, Meso-Melanesian; Admiralties; Southeast Solomonic; Nuclear Micronesian; Central-North Vanuatu; and New Caledonia-Loyalties. There are some 220 Oceanic languages in Papua New Guinea alone (Pawley and Ross 1993:436–7, 439–40; Tryon 1995:7–13; Ross 1995b). (See Figure 6.2.)

Polynesian is the best-known branch of this huge family. The Polynesian languages are so closely related that their family relationship is obvious even on rather casual inspection. In Robert Louis Stevenson's (1924[1888]:10) apt words, "the languages of Polynesia are easy to smatter, though hard to speak with elegance. And they are extremely similar, so that a person who has a tincture of one or two may risk, not without hope, an attempt upon the others." Still, even the recognition of the genetic relationship among Polynesian languages developed only over time. Before Cook's voyages little was known of Polynesian languages except for the short vocabularies published by the explorers Iacob Le Maire and Willem Cornelis Schouten, who passed through the center of Polynesia in 1616, visiting the outliers of Tonga, Futuna, and Alofi. These vocabulary lists included

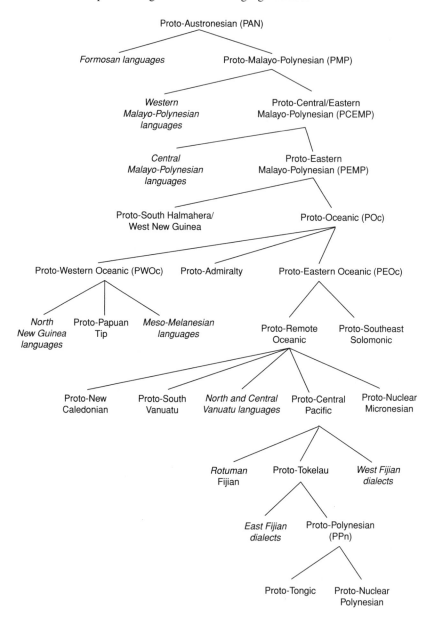

Fig. 6.2 The Austronesian family tree

32 words from East Futuna and 114 from Niuatoputapu (island of north Tonga). (They also collected vocabulary samples of some Melanesian languages.)

Cook and his naturalists, William Anderson and Johann Reinhold Forster, recorded vocabulary from Tahitian and Maori and then later from Easter Island (Rapanui), Marquesan, and Tongan (as well as from three other non-Polynesian Oceanic languages), and about 40 words from these five languages were presented in the comparative table at the end of Cook's account (Cook 1777:2.364). Johann Reinhold Forster, naturalist on Captain Cook's second voyage to the Pacific, collected a significant amount of material on Oceanic languages, but he had no significant impact on the understanding of language classification in this part of the world, since his linguistic materials were not published with accounts of the second voyage. Rather, Forster's three manuscripts containing the linguistic material from the voyage were found among Forster's books bought by the royal Prussian Library in Berlin when he died in 1798 (Rensch 1996:383). Forster was able to distinguish Polynesian – which he called the "same general language" – from non-Polynesian languages. As he says:

I took particular care in collecting the words of every peculiar nation we met with, that I might be enabled to form an idea of the whole, and how far all the languages are related to each other. I soon perceived, that in general, the five nations already enumerated [O-Taheitee (Tahiti), the Society Islands (Tahitian islands, French Polynesia), the Marquesas, Easter Island, and New Zealand], spoke a language differing only in a few words, and that for the greater part, the difference consisted in a few vowels or consonants, though the words still preserved a great affinity; nay, many were absolutely the same in all the dialects. I could therefore no longer doubt, that they were all descended from the same original stem, and that the differences in the language arose only from the difficulty of pronouncing consonants, which some sounded more easily, whilst others, either changed, or entirely omitted them. (Rensch 1996[1778]:185)

The L A N G U A G E of the Society Islands [Tahitian] was better understood by us than any other . . . We found, however, that the language spoken at Easter Island, the Marquesas, the Low, the Society [Tahiti], and Friendly-Islands [Tonga], and in New Zeeland, is the same, and that the differences are hardly sufficient to constitute dialects. The languages spoken at the New-Hebrides, New-Caledonia, and New Holland, are absolutely distinct from the above general language, and likewise differ among themselves. (Rensch 1996[1778]:249)

Forster had also observed connections with Malay, but did not know how to interpret them:

We likewise find a very remarkable similarity between several words of the fair tribe of islanders in the South Sea [Polynesians], and some of the Malays. But it would be highly inconclusive from the similarity of a few words, to infer that these islanders were descended from the Malays: for as the Malay contains words found in the Persian, Malabar, Braminic, Cingalese, Javanese, and Malegass [Malagasy]. (Rensch 1996[1778]:187)

In all the Philippines, the interior mountainous parts, are inhabited by a black set of people, with frizzled hair, who are tall, lusty, and very warlike, and speak a peculiar language different from that of their neighbours. But the outskirts towards the sea are peopled with a race infinitely fairer, having long hair, and speaking different languages: they are of various denominations, but the *Tagales*, *Pampangos*, and *Bissayas*, are the most celebrated among them. The former are the more antient inhabitants, and the latter are certainly related to the various tribes of Malays . . . Their language is likewise in many instances related to that of the Malays. (Rensch 1996[1778]:187)

The language of the Tagalas [Tagalog] having an undoubted relation to that of the Malays, as may be easily collected from the comparison of the words of both languages; it can be no wonder that Malayan words were found in the Taheitean [Tahitian] language, and in its various dialects. These general observations on the language are so far curious and interesting, as they afford a farther confirmation of the origin and migration of these islanders. (Rensch 1996[1778]:250)

(See also Ray 1926:12, 19; Schütz 1994:323; and Grace 1959:3.)

While Cook's naturalists were on the right track towards classification of the languages, Sir William Jones (1799c:10), as mentioned in Chapter 3, got things wrong. He mistook Malay as Semitic (based on Arabic books). He also mistakenly regarded other Austronesian languages as Indo-European, especially associated with Sanskrit (see quotes in Chapter 3).

Like Max Müller (1861:142) before him, Ray (1926:20) also attributes the first definite establishment of Malayo-Polynesian as a family to Lorenzo Hervás y Panduro (1784, see 1800–5:30), who gave a table of agreements in the numerals from the Cook specimens and from the Marianas, Philippines, Malay, Java, and Madagascar. Hervás y Panduro himself, however, cedes the credit for the discovery to Captain James Cook. William Marsden (1834), cited by Sir William Jones (Chapter 3), more clearly demonstrated the general language he called "Polynesian," which is found, he said, "from Madagascar, or, more obviously, from Sumatra, as its western, to Easter Island, in the Pacific Ocean, as its eastern limit" (Marsden 1834:3; see also Ray 1926:20). He says of their relationship:

there is a manifest connexion between many of the words by which the inhabitants of these islands express their simple perceptions, and in some instances of places the most remote from each other, a striking affinity; insomuch that we may pronounce the various dialects [languages], in a collective sense, to form substantially one great language [family]. (Marsden 1834:3)

Languages of the Malay archipelago Marsden called "Hither Polynesian" and others were called "Further Polynesian." Marsden distinguished races among Pacific peoples and associated his general language only with the lighter-skinned people (setting aside the "Negritos" and their languages, 1834: 3, but see 13–16). Assumptions about race complicated subsequent classificatory work in Austronesian languages significantly. Marsden rejects as "materially wrong" the notion some had of "Malayan" (Malay) as "the parent stock from which the other dialects have sprung," explaining that "on a superficial view, the Malayan might be thought to belong to a distinct family; yet a comparison of its most simple vocables with those of the less cultivated dialects, with attention to the structure of both, will furnish abundant evidence of their original consanguinity" (Marsden 1834:8). He also dismissed Sir William Jones' Sanskrit origin theory (Chapter 3), suggesting that "it is perhaps a more natural inference to conclude that they have all been modified by some general language, than, with Sir W. Jones, to determine that the parent of them all has been Sanskrit" (Marsden 1834:8).

Marsden (1834:11–12) gives us a fairly explicit statement of his methods:

My plan for the comparison of languages has been to adopt a limited number of words [i.e. 45], the most simple in their meaning and the least liable to misapprehension, to be used as an invariable and therefore an impartial standard: and if, upon comparing these lists, a reasonable proportion of their respective terms are found to bear a resemblance to each other, I have then felt justified in considering them cognate dialects. This mode appeared to me preferable to that of taking insulated [isolated] words, and seeking generally through vocabularies for such as may happen to resemble them in sound; because it is not from what may be termed chance coincidences, that a relationship can be inferred.

In short, Marsden relied on sound–meaning similarities in basic vocabulary. This approach may be inadequate for proof of controversial cases of disputed genetic relationship, but given the rather obvious relatedness of the languages he was comparing, it was sufficient for this particular case, which, of course, offers no room for doubt in the later more reliable applications of the comparative method. Moreover, Marsden did observe some sound correspondences, noting, for example that in "Madagash" (Malagasy), "the *v* uniformly tak[es] the place of the *b* [of "Malayan" and other related languages], as *r* often does of *d* and *l*" (Marsden 1834:33); several cognates are presented and discussed illustrating these; mention of other such seeming sound correspondences are found scattered through the work (for example, 1834: 42, 52, 55, 59–60, 68). He also made specific grammatical comparisons in several cases (see for example Marsden 1834:40–2, and elsewhere). Marsden presented a brief discussion of each of a large number of Pacific languages; his comparative word lists (of 34 words) are provided for nearly ninety languages, with multiple lists sometimes representing distinct dialects for several of these. Most are Austronesian, though there are also others, Chinese, Andaman Islands languages, and some Australian languages, for example, also in the lists.

As the following quotation from Lorrin Andrews (1836) shows, significant progress had been made in understanding the Polynesian subfamily by this date:

The origin of the language of the Polynesians, divided as it is into several different dialects, is buried in deep obscurity. The people themselves know not whence they are, as the fabulous accounts of their own origin sufficiently testify; and yet, on the slightest inspection and comparison of the different dialects, it cannot for a moment be doubted that they had one common origin. And a singular circumstance is, that the people at the extreme parts of Polynesia speak dialects of the general language the most resembling each other . . . no doubt a careful and thorough examination of the several dialects, and a comparison of one with the other with a view to ascertain the groundwork of the general language, and a comparison with the languages of the neighboring continents, would not only be a subject of inquiry full of interest, but would go far to indicate the probable origin of this people. (Andrews 1836:12–13 [quoted in Schütz 1994:322])

Ten years later, Horatio Hale (1846:58) could present a "comparative grammar of the Polynesian dialects [languages]." He catalogues the sound changes that the various Polynesian languages in his list have undergone (Hale 1846:231–2), in a table of sound correspondences labeled as "regular permutations." A set of eighteen cognates in eight languages is also presented (1846:235) which "show the changes which words undergo." Finally, there is a long "essay at the lexicon of the Polynesian language" (1846:291–339) in which a "primitive or radical form of the word" is established, where "in many instances . . . the primitive form of the word is not found in our vocabularies [of various Polynesian languages], but has been deduced from comparison of the variations" (1846:292). This is an early instance of reconstruction via the comparative method.

As for the wider Austronesian family beyond Polynesian, as mentioned above, several scholars credit Wilhelm von Humboldt with proving the Malayo-Polynesian genetic relationship in his famous work on the "Kawi" language of Java (Humboldt 1836–9; cf. Pedersen (1962[1931]:130), and Humboldt is also given credit for coining the name "Malayo-Polynesian" (Tryon 1995:18; see also Müller 1861:142). Humboldt (1836–9:207) recognized the general extent of the family:

All the languages of the olive-colored race which have been recognized until now betray by even a superficial comparison an unmistakable unity [Gleichförmigkeit] from the most western point, Madagascar, to the most eastern, Easter Island, and from south to north to the Asiatic mainland, and in the open sea to the Sandwich Islands [Hawaii].[8]

Nevertheless, Humboldt cited a number of earlier scholars (Marsden, Crawfurd, Raffles) who had recognized language relationships, and he discussed their evidence. George Grace (1959:3) reports that "Humboldt gave sketches of several Indonesian and Polynesian languages and established definitely that they were members of the same family" (see also Ray 1926:20–1). Humboldt (1836–9:241–8, 264) compared 131 words in nine languages of the Mayalan

---

[8] "Alle bis jetzt bekannt gewordenen Sprachen der olivenfarbigen Race aber verrathen, von dem westlichsten Punkte, Madagascar, bis zum östlichsten, der Osterinsel, und von Süden nach Norden bis zum Asiatischen Festlande, und im freien Meere bis zu den Sandwich-Inseln hin, eine auch bei flüchtiger Vergleichung unverkennbare Gleichförmigkeit."

and Polynesian regions: Malayisch (Malay), Javanisch (Javanese), Bugis (of Sulawesi, Indonesia), Madecassisch (Malagasy, from five different sources), Tagalisch (Tagalog), Tongish (Tongan), Neu-Seeländisch (Maori), Tahitisch (Tahitian), and Hawaiisch (Hawai'ian). He did not, however, rely only on vocabulary ("basic vocabulary," Humboldt 1836–9:209–10, 224–5) as proof of kinship, but also utilized phonological and grammatical comparisons, both individual traits and the whole grammar (cf. Humboldt 1836–9:208–10, 217, 221). He found the sameness of their words and roots, and of their grammatical structure, to be proof that these languages are related (Humboldt 1836–9:217). Humboldt's discussion of sound correspondences was not as sophisticated as that of later scholars, but he was certainly aware of their importance as "the most convincing proof of family relationship" (Humboldt 1836–9:219–20)[9] and of dealing with them in order to determine cognates accurately; he discussed at length some of the "best examples" of notable correspondences in these languages (Humboldt 1836–9:225–7). He pointed out that "in some cases each language shows its own regular 'shift of letters [sounds]'" (Humboldt 1836–9:225), for example, the correspondence between r, l, and d across several of the languages in several cognate sets, also <v> and <b>, with examples of cognates exhibiting a k to "absence" ($\emptyset$; actually glottal stop) across several languages, the s to h correspondence in several, among other examples. At the end of his discussion of these examples, he concludes, "from the cases presented here the sound change[s] that has taken place in these languages can be observed" (Humboldt 1836–9:227).

Humboldt presented a table of fifty-six lexical comparisons (plus words for the numbers 1–10, 100, and 1,000), of mostly cognate words from the nine languages mentioned above. This, perhaps more than anything else, impressed those who came after him.

Humboldt believed that the simplicity of Polynesian grammar proved its greater antiquity, the most archaic form of Malayo-Polynesian, and that the languages all belong to one grammatical system so that variations within the grammars are seen as consistent with that single grammatical system (Ray 1926:20–1). Unfortunately, this and similar evolutionary views of the nature of grammar and language change got the relationship of the Polynesian languages with respect to the rest of the family wrong for many years (see Chapter 8).

David Cargill in 1840 (mentioned in Chapter 1) called on several sorts of linguistic evidence (expressing also sympathy for non-linguistic evidence) in his answer to the request from the Wesleyan Methodist Society in London to discuss the relationship of Fijian to "the other Polynesian dialects." He compared words from Fijian, Tongan, Hawai'ian, Tahitian, and Samoan, first with a list showing no sound shifts among these languages involving the consonants

---

[9] "was überall der überzeugendste Beweis der Stammverwandtschaft ist."

t, l, m, n, and second with a list of "words which have evidently sprung from one stock, but which have assumed a different appearance in adaptation to the genious of the people," i.e. cognates exhibiting differences among consonant correspondences. His third source of evidence was that "they [Polynesian languages] are all characterized by the same peculiarities," i.e. mostly grammatical and phonological observations. Here he pointed out correspondence of grammatical particles and inclusive/exclusive pronouns. His final type of evidence he called "idiom," essentially overall typological congruences: "the different structures have been reared in imitation of one model," and "one spirit has infused the characteristic peculiarities of all the dialects of Polynesia" (cited in Schütz 1972:45–6).

As mentioned, van Driem (2001:306) credits Julius Klaproth (1823, 1826) for recognizing that the Formosan languages and Malayo-Polynesian languages were genetically related.

As languages of New Guinea and Melanesia came to be better represented in the information available, preconceptions about race complicated linguistic classification. Notions of distinct races correlated with language differences in Oceania had persisted almost from the earliest recordings. For example, Forster (1996[1778]:153), a naturalist on Cook's second voyage charged with collecting vocabularies from native peoples encountered, asserts vigorously:

We chiefly observed two great varieties of people in the South Seas; the one more fair, well limbed, athletic, of a fine size, and a kind benevolent temper; the other, blacker, the hair just beginning to become woolly and crisp, the body more slender and low, and their temper, if possible more brisk, though somewhat mistrustful. The first race inhabits O-Taheitee [Tahiti], and the Society Isles [western Tahitian islands], the Marquesas, the Friendly Isles [Tonga], Easter-Island, and New-Zeeland. The second race peoples New-Caledonia, Tanna [Vanuatu], and the New Hebrides [Vanuatu], especially Mallicollo [Malakula, Vanuatu].

Latham (1843) spoke of "Negrito languages," of "an older population of ruder manners, and darker colour than the Malays, the proper Polynesians, and the populations allied to them" (quoted in Ray 1926:21). Friedrich Müller's (1876–88) linguistic classification followed human physical traits, especially hair, and thus for him the Austronesian languages were a subdivision of the languages of the *straffhaarigen Rassen* [straight-haired races], a subdivision of the languages of the *schlichthaarigen Rassen* [smooth-haired races] (Grace 1959:4). Hans Conon von der Gabelentz (1861) published collections of grammatical sketches and vocabularies of languages of Melanesia (Fiji, the Loyalty Islands, Vanuatu [former New Hebrides], and the Solomons), compiled from work by missionaries. He thought the evidence proved that these Melanesian languages all belonged to a single stock and that Melanesian and Polynesian languages share more than can be explained by borrowing (Grace 1959:4). In his first work,

Gabelentz (1861) distinguished Melanesians (called black) from Polynesians (called brown); he accepted that Polynesian and Malayan languages belong to the same family, but in spite of recognition of many similarities between Melanesian and Polynesian languages, he was inclined to feel that a decision on their relationship would require more grammatical study (Ray 1926:22). He grouped the Melanesian languages together based on vocabulary, though they varied much in grammar. He was inclined towards Polynesian and Melanesian having a common origin, since he thought borrowing was not sufficient to explain the similarities (Ray 1926:22–3). However, Gabelentz, like others at the time, considered both the language and the people of Fiji to be a mixture between *braunen und schwarzen* [brown and black] (Schütz 1972:47).

Tryon (1995:19) reports H. N. van der Tuuk (1861, 1864, 1864/7) as "the first to apply the principles of Indo-European comparative linguistics to the Austronesian languages. His [van der Tuuk's] work on Batak, Batavian Malay, Malagasy, Old Javanese and Balinese provided a starting point for the next generation of Austronesian historical linguists."

Understanding of the family as a whole still remained unsettled. Robert Cordington's (1885a) reading of past attempts to classify languages of the region was perceptive. Noting that various "Ocean families" of languages do not "borrow from the other without good reason," he observed:

The Melanesian languages, which are very little known, come geographically between the Malay and Polynesian languages, which are well known. Any observer of the Melanesian languages who approaches from the West and sees in them much that is the same with the Malay, calls that a Malay element, and calls that which he does not recognise the native Melanesian or Papuan element. One who approaches the Melanesian languages from the East finds much that is common with the Polynesian, and he calls that the Polynesian element, and again what he does not recognise the Melanesian or Papuan. But suppose an observer to begin with the Melanesian languages, and, being familiar with them, to advance on the one side to the Polynesian regions and on the other to the Malayan. He will find in the islands of the Eastern Pacific people of brown colour, using a language very much of which is familiar to him, but one poorer in sounds, poorer in Grammatical forms. He will say that they speak a kind of Melanesian dialect. (Cordington 1885a:11)

Cordington asserted firmly that the Melanesian languages were Austronesian and he denied the relevance of the racial arguments:

There is no doubt a certain reluctance on the brown side to acknowledge the kindred of the black. The Melanesians are the poor relations, at the best . . . but a question of language must be discussed on its own merits, and degrees of complexion or cultivation may be put on one side. (Cordington 1885a:12–13)

Cordington accepted the genetic relationships between Indonesian, Polynesian, Melanesian, and Micronesian languages. He compared thirty-four "Melanesian" languages and showed vocabulary and grammatical agreements in Maori,

Malagasy, Malay, and these Melanesian languages (Cordington 1885a:18–24), preceded by a reasonable discussion of methodology "for the proof of kinship of languages" (e.g. mentioning that when "the changes and variations are regular, no one can doubt the identity of the word" [Cordington 1885a:23] and that "the proof of kindred afforded by the Grammar of languages is no doubt more effective than that given by Vocabulary" [Cordington 1885a:25]).

Hendrik Kern (1886, 1906), with background in Indo-European and Indonesian, compared the languages of the Melanesian area. He concluded that "Fijian and Polynesian are offshoots of one stem which led an independent life long, very long after it had separated from the parent trunk somewhere in the Indian archipelago." He debunked the claim of Polynesian influence on Fijian, saying, "I, myself, have not been able to discover a single trace of such an influence. There is, however, an obvious similarity throughout the grammar, such as there is, for example, between French and Italian grammar" (Kern 1916:247; quoted in Grace 1959:5).

Only from 1889 onward did significant information on the Papuan languages of New Guinea become available and these were shown to be distinct from the Austronesian languages (cf. Ray 1926:24). The name "Austronesian" was given to the broader family by Wilhelm Schmidt (1899).

Reconstruction of Proto-Austronesian phonology, grammar, and vocabulary started with Brandstetter (1893), although Otto Dempwolff (1934–8) is considered the first serious effort at reconstruction, and his work is the backdrop for all modern studies (cf. Clark 1987; Pawley 1974). (For Austronesian historical linguistics generally, see Ross 1995a.)

Understanding of the full range of Austronesian unfolded over time; nevertheless, except for the Polynesian languages with their high degree of similarity one to another, the relationships came to be recognized based on traditional criteria: basic vocabulary, grammatical agreements, and sound correspondences.

6.5   Dravidian

Dravidian is the family which embraces most of the languages of south India, as well as a few others elsewhere on the Indian subcontinent – some twenty-five languages spoken by about 200 million speakers (Krishnamurti 2001:370). Hindu grammarians had recognized the linguistic diversity found in India, but tended to ignore the distinction between Indo-Aryan and Dravidian, seeing the Dravidian languages as "'Prakrit' descendants related to Sanskrit in the same way that Hindi, Bengali, and Marathi are" (Emeneau 2000:546) – such a view has persisted into modern times in some quarters in India. Francis Whyte Ellis, British civil servant (then head of the Board of Superintendence for the College of Fort St. George), is conventionally credited as the first to recognize the Dravidian language family. Nevertheless, Ellis depended in part on Roberts (1798) for his material (Zvelebil 1990:xviii–xix). Ellis' *Disserta-tion on the Telugu language* was published as a "Note to the Introduction" in Alexander Duncan Campbell's *A grammar of the Teloogoo language com-monly called the Gentoo* in 1816. His primary goal was to show that the then common belief that Telugu and other Dravidian languages of south India were related to or descended from Sanskrit was wrong (cf. Emeneau 2000:546); Ellis said:

> It is the intent of the following observations to shew . . . that neither the Tamil, the Telugu, nor any of their cognate dialects [languages] are derivations from the Sanscrit; that the latter, however it may contribute to their polish, is not necessary for their existence; and that they form a distinct family of languages, with which the Sanscrit has, in latter times especially, intermixed, but with which it has not radical [genetic] connexion. (Ellis 1991[1816]:2)

He continued:

> The members, constituting the family of languages, which may be appropriately called the dialects [languages] of Southern India, are the high and low Tamil; the Telugu, gram-matical and vulgar; Carnátaca or Cannadèi [Kannada], ancient and modern; Malayálma or Malayálam . . .; and the Tuluva [Tulu] . . . [and others]. (Ellis 1991[1816]:3)

(See also Krishnamurti 1969:312, 2001:371; Zvelebil 1990x:xviii.)

Ellis did not discuss his methods explicitly, but the sort of evidence he used is clear from his treatment of his topic. He based his conclusion of genetic relationship mostly on lexical and grammatical evidence. He was also aware of sound correspondences, though it is not clear to what extent he may have viewed them as evidence for the genetic relationship. He said:

> The Telugu, to which attention is here more specially directed, is formed from its own roots, which, in general, have no connexion with the Sanscrit, nor with those of any other language, the cognate dialects [languages] of Southern India, the Tamil, Cannadèi &c. excepted, with which, allowing for the occasional variation of consimilar sounds, they generally agree; the actual difference in the three dialects [languages] here mentioned is in fact to be found only in the affixes used in the formation of words from the roots. (Ellis 1991[1816]:3)

In his exposition he shows that many verb roots compared in Sanskrit and Telugu are totally lacking in similarity, while compared roots from Telugu, Cannadèi (Kannada), and Tamil are very similar indeed. This is followed by comparison of additional words in order to show not just that "radical con-nection [genetic relationship] may be proved to exist" but to demonstrate just how "'intimate' the connection is" (Ellis 1991[1816]:11), showing that "the native terms in each, also correspond" (18). In his listing of compared verb roots and nouns, Ellis provided abundant commentary on morphological and phonological agreements and differences in the three languages which reveal something of his insights and methods. For example, in several cases, he points out sound correspondences, e.g. "when *P* begins a word in Tamil or Telugu, it is in Cannadèi changed to *H*, as in Tamil *Palli* Tel: *Palle*, Can. *Halli a small village*: but in old Can. all such words may, also, be written with a *P*" (19); "the consonant of this root . . . is pronounced *tsa* and *cha* in Telugu: *cha* in Can. and *sa, sha, cha*, and *ja* in Tam. according as it is final or medial, single or double" (8). He seems to rely most heavily on the overall agreements in morphology as evidence. He says: "With little variation, the composition of the Tamil [and] Cannadèi are the same as the Telugu and the same distinctions, consequently, are made by their grammatical writers" (21). He also provides a detailed comparison of syntax between Sanskrit, Telugu, Kannada, and Tamil, showing that "the Sanscrit differs in every point from the southern dialects" (25), while the other three hold much in common.

Ellis' methods are still a far cry from the more evolved ones of later times, but because Dravidian languages are reasonably closely related and easy to recognize, his approach was adequate to demonstrate their family relationship. Still, Ellis had little impact on the continuing development or even general recognition of Dravidian. As Emeneau (2000:547) points out, "[Ellis] dropped out of sight as the discoverer until his publication in a 'Note to the introduction' of A. D. Campbell's *A grammar of the Teloogoo language* was brought to modern attention again by N. Venkata Rao (1954–55) followed by Burrow and Emeneau (1961:v; 1984:vii), and Krishnamurti (1969:311–12)."

Others also made preliminary comparisons among the Dravidian languages. For example, Christian Lassen (1844) recognized that Brahui was related to the languages of south India. Valentin Christian Friedrich Rost (1790–1862) (1846) compared genitives in Dravidian languages, his "dekhanischen Sprachen." Walter Elliot (1847) made comparisons between the language of the "Gonds" (Gondi) and Telugu, Tamil, and Kannada (Zvelebil 1990:xix). R. Stevenson (1852) also compared the vocabulary of several of these languages.

However, it is Robert A. Caldwell, Church of England clergyman (later bishop), who is usually seen as providing the definitive founding work in comparative Dravidian (Caldwell 1856, subsequent editions 1875, 1913), written forty years after Ellis, seventy after Jones, and twenty before the Neogrammarians – when "comparative linguistics was still in its infancy" (Krishnamurti 2001:371). Caldwell coined the name by which the family is known, basing it on the Sanskrit word *drāviḍa-/dārmiḍa-* which presumably meant 'Tamil' (perhaps a wrong reading; cf. Zvelebil 1970:12, 1990:xx–xxi; said to be of "doubtful etymology," Krishnamurti 2001:370). (The family had been known earlier as "Tamilian"/"Tamulian" or "Dekhan," Bloch 1954:xxvi; Zvelebil 1970:12.)

The demonstration of Dravidian genetic relationship, as in the case of other language families, was not a once-and-for-all discovery of a kinship for all languages now known to be Dravidian. New Dravidian languages continued to be discovered, with several coming to light during the 1960s and 1970s from more remote jungle and mountainous areas (Zvelebil 1990:xxiv–xxv, 1994:1063). There are now more than twenty-five known Dravidian languages, although Caldwell dealt with only twelve, drawing mainly only from the literary languages, with primacy given to Tamil; his others were Malayalam, Kannada, Telugu, Kota, Toda, Tulu, Gondi, Kui-Kuvi, Kurukh (Kurux), Kodagu, and Malto, and a note on Brahui was added to Caldwell's second edition (1875). With limited sources, Caldwell proved the family relationship, relying on phonological and morphological evidence; he also disproved (as Ellis had done before him) the strongly held assumption of a Sanskrit origin for Dravidian languages (cf. Krishnamurti 1969:312). For a survey and history of later work further developing Dravidian comparative linguistics, see Krishnamurti (1969, 1985, 1994, 2001:370–81, 2001).

Caldwell's (1974[1875]:1) method relied on comparing "grammatical principles and forms"; he held the Dravidian languages to be related:

because of the essential and distinctive grammatical characteristics which they all possess in common, and in virtue of which, joined to the possession in common of a large number of roots of primary importance, they justly claim to be considered as springing from a common origin, and as forming a distinct family of tongues. (Caldwell 1974[1856/75]:3)

He found Brahui (a rather distinct Dravidian language located in modern Pakistan at a considerable distance from most of its relatives in south India) a bit trickier:

It is true that the great majority of the words in the Brahui language seem altogether unconnected with Dravidian roots; but it will be evident from the analogies in structure, as well as in the vocabulary, that this language contains many grammatical forms essentially and distinctly Dravidian, together with a small proportion of important Dravidian words. (Caldwell 1974[1856/75]:40)

Curiously, the written, classical Dravidian languages were generally treated as closely associated so that it was necessary to point out just how different they really were from one another. This led to a twist with regard to the "ruder" or "unwritten" Dravidian languages. Where it was necessary to demonstrate the differences among the written, classical Dravidian tongues, with regard to the others, Caldwell found it necessary to demonstrate evidence that these languages are related; as he said:

So many and great are the differences and peculiarities observable amongst these rude dialects [languages], that it has seemed to me to be necessary to prove, not that they differ, but that they belong, notwithstanding their differences, to the same stock as the more cultivated tongues, and that they have an equal right to be termed Dravidian. (Caldwell 1974[1856/75]:41)

While sound correspondences were not given any particular emphasis in Caldwell's study, he does cite them among the evidence for particular language relationships, e.g. "Gônd [Gondi] also like Canarese [Kannada] sometimes prefers *k* where the Telugu has *ch* and the Tamil *s*" (illustrated in examples of cognates) (Caldwell 1974[1856/75]:627).

Dravidian, therefore, like other language families, was established on the basis of grammatical evidence, especially morphological; lexical similarities, though not given excessive weight and wielded so as to be able to separate out Sanskrit loans; and sound correspondences, though not fully developed and not thought of in precisely the same way that modern historical linguists would.

Proposals to link Dravidian with various other language families abound. The best known of these involve Uralic, Ural-Altaic, Japanese, and Elamite; even Caldwell (1974[1856/75]:42, 62–3) recommended Uralic and "Altaic" connections, though the support for these is questioned (see Chapter 9).

6.6   Sino-Tibetan

In some senses Sino-Tibetan is of less interest for our purpose, since as an established language family it is very "young." As Matisoff (1991:469) says, "it is sobering to realize that ST [Sino-Tibetan] linguistics is only about 50 years old, and has been a flourishing field of inquiry for only the past 25 years." The classification has been and continues to be controversial; many Chinese scholars include in the family also Hmong-Mien (Miao-Yao) and Tai-Kadai languages, where most western scholars limit the family to the two branches, Chinese and Tibeto-Burman.[10] (For a thorough review of the field, see Matisoff 1991, 2003; see also van Driem 2001:333–462.) In other significant ways, however, Sino-Tibetan is instructive, for the challenges it offers to classification and to the application of the comparative method. For one, the predominance of monosyllabic roots makes it more difficult to distinguish inheritance from sheer chance when monosyllabic words are compared among the languages. There is just a higher chance of possible accidental similarity when it comes to compared short forms (see Nichols 1996a; Ringe 1999; Chapter 7). Another complication is the extensive borrowing among languages in the areas where Sino-Tibetan languages are found. Extensive borrowings from both within the family and from non-related languages make it difficult to distinguish between what is inherited from a common ancestor and what has been borrowed (see Migli-azza 1996:19). Areal linguistics in southeast Asia also complicates linguistic

---

[10] Interestingly, Greenberg (1996a:134) says of Sino-Tibetan that "it would seem that this [Sino-Tibetan] is one of the most solidly based and universally accepted linguistic stocks in the world."

classification (see Matisoff 2003:6–8). For example, some earlier classifications included Miao-Yao, Tai, and Vietnamese in Sino-Tibetan based on typological resemblances to Chinese, but it is now clear that the structural resemblances and shared vocabulary among these languages reflect areal linguistics and borrowing rather than shared inheritance from a common ancestor (see Delancey 1990.) Finally, the lack of written records for some of the languages and in particular the unphonological nature of the writing systems that do exist for a number of the languages have also been seen as hampering comparison (see Matisoff 1991:473–4).

While Sino-Tibetan as a whole is young as an established family, Tibeto-Burman (the largest subgroup of Sino-Tibetan) was established rather early. Julius Klaproth (1823:365) pointed out similarities between Burmese and Tibetan, observing also that Tibet has many roots in common with Chinese (Klaproth 1823:346), but he separated Vietnamese, Thai, and Mon from these. Brian Houghton Hodgson (1828) is credited by many as the first to recognize the unity of the Tibeto-Burman languages (Grierson 1909; Hale 1982:1). Grierson and Konow (1909:13) attributed to Max Müller (1854:97ff) the first attempt at classification; Müller divided Tibeto-Burman languages into two groups: his sub-Himalayan or Gangetic group and the Lohitic group, which included Burman, the dialects of North Assam, Naga, Bodo, Kachin, and Kuki-Chin (Hale 1982:1). Benedict (1972) gave the title of the first Tibeto-Burmanist to Wolfenden (1929), though not all agree (see Shafer 1955).

August Conrady (1896) was influential; Egerod (1976:51) says Conrady's is "a work the comparativist will never tire of reading and admiring." British scholars and colonial administrators were the first to study the local "tribal" languages in India and Burma, and in the Linguistic Survey of India, G. A. Grierson (1903) and Grierson and Konow (1904, 1909, 1927, 1928) presented a classification of Tibeto-Burman languages, the general characteristics of the family and its major subgroupings, and a set of word lists, with brief descriptions of about one hundred languages which include grammatical comments and texts with word-by-word and free translations (cf. Hale 1982).

Shafer (1966–73), Voegelin and Voegelin (1965–6), and Benedict (1972) all attempted to describe broader Sino-Tibetan. There is some contention among scholars about, on the one hand, the extent of the Sino-Tibetan family, and on the other hand about its very existence, or rather about whether Chinese (Sinitic) and Tibeto-Burman can justifiedly be placed together, though this last doubt seems not to be taken to be a serious problem (see Matisoff 2003).

A large-scale investigation was undertaken as a WPA (Works Progress Administration) depression relief project in the US, sponsored by Alfred Kroeber and headed by Robert Shafer, an "eccentric amateur comparativist" (Matisoff 2003:1), with a range of helpers, many non-linguists, including Paul Benedict (see below). Between 1935 and 1941 the project's task was to collate all the published material on Sino-Tibetan languages. The result was the unpublished manuscript (1939–41) called "Sino-Tibetan Linguistics." Benedict (1975b) saw Shafer as the first Sino-Tibetanist. Both Shafer and Benedict used this source in their later papers. Shafer sifted through the descriptive Sino-Tibetan sources and attempted to establish the sound correspondences upon which to base a classification of the languages, attempting a proper application of the comparative method. Despite the effort, Matisoff (1991, 2003) points out as problems the inadequate quality of the data then available for the various language groups and Shafer's distrust of phonemic representations. Hale (1982:6) notes that "Shafer's work has never received a very enthusiastic following . . . his methods have generally been considered inadequate and his handling of materials, lacking in insight and discrimination." Shafer (1955) included Tai in the Sino-Tibetan family, though Tai is not considered part of the family by most Western scholars in this field today. The work was finally published in five parts (Shafer 1966–73).

Using the same database, Benedict wrote *Sino-Tibetan: a conspectus* in 1942 or 1943, but the manuscript remained unpublished until (re-)discovered by Matisoff in 1968, who annotated and edited it, and published it as Benedict (1972). Matisoff (2003:32) sees this publication as laying "the foundations for modern Sino-Tibetan historical/comparative linguistics." Hale (1982:6) notes that although the *Conspectus* can be difficult to read and interpret, it "is easily the best book of its kind that we have." Though using the same data as Shafer, Benedict arrived at different conclusions. The work was widely accepted, though criticized by Miller (1974) for methodological peculiarities. For example, Benedict allowed considerable semantic shift coupled with phonological regularities, and Miller thought few of his cognate sets would be considered well behaved by strict standards.

Matisoff's (2003) *Handbook of Proto-Tibeto-Burman* constitutes the fullest treatment of the family, in particular the Tibeto-Burman side.

In short, the reliable work to establish Sino-Tibetan, though fraught by considerable difficulties, also relied on standard criteria, especially regular sound correspondences.

6.7   American Indian language families

There are some 180 different language families (and isolates) in the Americas. We do not, however, attempt to survey how these were established. Rather, in this section we deal only briefly with some of the better-known families which were established fairly early, concentrating on the methods used to establish them and on correcting confusing claims about how this was done. (See Campbell 1997a for details.)

6.7.1   Eskimo–Aleut

The relationship between Eskimo and Aleut was discovered by Rasmus Rask in 1820 (Thalbitzer 1922), was known to Latham (1850) and Buschmann (1856), and has subsequently been thoroughly confirmed (Bergsland 1959, 1978; Marsh and Swadesh 1951; cf. also Fortescue 1994). The connection between the two branches is remote, referred to as the "enormous gap between Eskimo and Aleut" (Woodbury 1984:62). The methods used to establish the family were reasonably straightforward; Rask relied on "grammatical proof," but also utilized lexical comparisons and phonetic evidence to support the relationship (see Thalbitzer 1922).

6.7.2   Algonquian

Algonquian as a recognized language family has a long, impressive pedigree. Roger Williams' (1643) *A key into the language of America*, on Algonquian languages of New England, was an influential contribution. He discovered the sound correspondence involving $n : l : r : y$ in several New England Algonquian languages (Williams 1643; Haas 1967:817). John Eliot (1604–90) (1666) observed the same correspondence (except for y). The significance of this sound correspondence for Algonquian relationships was discussed later by Pickering (1833):

An attention to these established differences [correspondences] is indispensable to a just comparison of the various dialects [languages], and the useful application of such comparisons [is indispensable] to the purposes of philology; and it will enable us to detect affinities, where at first view there may be little or no appearance of any resemblance. (Cited in Haas 1967:817)

This shows that the claim is erroneous which asserts that sound correspondences played no role in the recognition of American Indian language families.

As pointed out in Chapter 1, before Sir William Jones' "philologer" passage was published, Jonathan Edwards, Jr. (1745–1826) (1788[1787]) reported the relationship among Algonquian languages. Edwards, a native speaker of "Muhhekaneww" or Mohegan, began his paper with the following account of his knowledge of and association with Mohegan:

That the following observations may obtain credit, it may be proper to inform the reader, with what advantages they have been made. When I was but six years of age, my father [the famous theologian and missionary Jonathan Edwards] removed with his family to Stockbridge [Massachusetts], which, at that time, was inhabited by Indians almost solely; as there were in the town but twelve families of white or Anglo-Americans, and perhaps one hundred and fifty families of Indians. The Indians being the nearest neighbours, I constantly associated with them; their boys were my daily school-mates and play-fellows. Out of my father's house, I seldom heard any language spoken, beside the Indian. By these means I acquired the knowledge of that language, and a great facility in speaking it. It became more familiar to me than my mother tongue . . . This skill in their language I have in a good measure retained to this day.

After I had drawn up these observations, lest there should be some mistakes in them, I carried them to Stockbridge, and read them to Capt. Yōghun, a principal Indian of the tribe, who is well versed in his own language, and tolerably informed concerning the English; and I availed myself of his remarks and corrections . . .

As for Edwards' method for showing relationship among Algonquian languages, he compared "some 60 vocabulary items, phrases, and grammatical features" (Koerner 1986:ii; see Edwards 1823[1788]:9). On the basis of these he concluded that the languages were "radically the same [i.e. from the same family]," though he was fully aware also of their differences: "It is not to be supposed, that the like coincidence is extended to all the words of those languages. Very many words are totally different. Still the analogy is such as is sufficient to show, that they are mere dialects [sisters] of the same original language [family]" (Edwards 1823[1788]:11; cf. also Andresen 1990:45; Wolfart 1982:403; Koerner 1986:iii; Edgerton 1943:27). Moreover, Edwards concluded that "Mohauk [Mohawk, Iroquoian], which is the language of the Six Nations, is entirely different from that of the Mohegans [Algonquian]" (Edwards 1823[1788]:11). He knew whereof he spoke since, when he was ten, his father sent him "among the six nations [Iroquoian], with a design that I should learn their language, and thus become qualified to be a missionary among them" (Edwards 1823[1788]:6–7). He supported this observation with the comparison of a word list of Mohawk with Mohegan, similar to those he used to compare Shawnee and Ojibwa, and through a comparison of the Lord's Prayer in the two languages. That is, it cannot be suggested that Edwards was just given to seeing Indian languages as related, since he clearly distinguished Algonquian and Iroquoian (with which he also had first-hand experience) as different families based on his methods. Edwards' discovery was significant; his observations did not go unnoticed – this work went through several editions (cf. Benfey 1869:263).

Peter Stephen Duponceau (1760–1844), the most famous American Indian linguist of his times, recognized among others what he called "Lenni-Lenápe" or "la famille algonquine," by then long known and accepted. In his 1838 *Mémoire*, he compared words for forty-five basic glosses for thirty Algonquian languages and varieties (Duponceau 1838:271–411).

Most of the Algonquian languages are quite similar to one another and so recognition of their family relationship for the most part was not too challenging.[11] Very instructive for our purposes, however, is the "Ritwan hypothesis" and

---

[11] Languages of the Arapaho group have undergone extensive sound changes and so cognates in this group are not so obviously similar as those in the other Algonquian languages.

how Wiyot and Yurok were shown to be related to Algonquian – an instance of a proven distant genetic relationship. "Ritwan" was the name Dixon and Kroeber (1913b) gave to their grouping of Wiyot and Yurok together as one of their more remote Californian stocks. Their evidence was extremely scanty (see Campbell 1997a:67–8). Nevertheless, a Ritwan–Algonquian broader connection was proposed by Sapir (1913a). Sapir utilized standard methods: "There is good lexical, morphological, and phonological evidence to genetically relate Algonkin [Algonquian] to Wiyot and Yurok" (Sapir 1913a:646); he stressed the importance of regular sound correspondences (Sapir 1913a:639). His evidence was plausible but inconclusive and the hypothesis remained controversial for some time (see Michelson 1914, 1915; Sapir 1915a, 1915c). However, evidence accumulated, with clearer cognates and sound correspondences, and morphological agreements, and subsequently the relationship was demonstrated to the satisfaction of all (see Haas 1958a; Teeter 1964; Goddard 1975, 1990b). The family (Algonquian with Wiyot and Yurok) is called Algic (see Campbell 1997a:152–5). The submerged features Teeter (1964) gave as grammatical evidence for Algic are presented in Chapter 7.

6.7.3   Athabaskan

The relationship among Athabaskan languages had been recognized and the family well defined by the mid 1800s. Excellent early historical linguistic work was done by Emile Petitot (1838–1916) and Adrien Gabriel Morice (1859–1938) (Krauss 1986:149). Morice (1891, 1892; cf. also 1904, 1907) established sound correspondences among several of the Athabaskan languages, comparing the regularity of their development explicitly to that known in Indo-European, and "pleading for application to Athabaskan of the principles developed in Indo-European comparative philology" (Krauss 1986:150). Morice 1892 contains a comparative vocabulary of 370 items, cognate stems, with an attempt to reconstruct the Proto-Athabaskan root (or at least the initial consonant) for each (Krauss 1986:150). As Krauss (1986:151) points out, it was through his insistence that "Athabaskan consonant systems develop with the same regularity demonstrated to apply to languages of 'civilization' such as Indo-European, that Morice was able to interpret [correctly] the inadequate transcriptions" of others. Athabaskan linguistics had already been placed on a strong footing by Emile Petitot's (1876) dictionary and its comparative grammatical introduction, which documented Loucheux (Kutchin), Hare, and Chipewyan and also contained considerable lexical data on several other Northern Athabaskan languages. His 1907 paper gave cognates and sound correspondences among consonants which included also Navajo and Hupa, i.e. representatives of the major branches of Athabaskan. In brief, the methods which established the Athabaskan family were the standard ones from the beginning.

6.7.4   Uto-Aztecan

As pointed out in Chapter 4, **Johann Severin Vater** (1771–1826) recognized the genetic relationships among several Uto-Aztecan languages of Mexico using basic vocabulary and grammatical agreements. Others who recognized connections among various Uto-Aztecan languages were Buschmann (1859), Bancroft (1874–6), and Gatschet (1879–80). Brinton (1891) classified the various languages together as a family, coining the name "Uto-Aztecan." His family had three branches: Shoshonean, Sonoran, and Nahuatl/Nahuatlecan. Powell (1891), on the other hand, considered but rejected the proposed Uto-Aztecan family, separating the Shoshonean and Sonoran languages. Brinton and Powell's difference of opinion is of methodological interest. Brinton's approach consisted of comparing "primitive" words (short list), together with the overall grammar and with specific grammatical forms, especially the verb. Powell rejected grammar as evidence, believing it reflected merely the stage of development obtained in unilinear social evolution (see Chapter 8). Powell's method was the superficial inspection of short word lists, inadequate for showing genetic relationships among languages (see Chapter 7). The fact that Powell rejected Brinton's grouping of Uto-Aztecan languages because he did not accept Brinton's grammatical evidence places these two approaches in sharp contrast (Campbell 1997a:57, 62).

The true proof of the validity of the Uto-Aztecan family belongs to Sapir (1913b, 1915–19), who demonstrated the relationship to everyone's satisfaction in one of the first systematic demonstrations of the applicability of the comparative method to languages without long traditions of writing. He used absolutely standard methods, strictly those used in Indo-Europeanist linguistics which relied on vocabulary, sound correspondences, and morphological matchings. In contrast to Brinton and Powell, Sapir fully understood and applied the comparative method, believing systematic correspondences would help distinguish genetically inherited features from similarities which are due to diffusion. He believed his methods put Uto-Aztecan "on bedrock" and that it was "almost humorous" how quite dissimilar stems could be matched when phonetic laws were applied (Sapir to Kroeber, June 21, 1913; cited in Darnell 1969:369).

6.7.5   Mayan

The relationship among Mayan languages was also recognized early, long before formal linguistic procedures had been formulated; nevertheless, early comparative work in the history of Mayan linguistics is very true to these procedures.

For example, Francisco Ximénez (1667–1730[?]), a Dominican missionary, at this early time, had a clear understanding of the family relationship among Mayan languages and of the nature of linguistic diversification:

all the languages of this Kingdom of Guatemala, from the languages Tzotzil, Zendal [Tzeltal], Chañabal [Tojolabal], Coxoh, Mame [Mam], Lacandon, Peten [Itzá], Q'aq'chiquel [Kaqchikel], Q'aq'chi [Q'eqchi'], Poq'omchi [Poqomchi'], to many other languages, which are spoken in diverse places, were all a single one, and in different provinces and towns they corrupted them in different ways; but the roots of the verbs and nouns, for the most part, are still the same; and it is no miracle, since we see it in our own Castilian language – the languages of Europe being daughters of Latin, which the Italians have corrupted in one way, the French in another, and the Spanish in another; and even these different ways according to the different provinces, as one may see among the Galicians, the Montañese, and Portuguese, and even among the Castilians there may be differences according to the different cities and places. (Ximénez c.1702:1; translation from Fox 1978:4)

Hervás y Panduro (1800–5:304) had determined that several Mayan languages were genetically related (see Chapter 4); his evidence included words for numbers, many other words, and "not a little of their grammatical structure" (Hervás y Panduro 1800–5:304). Vater in volume 3 of Adelung and Vater (1816 [1806–17]) also recognized the genetic relationship among several Mayan languages (1816:5–6, 14–5, 106; cf. also Vater 1810); he presented a list of seventeen cognates and some structural comparisons (1816:22–3).

Charles Felix Hyacinthe, Le Comte de Charencey (1832–1916) (1870) used sound correspondences to classify and subgroup the languages of Mesoamerica, and he grouped into his "Yucatecan subgroup" of Mayan languages "Maya [Yucatec], Tzeltal, and their dialects, as well as Huastec" based on such "characteristics" as "the absence of the letter [sound] r, generally replaced by i or y [both phonetically y]" (Charencey 1870:35). Charencey (1872) and (1883) include several Mayan correspondences sets and sound changes. Otto Stoll (1849–1922) also presented a number of sound correspondences and associated sound changes among Mayan languages, some the same as presented by Charencey. His observations concerning these are methodologically interesting:

These changes follow regular phonetic laws and bear a strong affinity to the principle of "Lautverschiebung" (Grimm's law), long ago known as an agent of most extensive application in the morphology of the Indo-Germanic languages. (Stoll 1885:257)

When . . . it concerns . . . on which basis . . . I proposed the diversification of the Mayan family [Stoll 1884] . . . the following can here be mentioned . . . One of the most striking differences between the individual groups of Mayan languages is the regular sound shift from one group to the other [several examples of which are given]. (Stoll 1912–13:40)

Not only were sound correspondences an important part of the history of the classification of the Mayan languages, comparative syntax also played a role (Seler 1887), in the Indo-Europeanist methodological tradition.

6.7.6   Other American Indian linguistic classifications

Here we have only briefly touched on the history of a few of the c.180 different language families and isolates in the Americas (see Campbell 1997a). Nevertheless, the classification of many of these has utilized standard criteria and the work in several families is at an advanced state. There is general agreement on family-level classifications, and the methods used have been straightforward and for the most part standard. Where there is disagreement is about potential higher-order, more inclusive groupings; many of the more inclusive long-range groupings, especially the "Amerind" hypothesis, are rejected by most linguists (see Chapters 7 and 9).

Having surveyed how these well-known language families were established, we turn now to a consideration of the history of comparative linguistics and language classification in Africa and Australia. While uncertainties and disputes remain, there are also methodological lessons to be gained from seeing what was done, and sorting what worked from what did not. (For more detail on specific distant genetic relationships, see Chapter 9.)

6.8   Africa

Africa is characterized by extensive linguistic diversity, with some "1,200 languages at a conservative estimate" (Bender 1997a:7), or Nurse's (1997) 1,250–1,500 figure, or the 2,058 languages in the *Ethnologue*'s generous count (www.ethnologue.com). As in other areas of the world, Africa's language families came to be established only gradually, although many questions remain unresolved. Also like elsewhere, language, race, culture, and nation were not distinguished in early classifications of the languages. However, in African linguistics, failure to move beyond race–language equations and to discard non-linguistic factors from considerations for language classification persisted longer than elsewhere, into the mid twentieth century, and this proved a major problem until Joseph Greenberg put an end to it in his famous classification of African languages (Greenberg 1955, 1966[1963]). In general, "Africanists tended to be somewhat isolated from the main stream of linguistic thought" (Gregersen 1977:95) and historical linguistic research in Africa on the whole has lagged behind that of most of the rest of the world, for these and other reasons to which we will come directly. Broadly speaking, historical linguistics in Africa continues to differ from that of the rest of the world. As Childs (2003:19) points out, in their culture of language classification, "Africanists, for the most part, contrast sharply with their counterparts in Oceania and the New World" by preferring "a 'tidy' picture with every language classified and few isolates . . . 'lumping.'" As Mikkola (1998:63) observes, "In comparative linguistics long-range classifications are usually not accepted. Yet in Africa they are commonly seen as valid." Lumping as done in Africa relies on multilateral (mass) comparison (called "the method of resemblances" by Heine [1970:3]), a method which "does not have wide acceptance outside Africa" (Childs 2003:39). Moreover, many of the major classification efforts in Africa, as in other parts of the world, involved the typological–evolutionary orientation (see Chapter 8); however, classification based on typological criteria continued to characterize proposed African classifications and some of these typological considerations continue to lurk in the background in some Africanist work yet today (see below). As Heine (1975:27) explains, "since its beginnings in the nineteenth century, comparative linguistics in Africa has been based on the assumption that typological studies were a *sine qua non* for the establishment of language relationship."

In Pierre Alexandre's (1972) view, the history of African linguistics developed along two paths until late in the nineteenth century, one centered on the Cape of Good Hope moving northward and the other starting on the Atlantic Coast and going eastward. While this may be oversimplified, it is reasonably representative – "during the nineteenth century, at least, Africanists generally were either West Africanists or Bantuists – a dichotomy whose repercussions may still be felt today" (Alexandre 1972:21).

Some attribute the earliest linguistic classification in African to **Andrea Corsali**, who wrote in a letter from India in 1515, after a voyage from Lisbon to India, "[along] the whole coast from the straits of the Red Sea, as far as the Cape of Good Hope, . . . they are all of the same language; and from the Cape of Good Hope as far as the Cape de Verde Islands, they speak a different language" (quoted in Cole 1971:7; Gregersen 1977:92). We know little of Corsali's methods. A more serious beginning might be attributed to **Abbé Lievin Bonaventure Proyart**. As mentioned in Chapter 1, some Africanists see his *Histoire de Loango, Kakongo, et autres royaumes d'Afrique* (1776) as a rival to Sir William Jones' "philologer" passage for early recognition of the comparative method. Proyart pointed out that Kakongo and Laongo differ in many respects from Kikongo, but "several similar articles [presumably noun-class prefixes], and a great number of common roots, seem, however, to indicate that these languages had a common origin" (quoted in Gregersen 1977:97). His evidence seems to be based on both grammatical and lexical comparisons, and, if Proyart did have Bantu noun-classifier affixes in mind, he anticipated a feature which has loomed large in African research ever since (see below). As for the real beginnings of sub-Saharan linguistics, as Gregersen (1977:97) points out, the Bantu family seems to have been "discovered" independently several times.

Heinrich Lichtenstein (1808) grouped southern Africans into "two principal races, the Hottentots and the Kaffirs" (the latter speaking Bantu, prefixing languages), based on the "most complete lack of affinity of the two languages to one another" (Cole 1971:7); he maintained that "all those of the area were merely dialects of these two languages" (Gregersen 1977:97).[12] Adelung and Vater (1812[1806–17]) repeated Lichtenstein's position, and **Adelung** (in Adelung and Vater [1806–17]), based on short word lists, classified some languages together for the first time which are indeed genetically related: his Mandingo group, Amina (Akan) group, and Congo group (Williamson 1989:3). **William Marsden**, of Austronesian fame (above), had access to vocabularies from several Congolese languages and wrote in a letter in 1816 (published 1818) "that most of these Congolese languages were probably mutually intelligible" and that:

Between the Congo language and that of the tribes of the eastern side [i.e. the east coast of Africa], the affinity although radical [i.e. belonging to the same family] is much less striking . . . but following instances of resemblance, in words expressing the simplest ideas [basic vocabulary], may be thought sufficient to warrant the belief, that the nations by whom they are employed, at a remote period, have been more intimately connected. (Gregersen 1977:98)

James Prichard (1826) postulated the unity of the "Kaffrarian Family" (Bantu), which he divided into three main groups: Kaffers proper, Mosambique Nations, and the Kongo race (Cole 1971:8). For him, the "Family" included all the languages south of the Equator except Hottentot (Williamson 1989:4). In 1837, based on comparative vocabularies, Prichard concluded:

When we consider the nature of these words, common to the idioms of so many distinct nations, the supposition that they may have been borrowed by one people from another seems altogether untenable . . . no other hypothesis can explain indications of affinity . . . except the obvious one that the tribes themselves were originally subdivisions of the same stock. (Quoted in Cole 1971:8)

The first overall classification of African languages was published in 1826, by **Adrian Balbi**. In it he linked "Hottentot" with "Bushman" (as in the more modern but controversial Khoisan hypothesis, below) (Bender 1997a:57).

Horatio Hale (1817–96) (1846), better known for his work with North American Indian and Polynesian languages (Campbell 1997a:44–6; see above), and not normally recognized in the Africanist literature, did early historical linguistic work that deserves mention. He was a member of the Wilkes Exploring Expedition to the South Pacific charged with collecting data relating to "ethnology and philology." During a stop in Rio de Janeiro, he collected vocabularies

---

[12] The term "Caffre," "Kafir," etc., today is derogatory. It is from an Arabic word meaning 'infidel' (cf. Hale 1846:658); note that several Indo-Iranian languages of remote areas of Afghanistan and nearby regions are also often called "Kafiri" (Torday 1997:57).

from recently arrived slaves, speaking thirteen different southern African languages, with the goal of arriving at an "ethnographical map" of Africa south of the Equator. From a comparison of the vocabularies he obtained in Brazil and others already published, he found that:

from the equator to latitude 30° south, the continent of Africa is occupied by a single people speaking dialects [languages] of one general language [family] . . . it appears that this general language, or rather family of cognate languages, has two distinct subdivisions, which may be entitled . . . the *Congo-Makua*, and the *Caffrarian*, each including under it several dialects, or minor divisions. (Hale 1846:657)

John W. Appleyard (1847, 1850) distinguished a "Click Class" (composed of two "families," Hottentot and Bushman) and an "Alliteral Class" (including the Congo, Damara, Sechuana, and Kaffir families, and the "Unclassified Dialects") among the southern African languages. Appleyard utilized phonological correspondences as evidence of genetic relationships (Cole 1971:9). He presented comparisons, especially of "Kaffir" and "Sechuana," with tables of vowel, consonant, and other changes to account for the differences between these languages. For example, he reported that:

From the preceding tables, it will be seen that roots which appear totally different the one from the other, are in fact the very same, or rather, of the same origin. Thus no one, at first sight, would imagine that the Sechuana *reka* and the Kaffir *tenga* . . . were mere variations of the same "root." (Appleyard 1850:54; quoted in Cole 1971:9)

A major contribution to African linguistics was that of **Sigismund Wilhelm Koelle**, a German missionary. He interviewed Africans liberated from slave ships in Freetown, Sierra Leone (cf. Childs 2003:15), and was able to assemble material (word lists and phrases) from 156 languages; he presented a classification of them. Several of the groups in Koelle's (1854) classification correspond to linguistic groupings still accepted today: North-West Atlantic ((West) Atlantic), North-Western High Sudan/Mandenga (Mande), and North-Eastern High Sudan (Gur) (Williamson 1989:4). His work was also influential in subsequent investigations of "Sudanic" (see below). In some cases where his overall grouping differs from modern classifications, his subgroups still match recognized genetic units; for example, his three subgroups of "Upper-Guinea languages" fit modern Kru, Gbe, and Yoruboid (Williamson 1989:4). Koelle pointed out that his North-West Atlantic languages are "like those of South Africa" in that they have "prefixal changes or an initial inflection" (Williamson 1989:4). This appeal to the noun-class affixes, as we shall see, has played a major role in the classification of African languages, especially of Niger-Congo (Niger-Kordofanian) languages.

Wilhelm Bleek (1827–75) (1856, 1862[1869]), German librarian to the Cape governor, is often credited as the founder of Bantu linguistics, and his work had a lasting impact on the field (Mutaka 2000:8). He was aware of Koelle's work and spoke of the unity of "that great family which, with the exception of the Hottentot dialects [languages], includes the whole of South Africa, and most of the tongues of Western Africa; certainly the Oti, or Ashantee, the Bullom, and the Timneh of Sierra Leone" (Bleek 1856, quoted in Williamson 1989:4). This he called the "Bântu" family, with South African and West African divisions (Bleek 1858, 1862[1869]). This corresponds roughly to modern Niger-Congo. He distinguished this from the "Gōr" family (with Fula, Wolof, and Ga, plus "Ukuafi" and Tumale, now placed in Kordofanian) (Williamson 1989:4). His Gōr languages would be placed within Niger-Congo by many today, and he himself considered it "related to" or belonging to "the same class of languages" as Bantu, the class he named "the prefix-pronominal languages" (Williamson 1989:4). This noun-classification and concord system has been a major focus in the classification of African languages, especially of Niger-Congo tongues. Bleek's "Bantu" name (based on *ba-* 'noun-class prefix for the class which includes humans' + *-(n)tu* 'person') stuck, but came to be restricted to his "South African" division. Bleek built on Appleyard's findings and presented tables of phonological correspondences with "Kaffir" as the pivot (Cole 1971:9).

By the mid nineteenth century, there was general recognition in African linguistics of Bantu, Bushman, and Semitic language groups as independent and unrelated (Gregersen 1977:98). **Friedrich Müller**'s (1876) classification recognized the families: Semitic, Hamitic, Nuba-Fulah, Negro, Bantu, and Hottentot-Bushman, and **Robert Cust** (1883) followed this classification (Mutaka 2000:13). **Richard Lepsius** divided Africa into two main groups or types of languages based on structural traits – the noun-class languages of the Bantus and the gender languages of the "Hamites" (Köhler 1975:152). Lepsius' (1880:xvii–xviii) classification recognized the following groupings:

A. Proto-African Negro languages (*Urafrikanische Negersprache*)
  I. Bantu (*Bāntu-Negersprachen*)
      Western (*Westliche*) (e.g. Hereró, Pongue, Fernando Po)
      Eastern (*Östliche*) (e.g. Kāfir [||Osa, Zulu], Tswana, Swahili)
  II. Mixed (*Misch-Negersprachen*)
      Western (*Westliche*) (e.g. Efik, Ibo, Yoruba, Ewe, Gã, Twi, Kru, Vei [Mande], Temne, Bullom, Wolof)
      Central (*Mittlere*) (e.g. Fula, Songai, Kanuri, Teda, Hausa, Umale, etc.)
      Eastern (*Östliche*) (e.g. Dinka, Silluk, Bongo, Bari, Oigob, Nuba, Barea)
B. Hamitic (*Hamitische Sprachen*)
  I. Egyptian (Ancient Egyptian, Coptic)
  II. Libyan languages (*Libysche Sprachen*) (e.g. Imasheg, Tuareg; Tamasheq [i.e. Berber languages]); Hausa

III. Cushitic (*Kuschitische Sprachen*) (e.g. Bega, Agau, Galla, Somali, etc.)
IV. Hottentot (*Hottentottisch*) (Koinkoin)
C. Semitic (*Semitische Sprachen*)
    I. Habesh (Ge'ez, Tigre, Amharic, Harari)
    II. Arabic

The African classifications came to be characterized in large part by typological and racial considerations. Some grouped Hottentot together with Bushman because they shared "clicks," potentially just a typological trait (or perhaps an areal one, see below), while others placed Hottentot with so-called "Hamito-Semitic," characterized by the presence of a masculine–feminine gender distinction in nouns and pronouns, also a trait of Hottentot (Gregersen 1977:99–100). Friedrich Müller (1876–88) equated "races" and language groupings, and notions of race were his basis for separating "Negro" and Bantu languages from one another and "Nuba-Fulah" from both these (Williamson 1989:5). Bleek's notion of "prefix-pronominal" (cf. the well-known Bantu noun-classification concord system), with Bantu in southern Africa as the purest type, and "sex-denoting languages" (those with a grammatical gender distinction), represented by "Hamitic" languages of northern Africa, was followed by Lepsius (1880) and Cust (1883), and continues to be influential in some fashion even today. R. Lepsius (1810–84) (1880:xx) attributed greater weight to grammatical evidence in his classification, and in this context he gave twelve characteristics on the basis of which, he believed, one could distinguish languages of his classification from one another, especially Bantu languages from Hamitic languages (Lepsius 1880:xx–xxxii). Some of the more important of these were: (1) Bantu languages are prefixing, Hamitic suffixing; (2) Hamitic languages have grammatical gender; the "Negro" languages (*Negersprachen*) do not; (5) concord (where the Bantu noun-classification system is cited); (6) Bantu languages with prepositions, Hamitic with postpositions; (7) genitive after the possessed noun in Bantu, before it in Hamitic; (8) in southern languages the word order is SVO, in Hamitic either VSO or SOV; (12) tone ("Intonation," common to the "*Afrikanische Negersprachen*," essentially a Bantu trait absent in Hamitic, but with much mixing in the Central languages). Robert Cust's (1883) criteria for Hamitic membership were: (1) not being Semitic; (2) having grammatical gender; and (3) being located in north/northeast Africa. Ultimately, the attachment of a number of Africanists to racial and cultural criteria rendered many of their decisions about linguistic classification worthless, and typologically based groupings (based for example on the presence or absence of gender) proved problematic for others. Mixture among the groups in these racial-linguistic classifications was often assumed for the intermediate groups, giving us names such as "Bantoid, Bantuoid, Semi-Bantu," etc. (see Lepsius 1880, Meinhof [below]) (Williamson 1989:5–6). As Gregersen (1977:100) puts it:

The criteria used in some classifications were often tenuous. For example, extraneous racial or cultural attributes of a certain group seem to have been at least sometimes decisive in determining that group's linguistic affiliations. One of the most blatant examples of this was undoubtedly Meinhof's conception of what can be called "maximal Hamitic," developed in *Die Sprachen der Hamiten* (1912). Despite little linguistic evidence, Meinhof tried to expand the Hamitic language family by fairly vague typological resemblances until speakers of "Hamitic" in his sense were largely coterminous with cattle-herding peoples and members of a basically Caucasoid stock – in Meinhof's view a *Herrenvolk* ("master race"). His theory necessarily entailed a good deal of mixing, both of races and languages. He assumed that Fulani represented a survival of the most archaic kind of Hamitic, that Bantu was a mixture of a Fulani-like language and a western Sudanic one, that Hottentot had a Hamitic base strongly influenced by Bushman, and that Maasai was typologically an ancient Hamitic form influenced by eastern Sudanic languages.

Carl Meinhof, just mentioned, had a monumental impact on African linguistics, some of it good, much of it for the worse. The good part was that Meinhof (1899, 1906) applied Neogrammarian techniques in his comparative Bantu phonology and grammar, and these proved "quite successful and have survived essentially unchallenged until the present" (Gregersen 1977:101). However, Meinhof (1905) saw Bantu as the original type of noun-class languages, and regarded Ewe-type languages as being of a different linguistic type which he called "Sudanic." In his opinion, his "Semi-Bantu" languages came about as the result of Bantu influence on the genetically unrelated Sudanic languages (Williamson 1989:6). Menhof's (1912) "Hamitic" classification became notorious because it relied on the non-linguistic criteria of cattle possession, race (a master race of Caucasian stock, influenced by black Africans), and typological traits such as the presence of gender, so that, for example, Fula (Fulfulde, Fulani), "Hottentot," Maasai, and Somali were all classified as Hamitic, that is, with languages from each of Greenberg's (1966[1963]) four major phyla bunched into Hamitic on the basis of these unreliable, unfortunate criteria (cf. Bender 2000:57).

Diedrich Westermann set about to investigate the "Sudanic" languages; his "Eastern Sudanic" (Westermann 1911) became the basis for what is now usually called Nilo-Saharan, and his "Western Sudanic" (Westermann 1927) together with Bantu became the foundation of Niger-Congo (Greenberg 1963:7, 9). As for methods, Westermann (1911:3) applied Neogrammarian techniques and spoke elegantly on behalf of regularity of sound change and sound correspondences in African research, but also emphasized grammatical comparisons, together with lexical evidence. Westermann's work was significant since Greenberg took it as the starting point for his famed classification of African languages (cf. Greenberg 1955, 1966[1963]).

A scheme involving the four groupings, Bantu, Bushman-Hottentot, Sudanic, and Hamito-Semitic, dominated linguistic thought in Africa until the 1940s, when Greenberg began his reclassification. For greater detail on the pre-Greenberg classification of African languages, see Köhler (1975).

Joseph Greenberg's African classification has had wide support and is the undisputed starting point for any current consideration of linguistic classification in Africa. It has been called "one of the milestones of twentieth-century science" (Bengtson and Ruhlen 1997:4). Given its prominence, we examine it in some detail. Greenberg (1949a, 1949b, 1949c, 1950a, 1950b, 1950c, 1950d, 1954) classified 321 African languages into sixteen families: (1) Niger-Congo, (2) Songhai, (3) Central Sudanic, (4) Central Saharan, (5) Eastern Sudanic, (6) Afroasiatic, (7) Click languages, (8) Maban, (9) Mimi (of Nachtigal), (10) Fur, (11) Temainian, (12) Kordofanian, (13) Koman, (14) Berta, (15) Kunama, and (16) Kyangiya. These were reduced further to twelve in Greenberg (1955), where (8) Meban and (9) Mimi were combined, and a new "Macro-Sudanic" unit was created with (14) Berta, (3) Central Sudanic, and (15 + 5) Kunama-Eastern Sudanic. About half of these families contained six or fewer languages, and in a large-scale sweeping up operation Greenberg (1963, which included many additional language names) grouped all these in only four large-scale phyla, now well known: Niger-Kordofanian, Nilo-Saharan, Afroasiatic, and Khoisan. In this 1963 classification, (12) Kordofanian was combined with (1) Niger-Congo to give the Niger-Kordofanian phylum (today commonly referred to as Niger-Congo, intended to include Kordofanian as one of its branches). "Macro-Sudanic" was renamed "Chari-Nile" (part of Nilo-Saharan), and the Click languages were renamed "Khoisan."

As with Greenberg's (1987) classification of languages of the Americas, his African claims have been heavily criticized on methodological grounds – to mention just one example, the abundant errors in his African data are a constant lament in the literature (see Winston 1966:168; Fodor 1969[1966]). As Bender (1997a:18) reports, "Greenberg's pioneering African language classification is riddled by such errors, most of which could have been avoided by the simple expedient of checking and proofreading the work." However, unlike his Amerind hypothesis, many Africanists came to accept Greenberg's African classification. As Williamson (1989:8) says, "his major conclusions have by now become the prevailing orthodoxy," though his groupings continue to be contested and modified. As an aside, we register our astonishment that many Africanists profess loyalty to this classification, declaring it a major achievement, while at the same time they point out major problems with it. They readily admit that at least two of the big four phyla, Khoisan and Nilo-Saharan, are abandoned or very uncertain, and often point out flaws in the methods upon which the classification is based. To cite one example, Hayward (2000:86–7) makes the following seemingly inconsistent declaration:

Now it was on the basis of "mass comparison," rather than the comparative method, that the canon of AA [Afroasiatic] languages was established by Greenberg, and although this methodology avoids reliance on typological features, and has, in the present writer's view, come up with the right conclusion, a methodology that does not invoke the rigour [of disentangling traits of shared linguistic parentage from merely typological or geographical traits] . . . falls short of true theoretical status. Pragmatically, too, it is quite crude for it incorporates no filter for rejecting unrelated "look-alikes" nor any means of recognising highly dissimilar, albeit cognate, items.

In another case, we read that "the method [multilateral (mass) comparison] does not have wide acceptance outside Africa. Nonetheless, it certainly put things in order in Africa" (Childs 2003:39). As will be seen shortly, the classification of African languages based on Greenberg's four phyla is badly in need of major reinvestigation and reworking.

As has been pointed out frequently, much of Greenberg's African classification simply repeated the correct classifications of earlier scholars, especially that of Westermann and Köhler (see Childs 2003:38; Gregersen 1977; Nurse 1997:367–8; Welmers 1973; Winston 1966).[13] Greenberg differed from his predecessors in that he denied Meinhof's conception of Hamitic (and rather grouped Semitic, Egyptian, Berber, Cushitic, and Chadic as co-ordinate branches of his "Afroasiatic") and he rearranged various of Westermann's groups.

Given their importance, we discuss each of Greenberg's four large African groupings in turn.

Niger-Kordofanian (Congo-Kordofanian, "Niger-Congo"[14]) (c.900 languages, 1,489 according to the *Ethnologue* [www. ethnologue.org]). Greenberg grouped Westermann's "West Sudanic" and Bantu in a single large family,[15] which he called Niger-Congo, after the two major rivers, the Niger and the Congo, "in whose basins these languages predominate" (Greenberg 1963:7). This included the subfamilies recognized by Westermann of (1) West Atlantic (to which Greenberg joined Fulani, in a Serer–Wolof–Fulani [Fulfulde, Fula]

---

[13] Likewise, as frequently pointed out, much of Greenberg's (1987) American Indian classification repeats and relies on the earlier proposals of Edward Sapir for North America and Paul Rivet for South America. A difference, however, is that many of these repeated American proposals have not received acceptance and remain controversial, while some others have been shown to be completely wrong. Thus, the part of Greenberg's strategy that helped to secure a measure of success for his African classification – that of repeating earlier accurate proposals – has, ironically, contributed to lack of success for his American proposals (see Campbell 1997a:210–11, 253–7 for details).

[14] In Bendor-Samuel (1989) "Niger-Congo" replaces "Niger-Kordofanian" as the name of the overall phylum, and this appears to be the usage in a number of recent works (e.g. Williamson and Blench 2000, see especially p. 16). This causes confusion, however, between "Niger-Congo" as one branch of "Niger-Kordofanian" or as a substitute for the whole of "Niger-Kordofanian."

[15] This is a position Westermann held; he believed that "the Western Sudanic languages are genetically related to the Bantu languages" (Williamson 1989:7).

group), (2) Mande (Mandingo) (thirty-five or forty languages), (3) Gur (or Voltaic), (4) Kwa (with Togo Remnant), and (5) Benue-Congo (Benue-Cross), with the addition of (6) Adamawa-Eastern, which had not previously been classified with these languages and whose classification remains controversial (Williamson 1989:7; see Greenberg 1963:8–9). For Greenberg, Bantu was but a subgroup of Benue-Congo, not a separate subfamily on its own. In 1963 he joined Niger-Congo and the "Kordofanian" languages into a larger postulated phylum which he called Niger-Kordofanian. The Kordofanian languages are those "of the Nuba hills of Kordofan," which, says Greenberg, form a "single Kordofanian family" with five "clearly distinguishable subgroups of which the fourth (Tumtum) shows considerable divergence from the remainder" (Greenberg 1963:149): (1) Koalib group, (2) Tegali group, (3) Talodi group, (4) Tumtum (Kadugli-Krongo or Kadu) group, and (5) Katla group. This remains controversial, and modifications have been proposed and several accepted. For example, Schadeberg and Bender both removed Greenberg's Tumtum (Kadugli-Krongo or Kadu), placing it in Nilo-Saharan (Bender 2000:46, 56; Schadeberg 1981).

Niger-Kordofanian is not well established, in spite of the praise Greenberg's overall classification has received. "No comprehensive reconstruction has yet been done for the phylum as a whole, and it is sometimes suggested that Niger-Congo is merely a typological and not a genetic unity" (Williamson and Blench 2000:10), though most scholars do accept some form of Niger-Congo as a valid grouping. As Nurse (1997:368) points out, it is on the basis of general similarities and the noun-class system that most scholars have accepted Niger-Congo, but "the fact remains that no one has yet attempted a rigorous demonstration of the genetic unity of Niger-Congo by means of the Comparative Method" (see also Dimmendaal 2001:368). For example, working only with Greenberg's comparative word lists, Boyd (1978) has shown that it is impossible to determine where Adamawa-Ubangi belongs – recall that Greenberg added Adamawa-Ubangi to Westermann's West Atlantic family (within his Niger-Congo grouping). Boyd shows that Adamawa-Ubangi could just as well be placed with Nilo-Saharan on the basis of Greenberg's data (Williamson 1989:9).[16] Mous (2003:162) points out that the evidence for including Ubangi in Niger-Congo is very weak. The Kwa and Benue-Congo groups enjoy no consensus: "it has been doubted whether Ijo, Kru and the Togo Remnant languages, which Greenberg placed with Kwa, really belong there" (Williamson 1989:10; cf. Williamson and Blench 2000:24; Welmers 1973:17). Greenberg's "Kwa" has been revised, with Eastern Kwa going to Benue-Congo and Western Kwa becoming the "(New) Kwa" (Childs 2003:42). The position of Mande is disputed (Welmers 1973:17; Mous 2003:162), and most linguists feel at least

---

[16] Greenberg's (1963) Adamawa contained fourteen numbered groups; Bennett (1983) showed that group 3, Daka, belongs to Benue-Congo, not to Adamawa (cf. Williamson and Blench 2000:27).

that there is greater distance between the Mande languages and the rest of Niger-Congo than there is among other branches of Niger-Congo (Williamson 1989:13). Some see Mande (which lacks the noun-class system)[17] as affiliated with Nilo-Saharan or as a bridge linking Niger-Kordofanian and Nilo-Saharan together in some larger-order grouping. Within Mande, the place of Bobo-Fing (Sya) is in doubt. Atlantic (a main branch of Niger-Congo) has been abandoned by many as a "wastebasket group" (Childs 2003:47); some believe that individual languages in Atlantic "have closer genetic relationships with languages outside the group than with languages within" (Childs 2003:49).

The noun-class system, largely a typological trait, has played a major role in the setting up of Niger-Congo and broader Niger-Kordofanian. As Williamson and Blench (2000:12) explain:

Niger-Congo is remarkable for an elaborate system of noun classification which marks singular/plural alternations with affixes (most commonly prefixes, sometimes suffixes, and occasionally infixes), and often requires concord of other elements in the sentence with their governing noun. In some families or branches the system has been remodelled or indeed lost with virtually no trace; but in others, of which the best-known case is Bantu, it is retained in considerable detail.

Greenberg reported that "the trait of Niger-Congo morphology which provides the main material for comparison is the system of noun classification by pair of affixes, one for the singular, another for the plural" (Greenberg 1963:9). He says:

In fact, the resemblances in noun class systems, a grammatical set of criteria, played a major role in my first work on Niger-Congo, and the relation to Kordofanian was based more on these resemblances than on lexical items, few of which were available at the time. (Greenberg 1996b:534)

Nevertheless, as already mentioned, the position of these affixes is not consistent across the languages grouped in Niger-Congo (and in Niger-Kordofanian):

In the West Sudanic group these affixes appear sometimes in the form of prefixes, as in Bantu and the languages of the Benue-Congo in general as well as other subfamilies; sometimes as suffixes, as in many of the Gur languages, and sometimes as both simultaneously as in some of the Gur languages and sporadically elsewhere. Of the eastern languages, the Adamawa branch shows suffixes and the Eastern branch some uncertain traces of prefixes and for Mondunga and Mba a suffixal system. The drift in Niger-Congo has been in the direction of the simplification of the nominal classification system. This has reached its climax in Mande and some of the Kwa languages in which the affixes have been entirely lost and an isolating system results. Hence while the presence of these affixes is important evidence for affiliation with the Niger–Congo family, absence does not prove lack of connection. (Greenberg 1963:9–10; see also Greenberg 1999:629)

---

[17] Mande initial consonant mutation in nouns is suggested to be the result of conditioning by earlier prefixes, and this is compared to the noun-class system of Niger-Congo languages (Williamson and Blench 2000:38–9).

(See also Greenberg 1963:31 for noun-class markers as prefixed in some languages and suffixed in others.)

Such reliance on the noun-classifier concord system constitutes a serious problem for classification. This trait is not convincing as a "genetic marker." The well-known noun-classification concord system is said to be found "in a well-preserved, reduced or purely vestigial form . . . in every branch of the family, and hence must be reconstructed for proto-Niger-Congo" (Williamson 1989:31; cf. Williamson and Blench 2000:14; Mous 2003:162). However, as the citations above point out, it is marked by prefixes in some branches, suffixes in others, and is not present at all in still others (see Köhler 1975:243). Moreover, the noun-class markers are thought to originate from grammaticalized demonstratives "which in the proto-language could either precede or follow the noun" (Williamson 1989:32–3; see Greenberg 1977, 1978; Dimmendaal 2001:380). Thus, the concord affixes appear to have originated from independent words (or clitics) in the proto-language which were grammaticalized as suffixes in some languages and as prefixes in others. Moreover, this kind of classification system, based on independent words or particles, could be subject to diffusion by language contact – similar classification systems are found in some languages from the Nilo-Saharan and Khoisan groupings (see below).

This being the case, it would appear that this feature which has been so irresistible to those classifying African languages almost from the very beginning has been overrated. That is, if it is reconstructible to Proto-Niger-Congo, it must be as independent demonstratives, which became grammaticalized as suffixes in some languages and prefixes in others, after the split up of the proto-language (cf. Williamson 1989:31–40).[18] The typological trait of morphological noun-classification may not have even existed at the stage of the proto-language. Noun-classification systems are also found in the other African phyla, though they may differ in their nature. Afroasiatic has sex–gender classification. Southern African Khoisan languages (Sands 1998) have a complex noun-classification and concord system similar to that of many Niger-Kordofanian languages. Several putatively Nilo-Saharan groups also have Bantu-like noun-class systems. This appears to make the noun-class system look like an areally diffused trait in at least some instances, though this is not how most Africanists see it. Some, rather, take the sharing of this trait to be evidence of the common

---

[18] Some may imagine this developing by some other less direct means. For example, some imagine that some of the suffixing languages were in fact prefixing but the auxiliaries to which they were thought to be attached were lost and the prefixes to these now missing auxiliaries became attached as suffixes to the preceding main verbs. Williamson and Blench (2000:39) suggest that work in Southern Atlantic and Gur "shows that prefixing languages can change to suffixing ones by concord elements attaching themselves to a final demonstrative or article. This is part of the process of 'renewal' of demonstrative or definite markers which have weakened." (See also Dimmendaal 2001:379–80.)

origin of Niger-Kordofanian and Nilo-Saharan in a much larger genetic grouping (Williamson and Blench 2000:13; see below).

This morphological trait seems to involve the kind of typological features which can be diffused or can evolve independently against which Greenberg (1966[1963]) warned – only comparisons involving both sound and meaning (not merely a trait like the presence of gender or of noun classification) can be considered reliable.[19] (See Chapter 7.) However, the trait is absent from some languages classified as Niger-Kordofanian, e.g. Eleme, Yoruba, Igbo, Jukun, Gokana, most Mande languages, Dogon, Mumuye (Adamawa), and Gbaya (Ubangi) (cf. Williamson 1989:36). The trait is not especially diagnostic nor convincing as evidence of genetic relationship: "while the presence of these [noun class] affixes is important evidence for affiliation with the Niger-Congo family, absence of the affixes does not prove lack of connection" (Greenberg 1963:10). Nichols (1997a) sees Niger-Kordofanian, with its system of singular and plural concord classes, as a "type-defining example" of a "quasi-stock": "Niger-Kordofanian is a quasi-stock, defined by the gender prefixes . . . and consists of the outlier Kordofanian family in the eastern Sahara and several west African stocks." Nichols finds this system "is quite specific and rare worldwide," but reports that "systematic sound correspondences and regular lexical reconstructability are absent from Niger-Kordofanian" (Nichols 1997a:363).

In effect, without the sound–meaning isomorphism required by Greenberg's (1966[1963]) own principles, reliance on the noun-class system as evidence of genetic relationship violates the generally accepted principle which permits only comparisons which involve both sound and meaning together (see Chapter 7). True, there are sound–meaning correlations across a number of these languages with respect to the noun-classifier morphemes, but not in all of them, and in particular not for the most problematic of them. Similarities in sound

---

[19] Greenberg (1996a:134) seems to confirm this view of the treatment of the noun concord markers; he protests that he has "been incorrectly assigned to the lexical camp" and mentions his "African work in which resemblances among the noun-class markers played an important role in the establishment of Niger-Kordofanian." Mous (2003:163) is of the opinion that this is not the sort of typological trait which violates Greenberg's principle of both sound and meaning being required. Mous says:

> The fact that a language has a Niger-Congo type noun-class system or remnants thereof is considered not to be [just] a typological criterion because the presence of a Niger-Congo type noun-class system does not make reference to just function but rather to function in connection with form and paradigmatic systematicity and hence this *is* a valid criterion to posit genetic relatedness.

> This may be so in the cases when in fact form and function are both involved, but as seen in the discussion so far, the noun-classification markers in some of the putative Niger-Kordofanian languages do not share form, only function, which is part of the debate about the classification of some of these.

alone (for example, the presence of tonal systems in compared languages) or in meaning alone (for example, grammatical gender in the languages compared, or as in this case, of noun classification) are not reliable, since they often develop independent of genetic relationship, due to diffusion, accident, or typological tendencies. With only a functional match but without the form to go with it, the sounds coupled with the meanings, this amounts to little more than a shared typological trait (not even present in all the so-called Niger-Kordofanian groups), not in itself sufficient evidence of genetic relationship.

In conclusion, while many of the putative Niger-Congo groups probably are genetically related and belong together, the evidence presented for this so far is not especially heart-warming – no reconstruction, limited to fragments of morphological and lexical similarities (Williamson and Blench 2000:41), with heavy reliance on the noun-class system, not present in all the groups, and not of the same form in others, but with similar systems also found in some African languages outside Niger-Congo.

With the overall evidence for Niger-Congo (Niger-Kordofanian) not being especially compelling, and questionable for some of the groups involved, it is difficult to see the attraction of a wider proposed grouping to lump together Niger-Congo/Niger-Kordofanian and Nilo-Saharan. Nevertheless, the possibility of such a gigantic genetic grouping, called variously "Kongo-Saharan," "Niger-Saharan," is mentioned favorably by a number of Africanists (Bender 1997a:59, 66, 2000:60; Blench 1995; Gregersen 1972; Mikkola 1999:110–11; Williamson 1989:8–9; Williamson and Blench 2000:16–17; cf. Childs 2003:42–4). The very limited evidence cited is (1) mostly lexical and morphological look-alikes which do not eliminate other possible explanations (borrowing, chance, etc.), and (2) the presence of typological similarities such as ATR (advanced tongue root) vowel harmony and labiovelars, all possibly diffused areally (Childs 2003:44).

Nilo-Saharan (*c.*100 languages). Greenberg (1963) placed Westermann's (1911) "Eastern Sudanic" in his "Chari-Nile" family, part of his broader Nilo-Saharan phylum. The Eastern Sudanic family was said to have ten branches, of which "Nilotic" is but one (Greenberg 1963:85). In dismantling the inaccurate and racially biased "Hamitic," of which Nilo-Hamitic was held to be part, Greenberg demonstrated the inadequacy of those former classifications and argued for the connection between "Nilotic" and Westermann's "Eastern Sudanic." He noted that "the Nilotic languages seem to be predominantly isolating, tend to monosyllabism, and employ tonal distinctions. They conform to the 'Sudanic' stereotype and were at first classified by Westermann with his Sudanic" (Greenberg 1963:92). It will not go unnoticed how shared typology – isolating, monosyllabism, tones – is involved here; these are all traits that could be diffused areally. This typological consideration could have influenced this classification.

Nilo-Saharan "was the last phylum that Greenberg proposed and many are not convinced of the higher-level genetic relationships" (Mous 2003:162). "Nilo-Saharan is the most problematic case in Greenberg's (1966[1963]) classification" (Mikkola 1999:108). Nilo-Saharan is generally thought of as Greenberg's wastebasket phylum, where he parked all the otherwise unaffiliated languages, and as such it competes with Khoisan for "the least widely accepted" of Greenberg's four African phyla (Bender 2000:43). Harold Fleming's (1987) account of Nilo-Saharan reflects this:

> It [Nilo-Saharan] has also been called "Greenberg's waste basket," hence a collection of hard-to-classify languages and a very unreliable entity as a phylum. Vis-a-vis AA [Afroasiatic] or N-K [Niger-Kordofanian], N-S [Nilo-Saharan] is widely viewed as the more shaky of the three . . . It represents far less consensus, far less agreement on sub-grouping, and very little progress on reconstruction. (Fleming 1987:168–9; cf. also Bender 1991, 1993).

Mikkola (1999:130) came to a similar conclusion after his extended reinvestigation:

> The exact status of Nilo-Saharan remains unresolved until a comprehensive and systematic comparison with all Niger-Congo branches is conducted. Especially the position of Saharan languages remains obscure. The inclusion of questionable units, at least Songai and Kuliak, plus Gumuz, could not be sustained. (Mikkola 1999:130)

> The Nilo-Saharan "family" is best regarded as a superphylum, with hypothetically 12 member phyla . . . these terms are preferred because attempts at reconstruction using a historical-comparative method do not seem to give any results. (Mikkola 1998:71)

In approaching these languages, Greenberg recognized the linguistic diversity involved:

> Starting from two problems, the position of Bantu in relation to Westermann's West Sudanic and the validity of Meinhof's suggestions regarding the extension of Hamitic, four extensive linguistic stocks have been defined: Niger–Congo, Afroasiatic, Khoisan and Eastern Sudanic. This, however, still leaves a considerable number of languages unaccounted for, chiefly in the eastern portion of the area formerly reckoned as Sudanic. (Greenberg 1963:108)

He grouped most of these leftover languages, together with "Eastern Sudanic," in what he called "Chari-Nile" (but not the Kordofanian languages, which he placed with Niger-Kordofanian). In the end, he grouped all the remaining unaccounted for languages into his Nilo-Saharan group, with six branches: (1) Songhai (Songay), (2) Saharan, (3) Maban, (4) Fur, (5) Chari-Nile (which includes Eastern Sudanic and Central Sudanic, together with Berta and Kunama), and (6) Coman (Greenberg 1963:130). Of the sixteen genetic groups in Greenberg's African classification before 1955, twelve of these – the isolates and very small families – ended up in Nilo-Saharan in Greenberg's (1966[1963]) classification (cf. Bender 2000:52) – small wonder it was considered his wastebasket phylum. Tucker and Bryan (1956, 1966) rejected Greenberg's "Eastern Sudanic" (underlying Chari-Nile and eventually Nilo-Saharan, with its several additions); they say:

There is insufficient grammatical correspondence to justify any grouping together of these languages. We therefore treat the languages of Greenberg's Eastern Sudanic family, other than Nilotic and Nilo-Hamitic, as Isolated Units or members of Isolated Language Groups. (Tucker and Bryan 1956:153)

Heine (1970:9) also challenges this part of Greenberg's African classification and advocates treating the ten branches of Greenberg's Eastern Sudanic Family as isolated languages or language groups.

As Bender (1997a:9) explains, there are "reservations about the membership of several groups: notably Songay (= Songhai), the westernmost member, the Kuliak family in northeast Uganda, and the Kado [Kadu] group in the Kordofan Hills of south-central Sudan." (See also Dimmendaal 2001:358; Mikkola 1998, 1999:130; Mous 2003:162; Nicolaï 2003.) Kuliak (Nyangiya, one of Greenberg's ten East Sudanic members) is highly disputed. Some place Kuliak in Afroasiatic with "Fringe Cushitic"; Bender (2000:55) finds it very distinctive, but influenced by Nilotic languages. Some see it as an independent non-aligned language family, some hold that it is an "Outlier" or an early branch of Nilo-Saharan, and some believe it is a branch of Eastern Sudanic within Nilo-Saharan (Childs 2003:45; cf. Mikkola 1998, 1999:130). The position of Gumuz and Koman is also disputed (Mous 2003:162; Mikkola 1998, 1999:130). The position of Songhay is also very disputed (Nicolaï 1992, 1995, 1996, 2002, 2003). Greenberg (1955) had it as an isolate (a position some still hold), then considered a possible Niger-Congo affiliation for it, before ultimately putting it in his Nilo-Saharan phylum of leftovers in Greenberg 1966[1963]. Several others argue that Songhay should be with Niger-Congo, closer to the Mande group (whose Niger-Kordofanian status itself is none too clear; see above) (see Bender 1997a:59); some link it more closely with Chadic, some wth Gur. Songhay is geographically separated from the other Nilo-Saharan languages and has undergone heavy influence from Mande languages and Berber languages; some even interpret it as a post-creole with a Berber base (Bender 2000:54) or as a mixed language (Childs 2003:46).

Still others see the uncertainty of Songhay between Nilo-Saharan and Niger-Kordofanian as reason for suspecting an even larger grouping embracing all the languages of these two big phyla, a vast "Kongo-Saharan" (see Bender 1997a:59, 66 for details; Gregersen 1972; Williamson 1989:8–9). A number of scholars criticized Greenberg's grouping of East Sudanic, Central Sudanic, Berta, and Kunama as "Chari-Nile" (earlier "Macro-Sudanic"), finding the evidence unconvincing (Bender 1997a:60, 2000:55), and Greenberg himself appears to have revised this, considering Central Sudanic and East Sudanic as independent branches of Nilo-Saharan (with Berta and Kunama closer to East Sudanic) (Greenberg 1983:18; Mikkola 1998:63; Ruhlen 1987a:111; Bender 1997a:60).

A sense of the extreme linguistic difference among the groups which came to be united in Nilo-Saharan can be gained from a consideration of the claim that combining East Sudanic and Central Sudanic was comparable to combining Indo-European and Ural-Altaic (Bender 1997a:58). "Nilo-Saharan is arguably the least-known of the four proposed African phyla, and the one for which the questions of integrity and composition are most open" (Bender 1997a:10). Bender's (1997a:10) work splits up Chari-Nile, adds Kado (or Kadu) (Kadugli-Krongo) which Greenberg had assigned to his Kordofanian family in the Niger-Kordofanian phylum, and removes Kuliak from Greenberg's Eastern Sudanic and considers it a separate family within Nilo-Saharan; Greenberg's Koman was divided into two separate families in the phylum, Koman and Gumuz. The Chari-Nile hypothesis has been especially controversial (Goodman 1970, 1971; Thelwall 1982:44; Bender 1991, 1993). The "Mao" languages (placed with Koman and Gumuz) are not Nilo-Saharan at all, but have been reclassified as part of Omotic (Bender 1983:259; Dimmendaal 2001:358). Schadeberg (1981) indicates that there is as much evidence for placing Kadugli languages in Nilo-Saharan as there is for Greenberg's assignment of them to Kordofanian, and Bender (1983:289) wondered whether Koman and Kadugli may be connected, reassigning Kadugli to Nilo-Saharan.

Thus, we concur with Cyffer (2000:42) that, "as the Nilo-Saharan phylum is the most disputed one among the African language phyla [after Khoisan, LC/WP], it is not surprising that several attempts of new proposals for reclassifications were made." In Nichols' (1997a:376) opinion, "Nilo-Saharan is probably not a genetic grouping and not even a structural pool but is simply a residual grouping. A core set of its stocks identified by Bender (1983) – Nilotic, Nubian, Central Sudanic, Kunama-Ilit, Koman-Gumuz, and Kadugli – may constitute a structural pool or even a quasi-stock. The other Nilo-Saharan groups are probably unrelated families and isolates found across the Sahel and central to eastern Sahara." (See also Nicolaï 2002, 2003.)

Thus, Nilo-Saharan is disputed, after Khoisan (see below) the most controversial of Greenberg's African big-four groupings (Bender 2000:43; Gregersen 1977:121; Fleming 1987:168–9). We do not find the evidence presented for Nilo-Saharan so far compelling.

Afroasiatic (also Afro-Asiatic, Afrasian; older related names: Hamito-Semitic, Erythraic, Lisramic) (*c*.370 languages, about 150 in Chadic alone; not including some 50 extinct varieties of Semitic). The Afroasiatic hypothesis had various incomplete antecedents in the guise of Hamito-Semitic and the like. Cohen (1924, 1947) was instrumental in gaining support for the classification, though Chadic was not yet included. Meinhof's controversial "Hamitic" has already been mentioned. Most, however, would assign the true beginning of Afroasiatic to Greenberg. For Greenberg (1963) Afroasiatic included: Semitic, Berber, Egyptian, Cushitic, and Chad[ic]. Today most would list Omotic (Greenberg's "West Cushitic") as a separate group, distinguished from Cushitic.

Afroasiatic enjoys reasonably wide support among linguists, but it is not uncontroversial, especially with regard to the groups assumed to be genetically related to one another as members of the phylum (Hayward 2000:74). In particular, there is disagreement concerning Cushitic (Hayward 2000:75), and Omotic (formerly called Sidama or West Cushitic) is disputed (Fleming 1976b; Hetzron 1980; Bender 1987). The great diversity within Omotic makes it a questionable entity for some. Chadic is held to be uncertain by others (cf. Newman 2000:262). As we shall see, typological and areal problems contribute to these doubts. Orel and Stolbova (1995) abandon Cushitic and treat it together with Omotic rather as a linguistic area (*Sprachbund*) of seven families within Afroasiatic; Bender (1997b) on the other hand proposes a "Macro-Cushitic" composed of Berber, Semitic, and Cushitic (proper) (and also speculates about possible accommodation for Indo-European within this group) (Hayward 2000:86). Many believe there is some closer connection between Berber, Semitic, and either Egyptian or Cushitic than among the other groups in Greenberg's Afroasiatic classification, though it is not certain yet whether this is indeed a closer genetic subgroup or whether these three merely share more diffused areal features. Porkhomovsky's (1988:102) view reflects these doubts and difficulties:

Chadic and Cushitic languages are extremely diverse. As a matter of fact, it would be correct to consider these language groups up to the second half of the 20th century, as areal, but not genetic communities, viz.: Chadic as non-Berber and non-Semitic Afrasian languages of the Western and Central Sudan, and Cushitic as a similar group in North-East Africa south of Sahara.

Comparison among Afroasiatic languages is complicated by long-term language contacts and borrowing, where Berber and Chadic have influenced one another; Chadic has also been influenced by both "Niger-Congo" and "Nilo-Saharan" languages; Omotic and Cushitic share areal traits; Egyptian influenced Semitic and was itself influenced; Cushitic has influenced Semitic; and Semitic, especially through Arabic in the last millennium, has influenced many others.

The Afroasiatic union has relied mainly on morphological agreements in the pronominal paradigms and the presence of a masculine–feminine gender distinction. This evidence is attractive, but not completely compelling. As for the lexical comparisons, Afroasiatic scholars are in general agreement that the findings have been more limited and harder to interpret. Indeed, the two recent large-scale attempts at Afroasiatic reconstructing and assembling large sets of cognates, Ehret (1995) and Orel and Stolbova (1995), are so radically different from one another, with little in common, that they raise questions about the possibility of viable reconstruction in Afroasiatic. As Newman reports, "the lists of supposed cognate lexical items between Chadic and other Afroasiatic languages presented in the past have on the whole been less reliable" (Newman 1980:13). Newman (2000:262) recognizes that "in the opinion of some scholars, the evidence supporting the relationship between the Chadic language family and other language groups in the Afroasiatic phylum, such as Semitic and Berber, is not compelling." Jungraithmayr's (2000:91) conclusions raise even graver doubts about being able to classify Chadic successfully:

To sum up: As long as there are deep-rooted properties – like pronominal morphemes – existant in a given language that hint at a certain genetic origin, these properties ultimately determine the classification of that language. However, since most of the ancient (Hamitosemitic) structures and properties of the Chadic languages have been destroyed or at least mutilated and transformed to the extent that they can hardly be identified as such any more, it is crucial to study these languages as deeply and thoroughly as possible.

He notes "the enormous degree of linguistic complexity we encounter in the Chadic languages," with the observation that

the degree of "africanization" has sometimes reached the point where, structurally speaking, the similarities between Chadic and Niger-Congo and/or Nilo-Saharan languages spoken in their immediate vicinity have become more striking than those between Chadic and other Hamitosemitic languages, particularly Berber or Semitic. These obvious surface similarities between Chadic and non-Chadic languages in central Sudan put an additional task load on the researcher's shoulders. (Jungraithmayr 2000:91)

Nevertheless, Newman is of the opinion that "some points of resemblance in morphology and lexicon are so striking that if one did not assume relationship, they would be impossible to explain away." There is a methodological lesson to be gained in examining Newman's (1980) argument, which has been considered strong evidence for Afroasiatic. Newman (1980:19) argued that in

a range of Afroasiatic languages from whatever branch, one finds that the words for 'blood,' 'moon,' 'mouth,' 'name,' and 'nose,' for example, tend to be masculine; 'eye,' 'fire,' and 'sun,' feminine; and 'water,' grammatically plural . . . where the overall consistency in gender assignment contrasts strikingly with the considerable diversity in form.

He compared fourteen words which have the same gender across the branches of Afroasiatic and assumed this coincidence proves the genetic relationship. (Newman's table has fifteen items, but 'egg' is listed as doubtful, and in any case, there may be a non-arbitrary real-world connection between 'egg' and female gender.) There are several problems with this claim. First, it violates the principle of permitting only comparisons which involve both sound and meaning (see Chapter 7). Newman's comparisons involve only meaning (gender) and the forms compared are not for the most part phonetically similar. Second, it assumes that the choice of the gender marking is equally arbitrary for each of the forms involved, but this is clearly not the case. For example, 'sun' and 'moon' tend to be paired cross-linguistically in a set where the two have opposite genders, one masculine, one feminine – Newman's Afroasiatic masculine 'moon' and feminine 'sun' parallels Germanic and many other languages. In many languages, including some of the ones compared here, feminine gender is associated with 'diminutive'; this may explain why the larger animals of the list, 'crocodile' and 'monkey,' have masculine gender. In any case, of Newman's fourteen, only four are feminine; perhaps, then, masculine is in some way the unmarked gender, the gender most likely to be found unless there is some reason for a morpheme to be assigned to the feminine class. As for 'water' being in the "plural," in three of the language groups compared, masculine and plural have the same form, so that it would be just as accurate in these to say that 'water' was "masculine." Also for 'water,' plurality and mass noun may be associated in some non-arbitrary way. The most serious problem is that of probability. As Nichols (1996a) shows, even if there were an equal probability for any word in the set to show up either as masculine or feminine (and as just argued, this is not the case), for Newman's argument to have force, it would need to involve a closed set with exactly these words with no others being tested for gender parallels. The probability of finding this number of forms with identical gender across the six branches of Afroasiatic when an open sample of basic nouns is searched comes out to be roughly equivalent to the fourteen in Newman's table – the number he found is about what should be expected. The argument, then, has no force.

Nichols (1997a:364) sees Afroasiatic as "an atypically stock-like quasi-stock." She says it is "routinely accepted as a genetic grouping, though uncontroversial regular correspondences cannot be found," though she thinks it has a "distinctive grammatical signature that includes several morphological features at least two of which independently suffice statistically to show genetic relatedness beyond any reasonable doubt." As pointed out above, some Afroasiatic languages lack these, while some neighboring non-Afroasiatic languages which have been influenced by them have these traits. This being the case, these traits are neither necessary nor sufficient to show the genetic relationship. Afroasiatic probably is a valid genetic grouping, at least large parts of what is postulated to belong in it, even though we are reticent to accept traits that may have other explanations and thus are not fully persuasive of that relationship.

Khoisan (*c.* thirty languages still extant). Greenberg originally called his Khoisan grouping "the Click Languages" until he changed the name, "compounded of the Hottentot's name for themselves (Khoi) and their name for the Bushmen (San)" (Greenberg 1963:66). Others had argued for joining the "Khoi" and "San" languages in a single family long before Greenberg (for example, Schils 1895; Planert 1905, 1926). Khoisan is defined as "those African languages which use clicks as regular speech sounds and which are not obviously members of one of the other families" (Sands 1998:17; cf. Greenberg 1963:66). The classification of these languages has almost from the beginning been complicated by inappropriate reliance on certain typological traits. As Mutaka points out, "some grouped Bushman and Hottentot [together] because of clicks. Others grouped Hottentot with Hamito-Semitic because of the presence of the masculine/feminine distinction in nouns and pronouns" (Mutaka 2000:244), mentioned above. For Greenberg, the phylum consisted of the Southern African Khoisan branch, with its three groups: Northern (Ju or !Xu) family (Zhu, !Kung), Central (Khoi, "Hottentot"; Nama, Nharo, Korana), and Southern (!Xóo), plus two other branches, Sandawe and Hadza (Hatsa).[20]

Khoisan is the least accepted of Greenberg's four African phyla, and is now rejected by many as a genetic relationship (see Heine and Nurse 2000a, 2000b:5, Güldemann and Vossen 2000:99–104; Mous 2003:163, Sands 1998). As Güldemann and Vossen (2000:99) say, "none of the several attempts at proving the genetic relatedness of all putative Khoisan languages has been convincing, and the evidence appears to be extremely meagre." Many have suspected that Sandawe and Hadza (of Tanzania) belong together in an Eastern African Khoisan branch, though there is no real evidence for this. In fact, nearly all have doubts about the inclusion of Hadza (Hatsa), most have doubts also about Sandawe, and many are dubious about the classification in general, doubting even that the Southern African Khoisan groups are genetically related to one another (see Bender 1997a:8; Sands 1998; Westphal 1971). Several scholars agree in using the term "Khoisan" not to reflect a genetic relationship among the languages, but rather as a cover term for all the non-Bantu and non-Cushitic click languages of eastern and southern Africa (Güldemann and Vossen 2000:102; Sands 1998).

Until Greenberg, the various comparative works on these languages typically relied on various non-linguistic considerations, physical or cultural criteria (Güldemann and Vossen 2000:101). For example, difference in subsistence patterns, with cattle-herding "Hottentots" on one side and hunter–gatherer "Bushmen" on the other, prevented scholars from considering the possibility of them being linguistically related (Güldemann and Vossen 2000:101).

Khoisan is a peculiar linguistic grouping, in any event, since it relies heavily on the single typological trait of clicks. This violates the spirit of Greenberg's

---

[20] Kwadi, an isolated click language of Angola "almost unknown to linguists," not listed among Greenberg's Khoisan languages, has been added as a separate branch in the phylum (Güldemann and Vossen 2000).

own principle that typological traits are not enough (like, for example, sharing the presence of tonal contrasts or of gender), since these can be shared by sheer accident or by diffusion. By this principle, both sound and meaning together are required for something to stand as evidence of genetic relationship (see Chapter 7). Clicks alone, then, are not sufficient evidence by this principle. Moreover, not all languages with clicks belong to Khoisan; as is well known, several neighboring Bantu languages (e.g., Sotho, Swazi, Xhosa, Zulu, etc.) have borrowed clicks from Khoisan languages, and Dahalo (Cushitic) clicks are attributed to influence from East African Khoisan (Hadza and Sandawe). Thus the presence of clicks in Khoisan languages, while potentially inherited from a common ancestor and therefore evidence of a genetic relationship, could have been acquired independently or through borrowing. Therefore, the principal basis of the proposed family is shaky. As Childs (2003:51–2) says, "the general lesson to be learned from this section [on Khoisan] is that a typological feature, however distinctive, cannot genetically define a linguistic group."

The actual evidence presented for Khoisan is not very compelling. In part this reflects the structure of the languages compared. Morphemes in southern African "Khoisan" languages are typically monosyllabic, and with the very large segmental inventories of these languages where the frequency of clicks in the vocabulary is extremely high, this means that many sounds do not recur with much frequency in the compared vocabulary, making detection of any potential sound correspondences difficult. As Sands (1998:36) points out, "the regularity of even 'transparent' correspondences between Khoisan languages remains in question as there are typically no more than two or three examples of any correspondence between any two languages in any given study." The canonical pattern of morphemes is typically CV(C(V)), where the first consonant is typically a click, and the second consonant is restricted to a small set: /r/, /n/, /m/, and /b/ or /p/. There is internal evidence to suggest that the second C(V) may very likely have been a separate morpheme, part of the noun-class concord system. This means lots of comparisons of CV shaped morphemes, where their shortness must compete with chance (accidental similarity) as a potential explanation for any similarities detected. We share Sands' (1998:37) view that "ignoring the second syllable may be a necessary technique in Khoisan comparisons at present, but it does leave a lot of linguistic material unaccounted for." Moreover, Sandawe and Hadza do not follow the Southern African Khoisan pattern, allowing the full range of consonants in the non-initial consonant position, including clicks. Sands could find no reliable sound correspondences involving clicks (Sands 1998:161, 165). She says, "given that the unity of Southern African Khoisan *is* in question, it is important to consider the number of cognates proposed between each major group" (Sands 1998:42). For example, between Hadza and Sandawe, Greenberg (1963) proposed less than a dozen! Out of Greenberg's 116 proposed Khoisan cognate sets, only 67 involve more than two Khoisan groups (Sands 1998:43). Sands' (1998:53) conclusion is telling:

Previous Khoisan comparisons have typically noted numbers and types of similarities which are suggestive of genetic relationship. If the languages are related, then the evidence points to a remote relationship at best. However, none of these studies has sufficiently demonstrated that the similarities are such that they *must* be due to genetic relatedness. Similarities are often noted without rigorous analysis of their significance. The role of chance in contributing to the number of similarities is typically overlooked or underestimated in these studies. Comparisons that do not constrain the semantic or phonological similarity, or the number of comparisons made make it difficult to evaluate the possible role that chance plays in contributing to the number of similarities.

Thus, while several studies present lexical similarities, none has demonstrated sound correspondences that are regular and repeated in the languages (Sands 1998:20). This is compounded by the fact that until recently many of the earlier sources commonly used were notoriously unreliable phonetically, making Greenberg's comparisons "particularly suspect" – Sands (1998:31–2) finds errors in one-third of the Hadza forms Greenberg (1963) cited as potential cognates.

In a careful statistical study of a 100-word list, Sands (1998:72) concludes, "the statistical analysis shows that the numbers of similarities between stem initial consonants and following vowels across major Khoisan groups and between Khoisan and the non-Khoisan languages are not greater than what might be predicted due to chance resemblance." In a second study of 100 words of basic vocabulary where the semantic range compared is loosened considerably, Sands (1998:77) found that all five of the major Khoisan groups do appear to share lexical items not merely by coincidence, though the source of the similarity is not apparent and could be due to borrowing and chance; significantly, this study revealed that Xhosa and Zulu (Bantu languages) also "share [with Khoisan] a number of items whose presence does not appear to be due to chance alone" (Sands 1998:77), suggesting to us that borrowing may be an important factor in explaining these similarities and those among Khoisan languages themselves (see Sands 1998:164). Perhaps the best evidence involves Sands' comparison of noun-class markers among some of the Khoisan languages. As she points out, "the synchronic noun class systems of the major Khoisan languages do not bear striking resemblances with each other" (Sands 1998:128), but there are some suggestive commonalities and Sands is optimistic that additional work may "uncover more substantial traces of an earlier, shared system" (1998:129). In any case, Hadza shows little similarity and is excluded from the other Khoisan languages (1998:165), while Sandawe does show some affinities with the other Khoisan branches. Sands' (1998:166) overall conclusion is:

At present, it is not possible to determine which of the identified possible cognates are actual cognates and which owe their similarity to borrowing or chance. Despite the present inability to validate a significant number of cognate sets through the illustration of regular sound correspondences, the similarities seen between all major Khoisan groups with the exception of Hadza, particularly as seen in the comparison of noun class markers . . . indicate that there are similarities which go beyond what can be explained due to chance or borrowing. On balance, from the evidence we now have on hand, it seems a little more likely than not that the Northern, Southern, Central Khoisan groups along with Sandawe are related but that additional data and further research is needed to elucidate the relationship.

Others are not so optimistic, opting more for areal explanations. Heine and Nurse (2000b:9) suggest that "it may well turn out that Khoisan could be more appropriately defined as a convergence area rather than as a genetic unit" (cf. Güldemann and Vossen 2000; Dimmendaal 2001:358). Nichols (1997a:375) sees "Khoisan" not as a genetic group, rather "the click languages include the Khoisan family in southern Africa and two or three isolates – Hadza and Sandawe in Kenya, possibly Kwadi in the southwest – and constitute a structural pool." M. Lionel Bender (personal communication) thinks Khoisan "may well be two or three phyla rather than a single one . . . the evidence is minimal and may be insufficient to answer this."

African isolates?   The usual picture of African language classification sees all the languages as belonging in some way to one or another of Greenberg's big four phyla – recall Greenberg (1966[1963]) essentially pushed all the isolates and leftovers into his Nilo-Saharan grouping. However, some scholars find new isolates, unclassified languages in Africa:

in south-western Ethiopia . . . there are – what appear to be – two linguistic isolates, Ongota (Biraile) and Shabo. These two highly endangered languages, which were not listed by Greenberg (1963), may constitute the last representatives of independent African stocks. Finally, a language called Laal (Chad), whose existence was not known among Africanists at the time of Greenberg's classification, has defied genetic classification so far, although some Africanists claim it is an Adamawa-Ubangian (Niger-Congo) language. (Dimmendaal 2001:358)

Other isolates mentioned are Hadza (Tanzania, formerly thought to be Khoisan), Jalaa (Nigeria), Pre (Ivory Coast, maybe Kwa with much Mande material), and Mpre (Ghana) (Mous 2003:164). A sober reassessment of Nilo-Saharan (and others) would probably require the recognition of several other isolates. (See Köhler 1975:338–44 for a list of isolates and poorly classified languages of Africa.)

Overall assessment of Greenberg's African classification   It is true that "despite . . . complexities . . . and resultant analytical shortcomings, there is considerable agreement [among many Africanists], *perhaps unwarranted*, on how African languages should be classified" (Childs 2003:31; our emphasis, LC/WP). We also agree with Winston (1966:160) that Greenberg's African classification "now require[s] considerable refinement, both in specific points of the classification, and in the underlying conceptual scheme." As Dixon (1997:35) points out, Greenberg's criteria are so "transparently inadequate" in his treatment of American Indian languages (Greenberg 1987), that it is causing linguists to reassess their thinking on his African classification, and several who formerly were supportive now have doubts concerning the African classification and in particular the methods upon which it is based. In short, acknowledging Greenberg's African success – realistically – does not deny fallibility. It is necessary to speak again of the African classification's methodological shortcomings due to its reliance on superficial lexical similarities:

Although Greenberg's work represents considerable progress over that of previous writers, it leaves a number of questions open. His approach is largely inadequate for the PROOF of genetic relationship; it can do little more than offer initial hypotheses, to be substantiated by more reliable techniques like the comparative method. In a number of instances, languages or language groups have been placed in a given family solely on the basis of a handful of "look-alikes," i.e. morphemes of similar sound shape and meaning. The Nilo-Saharan family, in particular, must be regarded as a tentative grouping, the genetic unity of which remains to be established. (Heine 1992:32)

I would suggest that parts of Greenberg's famous classification of African languages, which was posited on the basis of multilateral comparison and more or less achieved the status of orthodoxy . . . urgently needs to be reinvestigated by reliable methods. (Ringe 1993:104)

As several have recently pointed out, "so far, it has not been possible to apply the comparative method appropriately to any of the four African language phyla" (Heine and Kuteva 2001:394; see also Bender 1987; Köhler 1975:144; Welmers 1973:16–19; cf. Hymes 1959:53, Winston 1966:163–4), and "controversies remain in the case of all four phyla established by Greenberg" (Bender 1989:1). Greenberg's African phyla involve such depth and internal diversity that they remain unproven and probably can never be demonstrated.

Africa and areal linguistics   It is important to bear in mind that areal linguistics has not played much of a role in African historical linguistics – "contact-induced language change and the implications it has for language classification in Africa are still largely *terra incognita*" (Heine and Kuteva 2001:392) –, though serious areal linguistic problems are known to exist and to complicate the classification (see Appleyard 1999; Bryan 1959; Childs 2003; Dimmendaal 2001; Ferguson 1976; Fleming 1976a:307; Heine 1970, 1972:7, 1992:33; Heine and Kuteva 2001; Jungraithmayr 2000; Sasse 1986; Zima

2000; cf. also Greenberg 1999). For example, in the Ethiopian linguistic area, "Cushitic, Omotic, and Ethiopian Semitic show a number of features which are virtually absent from Afro-Asiatic languages outside the area, but which are shared by non-Afro-Asiatic languages within it, e.g. the presence of ejective consonants and of Subject-Object-Verb syntax" (Heine 1992:33). Several cases are documented in which Cushitic and Bantu languages have converged extensively, so much so that accurate classification is made difficult (Mous 1994; Nurse 1991, 1994; Thomason and Kaufman 1988:202–4, 223–8). Wedekind (1985) discovered convergence areas involving tonal properties in Africa. Bender (1997a:40) points out:

Wedekind (1985:109) presents a map showing three foci of languages which are analyzed as having five contrastive tone levels. These are in Omotic of southwestern Ethiopia, Mande and Voltaic of Ivory Coast, and Kwa and Benue-Congo of Nigeria-Cameroon (ibid. 112). The coincidence with Heine's [1975] three areas of recessive word-order-influence is impressive.

"The distribution of V[erb]-initial languages among adjoining groups in East Africa is not random" (Bender 1997a:37). And so on. This neglect of areal linguistics is unfortunate, and progress in the future will depend on bringing such considerations seriously into the picture.

In summary, those African families which have been clearly established and are not in dispute were established on the basis of more or less standard criteria. Those proposals which remain controversial have relied on questionable criteria, typological traits or inadequate methods such as mass (multilateral) comparison. In short, it is, we believe, best to view Africa in terms not of Greenberg's phyla, but in terms of the fifteen to twenty more established genetic groupings and perhaps several isolates. In like vein, Nichols (1997a:376) sees Africa as having "as many as 30 stocks and as few as 17 combined stocks and quasi-stocks" (Nichols 1997a:376).

6.9   Australia

In one sense, the classification of Australian languages is less relevant to our interests than research in other parts of the world. This is because little comparative linguistic research was undertaken on Australian languages before the twentieth century, meaning that standard methods were already fully developed and well understood before language classification was seriously undertaken there. Moreover, less "systematic reconstruction" has been attempted in Australia than in many other parts of the world, leaving much work yet to be done (Blake 1990:435). In another sense, however, Australia is quite relevant to us, for two reasons. First, some scholars have assumed that Australia is a special case, that language change in Australian languages is somehow different from elsewhere and that it challenges the standard comparative method (see, for example, Dixon 2002:699). In this section we show that this assumption is misguided (see also Bowern and Koch 2004a and Evans 2003a). Second, it is very often assumed that all mainland Australian languages are genetically related (of which c.250 are attested, among some 600 tribes) – a controversial claim of remote linguistic kinship (cf. Capell 1956; Dixon 1980:222; see Micelli 2004). Therefore, it is worth focusing some attention on the classification of Australian languages and especially on the controversies about the nature of language change and claims about how this might affect classifications and claims of relatedness. (For a historical overview of the methods utilized in Australia, see Koch 2004.)

6.9.1   History of language classification in Australia

It has been an article of faith, starting at least as early as 1841 with Sir George Grey,[21] that all the languages of mainland Australia are probably genetically related. This assumed unity plays a major and misleading role in how language relationships in Australia have been faced. We shall see how it plays itself out in the history of this field (below).

One of the earliest comparative linguistic studies involving Australian languages was that of Horatio Hale (1846:479–532) (better known for work in American Indian linguistics, but mentioned earlier in this book also in connection with Polynesian and African language classification). He notes that at first "the great differences observed between those [languages] spoken by tribes in close vicinity to one another led to the impression that a multitude of totally dissimilar idioms were spoken in the country" (Hale 1846:479), but he goes on to report the general opinion at the time "that the tribes of Australia are of one stock, and speak languages which, though differing in many respects, yet preserve sufficient evidence of a common origin." He notes, however, that this opinion "is founded rather [more] upon the resemblance of a few of the most common words, and a general similarity of pronunciation, than upon any careful comparison of the various languages, more especially with reference to their grammatical characteristics, on which alone any positive conclusion can be founded" (1846:479). Hale's reading of Australian opinion at that time could aptly be repeated of much opinion today.

Hale's own study was limited to the colony of New South Wales (which then included Victoria and Queensland), where he concluded: "that, within this region, the dialects [languages] of all the native tribes are nearly akin, cannot be doubted." He presented a list of some thirty-three probable cognates in nine

---

[21] It probably started even earlier than with Sir George Grey in 1841 (David Nash, personal communication).

languages of the region (1846:479–81). But, since Hale found lexical similarities not as compelling as grammatical evidence, he went on to examine the "degree of resemblance . . . apparent in the grammatical structure of the different languages" (1846:481), noting many close grammatical similarities between Kāmilarai (Gamilaraay) and Wiradurei (Wiradhurri). These two, we now know, are members of the reasonably close-knit Central New South Wales family.

Hale had no lasting impact on Australian language classification, but it is significant to note his report of a generally shared belief in "one stock," in the genetic unity of all Australian languages. This has been a pivotal problem in historical linguistic research in this area.

Father Wilhelm Schmidt (1919), associated with the *Kulturkreis* diffusionist school in anthropology, was the first to offer a general classification of Australian languages, as part of his worldwide classification of languages. Schmidt's view is relatively consistent with views still held today,[22] with one notable difference: he rejected the view that all the Australian languages were genetically related. He said:

The Australian languages do not, as had always been believed, represent an essentially homogeneous group of languages . . . the whole of the north of Australia contains languages which do not present any lexical relationship and only very few grammatical relationships with that larger ["South Australian"] group or even with each other. (Schmidt 1972[1919]:4, quoted in Koch 2004:19)[23]

Schmidt was the first to attempt to establish a large family of languages (his "South Australian") within Australia based on the linguistic evidence. He separated "southern languages" from "northern languages," and he successfully recognized some lower-level family groupings which were "fairly obvious because of the masses of shared vocabulary and grammatical forms" (Koch 1997:40).

Schmidt's methods were far from standard, however. According to Dixon (1980:21), he utilized some "quite superficial features" in his classification, "for instance, which sounds could occur at the end of a word – that are seldom good criteria for genetic grouping." For establishing his Victoria group, he used three typological features shared by these languages but absent from neighboring languages, namely words could begin with *l*, words could end in stops and consonant clusters, and the possessor follows the possessed noun; eight shared

---

[22] That is, except for those languages which have undergone considerable phonological reduction (for which Kenneth Hale 1964, 1976 nevertheless demonstrated "Pama-Nyungan" connections).

[23] A quite differently worded version of this quotation from Schmidt is cited by Dixon (1980: 220–1):

Although most of Australia contains languages which despite many differences are nevertheless related through a number of common features, nevertheless the whole of the north of Australia contains languages which do not show any lexical relationship and only very few grammatical relationships with the larger group and even with each other. Here in the north we find a wealth of languages comparable with the diversity found in New Guinea.

vocabulary items offered supplementary support (Koch 2004:20–1). Rarely, Schmidt also relied on shared phonological changes, for example when he grouped Thangatti-Yukumbul based on vocabulary items and the replacement of medial *l* with *t* (Koch 2004:21; see Schmidt 1919:124). For major groupings, his only evidence was vocabulary. Koch (2004:23) points out that of Schmidt's (1919:27) twelve "characteristic words" for his Southwestern group, Schmidt himself admits that five also occur in his South-Central group, and Koch finds problems with all the rest involving phonological difference, restricted distribution, and occurrence in various other languages outside the group, so that "*none* of the characteristic lexemes are exclusive to the Southwestern Group" (Koch 2004:23).

The next scholar of significance in Australian linguistics was Gerhardt Laves, a graduate student from the University of Chicago. Though often overlooked in historical accounts, he left behind an extensive collection of good-quality material on a number of the languages, little of which has been published, though it has been consulted with profit in recent years. He reported that he was "working under the auspices of the Australian National Research Council during the period August 1929 to August 1931" and chose "six languages in representative areas for intensive study."[24] Laves said of the state of study of Australian Aboriginal languages then:

Up to the present date, a fairly large body of material on Australian languages has appeared in print. Unfortunately, however, the greatest part of this literature is so fragmentary and phonetically inaccurate as to be of little use for either specific or for comparative studies.

Of his own findings, he reported:

Phonetically, I have been able, on the basis of my material, to group together all of the Australian languages. With respect to morphology, however, it is necessary to separate them into three major groups. The first and by far the largest in area, would seem to occupy the entire south of the continent, project to the north coast in the eastern Northern Territory and cover all of the continent to the eastward except for a few languages in northern Cape York Peninsula of northern Queensland. This large group I propose to name the Transcontinental Languages. The second is to be found in northern Western Australia to the north of Broome and extends over into the north-western part of the Northern Territory including the lower reaches of the Victoria, the Fitzmaurice and the Daly Rivers. This group I shall designate as the Northwestern Languages. The third, and smallest, group embraces a few languages in the northern extremity of Cape York Peninsula, northern Queensland; I shall call them the Cape York Languages despite the fact that there are also Transcontinental languages in the peninsula . . .

---

[24] These are, (1) Kumbaingeri of Northern New South Wales, (2) Karadjeri, near Broome, Western Australia, (3) Barda, of Cape L'Eveque peninsula, north of Broome, (4) Kurin, near Albany, southern Western Australia, (5) Hermit Hill, Daly River, Northern Territory, and (6) Ngengumeri, also on the Daly River.

It remains to be seen how these genetically related groups are to be further subdivided and whether the criss-crossing of the lines of division will materially alter the present grouping.[25]

Unfortunately, Laves also had no significant impact on the later development of Australian linguistic study.

Arthur Capell (1956, cf. also 1962), in the next general classification of Australian languages, set up typological groupings and considered schemes by which one type might change into another type. His classification of the languages into "prefixing" and "suffixing" (i.e. "non-prefixing") languages became influential in the subsequent Australianist literature, and the genetic classification was assumed to correspond reasonably well to this typological one (Blake 1990:436), though the genetic relationships have not yet been fully determined. In Dixon's (1980:21) view, the prefixing languages form a solid geographical block in the north, the prefixing being but a widely shared areal trait with no genetic implications. Capell, unlike Schmidt, at first advocated the idea of all the Australian languages belonging to a single language family – "the Australian languages are ultimately one" (Capell 1956:95). (See also Capell 1956:2–3; Koch 2004:27.)

As for his methods, he utilized both structural comparison and shared vocabulary, with primacy given to the structural evidence (Koch 2004:27). He supported his "Common Australian" with presumed cognate sets representing thirty-five meanings; he considered the widespread shared verbs especially "important . . . in establishing the idea of 'Common Australian' in regard to vocabulary" (Capell 1956:81, cited in Koch 2004:28). Views similar to his on the nature of cognate identification and the role of sound changes in Australia still characterize much Australian work:

Usually in the Australian field words are either fairly obviously cognate as between languages, or equally obviously non-cognate. There has not appeared the same necessity of establishing sound laws to prove connections . . . The establishment of sound laws in Australia is not so much to be used to determine relationships of words as to fit related words into sub-groups not to decide whether a word is C[ommon] A[ustralian] or not. (Capell 1956:83, quoted by Koch 2004:29)

We return to this view below.

Later, Capell gave up his belief that all Australian languages are genetically related, opting instead for several "Early Australian" languages together with a later widespread Common Australian which he saw as the ancestor of many

---

[25] These citations, on www.anu.edu.au/linguistics/nash/aust/laves/intro.html, are taken from a manuscript, "A Preliminary Report on the Languages of Australia" by Gerhardt Laves (which indicates it was to be presented before Section L of the AAAS [American Association for the Advancement of Science] at Atlantic City, December 31, 1932), in draft in Section 7.2.1 of the Laves Papers.

but not all Australian languages (Capell 1975, 1979; Koch 2004:29). This view was much more like Schmidt's (above).

Dixon (1980:21) attributes the next classification, which forms the foundation of the most widely held classification today, largely to the work of Kenneth Hale. This classification came from the survey of Australian languages by Hale, O'Grady, and Wurm in the 1950s and 1960s (published in O'Grady, Voegelin, and Voegelin 1966; Wurm 1972). Unfortunately, it was based mostly on lexicostatistics, now dismissed by most linguists (see Chapter 7). Wurm (1972:109) reports that "though the basis of classification was admittedly lexicostatistic in nature, typological criteria [were] taken into consideration in arriving at the results and [were] regarded as decisive in doubtful cases." They were firmly committed to the view that all the Australian languages were related in a single Australian macro-phylum. It contained twenty-nine families (covering 502 community dialects), twenty-nine in the north plus widespread Pama-Nyungan. Their classification was offered as preliminary and tentative, but nevertheless was widely accepted and often repeated, still the foundation of much contemporary discussion of Australian language relationships. The attitude that the discernible language "families" probably belonged together as genetically related members of an Australian macro-phylum contributed significantly to the persistent confusion surrounding what below we call "the subgrouping problem," since if these groups (which we call "families" if their relationship to one another is unconfirmed) belong together in some high-order genetic grouping, then they could be considered "subgroups" of "Proto-Australian"; however, if no such higher-order grouping is yet established on legitimate evidence, then the persistent discussion of Australian families as "subgroups" is just misleading, particularly for those who are not specialists in Australian linguistics. (See below.)

The terminology stemming from this classification became basic in subsequent discussions. For example, it recognized "Pama-Nyungan" (a name composed by Hale, based on the words *pama* 'man' in the far northeast and *nyuŋa* 'man' in the southwest), which is the largest "family" in Australia. Languages assigned to Pama-Nyungan extend over four-fifths of Australia, i.e. most of the continent except northern areas. Pama-Nyungan is accepted among most Australianists as a legitimate language family, but not uncritically and not universally. It is rejected by Dixon (2002); it is held by some to be plausible but inconclusive, based on current evidence (cf. Micelli 2004, for discussion; see also Dench 2001). Dixon believes it does not constitute a valid family, but rather reflects areal and other influences. Many Australianists have a strong intuitive feel for the structure of Pama-Nyungan, but the phonology (and hence also the lexicon) has not been reconstructed via the comparative method (see, for example, Dixon 1980:150–9). Though not established beyond dispute through traditional reconstruction, several scholars have presented extensive evidence that Pama-Nyungan is a legitimate genetic unit, a real language family (see Alpher 1990, 2004; Blake 1988; Evans 1988; Koch 2003; O'Grady 1998;

O'Grady and Hale 2004). Dixon (2002:44–54) discounts arguments in favor of Pama-Nyungan, including Blake's pronoun evidence (which includes widely distributed forms such as *nhurra/nyurra* 'you plural'), Evans' claim of a Pama-Nyungan shared innovation where initial apical stops and nasals in non-Pama-Nyungan languages correspond to laminal stops and nasals in Pama-Nyungan languages,[26] and Blake's and Evans' evidence from allomorphy in the ergative and locative case suffixes. Dixon believes all these involve areal diffusion (occasionally independent parallel development). The recent work by Alpher (2004) and O'Grady and Hale (2004), with abundant Pama-Nyungan cognate sets and discussion of sound correspondences, may contribute to establishing the family and resolve the dispute (see also Koch's 2003 morphological evidence).

In addition to Pama-Nyungan, the lexicostatistical classification of Australia had some twenty-eight families of non-Pama-Nyungan languages in northern Australia. Koch (1997:41) speculates that on-going work with these languages may bring the figure down to eight or ten major genetic groupings; proposals in Evans (2003a:14) would reduce the number of non-Pama-Nyungan groups to around twenty. There are plausible but inconclusive hypotheses which would link various, maybe all, of the non-Pama-Nyungan languages, of the north of Australia. Blake's (1988) "Proto-Northern" is suggested on the basis of proposed proto-forms to account for most of the free pronouns in the non-Pama-Nyungan languages; others see similar things in the person-marking prefixes and shared verb inflections (see Koch 2004:45 for details). Evans (2003b) and the papers of Evans (2003a) are optimistic about the prospects of eventually demonstrating the unity of the northern, non-Pama-Nyungan languages, perhaps all Australian groups, as are some of the articles in Bowern and Koch (2004a). (We return to this below.)

Dixon's (1980) classification was more complete but did not differ markedly from others to that time. Its highlights, it could be said, were Dixon's judgments on the validity of various proposed genetic groupings, opposition to the Pama-Nyungan hypothesis, and defense of "Proto-Australian." He believed Pama-Nyungan involved areal and typological traits, and was not a genetic unit, and anything genetic about it was due to "Proto-Australian" and not limited just to Pama-Nyungan:

[Pama-Nyungan] has not yet been shown to have any genetic significance . . . There is nothing that could be attributed to a putative proto-Pama-Nyungan which could not equally validly be assigned to proto-Australian. There is no evidence of any shared innovations which would justify a period of common development for language of the PN [Pama-Nyungan] type. (Dixon 1980:255–6)

About Proto-Australian, Dixon (1980:xiv) tries "to provide the beginnings of a proof that all the languages of Australia (except perhaps two or three

---

[26] Evans' (1988) argument was supported by only eleven etymologies which show the correspondence in question.

northern tongues such as Tiwi and Djinili) are genetically related." We look at the evidence for this presently. This pervasive hypothesis has by no means been established or even investigated squarely by normal linguistic means (cf. Micelli 2004). Indeed, it is generally accepted that Australian Aborigines arrived in Australia by at latest c.40,000 years ago (some present evidence for as early as 50,000 and 60,000 years ago). Given such a deep time depth and the limitations of standard historical linguistic methods (see Chapter 11), it may well be beyond our means to be able to establish a genetic relationship on the basis of the linguistic evidence available today among languages which began to diversify in such a very remote past, even if these languages were all descendants from a common ancestor at such an early date. Moreover, though it is commonly believed that humans entered Australia only once, bringing a single language (which later diversified into many), there is no compelling reason to think that different groups with different languages could not have migrated to Australia at different times – the land bridge between Australia and New Guinea lasted until c.7,000–10,000 years ago, and in any event the distance is short and ocean travel between the two is by no means ruled out (cf. Dixon 1980:227, 2002:35, 690) – the dog (from whence today's dingos) did not arrive until some 3,000 to 5,000 years ago (depending on sources).

Dixon's (1980) original evidence for the genetic unity among all the mainland Australian languages was somewhat scant and has been disputed. Even Dixon himself now appears to view much of this as areally diffused and not as evidence of genetic relationship (Dixon 2002). In particular, it has been pointed out that the forms Dixon placed in evidence for Proto-Australian reflect essentially only Pama-Nyungan languages. As Blake (1988) showed, the functional roots such as pronouns, case markers, verb inflections, and interrogative roots that Dixon attempted to reconstruct for Proto-Australian are mostly not found among the prefixing northern languages. That is, Dixon denied that there was a difference between Proto-Australian and Proto-Pama-Nyungan, but nevertheless the evidence presented as Proto-Australian came mostly only from Pama-Nyungan languages (cf. Heath 1990:403). As Alpher (1990:167) explains, "Dixon's decision to reject 'Proto-Pama-Nyungan' out of hand as against 'Proto-Australian' would be expected to lead naturally to the rejection of features limited to Pama-Nyungan languages. In fact, his discussion is almost exclusively limited to putative Pama-Nyungan languages."

It should be added that many Australianists share the gut-level feeling that all the Australian languages are genetically related and this is seen as tacit support for Proto-Australian. For example, many see the presence of a number of shared verb roots and seeming shared pronominal material as evidence of the original unity of all the Australian languages. There is generally optimism for the prospects of gradually building up a solid case for the relatedness of most and perhaps all Australian languages by gaining greater insights into the individual language families within Australia and then comparing them further in a bottom-up fashion, but vigorous work of this sort has been pursued only for the last decade or so, so that much remains to be discovered. Some point to Crowley (1997) as symptomatic of a turning point towards more traditional reconstruction research and away from the notion of Australia as a special case. We turn now to evaluate the evidence for a genetic relationship uniting all the Australian languages.

Dixon's (1980) evidence consisted of some verb roots, some presumed inflections of these verb roots, some pronominal (and interrogative) roots, some nominal case suffixes, and some vocabulary, but "little in the way of comparative wordlists" (Koch 2004:49). We consider these in turn.

(1) The case-marker evidence and other affixes. Dixon (1980:381) proposed several Proto-Australian suffixes: *-gu 'purposive' (now generally spelled -ku), *-ga 'imperative' (alternative preferred spelling -ka), *-NHu 'past.' Pama-Nyungan languages share cognate case markers for these, which is part of the evidence of their genetic relatedness, but case markers and these verb suffixes are mostly absent from the non-Pama-Nyungan languages. Under the assumption of an overall Australian genetic unity, the majority of the non-Pama-Nyungan languages would be seen as having undergone a typological change, from the case-marking-type languages to the cross-referencing and adpositional type (lacking case marking). This constitutes a many-sided problem for attempts to get at Australian linguistic unity. On the one hand it means there may be little or nothing in the non-Pama-Nyungan languages with which to compare the case endings of such importance within Pama-Nyungan linguistics; on the other hand, this change could have spread through diffusion, and, whether inherited or diffused, the results of the loss of case would have complicated comparison (cf. Blake 1988).

As for the actual case forms that have been proposed, *-ku 'dative' (in alternative spelling *-gu) is perhaps the most widespread, or at least the most frequently cited, as potentially Proto-Australian (see Evans 2003b:9). The -ku dative/locative forms are short, perhaps involve diffusion, perhaps reflect independent grammaticalizations from different independent roots, and would be more impressive if similar forms were not also found in so many languages elsewhere, e.g. Dravidian (Dixon 1980:237), American Indian languages, and others, presumably by accident. The *-la 'locative' has no clear reflexes in the north; *-ngu as a case marker (genitive) is found exclusively in Pama-Nyungan languages. Dixon's *-lu 'ergative-instrumental' is said to have some reflexes in the northern area, but again, this is not altogether clear, and given the frequency of these unmarked consonants, l and n, in grammatical affixes in languages in general, such an example may owe its explanation to chance.

(2) Pronoun evidence. Blake (1988, 1990), on the basis of pronominal forms, argues for two proto-languages in Australia, a proto-southern (Pama-Nyungan) and a proto-northern (non-Pama-Nyungan) pronominal set (which could perhaps ultimately be related at a deeper level). While Blake may be

onto something, we would reserve judgment until this classification can be supported by evidence in addition to just pronoun distributions and the typological cohesion of Pama-Nyungan languages as non-prefixing. A pronoun approximating ŋali 'first person dual' is widespread in Pama-Nyungan languages (but not found in all of them), and has been taken as evidence of the Pama-Nyungan genetic unity (see Blake 1988). Dixon (2002:26, 277–84), who rejects Pama-Nyungan as a genetic unit, favors the explanation that ŋali has simply diffused over a wide continuous area. Given the similarity among forms for 'first person' among the pronouns of the world's languages, where nasals predominate (Campbell 1994a, 1994b; cf. Nichols 1996a, 2003), the Australian forms listed as similar to ŋay turn out to be less impressive.

The pronoun *ngay (/ŋay/) 'first person singular' is an exception, with wider distribution.

(3) Monosyllabic verbs.[27] For example bum 'to hit, to kill' (actually bu-m), found in Pama-Nyungan (where -m is analyzed as a Pama-Nyungan conjugation marker) and among languages of the north (lacking -m), appears to be onomatopoetic (the noise of 'hitting,' 'pounding', cf. English pow, boom, bam, bang, and the pu-/bu-like forms for hitting words in so many languages). Dixon's *ma 'take, get' (a lexical root which also shows up as an auxiliary verb, verb suffix, sometimes causative) is similarly unimpressive, given that it is short, involves an unmarked consonant, and could be subject to diffusion, and similar forms are not uncommon elsewhere in the world, as for example with the so-called pan-Americanism for 'hand, give, take.'[28] (See Blake 1990, Koch 1997 for general discussion of Dixon's Proto-Australian forms.)

(4) Verb conjugation markers. Dixon (1980:398) identifies the specific conjugations of one language with specific conjugations in another mostly according to the form of affixes, according to the predominance of transitive over intransitive roots, and according to the actual verbs (almost exclusively monosyllabic roots) inflected according to the relevant paradigm. He argues that conjugation markers were present in every inflectional category of the relevant verbs and that these markers were originally part of their respective roots, for example, that the -l- of *patja-l-ku 'purposive or future of bite' (Pama-Nyungan *patja 'bite') and the *-n- of *ya-n-ku (Pama-Nyungan *ya 'go'), now seen in some inflectional suffixes of the conjugations of these respective verbs but not in all the affixal morphemes, were once part of the respective verb roots. Alpher (1990) shows that these assumptions are not supported, that the conjugation markers (such as -l- and -n- in these examples) are not part of the original roots

---

[27] Foley (1986:265–79) considers a possible connection between Papuan and Australian languages based on perceived similarities in these monosyllabic verb roots, which to our way of thinking weakens the evidence for Australian unity rather than supports a case for vastly more remote connections. (See Chapter 7 for the problems of comparisons among short forms.)

[28] See Greenberg (1987:58) and Swadesh (1954:309), for example.

(relics of root-final consonants), but have their origin in grammatically significant morphemes and involve considerable analogical shifting within various parts of the verb morphology, but were never general throughout the assembly of inflectional suffixes of the verbs in question.

On the non-Pama-Nyungan side of the equation, a growing tendency among Australianists is to see evidence of genetic relations among various of the non-Pama-Nyungan northern language groups, seen in pronominal prefixes, verbal inflections, verb structure, and details of noun-class morphology. Evans (2003a:7) says of these, "for at least a large subset of the non-Pama-Nyungan languages, the growing number of such formal features, often highly idiosyntactic, increasingly point to deep-level shared inheritance rather than just typological convergence."

"Proto-Australian" and the "subgrouping" problem   As mentioned, the widely held view of the genetic unity of all Australian languages has strongly influenced how language relationships have been approached among Australian Aboriginal languages. Under this assumption, the individual families in Australia are commonly called "subgroups" (that is, assumed to be subfamilies of Proto-Australian), and it is often assumed that an appropriate way to demonstrate that a certain set of languages belongs together in a family is to seek shared innovations – the standard criterion for subgrouping languages within known language families. However, if there is no legitimate Proto-Australian, or if Proto-Australian existed but cannot be reconstructed, then it is in effect impossible to determine what a shared innovation, a departure from Proto-Australian traits, would be. This means this common outlook on how to establish the families within Australia is inadequate. Fortunately, standard historical linguistic research is also being done in Australia and many families are well established (see Bowern and Koch 2004; Evans 2003a). When the assumed genetic unity of all Australian languages is given up (or at least not made the starting assumption), the standard methods (see Chapter 7) for establishing families among Australian languages can prevail. Ironically, though Dixon (2002) has given up the search for Proto-Australian, he nevertheless continues his old practice of speaking of Australian "subgroups" instead of "families," because, as he says, this "leaves open the possibility that some of these subgroups [n.b.] may eventually be shown to be linked together in higher-level genetic groupings" (Dixon 2002:xxiv). This practice strikes us as about as legitimate as arbitrarily deciding to call all language families and isolates of any large geographical region selected at random "subgroups" under the assumption that perhaps one day they may be found to belong together with others in a higher-order genetic grouping. Dixon (2002) recognizes over thirty "clearly defined low-level genetic subgroups [i.e. families], to which about half of the *c*.250 Australian languages are assigned" (Dixon 2001, cf. Koch 2004:51); only fifteen of these are

actually discussed in his book (Dixon 2002:658–68). His classificatory list (Dixon 2002:xxx–xlii) contains fifty groupings, though there are "subgroups," "areal groups," and isolates among these. That is, this is *not* a genetic classification, and it reflect Dixon's current decision to privilege areal diffusion over genetic relationship (see Chapter 10).

6.9.2   How Australian languages have been classified

Australian classification has been rife with methodological disagreements, and putative challenges to the comparative method have been based on beliefs about the character or behavior of Australian languages. It is to this issue we now turn. Some scholars have maintained that lexical borrowing has been so intense among Australian languages that lexical comparison cannot be a sound basis for determining the genetic affinities (see Dixon 1980:254, 1997, 2001, 2002; Johnson 1990:430). As Dixon (1990:393) explains:

The hardest task in Australian comparative linguistics is to distinguish between similarities that come from areal diffusion and those that are due to genetic retention . . . grammatical reconstruction has progressed . . . but . . . we are still groping to separate the inherited from the borrowed.

Also, some scholars insist that the taboo avoidance of words homophonous or nearly homophonous with a dead person's name contributes to lexical diversity among related languages. On the other hand, the value of grammatical information has also been challenged. Blake (1988) points out that in the extensive multilingualism of Aboriginal Australia, some grammatical traits were easily calqued from language to language, as in the case of the use of clitic pronouns and switch-reference markers which have wide distributions within continuous geographical areas thus uniting languages that are otherwise not similar. (See Heath 1978.) The borrowability of phonological traits is also brought into the picture. In contrast, Blake (1988) argues that pronouns are not known to be borrowed among Australian languages and, as mentioned above, he uses evidence of similarities among pronoun systems as evidence of a genetic connection among all Australian languages. We find this shaky ground for faith in the classification of Australian languages in the absence of other corroborating evidence, since numerous cases of borrowed pronouns from elsewhere in the world are known (see Campbell 1994b, 1997a:245–6; Chapter 7), and Dench (1994, 2001) presented evidence of patterns of diffusion among pronouns in the Pilbara, showing the problems the failure to recognize this cause for claims about classification of these Australian languages.

Australian languages have often been involved in disputes concerning historical linguistic methods. Some linguists have doubted the applicability of the comparative method to so-called exotic languages, especially Australian languages, stemming from an imprecisely articulated belief that change in exotic languages may somehow be fundamentally different from that typical of Indo-European and other languages with a long written tradition. For example, Sommerfelt (1938:187–8) believed:

Of course, the comparative grammar of Aranta calls for special methods. While Indo-European comparative grammar is chiefly built on the foundations of grammatical forms more or less devoid of concrete meaning, in A[ranta] all the derivational elements are roots with concrete meaning.

(Cf. Hoenigswald 1990b:376.) Boretzky (1982, 1984) made similar claims, which have been cited approvingly by some (see Mühlhäusler 1989; cf. also Baldi 1990:11). Boretzky contrasts Aranta (in Australia) and Kâte (in New Guinea) with Slavic and Romance – "exotic" with "European." Boretzky claims that in exotic languages semantic slots are likely to be filled either by difficult-to-relate morphs, or, conversely, that the phonological differences are so small (in Arandic) that there is no scope for reconstruction; he thinks that change in the Arandic languages proceeds more by abrupt lexical replacement through borrowing than by gradual phonological change (cf. Hoenigswald 1990b:377). Baldi (1990:11) asks:

The comparative method relies on sound correspondences; what, then, can it do in language families where sound correspondences are irregular and inconsistent? Boretzky (1984), for example, has argued that change in the Arandic languages of central Australia seems to proceed more by abrupt lexical replacement through borrowing than by gradual phonological change.

This, however, does not invalidate the comparative method for these languages. Dixon (1990:398) showed that "it is quite clear that Australian languages change in a regular fashion, in the same way as Indo-European and other families." In fact, it was through a demonstration of regular changes that Hale (1964, 1976) was able to show that the languages of northeastern Queensland formerly thought to be quite aberrant, with many short monosyllabic words, in fact developed regularly from a normal Pama-Nyungan-type language. Vocabulary may be difficult to deal with in Australia, but lexical borrowings are a fact of linguistic life that historical linguists have to contend with everywhere, not just in Australia or New Guinea (see Dixon 1980:254; Johnson 1990:430; cf. Alpher 1990:155, 169). Moreover, as Hoenigswald (1990b) points out, Boretzky's assumption is wrong that the comparative method was developed only in work on Indo-European languages and applies well only to these languages (see Chapters 2 and 10). Comparative work in numerous families (Algonquian, Austronesian, Dravidian, Mayan, Uralic, Uto-Aztecan, among others) has contributed to the development of the comparative method and to greater understanding of linguistic change in general, as we have seen above and in previous chapters.

More recently, Dixon (1997, 2001, 2002) has changed his thinking about the classification of Australian languages. He believes that "the language situation in Australia is unique and just not like that characteristic of the well-known language families such as Austronesian, Indo-European, Uralic and so on" (Dixon 2001:88, 2002:699). (See Chapter 10.) He no longer attempts to explain the widespread similarities by appeal to Proto-Australian; he says "the question of whether all Australian languages go back to a single ancestor is not answerable, because of the great time-depth involved" (Dixon 2002:xix). We agree. He also allows for the possibility that "languages from several different families came into the Australian area" (Dixon 1997:92). Again, we agree. Instead, Dixon favors areal diffusion as the explanation for the more widespread similarities among Australian languages, seeing the diffusion as so pervasive as to challenge the applicability of the traditional comparative method in Australia. This view reinforces his opposition to Pama-Nyungan: "The 'Pama-Nyungan' idea . . . is totally without foundation and must be discarded if any progress is to be made in studying the nature of the linguistic situation in Australia" (Dixon 2001:98), and "the putative division between 'Pama-Nyungan' and 'non-Pama-Nyungan' . . . has had a deleterious effect on the study of Australian languages" (Dixon 2002:53). (See the papers of Bowern and Koch 2004 for substantial support of Pama-Nyungan.) Dixon now favors a view of Australia seen through his much-criticized model of "punctuated equilibrium" (see Chapter 10). He believes that when humans first entered Australia 40,000 or more years ago, "the first occupation of a new territory" was a punctuation, producing many language splits and expansions. Then an equilibrium of many millennia set in, as these languages formed a large diffusion area with extensive borrowing, which blurred genetic affiliations (Dixon 2002:34). The concluding paragraph of his 2002 book reads:

The Australian linguistic area poses problems of investigation and analysis unlike those found anywhere else in the world. The established methods of historical and comparative linguistics, which can be applied so successfully elsewhere, have limited appropriateness in Australia. The special nature of the Australian situation must be acknowledged for real progress to be made in describing the nature of this linguistic situation, and for an understanding to be attained concerning the nature of interrelations between its constituent languages. (Dixon 2002:699)

Dixon, nevertheless, is essentially alone among specialists in Australian linguistics in this view of Australian language classification and of the assumed problems for comparative linguistics and standard methods. (For a critique see Chapter 10.) For a more realistic, more mainstream view which shows the applicability of the comparative method to numerous Australian cases, see the papers of Bowern and Koch (2004) and Evans (2003a). After presenting a review of numerous productive applications of the comparative method to Australian language groups, O'Grady and Hale (2004:70) conclude that "this is the stuff of Comparative Method linguistics *par excellence*! Asserting that the Comparative Method doesn't work in Australia would appear to be ridiculous in the extreme." Still, it is likely true that it may not always be possible to distinguish inherited elements from diffused material successfully in some Australian instances. This may leave some questions unanswered, but it does not invalidate the methods. In Australia and everywhere, we do the best we can with the evidence available. If the evidence is inconclusive, then we must be prepared to live with that. But this does not mean the methods are wrong. In Australia, contrary to Dixon's claim of the inapplicability of the comparative method there, the comparative method has been applied successfully in numerous cases and much comparative work is currently underway (see Bowern and Koch 2004; Evans 2003a).

The "Oz paradox" Let us turn now to what we might call the "Oz paradox" – the Australian paradox. When Australian linguists talk about historical relationships among Australian languages, it appears to outsiders that a kind of paradox is involved. It goes like this. Australian linguists do not really trust the vocabulary very much in their historical work because one cannot be certain, in many cases, whether vocabulary items are borrowed or not because the historical reconstruction by the traditional comparative method has not yet been done which would provide some means of distinguishing loanwords, those items which do not fit the regular sound correspondences. On the other hand, the phonology is rather similar across groups of languages in Australia and so even if the regular sound correspondences had been worked out, it would not always be clear whether borrowed lexical items might not exhibit those sound correspondences anyway, meaning that some Australianists do not trust the standard tool (reconstruction and sound correspondences) for distinguishing borrowed from inherited forms. So, we get a paradox where Australianists may not trust the vocabulary (because of potential borrowings), and yet they do not do the historical reconstruction needed in order to be able, in principle, to distinguish loans and thus trust the compared vocabulary.

Given this situation, in much Australian comparative work there is instead a predilection toward investigating morphological similarities rather than shared vocabulary (with sound correspondences) as evidence of relationship. However, to outsiders looking on, work of this sort appears to be skipping a crucial step. Morphological paradigms are set up and compared across some subset of languages and lots of exciting similarities in them are discovered – lots of pronouns, lots of cases, lots of verb affixes –, and because one can see a lot of similarity, one rushes on, skipping traditional parts of the comparative method. That is, in these superficial morphological comparisons, the sounds seem to line up and the functions often match, and so when the morphological comparisons are just superficially scanned, they seem convincing: these seem similar enough that the Australian linguist concludes they must be related and so calls them "cognates," though the standard comparative method has not been applied to demonstrate cognacy based on recurrent regular sound correspondences (and thus it is not possible to eliminate any of the presumed morphological "cognates" that might be due to borrowing, accident, etc.). Australianists call what they see in common in this kind of superficial morphological comparison a "reconstruction," even though this notion of reconstruction is not what scholars outside the Australian field do in comparative reconstruction. When others reconstruct, they provide sets of sound correspondences, reconstruct the proto-sounds, and then reconstruct the vocabulary and the morphology only to the extent that the compared forms exhibit the corresponding sounds. When Australianists scan the paradigms of sets of compared Australian languages, they can often see enough similarity to allow a guess about what the earliest form and function of individual morphemes might have been. However, such a procedure is unlikely to convince outsiders. In the "Oz paradox," lexical cognates are distrusted to the point that phonological reconstruction is not done, but the phonological reconstruction is necessary to convince the skeptics; morphological reconstruction is attempted without the sound correspondences needed to confirm the morphological reconstruction.

Perhaps, given the difficulties of reconstruction inherent in the "Oz paradox," this morphological comparison might make sense as a preliminary approach to the problem. Nevertheless, we believe this should be engaged in only with abundant warnings and qualifiers. When given these paradigms and told that based on similarities seen in them the Australian linguist would "reconstruct" such and such, a skeptical outsider might say "not too bad as a start, but where are the sound correspondences upon which the reconstruction is based?" In particular, the outsiders become uneasy about such reconstruction based on this kind of inspection of morphological paradigms when they hear things such as, "in spite of the genetic relationship posited for these particular languages, particular pronominal affixes here and there appear to have been taken over from another group of languages which is not related (at least not closely), and this case suffix was borrowed from this other unrelated group," and so on. Knowing that some of the morphological similarities do not fit and are thought to be borrowings, outsiders start doubting what initially looked like a plausible reconstruction though the full comparative method with sound correspondences had not yet been applied. Once the floodgates of morphological borrowing of pronouns and case markers are opened, where does it stop? Couldn't many more, perhaps all, of the similarities in the postulated morphological comparisons be borrowed or due to areal diffusion? In short, the skeptics cannot be appeased when the reconstruction of the phonology from the ground up has not been done. The striking similarities in paradigms can be pointed to as evidence, but too many people already believe that nearly everything in Australia is borrowed anyway, and the Australian linguist is aiding and abetting this inappropriate view of these languages by pointing out affixes and pronouns that are borrowed from different languages or language groups.

The comparative method is operable in Australia, and much remains to be done, though considerable progress has been made recently (see Evans 2003a; Bowern and Koch 2004).

6.10   Conclusions

We have seen in this chapter something of the history of language classification in a number of important language families beyond Indo-European that were established early, as well as some of the history of language classification in Africa, Australia, and the Americas. We paid particular attention to the methods used to establish these families and to the criteria and principles involved. Finno-Ugric and Uralic were established early, and work in this family had a major impact on the development of the comparative method and on the study of relationships among Indo-European languages. Semitic too was recognized as a language family quite early, and while this was not particularly challenging, given the closeness of the relationship and the obvious commonalities among the languages, nevertheless, the methods utilized were consistent with those utilized to establish other language families. The fuller understanding of Austronesian developed gradually (as did understanding of most language families), though several important language relationships in the family were recognized very early. Dravidian was also recognized fairly early, and standard comparative techniques were employed to work out the classification of the family. Sino-Tibetan, on the other hand, was recognized quite late, and had no role in the development of historical linguistic methodology, though some of the problems it poses call for careful deployment of these techniques. The classification and historical linguistic work in a number of American Indian language families reveals that solid methods were employed, in several instances early in history. Work in these languages demonstrated conclusively, for example, that the comparative method is equally applicable to so-called "exotic," non-written languages. The history of linguistic classification in Africa and Australia was surveyed, and in both instances we find some solid historical linguistic research but also numerous problems, in particular involving assumed larger groupings which are not demonstrable on the basis of reliable standard methods, as well as unfounded claims for alternative methods (see Chapters 9 and 10).

This survey has been valuable for determining what methods have worked and what has not in past attempts to establish genetic relationships among various languages. In the following chapter, we turn to an in-depth examination of the methods for investigating possible genetic connections among languages.

7 How to show languages are related: the methods

> A man's foes, it has been said, are those of his own household. Comparative Philology has suffered as much from its friends as from its opponents.
>
> (Sayce 1874–5:5)

7.1 Introduction

Scholars appear to agree that a successful demonstration of linguistic kinship depends on adequate methods. Unfortunately, there is disagreement and confusion concerning what these methods are, and hence discussions of methodology frequently assume a central role in considerations of possible remote relationships. Given this state of affairs, it is important to appraise the various methodological principles, criteria, and rules of thumb, as well as pitfalls, relevant to investigating distant genetic relationships. That is the goal of this chapter. We provide guidelines for both framing and testing proposals of distant linguistic kinship, and we point out the frequent errors that need to be avoided.[1] (In Chapter 9 we evaluate several of the more prominent hypothesized distant genetic relationships on the basis of the methods surveyed here.)

In practice, the successful methods for establishing distant linguistic affinity have not been different from those used to validate any family relationship, whether close or distant. The comparative method has always been the primary tool for establishing these relationships. Because the methods for investigating potential distant genetic relationships are not essentially different from those utilized to work out the history and classification of more closely related languages, this has resulted in a continuum from established and non-controversial families (e.g. Austronesian, Bantu, Indo-European, Finno-Ugric, Mayan), to more distant but solidly demonstrated relationships (e.g. Uralic, Siouan-Catawban, Benue-Congo), to plausible but inconclusive proposals (e.g. Indo-Uralic, Proto-Australian, Macro-Mayan, Niger-Congo), to doubtful but not implausible ones (e.g. Altaic, Austro-Tai, Eskimo–Uralic, Nilo-Saharan),

---

[1] The discussion in this chapter is based on Campbell (1997a:206–59) and Campbell (2003a). See also Hock (1986:556–66).

and on to virtually impossible proposals (e.g. Basque–Na-Dene, Indo-Pacific, Mayan–Turkic, Miwok–Uralic, Niger–Saharan, and so on). It is difficult on the basis of standard historical linguistic methods to segment this continuum so that plausible proposals based on legitimate procedures fall sharply on one side of a line, distinguished from obviously unlikely hypotheses on the other side.[2] This leads to disagreements, even by those who profess allegiance to the same methods. As Greenberg (2000b:163) explained:

> The view of genetic linguistics as concerned with proving relationships and the notion of certain procedures as providing such proof are shared by the "conservatives" who believe that there are a large number of independent, or at least not provably related families in the world, and those who undertake long-range comparisons . . . It is just that the "proofs" of the latter are not accepted by the former as adequate.

A firm understanding of methodology becomes crucial if supporters of fringe proposals can pretend to apply the same kinds of methods as those employed in more plausible hypotheses. For this reason, careful evaluation of the evidence presented on behalf of any proposed distant linguistic relationship and of the methodological precepts that are employed is called for. Also, while some methods are more successful than others, even successful ones are sometimes applied inappropriately. As is well known, excessive zeal for long-range relationships can lead to methodological excesses: "the difficulty of the task of trying to make every language fit into a genetic classification has led certain eminent linguists to deprive the principle of such classification of its precision and its rigor or to apply it in an imprecise manner" (Meillet 1948[1914]:78).[3] As pointed out by Janhunen (1989:28):

> The essence of the problem [of why the work of most long-rangers fails to convince critical people] is that most long-rangers allow themselves a rather extravagant negligence of the established principles of comparative and diachronic linguistics. It is clear that the looser the theoretical apparatus is, the easier it is to "establish" new distant relationships.

Therefore, our goal in this chapter is to appraise the methods, techniques, and procedures utilized in the investigation of potential distant genetic relationships.

It will be helpful to keep in mind two outlooks, or stages in research, concerning potential distant genetic relationships, each with its own practices. The

---

[2] Janhunen (1989:28) correlates the least defensible proposals of distant linguistic relationships with the least able scholars:

> Typically, some of the boldest long-range comparisons, such as, for instance, those underlying Uralo-Japanese or the Ob–Ugric–Penutian hypotheses, have mainly been propagated by people who can hardly qualify as serious linguists. Unfortunately, the difference between the professionals and the non-professionals is not always easy to determine.

[3] English translation from Rankin (1992:324).

quality of the evidence typically varies with the proposer's intent. Where the intention is to call initial attention to a possible but as yet untested connection, one often casts a wide net in order to haul in as much potential evidence as possible. When the intention is to test a proposal that is already on the table, those forms gathered initially as possible evidence are submitted to more careful scrutiny. Unfortunately, the preliminary, more laissez-faire setting-up-type proposals are not always distinguished from the more cautious hypothesis-testing type. Both orientations have their purpose. Nevertheless, long-range proposals which have not been evaluated carefully cannot move to the more established end of the continuum of proposed language families.

Even among those who profess faith in the traditional techniques, in the comparative method in particular, for determining genetic relationships among languages, there are conservatives and liberals (often labeled in the literature as "splitters" and "lumpers," respectively – though not all lumpers favor or apply the comparative method). Splitters are not necessarily against new cases of genetic relationship, but rather tend more towards a "show-me" attitude. That is, their demands for supporting evidence are higher. Lumpers tend to be more generous with the evidence, often willing to embrace hypothesized distant genetic relationships when the evidence is only suggestive, in their zeal to push ahead. Paul Newman (2000:260–1), an Africanist and Chadic specialist, defends this latter position:

> The job of the comparative linguist is to provide the best explanation possible consistent with the facts. In proposing a classification, it is *not* necessary that the linguist "prove" that the classification is absolutely certain by the presentation of conclusive evidence. In response to widely speculative classifications that had been offered at various times by irresponsible scholars [as well as by famous respectable ones, e.g. Sir William Jones, Franz Bopp, Edward Sapir, etc., LC/WP], many careful, empirically based linguists jumped to the opposite extreme and took the position that all languages should be treated as unrelated unless and until proved otherwise. However, on closer inspection, this requirement turns out to be untenable and not in keeping with standard linguistic procedures . . . *the linguist is justified in postulating a genetic relationship even if the evidence is still somewhat on the weak side.* For example, in the opinion of some scholars, the evidence supporting the relationship between the Chadic language family and other language groups in the Afroasiatic phylum, such as Semitic and Berber, is not compelling. Nevertheless, some points of resemblance in morphology and lexicon are so striking that if one did not assume relationship, they would be impossible to explain away. The classification of Chadic within Afroasiatic is thus fully justified, not because it has been "proved" as in a court of law, but because it is the explanation most consistent with the facts as a whole. (Our emphasis, LC/WP)

We maintain that neither stance is wrong; both have a place. It is not a matter of yes-or-no, related-or-not-related, but rather a question of how strong an inference of probable genetic affiliation is warranted by the evidence presented. In preliminary stages of the investigation or when the goal is to call attention to the possibility of a relationship, it is appropriate to cast a wide net and consider as possible evidence any similarities or shared patterns one encounters. However, when the goal is to satisfy skeptics or to test these initial proposals, then the rough and ready evidence collected in the initial scouting-expedition stage is submitted to much more careful scrutiny. Some cases, when tested, reveal strong support for the hypothesis of genetic relationship. In other cases, the evidence may not reach a level of conviction, but may still remain suggestive, warranting further investigation. Such hypothesized relationships are not to be embraced with full enthusiasm, and are to be reported only with appropriate warnings and qualifications, and encouragement to investigate further. Some proposals, of course, may be found lacking and abandoned for lack of sufficient evidence to guarantee even a minimum plausibility for the proposed genetic connection. (For examples and discussion, see Chapter 9.)

Many have assumed that demonstrations of linguistic kinship rely mostly on observation of similarities among compared languages, but this is not sufficient, since similarities can be due to several things, accident (chance), borrowing, onomatopoeia, sound symbolism, nursery forms, and universals and typologically commonplace traits, as well as genetic relationship (inheritance from a common ancestor). This being the case, the burden of proof on anyone proposing a genetic relationship among languages is to show that the evidence presented in favor of the hypothesized relationship cannot as easily be explained by these other non-genetic factors. Unfortunately, as we shall see, many proposals fail to meet this burden of proof.

We turn now to the criteria, techniques, rules of thumb, and procedures generally held important, and to things to avoid, if one is to meet the burden of proof for proposals of distant genetic relationship.

7.2   Lexical comparison

As seen in earlier chapters, throughout history word comparisons have been employed as evidence of family relationship. However, "given a small collection of likely-looking cognates," we ask with Swadesh (1954:312), "how can one definitely determine whether they are really the residue of common origin and not the workings of pure chance or some other factor? This is a crucial problem of long-range comparative linguistics." The results of lexical comparisons have seldom been considered convincing without additional support from other criteria, e.g. sound correspondences or compelling morphological agreements (cf. Haas 1969). As we have seen, the use of lexical material alone (or as the primary source of evidence) often led to incorrect proposals. Therefore, lexical-based approaches require discussion.

7.2.1   Basic vocabulary

As seen in earlier chapters, in lexical comparisons most scholars have insisted that basic vocabulary (*Kernwortschatz, vocabulaire de base, charakteristische Wörter*, "non-cultural" vocabulary) be given prominence. Basic vocabulary has been understood intuitively to contain terms for common body parts, close kin, frequently encountered aspects of the natural world, and low numbers. It is assumed that since, in general, basic vocabulary is more resistant to borrowing, similarities found in comparisons involving basic vocabulary are unlikely to be due to diffusion and hence stand a better chance of being the results of inheritance from a common ancestor, evidence of a genetic relationship. Of course, basic vocabulary can also be borrowed (see examples below), though less frequently, so that its role as a safeguard against borrowing is useful but not foolproof.

Moreover, some things in "basic vocabulary" seem quite subject to borrowing or lexical replacement, for example, the terms for 'head' in well-known European languages. Proto-Indo-European **kaput* 'head' gave Proto-Germanic **haubidam/*haubudam* (hence Old English *hēafod*, Modern English *head*) and Proto-Romance **kaput*. However, several Germanic and Romance languages no longer have cognates of these terms as their basic word referring to the human head. For example, German *Kopf* 'head' originally meant 'bowl'; the German cognate from Proto-Indo-European **kaput* is *Haupt*, which now means basically only 'main,' 'chief,' as in *Hauptbahnhof* 'main/central train station.' French *tête* and Italian *tèsta* 'head' both originally meant 'pot' (cognate with Spanish *tiesto* 'potsherd'); the French cognate from **kaput* is *chef*, but this means now 'main, principal, chief,' not a human head; the Italian cognate *capo* now means 'top, chief, leader.' Similar replacements are known from languages around the world. For example, in Pipil (a Uto-Aztecan language of El Salvador) *tsuntekumat* 'head' comes from *tsun* - 'top, hair' (in compounds) + *tekumat* 'bottle gourd,' and has replaced Proto-Aztecan **kʷāyi-* for 'head.' Terms for 'face' often vary greatly within the related languages of a language family, reflecting frequent lexical replacements – for example, compare English *face* (a loanword from French *face* 'face') and German *Gesicht* (from 'sight, look'), or Spanish *cara* (etymology uncertain, possibly from Greek *khara* 'head') and French *face* (from Vulgar Latin *facia* < Latin *facies* 'form, shape, look, face'). Words for 'face' can vary widely even within a single language, as seen in English *face, visage, countenance, mug, kisser*, etc. Words for 'sun' and 'moon' are charged with religious symbolism in some areas of the world, especially in south and east Asia, and words for them often turn out to be loans from other languages or are replacements of earlier words, for religious reasons. The pronouns 'I' and 'you' not only reference persons, but in many places also involve social stratification and levels of deference, and as a result the forms for 'I' and especially for 'you' have changed radically and rapidly in many instances, for example, well-known European cases such as Spanish *usted* 'you' (formal) from *vuestra merced* 'your grace,' a well-documented change after the fifteenth century. Corresponding forms in related languages are often not cognates, as in the case of Spanish *usted*, German *Sie*, French *Vous*, Italian *lèi*, Polish *pan, pani*, and so on, all meaning 'you' (formal).

In short, even in the domain of basic vocabulary, as seen here in a few basic terms, some concepts seem much more subject to borrowing and lexical change than others.

7.2.2 Glottochronology[4]

Glottochronology – a putative means of dating the length of time related languages have been separated – depends on basic, relatively culture-free vocabulary, which is why it is mentioned in this section. It has, however, been rejected by most linguists, since all its basic assumptions have been challenged (see Campbell 2004:201–10) and therefore it warrants little discussion here. Suffice it to say that glottochronology does not find or test family relationships, but rather just assumes them. That is, built into its application is the assumption that the languages compared are related. In the application of glottochronology the basic vocabulary of any two (or more) languages, related or not, is compared and similar words on the core vocabulary list are checked off. Glottochronology proceeds to attach a date based on the number of core vocabulary items that were deemed similar, thus presupposing that the languages are related and that they separated from one another at the time indicated in the date given. This, then, is no method for determining whether languages are related or not.

Glottochronology does, however, raise an important question for the use of lexical evidence in long-range relationships. It is commonly believed that "the greater the time depth of the data examined, the smaller the attested data that can be useful for this work" (Gurevich 1999:119), or, in other words, "comparable lexemes must inevitably diminish to near the vanishing point the deeper one goes in comparing remotely related languages" (Bengtson 1989:30). This is suggested by, but in no way depends on, glottochronology's assumed constant rate of basic vocabulary loss through time and across languages. In general, related languages long separated may have undergone so much vocabulary replacement (forgetting now any claims of constant rates of retention and loss) that the number of original shared vocabulary items which remains may be insufficient for an ancient shared kinship to be detected.[5] This constitutes a

---

[4] The term "lexicostatistics," while given a technical distinction by some, is usually used as a synonym of glottochronology.

[5] By glottochronological counts, after about 14,000 years of separation, two related languages will share only about 5 percent of the original basic vocabulary, and it is generally considered that

serious problem for those who believe in deep relationships supported solely by lexical evidence. (It is especially crucial in considerations of Proto-World, see Chapter 10.)

7.2.3   Multilateral comparison

The best-known approach which relies on inspectional resemblances among compared lexical items is Greenberg's multilateral (or mass) comparison (Greenberg 1963, 1987, 2005). It is based on lexical look-alikes determined by visual inspection, "looking at . . . many languages across a few words" rather than "at a few languages across many words" (Greenberg 1987:23), where the lexical similarities shared "across many languages" alone are taken as evidence of genetic relationship. As Newman (2000:262), a supporter of the method, points out, "in this method, there is no requirement that regular sound correspondences have been established by the comparative method . . . only that words look alike." Greenberg (1996b:535) argued that "the observation of 'surface resemblances' leads to the correct classification." However, as has been repeatedly pointed out, where Greenberg's method stops (after having identified superficial lexical resemblances) is where standard approaches start. The inspectional resemblances must still be investigated to determine whether they are due to inheritance from a common ancestor or to borrowing, accident, onomatopoeia, sound symbolism, nursery formations, and other things. As founding figures of our field frequently pointed out:

> Upon how narrow and imperfect a basis those comparative philologists build who are content with a facile setting side by side of words; whose materials are simple vocabularies, longer or shorter, of terms representing common ideas . . . *surface collation without genetic analysis, is but a travesty of the methods of comparative philology.* (Dwight Whitney, cited in Trumbull 1869–70:58–9; our emphasis, LC/WP)

> In dealing with related languages that have ceased to be very much alike among themselves, a strong superficial resemblance between two words is, for the linguist, reason to doubt that they represent a single proto-language expression. French feu ['fire'] has nothing to do with German feuer ['fire']; . . . [however] it is easy to show the relationships that exist between French cinq . . . and the equivalent English five, Russian piat', (and) Armenian hing; but at first glance these words hardly look alike at all. But it is not outward resemblances on which linguists rely when they compare words and establish etymologies for them; rather it is on formulae of regular correspondences. (Meillet 1948[1914]:92–3)

Since multilateral comparison does not go beyond this preliminary step of assembling superficially similar lexical items, the results frequently have proven

---

5 to 6 percent of basic vocabulary may be shared by sheer accident. That is, after so long a separation, if glottochronology were accurate, it would be impossible to distinguish the languages which were truly related from those which merely have accidental similarities.

erroneous and controversial. Greenberg believed that a sufficient number of morphemes which show similarities in their phonetic shape and meaning can be proof of genetic relationship, though he did not make clear how many morpheme matchings were necessary in order to be "sufficient," nor did he specify explicitly what constituted phonetic similarity or how it was determined. In fact, in numerous cases, his conclusions of relationship were based on very few examples (see Campbell 1988). For example, Greenberg placed Nyangiya-Teuso in his Eastern Sudanic on the basis of only ten similar words in these languages. As Heine (1970:4) points out, "none of these word correspondences [matchings] is convincing. In particular, the difference in phonetic shape is often so great as to make it implausible that we are dealing with possible cognates. Most of the words compared have only one sound, some even none, in common." The Temein group's inclusion in Eastern Sudanic was based on only seven word comparisons, only two of which are regarded by Heine (1970:4) as possible. Similar numbers can be cited for several other of Greenberg's classifications.

Greenberg's (1949a, 1949b, 1949c) earlier discussion of methods was much more conventional than his later work, particularly that of Greenberg 1987. Moreover, his conception of multilateral (or mass) comparison underwent telling mutations, from a rather standard stance to one rejected by almost all mainstream historical linguists. Greenberg (1957:45) advocated standard criteria, for example, "semantic plausibility, breadth of distribution in the various subgroups of the family, length [of compared forms], participation in irregular alternations, and the occurrence of sound correspondences" (all discussed below). Still, his emphasis was on vocabulary. In his 1957 conception of it, mass comparison was seen as only supplementary to the standard comparative method. However, by 1987 he saw multilateral (mass) comparison as superior to and replacing the standard procedures. Unlike Greenberg's later conception of multilateral comparison, the 1957 version concentrated on a language (or group of related languages taken as a unit) whose relationship was yet to be determined and compared this language with other languages whose family relationships were already known:

Instead of comparing a few or even just two languages chosen at random and for linguistically extraneous reasons, we proceed systematically by first comparing closely related languages to form groups with recurrent significant resemblances and then compare these groups with other similarly constituted groups. Thus it is far easier to see that the Germanic languages are related to the Indo-Aryan languages than that English is related to Hindustani. In effect, we have gained historic depth by comparing each group as a group, considering only those forms as possessing likelihood of being original which are distributed in more than one branch of the group and considering only those etymologies as favoring the hypothesis of relationship in which tentative reconstruction brings the forms closer together. Having noted the relationship of the Germanic and Indo-Aryan languages, we bring in other groups of languages, e.g. Slavonic and Italic. In this process we determine with ever increasing definiteness the basic lexical and grammatical morphemes in regard to both phonetic form and meaning. On the other hand, we also see more easily that the Semitic languages and Basque do not belong to this aggregation of languages. *Confronted by some isolated language without near congeners, we compare it with this general Indo-European rather than at random with single languages.* (Greenberg 1957:40–1; our emphasis, LC/WP)

Greenberg's multilateral comparison after 1987 is no longer of the gradual build-up sort that it was in his 1957 work, where the method was based on the comparison of an as yet unclassified language with a number of languages previously demonstrated to be related to one another. An array of cognate forms in languages known to be related might reveal similarities with a form compared from some language whose genetic affiliation we are attempting to determine, where comparison with but a single language from the group of related languages may not. Given the possibilities of lexical replacement, a language (one already known to be related to others) may or may not have retained a particular cognate which may, however, still be seen in some of its sisters which did not replace the word. This being the case, in a pair-wise comparison of just one language from a set of related languages with one whose affiliation is yet unknown, we may fail to find a cognate (even if the languages were related) in comparison of a particular lexical item, because it was replaced in the single language under scrutiny. However, cognates of this particular lexical item might be preserved in other sister languages of the family; we may be able to detect this if a wider array of the related languages were brought into the comparison with the as yet unclassified language. Nevertheless, this kind of comparison (involving several sister languages at once) is equivalent to the "tentative reconstruction" Greenberg mentioned (above) which "brings the forms closer together." It is, in essence, a recommendation that we reconstruct accessible families – where proto-forms can be reconstructed on the basis of the cognate sets, although for some cognate sets some individual language or languages of the family may have lost or replaced the cognate word – before we proceed to investigate potential higher-level, more inclusive families. A validly reconstructed proto-form is like the "multilateral comparison" of the various words in a cognate set from across the languages of the family upon which the reconstruction of that form is based, since a sort of "mass" comparison is embodied in the procedure which leads to the reconstructed form based on cognate words among the various languages compared which reflect the proto-form. For attempts to establish more remote genetic affiliations, comparison with the reconstructed proto-form (as a representative of the cognates in the cognate set from across the related languages) and comparison with the individual words in the family-wide cognate set upon which the reconstruction would be based are roughly equivalent. Even so, Greenberg (1987) has abandoned this view of his method, now comparing "a few words" in "many languages" potentially of uncertain genetic affiliation. The drawbacks of this procedure have been pointed out many times and will become increasingly clear throughout this chapter.

Even within the study of Indo-European, scholars have been wary of mere vocabulary similarities as evidence for grouping. Meillet and Leskien taught "that the number of watertight etymologies is small, and that the possibility of borrowing is great" (Clackson 1994:4). In short, no technique which relies solely on inspectional similarities has proven adequate for supporting relationships:

It is widely believed that, when accompanied by lists of the corresponding sounds, a moderate number of lexical similarities is sufficient to demonstrate a linguistic relationship . . . However, . . . the criteria which have usually been considered necessary for a good etymology are very strict, even though there may seem to be a high a priori probability of relationship when similar words in languages known to be related are compared. In the case of lexical comparisons it is necessary to account for the whole word in the descendant languages, not just an arbitrarily segmented "root," and the reconstructed ancestral form must be a complete word . . . The greater the number of descendant languages attesting a form, and the greater the number of comparable phonemes in it, the more likely it is that the etymology is a sound one and the resemblances not merely the result of chance. A lexical similarity between only two languages is generally considered insufficiently supported, unless the match is very exact both phonologically and semantically, and it is rare that a match of only one or two phonemes is persuasive. If the meanings of the forms compared differ, then there must be an explicit hypothesis about how the meaning has changed in the various cases. Now, if these strict criteria have been found necessary for etymologies within KNOWN linguistic families, it is obvious that much stricter criteria must be applied to word-comparisons between languages whose relationship is in question. (Goddard 1975:254–5)[6]

Ringe (1999:219) points out a fatal flaw in the logic of multilateral comparison. With constraints on what sounds can be matched (e.g. a b to labial consonants b, p, or v in other languages) essentially the same as Greenberg (1987) utilized, Ringe shows that for CVC-roots:

if we compare on 13 languages[,] the probability of finding a match is $1 - .481952 = .518048$, or better than fifty-fifty, and if we compare 23 languages [and recall that the multilateral comparison in "Amerind" involved several hundred Native American languages][,] the probability is $1 - .086428 = .913572$, or greater than 90%. Thus in comparing 23 wordlists we expect to find at least one CVC-match, on the average, for more than nine of every ten meanings on the list using these criteria for a match.

Ringe (1999:229) concludes: "the foregoing demonstrates conclusively that a famous claim of Joseph Greenberg, namely that as one compares an increasing number of languages the probability of a match in sound and meaning quickly

---

[6] Hock (1986:561) recommends even stronger constraints, that "evidence for possible genetic relationship thus should consist of correspondences which pervade the vocabulary and which include most of the basic vocabulary."

falls to the point where it can be ignored (Greenberg 1963:3; cf. also Greenberg 1987:22ff.), is false, indeed, its falsity ought to have been obvious."[7] (Additional problems with multilateral comparison are considered in Chapter 9.)

In short, comparative linguists through many and varied experiences have come to a very clear understanding that mere lexical similarities alone are generally not sufficient to show genetic relationship.

7.3   Sound correspondences

It is important to emphasize the value and utility of sound correspondences in the investigation of linguistic relationships. Some linguists hold recurring regular sound correspondences necessary for the demonstration of linguistic affinity, and nearly all consider them strong evidence for genetic affinity. Since his method of multilateral comparison dismisses the need for sound correspondences, Greenberg (1987, 2000b) attempted, unsuccessfully, to cast doubt on their utility as evidence of relatedness among languages by claiming they have "so many alternative explanations," citing especially analogy and borrowing (Greenberg 2000b:167). Unlike Greenberg, other historical linguists recognize that a full picture of the past requires sorting out the effects of analogy and borrowing (not done in multilateral comparison), but, in fact, it is by working out regular sound correspondences that we are able to do this. Nearly all historical linguists recognize that if regular sound correspondences can be established, then complicating factors from analogy and borrowing can generally be detected, and that the sound correspondences have value for determining genetic affiliation.

While sound correspondences are a staple of traditional approaches to determining language families, it is important to make clear how their use can be perverted in order to understand why some proposed distant genetic relationships which are purportedly based on sound correspondences nevertheless fail to be convincing (see also Nichols 1997a:362).

First, it is important to keep in mind that it is systematic correspondences which are crucial, not mere similarities, and that such correspondences do not necessarily involve sounds which are phonetically similar to one another. It is surprising how the matched sounds in most questionable proposals of remote relationship are typically very similar, often identical, while among the daughter languages of well-established non-controversial older language families such identities among the corresponding sounds are not so frequent and a number of the correspondences which have been firmly established involve some

---

[7] In Janhunen's (1989:29) words, "after all, it is three times easier to compare a language with three language families than with one" (speaking of attempts to classify Korean and Japanese).

sounds which are in fact not very similar to one another. While some sounds may stay relatively unchanged over time, many others undergo changes which produce phonetically non-identical correspondences. One wonders why systematic correspondences involving sounds that are not so similar are not more common in proposals of remote relationships. The sound changes that lead to such non-identical correspondences often change cognate words so much that their cognacy is not easily recognized until the systematic correspondences are understood. These true but non-obvious cognates are missed by methods which seek merely inspectional resemblances, such as multilateral comparison. For example, the true English–Hindi cognates such as the following would be missed: *wheel* : *cakkā* (< Sanskrit *cakra-* < PIE *k^wek^wlo-* 'wheel'); *horn* : *sīg* (< Sanskrit *śṛṅga-* < PIE *$\check{k}er$/*$\check{k}ṛ$-* 'horn'); and *sister* : *bahan* (< Sanskrit *svasar* <PIE *swesor-* 'sister') (Hock 1993:218). A method which scans only for phonetic resemblances misses such well-known true cognates as French *cinq*/Russian *p^jat^j*, Armenian *hing*/English *five* (all easily derived by straightforward changes from original Proto-Indo-European *penkwe* 'five'), or French *bœuf*/English *cow* (< PIE *g^wou-*), French /nu/ (spelled *nous*) 'we, us'/English *us* (< PIE *nes-*; French through Latin *nōs*, English *us* from Germanic *uns* [Indo-European zero-grade *$\underset{\circ}{n}$s]) (Meillet 1948[1914]:92–3). None of these common cognate sets involves cognate words which are visually similar to one another. Nevertheless, they do involve systematic sound correspondences detected in the standard application of the comparative method which help us to determine the real historical relatedness among such forms. For example, in the case of Armenian *hing* 'five,' which does not appear very similar phonetically to the words for 'five' in the other Indo-European languages cited, it is the regular correspondence which demonstrates the historical relationship – the correspondence of, for example, Armenian *h* to Greek and Latin *p* as a result of the sound change of *p* > *h* in Armenian, exhibited in a range of other cognate sets, e.g. Armenian *het* : Greek *ped-* 'foot,' *hour* : *pyr* 'fire,' *hayr* : *pater* 'father,' etc. Cognates of this sort which are phonetically not so similar but involve regular sound correspondences are typically missed by methods of lexical inspection, such as Greenberg's multilateral comparison. This point was made also by Winston (1966:167), who points out its consequences for mass (or multilateral) comparison:

there is a measure of conflict between the concepts of "resemblance" and "regular correspondence." While not all resemblances involve regular correspondences, regular correspondences may occur between quite dissimilar items. Thus, English *care* does not correspond regularly to Latin *cura*, and English *hundred* does correspond to Russian <cto> [sto]. It is *a priori* virtually certain, therefore, that some of Greenberg's [African] etymologies are incorrect, and Tucker has noted a few cases where they do in fact conflict with regular correspondences as far as known at present.

As these examples show, sound correspondences do not necessarily involve similarities, but rather systematic correspondences, this in spite of Greenberg's (1996a:133) claim that "sound laws are based on perceived resemblances."

There are a number of ways in which the criterion of sound correspondences can be misapplied. True sound correspondences usually indicate a historical connection, though sometimes it is not easy to determine whether this is due to inheritance from a common ancestor or to borrowing. Regularly corresponding sounds may sometimes also be found in loans. For example, we know from Grimm's law that real French–English cognates should exhibit the phonological correspondence *p* : *f*, as in *père/father*, *pied/foot*, *pour/for*. However, French and English appear to exhibit also the correspondence *p* : *p* in cases where English has borrowed from French or Latin, as in *paternel/paternal*, *piédestal/pedestal*, *per/per*. Since English has many such loans, examples illustrating this bogus *p* : *p* sound correspondence are frequent. Greenberg (1957:40) was correct that "the presence of recurrent sound correspondences is not in itself sufficient to exclude borrowing as an explanation. Where loans are numerous, they often show such correspondences." In comparing languages not yet known to be related, we must use caution in interpreting sound correspondences to avoid the problems of undetected loans. Generally, sound correspondences found in basic vocabulary warrant the confidence that the correspondences are not found only in loans, and this would help us identify the *p* : *f* correspondence (above) as native, found in basic vocabulary, and the *p* : *p* correspondence as the result probably of borrowing, found mostly in non-basic vocabulary.

However, even here one must be careful, since as mentioned above, basic vocabulary also can be borrowed, though more rarely. For example, Finnish *äiti* 'mother' and *tytär* 'daughter' are borrowed from Indo-European languages; if these loans were not recognized, one would suspect a sound correspondence of *t* : *d* involving the medial consonant of *äiti* (cf. Germanic **aidī*) and the initial consonant of *tytär* (cf. Germanic **dohtēr*) based on these basic vocabulary items (but found also in many other loans).[8] While basic vocabulary is borrowed less frequently than other kinds of lexical items, examples of borrowed basic vocabulary are not uncommon in the literature. For example, Udmurt (Votyak, a Finno-Ugric language) borrowed many items of basic vocabulary from Tatar (Turkic), terms for 'mother,' 'father,' 'grandmother,' 'grandfather,' 'brother/sister,' 'elder brother,' 'elder sister,' 'uncle,' 'strong,' 'healthy,' 'deaf,' 'blind,' 'sick,' 'illness,' 'love,' 'land,' 'people,' 'person,' 'cool,' etc. (Csúcs 1990:69–70). Foley (2000:392) points out that Warembori, an isolate in Papua New Guinea, "exhibits extensive borrowing from Austronesian in basic vocabulary such as kin terms, body parts, and even pronouns."

---

[8] Actually, *tytär* 'daughter' is usually held to be a loan from Baltic (cf. Latvian *duktē-*, genitive *dukteřs*) rather than Germanic, but this does not affect the argument here, since the question is about Indo-European not its individual branches.

In addition to borrowings, there are other ways by which proposals that purport to rely on sound correspondences come up with phony correspondences. Some apparent but non-genuine correspondences come from accidentally similar lexical items among languages – the so-called *Sirene des Gleichklangs* [sirens of harmony] (cf. Diakonoff 1990:59). A few examples of similar forms shared due to accident are: Proto-Jê **niw* 'new'/English *new*; Kaqchikel dialects *mes* 'mess, disorder, garbage'/English *mess*; Jaqaru *aska* 'ask'/English *ask*; Lake Miwok *hóllu* 'hollow'/English *hollow*; Seri *ki?*/French *qui* (/ki/) 'who?'; Yana *t'inii-* 'small'/English *tiny, teeny*; Teda (Saharan) *kulo* 'anus'/Spanish *culo* /kulo/ 'anus'; Thai *rim¹* /English *rim*, Thai *fay¹*/English *fire*; Songay (putatively Nilo-Saharan) *mana* 'no'/Quechua *mana* 'no'; Mbabaram (Australia) *dog* 'dog'/English *dog* (Dixon and Aikhenvald 1999:11); Gbaya (Niger-Congo) *te* 'tree'/Cholan (Mayan) *te?* 'tree'; Proto-Tibeto-Burman ***bwuik* 'belly'/Dutch *buik* 'belly'; Turkish *tepe* 'hill'/Nahutal *tepe:-* 'mountain'; not to mention those of handbook fame such as Farsi *bad*/English *bad*, and Malay *mata* 'eye'/Modern Greek *mati* 'eye', to which we could add also Dura (Tibeto-Burman) *mata* 'look, watch' (van Driem 2001:812); Romanian *fiǔ* 'son' (< Latin *filius* 'son')/Hungarian *fiú* 'son, boy' (<Proto-Finno-Ugric **poji* 'boy'); etc. It is easy to see how non-real sound correspondences might turn up in compared languages if more than one set of such accidental similarities of this sort should turn up involving the same sounds. For example, Maori (Polynesian branch of Austronesian) and Finnish (Uralic) share accidentally similar forms suggestive of a $k : k$ and an $r : r$ sound correspondence, as in: Maori *kurī* 'dog'/Finnish *koira* 'dog'; Maori *kiri* 'bark, skin'/Finnish *kuori* 'bark, skin, peel'; Maori *kuru* 'greenstone ornament'/Finnish *koru* 'ornament, jewelry'; Maori *kiri* 'basket'/ Finnish *kori* 'basket'; etc. Such forms show how accidentally similar lexical items can exhibit bogus correspondences – no respected linguist has proposed that Maori and Finnish are related. In these Maori–Finnish comparisons it will be noticed that the consonants are identical but the vowels can differ. We have in fact selected such forms purposefully to mimic the examples presented in Greenberg's (1987) application of multilateral comparison. Greenberg nowhere told explicitly what principles he followed to determine which forms are to be treated as sufficiently similar and therefore as probable cognates, but a look at the actual forms he grouped in his putative "etymologies" shows that in his lexical sets, vowels are mostly ignored and consonants are accepted as sufficiently similar if they are either identical or occupy similar points of articulation (for example, any consonant from the set of q/k/x/č/ts/ʃ/s can show up in one of his equations). That is, it is precisely such accidentally similar lexical matches as seen in these Maori–Finnish comparisons (save Greenberg does not require sound correspondences nor recurrent matching of consonants as with the $k : k$ or $r : r$ of these forms) which make up the bulk of Greenberg's "evidence."

Other cases of non-genuine sound correspondences can turn up by accident if one permits generous semantic latitude in proposed cognates, such that phonetically similar but semantically disparate forms are equated (Ringe 1992, 1999). Gilij (1965[1780–4]:132–3) showed this long ago with several examples of the sort *poeta* 'drunk' in Maipure but 'poet' in Italian; *putta* 'head' in Otomaco, 'prostitute' in Italian. The phonetic correspondences in such cases are due to accident, since it is always possible to find phonetically similar words among languages if their meanings are ignored. When one sanctions semantic liberty among compared forms, one easily comes up with the sort of spurious correspondences as seen in the initial $p : p$ and medial $t : t$ of Gilij's Amazonian–Italian 'drunk–poet' and 'head–prostitute' comparisons. Additional non-inherited phonetic similarities crop up when onomatopoetic, sound-symbolic, and nursery forms are compared (see below). A set of proposed cognates involving a combination of loans, chance enhanced by semantic latitude, onomatopoeia, and other such factors may exhibit seemingly real but false sound correspondences. For this reason, many proposed remote relationships whose backers profess allegiance to regular sound correspondences nevertheless fail to be convincing. (See Ringe 1992.)

Most scholars hold sound correspondences to be strong evidence of relationship, but many neither insist on them solely nor trust them fully (see Watkins 1990). While the comparative method is often associated with sound change, and hence with regularly recurring sound correspondences, this is not essential for its application. As some are fond of reminding us, Antoine Meillet (1967[1925]:13–14) introduced the comparative method in his book on the topic, not with examples of phonological correspondences, but with reference to comparative mythology. Some introductions to the comparative method illustrate it with the ancestry and development of various forms of football games. Thus, many have relied also on grammatical comparisons of the appropriate sort, seen also as involving the application of the comparative method but not necessarily established sound correspondences. As we saw in previous chapters, grammatical evidence has been the most persistent preference of many in their attempts to show languages to be related. It is important to consider its use in more detail.

7.4   Grammatical evidence

Scholars throughout linguistic history have held morphological and grammatical evidence to be important for establishing language families. Given that inspectional resemblances among lexical items are often not sufficient to rule out chance and other possible explanations, and given that spurious sound correspondences can be assembled if loans, onomatopoeia, accidentally similar forms, and the like are not taken out of the picture, many scholars feel that additional evidence is necessary, or at least desirable, to remedy this situation, and grammatical evidence fits the bill for many linguists. Some have utilized as their principal grammatical evidence similarities in compared languages seen against the backdrop of a language's overall morphological game plan (typology) (as, for instance, Rask in part, see Chapter 4), while many others have required idiosyncratic, peculiar, arbitrary morphological correspondences (Meillet's "shared aberrancy," below), instances so distinctive they could not easily be explained by borrowing or accident. This deserves a closer look.

7.4.1 "Submerged features"

It has been repeatedly pointed out that Edward Sapir's classification of the native languages of North America with its six superstocks relied very heavily on general morphological (typological) traits, and secondarily on lexical evidence.[9] His Subtiaba–Hokan article (Sapir 1925a) is repeatedly cited as a model of how distant genetic relationships can be approached, or at least of Sapir's method of doing so – perhaps ironical, since Subtiaba is now known to be an Otomanguean language, not connected with putative Hokan languages as Sapir argued (Campbell 1997a:157–8, 208, 211, 292, 296–8, 325). In particular, the "submerged features" passage from Sapir's article has received much attention. We cite the passage here, and then consider the interpretations it has been given:

When one passes from a language to another that is only remotely related to it, say from English to Irish or from Haida to Hupa or from Yana to Salinan, one is overwhelmed at first by the great and obvious differences of grammatical structure. As one probes more deeply, however, significant resemblances are discovered which weigh far more in a genetic sense than the discrepancies that lie on the surface and that so often prove to be merely secondary dialectic developments which yield no very remote historical perspective. In the upshot it may appear, and frequently does appear, that the most important grammatical features of a given language and perhaps the bulk of what is conventionally called its grammar are of little value for the remoter comparison, which may rest largely on *submerged features* that are of only minor interest to a descriptive analysis. (Sapir 1925a:491–2; our emphasis, LC/WP)

[9] It should be pointed out that Sapir intended his six-super-stock classification as only "suggestive but far from demonstrable in all its features" (Sapir 1929a:137), and that, in spite of its heavy morphological–typological leanings, Sapir also felt that he had both morphological and lexical evidence for the groupings, and believed and hoped that in the future more rigorous comparison of the traditional sort with phonological evidence would increasingly support his preliminary proposals (Sapir 1990[1921a]:93, 1925a:526; cf. Campbell 1997a:69–72, 74–6). In spite of this classification of Sapir's being associated with broad typological traits, Sapir himself insisted on sound correspondences for definitive proof of genetic relationship: "there may be some evidence for considering distinct languages related – for example, the general form of their grammar may seem to provide such evidence – but the final demonstration can never be said to be given until comparable words can be shown to be but reflexes of one and the same prototype by the operation of dialectic phonetic laws" (Sapir 1949[1931]:74).

What Sapir intended by "submerged features" appears to be illustrated in his example: "Thus, Choctaw *la^{n}sa* 'scar'/*mi^{n}sa* 'scarred' is curiously reminiscent of such alternations as Subtiaba *daša* 'grass'/*maša* 'to be green' and suggests an old nominal prefix *l*" (Sapir 1925a:526). Several have interpreted Sapir's submerged features to be like the fine-grained, idiosyncratic facts so often emphasized in language comparisons (for example, by Meillet, below). This is the interpretation given by Mary Haas (1941:41) and Harry Hoijer (1954:6), both students of Sapir's, and by Bright (1984:12), Campbell (1973), Campbell and Mithun (1979), Goddard (1975), Teeter (1964), and Liedtke (1991:87–92), among others. As Krauss (1969:54) put it, "we often find our most valuable comparative evidence in certain irregularities in fundamental and frequent forms, like prize archaeological specimens poking out of the mud of contemporary regularity." A particularly clear example which illustrates this is Teeter's (1964:1029) comparison of Proto-Central-Algonquian (PCA) and Wiyot possessive formations, where in PCA a -*t*- is inserted between a possessive pronominal prefix and a vowel-initial root, while in Wiyot a -*t*- is inserted between possessive prefixes and a root beginning in *hV* (with the loss of the *h*-), e.g.:

PCA **ne* + **ehkw-* = **netehkw-* 'my louse'
Wiyot *du-* + *híkw* = *dutíkw* 'my louse'

Sapir (1913a) had proposed that Wiyot and Yurok of California were related to the Algonquian family in what he called Algonkian-Ritwan (now called Algic). This proposed relationship was very controversial, but evidence such as Teeter's and new cognates ultimately helped to prove the hypothesis to the satisfaction of everyone (cf. Haas 1958a; Goddard 1975).

This interpretation of Sapir's submerged features would seem to be confirmed in Sapir's own characterization of his method, where he spoke of "peculiar details": "I have even unearthed some morphological resemblances of detail which are so peculiar as to defy all interpretation on any assumption but that of genetic relationship" (1912 letter from Sapir to Kroeber, in Golla 1984:71).

On the other hand, there is another interpretation of what Sapir meant. Some scholars see Sapir's use of typological information in setting up his more inclusive groupings as a claim that the overall morphological plan of compared languages may constitute evidence of their relatedness. The assumption here is that "languages which have been demonstrated as historically related almost invariably show a great many structural features in common. That is, their basic morphological patterns prove to be alike" (Kroeber 1940:465; cf. 465–6). Tom Smith-Stark (1992) challenges the interpretation that Sapir's *submerged features* and his approach to distant genetic relationships rely primarily on "peculiar details." He points out that in Sapir's view each language has a type or determining structural nucleus, spoken of in terms such as "basic plan," a "determined cut," a "general form," a "structural genius," a "great underlying ground-plan," which he qualified with adjectives such as "internal," "basic," "fundamental," "deep," "profound," "general," "underlying," and, in particular, "submerged."[10] Sapir (1949[1921b]:144) contended that "languages are in constant process of change, but it is only reasonable to suppose that they tend to preserve longest what is most fundamental in their structure." He conceived of this in terms of gradual changes in morphological type:

Now if we take great groups of genetically related languages, we find that as we pass from one to another or trace the course of their development we frequently encounter a gradual change of morphological type. This is not surprising, for there is no reason why a language should remain permanently true to its original form. (Sapir 1949[1921b]: 145–6)

Nevertheless, he held that the conceptual type, one of his typological classification scales, tended to persist longer (Sapir 1949[1921b]:145), and Smith-Stark (1992:22) sees this as what is fundamental to Sapir's program for the investigation of remote genetic relationships, typological and geographical at the same time, with Sapir identifying what was most fundamental synchronically with what was most stable diachronically. Smith-Stark emphasizes Sapir's references to the aggregate of compared morphological features as evidence, although it is Sapir's mention of the importance also of "specific resemblances" that others have highlighted.

Morris Swadesh (1951:7), another of Sapir's students, attempted to test the ability of Sapir's method to distinguish between borrowed and inherited features (the basis of the disagreement between Sapir and Franz Boas; see Boas 1920, 1929; Campbell 1997a:217–18) by applying it to French and English. Swadesh was taking up the test which Sapir had suggested:

It would be an instructive experiment in method to compare English grammar with that of the Indo-European language reconstructed by philologists. Whole departments of Indo-European grammar find no analogue in English, while a very large part of what English grammar there is is of such secondary growth as to have no relevance for Indo-European problems. (Sapir 1925a:492)

Swadesh listed several shared structural features, mostly of a rather general sort (e.g. presence of inflectional categories of singular and plural; past and present tenses) "which go back to their ancient common form, that is Indo-European," and a few "which reflect diffusional influences" (Swadesh 1951:8). He acknowledged the number of his "residual common traits" was "not so great," but he was impressed that some "involve formational irregularities that could hardly come over with borrowed words" (Swadesh 1951:8). Based on this, he speculated about what this might mean for more remote relationships:

But what would happen after a much longer time [than 5,000 years]? Suppose twelve or twenty-four thousand years had elapsed since the common history of the two languages.

---

[10] Here, parallels to the notion of "inner form," the "genius of a language," and the like, so pervasive in nineteenth-century thinking on language, are in evidence (see Chapter 8).

Would not the structural similarities become less and less in number and more and more attenuated in form until they are reduced to perhaps only one recognizable but very vague similarity? In this case, would the situation be indistinguishable from one in which a single trait had been taken over by borrowing? Not necessarily. If the last vestigial similarity involved a *deep-seated coincidence in formation*, such as that between English *I-me* and French *je-moi*, then even one common feature would be strongly suggestive of common origin rather than borrowing . . . However, it could also constitute a chance coincidence with no necessary historical relationship at all. (Our emphasis, LC/WP)

Buoyed by this English–French comparison, Swadesh proceeded to test "the case which Boas regarded as probably unresolvable, the relationship between Tlingit and Athabaskan" (Swadesh 1951:10), listing Sapir's nine shared structural similarities. He concluded:

The foregoing list of common structural features bears out Boas' statements that "There is not the slightest doubt that the morphology of the two groups shows the most far-reaching similarities" and further that "the inference is inevitable that these similarities must be due to historical causes" [Boas 1920:374]. However, in the light of our control case we no longer need have any doubts as to the kind of historical causes which gave rise to this array of structural similarities. It is clearly of the same general order as that shown by the residual similarities of English and French. In fact, Tlingit and Athabaskan show a distinctly closer structural affinity than English and French. (Swadesh 1951:11)

Here, Swadesh appears to rely on the aggregate of shared structural features, rather than the irregular and arbitrary correspondences of individual "submerged" traits such as his English–French *I-je*, *me-moi* sort.[11] Swadesh's use of both individual striking grammatical correspondences and similarities shared in the overall morphological patterns appears to mirror Sapir's methods well.

We believe that both interpretations of Sapir's methods are essentially correct. That is, we find instances where Sapir argued from the weight of the overall pattern of shared morphological similarities, i.e. correspondences in basic morphological plans; but we also find instances where he argues from the strength of individual or peculiar shared traits, such as those favored by Meillet

---

[11] Incidentally, Swadesh's (1951) own methodological recommendations in this article did not stop with Sapir's shared structural features of morphology, but (as we might by now expect from tradition) also included lexical and phonological evidence:

Highly dependable separate tests can be developed in the three areas of structure, basic vocabulary, and phonology. These three criteria, moreover, are mutually confirmatory. (Swadesh 1951:21)

Phonology, besides being a necessary concomitant of any effective study of vocabulary correspondences, constitutes an additional criterion for the differentiation of residual and cumulative similarities. If the phonologies of compared languages are such as to admit their being derived by realistic regular formulas of change from a realistic reconstructed prototype language, one cannot doubt the fact of common origin and residual relation. The interwoven fabric of a reconstructed speech-sound pattern is too complex to be pulled out of thin air. (Swadesh 1951:20)

Table 7.1 *Matching forms of the verb 'to be' across Indo-European languages*

	3rd pers sg	3rd pers pl	1st pers sg
Latin	est	sunt	sum
Sanskrit	ásti	sánti	asmi
Greek	esti	eisi	eimi
Gothic	ist	sind	am
Hittite	ešzi (<z> = [ts])	ašanzi	ešmi
PIE	*es-ti	*s-enti (Ø-grade)	*es-mi

(below). William Bright's (1991) interpretation of Sapir's procedures was that Sapir liked to use broad typological similarities of form (such as those on which he based the six superstocks in North America), but that by 1929 he had zeroed in on idiosyncratic, "submerged" traits as a way of moving beyond hypothesis to proof.

In the area of grammatical evidence, Antoine Meillet has been even more influential than Sapir, and we turn now to Meillet, with whom there is general methodological agreement today.

7.4.2 Meillet

Antoine Meillet (1866–1936) employed the three standard sources of evidence for establishing family relationship – morphological agreements, phonological correspondences, and basic vocabulary. He favored morphological proofs in particular (Meillet 1967[1925]:36), though his discussions of regular phonological correspondences and "phonetic laws" are also well known. His sort of grammatical evidence, his "shared aberrancy," is illustrated by forms of the verb 'to be' in branches of Indo-European, in the matchings of the suppletive forms across the branches compared, seen in Table 7.1.

Meillet also occasionally spoke of language "type" in terms reminiscent of Sapir's type or basic plan discussed above; however, Meillet found the general type of little value for establishing genetic relationships:

Although the usage made of some type is often maintained for a very long time and leaves traces even when the type as a whole tends to be abolished, one may not make use of these general types at all to prove a "genetic relationship." For it often happens that with time the type tends to die out more or less completely, as appears from the history of the Indo-European languages. (Meillet 1967[1925]:37)

Common Indo-European presented in the most extreme way the type which is called "inflectional" ... even the most conservative Indo-European languages have a type completely different from Common Indo-European ... Consequently, *it is not by its general structure that an Indo-European language is recognized.* (Meillet 1967[1925]:37–8; our emphasis, LC/WP)

Thus, it is not with such *general features of structure*, which are subject to change completely in the course of several centuries . . . that one can establish linguistic relationships. (Meillet 1967[1925]:39; our emphasis, LC/WP)

Meillet, rather, favored "particular processes," "singular facts," "local morphological peculiarities," "anomalous forms," and "arbitrary associations" (i.e. "shared aberrancy"):

The more singular the facts are by which the agreement between two languages is established, the greater is the conclusive force of the agreement. *Anomalous forms are thus those which are most suited to establish a "common language."* (Meillet 1967[1925]:41; our emphasis, LC/WP)

What conclusively establish the continuity between one "common language" and a later language are the particular processes of expression of morphology. (Meillet 1967[1925]:39; our emphasis, LC/WP)

Meillet's use of "shared aberrancy" in grammatical evidence is now standard practice among Indo-Europeanists and historical linguists generally (cf. Hock 1986:563–4; P. Newman 1980:21).

7.4.3   Greenberg's use of grammatical evidence

Earlier in his career Greenberg had advocated Meillet's approach:

The natural unit of interlingual comparison is the morpheme with its alternate morphs. The presence of similar morph alternants in similar environments is of very great significance as an indication of historical connection, normally genetic relationship. This is particularly so if the alternation is irregular, especially if suppletive, that is, entirely different. The English morpheme with alternants *gud-*, *bet-*, *be-*, with the morph alternant *bet-* occurring before -ər, "comparative," and the alternant *be-* before -*st*, "superlative," corresponds in form and conditions of alternation with German *gu:t-*, *bes-*, *be-*, with *bes-* occurring before -ər, "comparative," and *be-* before -*st*, "superlative." We have here not only the probability that a similar form is found in the meaning "good" but that it shows similar and highly arbitrary alternations before the representatives of the comparative and superlative morphemes. The likelihood that all this is the result of chance is truly infinitesimal. (Greenberg 1957:37–8)

Given Greenberg's endorsement of such irregular morphological correspondences, it is puzzling that arbitrary or irregular or suppletive alternations play no significant part in the evidence for his Amerind proposal, though he does attempt to marshal some arguments of this sort in the evidence he presents for his Eurasiatic hypothesis (Greenberg 1991, 2000a, evaluated in Chapter 9). Greenberg gave lip service in his methodological pronouncements in the 1987 book to this sort of grammatical evidence which he had advocated in 1957, but seems to go out of his way to play down its importance:

Agreement in irregularities and evidence from survivals of grammatical markers that have become petrified are worthy of special attention and are used in the present work. An agreement like that between English 'good'/'better'/'best' and German *gut/besser/best* is obviously of enormous probative value. However, subject as such agreements are to analogical pressure, their absence is not negative evidence, and their presence tells us that there is a relationship, but not at what level. They are psychologically reassuring in showing that we are on the right track and inherently interesting, *but not really necessary*. (Greenberg 1987:30; our emphasis, LC/WP)

Greenberg (1987:30) continues to advocate Meillet's "agreements in irregularities," but seemingly grudgingly. He seems to cancel its importance by offering multilateral (mass) comparison as a substitute, saying that Meillet "never thought of the simple expedient of mass comparison." The morphological comparisons in Greenberg (1987) are handled for the most part in a fashion completely parallel to his treatment of vocabulary comparisons – only these involve shorter forms –, treated as the lexical look-alikes assembled in what he calls his "etymologies." Here, what he calls morphological or grammatical evidence is in fact just phonetic resemblances observed among bound morphemes and includes almost nothing of grammatical patterns nor of the shared "peculiarities" that Meillet sought. He interpreted as a Meillet-like example the pattern of pronouns with *i-*, *a-*, *i(?)-* 'first,' 'second,' 'third person,' respectively, which he argued crosses several South American families (Greenberg 1987:44–6). He contended that this is an interesting example because the last, but not the first, does not cause following consonants to palatalize and shows up as *e* in some languages. He sees this sort of feature as evidence for a more inclusive Gê-Pano-Carib grouping. However, by his own account, this example does not involve idiosyncratic alternations at all, and therefore, while it might constitute a small paradigm (if the facts were correct), it does not have anything like the force of an example such as, say, the *r/n* alternation exhibited by the *-r* stem nouns in several Indo-European languages, as illustrated by words like Hittite *wâdar* 'water' (nominative sg)/*wedenas* (genitive sg), cognate with Greek *hudōr* (nominative sg)/*hudatos* (< *hudn̥tos*) (genitive sg) – this irregular and unexpected alternation is among the sort of facts which convinced the linguistic world that Hittite was indeed an Indo-European language (Chapter 5). The South American *i/a/i* pattern is not like this, and not like Swadesh's *I/me-je/moi* example; it is not the sort of example of which Meillet and Sapir spoke.

When Greenberg (1949a:79–80) said that "lexical resemblances, whether in root or inflectional morphemes are *sine qua non* for the establishment of all relations," he seems to equate lexical and grammatical morpheme comparisons with each other, as seems quite apparent in his later procedures (as pointed out by Rankin 1992), though he attempts to portray the grammatical comparisons as somehow different in kind from his lexical equations. Also, in 1949 he relied on "correspondences" in sound in order to reduce the possibility of chance accounting for the similarities; by 1987 he denied the relevance of sound correspondences. Finally, his leanings towards favoring lexical evidence are seen in his favorable citation of Powell's lexically based method of classifying of North American Indian languages; by 1987 raw lexical similarities had become nearly his only evidence, his lip service to grammatical evidence notwithstanding.

Given that chance coincidences can sometimes result in morphological similarities, the question is raised, just how does one interpret grammatical evidence, and how many and what sort of examples are necessary to deny chance and borrowing as the possible explanations of the similarities? We turn now to this question.

7.4.4   Cautions in the interpretations of "shared aberrancy"/ "submerged features"

Grammatical evidence in the investigation of distant relationships is to be highly recommended, particularly the idiosyncratic sort advocated by Meillet, Sapir, and their followers. In some instances such grammatical evidence alone may be sufficient to support the probability of a genetic relationship, though proposed distant genetic relationships naturally receive their strongest support when, in addition to such grammatical evidence, there is also support from basic vocabulary and sound correspondences. However, one must be cautious in the interpretation of this sort of grammatical evidence. That is, there are reasonably strong cases of what appear to be idiosyncratic grammatical correspondences which in fact have non-genetic explanations due to accident or borrowing. We cite examples to illustrate this, though we do not wish these examples to bear negatively on the general importance of seeking shared aberrancies or submerged features as strong support for distant genetic relationship.

Peripheral Quechua and K'iche' (Mayan) share seemingly "submerged" or arbitrary and idiosyncratic features. Both languages have two different sets of pronominal affixes in distinct contexts, and they are strikingly similar in their first person singular forms: Peripheral Quechua *-ni-* and *-wa-*, K'iche' *in-* and *w-* (from Proto-Mayan *in-* before consonant-initial roots, and *w-* before vowel-initial forms). Closer scrutiny, however, shows that this striking and idiosyncratic similarity is just spurious. The *-ni-* of Peripheral Quechua (the dominant languages in the Quechuan family) is derived historically from the empty morph *-ni-* which is inserted between two morphemes when otherwise two consonants would come together. The first-person singular morpheme originally was *-y*, as it still is in many circumstances (e.g. *-y* '1st sg possessive') (Parker 1969:150; ultimately *-ya* by Cerrón-Palomino's [1987:141–2] reconstruction); it followed the empty morph -*ni*- when attached to consonant-final roots (e.g. *C+ni+y*). Ultimately the final -*y* was swallowed up as part of the *i* in -*ni*- and the first-person suffix on verbs was then reanalyzed as -*ni* (e.g. -*ni+y* > -*ni*) (cf. Adelaar 1984:42; Cerrón-Palomino 1987:124–6, 139–42). Furthermore, the -*wa*- '1st pers object' of Peripheral Quechua comes from Proto-Quechua *ma, as seen in its cognates in Central Quechua (Parker 1969:193). Thus, the picture that seemed to present a striking and idiosyncratic similarity for 'first person' (Peripheral Quechua *ni/wa*, K'iche' *in/w* – recall Swadesh's *I-me/je-moi* example, above) is actually rather Quechua *-*y*/*-*ma*, K'iche' *in/w*, not very similar at all.

The second example of a seemingly "submerged" or strikingly idiosyncratic grammatical feature shared by Quechua and K'iche' involves the phonetically similar discontinuous negation construction in the two languages: Quechua *mana . . . -ču*, K'iche' *man . . . tah*. This example, too, dissolves under closer scrutiny. Proto-Mayan negation had only *ma, and K'iche' acquired the discontinuous construction when the optative particle *tah was grammaticalized and became obligatory in the context with negatives. The *man* negative apparently comes from *ma* 'negative' + *na* 'now, still, yet, later, first.' Thus the more accurate comparison would be between *ma* and Quechua *mana . . . -ču*, but this is not nearly as striking a similarity as it had initially appeared to be. Moreover, the remaining phonetic similarity between the K'iche' and Quechua negatives is not compelling, given the many other languages in the world with *ma* negatives (see below). Moreover, discontinuous (flanking) negative constructions are actually quite common among the world's languages (as for example French *ne . . . pas*; see Campbell 1997a:220 for several others).

Another example involves some idiosyncratic, arbitrary, seemingly chance-defying similarities shared by Quechua and Finnish (see Campbell 1973[1993]).

Table 7.2 *Quechua–Finnish accidental morphological similarities*

Quechua	Finnish	
-ču	-ko/-kö	'Question morpheme'
-ču	-ko/-kö, -ka/-kä	'Negative morpheme'
-ču	-k, -ka/-kä	'Imperative morpheme'

These grammatical morphemes seem to share the recurrent sound correspondence of *č* : *k*, which suggests the plausible sound change of *k* > *č*, for example, and given that languages rarely have all three of these morphemes as clitics or suffixes, this combination of facts might seem to support a genetic relationship. Presumably this combination is unlikely to occur by chance alone (though chance is not outside the realm of possibilities). Nevertheless, the explanation for the shared similarities need not be one of inheritance from a common ancestor. In many languages there is a morphosyntactic connection between negation and yes/no questions (e.g. Mandarin, Somali, certain versions of formal logic, etc.); therefore, languages which show such a morphosyntactic connection are not odd; Finnish and Quechua can each easily have similar question and negative markers independently of any historical connection between the two languages. It is possible that the similarity which the imperative markers share with the questions (and negatives) in these two languages also has some internal motivation (for example, both involve irrealis situations). In any case, such a correspondence is not outside the realm of possible accidental similarity. Thus, this seemingly "submerged" set of correspondences does not provide a persuasive example of linguistic affinity.

In these cases, what at first seemed like strikingly idiosyncratic grammatical correspondences turn out to be merely accidental similarities. Examples such as these show why care should be exercised in interpreting "submerged" or idiosyncratic morphological and grammatical features. This notwithstanding, however, with appropriate cautions in place, shared aberrancies/submerged features, idiosyncratic patterns, remain an extremely powerful source of evidence for ancient linguistic kinship among languages.[12]

We end this section with a reminder. Namely, while the evidence of shared aberrancies, idiosyncratic patterns, shared suppletion, or submerged features is excellent and we would hope for proposals of distant genetic relationship to have such evidence in abundance, it is not realistic to expect to find such cases with great frequency. These sorts of irregularities in language are precisely the ones that tend to get leveled out by analogy over the long run, so, they constitute great evidence when we have them, but they often do not survive especially well and therefore they are not as frequently found as we would like.

7.4.5   Nichols' use of grammatical and other evidence in distant genetic relationships

Johanna Nichols (1996a) speaks of "individual-identifying evidence" to establish genetic relationship, and she discusses "descent-proving features," called "genetic markers" (Nichols 1997a:360), of which there are three types, each

---

[12] We hasten to point out that instances of shared aberrancy or submerged features are not generally the sort that violate the requirement for only comparisons involving both sound and meaning. The sorts of irregularities identified in such examples do involve similarity in both sound and meaning, not the sort of gross comparison of just the presence of some phonological trait (say tones or glottalized consonants) or just some meaning (say gender), but the identification of shared similarities involving both sound and meaning, as in the suppletive paradigm for the verb 'to be' with its various phonetic realizations in Indo-European languages, or the 'good/better/best' comparison in Germanic languages.

with connections to grammatical evidence for relationships. These are worth consideration. With regard to the first she speaks of:

an ordered sequence or other patterned set of form-function pairings whose overall probability of occurrence is about two orders of magnitude less than the probability of any one language turning up in a random draw. (There are some 5000–6000 languages, hence $1/5000 \times 0.01 = 0.000002$ or two in a million.) A four-consonant sequence or ordered set meets this threshold. The person prefix paradigm of the Algonquian family of North America, for example, consists of first person *ne-, second person *ke-, third person *we-, and indefinite *me- . . . This small but highly structured paradigm meets the threshold and is a strong genetic marker . . . Another genetic marker is the gender–number suffixes masculine -n, feminine -t, plural (masculine = feminine) -n in certain pronominal paradigms, which is diagnostic of Afroasiatic genetic reality. (Nichols 1997a:360–1)

It would be wonderful if it were so easy to establish genetic relationships. One complicating factor is that the 5,000–6,000 languages are not all independent of one another, but fall into, by Nichols' (1997a) count some 250 "stocks," and therefore the chances of finding such a match may be far more frequent than just two in a million, since related languages often exhibit commonalities due to retention of inherited forms. This in effect reduces her formula from 1/5,000 to something much smaller, closer to 1/250 (or 1/350 by our count). More importantly, since languages can undergo change, there are Algonquian languages which do not have all of these four "form–function" pairings. For example, as reflexes of the Proto-Algonquian *ne- 'first person,' *ke- 'second person,' *we- 'third person,' and *me- 'indefinite' pronoun paradigm (for dependent possessed nouns), Arapaho has ne-, he-, hi-, be-, respectively, while Cheyenne (for possessed nouns) has na-, ne-, he-, ma- (Goddard and Campbell 1994:198–9; Ives Goddard personal communication). It is not certain how these might be counted, but it is certain that we no longer have four points of matching in the paradigm for these two languages – Arapaho hi- for *we- and Cheyenne ne- for *ke- are not clear matches by any means. In fact, we see the sort of alliteration (he-, hi- in Arapaho and na-, ne- in Cheyenne) which Nichols (2003) expects in such paradigms, but here the development of the alliteration has eroded the points of contact which would have been needed for this structured paradigm to reach the threshold as a genetic marker. In like manner, there are languages classified as Afroasiatic which lack its gender pattern. Nichols (1997a:362) acknowledges that such tests give "false negatives," that the gender–number paradigm is fully present in the Semitic, Berber, and Chadic branches of Afroasiatic, but not in others. This means that absence of a "descent-proving feature" does not necessarily disqualify a language, in these cases, from possibly being Algonquian or Afroasiatic. On the other hand, languages can influence one another and borrow from one another, and consequently there are adjacent languages classified as Nilo-Saharan or as Niger-Kordofanian which exhibit similarities to the Afroasiatic gender pattern (see Chapter 6). That is, presence of the "diagnostic" feature may be insufficient to guarantee the "correct" classification. Moreover, both these examples involve short morphemes with unmarked consonants, the sort that are encountered over and over in the short grammatical morphemes of the world's languages, aligned in paradigmatic sets with iconic/deictic oppositions. There appear to be reasons motivated by ease of perception and iconicity of functional oppositions for why nasals recur so frequently in pronoun markers across languages (as indicated also by Nichols 2003; Campbell 1997a:243–4). Thus, in these two examples, it is not so straightforward as just a patterned set in which four components match one another arbitrarily and independently without other factors potentially influencing the sort of consonants involved or the sort of opposition extant in the patterned set.

Finally, it is to be recalled that matchings containing even more than four points of contact are known to occur sometimes by accident, as in the case of the remarkable congruences between Proto-Eastern Miwokan and Late Common Indo-European pronominal affixes pointed out by Callaghan (1980:337):

Table 7.3 *Coincidences between Proto-Eastern Miwokan and Late Common Indo-European*

	Proto-Eastern Miwokan	Late Common Indo-European
	Declarative suffixes	*Secondary affixes (active)*
1 sg	*-m	*-m
2 sg	*-ṣ	*-s
3 sg	*-Ø	*-t < **Ø
1 pl	*-maṣ	*-me(s)/-mo(s)
2 pl	*-to-k	*-te

In spite of the caution urged with respect to this methodological desideratum, evidence of the sort advocated by Nichols is appropriate and important, though not always as conclusive as she holds it to be. Nichols' (1997a:361) second "genetic marker" is: "Significantly greater than chance frequency of phoneme matchings in semantically identical words from a standard 100-word list." Various scholars have proposed mathematical approaches to the threshold of phonological matchings or correspondences that might be expected by accident (e.g. Ringe 1995a, 1995b, 1996, 1999; see also Bender 1969; Justeson and Stephens 1980). They reveal generally that the constraints on what is required in order to show higher than chance phoneme matchings (so as to constitute evidence of distant genetic relationship) are on the whole much higher than thought by many enthusiasts of distant genetic relationships – that is, the burden of proof has turned out to be rather high. It is difficult to demonstrate a genetic relationship in this manner for languages whose relatedness is otherwise in question. As many point out (see above), it is very difficult to demonstrate genetic relationship on the basis of compared vocabulary from a short list for languages which separated so long ago that most of the vocabulary items on the list will have been lost and replaced or will have changed semantically and/or phonologically beyond recognition (see Chapter 10).

Nichols' (1997a:361) says of her third kind of "genetic marker":

> in principle a set of features – none a genetic marker by itself but all of known diachronic stability and relatively low frequency worldwide, and all demonstrably independent of each other – could as a set reach the threshold of genetic markers and serve as a diagnostic of deep genetic connection.

We agree with this, though we see it also essentially as the traditional search for compelling grammatical evidence of distant genetic relationship. We would expect the "set of features" to be sufficient to deny chance and borrowing, and, as pointed out earlier, we find these demands to be fairly high, since so often errors have been made and since striking cases due to sheer accident (as pointed out above) are known.

7.4.6   Additional cautions in morphological comparisons

There are several ways in which the comparison of bound grammatical morphemes differs from compared lexical material, and care is needed in the interpretation of similarities among these. The first caution is that grammatical affixes tend to utilize only a subset of the consonants and vowels available within a language, and typically this subset is made up of the less marked segments of the language (Floyd 1981; Goddard and Campbell 1994:196–7; see below). Since these typically unmarked consonants involved in grammatical affixes are those which recur with the greatest frequency across languages, it is to be expected that numerous similarities which are purely accidental will be encountered in comparisons of such morphemes across languages, particularly since grammatical affixes are usually quite short (e.g. C, CV, VC, or V in shape; cf. Meillet 1948[1921]:89–90).

For a second caution, bound morphemes in many languages often have more than one function; a single affix form F_1, in language L_1, might have several grammatical meanings, $M_1, M_2 \ldots M_n$, which in another language L_2 may each be signaled by distinct morphemes, $F_1, F_2 \ldots Fn$, each with only one of the meanings from the set of meanings F_1 has in L_1.[13] For example, in most modern

---

[13] The various forms/affixes of L_2 could have one or more of the meanings of F_1 of L_1, but not all of them, in the situation described here.

Balkan languages both the dative and genitive case functions are signaled by a single affix; if a Balkan language, L_1 (with a single morpheme which has multiple meanings, F_1-M_1 = Dative /M_2 = Genitive), were compared with some other language, L_2, in which the case endings for genitive and dative are formally distinct (i.e. L_2 has two separate case markers each with a single function, F_1-M_1 = Dative, and F_2-M_2 = Genitive), the result would be multiple possible target matchings in L_2 for the single Balkan suffix of L_1. This is a rather straightforward demonstration of the very common one-to-many target ratio that can exist when a single marker (with multiple meanings/functions) of one language is compared to multiple markers each with some of the meanings corresponding to some of those of the single marker of the other language. This many-to-one target ratio increases the chance of accidental matchings. It is not an uncommon situation.

A third caution involves the inverse of this last one. Languages can employ a number of different markers to signal the same function (i.e. $F_1/F_2/F_n$-M_1), for example, German 'plural' markers -∂r, -n/-∂n, -∂ (with or without umlaut). In this case, r and n are among the most common consonants, and German offers multiple common targets for comparison with 'plural' markers from other languages, and, not unexpectedly, easy matches turn up in languages known not to be demonstrably related, e.g. Nahuatl -n 'plural' (one of several), Uralic -n 'plural' (one of several, Laanest 1982:152–3), Greenberg's -l or -r 'plural' of putative Macro-Panoan and Chibchan-Paezan (Greenberg 1987:294–5), etc. This, too, is a common situation, and the many-to-one ratio again increases the number of possible targets of comparison which in turn increases the likelihood of finding matchings which are only accidentally similar.

A final caution about the use of grammatical evidence has to do with typologically commonplace features. Comparison of grammatical traits that are typologically common and thus found with considerable frequency in the world's languages does nothing to enhance a proposal of genetic relationship. We illustrate this by considering some of Swadesh's (1953a) proposed evidence for the Mosan hypothesis (which hypothesized a genetic connection between the Salishan, Wakashan, and Chimakuan language families). Sapir (1929a) accepted Mosan as a genetic grouping (which he made part of his even more inclusive Algonkian-Mosan), and Swadesh (1953a, 1953b), his student, attempted to provide supporting evidence for Mosan. Swadesh (1953a:29–30) also listed sixteen shared structural similarities, but these prove unimpressive today, since most are typologically commonplace traits (several are also general areal traits of the Northwest Coast linguistic area; see Campbell 1997a:332–4, 1997c). Swadesh's traits included:

1. "Extensive use of suffixes." This is typologically commonplace; many languages are exclusively suffixing though not genetically related (especially SOV languages). This is also a Northwest Coast areal trait.

2. "Nearly complete absence of functioning prefixes in Chimakuan and Wakashan, minor role as compared with the suffixes in Salish." Again, this is a commonplace typological feature, found easily in languages that are not related to one another (see Altaic, Chapter 9). It is also an areal trait characteristic of Northwest Coast languages.
3. "Changes in stem vowel, including lengthening and i-mutation." Ablaut and umlaut vowel mutations are not uncommon cross-linguistically, found in Indo-European, Semitic, Jicaque, Sapir's "Penutian," and many more. They are not typologically uncommon.
4. "Aspect, including at least the dichotomy of momentaneous and durative." Such aspect distinctions can also easily evolve independently in unrelated languages. This is also a feature of the linguistic area.
5. "Tense is an optional category." That aspect is much more important than tense is true of many, many languages throughout the Americas and elsewhere in the world. It is typologically common.
6. "Use of demonstratives or articles to substantivize verbs." This feature could easily be the result of independent parallel grammaticalizations in these and other languages which have this. It is not unusual typologically; see, for example, Spanish *el andar* 'walking' (noun), literally 'the to.walk [infinitive]').
7. "Predicative use of nouns, with personal [i.e. pronominal] predicative affixes added directly." For example, 'I am chief' in Nootka and in Kalispel may be expressed by adding the appropriate personal affix to the word for chief. This is not a particularly unusual grammatical feature, particularly in American Indian languages; it is typical of the Mesoamerican linguistic area, for example, Nahuatl *ni-tla:katl* [I-man] 'I am a man,' Q'eqchi' (Mayan) *kwinq-at* [man-you] 'you are a man,' and found in South America, for example, Chulupí (Matacoan) *ya-niwakle* [I-person] 'I am a man/person.'
8. "Demonstrative distinctions such as the present versus absent, or visible versus invisible." This is also typologically not uncommon, a contrast known in numerous other languages around the world, for example, Chulupí (Matacoan) *na niwakle* 'this man' (present, visible); *xa niwakle* 'that man' (known but not visible); *pa niwakle* 'that man' (unknown, unseen). This trait, too, is a general areal feature in Northwest Coast languages.

Some of these traits are also not typologically independent of one another (for example (1) extensive use of suffixes and (2) nearly complete absence of prefixes).

As might be guessed from evidence such as this, Mosan is now largely abandoned. Several of these traits are so typologically commonplace that they could easily have developed independently in the languages which share them. Such traits need to be avoided in proposals of distant genetic relationship.

7.4.7   Positional analysis

Dell Hymes (1955, 1956) argued that in languages with complex affix systems, the positional analysis of "cognate categories" could constitute important evidence for genetic relationship. By this he meant that the shared patterns of morphological structure, in particular shared ordering of functionally equivalent morphemes in strings of affixes in compared languages could be taken as evidence of genetic relationship, where the phonological substance of the morphemes themselves was considered irrelevant (a violation of the isomorphism requirement that form and function both need to be present in comparisons). He illustrated this claim with the Na-Dene hypothesis. This approach turned out not to be valid for establishing genetic relationships, as shown by Bartholomew (1967:77–8), Thomason (1980), Campbell (1997a:222–4, 282–3), and others.

Thomason (1980:360) showed that "morphology is by no means so stable as to justify the assumption that lexical cognates may vanish almost entirely while the morphology holds firm," and contrary to the assumption of positional analysis, "the morphology may be restructured to a considerable degree through the influence of another language." She pointed out that "all the evidence available from well-documented language families indicates that morphological diversification goes along with diversification elsewhere in the grammar" (Thomason 1980:368). Unrelated languages can acquire new morphological positions through grammaticalization which independently correspond to the pattern of these in other languages due to the typical directionality of many such changes and to general iconic/semantic constraints on the order of morphemes. To mention just one telling factor, it is a generally accepted universal that derivational affixes are found closer to the roots than inflectional affixes. Any shared affix order which reflects this general positioning of derivational and inflectional affixes with respect to one another would not count as evidence of genetic relationship.

Not only can non-related languages come independently to share positional categories through morphological changes, related languages not infrequently come to have morphological categories whose positions do not match. For example, in some Finno-Ugric languages the order among suffixes on nouns does not correspond to the order in other languages of the family; some have *case + possessive* order where others have *possessive + case*, as seen in the comparison of Finnish *kodi-ssa-ni* [home-in-my] with Hungarian *ház-am-ban* [house-my-in], both meaning 'in my house'. Even in so-called "Na-Dene" languages there are significant positional differences among the grammatical affixes (Krauss 1969:76).

In short, since non-related languages can develop impressive agreements in positional categories while genetically related languages often do not exhibit such agreements, the positional analysis approach to detecting genetic relationship proves not to be reliable.

7.4.8   Another red herring: reconstruction as proof of relationship

A number of advocates of long-range relationships accuse the conservatives ("splitters") of insisting on sound correspondences as proof of relationship. This is not true of all conservatives. As pointed out, some are quite content to see certain patterned morphosyntactic agreements of the appropriate sort as evidence of relationship even without strict sound correspondences and lexical cognates, though naturally they are happiest when these different sources of evidence coincide. Another claim made by some enthusiasts of remote relationships is that the conservatives require reconstruction by the comparative method for proof of relationship among languages (see for example, Greenberg 2000b:168–9). This is not true for a good number of the conservatives. Certain patterned morphosyntactic agreements, such as submerged features, shared aberrancies, or individual-identifying evidence, do not require reconstruction. Even identifying sound correspondences does not require reconstruction; in some instances, it is possible to recognize recurrent sound correspondences in cognates of basic vocabulary without necessarily being able to reconstruct fully, and yet this, too, is accepted as evidence of relatedness by many.

Greenberg argued that relationships are discovered first by observing lexical similarities, the classification established, and then subsequently sound correspondences may be worked out and reconstruction undertaken. Specifically, he saw "three stages, which are in order of logical and usually historical priority": "(1) Recognition of a family of related languages [mostly on observation of lexical similarities]; (2) The discovery of sound laws; (3) The application of the comparative method, starting with sound laws" (Greenberg 2000b:170). Greenberg and like-minded thinkers fail to recognize that the lexical similarities are not, ipso facto, etymologies, but require the application of historical linguistic techniques to sort out borrowings, accidents, onomatopoeia, etc. from possibly inherited words. They forget that other linguists live by Meillet's dictum that languages are systems "ou tout se tient," where the pieces are interconnected and work in concert. Thus, the lexical items do not stand apart from the phonological segments of which they are composed and the sounds are observed only in the context of the lexical items in which they are found. Thus, it is not so easy as first observing some similar words, calling them etymologies, classifying the languages, and then belatedly seeking sound correspondences and attempting reconstruction. Rather, given the interrelatedness, both recognizing possible cognates and working out sound correspondences are necessary to confirm each other. To show words compared in different languages are true "etymologies" (cognates), it is necessary to show support of regular sound correspondences, since otherwise it is not possible to know whether the similarities exhibited might not be due to some other factor than inheritance. Similarly, true sound correspondences can be established only by comparing cognate forms. Since these depend on one another, it becomes necessary to work back and forth, checking correspondences within probable cognates and refining cognates against their fit with sound correspondences until in the end both are understood and mutually support one another, and exclude material that does not fit the system. This is not circular, but rather requires both to be worked out before final judgments are warranted. It is certainly not the case, as Greenberg asserted, that the classifications are clear before the sound laws are established or before reconstruction starts.

7.5   Borrowing

Since it is generally recognized that borrowing, a source of non-genetic similarity among languages, can complicate evidence for remote relationships, it should be sufficient just to mention that efforts must be taken to eliminate borrowings from evidence presented for cases of distant genetic relationship. However, too often scholars well aware of this problem still err in not eliminating loans from their proposed evidence of distant genetic relationships. We mention a couple of cases just to exemplify the problem. A good illustration is Greenberg's (1987:108) 'axe' "etymology," which he presented as evidence for his "Chibchan-Paezan" hypothesis. Forms from only four languages were cited, two of which are loans: Cuitlatec *navaxo* 'knife,' borrowed from Spanish *navajo* 'knife, razor'; Tunebo *baxi-ta* 'machete,' from Spanish *machete*.[14] Clearly the failure to eliminate these loans devastates this proposed cognate set, and weakens the overall evidence for the hypothesis. In the case of the Nostratic hypothesis (see Illich-Svitych 1989a, 1989b, 1990; Kaiser and Shevoroshkin 1988), given central Eurasia's history of wave upon wave of conquest, expansion, and trade, it is not surprising that some of the forms cited as evidence are confirmed loans, others probable borrowings, e.g. 'vessel,' 'practice witchcraft,' 'honey,' 'birch,' 'bird-cherry,' 'poplar,' 'conifer,' etc. (see Campbell 1998, 1999 for details).

It is frequently suggested that "the borrowing factor can be held down to a very small percentage by sticking to non-cultural words" (Swadesh 1954:313). That is, in case of doubt, more reliance should be placed on basic vocabulary because it is less likely to be borrowed. While this is good practice, it must be remembered (as mentioned above) that even basic vocabulary can sometimes be borrowed. Finnish borrowed from its Baltic and Germanic neighbors

---

[14] Tunebo [x] alternates with [š]; nasal consonants do not occur before oral vowels; the vowels of the Tunebo form are expectable substitutes for Spanish *e*.

various terms for basic kinship and body parts, e.g. 'mother,' 'daughter,' 'sister,' 'tooth,' 'navel,' 'neck,' 'thigh,' 'fur,' etc. Based on approximately 15 percent of the 3,000 most common words in Turkish and Persian being Arabic in origin, it has been claimed that, "if Arabic, Persian, and Turkish were separated now and studied 3,000 years hence by linguists having no historical records, lists of cognates could easily be found, sound correspondences established, and an erroneous genetic relationship postulated" (Pierce 1965:31). Closer to home, even English has borrowed basic vocabulary items, from French, Latin, and Scandinavian: 'stomach,' 'face,' 'vein,' 'artery,' 'intestine,' 'mountain,' 'navel,' 'pain,' 'penis,' 'person,' 'river,' 'round,' 'saliva,' 'skin,' 'sky,' 'testicle,' 'they'/'them'/'their,' 'vagina,' and 'vein'. The problem of loans and potential loans is very serious.

7.6   Semantic constraints

It is dangerous to assume that phonetically similar forms with different meanings may have undergone semantic shifts and then to compare them as possible/probable cognates in proposals of distant genetic relationship. Meaning can shift, for example, Albanian *motër* 'sister,' from Indo-European 'mother.' However, in hypotheses of remote relationship the assumed shifts cannot be documented, and the greater the semantic latitude permitted in compared forms, the easier it is to find phonetic similarity, albeit fortuitous similarity, between compared forms. When semantically non-equivalent forms are compared, the possibility that chance accounts for the phonetic similarity is greatly increased. As Ringe has shown, "admitting comparisons between non-synonyms cannot make it easier to demonstrate the relationship of two languages . . . it can only make it more difficult to do so" (Ringe 1992:67; see also Nichols 1997a: 362).

The reason for preferring semantically equivalent forms in comparisons certainly is not, as Greenberg (2000b:172) alleges, "to make it as difficult as possible to prove that anything is related to anything else." Rather, it is because otherwise it is difficult to surpass chance as the possible explanation of the similarity. This point is made bluntly clear in the following comparison of phonetically similar but semantically disparate forms in Finnish (Uralic family) and Pipil (Uto-Aztecan family): Pipil *teki* 'to cut' : Finnish *teki* 'made'; *te:n* 'mouth' : *teen* 'of the tea'; *tukat* 'spider' : *tukat* 'hairs'; *tila:n* 'pulled' : *tilaan* 'into the space'; *tu:lin* 'cattail, reed' : *tuulin* 'by the wind'; etc. In these comparisons we notice a recurring $t : t$ correspondence, also $k : k$ and $l : l$ correspondences. However, the sound correspondences in these words are accidental, since it is always possible to find phonetically similar words among languages if their meanings are ignored, as in these sets. With semantic permissiveness it is easy to come up with spurious correspondences such as the Finnish–Pipil $t : t$.

Only after a hypothesis has been seen to have some merit based on semantically equivalent forms could one entertain the idea of semantic shifts, and even then it should be borne in mind that etymology within families where the languages are known to be related still requires an explicit account of any assumed semantic changes. The following advice is sound: "count only exact equivalences" (Swadesh's 1954:314); "the closer the meaning, the surer the results of comparison" (Shirokogoroff 1979[1931]:170). If one cannot prove a relationship "comparing only words that translate each other, one will not be able to do so by allowing the comparison of approximate synonyms as well, since that increases the number of comparisons without increasing the cognate resources (if there are any)" (Ringe 1999:215).

The problem of semantic promiscuity in lexical comparisons is one of the most common and most serious in long-range proposals; we mention but a few random examples for illustration's sake (citing only the glosses of the various forms compared). In Greenberg's (1987) Amerind: 'excrement/night/grass,' 'body/belly/heart/skin/meat/be greasy/fat/deer,' 'child/copulate/son/girl/boy/ tender/bear/small,' 'field/devil/bad/underneath/bottom.' In Benedict's (1990) Japanese–Astro-Tai: 'wing/flutter/beat/drive in a nail/ears/fly/feather/flege,' 'bottom/stomach/belly/abdomen/calf/base/foundation/root,' 'bast/pubic hair/ feather/hair/hemp/hairy/coarse/eyebrow,' 'anus/den, lair/womb/room/hog's den/transplant/opening.' In Illich-Svitych's (1990) Nostratic: 'lip/mushroom/ soft outgrowth,' 'grow up/become/tree/be,' 'crust/rough/scab' (also Kaiser and Shevoroshkin 1988). In Ruhlen's (1994a:322–3) global etymology for 'finger, one': 'one/five/ten/once/only/first/single/fingernail/finger/toe/hand/palm of hand/arm/foot/paw/guy/thing/to show/to point/in hand/middle finger.'[15]

The more semantic non-equivalence in the forms compared, the greater the possibility that chance alone accounts for any perceived phonetic similarity, and not inheritance from a common ancestor.

7.7   Onomatopoeia

Onomatopoetic forms may be similar because the words in different languages have independently approximated the sounds in nature, and such cases must be eliminated from proposals of distant genetic relationship, since the similarity may be explained by onomatopoetic mimicry rather than inheritance from a common ancestor. "A simple way to reduce the sound-imitative factor to a negligible minimum is to omit from consideration all such words as 'blow, breathe, suck, laugh' and the like, that is all words which are known

---

[15] Mikkola (1998:68) finds that 81 percent of Greenberg's Nilo-Saharan word comparisons were semantically matched with the main meaning of each "etymology," something he sees as Greenberg being cautious about semantics shifts – many would not see this as so cautious.

to lean toward sound imitation" (Swadesh 1954:313). Judgments of what is onomatopoetic are subjective; however, possible onomatopes to be eliminated are forms whose meaning plausibly lends itself to mimicking the sounds of nature which frequently are seen to have similar phonetic shapes in unrelated languages. For example, one finds in many proposals of distant genetic relationship words for 'blow/wind' being compared which approximate *p(h)u(h/x/w/f)* phonetically, and for 'breast/suckle, nurse/suck' *(V)m/nVm/n, s/š/ts/č/Vp/b/k,* or *s/š/ts/č/Vs/š/ts/č,* as seen in forms presented as Nostratic, **p[ʰ]uw-/*p[ʰ]ow-* 'to blow,' **mun-at ʸ* 'breast, to suckle,' **mal-* 'to suck' (Bomhard and Kerns 1994); among forms for the Austro-Thai hypothesis **piyup, *piuᶜ, *pyom* 'to blow/breath/wind,' **tśitśi, *tśi, sê* 'breast,' **(n)tšuptšup, *suup, sui, sop-i* 'suck' (Benedict 1990); and in Amerind *pusuk, puti, pōta* 'to blow,' *puluk* 'wind,' *mana, neme, nano, ču, ʔiču, si* 'breast' (Ruhlen 1994a). A few others which frequently are similar across languages due to onomatopoeia are: 'cough,' 'sneeze,' 'break/cut/chop/split,' 'cricket,' 'crow,' 'frog/toad,' 'lungs,' 'baby/infant' (imitative of crying, e.g. Peripheral Quechua *wawa,* Finnish *vauva*), 'beat/hit/pound,' 'call/shout,' 'breathe,' 'choke,' 'cry,' drip/drop,' 'hiccough,' 'kiss,' 'shoot,' 'snore,' 'spit,' 'whistle,' and many bird names (see, for example, Hunn 1975).

7.8   Sound symbolism

"Sound symbolism" involves a direct association in a language between sounds and meaning, where the meaning typically involves the semantic traits of "size" or "shape." Size–shape sound symbolism is related to expressive/iconic symbolism in general, though sound symbolism can become part of a language's structural resources.[16] For example, in English, lengthened vowels can be used to indicate an emotive/expressive sense of intensity or size, as in instances where attempts to write them are given as, for example, "it was soooo ugly," "it was reeeaaally wonderful," "it was biiig and looong." Nevertheless, a long–short vowel opposition is not a formal grammatical marker of bigger versus smaller things in English grammar; however, it is in some languages. Productive sound symbolism is attested in many languages (cf. Nichols 1971; see the papers of Hinton et al. 1994; Campbell 1997a:226–7). Regular sound correspondences can have exceptions in cases where sound symbolism is involved, and this can complicate historical linguistic investigations, including proposals of distant genetic relationship (for several examples, see Campbell 1997a:227). Caution

---

[16] Hinton *et al*'s (1994:1) definition is: "Sound symbolism is the direct linkage between sound and meaning." This is perhaps more inclusive than what we have suggested here and would include additionally various expressive/iconic, onomatopoetic, and phonesthematic sorts of symbolism as well.

must be exercised to detect similarities among compared languages not yet known to be related which may stem from sound symbolism rather than from common ancestry.

7.9   Nursery forms

It has been recognized for centuries that nursery formations (so-called *Lallwörter*, the *mama-nana-papa-dada-kaka* sorts of words) should be avoided in considerations of potential linguistic affinities, since these typically share a high degree of cross-linguistic similarity which is not due to common ancestry (cf. Greenberg 1957:36). Nevertheless, examples of such words are frequent in the evidence put forward for many hypotheses of distant genetic relationship. The forms involved typically mean 'mother,' 'father,' 'grandmother,' 'grandfather,' and often 'brother,' 'sister' (especially elder siblings), 'aunt,' and 'uncle,' and have shapes like *mama, nana, papa, baba, tata, dada*, and less frequently *kaka*, etc.

Murdock (1959) investigated 531 terms for 'mother' and 541 for 'father' to test for "the tendency of unrelated languages to develop similar words for father and mother on the basis of nursery forms," concluding that the data "confirm the hypothesis under test – a striking convergence in the structure of these parental kin terms throughout historically unrelated languages" (cited by Jakobson 1962[1960]:538). Jakobson (1962[1960]) explained the non-genetic similarity among such terms cross-linguistically as nursery forms which enter common adult vocabulary:

Often the sucking activities of a child are accompanied by a slight nasal murmur, the only phonation which can be produced when the lips are pressed to mother's breast or to feeding bottle and the mouth is full. Later, this phonatory reaction to nursing is reproduced as an anticipatory signal at the mere sight of food and finally as a manifestation of a desire to eat, or more generally, as an expression of discontent and impatient longing for missing food or absent nurser, and any ungranted wish . . . Since the mother is, in Grégoire's parlance, *la grande dispensatrice*, most of the infant's longings are addressed to her, and children . . . gradually turn the nasal interjection into a parental term, and adapt its expressive make-up to their regular phonemic pattern. (Jakobson 1962[1960]:542–3)

The forms with nasals are found more frequently in terms for females, stops for males, but not exclusively so. Jakobson reported a "transitional period when *papa* points to the parent present [mother or father], while *mama* signals a request for fulfillment of some need or for the absent fulfiller of childish needs, first and foremost but not necessarily the mother," and eventually the nasal–mother, oral–father association becomes established and then extends to terms not confined to just parents (Jakobson 1962[1960]:543). This helps explain frequent spontaneous symbolic, affective developments, seen when inherited *mother* in English is juxtaposed to *ma, mama, mamma, mammy, mommy, mom, mummy*, and *mum*, and *father* is compared with *pa, papa, pappy, pop, poppy, da, dad, dada*, and *daddy*.

Because these kinship terms are often found to be phonetically similar across genetically unrelated languages, and because this similarity has plausible explanations, as that offered by Jakobson, such nursery words are not considered viable evidence in proposals of distant genetic relationship.

While most historical linguists accept the need to set such forms aside from evidence presented in favor of distant genetic relationships, Ruhlen (2000b) does not. He doubts what he takes Jakobson's explanation to be and claims that Jakobson "suggested an answer based on the order of development of consonants in child language." He says that "Jakobson argued that since *m-* and *p-* are among the earliest consonants produced by children learning language, they would quite naturally come to be associated with the mother and father regardless of the specific language being learned" (Ruhlen 2000b:521). He reasons that since there are other nursery words that do not seem to have this distribution, Jakobson's explanation should be doubted, and he presents a list of *kaka*-like forms meaning 'older male relative,' 'older brother,' 'uncle' and *aya*-like forms for 'older sister,' 'aunt,' 'grandmother,' 'mother' found in various languages to show this. He says:

If we are to extend Jakobson's explanation to take care of these examples, we must hypothesize that older male relatives somehow appear on the scene at the moment the child is learning velar consonants, which are not particularly early in their development, while older female relatives somehow come to be associated with *aya* – as to account for these regularities. Furthermore, there are the other well known examples that have to be accounted for, *tata* ~ *dada* 'father,' *nana* 'older female relative.' That all of these specific sound/meaning relationships are due to the order of development of consonants in child language seems to me unlikely. Rather I believe we must recognize that similarities among such forms have a much higher genetic component than has previously been recognized. There may well be a germ of truth in Jakobson's explanation of *mama* and *papa*, but this explanation cannot reasonably be extended to *kaka* and *aya*, and because of this even its appropriateness for *mama* and *papa* is suspect. (Ruhlen 2000b:524)

As can be seen from the quote above from Jakobson, this is not an accurate representation of Jakobson's account, and leaves out the most relevant parts having to do with phonation while nursing and so on. Jakobson's account does not leave out the *tata/dada* and *nana* forms, and there is no necessary connection between the order of acquisition of consonants in child language and the existence of a certain small number of nursery words found in many independent languages, that is, words whose phonetic similarity is not due to inheritance from an earlier common ancestor but rather is due to the linguistic behavior of small children, and this covers the *kaka* and *aya* cases as well (see also Campbell 1997a:227–9).

In sum, nursery words do not provide reliable support for proposals of distant genetic relationship.

7.10   Short forms and unmatched segments

The length of proposed cognates and the number of matched segments within them are important considerations, since the greater the number of matched segments in a proposed cognate set, the less likely it is that accident may account for the similarity (cf. Meillet 1948[1921]:89–90); as Greenberg (1996a:134) puts it, "the longer an item, the greater its weight" (see also Ringe 1992, 1995a, 1995b, 1996, 1999; Nichols 1996a). Monosyllabic CV or VC (or V) forms may be true cognates, but they are so short that their similarity to forms in other languages could also easily arise due to chance. Likewise, if only one or two segments of longer forms are matched (and other segments in the words unmatched), then chance remains a strong candidate for the explanation of the similarity. Unfortunately examples of both are frequent in many proposals of distant genetic relationship. Such forms will not be persuasive; the whole word must be accounted for. (See Ringe 1992, 1996, 1999 for mathematical proof.)

7.11   Chance similarities

Chance (accident), mentioned several times already, is another possible explanation for similarities in compared languages, and its avoidance in questions of deep family relationships is crucial. "Any claim that a similarity between two human languages is significant must be supported by a demonstration that it could not be the result of sheer chance" (Ringe 1999:213). A principal reason why a number of the proposed distant genetic relationships have not been accepted is because their supporters have not demonstrated that the evidence presented could not be accounted for by chance. As Ringe (1992:81) explains:

Resemblances between languages do not demonstrate a linguistic relationship of any kind unless it can be shown that they are probably not the result of chance. Since the burden of proof is always on those who claim to have demonstrated a previously undemonstrated linguistic relationship, it is very surprising that those who have recently tried to demonstrate connections between far-flung language families have not even addressed the question of chance resemblances. This omission calls their entire enterprise into question.

Therefore, insight on what similarities might be expected by chance can be beneficial to the comparativist. Conventional wisdom holds that 5 to 6 percent of the vocabulary of any two languages may be accidentally similar (Bender 1969). Greenberg believed the value for accidental similarities between unrelated languages was 4 percent; he held the figure was 4 percent among languages with "unlike phonemic systems" and 7 percent for languages with "like phonemic systems" (Greenberg 1953; Croft 2005:xv). Nichols (1998b:128) holds that "7% represents the lowest number of resemblant items that can safely be considered distinct from chance." Ringe explains why chance is such a problem in multilateral comparison:

> Because random chance gives rise to so many recurrent matchings involving so many lists in multilateral comparisons, overwhelming evidence would be required to demonstrate that the similarities between the languages in question were greater than could have arisen by chance alone. Indeed, it seems clear that the method of multilateral comparison could demonstrate that a set of languages are related only if that relationship were already obvious! Far from facilitating demonstrations of language relationship, multilateral comparison gratuitously introduces massive obstacles . . . most similarities found through multilateral comparison can easily be the result of chance . . . a large majority of his [Greenberg's Amerind] "etymologies" appear in no more than three or four of the eleven major groupings of languages which he compares; and unless the correspondences he has found are very exact and the sounds involved are relatively rare in the protolanguages of the eleven subgroups, it is clear that those similarities will not be distinguishable from chance resemblances. When we add to these considerations the fact that most of those eleven protolanguages have not even been reconstructed (so far as one can tell from Greenberg's book), and the fact that most of the first-order subgroups themselves were apparently posited on the basis of multilateral comparisons without careful mathematical verification, it is hard to escape the conclusion that the long-distance relationships posited in Greenberg 1987 rest on no solid foundation. (Ringe 1992:76)

Phoneme frequency within a language plays a role in how often one should expect chance matchings involving particular sounds in comparisons of that language with other languages. For example, 13 to 17 percent of English basic vocabulary begins with s, while only 6 to 9 percent begins with w; thus, given the greater number of initial s forms in English, one must expect a higher possible number of chance matchings for s than for w when English is compared with other languages (Ringe 1992:5). As Ringe demonstrates, the potential for accidental matching increases dramatically in each of the following: when one leaves the realm of basic vocabulary or when one increases the number of forms compared or when one permits the semantics of compared forms to vary even slightly. As Winston (1966:166–7) pointed out, there is a special problem here for Greenberg's application of mass (or multilateral) comparison:

> His [Greenberg's 1955, 1963] usual unit of comparison seems to be the sub-group rather than the individual language; but this is open to two objections. In the first place, Greenberg himself states that the establishment of correct sub-groups is more difficult than that of the main families, so that it can hardly be legitimate to let the latter depend upon the former. Secondly, even if it is granted that the sub-groups are correctly set up, if it is admissible to find correspondences in any of the languages of a sub-group and not in a single one throughout, the chances of accidental similarity occurring are clearly

considerably increased, and the value of the mass comparison method as a means of correcting for this correspondingly reduced. Greenberg's application of this method to the Afroasiatic family is worth considering. Of the seventy-eight suggested etymologies, fifty-seven extend to only two or three of the five proposed subgroups, and for the reasons given above have comparatively little evidential value. Of the remaining twenty-one, sixteen cover four sub-groups and only five cover all five; moreover, correspondences with Niger-Congo can be quoted for at least four of these critical twenty-one.

The possibility of accidental similarities in the application of multilateral comparison is greatly increased by the fact that Greenberg nowhere specifies precisely what constitutes an admissible resemblance or what criteria are used for deciding what constitutes sufficiently similar forms. This subjectivity in the methodology means that even greater accidental similarities will turn up in its application than would be the case if criteria for determining resemblance/similarities were made explicit (cf. Winston 1966:168).

Doerfer (1973[1963–75]:69–72) discusses two kinds of accidental similarity. His "statistical chance" has to do with what sorts of words and how many of them might be expected to be similar by chance. For example, the many names of American Indian languages which begin with *na-* (for example, Nahuatl, Nambicuara, Nanticoke, Naolan, Narragansett, Naskapi, Nass, Natchez, Natick, Navajo, etc.) are similar in their first syllable by sheer happenstance, statistical chance. His "dynamic chance" has to do with forms becoming more similar through convergence, that is, lexical parallels (known originally to have been different) which come about due to sounds converging through sound change. Cases of non-cognate similar forms are well known in historical linguistic handbooks, e.g. French *feu* 'fire' and German *Feuer* 'fire' (Meillet 1948[1914]:92–3) (French *feu* from Latin *focus* 'hearth, fireplace' [-k- > -g- > -Ø-; o > ö]; German *feuer* from Proto-Indo-European **pūr* [< **pwer-*, cf. Greek *pūr*] 'fire,' via Proto-Germanic **fūr-i* [cf. Old English *fȳr*]). As is well known, these cannot be cognates, since French *f* comes from PIE **bh*, while German *f* comes from PIE **p* (as prescribed by Grimm's law).[17] The word pair with English

---

[17] Greenberg (2000b:172–3) tries to dismiss this example of Meillet's, failing to grasp how serious it is for his approach. He says, "what Meillet fails to consider is how we know that French *feu* is only accidentally similar to German *Feuer*." He asserts that it is through mass comparison that we know; he says that it is by aligning the French word with its Spanish and Italian cognates (noticing also the velar consonant in these other languages in this word and also in *peu/poco* 'little, few') and then seeing so many other similarly aligned words in these languages which shows they are related. He adds that "German *Feuer*, English *fire*, etc. are not all that different from *pur* and *hur* since *p>f>h* is a very commonly encountered form of change and they agree in their final *r*." But this utterly misses the point. First, here he calls upon sound correspondences (at least a rudimentary notion thereof) in referring to the velars in the Romance languages and the agreeing final *r* in the others. Unless these are regular correspondences, however, the similarity will not help much. The French form *feu* without final *r* could easily be a cognate if loss of final *r* in that language, a commonly enough encountered change in other languages, were regular, while the *h* of *hur* could just as easily be an accident in spite of a commonly observed *p>f>h*

much: Spanish *mucho* 'much' is another well-known example. Spanish *mucho* is from Latin *multus* (< Indo-Europan *ml̥-to-*, suffixed form of *mel-* 'strong, great'), which underwent the well-known Spanish sound changes, *l* > *y* before *t*, then *yt* > *yč* > *č* (*multo-* > *muyto* > *muyčo* > *mucho*); English *much* is from Old English *micel, mycel* 'great,' 'much' (< Germanic *mik-ila* < Proto-Indo-European *meg-* 'great'; cf. Latin *magnus*, from the same root). Another case is English *day* : Spanish *día* 'day' (where these do not obey Grimm's law as true cognates do; English *day* < Old English *dæg* < Germanic *dagaz* 'day' < Proto-Indo-European *agh* 'day'; Spanish *día* < Latin *dies* 'day' < Proto-Indo-European *dyē-*, variant of *deiw-* 'to shine'). Another is Hungarian *fiú* 'boy': Romanian *fiú* 'boy, son' (Hungarian < Proto-Finno-Ugric *poji* 'boy, son'; Romanian *fiú* < Latin *filius* 'son' < Proto-Indo-European *dhi:-lyo-* derived from *dhe(i)-* 'to suck, suckle'). Others are Persian *bad* : English *bad*; Hindi *path* : English *path*, and so on. (See also Hock 1986:561.)

These phonetically similar words from basic vocabulary owe their resemblance to dynamic-chance convergence through subsequent sound change, not to inheritance from any common ancestral form. Swadesh (1954:314) made a similar point with respect to similarities among sounds due to convergent developments in sound changes. This underscores the importance of systematic correspondences over sheer similarities in sound, and it highlights the role of phonological typology. Languages with relatively simple phonemic inventories and similar phonotactics easily exhibit accidentally similar words, explaining, for example, why Polynesian languages, with simple phonemic inventories and phonotactics, have been proposed as the relatives of languages all over the world. True cognates, however, as mentioned earlier, need not be phonetically similar, depending on what sorts of sound changes the languages involved have undergone. Matisoff's (1990:111) example is telling: in a comparison of Mandarin Chinese *èr*/Armenian *erku*/Latin *duo*, all meaning 'two,' it is Chinese and Armenian (unrelated) which bear the greatest phonological similarity, but by accident, while Armenian and Latin (related) exhibit true sound correspondences (*(e)rk* : *dw*, seen to recur systematically, for example in Armenian *erku* 'two' : Greek *duo* 'two,' *erki-ul* : *dweid-* 'to fear') which witness their genetic relationship.

That through the action of sound changes originally distinct forms in related languages can become similar due to convergence is not surprising, since even within a single language originally distinct forms can converge, as in examples such as: English *son/sun* (Germanic *sunuz* 'son,' PIE *sewə-* 'to give birth,' *su(ə)-nu-* 'son' / PIE *seəwel-/*s(u)wel-/*s(u)wen-/*sun-*, Germanic

---

change, if it is not discovered to recur regularly. Also, the procedures used by Greenberg do not allow us to know that French *feu* fits with the other Romance languages rather than being, say, a loanword from German or even an accident.

sunnōn̄- 'sun'); English *eye/I* (Germanic **augōn* 'eye,' PIE **okʷ-* 'to see'; Germanic **ek* 'I,' PIE **egō* 'I'); English *lie/lie* (Germanic **ligjan* 'to lie, lay,' PIE **legh-* / Germanic **leugan* 'to tell a lie,' PIE **leugh-*) (see Rask 1993[1818]:14–15 for additional examples). A sobering example of dynamic chance is seen in the striking but coincidental similarities shared by Proto-Eastern-Miwokan and Indo-European personal pronominal affixes, cited above.

The manner in which comparisons are presented can encourage the appearance of greater phonetic similarities in putative cognate sets, though by accident. This happens when forms are compared in a chain where not all are equally similar to one another, but they are ordered visually to suggest greater similarity. When in a potential cognate set, say, three forms (F_1, F_2, F_3) are compared from three languages (L_1, L_2, L_3), one frequently notices that each neighboring pair in the comparison set (say F_1 with F_2, or F_2 with F_3) is arranged to exhibit the most similarities, but as one goes along the chain, forms at the extremes (e.g. F_1 with F_3) may bear little or no resemblance (Goodman 1970:121). An illustration of this is Greenberg's (1963:20–1) Niger-Congo set for 'mouth,' with *nyeŋ* near the beginning and *mu* at the end, not very similar to one another, but with such forms as *nyā, nyo, nu, inua, nwa, mwa*, etc. listed along the way, ordered so that adjacent pairs appear more similar phonetically, but with the extremes in the chain hardly so. Another example is from the Nilo-Saharan set for 'hair': *hambiri, hamni, kamur, amur, mul, muli* (Greenberg 1963:139), where the extremes, *hambiri* and *muli*, exhibit much less similarity than the adjacent forms in the chain. Thus, as Goodman (1970:121) says, "the more forms which are cited, the further apart may be the two most dissimilar ones, and the further apart these are, the greater the likelihood that some additional form from another language will resemble [by sheer accident] one of them." (For other examples involving European languages, see Gurevich 1999:126.)

Ruhlen's (1994a:183–206) proposed Proto-Amerind etymon **t'ana* 'child, sibling' shows how easy it is to find similarities by chance. The semantics of the glosses range over 'small,' 'person,' 'daughter,' 'woman,' 'old,' 'sister-in-law,' 'brother-in-law,' 'son,' 'father,' 'older brother,' 'boy,' 'child,' 'blood relative,' 'aunt,' 'uncle,' 'man,' 'male,' 'mother,' 'grandfather,' 'grandmother,' 'male of animals,' 'baby,' 'grandchild,' 'niece,' 'nephew,' 'cousin,' 'daughter-in-law,' 'wife,' 'girl,' 'female,' 'friend,' 'old woman,' 'first-born,' 'son-in-law,' and 'old man.' While many of the forms cited have some *t*-like sound + Vowel + some *n*-like sound, some do not share all these phonetic properties. For example, the *n*-like sound is apparently not necessary (given such forms as *tsuh-ki, u-tse-kwa*), while the *t*-like sound can be represented by *t', t, d, ts, s*, or *š*. Ruhlen's target template appears to be *TV(N)* (where *T* is any dental, alveolar, or alveopalatal sound vaguely similar to *t, V* is any vowel, and *(N)* is an optionally present nasal). It is not hard to find forms of the shape *TVN* or *TV* (more precisely *t/d/ts/s/čV(w/y)V(n/ŋ)*) with a gloss equivalent to one of those in the list above (e.g. a kinship term or a person of some sort) in virtually any language anywhere, e.g. English *son*; Finnish *tenava* 'kid, child'; German *Tante* 'aunt'; Japanese *tyoonan* 'eldest son'; Malay *dayang* 'damsel'; Maori *teina* 'younger brother, younger sister'; Somali *dallàan* 'child'; and so on.[18]

In short, the problem of chance/accident is extremely serious, one not properly attended to in numerous proposals of deeper family relationships.

7.12 Sound–meaning isomorphism

Meillet advocated permitting only comparisons which involve both sound and meaning together (urged also by Greenberg 1957, 1963, 1987), and this is held by historical linguists to be an established principle. Similarities in sound alone (e.g. presence of a tonal system in compared languages) or in meaning alone (e.g. grammatical gender in compared languages) are not reliable, since they are often independent of genetic relationship, due to diffusion, accident, typological tendencies, etc. In Meillet's (1948[1921]:90) words:

Chinese and a language of Sudan or Dahomey such as Ewe, for example, may both use short and generally monosyllabic words, make contrastive use of tone, and base their grammar on word order and the use of auxiliary words, but it does not follow from this that Chinese and Ewe are related, since the concrete detail of their forms does not coincide; *only coincidence of the material means of expression is probative*. (Our emphasis, LC/WP)

This principle, and in particular violations of it, have played an important role in the history of African linguistics (see Chapter 6).

7.13 No non-linguistic evidence

Another valid principle permits only linguistic information, and no non-linguistic considerations, as evidence of genetic relationship among languages (Greenberg 1957, 1963). As Gabelentz (1891:157) put it, "the only sure means for recognizing a [genetic] relationship lies in the languages themselves."[19] Shared cultural traits, mythology, folklore, technologies, and human biological traits must be eliminated from arguments for linguistic kinship. The wisdom of this principle is seen against the backdrop of the many outlandish proposals based on non-linguistic evidence. For example, some earlier African classifications proposed that Ari (Omotic) belongs to either Nilo-Saharan or Sudanic "because the Ari people are Negroes," that Moru and Madi belong to Sudanic because they are located in central Africa, or that Fula is Hamitic because the

---

[18] Even English *daughter* (Old English *dohtor*, PIE **dhughəter*) fits in view of such forms as *tsuh-ki* and *u-tse-kwa* in the list.

[19] "Das einzig untrügliche Mittel, eine Verwandtschaft zu erkennen liegt in den Sprachen selbst."

Fulani herd cattle, are Moslems, and are tall and Caucasoid (Fleming 1987:207; cf. Clackson 1994:12–14.)[20]

It is too frequently assumed in recent work seeking correlations between languages and genes that somehow the phylogenetic classification of human genetic groups may help sort out difficulties in the genealogical classification of the languages. But the frequent expectation of a direct association between language and genes (assumption of parallel descent, following, for example, Cavalli-Sforza *et al.* 1988, 1989, 1992) is wrong. Work on phylogenetic linguistic–human genetic comparisons needs to take seriously into account (1) that while a person has only one set of genes (for life), a person can be multilingual, representing multiple languages; (2) that individuals (and communities) can abandon one language and adopt another, but people do not abandon their genes nor adopt new ones – *language shift* (language replacement) is a common fact of linguistic life; there is no deterministic connection between languages and gene pools. Languages become extinct in populations which survive genetically (language replacement and extinction are frequent). We cannot assume, *a priori*, that linguistic history and human biological history will correlate (Blount 1990:15; Boas 1911:6–10, Moore 1994; Spuhler 1979). Since human genetic and linguistic lines of descent very often do not match, it cannot be assumed that non-linguistic facts from human biology can be reliable evidence of genetic relationships among languages.

7.14   Erroneous morphological analysis

Where compared words are assumed to be made up of constituent morphemes, it is necessary to show that the segmented morphemes (roots and affixes) in fact exist in the particular language. Unfortunately, unmotivated morphological segmentation is found frequently in proposals of remote relationship. Similarly, undetected morpheme divisions cause difficulties and are also a frequent problem. Both of these can make the compared languages seem to have more in common than they actually do. To cite one example, Greenberg compared Tzotzil (Mayan) *ti ʔil* 'hole' with Lake Miwok *talokh* 'hole,' Atakapa *tol* 'anus,' Totonac *tan* 'buttocks,' Takelma *telkan* 'buttocks' as evidence for his Amerind hypothesis (Greenberg 1987:152); however, the Tzotzil form is *ti ʔ-il*, meaning 'edge, border, outskirts, lips, mouth,' but not 'hole,' from *ti ʔ* 'mouth' + *-il* 'indefinite possessive suffix.' The appropriate comparison, the root *ti ʔ* 'mouth,' bears no particular phonetic resemblance to the other forms listed. Failure to take the morpheme boundary into account in this example results in a seeming

---

[20] Violations of this principle have been particularly frequent in classifications of American Indian languages, and when it came to defending his Amerind proposal, even Greenberg himself seems to have forgotten his principle in numerous publications of his. (See Bolnick *et al.* 2004.)

but unreal lexical matching based on superficial similarity which cannot tell its 'anuses' from a 'hole in the ground.' (See Chapter 9 for other examples.).

The other problem is that of inserted morpheme boundaries where none is justified. For example, Greenberg (1987:108) arbitrarily segmented Tunebo *baxi-ta* 'machete' (a loan from Spanish *machete*, mentioned above); this erroneous morphological segmentation falsely makes the form appear more similar to the other forms cited as putative cognates, Cabecar *bak* and Andaqui *boxo-(ka)* 'axe.'[21] In another instance, as Poser shows, Greenberg (1987:214, 246), following Rivet, segmented Yurumanguí (a language of Colombia which he takes to be connected with "Hokan") *joima* 'saliva' as *jo* 'mouth' + *ima* 'water,' but there is no evidence in the data on Yurumanguí that *joima* is morphologically complex (Poser 1992:218). Greenberg had assumed a connection between *joima* 'saliva' and *čuma* 'to drink,' which he then segmented as *č-uma*, but "again there is no language-internal evidence that *č* is a prefix" (Poser 1992:218). There is no basis for any of the four morphemes posited, *jo* 'mouth,' *ima* 'water,' *č-* 'prefix,' and *uma* 'drink,' though such unmotivated segmentation does suggest greater similarity with some of the forms in other languages to which Greenberg compared them.

7.15   Non-cognates

Often unrelated forms from related languages, joined together in the belief that they might be cognates, are then compared further with forms from other language families as evidence for even more distant relationships. However, if the forms are not even cognates within their own family, any further comparison with forms from languages outside the family is untrustworthy.[22] Cases from Olson's (1964, 1965) well-known Chipaya–Mayan hypothesis illustrate the difficulty (see Campbell 1973[1993]). Tzotzil *ay(in)* 'to be born' (actually from Proto-Mayan **ar-* 'there is/are,' Proto-Tzotzilan **ay-an* 'to live, to be born') is not cognate with *ya?* (actually *yah*) 'pain' of the other Mayan languages listed in this set (from Proto-Mayan **yah* 'pain, hurt'), though its inclusion makes Mayan seem phonetically more like Chipaya (of Bolivia) *ay(in)* 'to hurt.' Yucatec Maya *čal(tun)* 'extended (rock)' is compared to non-cognate *č'en* 'rock, cave' in other Mayan languages; the true Yucatec cognate would have been *č'e?en* 'well' (and 'cave of water') (from Proto-Mayan **k'e?n* 'rock,

---

[21] The only other form in this set, Cuitlatec *navaxo* 'knife,' as mentioned earlier, is also borrowed from Spanish.

[22] It is possible that some of the non-cognate material within erroneously proposed cognate sets may have a more extended history of its own and therefore could turn out to be cognate with forms compared from languages where one suspects a distant genetic relationship. However, such forms do not warrant nearly as much confidence as do real cognate sets which have a demonstrable etymology within their own families and therefore, due to their attested age in that group, might be candidates for evidence of even more remote connections.

cave'). Yucatec *čal(tun)* means 'cistern, deposit of water, porous cliff where there is water' (from *čal* 'sweat, liquid' + *tun* 'stone,' cf. Proto-Mayan **to:n* 'stone'). The non-cognate *čaltun* suggests greater similarity to Chipaya *čara* 'rock (flat, long)' with which the set is compared than the **k'eʔn* etymon does, though most of the phonetic similarity is borne by the much less plausible *čal* 'sweat, liquid.'

7.15.1 Forms of limited scope: "reaching down"

Related to the appeal to non-cognate forms from a language family is the tendency for distant genetic relationship enthusiasts to compare a word from but one language (or a very few languages) of one family with some word thought to be similar in one (or a few) languages in some other family – Larry Trask (1999) called this "reaching down." A form which has a clearly established etymology in its own family by virtue of having cognates in a number of sister languages stands a better chance of perhaps having cognate associations with words of languages that may be even more remotely related than some isolated form does in some language which has no known cognates elsewhere within its family and hence no *prima facie* evidence of potential greater age. Inspectionally resemblant lexical sets of this sort are not convincing. Meillet's etymological principle for established families should be considered an important heuristic for distant genetic proposals as well:

> When an initial "proto language" is to be reconstructed, the number of witnesses which a word has should be taken into account. An agreement of two languages, if it is not total, risks being fortuitous. But, if the agreement extends to three, four or five very distinct languages [of the same family], chance becomes less probable. (Meillet 1925:38; Rankin's 1992:331 translation)

Meillet's heuristic is that evidence is needed from more than one branch and the more languages and branches represented the better (see Salmons 1992a, 1992b, 1997; Trask 1996:394). Numerous examples of "reaching down" are seen in Chapter 9 in forms presented in favor of the Nostratic hypothesis.

7.15.2 Neglect of known history

Another related problem is that of isolated forms which appear similar to forms from other languages with which they are compared, but when the known history is brought into the picture, the similarity is shown to be fortuitous. For example, in a set labeled 'dance' Greenberg (1987:148) compared Koasati (Muskogean) *bit* 'dance' with Mayan forms for 'dance' or 'sing' (e.g. K'iche' *bis* [actually *b'i:š*], Huastec *bišom*, etc.); however, Koasati *b* comes from Proto-Muskogean **kʷ*; the Muskogean root was **kʷit-* 'to press down,' where 'dance' is a semantic shift in Koasati alone, applied first to stomp dances (Kimball 1992:456). Only neglect of Koasati's known history (that *b* historically comes from k^w) permits the Koasati form to be seen as similar to Mayan. It is not uncommon in proposals of distant genetic relationship to encounter forms from one language which exhibit similarities to forms in another language where the similarity is known to be due to recent changes in the individual history of one of the languages – in effect anachronisms. In such cases, when the known history of the languages is brought back into the picture, the similarity disappears. (For other examples, see Chapter 9.)

7.16   Spurious forms

Another problem found in a number of proposed distant genetic relationships is that of non-existent "data," i.e. the "bookkeeping" problems and "scribal" errors that result in spurious forms being compared. For example, Brown and Witkowski (1979:41) in their Mayan–Mixe-Zoquean hypothesis compared Mixe-Zoquean forms meaning 'shell' with K'iche' *sak'*, said to mean 'lobster,' but which actually means only 'grasshopper' – a mistranslation of the Spanish gloss *langosta* given for the meaning of K'iche' *sak'*, where Spanish *langosta* means 'grasshopper' in Guatemalan Spanish, not 'lobster' as in other varieties of Spanish. While a 'shell'–'lobster' comparison is already somewhat stretched semantically, the 'shell'–'grasshopper' connection that would be required for this set to work is out of the question. In another instance, Gurov (1989) suggested Kusunda (an isolate) is related to Yenisseian languages on the basis of only nineteen unclear lexical parallels, one of which was Kusunda *tou* 'snake,' the gloss for which was misread as 'smoke' and compared to Proto-Yenisseian *du(h)* 'smoke' (cited in van Driem 2001:260). Errors of this sort can be very serious, such as in the instance where "none of the entries listed as Quapaw [in Greenberg 1987] is from that language," but rather are from Biloxi and Ofo (Rankin 1992:342). Poser (1992) points out that of the forms Greenberg (1987) presented as "Salinan," four are actually from Chumash (an unrelated language) and eight of the others are just spurious. Skewed forms also often show up due to philological mishandling of the sources. For example, Greenberg (1987) systematically mistransliterated the <v> and <e> of his Creek source as *u* and *e*, although these symbolize /a/ and /i/ respectively. Thus Greenberg gives <vne> 'I' as *une* rather than the accurate *ani* (Kimball 1992:448).

Trask (2001) presented an interesting example in which a proposed genetic relationship between Basque and Etruscan fails because the evidence on both sides is spurious. Both Basque and Etruscan, at least to the present, have no known relatives. In this example, a Spanish scholar announced a "breakthrough" showing these two languages to be related, uncritically reported in leading newspapers, including *Le Monde* in Paris and *The Times* in London. The single pair of words reported which he supposed demonstrated the relationship was Basque *dulla* 'scythe' and Etruscan *dula* 'scythe,' which he regarded as "practically identical," and therefore strong evidence for joining these two languages. As Trask points out, the alleged Etruscan word *dula* does not exist. No word of this form is found in the Etruscan corpus, regardless of meaning, and moreover, such a word would be impossible: Etruscan had no /d/; the Etruscan alphabet, taken from Greek, eliminated the letter "D" – they could not even write a word such as *dula*. Worse, Basque has no word *dulla* either. In Trask's words, "these scholarly breakthroughs are so much easier to achieve, of course, if you're allowed to invent your own data. Real data can be so tiresomely unhelpful." As Poser (1992:224) observes, spurious forms "are of no comparative value, no matter what methodology one may favor."

7.17   A single etymon as evidence for multiple cognate sets

Another common error in proposals of distant genetic relationship is that of presenting a single form as evidence for more than one proposed cognate set. A single form/etymon in one language cannot simultaneously be cognate with independent multiple forms in another language. The only exception – not a true exception – is when the two or more words of the one language (which are compared to but a single word in another) are derived historically or synchronically from a single original linguistic element, meaning that in reality only one cognate set is involved. An example (somewhat forced) would be, for instance, if, say, English *eyeball* were compared to German *Auge* 'eye' in one proposed cognate set and then *eyelash* were compared to German *Auge* 'eye' in an entirely different cognate set. Since both the English forms are based historically on the root *eye-* (the only part of *eyeball* and *eyelash* that is cognate with German *Auge*), this constitutes not two independent votes for the English–German kinship, but only one.

For an actual example in a proposed "macro-family," Greenberg (1987:150, 162) cites the single Choctaw form *ati* in two separate sets; he gives *ti* 'wing,' actually *ati* 'edge, margin, a border, a wing (as of a building),' in a cognate set labeled 'feather,' and then he gives *əti* (misrecorded for *ati*) in the set labeled 'wing.' In this case the Choctaw form can scarcely be cognate with either one (and impossible logically to be cognate with both), since 'wing' could enter the picture only if it were a wing of a building that was intended (Kimball 1992:458, 475).

Closely related to this is the mistake of separating different forms which are known to be cognates within their own families in order to compare them in sets assumed to be different, assuming them to be multiple pieces of evidence for the proposed distant genetic relationship. For example, under M A N ₁ Greenberg (1987:242) listed Central Pomo *čač* (i.e. *ča:č'*), but he put the Eastern Pomo

Table 7.4 *The* FIRE *'word family' in Sahaptian–Klamath–Tsimshian comparison*

	fire	make fire	burn	wood	sun, sky	warm
Nez Perce			ʔaalik		hawlaxhawlax	luʔuq-'ic
Sahaptin	ilkw-S	ilk	ilkw-as			
Klamath	loloG-s	s-likw-			Galo:	loqwa
Coast Tsimshian	læk	s-lkəs	gwælək	læk/ʔoɬg	laxa	
Nass-Gitksan	lakw			*kwælkw	ɬoq-s	

cognate *ka:kʰ* in a different "cognate" set, MAN₂ (Greenberg 1987:243) (see Mithun 1990:323–4).

7.18 "Word families" or "oblique cognates"

A strategy sometimes employed is to look for lexical doublets or "families" of lexically related forms which are presented as sets of interconnected cognates in the languages compared and thought somehow to be more powerful witnesses of genetic relationship than isolated cognate sets might be. Some assert that when comparable interrelated lexical sets are found across compared languages, the likelihood of chance accounting for this occurrence is significantly reduced (for example, see Pinnow 1985; DeLancey *et al.* 1988). When whole sets of seemingly interrelated words appear independently in the languages compared, it creates more sympathy towards them as possible cognates than for individual isolated lexical resemblances, and this is potentially valuable evidence. Nevertheless, the sort of examples that are sometimes presented fall short of being compelling. DeLancey *et al.* (1988) illustrate this strategy in their comparison in Sahaptian, Klamath, and Tsimshian of words in what they call "the FIRE family" (DeLancey *et al.* 1988:205–6); the glosses of the forms compared include 'fire,' 'make fire,' 'burn,' 'wood,' 'sun/sky,' 'cook/dry,' 'warm,' and a few others. The example in Table 7.4 is sufficient to review what the problems with the strategy may be.

We note that if compared languages had a word that was similar for non-genetic reasons (accident, borrowing, onomatopoeia, etc.), it is quite likely that through normal word-formation processes, the languages could end up with a series of interconnected forms internal to each of the compared languages which would constitute a single comparison set for purposes of seeking genetic relationships. For example, the English noun *light* (derived from Proto-Indo-European **leuk-*) is similar to the forms of the Sahaptian–Klamath–Tsimshian "fire" word family. We could see English *to light* as a second point of contact in an English word family. However, given that *to light* is presumably independently derived from *light*, these multiple words in the comparison set still constitute but a single point of comparison with the words of the Sahaptian–Klamath–Tsimshian "fire" word family. As pointed out in Campbell (1997a:240), Finnish has various similar forms with similar meanings which could be compared to those of the words of the Sahaptian–Klamath–Tsimshian "fire" word family: *liekki* 'flame, small fire,' *liekehti-* 'to burn, flame,' *liekehdintä* 'blazing' (cf. 'warm'), *lieska* 'flame (fire),' *liesi* 'hearth, stove,' *leisku-* 'to burn, blaze, flash, flare,' *leiskahta-* 'to flame, blaze.' However, this Finnish FIRE word family does not indicate several points of comparison with the "fire" word family words of Sahaptian, Klamath, and Tsimshian. It reflects an accidental similarity with a root, which happens to have several related words derived from it.

Another way where word families might match in genetically insignificant ways is when expressive symbolism is involved, as, for example, presumably with what is behind the similarity among the English words *sleek, slick, slide, slime, slink, slither, slip* or among *shine, shimmer, sheen*. The word-family strategy can also lead to comparisons of forms which have no etymological connection among themselves, in spite of assumptions that this is the case (see Campbell 1997a:240 for examples from Pinnow's 1985 comparisons of "Na-Dene" forms).

Given these sorts of problems, the word-family approach to comparison is not successful. Since many of the same problems of identifying ordinary cognates carry over into attempts to identify word families as interlaced cognate sets, caution is called for in dealing with examples of this sort proposed as evidence of distant genetic relationship.

7.19   Pronouns and proposals of distant genetic relationship

In recent years, what seems like a cottage industry of papers dealing with pronouns in various proposed distant genetic relationships has arisen (see Campbell 1994b; Gordon 1995; Nichols 2003:292–5; Nichols and Peterson 1996, 1998; Ruhlen 1994a, 1994b, 1995a; Willerman 1994). While it is good that the matter is getting a hearing, there is considerable confusion concerning the role of pronouns as possible evidence of genetic affiliation and the claims made about them, and for that reason we attempt to clarify the situation here.

We begin by exposing problems with two popular claims frequently encountered in writings favoring long-range comparisons: (1) that pronouns are rarely borrowed, and (2) that shared pronoun patterns defy chance. We follow this with discussion of claims about pronoun evidence for the Amerind hypothesis, since it has received the most attention.

The claim that pronouns are rarely borrowed is common. For example, Greenberg and Ruhlen (1992:97) assert "pronominal affixes are among the most stable elements in language: they are almost never borrowed." Shevoroshkin (1989a:6) is sure that "pronouns of the sort 'I,' 'me,' 'thou,' 'thee' are not borrowed from language to language; they are inherited." Nichols and Peterson (1996:337) also assert that "pronouns are almost always inherited," not borrowed.

This common perception is nevertheless a misconception. Many instances of pronoun borrowing are known. It is well known that English *they, their, them* are borrowed from Scandinavian (replacing Old English *hie, hiera, him,* respectively; cf. Baugh 1957:120, 194). Surely we cannot deny the borrowing of pronouns elsewhere, when we have clear examples in our own linguistic backyard. Examples of borrowed pronouns are not uncommon in languages of southeast Asia. For example, Indonesian *saya* 'I' and *kalian* 'you (pl)' are borrowed from Sanskrit (Tadmor 2003); Thai *khun* 'you' is from Sanskrit (Suthiwan 2003); in Chamic languages afer the breakup of Proto-Chamic *BiN* 'we' and *ih* 'you, thou' were both borrowed from Mon-Khmer (Thurgood 1994:337, 338, 351, 356). Thomason and Everett (2001) cite many other case of borrowed pronouns, including cases where pronominal suffixes have been borrowed, and they argue that Pirahã has borrowed a majority of its pronouns. For other examples of borrowing of pronouns see Gedney (1989[1976]:124), Kinkade (2005), Matisoff (1990:113), Newman (1977:306–9, 1979a:218–23, 1979b:305–7, 1980:156), Rhodes (1977:9), and Thomason and Kaufman (1988:219–20, 223–8, 235); Campbell (1997a:244–5) presents several examples from various American Indian languages. Dixon (2002:26) believes that pronouns "are frequently borrowed" in Australia, and others document borrowing in a number of specific Australian languages (see Dench 1994, 2001). Even Ruhlen (1994a:257) allows for the possibility that Nahali borrowed 'you sg' from Dravidian. As Gedney (1989[1976]:123) points out:

pronouns in Southeast Asian languages are especially susceptible to change and innovation. Apparently, in the traditional, stratified, social situation, polite pronouns rather rapidly become "worn out," so to speak, tending to become less polite, with the result that new, fresher, more polite pronouns had to be introduced from time to time . . . The Thai languages of Kwangsi and adjacent parts of North Vietnam have adopted the Cantonese words for 'you' and 'I.' One suspects that this drastic change involved a rejection of the traditional social structure.

The result of all this is that each Thai language shows differences from the others in its inventory of pronouns. (Gedney 1989[1976]:124)

Warembori (an isolate in Papua New Guinea) has borrowed its pronouns: "the first- and second-person singular are transparent Austronesian loans, with even the inclusive-exclusive distinction being taken over: PAN [Proto-Austronesian] *kami* (1PL EXCL) > War[embori] *ami*; PAN *kita* (1PL INCLU) > War *ki*" (Foley 2000:392).

Moreover, it is well established that certain aspects of pronominal systems are quite easily influenced by contact from other languages, e.g. the widespread diffusion of the inclusive/exclusive pronominal category in a number of languages of Western North America (Jacobsen 1980), and the shift from independent plural pronominal affixes to ones structurally composed of the singular pronominal marker plus a plural affix (cf. Robertson 1992).

A second misconception, also prevalent but not as common as the first, is that shared pronoun patterns/paradigms defy chance and therefore qualify as evidence of genetic relationship. This is a common argument presented on behalf of Altaic and Nostratic, for example (see Chapter 9), where subject and object forms of pronouns seem to have differences which recur in various of the languages thought to be related to one another. Patterned grammatical material can constitute strong arguments for genetic relationship if nothing else accounts for the shared patterns, but that is often not the case in pronominal paradigms. It is well established also that pronominal systems seem to be subject to analogical reformations, and are also dominated by tendencies towards iconic symbolization, as other deictic markers are (cf. Gedney 1989[1976]; Nichols 2003). Meillet (1948:89–90, cited in Nichols 2003:292) pointed out early that the pronouns of Indo-European languages resemble each other less than cognate nouns and verbs do. Nichols (2003) explains the problems here very well. She points out that pronouns are "prone to analogical reshaping, restructuring due to the pragmatics of deference and respect, phonosymbolic pressures, etc." (Nichols 2003:292). Viewed as a set rather than as individual elements, the paradigm is often affected by its own phonological and morphological structure. Aspects of phonology such as alliteration and rhyme link and affect elements in the set. These properties, called "resonance" (Nichols 2003:292), phonosymbolize elements of the meaning in deictic systems, and resonance in pronominal systems typically has recurrent phonological properties that connect with meanings in the system (person, number, case), for example "they make crucial use of nasals; and they oppose labial (often [m]) to dental articulations" (Nichols 2003:292). "The resonant patterns and resonant devices [e.g. rhyme, alliteration, shared vowels to link forms] differ from language to language" (Nichols 2003:292), but they typically are secondary developments, not original and thus not good evidence of genetic relationship. These phonosymbolic resonance properties are not limited merely to pronominal systems, but characterize other deictic oppositions and nursery-word oppositions ('mama–papa') (see Nichols 2003:294).

Given that pronouns can indeed be borrowed and that similarities among pronominal systems may involve the "resonance" factors Nichols (2003) speaks of, it is not surprising that prominent historical linguists have spoken against similarities among pronouns as evidence of genetic relationship. Meillet (1948[1921]:89–90) explains this:

It goes without saying that in order to establish genetic relatedness of languages one must disregard everything that can be explained by general conditions common to all languages. For instance, pronouns must be short words, clearly composed of easily pronounced sounds, generally without consonant clusters. The consequence is that *pronouns are similar in almost all languages*, though this does not imply a common origin. On the other hand, pronouns often show little resemblance in languages that are otherwise quite similar . . . Even forms that descend from the same protoform, like French *nous* and English *us*, may no longer have a single element in common (the French s is purely graphic). *Therefore, pronouns must be used with caution in establishing relatedness of languages*. (Our emphasis, LC/WP)

7.19.1   Amerind pronoun arguments

It is claimed that there is a widespread pronominal pattern among American Indian languages with *n* for 'first person' and *m* for 'second person,' and it is claimed that this constitutes evidence for Greenberg's (1987) Amerind hypothesis. Proponents of Greenberg's classification believe the pronoun argument convincing, that the putative *n*/*m* pronoun pattern is "the most telling datum favoring the Amerind phylum" (Ruhlen 1994a:123, also 1994a:21; cf. Fleming 1987:196, Ruhlen 1994a:41, 253, 271–2, 1994b:178), and they repeat it frequently. Greenberg and Ruhlen contrast this with pronouns elsewhere:

The enormously widespread *n* first person and *m* second person in the Americas as against *m* first person and *t* second person in Europe and Northern Asia is powerful evidence which requires explanation. (Greenberg 1990c:19)

it [the *n*/*m* pattern] also serves to distinguish the Amerind family from the world's other language families. In a recent study of personal pronouns in the world's languages (Ruhlen [1994a:252–60]) I found that the Amerind pattern (*n*- 'I' vs. *m*- 'thou') is virtually nonexistent elsewhere in the world. (Ruhlen 1994b:178)

Here Greenberg and Ruhlen appear to forget the 'first-person' *m* which they find in several "Amerind" groups (Greenberg 1987:276; Ruhlen 1994a:141, 228–9, 258) and do not acknowledge the widespread **ta/tu* 'thou' suggested by Swadesh (1960:909) as Proto-American. That is, if the *n*/*m* pattern distinguishes Amerind from Europe and northern Asia with an alleged *m/t* pattern, then why do several Amerind groups exhibit the pronoun forms *m* 'first person' or *t* 'second person' that Greenberg attributes to Eurasiatic? Moreover, in spite of the supposed clear distinction in pronouns between Amerind and other languages of the world, Ruhlen could nevertheless equate several putative Amerind pronouns with Nostratic counterparts, specifically Amerind **na* 'I, we' with Nostratic **na* 'we,' Amerind *ma 'we' (and 'I') with Nostratic *mä 'we inclusive' (and 'I'), and Amerind *na 'we, I' with Nostratic *ni 'we exclusive' (Ruhlen 1994a:228–9, 231). This makes the "Amerind" pronoun claim less "powerful," but no less in need of an "explanation." In short, the claimed distribution has been overstated (see Goddard and Campbell 1994). A brief review of the history of claims about these pronoun patterns, together with the varied explanations proposed to account for them, will help to put the matter in perspective.

7.19.2   Some history

The observation that there are pronoun similarities among many American Indian (and other) languages is by no means new (see Edwards 1823[1787]:18, Gilij 1965[1780–4]:274; Brinton 1859:12, etc). By 1870, the widespread n of 'first person' in various American Indian languages was well known (Sayce 1874–5:216; Tolmie and Dawson 1884:128–9; Brinton 1890[1888]:396.) Boas (1917:5) knew the American Indian pronoun facts, but thought they would submit to "psychological explanations" (Haas 1966:102). Boas cited Gatschet, who also did not attribute these necessarily to genetic inheritance (Haas 1966:102). Kroeber (1913:399), too, was aware of the American distribution of the n/m pronominal markers (stating it was a well-known example); he realized that a genetic explanation was not necessarily required; he opted for diffusion/language contact as the probable explanation. The alleged n/m pronoun pattern was also cited by Trombetti (1905) and it became well known through the Sapir–Michelson debates (Michelson 1914, 1915; Sapir 1915a, 1915c) and Sapir's (1918) review of a book on Mosetén in the first volume of the *International Journal of American Linguistics*. In 1920 Sapir listed "persistence of n- 'I' [and] m- 'thou'" as "Proto-American possibilities" (Sapir 1990[n.d.]:86; Golla 1984:452). Sapir (1918:184) spoke of "the curiously widespread American second person singular in m-," and said of the widely talked about widespread n for 'first person,' "how in the Hell are you going to explain general American n- 'I' except genetically?" (letter from Sapir to Speck in 1918, Darnell 1990:122; cf. also his letter to Kroeber in October of 1920, Golla 1984:316). Bertolazo Stella (1929[1928]:98–109) discussed at length "o typo n- do pronombre da primeira pessoa" [the n- type of the first-person pronoun] and the "typo m- do pronombre da segunda pessoa" [m- type of the second-person pronoun], with examples from many American Indian languages, similar to Greenberg's (1987) presentation.

As these citations show, the observations about pronouns were not new arguments when Greenberg (1987) presented them as evidence of his "Amerind" hypothesis, but rather were old controversies (Ruhlen 1987a:222, 1994a:253). Although the pronoun pattern was widely recognized, it was not generally assumed that a common genetic heritage was necessarily the explanation:

Many American Indian languages, North as well as South, show resemblance in the pronominal system, often *n* for the first person, *m* or *p* for second person. Whether this is the result of common origin, chance, or borrowing has never been proved, but the resemblance should not be used as evidence of genetic connection between any two languages. (Mason 1950:163)

There were also genetic claims, as well,:

At least two short elements, *n* for the first person pronoun and *m* for the second . . . are so numerous as to virtually eliminate the chance factor despite their brevity. In fact, even if one disregarded the cases which have one or the other and included only the languages which have both *n* and *m* for first and second person respectively . . . the list of language groups would still be fairly impressive. It would include families of the Penutian and Hokan-Coahuiltecan phyla, Aztectanoan, Chibchan, and Mapuche. (Swadesh 1954:311–12)

Others had also noticed these similarities among the pronouns also in diverse languages of the world, but denied the genetic explanation, e.g. Wundt (1900:33) and Trombetti (1905:44). It will pay us to look at the alternative explanations offered.

7.19.3   Proposed explanations of the American Indian pronoun patterns

Greenberg (1989:113) asserts of the alleged pronoun pattern that since "a highly improbable event should have recurred more than a hundred times exceeds the bounds of credibility . . . [it] cannot be explained plausibly except as the result of genetic inheritance." However, the assumption of genetic inheritance is by no means necessary nor is it the only explanation available. Boas (1917:5) asked whether the pronoun pattern could be "due to obscure psychological causes rather than to genetic relationship." The following are a few factors which have been proposed which may make Boas' "psychological causes" less "obscure."

(1) Certain sounds, especially nasals, are to be *expected in grammatical morphemes*, in particular in pronoun markers:

The repeated appearance in different languages of the same consonants in grammatical functions is a real phenomenon of human language and as such requires an explanation. One contributing factor is the well known general linguistic trait that a single language typically uses only a fraction of its full complement of consonants to form its primary grammatical morphemes and hence must use the same consonants over and over in different functions (Floyd 1981). The consonants that are used tend to be the ones that are least marked . . . specifically, the least marked consonants of the languages of the world include *m, n, t, k*, and *s* (cf. Ruhlen 1987a:11). As a result of this economy and, so to speak, lack of originality in the use of consonants, there is a much greater than chance agreement among the languages of the world on what consonants are used in grammatical elements. It is thus to be expected a priori that these consonants will show up again and again in different languages and language groups marking, say, first or second person, and many languages will therefore come to have similar pronominal systems by this factor alone. (Goddard and Campbell 1994:196–7)

German inflectional endings are constrained such that the only vowel found is schwa, the only consonants /d, m, n, r, s, t/. Of Latin's fifteen consonants, only /b, d, m, n, r, s, t, w/ occur in inflectional endings; Hebrew permits only eight of twenty-two; of Ancient Greek's fifteen consonants, only /t, θ, k, m, n, r, s/ occur in inflectional morphemes (Floyd 1981). Even Trombetti (1905:89) had realized something of the limited sounds encountered in pronominal forms in the world's languages: "In all these old pronominal forms only the vowels *a, i, u*, the stop consonants *k, t* and the nasals *n, m* are found. These are certainly primordial sounds."[23] The likelihood of finding non-significant phonological matchings in pronominal markers was emphasized by Meillet (1948[1921]:89–90), cited above (cf. Matisoff 1990:9).[24] These limitations mean that consonants from the same small set recur frequently in grammatical affixes of the world's languages, and therefore the probability of an accidental agreement in compared grammatical morphemes is high, and frequently attested. (Cf. Nichols 2003.)

(2) Nasals in particular are found in grammatical morphemes precisely because they are the most *perceptually salient* of all consonants (Maddieson 1984:70). "[T]he more distinctive speech sounds . . . achieve the most successful transmission of a message." Nasals "are rarely subject to confusion with other types of consonants," and "there is value in incorporating such sounds [nasals] into any language" (Maddieson 1984:70).[25] The dental/alveolar nasal (*n*) is most common, with the bilabial (*m*) also common; most languages have both (Maddieson 1984:60, 69). These facts would seem to explain why nasals, especially *n* and *m*, show up in markers of pronouns so frequently in languages everywhere.[26] This is borne out in, for example, in Ruhlen's (1994a:252–60) survey of first- and second-person pronouns in the world's languages. He assembled examples for 34 distinct genetic groupings (many of which represent very

---

[23] "In tutte queste antichissime forme pronominali si trovano soltanto le vocali *a, i, u*, le consonanti esplosive *k, t* e le nasali *n, m*. Questi sono certamente suoni primordiali . . ."

[24] Another source of new consonants in pronouns is reanalysis, where a consonant from another word or element that happens to be adjacent to the pronoun may be reinterpreted as part of the pronoun (Campbell 1988:601–2). For example, Swedish replaced the old 'second-person- plural pronoun' *i* with *ni*; the added *n-* was from the second-plural suffix *-en* of verbs, which preceded the pronoun in many instances (Haugen 1976:375, 304). A parallel example mentioned above is the Quechua reanalysis which resulted in *-ni-*, formerly the empty morph used to separate consonants that otherwise would come together over morpheme boundaries, reanalyzed as the 'first-person-singular pronoun.' Note the *n* in both cases.

[25] This may explain such observations as, "Thus, word-initial nasal consonants such as *m-* and *n-* often remain intact for millennia" (Ruhlen 1990:76), and "the old *n* of proto-Indo-European [was] retained in English practically intact" (Swadesh 1960:898).

[26] We suspect that the perceptual salience of nasals and the importance in communication of being able successfully to distinguish negative utterances from affirmative ones combine to help explain why negative markers in languages around the world so typically have *n* or *m*, why *ma* and *nV* or something very similar are so frequent.

long-range and controversial proposals). For 'I' we find 26 of the 34 exhibiting a nasal as the sole or primary consonant of one of the pronouns given, with 3 others which also contain a nasal but not as the main consonant; only 6 of the 34 have no nasal. Similarly for 'thou,' 16 of the 34 have a nasal as the sole or primary consonant, 3 others also contain nasal consonants, and only 13 have no nasal (for some, e.g. Etruscan, Sumerian, no forms are given); in some instances constituent language groups inside the 34 groupings exhibit nasals while the general form offered to represent the overarching genetic unit containing them does not; for example, Na-Dene, represented by *wǐ 'thou,' contains Athabaskan as a subordinate unit, which has *nani* ∼ *nine* ∼*niŋ* ∼ *nì*; Ruhlen's Caucasian pronoun forms lack nasals, but its constitute East Caucasian is represented by *mi(n)/me(n)*. Specifically, for 'I,' 11 of the 34 exhibit the nasal *n*, as claimed for Amerind. (The other consonants exhibited in the non-nasal cases for 'I' are predominantly *t*, *s*, and *k*, also highly unmarked sounds; for 'thou,' among those lacking nasals, the predominating consonants are *t*, *s*, *č*, and *w*.) For 'thou' 8 of the 34 have *m*; an additional 2 can be added if 'you' ('you plural') forms are included, as Greenberg does in his treatment of Amerind pronouns. Finally, one finds a full 8 in addition to Amerind of the 34 which have both *n* among the first-person forms ('I' or 'we') and an *m* among the second-person forms ('thou' or 'you plural'), counted in accordance to Greenberg's (1987) treatment of "Amerind" pronominal forms. Clearly, there is nothing unique about the assumed *n/m* pattern among American Indian languages, in spite of Ruhlen's claims to the contrary, as shown by his own data. Moreover, these recurrent sounds in the world's pronoun systems are not accidental, but are predictable based on the perceptual saliency of the sounds employed and "resonance" patterns involved (see Nichols 2003).

(3) Nichols (2003), as mentioned above, calls attention to the prevalence and role of nasals in pronominal markers due to their deictic functions and roles in paradigmatically arranged morphological subsystems.

(4) Borrowing is another possibility. Some consider the possibility of *areal diffusion*, including pronouns, among the various early groups which came into America, borrowing from one another either before they crossed the Bering Straits, or after, or both (cf. Bright 1984:15–6, 25; Milewski 1960, 1967:13–14; Kroeber 1913:399). Diffusion of pronouns is not so unusual as some prefer to think (examples above). There are also a number of documented cases of borrowed pronouns in Native American languages. For example, Miskito borrowed its independent personal pronouns from Northern Sumu in relatively recent times: Miskito *yaŋ* 'I' (cf. Sumu *yaŋ*), *man* 'you' (cf. Sumu *man*) (Hale 1997:154). In another example, Mednyj Aleut (Copper Island) borrowed its verb morphology, including pronominal endings, from Russian (Thomason and Kaufman 1988:234–5, cf. Comrie 1989:87, Golovko 1994, Campbell 1997a:245). The full Russian pronominal system was borrowed.

Alsea (isolate, in Oregon) appears to have borrowed a whole set of Salishan pronominal suffixes (Kinkade 2005), as shown in Table 7.5:

Table 7.5 *Borrowings of Salishan pronominal suffixes into Alsea*

Alsea	Proto-Salishan	
-an	-n	first person singular
-ax	$-x^w$	second person singular
-ø	-ø	third person singular
-al	-ł	first person plural
-ap	-p	second person plural
-ałx	(lx)	third person plural

Mary Haas (1976:358) concluded from her comparison of languages in northern California that the *n/m* pattern is widely borrowed:

There are clear *evidences of diffusion* in pronominal forms in northern California . . . belonging to a single diffusion area . . . The most prominent feature is *n-* in the first person paired with *m-* in the second person . . . But the total picture of *diffusion* of *n-* and *m-* in the first and second persons goes beyond the area being studied in this paper [Haas 1976] and so the problem really needs to be attacked on a larger scale. [Our emphasis, LC/WP]

(5) Another explanation that has been offered involves child language. In this view, child-language expressions around the world abound in self-directed and other-directed words containing nasal consonants. The ultimate reason for this is the universal physical fact that a gesture equivalent to that used to articulate the sound *n* is the single most important voluntary muscular activity of a nursing infant. As Goddard (1986:202) points out, possibly this factor and the tendency for primary grammatical morphemes to consist of a single, unmarked (phonetically commonplace) segment account for the widespread appearance of *n-* in 'first-person' pronouns. In many societies, particularly among hunting and gathering groups, infants may continue to nurse until the age of five or longer, well into and beyond the age of language acquisition (cf. Goddard and Campbell 1994).[27]

(6) More to the point, the claim for the ubiquity of 'first-person' *n* and particularly for 'second-person' *m* in "Amerind" is overstated. We need to ask also

---

[27] Greenberg and Ruhlen in several reports singled out this possible explanation for the nasal pronoun pattern, neglecting the others Campbell and Goddard had offered (Greenberg 1990a:11; Ruhlen 1994a:253), misrepresenting the claim and implying it is an unreasonable hypothesis without stating why. Their caricature of it as "infant sucking reflexes" is garbled and fails to mention the other more relevant and damaging facts.

about all the American Indian languages which lack 'first-person' *n* or 'second-person' *m*, or both. Also, what of all the non-American Indian languages which have one or both of these? The second-person *m* is not nearly so common among American language groups as asserted to be. Thus, in spite of the claimed generality for 'first-person' *n* and 'second-person' *m*, Greenberg finds South America typified by *i* 'first person,' *a* 'second person,' *i* 'third person' (Greenberg 1979, 1987:44–9, 273–5, 277–81; cf. Swadesh 1954:312) – a distinct pattern, with second-person *m* absent. If the *i/a/i* pattern is the hallmark of South America, then the *n/m* pattern is not as diagnostic for Amerind as a whole as claimed. Moreover, Greenberg (1987:276) presented in support of Amerind also a 'first-person' *m* which he believes is characteristic of several Amerind groups – but recall that *m* 'first person' is what Greenberg and Ruhlen expect of Eurasiatic; at the same time, several other of his "Amerind" groups exhibit widespread 'second-person' *ka* or *s*, not the expected "Amerind" *m* (Greenberg 1987:278; cf. Ruhlen 1994a:252–60). In brief, the distribution of pronouns in American Indian languages has been overstated and misunderstood.

Furthermore, in many languages outside the Americas 'first-person' *n* abounds, and it is not difficult to find non-American languages with both 'first-person' *n* and 'second-person' *m*. For example, Rivet (1957[1943/1960]:127) compared Malayo-Polynesian *inya* / Hokan *inyau, nyaa* 'I,' and *ma, mu, me, mo* / *maa, ma, mo', me, mi, mu* 'you,' in his attempt to relate Malayo-Polynesian and Hokan – it has been known for at least fifty years that the pattern with first-person *n* and second-person *m* exists also outside the Americas (see Campbell 1994b; Trombetti 1905:80–90; Benjamin 1976; Matisoff 1990). Dryer found in his sample of 333 languages that 7 percent of the languages (excluding Amerind; i.e. 17 out of 252 languages) had both an *n* in first person and an *m* in second person, with both either singular or both plural (cited in Campbell 1997a:246–7). These include Enga, Chuave (Papuan); Chrau (Mon-Khmer); Akan (Niger-Congo); seven Bantu languages; Tamazight (Berber); and Hebrew, Arabic, and Tigrinya (Semitic); among others. In Dryer's research, only 17 percent of the languages from Greenberg's Amerind (14 out of 81 languages) had this pronoun pattern. Dryer found from pronoun data on 289 languages that 118 had more nasals in first person singular than in third person singular, 128 had the same number of nasals in both, and in only 47 were there more nasals in third person singular than in first person singular. At the same time, 74 of these languages had more nasals in second person singular than in third person singular, while 48 had more nasals in third person singular than in second person singular.[28]

---

[28] Dryer (personal communication) cautions that, while the overall numbers support his test hypotheses about nasals in pronouns, the nature of the sample precludes applying statistics to test for significance. He also is inclined to believe that the *n/m* pattern in American Indian languages may suggest genetic relationship, but points out that if Hokan and Munda can share *n/m* due to chance, then why can't Hokan and Penutian?

It is sobering to recall Callaghan's (1980:337) presentation of the accidental coincidences in Miwokan and Indo-European pronominal affixes (cited above). It is interesting in the context of accidental similarities to point out also that Atakapa has two Indo-European-like 'first-person' pronominal markers, *wi* 'first-person-singular' independent pronoun, and *-o* 'first-person-singular' verbal ending (as in Spanish, or Greek). The K'iche'–Quechua pronominal forms which are accidentally similar should also be recalled (discussed earlier in this chapter).

Moreover, as Ringe (1993:103) demonstrated mathematically, even without reference to the typical presence of unmarked consonants in pronominal markers, "the two or three pronouns invoked by Greenberg . . . are obviously inadequate as a mathematical basis for anything." Greenberg's case is also not helped by languages which behave in ways opposed to his expectations, for example "Amerind" cases with *n* 'second person', e.g. Cayuse *-n*, Cherokee *nihi*, Atakapa *na*, Tonkawa *na-*, Siuslaw *-nx*, Cheyenne *ne-*,[29] Proto-Guajiboan **ni-hi*, Guambiano *ni*, Tupinamba *ené*, Proto-Tupi–Guarani **ne*, etc., and cases with the reverse of expectations, i.e. *n* 'second person' / *m* 'first person,' as in Lakota *miye* 'first person singular,' *niye* 'second person singular.' Greenberg's case is also not helped by "Amerind" languages which have neither *n* nor *m* in first- or second-person forms (e.g. Chumash, Zuni, Kuikuro [Amonap], Muskogean languages, etc.).

Whatever the explanation for the frequency of 'first-person' *n*, and for the recurrence of 'second-person' *m*, it will not do to look only at American languages which contain them, ignoring the many American tongues which lack them and the numerous non-American languages where they are attested. The *n* 'first person' / *m* 'second person' pattern is by no means unique to, diagnostic of, or ubiquitous in American Indian languages. The pronoun evidence for Amerind has been misleadingly simplified and overstated. The use of pronouns in general in attempts to establish genetic relationships between languages is tricky at best, and is rejected as bad methodology by many, as seen here.

7.20   Conclusion

Given the confusion surrounding a number of proposed distant genetic relationships, it is important to consider carefully the methodological principles and procedures involved in the investigation of possible distant genetic relationships,

---

[29] Interestingly, Siuslaw, Miluk, and Cheyenne have *n* in both first- and second-person pronouns, i.e. Cheyenne *na-* 'I,' *ne-* 'you' (from Proto-Algonquian **ne-* and **ke-* respectively); Siuslaw has *-n* 'I,' *-nx* 'you'; Miluk has *-enne'-* 'first-singular subject', *-ne-* 'second-singular subject'; in Proto-Salish we find **n-* 'first-person possessive,' **ʔən-* 'second-person possessive' (Newman 1979a:211, Goddard 1988, Pierce 1965:383). Chimane has nasals in its pronouns for all three persons, both singular and plural (Martín and Pérez Diez 1990:576).

that is, in how family relationships are determined. Principal among these are reliance on regular sound correspondences in basic vocabulary and patterned grammatical evidence involving "shared aberrancy" or "submerged features," with careful attention to eliminating other possible explanations for similarities noted in compared material (e.g. borrowing, onomatopoeia, accident, nursery forms, etc.). We feel safe in predicting that most of the future research on possible distant genetic relationships which does not avoid the methodological problems discussed here and follow the recommendation contained in this chapter will probably remain inconclusive. On the other hand, investigations informed by and guided by the methodological considerations surveyed here stand a good chance of advancing understanding, by either further supporting or denying proposed family connections. (For examples of promising proposals of distant genetic relationship, see Chapter 13.)

8 The philosophical–psychological–typological–evolutionary approach to language relationships

> The founders of modern mind are philologists.
>
> (Ernest Renan 1890:141 [Said 1979:132])

8.1 Introduction

For most of this book we have been dealing with language classification as viewed in the dominant current of comparative linguistics. However, there is, or better said, there was, another once influential orientation, which involves *philosophical–psychological(–typological–evolutionary)* outlooks concerning the general nature and evolution of language, including the classification of languages. Both approaches reflect the nineteenth-century search for origins and the belief in "progress" (unilinear evolution). The two currents were partially overlapping and intertwined, and partially conflicting theoretical lines of historical linguistic thought. The other approach was still remembered and addressed, for example, by Sapir (1921b) and Bloomfield (1933) (see also Pedersen 1962[1931]), but is largely forgotten by current generations of linguists – though important unrecognized repercussions still affect historical linguistic work today, particularly in typological arguments. This difference has to do with the frequent nineteenth-century clash between linguistics viewed as a *"Naturwissenschaft"* and as a *"Geisteswissenschaft." Geisteswissenschaft* was often translated as 'moral [or spiritual] science' (linked with modern humanities), *Naturwissenschaft* as 'natural or physical science.' This dichotomy is usually mentioned in connection with August Schleicher's attempt to place linguistics in the natural sciences, denying linguistics as a branch of the humanities or of the more spiritual/mental/"sentimental" intellectual pursuits (see Schleicher 1861–2). Bloomfield (1933:17–18) repeated the by then received opinion that there was both a nineteenth-century "main stream" represented by the Neogrammarians and a "small current," the psychological–typological–evolutionary orientation represented by the Humboldt–Steinthal–Wundt tradition. Of course Schleicher was not the first to see linguistics as a natural science rather than a "sentimental," "ideologic" enterprise. The close analogy of linguistics with biology had been insisted upon by Friedrich von Schlegel

(1808); Rasmus Rask held that language is an "objet de la nature" which "ressemble à l'histoire naturelle" (Hjelmslev 1966[1950–1]:185). Many shared this outlook. It is necessary to understand both approaches to comprehend the methods and practice of many scholars important in the development of comparative linguistics, since the work of many involved both outlooks. Our purpose in this chapter is to examine this other orientation and to see how it impacted the methods we utilize today, and why it did not prove effective for establishing family relationships.

8.2   Background

After John Locke's (1690) *An essay concerning human understanding*, language came to be considered "a material expression of human genius, as exercised over the centuries in a progressive, evolutionary fashion that revealed in its very form the historical movement of nations" (Gray 1999:86). Most eighteenth-century language philosophy depended on Locke's basic premise that "language is the material expression of mind, and mind has a uniform and progressive history" (Gray 1999:96). In the framework of many scholars (see Chapters 1–4), language, race, nation, and culture were often not clearly separated. Sir William Jones, Gottfried Wilhelm Leibniz, Lorenzo Hervás y Panduro, Johann Christoph Adelung, Rasmus Rask, and others believed they were working out the history of races and nations rather than that of mere languages. As Rask put it:

the human races about which I think I have a clear idea from their languages are: (a) Caucasian (ours), (b) Scythian (Greenlandic [or Polar]), (c) Malayan (Australian), (d) the Chinese (Seric) . . . To this may be added with relative certainty (e) the Negritic, (f) the American; but it is quite possible that there may be more. (In a letter from 1818, in Benediktsson 1980:21)

In this view, "to establish distinct families of languages is tantamount not only to establishing the ancient state of nationalities, but of racial discrepancies among tribes" (Gatschet 1882:261). Folk (or national) psychology, coupled with the assumed stage of social evolution attained – often called "progress" –, was thought to determine a language's structure or typology, how the language evolved. For example, the stage of savagery in social evolution was thought to be correlated with isolating typology in languages, barbarism with agglutination, and civilization with flectional languages. That is, it was assumed, for example, that a nation classified as barbarians would be speakers of an agglutinative language. This was the sort of macro-level linguistic history rejected by followers of the mainstream approach as too psychological.[1]

---

[1] The notion of unilinear social evolution from savagery to barbarism to civilization (reflecting European ethnocentrism) was an old one. It was already common in the late 1700s, and as stated, many were influenced in this direction by Locke. Sir William Jones' thinking along these lines was influenced by William Robertson's (1769) typology with this view of social evolution.

Peter Stephen (Pierre Etienne) Duponceau (1838), famous for contributions to American Indian linguistics and to typology (see Chapter 6), recognized these two different orientations to language and referred to them as the "etymologic" (i.e. genetic or historical–comparative) and "ideologic" (i.e. philosophical–psychological–typological–evolutionary) divisions. Aspects of both the "ideologic" and the "etymologic" approaches endured into the twentieth century, although the former was played down in the official histories, written mostly by Neogrammarians (such as the well-known one by Pedersen [1962(1931), 1983(1916)]), and hence current generations of linguists have lost sight of its impact. "Etymology" for Duponceau was the mainly historical comparison of word forms, by which the affinities of languages could be established; genetic classification belonged to this subdivision. "Ideology" embraced the various forms, structures, and systems of languages and the means whereby they differently group and expound the ideas of the human mind. It governed the broader evolution of language and thus also had implications, at a more abstract level, for language classification. Typology and its psychological implications, as viewed in the eighteenth and nineteenth centuries, belonged to this subfield (Robins 1987:437–8; Campbell 1997a:37–62). Duponceau's labels for the two approaches are convenient and we utilize them in this chapter, alternating reference to the two approaches also with longer more descriptive designations.

8.3   Inner form

The notion of the "inner form" (or "inner structure") was a persistent theme. Ideas embodying such notions as "inner form" and "basic plan of thought" had been part of the European linguistic heritage essentially from classical times and in any event since the Modistae and the speculative (i.e. logical, semantic-based) grammars of the Middle Ages, later found again in the various guises of universal grammar, from at least as early as Sanctius (1585/1587; see Breva-Claramonte 1983). Herder (1772), with his *innere Entstehung der Sprache* [the inner development of language], distinguished *innere* [internal] and *äussere* [external] developments (Aarsleff 1982:196). The notion was prominent in the work of Adelung, Friedrich von Schlegel, Franz Bopp, Wilhelm von Humboldt, Heymann Steinthal, and others. In American linguistics, Daniel Brinton (1885b, 1891) followed and attempted to promote Humboldt's "inner form" (Andresen 1990:200; Campbell 1997a:56), and Franz Boas, much influenced also by Steinthal (1855, 1860), also used Humboldt's concept of "inner form" to deal with the diversity of American Indian languages, seeing languages as conditioning the worldview of their speakers (Andresen 1990:214; Koerner 1990b:114; Campbell 1997a:42, 65, 382). Edward Sapir, who was influenced both by Boas and by his study of Germanic linguistics (cf. Sapir 1907–8; Sapir's MA thesis was on Herder), thought along similar lines, and it was from

Sapir that Benjamin Lee Whorf took up the notion, where it was to become the foundation of the much discussed Sapir–Whorf hypothesis.

8.4   Influential protagonists

Some powerful personalities in the history of linguistics embraced this "ideologic" orientation in attempts to get at linguistic prehistory. We look briefly at a few of these and at those who influenced this line of philosophical thinking.

8.4.1   Leibniz and others

Gottfried Wilhelm Leibniz (1692) brought the two orientations and the various linguistic and philosophical currents of his time together in an integrated focus on language history (see Chapter 2). For Leibniz, word–thought correspondences afforded implications for historical relationships among languages. Any assumption of genetic relationship presupposed common features of thought, as manifested by shared features of linguistic form, emanated from shared historical development and was by no means the result of a universal logical patterning – *"those who study the march of the human mind must march at every moment with the torch of etymology in hand"* (emphasis added, LC/WP; quoted in Aarsleff 1982:69; see Leibniz 1697, 1710a, 1710b, 1717, 1768; cf. Aarsleff 1982:84, 169).

Nicolas Beauzée (1717–89), famous for his contributions to the well-known *Encyclopédie*, held there was a "thorough-going isomorphism between language, thought, and reality" (Eco 1995:108), and under the entry "language" in the *Encyclopédie*, he said languages were reflections of the "genius" of the peoples who spoke them and this "genius" explained how each language "contains its own particular vision of the world" (Eco 1995:110). Condillac and Herder held similar views, and similar thinking was developed further by Wilhelm von Humboldt, with whom this view is especially associated in histories of linguistics. As mentioned earlier, most eighteenth-century language philosophy depended on Locke's basic premise that "language is the material expression of mind, and mind has a uniform and progressive history" (Gray 1999:96).

8.4.2   Adelung and glottogonic thought

Johann Christoph Adelung (1806[1806–17]) proposed a typological classification of languages in what came to be known as a "glottogonic" interpretation, which saw modern languages as mere "decayed" versions of the more "perfect" classical languages. So-called glottogonic views linked notions of typology and language evolution ("progress"), both usually associated with assumptions about the development of thinking and "mind" (hence the psychological and philosophical connections). Adelung distinguished two language types: "monosyllabic" and "polysyllabic" languages (types often mentioned in other works both before and after Adelung). The glottogonic interpretation, later associated with Bopp and especially with Schleicher – and vigorously attacked by the Neogrammarians –, was that languages of the monosyllabic type were primitive while the polysyllabic languages were more highly evolved. Frequently it was asserted that originally there were only vowels, then consonants and monosyllabic roots emerged; only later in the polysyllabic phase was there effective progress. This developmental sequence was associated with the evolution of reason, the belief that language and reason evolved together (Coseriu 1977:149; cf. Schleicher 1983[1863], 1983[1865]), and was abetted by study of the ancient Hindu grammatical tradition – well known to nineteenth-century linguists – with its emphasis on developments beginning with original simple roots.[2]

8.4.3   Schlegel

"Grammatical structure" was Friedrich von Schlegel's criterion of genetic relatedness. As seen in Chapter 4, for Schlegel, two languages were to be considered truly related when their morphological systems and "the inner [internal] structure" presented distinct resemblances. Schlegel compared case endings, particles, and pronouns, among other things. His historical inquiry into the internal structure of language was followed and further urged by Jacob Grimm (1818:xvi) and Wilhelm von Humboldt (cf. F. Schlegel 1808:6–7, 28; see Hoenigswald 1963:4; Jankowsky 1972:53). In this way, inner form and the overall morphological ground plan or typology came to be a core concept in "comparative grammar," so important in the development of the comparative method and historical linguistics in general (see Chapter 4).

8.4.4   Bopp

Franz Bopp's (1816, 1833[1833–52]) approach (see Chapter 4), followed by many, was also "glottogonic." It is illustrated in his treatment of verb endings, where his reconstruction of 'first person singular' in Indo-European was -*ma*, 'second person singular' -*tva*, with reconstruction of the rest of the system based on semantic components. Plurals were derived from combinations of these, with 'first person plural' -*ma-tva* and 'second person plural' -*tva-tva*; other plurals were formed from the repetition of singular endings, and the middle by repeating active endings. Thus for Curtius (1871), extending Bopp's

---

[2] Delbrück (1989[1880]:56) characterizes "*glottogonic* hypotheses" as "attempts to explain the forms of the parent speech and to build up a history of inflection upon them."

scheme, plural middle-voice forms were reconstructed for 'first person plural' as *-ma-tva-tva* and 'second person plural' as *-tva-tva-tva*; for Schleicher (1861–2[1871]), these were *-ma-tva-ma-tva* and *-tva-tva-tva-tva* respectively (Curtius 1870, 1871; Kiparsky 1974:334). This sort of treatment was later abandoned because of the Neogrammarian criticism of glottogonic theory. (See Chapter 4.)

8.5   The fate of "glottogonic" thought

August Schleicher's (1861–2) *Compendium der vergleichenden Grammatik der indogermanischen Sprachen* is the acknowledged synthesis of historical and comparative linguistics for its time (Koerner 1983:xvi; cf. also Schleicher 1848, 1983[1863], 1983[1865]). Schleicher classified languages as "monosyllabic," "agglutinating," and "flectional," following Humboldt. Schleicher expounded the view that languages evolve, or "progress," from isolation to agglutination (with affixes arising from earlier lexical roots) and move onward to flexion, with gradual progress in the direction from simple to complex forms. However, for Schleicher "growth" (through agglutination) was assumed to take place only in the prehistoric phase when languages were still young and capable of word formation (the period of *Sprachbildung*), whereas only changes of "decay" (by sound change and analogy) took place in the later historical period, after the growth process was assumed to have entirely ceased (in the period of *Sprachgeschichte*) (Schleicher 1869:31; Müller 1862–5:331; Bynon 1986:131). Many linguists at this time followed the glottogonic view: "This prejudicial view of modern languages [i.e. that modern languages are but decayed skeletons of former perfection] as but dim reflections of their more perfect progenitor pervades the work of the early comparativists" (Christy 1983:13).

The Neogrammarians rejected Schleicher's (and others') "growth process," which they held up as a primary example of "glottogonic speculation" – and this was perhaps the principal distinction between the Neogrammarians and their predecessors. Karl Brugmann (1849–1919), a principal founder of neogrammarianism, rejected this separation of stages (see Osthoff and Brugmann 1878). For Brugmann, the same kinds of language changes applied to all phases of linguistic history (cf. Paul 1920[1898]:174; Christy 1980, 1983:74–5; Hock 1986:629); analogy and sound change were needed at all stages (Davies 1986:154). This reflects the impact of Sir Charles Lyell's (1830) uniformitarianism (in geology) – "that all past events – yes, every single one – could be explained by the action of causes now in operation. No old causes are extinct; no new ones have been introduced" (Gould 1987:105).

It is instructive to contrast Brugmann's Neogrammarian (uniformitarian) treatment of verbal endings with that of Bopp and Schleicher (above), who viewed personal endings as having developed from pronouns (or other roots) which became attached to the verb. Schleicher (1871[1861–2]), following Bopp, had reconstructed *ma* for the 'first-person-singular active pronoun'; Bopp postulated that this form (1) was weakened to *mi* (in the pronominal suffix in, for example, Sanskrit *ásmi*, Greek *eimi* 'I am'; Sanskrit *bhárāmi* 'I carry'); (2) it was lost in Greek *phérō* 'I carry'; (3) it lost its *m* in the Greek perfect *léloipa* 'I have left' (assumed to be from *léloipma*); (4) it lost the *a* in Greek *épheron* 'I was carrying' (with -*m* > -*n*, i.e. *épheron* < *épherom* < *épheroma*); and (5) it lost both the *a* and the *m* in the Greek 'aorist' *étupsa* 'I beat' (assumed to be from *étupsama*). However, none of the "sound changes" necessary to derive these different forms from the assumed original *ma* (except -*m* > -*n*) is found in other Greek forms. Brugmann, in contrast (in Osthoff and Brugmann 1878), reconstructed four different first-person endings: -*mi* and -*ō* for 'present' (in different verb classes); -*m* (-*m* > Greek -*n*), and -*m̥* (postconsonantal, which became Greek -*a*) for 'past'; and -*a* for 'perfect.' (He held Sanskrit *bhárāmi* [< **bher-ō*] to be due to "contamination," i.e. analogy, between the -*ō* and -*mi* class verbs.) Brugmann's motivation for this reconstruction was the principle of exceptionless sound changes (the basis of the oft-repeated Neogrammarian slogan that sound laws suffer no exceptions). In this way the attested forms are accounted for without postulating sound changes which do not recur in other forms in the language (i.e. are not regular, not exceptionless). The result is that some of Brugmann's reconstructed pronominal endings show no clear similarity to the independent pronouns (from whence they were assumed to have evolved in the Bopp approach). Therefore, according to Brugmann, it was not warranted to assume that personal endings were necessarily independent pronouns in origin (Davies 1986:157). The processes of change (sound change, analogy) were the same from the proto-language onward, and there was no need to assume independent lexical roots lying behind grammatical endings and certainly no separation of stages of "progress" versus "decay." The glottogonic view of language development was dismissed (Delbrück 1901:47, 1989[1880]:61–73).

The traditional typology (as in Schleicher's view), with its separation of stages of development, was further seriously discredited by Gabelentz's (1891:252) presentation of evidence that the isolating structure of Chinese (note that Chinese was considered the archetypical example of the "primitive" isolating languages, Chinese early high culture notwithstanding) was a later development in history, that Chinese showed evidence of earlier agglutination and even inflection (Greenberg 1973:170). Jespersen (1894:378) also presented arguments against the agglutination theory.

8.6   Duponceau

Peter Stephen (Pierre Etienne) Duponceau (1819, 1838), important in the history of American Indian linguistics (see Campbell 1997a:37–40), deployed and intertwined both approaches. As mentioned above, a dominant framework (from before Duponceau to the early twentieth century) was one where folk (or national) psychology (usually coupled with assumptions about the assumed stage of social evolution attained by speakers of the language) was thought to determine language typology, and so Duponceau, like many others of his day (e.g. Schlegel, Bopp, Humboldt, and later Schleicher), was involved with language typology, making significant contributions.[3] It was Duponceau who first defined *polysynthesis* (essentially referring to long words composed of many morphemes each) and applied it to what he believed to be the structure of Native American languages (Duponceau 1819:399–402, 430). Humboldt (below) adopted Duponceau's "polysynthesis," and through Humboldt, the concept became well known (see Duponceau 1838:84; cf. Leopold 1984:67).

8.7   Wilhelm von Humboldt

Humboldt was probably the most influential linguistic thinker of his time (see Chapter 4). His methodology concerning language genealogy was complex, but included the criteria for establishing languages families accepted throughout the history of linguistics (basic vocabulary, sound correspondences, and grammatical agreements), but with an emphasis on grammar, which for him was largely an "ideologic" concern, so that Humboldt (1822, 1836) emphasized typology and aspects of universal grammar. His typology classified languages as isolating, agglutinative ("mechanical affixing"), and flexional (August Schlegel's three types), plus "incorporating" (*einverleibende*), a fourth type which Humboldt added, which he found exhibited by most American Indian languages, Basque, and Malaysian languages.[4] As mentioned in Chapter 1, Humboldt distinguished three aspects of "comparative grammar," and his approach to genetic affinity helps to explain the welding of "ideologic" (philosophical–psychological– typological–grammatical–evolutionary) concerns with the more "etymologic"

---

[3] Aarsleff (1988) argues that Humboldt's typology owes much to influence from Adam Smith, and that both were influenced by Diderot and other French *idéologues* (Humboldt had spent four years in Paris, 1797–1801). Duponceau was also familiar with the work of these French *Philosophes* (cf. also Leopold 1984:67).

[4] The relationship between "incorporating" and "polysynthesis" may not be clear, since many subsequently assumed them to refer to the same thing. Leopold (1984) argues that Humboldt arrived at his notion of *Einverleibung* [incorporation] early in his career, before contact with Duponceau, and while it was exhibited by many American Indian languages, for Humboldt it was not a special type of language, but was a construction that all "nations" could employ (Leopold 1984:69–70). In any case, it is clear that Humboldt was influenced significantly by Duponceau's views. Pott (1840:24, 1870:xvii) used Duponceau's polysynthesis as equivalent to or as a subdivision of the German term for incorporation, but reserved his use of the term polysynthesis basically for American Indian languages. In the works of Müller, Whitney, and others, incorporating and polysynthesis became synonymous (Leopold 1984:71).

(lexically based comparative–historical) considerations better known to linguists today.[5]

Humboldt's typology was fundamental to his philosophy of language and reflected German Romanticism. The language types were taken as outward symptoms of the "inner form" of language, which itself was an expression of the "spirit" (*Volksgeist*) of the speakers and the "genius" of the language and nation (cf. Drechsel 1988:233). However, Humboldt's writing was notorious even among his friends for "lack[ing] form, [getting] stuck in too many details, laps[ing] into excursions, and mov[ing] on a level that was too high and abstract" (Aarsleff 1988:xv). This is certainly true of his writing on "inner form" (Aarsleff 1988:xvi). Perhaps the clearest concise statement in Humboldt's own words, which reveals how the different ingredients are interconnected in his overall approach, is that in an 1830 letter to his friend F. G. Welcker:

> My aim is much simpler and also more esoteric, namely a study that treats the faculty of speech in its inward aspects, as a human faculty, and which uses its effects, languages, only as sources of knowledge and examples in developing the argument. I wish to show that what makes any particular language what it is, is its grammatical structure and to explain how the grammatical structure in all its diversities still can only follow certain methods that will be listed one by one, so that by the study of each language, it can be shown which methods are dominant or mixed in it. Now, in these methods themselves I consider of course the influence of each on the mind and feeling, and their explanation in terms of the causes of the origins of the languages, in so far as this is possible. Thus I connect the study of language with the philosophical survey of humanity's capacity for formation [Bildung] and with history. (Quoted in Aarsleff 1988:xiv)

Humboldt maintained that the recovery of the "different possibilities of historical connection among languages" involved generalizations concerning the role of grammatical type, words, and affixes (Hoenigswald 1974:350). For him, "the science of languages is the history of progress and evolution of the human mind" (quoted in Aarsleff 1988:lxv), a phrase used also by Duponceau; in Humboldt's words (in translation), "the *comparative study of languages* . . . loses all higher interest if it does not cleave to the point at which language is connected with the shaping of the *nation's mental power*" (Humboldt 1988[1836]:21). This thinking is reflected more clearly by Noah Webster:

---

[5] As Robins (1990:97) explains:

Comparison [was] of the semantic content of grammatical classes and categories (e.g. whether the verbs of a language have a passive voice), the means whereby grammatical distinctions are maintained (e.g. affixes, vowel alternations, etc.), and the actual inflectional morphs themselves . . . and it was this last that carried the greatest weight in historical affiliation. This clarifies Friedrich Schlegel's . . . reference to 'die innere Struktur der Sprachen oder die vergleichende Grammatik' [the inner structure of the languages or the comparative grammar] (1808:28). But it was still comparative grammar, the comparison of inflectional morphs, rather than general lexical etymologies, that constituted the key, in Humboldt's eyes, to genetic relations.

(Cf. also Hoenigswald 1990:127a.)

the wonderful structure of language and its progress from a few simple terms expressive of natural objects, which supplied the wants or effected the senses of unlettered men, thro [*sic*] a series of ingenious combinations to express new ideas, growing with the growth of the human mind to its highest state of refinement, are yet to be charted and elucidated. (Cited in Gray 1999:126)

Humboldt's outlook had an exceptionally strong impact on "ideologic" discussions and on the subsequent history of linguistics.[6]

8.8 Conclusion

After Sapir (1921b), Bloomfield (1933), and Pedersen (1962[1931]), the "ideologic" philosophical–psychological–typological–evolutionary orientation essentially dropped out of the consciousness of contemporary linguists. Viewed from today's perspective, it is not difficult to see why this would be the case. The "ideologic" approach, to the extent that it concerned itself with attempts to establish genetic relationships among languages, basically relied on the same combination of standard criteria, of basic vocabulary, sound correspondences, and grammatical agreements – though individual practitioners attributed different strengths to these. Most of the contents of the "ideologic" orientation – aspects of philosophy, psychology, typology, and evolution – did not impinge directly on fundamental assumptions of comparative linguistics, which many of the ideologically minded supported and to whose development they also contributed. Rather than denying or competing with such evidence for language relationships, the "ideologic" trappings usually involved a level of abstractness above or beyond these sorts of data. From today's perspective, we might legitimately see aspects of universal grammar and human cognition in theoretical thinking as something like the current analogue of the "ideologic" outlook of then, relevant only in a very broad sense to determining genetic relationships among languages, particularly in how grammatical evidence might be viewed, but not changing the basic fact that basic vocabulary, sound correspondences, and grammatical agreements constitute the evidence upon which such hypotheses of linguistic kinship must be founded. Today's theorizing about general language typology, universals, and aspects of human cognition should contribute to, rather than compete with or detract from, our ability to distinguish doubtful comparisons among languages not yet known to be related.

---

[6] For a full discussion of the "ideologic" orientation in American Indian linguistics, and the role of Duponceau, Humboldt, Brinton, Powell, Boas, and others, see Campbell (1997a:29–62).

9 Assessment of proposed distant genetic relationships

> The difficulty of the task of trying to make every language fit into a genetic classification has led certain eminent linguists to deprive the principle of such classification of its precision and its rigor or to apply it in an imprecise manner.
> (Antoine Meillet 1948[1914]:78)[1]

9.1 Introduction

Throughout this book, we have concentrated on methodological considerations which need to be taken into account in attempts to determine family relationships among languages, and we have looked at successful cases where it has been possible to demonstrate that languages are related and thus to establish different language families (Chapters 4, 5, and 7). In this chapter the goal is to examine several of the best-known hypotheses of long-range relationships, so-called "macro-families" – proposed distant genetic relationships where it has not yet proven possible to demonstrate convincingly the postulated relationship among the languages. These include Altaic, Ural-Altaic, Nostratic, Eurasiatic, Amerind, Na-Dene, proposed Dravidian external connections, and Indo-Pacific. (Some contested proposals in Africa, Australia, and the Americas were considered in Chapter 6, and Proto-World is considered in Chapter 12.) We concentrate here on methodological principles. Our intent in this chapter is to try to explain why these hypotheses of remote linguistic kinship remain in doubt and why most historical linguists do not accept them. These case studies should contribute to clarifying the methods and procedures employed in the investigation of distant genetic relationships and what it takes to support a case for linguistic kinship. We believe, also, that when the nature of the evidence and the methodological problems involved in these proposed long-range relationships are laid out clearly, it will contribute to the resolution of some

---

[1] "La difficulté de fait qu'on éprouve à faire entrer toutes les langues dans la classification généalogique a conduit certains linguistes éminents à ôter au principe de cette classification sa précision et sa rigueur ou à l'appliquer d'une manière inexacte."

issues, perhaps to the abandonment finally of some indefensible hypotheses of remote linguistic kinship, and to the establishment of others.

We note that "many new classificatory proposals have been proposed in recent years," but "not all of them can be correct, since some are mutually exclusive" (Michalove *et al.* 1998:461), or, put somewhat differently, "a fact which even the most fervent long-rangers cannot deny is that the conclusions drawn from long-range comparisons are often mutually contradictory" (Janhunen 1989:28). We by no means attempt to evaluate all hypothesized macro-families and proposed distant genetic relationships (see the Appendix for a list of most of these). We focus, rather, on several of the most widely known and influential proposals in this chapter.

9.2   Altaic

The core of the Altaic hypothesis holds that Turkic (Chuvash-Turkic), Mongolian (some ten languages), and Tungusic (Manchu–Tungusic, some twelve languages), together comprising some forty languages, are genetically related. More extended versions of the Altaic hypothesis would include other languages, Korean and Japanese, sometimes also Ainu. Some speak of the "core" Altaic hypothesis, which would connect Turkic, Mongolian, and Tungusic languages, called "Micro-Altaic," and of the hypothesis which would connect these "Micro-Altaic" languages with Korean and Japanese as "Macro-Altaic" (Georg *et al.* 1999). Our use of the term "Altaic" is intended to refer to the "Micro-Altaic" grouping; where clarification is necessary, we specify directly whether the broader or narrower hypotheses are intended. A number of scholars support the inclusion of Korean also as core Altaic (started by Ramstedt 1924). In spite of the recent focus on Japanese in literature deailing with Altaic, fewer support its inclusion in Altaic.

The Altaic hypothesis emerged gradually in history. Various scholars in the early and mid 1800s proposed various groupings which would include some or all of the "Micro-Altaic" languages, but typically these were included in larger more poorly defined proposed affiliations. Klaproth (1823:295) is credited with early mention of a specific connection among the Micro-Altaic language groups. Castrén (1847, 1850, 1857) is sometimes cited as the first to attempt to group these languages based on linguistic criteria, though what he called "Altaic" included also Samoyed (a branch of Uralic; see Tekin 1994:82). Georg *et al.* (1999) argue that it was the conclusive demonstration of Uralic – that Samoyed and Finno-Ugric constitute a single family – that led almost by default to the view of "Altaic" as containing those language groups that were left over from earlier more inclusive views, such as the now abandoned Ural-Altaic hypothesis. Work by Ramstedt (1914–15, 1915–16, 1946–7, 1952, 1957), and later by Poppe (1960, 1965, 1973, 1974), is seen as the foundation of the Altaic proposal, though many have criticized these works for various reasons (Georg *et al.* 1999).

While "Altaic" is repeated in encyclopedias and handbooks, "most specialists in the Altaic languages no longer believe that the three groups of traditional Altaic, Turkic, Mongolian, and Tungusic, are related" (Greenberg 1997:88). Leading "Altaicists" have abandoned the Altaic hypothesis, showing that the evidence mustered on its behalf does not support the genetic affinity among the groups usually identified as "Altaic" (Austerlitz 1982, 1983; Clauson 1956, 1959a, 1959b, 1962, 1969; Doerfer 1963–75, 1968, 1973; Janhunen 1989; Nichols 1992:269; Róna-Tas 1986; Sinor 1988; and Unger 1990a). Even some supporters of Nostratic now no longer accept a unified Altaic, though they may still believe that Turkic, Mongolian, and Tungusic, and sometimes also Korean and Japanese, are related, but as independent branches of a broader Nostratic superfamily (Markey and Shevoroshkin 1986:xviii–xix; Starostin 1986, 1989:42; cf. Manaster Ramer 1993b:215). Even Greenberg (2000a:12), who maintained "Altaic," admitted that "it appears that most, if not all, of the younger specialists in one or more of the traditional branches of Altaic (Turkic, Mongolian, and Tungusic) no longer believe there is an Altaic family" (see also Greenberg 1997:88).[2] In spite of this, Altaic does have some supporters (see Starostin 1991b; Georg *et al.* 1999). It is highly controversial and it deserves more careful attention than we are able to give it here, though we can present some of the main reasons many find it unacceptable.

The most serious problems for the Altaic proposal are the extensive lexical borrowing across inner Asia and among the "Micro-Altaic" languages, lack of significant numbers of convincing cognates, extensive areal diffusion, and typologically commonplace traits presented as evidence of relationship. The shared "Altaic" traits typically cited include vowel harmony, relatively simple phoneme inventories, agglutination, their exclusively suffixing nature, (S)OV word order, and the fact that their non-main clauses are mostly non-finite (participial) constructions. These shared features are not only commonplace typological traits which occur with frequency in unrelated languages of the world, but they are also areal traits, shared by a number of languages in surrounding regions whose structural properties were not well known when the hypothesis was first framed: "the comparative evidence once presented in favour of the genetic relationship between the three basic 'Altaic' language families [Turkic,

---

[2] Greenberg (2000a:12–13) asked, "are the [hypothesized] Altaic languages related to one another?" and "do they form a valid genetic node, that is, a set of languages more closely related to each other than to any others?" He finds the answer to the first question "overwhelmingly positive"; he believes the answer to the second is also "obvious" based on "personal, demonstrative, and interrogative pronouns" (2000a:13). Greenberg's Altaic does not include Japanese, Korean, or Ainu, which he holds to be members of his Eurasiatic stock, independent of Altaic itself but related to it within this broader classification.

Mongolian, and Tungusic] can only be explained in terms of a complicated network of areal interaction" (Janhunen 1989:29).

The hypothesis, in spite of its long history, has been controversial almost from its beginning (cf. Shirokogoroff 1970[1931]:89). Strahlenberg (1730) noted structural similarities among a number of tongues which he called "the Tatar languages." He classified these languages and their speakers in six groups: (1) Uighurs (which he placed with Finno-Ugric peoples), Baraba Tatars, and Huns; (2) Turco-Tatar peoples; (3) Samoyeds; (4) Mongols and Manchu; (5) Tungus; and (6) "the tribes living between the Black and Caspian seas" (including Turks, Iranians, and Caucasians) (Poppe 1965:125). There are several inaccuracies in this classification, for example, Finno-Ugric, Uighur, and Baraba Turkic do not belong together; and Manchu and Tungusic go together, not Manchu with Mongolian. Rasmus Rask (1834) included in what he called "the Scythian languages" those of Strahlenberg's "Tatar languages" as well as some others from Greenland, North America, Northern Asia and Europe, the Caucasus, and even Basque (cf. Poppe 1965:125). Max Müller's (1855, 1869) proposed "Turanian languages" expanded Strahlenberg's and Rask's collection of languages more broadly to include also Thai, Tibetan, Dravidian, and Malayan. This name is based on Turan, the hypothetical homeland of the Turks in Inner Asia. This was not a classification arrived at through the application of comparative linguistic methods, but rather represented the non-Indo-European and non-Semitic languages which shared agglutinative structure, which Müller held to be associated with a particular stage in the assumed unilinear social evolution of society (see Chapter 8), and were hence called "nomadic languages" (cf. Poppe 1965:125). Müller's (1861:413) "Northern Division" of the "Turanian Family" included: "Tungusic, Mongolic, Turkic, Samoyedic, and Finnic [Finno-Ugric]"; the "Southern Division" comprised: "Taïc, Malaic, Gangetic, Lohitic, Munda, and Tamulic." In Müller's (1861:300–1) words:

The whole of what is called the *Turanian* class consists of Terminational or Agglutinative languages, and this Turanian class comprises in reality all languages spoken in Asia and Europe, and not included under the Aryan [Indo-European] and Semitic families, with the exception of Chinese and its cognate dialects [members of the "Monosyllabic or Isolating Stage"] . . . This Turanian class is of great importance in the science of languages. Some scholars would deny it the name of a family; and if family is only applicable to dialects so closely connected among themselves as the Aryan and Semitic, it would no doubt be preferable to speak of the Turanian as a class or group, and not as a family of languages. But this concession must not be understood as an admission that the members of this class start from different sources, and that they are held together, not by genealogical affinity, but by morphological similarity only . . . The name Turanian is used in opposition to Aryan, and is applied to the nomadic races of Asia as opposed to the agricultural or Aryan races.

In Müller's actual treatment of his Turanian languages, "morphological" (typological) similarity forms the basis of the grouping. This raises doubts about its validity, doubts that have persisted from the earliest classifications to this day.

"Altaic" was separated only gradually from notions that joined Uralic and "Altaic" together.

Ramstedt, unlike the others, left a legacy of postulated sound correspondences, morphological matchings, and the version of the hypothesis that has been the most influential. Ramstedt, Poppe, and Aalto were the leading supporters of the proposed Altaic unity, though, as explained above, the balance of opinion has shifted to opposing the proposed Altaic affinity (cf. Sinor 1988, 1990b).

There have been several kinds of criticisms of the evidence presented in favor of Altaic. One is the claim that lexical comparisons among the putative (Micro-)Altaic languages lack basic vocabulary. For example, it has been argued (and disputed) that most body-part terms and low numbers are lacking from among the proposed Altaic cognates (cf. Clauson 1956; Doerfer 1988; see Georg *et al.* 1999 for opposing views). Lack of basic numbers is not a serious fault, but the near absence of body-part terms is grounds for raised eyebrows with regard to the hypothesis. Others, however, argue that there are some significant body-part terms among the putative cognates, making this particular argument inconclusive at the moment. The biggest difficulty, all agree, has been the problem of the extensive borrowings. Even supporters of the Altaic hypothesis have abandoned instances formerly thought to be cognates due to recognition of borrowing (see Poppe 1974).

Some of the criticism of Altaic involves the putative sound correspondences that have been suggested among the Micro-Altaic languages. One major point of dispute has to do with reconstructions of Turkic sounds and how they might correspond to Mongolian and Tungusic. As seen by many, Proto-Turkic *s split into s and z, while *$š$ split into $š$ and $ž$, in specific environments (involving roots of two syllables and with long vowels), and then in the highly influential Bulgaric or Chuvash branch of the family $z > r$, and $ž > l$. As a result, words in Mongolian (and Tungusic) which have an r or l (as in Chuvash) corresponding to s, z, $š$, or $ž$ in other Turkic languages are seen as borrowings from the Chuvash branch of Turkic, not as cognates to the compared forms in the other "Altaic" languages (or they are taken to be accidental similarities). There is a sizeable number of examples of this sort in the lexical comparisons, many of them projected further on into Nostratic, as well (see below). Nevertheless, some scholars (primarily those who support the inclusion of "Altaic" as a subbranch of Nostratic) prefer reconstructions of Proto-Turkic which hold that these sounds were originally liquids (not sibilants). Given this reconstruction, they deny that borrowing is a problem for the proposed cognates when these Turkic forms are compared with forms from other putative "Altaic" languages. This interpretation requires the assumption that the liquids (*l/r*) were original in Proto-Turkic and that they changed to sibilants in several Turkic languages (all but the Chuvash branch). One problem for this interpretation is that it requires a sound change of liquids to sibilants, which is not common in the world's languages, although changes in the other direction (of voiced sibilants to liquids) are not uncommon (as in rhotacism). Among Turkologists, those who believe in the Altaic hypothesis (as well as Doerfer, who opposes Altaic and holds Mongolian forms in these comparisons to be Turkic loans) postulate original liquids (which then would make the sibilants of other Turkic languages the results of later sound changes). Those who oppose the Altaic hypothesis (with the exception of Doerfer) hold the sibilants to be original (which makes the liquids the results of later sound changes). That is, some charge that those who have an understanding of phonological systems and phonetic plausibility all postulate a change of *$*s > z >$ r and $*š > ž > 1$ (in the Chuvash branch), where the steps in the change are seen as incremental, intimately interrelated, and natural; these scholars believe that the reverse, the changes of $*r > z/s$ and $*1 > ž/š$ (in non-Chuvash Turkic languages) are unnatural and implausible (Shherbak 1986b; Janhunen personal communication). Thus, for example, the Altaic *p'ok'ü- 'bovine animal, bull,' supported by Nostraticists, is held by opponents to be a clear example of a loanword. It is based on Proto-Turkic *pöküs 'bovine,' borrowed from Bulgaric Turkic into Mongolian and from there on into Tungusic (Janhunen 1996:240–1, 255). This set would be questionable as a possible loan in any case, given the important role of cattle in the associated cultures and in the territory of the various "Altaic" languages. Janhunen (1996:256) argues that Proto-Turkic *pöküs (< *peküs) is probably borrowed from Indo-European (cf. Latin *pecus* 'cattle'), connecting it with the corpus of Indo-European loanwords in Turkic from Pre-Proto-Tocharian. (For other problems with the forms compared in this putative Altaic cognate set, see Clauson 1956:186; Sinor 1999:390; Starostin 1999c:146, cf. p. 145.)

A second dispute having to do with proposed sound correspondences among putative Altaic languages is what we may call the many-to-one target ratio problem (see Chapter 7). Thus, for example, in Poppe's (1960) scheme, several postulated Proto-Altaic initial sounds – *d-, *ʒ-, *n-, and *ḷ- – all merged to *y- in Proto-Turkic. While this could have happened in this way, this scheme has the decided disadvantage of increasing the targets for searching for potential matches with Turkic words in *y-*, and this in turn dramatically increases the number of potential matches – that is, matches in Mongolian or Tungusic to a Turkic *y-* word could be sought from a wide range of forms, beginning with the reflexes of any of these various "Altaic" proto-sounds, increasing the probability of finding accidental matches. To put the problem in clearer perspective, imagine a claim that said all the initial consonants of some language were lost; this would permit searches for cognates which would pair vowel-initial words in this language with any of the many words beginning in any of the consonants of suspected sister languages. This many-to-one target ratio means many searches will produce accidental matches. Thus, if Turkish really did change in this way (merging numerous originally distinct sounds to *y*), it would make it much more difficult to distinguish real cognates from accidental matchings.

Traits sometimes mentioned as characteristic of Altaic languages, and thus as possible evidence for the hypothesis, include the following (see Tekin 1994):

1. Vowel harmony. This is possibly an areal trait, diffused; it is typologically quite common; as proposed evidence of genetic relationship, it violates the sound–meaning isomorphism requirement.
2. SOV word order, with modifiers before heads. This is also commonplace typologically, and subject to areal diffusion.
3. Postposition. This is expected of SOV word-order languages – it is not an independent feature. It is also common typologically.
4. Agglutinative. This is also common typologically, also possibly an areal linguistic trait.
5. Comparatives based on adjectives in ablative case. This is not uncommon typologically and is correlated with SOV word order.
6. Relatively simple phoneme inventories, absence of initial consonant clusters. This is another trait which is not uncommon and potentially due to areal influence.
7. No verb 'to have' for possession – very common cross-linguistically.
8. No articles, no gender. This, too, is common, potentially areal, and violates the sound–meaning isomorphism requirement for evidence of genetic relationship.

The pronoun similarities among putative "Altaic" languages have been held the strongest evidence for the hypothesis. Greenberg (1997:89–90) believed that the probability of the patterns among pronouns he noted occurring "by accident is infinitesimal"and that borrowing is improbable, since, in his opinion, "one has literally to scour the earth to find a few instances of a borrowed pronoun, much less an entire irregular alternation in pronouns." He saw this as sufficient by itself "to show that the Altaic languages are related" (1997:90). Georg *et al.* (1999) also see the similarities in the first- and second-person pronouns in Turkic, Mongolian, and Tungusic, which share not only similar nominative forms but also a suppletive pattern, as strong support. They assert this could not be due to borrowing (see also Doerfer 1965[1963–75]). However, pronouns are far easier to borrow than they and Greenberg believe, and patterns of the type cited for Altaic are also not unexpected, given the "resonance" factors cited by Nichols (2003; see Chapter 7).

In short, these traits are not persuasive evidence of genetic relationship. This, coupled with the serious doubt about the lexical comparisons, makes it clear why so many reject the "Altaic" hypothesis. In saying this, we do not mean that the Altaic hypothesis is impossible, rather only that it has not been demonstrated on the basis of the evidence presented so far.

9.3   Ural-Altaic

Ural-Altaic is the name of a proposed genetic grouping which would join the uncontested Uralic family and the various "Altaic" languages, of disputed genealogy. Given the problems with "Altaic," the formerly widely accepted Ural-Altaic hypothesis has basically been abandoned. Even the name of the journal *Ural-Altaische Jahrbücher*, influential in this area, was changed a few years ago to *Eurasian Studies Yearbook*.[3] The Ural-Altaic hypothesis has a long history, but, like "Altaic," it was controversial from the beginning (cf. Ramstedt 1903:iii; Kroeber 1913; Shirokogoroff 1970[1931]:89). Ideas to group the languages involved were suggested by Strahlenberg (1730), Rask (1834), Müller (1869), and others, but the hypothesis' real inception is generally attributed to M. A. Castrén (1856, 1862), the first to apply comparative linguistic criteria to the languages assumed to belong together as Ural-Altaic. Though other scholars had been attracted to the shared agglutinative structure (and vowel harmony), Castrén held that this was insufficient for proof of genetic relationship. He included only Finno-Ugric, Samoyed, Turkic, Mongolian, and Tungusic languages in his hypothesized genetic grouping, excluding other languages that Strahlenberg, Rask, and Müller had grouped together (above). He saw the identity of the personal suffixes and similarity among grammatical morphemes of the languages as favorable. (His term "Altaic" embraced what would later be called "Ural-Altaic.")

Castrén's less influential contemporary W. Schott (1849, 1853, 1860) based his conclusions on similarities in vocabulary and morphology, grouping his "Chudic" (i.e. Finno-Ugric, to which he closely related Samoyed) and his "Tatar" (Turkic, Mongolian, and Manchu–Tungusic) groups in what he called "Altaic" or "Chudic-Tatar" (equivalent to later "Ural-Altaic").

Alfred Kroeber (1913) was particularly critical of the Ural-Altaic hypothesis, since he saw it as based primarily only on broad typological features of shared morphology. Aurélien Sauvageot (1930) saw as weaknesses of the hypothesis the simplicity of the structure of the languages involved, the insufficiency of the pronoun evidence, and the error of founding the hypothesis on vowel harmony. In its favor, however, he cited the sharply defined geographical area, the persistence of language groups not different from ancient times, and the closeness

---

[3] Interestingly, earlier it was considered a serious problem for the Altaic hypothesis that the Ural-Altaic hypothesis was then held to be better established than (Micro-)Altaic, leading many to doubt the narrower Altaic hypothesis (cf. Georg *et al.* 1999).

of the geographical territory corresponding to structural unity of the languages (cf. Shirokogoroff 1970[1931]:90–3). In 1931 Shirokogoroff summarized the hypothesis with, "There remain very few parallels [between Uralic and "Altaic"] which are not contested" (Shirokogoroff 1970[1931]:89), and this situation has changed little since then. As Shirokogoroff (1970[1931]:163) pointed out, the remarkable thing about the Ural-Altaic hypothesis has been "the persistence of a tendency to find proofs [evidence] in spite of previous attempts which subsequently failed." Ramstedt, a founder of the Altaic hypothesis, was also skeptical about joining Uralic and Altaic together (Tekin 1994:82). Other works on Ural-Altaic include Collinder (1952, 1955a, 1965b, 1970, 1977), Menges (1945), Räsänen (1955, 1965), Sauvageot (1930), and Winkler (1884, 1886, 1909, 1914).

There seems to be general recognition that the shared structural–typological similarities, which have been the main arguments in favor of this hypothesis, no longer suffice for demonstrating a genetic relationship, although defenders of the hypothesis do not abandon them. For example, Collinder (1977:69) held that "Die strukturelle Ähnlichkeit hat zwar keinen Beweiswert, sie erleichtert aber die etymologische Vergleichung" [The structural similarity has no value as evidence, but it facilitates etymological comparison] – whatever that means. Of Collinder's (1977) 62 lexical sets presented as evidence for Ural-Altaic, there are "only 8 UA [Ural-Altaic] comparisons, 25 are U[ralic] and present in two of the A[ltaic] languages and the remaining 29 are either PFU [Proto-Finno-Ugric] or PS [Proto-Samoyed] and are present only in one of the A[ltaic] languages" (Róna-Tas 1986:237). That is, "about half of his [Collinder's] comparisons are either only in FU [Finno-Ugric] or only in S[amoyed]." As Róna-Tas (1986:237) points out, "this itself should have raised the possibility of early contacts among FU [Finno-Ugric] and S[amoyed] on the one side and some A[ltaic] languages on the other." Collinder himself called into question the words in his list which reflect a so-called "elementare Verwandtschaft" [a basic relationship], 'father,' 'mother,' and 'suck,' and three "Kulturwörter," 'needle,' 'ski,' and 'sleigh' (possible loans). Of Collinder's 8 Ural-Altaic comparisons, 4 are pronouns, and Róna-Tas (1986:237) puts these aside, saying that "the phonetic history of deictics [which for him include these pronouns], just because of their emphatic character, does not always follow the general lines of linguistic history." Of Collinder's 4 remaining Ural-Altaic forms, 2 deal with reindeer breeding (possible "eurasisches Wanderwörter"), and only 2 involve "basic concepts," one of which Róna-Tas (1986:238) challenges because of semantic problems, the other because the reconstruction in Uralic is wrong (problems of contradictory correspondences). Several of the other forms turn out to be loans, making early contact the explanation for many of Collinder's Ural-Altaic comparisons.

Given the general recognition of the shakiness of the Altaic hypothesis, we do not go into detail concerning broader proposals which rely on it, such as those which would include also Japanese, Korean, Ainu, etc. (See Kim 1976; Krippes 1990b; Lewin 1976; Martin 1966, 1968, 1975, 1990, 1991; Menges 1975, 1984; Miller 1968, 1971a, 1971b, 1975, 1976, 1977, 1979a,1979b, 1981, 1984, 1991; Murayama 1966, 1975, 1977; Lee 1958; Ramstedt 1924; Street 1973, 1981, 1985; Whitman 1985. For arguments and assessments see Comrie 1993; Doerfer 1974; Janhunen 1989; Janhunen and Kho 1982; Róna-Tas 1974; Shirokogoroff 1931[1970]; Sinor 1988, 1990; Unger 1990a, 1990b.)

9.4 Nostratic[4]

The Nostratic hypothesis has received considerable attention in recent years (see for example Joseph and Salmons 1998; Renfrew and Nettle 1999.). It is better known than most other proposed macro-families, but it remains controversial. Most historical linguists either reject it (see Campbell 1998, 1999; Ringe 1995a; Trask 1999; Vine 1991) or ignore it. The hypothesis, as advanced in the 1960s by Illich-Svitych in its best-known form, held Indo-European, Uralic, Altaic, Kartvelian, Dravidian, and Hamito-Semitic (later Afroasiatic) to be genetically related. Dolgopolsky's version (cf. 1964a, 1964b), from about the same time, includes most of these but excluded Dravidian, while being sympathetic to "Chuckchi–Kamchatkan" possibly being included. Starostin (1989:43, 44) wanted to exclude Afroasiatic, believing Nostratic and Afroasiatic to be related, but at a deeper level, although he included Eskimo–Aleut within Nostratic itself. Bomhard's Nostratic macro-family embraces Indo-European, Afroasiatic, Uralic–Yukaghir, Elamo-Dravidian, Altaic, and possibly Sumerian, with genetic links also to Chukchi–Kamchatkan, Eskimo–Aleut, and Gilyak (Nivkh) (see Bomhard 1984, 1990; Bomhard and Kerns 1994). Other proposals would expand Nostratic variously to include, or at least be related with in higher-order genetic units, also Eskimo–Aleut, various American Indian groups, Yeniseian, Gilyak (Nivkh), Sumerian, Elamite (with Dravidian), Sino-Tibetan, North Caucasian, and others, thus connecting Nostratic with major segments of the world (see Bomhard and Kerns 1994:3, 34; Ruhlen 1994a; Shevoroshkin 1989c; Starostin 1989:43, 1991a). The question is, then, what version of Nostratic is most credible, if any?[5]

Greenberg's (1990b, 1991, 2000a, 2002) Eurasiatic hypothesis was not intended to be equated with Nostratic, but rather is presented as a competing

---

[4] This discussion of Nostratic is based on Campbell 1998 and 1999.

[5] It is worth recalling that the Nostratic hypothesis had antecedents before Illich-Svitych's work. For example, it is often noted that over 50 percent of Illich-Svitych's sets had been noted in some preliminary fashion in Collinder's work (Collinder 1934, 1954, 1965b). Other precursors include Cuny 1912, 1924, 1943, 1946, Dolgopolsky 1964a, 1964b, 1965 (cf. also Dolgopolsky 1969, 1970, 1971, 1972, 1974, 1984, 1989), and Pedersen 1933, 1935, among others.

hypothesis. Nevertheless, it overlaps Nostratic to a considerable extent, including Indo-European, Uralic, Yukaghir, Altaic, Ainu, Korean, Japanese, Nivkh, Chukotian, and Eskimo–Aleut. Of these, Indo-European, Uralic, Yukaghir (under Uralic or Yukaghir–Uralic), Altaic, and Korean (under Altaic), and often Japanese (as a putative further member of Altaic), are typically considered to be members of Nostratic by its supporters, and the others (except Ainu) have from time to time been thought by various Nostraticists either also to belong to Nostratic or to be related to Nostratic as coordinate members of some higher-order grouping. Greenberg's Eurasiatic, on the other hand, excludes the presumed Nostratic (sub)families Kartvelian, Dravidian, and Afroasiatic. However, Greenberg still held that these and the other putative Nostratic languages are related, but more distantly: "I am by no means denying the relationship of these groups: namely Afroasiatic, Kartvelian and Dravidian, but I believe these relationships are more remote" (Greenberg 1990b:88). While there is considerable overlap in the members of Eurasiatic and Nostratic, there are also differences, and therefore both hypotheses cannot be correct where they make contradictory claims.

Strongly worded polemic from the dedicated among the former Soviet inner circle of Nostraticists has been aimed at Bomhard's view of Nostratic (see Kaiser and Shevoroshkin 1987; Markey and Shevoroshkin 1986), and Bomhard responds with criticisms of "Muscovite views on Nostratic," those of the "Moscow School." Debate centers on the methods employed (essentially techniques of standard comparative linguistics though applied somewhat liberally), on which families are to be included within the larger Nostratic construct, and especially on alternative reconstructions of Nostratic phonology differing largely on the acceptance or rejection of the glottalic theory for Indo-European stop consonants. For Illich-Svitych and Dolgopolsky (letting Indo-European D represents the whole series of voiced stops, T voiceless stops, T' glottalized stops, D^h voiced aspirates), Indo-European D < Nostratic T, Indo-European T < Nostratic T', Indo-European D^h < Nostratic D, but for Bomhard, who holds the glottalic theory for Indo-European, the traditional Indo-European D (glottalic theory T') < Nostratic T', Indo-European T (given as T[^{h}], phonetically aspirated) < Nostratic T (also phonetically aspirated), and Indo-European D[^{h}] < Nostratic D. (See Palmaitis 1986.) However, since the glottalic and traditional views of Indo-European obstruents are incommensurate, the correspondence sets and associated cognates proposed by Bomhard differ from those of Illich Svitych and others; thus for forms involving these sounds, the same Indo-European etymon may find itself in totally different proposed Nostratic cognate sets in these different approaches. Few of the sets actually match, however, though both the Moscow School and Bomhard each present a large number of lexical sets they believe to be cognates. To us this suggests how easy it is to find accidental matches.

It is important to remember that some families in the large Nostratic construct (or set of interconnected constructs) could prove to be related to one another while others might not (Campbell 1998). Thus, for example, it is plausible that the evidence could perhaps show Indo-European and Uralic (as in the Indo-Uralic hypothesis) to be related to one another, but fail to demonstrate that these are related to, say, Dravidian (as would be consistent with Dolgopolsky's version of Nostratic). This being the case, the status of each member family and its possible relationship with each of the other proposed families within this hypothesis are to be determined individually. It is not so simple as just determining whether there either is or is not a valid Nostratic family; rather, at stake is a whole set of intersecting hypotheses involving a possible relationship between each individual family and each other family implicated in the various Nostratic proposals.[6]

Also, even if one were to be able to show numerous of the proposed Nostratic cognates invalid, there might remain enough other proposed cognate sets which conceivably could still uphold the hypothesis (Manaster Ramer 1993b:227). Illich Svitych (1989d) had 607 lexical sets, and the volumes of his etymological dictionary have 378 proposed etyma (Illich Svitych 1971a; cf. 1989a, 1989b, 1989c, 1989d, 1990); Bomhard and Kerns (1994) have 601 lexical sets. The solution to this problem adopted here is to concentrate on those forms considered by proponents of the hypothesis to be the strongest (those of Dolgopolsky 1964a[1986] and Kaiser and Shevoroshkin 1988). If those considered to be the strongest do not hold up, the sets considered to be of less strength will not be persuasive.

The large number of proposed cognate sets together with the many languages in Nostratic hypotheses could make it seem impossible for individuals without a strong background in all the language families involved to be able to evaluate the proposal (cf. Manaster-Ramer 1994:157). However, this is not the case. Individuals can evaluate numerous aspects of the evidence presented. For example, one can check whether the forms presented match the sound correspondences that have been postulated without firsthand experience with the languages. One can determine to what extent the proposed reconstructions correspond to typological expectations and linguistic universals, whether the proposed cognates are too permissive in semantic associations, when onomatopoetic forms are involved, when the forms are too short to deny chance as a possible explanation, etc. That is, an individual who is not an expert in the language families involved can still apply many of the standard criteria (Chapter 7) to determine whether the evidence presented is supportive or problematic. This we do in part here.

---

[6] Of course, it is also possible that some of these families may actually have descended from a common ancestor so long ago but have undergone so much linguistic change that it is impossible now with legitimate methods ever to demonstrate such a relationship.

Ultimately areal linguistic issues must also enter the discussion, since a number of well-known language areas in the linguistic literature involve several of the Nostratic families. As Sinor (1990:16) puts it in his discussion of Inner Asia:

> While there are those scholars who aver that some or even all of them [Uralic and "Altaic" (or Turkic, Mongolian, and Tungusic)] are genetically related – that is, that they descend from a common, ancestral *Ursprache* – others, including myself, believe that the elements which they unquestionably have in common are due to constant interaction over the centuries if not millennia, and that they result from convergent rather than divergent development. Beyond purely linguistic arguments . . . the historically documented absorption by either Uralic or Altaic languages of many of the so-called Paleoasiatic tongues would support such a theory.

(Cf. Campbell 1997c; Hajdú 1979; Jakobson 1931; Masica 1976; Pusztay 1980; Starostin 1989:43.) To date, work in Nostratic has avoided the areal linguistic issue, but as recent work shows, it is almost always necessary in questions of remote linguistic kinship to take areal linguistic considerations carefully into account.

9.4.1   Nostratic methodologically viewed

There is considerable agreement among both protagonists and opponents of Nostratic with respect to methodology. Here we call upon some of the standard criteria for evaluating methodological aspects of the hypothesis (see Chapter 7). We concentrate on Illich-Svitych's (henceforth IS) version of Nostratic, since it is the most widely acknowledged. When one brings these general methodological considerations to bear upon the evidence presented in favor of his Nostratic hypothesis, one finds difficulties with a large number of the forms presented as potential cognates. We illustrate this here, not by presenting a detailed commentary on all the data, but rather by counting forms which exhibit various methodological problems. (See Campbell 1998, 1999 for details.)[7]

9.4.1.1 "Descriptive" forms IS forthrightly labeled 26 of the 378 forms of his etymological dictionary as "descriptive," by which he means onomatopoetic, affective, expressive, ideophonic, or sound-symbolic forms, i.e. 7 percent of the total number of forms. Moreover, we find 16 additional

---

[7] Here we follow Kaiser and Shevoroshkin's (1987) diacritic conventions (and those of IS 1989c utilized by Parkinson in his translation) in representing glottalized consonants as *C'*, rather than with a dot under them as IS does. This, however, necessitates representing Indo-European palatalized consonants as C^y, rather than with IS's *C'*, to avoid confusion with glottalized consonants. We follow Kaiser and Shevoroshkin also in writing *V* rather than IS's small upside-down *v* for vowels of unknown quality. We also have utilized *w* and *y* instead of the *u* and *i* with circumflexes under them, respectively.

onomatopoetic, affective, or sound-symbolic forms, not so labeled by IS, which we attribute to this category (nos. 4, 5, 12, 53, 64, 84, 94, 109, 139, 189, 196, 199, 202, 205, 218, 291), making the total 42, or about 11 percent of the total. A less conservative count might add several others (e.g. nos. 16, 19, 33, 37, 145, 148, 302, 350).

9.4.1.2 Questionable cognates IS himself indicated that 57 of the 378 sets are questionable (i.e. 15 percent), which he signaled with a question mark. We would add the other sets questioned in this chapter also to this category – a large number, indeed. However, this number could be increased many times over, since in numerous forms IS points to problems, things not conforming to expectations, which he lists in slanted lines (/ /), in forms given with question marks, and in reconstructions with upper-case letters (which indicate uncertainties).

9.4.1.3 Sets with only two families represented One of Illich-Svitych's (1989a[1971a]) criteria was that only cognate sets with representatives from at least three of the six families proposed as members of Nostratic would be considered as supportive of the hypothesis:

Clearly, a special proof is necessary to show that the similarities found between compared languages are not accidental, but rather point to a distant linguistic relationship ... Toward this end, we propose the following method of evaluating the character of the similarities collected . . . We will take the similarities between three pairs, made up of any three of the six proto-languages being compared . . . (Illich-Svitych 1989a:112; cf. Kaiser and Shevoroshkin (1987:35)

Nevertheless, 134 sets from the 378 involve forms from only two families. That is, 35 percent of the forms are questionable on IS's own grounds.

9.4.1.4 Non-corresponding sound correspondences[8] Nostraticists maintain that they follow standard principles of historical linguistics and rely on "exacting phonological correspondences" (Markey and Shevoroshkin 1986:xiv). As Starostin (1999b:4) put it:

What is the method of establishing and proving ancient genetic relationships between language families? To this, evidently, there can be only one answer: the classical method of comparative historical linguistics, that is the discovery of a system of regular sound correspondences between proto-languages that is valid for the majority of lexical and morphological items, and the reconstruction of an earlier system based on those correspondences. It is precisely this method that was used by Illič-Svityč in his reconstruction of Common Nostratic.

---

[8] A double asterisk (**) is used here to signal postulated Proto-Nostratic forms and to distinguish these from forms reconstructed in the proto-languages that are thought to make up Nostratic, such as Proto-Indo-European, Proto-Uralic, etc., signaled by a single asterisk (*).

Nevertheless, frequently the forms presented as evidence of Nostratic do not exhibit the proposed sound correspondences, i.e. they have sounds at odds with those that would be required according to the Nostratic correspondence sets (given in Dybo 1989b, 1990). Campbell (1998), looking mostly only at stops and only at the Indo-European and Uralic forms, found 25 cases of postulated cognates that did not follow the proposed Nostratic correspondences. For example, in (30) **$bVnt'V$ 'to tie, bind,' with Afroasiatic *bn* and Indo-European *bhendh* 'tie,' only two constituent language families are represented, but in neither are the actually occurring sounds those predicted by the expected sound correspondences. Rather, the Afroasiatic reflex of Nostratic **t' should be $t^1(t^2)$, and the Indo-European reflex should not be *dh*, but rather *t*. In (12) **$bič'V$ 'to break,' Indo-European *peis-* 'smash, crush, press,' is given, although the sound correspondence charts show that the only expected Indo-European reflex of Nostratic **b- is Indo-European *bh-*. The **k' of (25) should be reflected by some form of Indo-European *k*, not the *g/gh* found in the proposed Indo-European cognate listed in this set. The **d of (174) should be reflected by Uralic *t* instead of the δ that occurs in the Uralic form listed. In (205) with **-t'-, the Dravidian form should actually have -*t(t)*-, and Afroasiatic should be -$t^1(t^2)$- rather than the actually occurring sounds, according to the sound correspondences. A thorough check would, we assume, turn up many more examples. (For a critique of the Nostratic vowel correspondences, see Serebrennikov 1982[1986], Bomhard and Kerns 1994:18.)

There is also another way in which IS's putative sound correspondences are not consistent with standard procedures of the comparative method. In the correspondence sets compiled by Dybo (1989b, 1990) from IS's material, several of the putative Nostratic sounds are not in fact reflected by regular sound correspondences among the languages. For example, we are told that "in Kartv[elian] and Indo-European, the reflexes of Nostratic *[**]p* are found to be unstable" (Illich-Svitych 1990:168); a brief look at Nostratic forms beginning in **p reveals that both the Indo-European and the Kartvelian forms arbitrarily begin with either *p* or *b*, but this is not regular sound change and is not sanctioned by the standard comparative method. Similarly, we are told that glottalization in Afroasiatic occurs "sporadically under other conditions still not clear" (Illich-Svitych 1990:168). In the correspondence sets, several of the languages are listed with multiple reflexes of a single Nostratic sound, but with no explanation of conditions under which one versus the other reflex might appear. For example, for Nostratic **ń the Indo-European box lists both *y* and *n-*, but an examination of the forms beginning with **ń shows that it is arbitrary when the postulated Indo-European cognate has *y and when *n.

9.4.1.5 Short forms It is easy to find accidental matchings in short forms among unrelated languages (forms of the shape CV, VC, C, or V) (see Nichols 1996a; Ringe 1992, 1993). Therefore, while short forms may represent true cognates, in a preliminary hypothesis involving languages not yet shown to be related, there is also a high probability that they may be due to chance. This being the case, such short forms do not help significantly to establish an as-yet undemonstrated relationship. Of IS's 378 forms, 57 (or 15 percent) involve such short forms.

9.4.1.6 Semantically non-equivalent forms We count 55 forms (i.e. 16 percent) which involve comparisons of forms in the different languages that are fairly distinct semantically. Semantic latitude makes it easier to find phonetically similar forms, increasing the possibility that chance rather than common ancestry explains the perceived similarity (see Chapter 7; also Ringe 1992; Campbell 1998, 1999). While some of these 55 cases are not so implausible in their semantic differences, a number stand out as problematic, e.g. (19) 'to grow up'/'become'/'tree'/'be'; (47) 'hardened crust'/'rough'/'scab'/'crust'; (70) 'see'/'day'/'bright, light'; (158) 'lip'/'mushroom'/'soft outgrowth'/'outgrowth'; and others.

9.4.1.7 Diffused forms Given the history of central Eurasia, with wave after wave of conquest, expansion, migration, trade and exchange, and of multilingual and multiethnic states, it is not at all surprising that some forms turn out to be borrowed among the languages in this broad area. Joki (1973) has identified many, and several of the forms cited by IS as Nostratic cognates have been identified by others as loans or probable loans; these include forms for 'sister-in-law,' 'water,' 'do,' 'give,' 'carry,' 'lead,' 'to do'/'put,' 'husband's sister,' and others (see Campbell 1998; Gamkrelidze and Ivanov 1984:1.224, 295, 1984:2.941–2, 1985:14–21; Joki 1973; Koivulehto 1991; Manaster Ramer 1993b:224). We would add the following from IS's 378 proposed etyma which involve probable or possible loans: (78) 'conifer, branch, point,' 'thorn'; (117) 'poplar'; (126) (Uralic *arpa*, "Altaic" *arba-*, both meaning 'practice witchcraft,' not an unlikely loan among the intermarrying shamanistic peoples of this region); (135) 'deer'; (142) 'relative pronoun/interrogative pronoun' (identified as borrowed in Uralic sources, cf. Joki 1973:264); (154) 'vessel'; (170) 'birch'; (274) 'bird cherry'; and (276) 'honey (sweet tree juice)' (cf. 'mead'; similar forms are widely diffused; see Hajdú 1975:33; Joki 1973:281–2, 283–5, 1988). As shown in Campbell (1990), a number of tree names have been borrowed among Uralic, Indo-European, and also so-called Altaic languages (see also Friedrich 1970; Hajdú 1975; Róna-Tas 1988:745–6; Suhonen 1988:605–6). An example is IS (1989d:159) ****p'ulV* 'poplar,' exemplified in his evidence only by "Altaic" *pula* 'poplar, ash' and Indo-European *pel-* 'poplar' (contrast Friedrich's [1970:49] Indo-European reconstruction *osp-*, Mallory and Adams' [1997:599] *$h_{2/3}osp$-* 'poplar, aspen') (see Campbell 1990:158–9). Given the close phonetic similarity among the forms IS gives for the tree names in his lists, there is good reason to suspect borrowing for a number of them.

9.4.1.8 Typological problems   As several have shown, Nostratic as traditionally reconstructed (by IS and others) is typologically flawed. For example, Manaster Ramer (1993b:211) points out that counter to typological expectations, there are "very few cases of [Nostratic] roots containing two voiceless stops" (where "in almost all of these the second voiceless stop is clustered with a preceding sonorant"). Given that voiceless stops are less marked, they should occur more freely and with greater frequency than is the case in IS's reconstructions. Similarly, Bomhard and Kerns (1994:13) direct attention to the fact that in IS's version of Nostratic, glottalized stops are considerably more frequent than their plain (unmarked) counterparts (where Proto-Indo-European plain voiceless stops are assumed to reflect Nostratic glottalics). Another example of IS's typologically inappropriate assumptions is his change from Nostratic affricates to clusters of fricative + stop in Indo-European (Doerfer 1973).

Additional examples in all these categories, as well as other classes of difficulties, are given in Campbell (1998), which deals with the Uralic data in IS's papers. This is telling, since Uralic is thought by proponents to hold a key position within Nostratic. Indeed, many of the proposed Nostratic reconstructions pay special heed to Uralic forms; Shevoroshkin (1989b:14) says that in some aspects "Uralic is the most archaic Nostratic language." It is said that more than 50 percent of IS's forms contain proposed Uralic cognates, a much higher percentage than from any other member family; as is frequently pointed out, IS's reconstruction of Nostratic vowels is nearly identical with Finnish (cf. Bomhard and Kerns 1994:18; Serebrennikov 1986[1982]79). Therefore, because the Uralic evidence utilized in IS's Nostratic comparisons was found problematic, serious doubt is cast on the Nostratic hypothesis as a whole.

9.4.2   Evaluation of the strongest lexical sets

A proper evaluation of Nostratic, given the several hundred proposed etymologies, is difficult, but not impossible. Not all the proposed etyma are held to be of equal weight. For example, as mentioned, IS overtly marked many of his proposed cognate sets as doubtful or problematic in some way. To avoid the

problem posed by the sheer number of proposed Nostratic sets, we emphasize
those which are held to be the strongest, most secure. These include those
which correspond to Dolgopolsky's (1964a[1986]) calculation of the fifteen
most stable lexemes, thought to be most resistant to replacement and/or borrowing cross-linguistically, and the Nostratic examples presented by Kaiser
and Shevoroshkin (1988) (henceforth K&S). If those examples held to be the
strongest evidence by proponents of the hypothesis prove problematic, then it
is clear that reservations concerning Nostratic are in order.

In our evaluation, we concentrate mostly on Uralic and Indo-European forms
given in support of putative Nostratic cognate sets. The numbers we give in
brackets ([]) are from K&S, those in parentheses are from Illich-Svitych (1990).
The latter contains translations of the headings from the three volumes of IS's
Nostratic dictionary (Illich Svitych 1971a), all that is published to date. Unfortunately, these 378 forms go only up to *p* in the alphabetic listing, where IS
reached in his preparation of the material before his death, with only a very few
forms listed from beyond that point in the alphabet. K&S sets which lack Uralic
material are not discussed here; this explains the missing numbers involving
K&S's examples. When the same (or an overlapping) lexical set is given in two
different K&S sets, the numbers for both are given.

Abbreviations:

D   = Dolgopolsky (1964a[1986])
FU   = Finno-Ugric
IS   = Illich-Svitych
K&S   = Kaiser and Shevoroshkin (1988)
SKES = *Suomen kielen etymologinen sanakirja* [Etymological dictionary of
         the Finnish language] (Toivonen *et al.* 1955–81)
SSA = *Suomen sanojen alkuperä: etymologinen sanakirja* [The origin of
         Finnish words: etymological dictionary] (Kulonen 1992–2000)
PFP   = Proto-Finno-Permic
PFU   = Proto-Finno-Ugric
PU   = Proto-Uralic
R   = Uralic forms from Rédei (1986–8)
S   = Uralic forms from Sammallahti (1988)

K&S [1] through [13] are monosyllabic forms, most *CV* in shape. (Sammallahti provides reconstructions only for forms which are dissyllabic or longer.)
A general methodological principle of distant genetic relationships (Chapter
7) is to avoid such short forms, since they do little to defy chance as a possible explanation for any phonetic similarity such forms might share among the
languages compared.

We begin with forms representing Dolgopolsky's (1986[1964a]:34–5) list of most stable lexemes, with the lexemes given here in order, signaled by D plus a number representing its rank in Dolgopolsky's list, where D1 represents the highest in stability, D2 next highest, and so on.

D1 'first-person marker.' [1a] (299) 'I': Uralic *mi. [1b] (299) 'I' (oblique stem built by adding the suffix **-nV to **mi-): Uralic *mi-nV-. [1c] (289) 'we' (inclusive): Uralic *mä-/*me- 'we.' R PU *më 'I, we'; Janhunen (1981:232) PU *mun 'I', PU ? *me (? *mä) 'we.' These forms for 'first person' are short and involve the nasals *m* and *n*; since pronominal forms with these nasals are found in languages throughout the world with rather high frequency, they by themselves are not particularly persuasive (see Campbell 1994b, 1997a:243–52). Nasal sounds in particular are found in grammatical morphemes precisely because they are the most perceptually salient of all consonants (Maddieson 1984:70), explaining why nasals, especially *m* and *n*, show up so frequently in the world's languages in markers of pronouns. (See Chapter 7.)

D2 'two.' No Nostratic representative of 'two' is given in K&S or IS 1990; however, IS 1989d:167 has **to 'two': Uralic *to-ńć-e 'second.' Neither Sammallahti nor Rédei reconstruct this, and Uralic has another clear form for 'two,' S PU **kektä. The IS form is based on Finnish *toinen* 'second, other,' which, however, is derived from the demonstrative pronoun root *tō* (Finnish *tuo*) 'that (one)' *(-inen* 'adjectival suffix') (*SKES* 4:1329, *SSA* 3:304). This is a short form, hence subject to a higher probability of chance explaining it. This is not a persuasive set. It also illustrates the point that IS often relied too heavily on Finnish.

D3 'second-person marker.' [2a] 'thou': Uralic *ti (oblique form *t). [2b] 'you' (plural): Uralic *tä. R (5:539) PU *të 'you singular, you plural.' Janhunen (1981:232) PU *tun 'you sg.,' PU ? *te (? *tä) 'you pl.' This, too, is a short form. Given that grammatical morphemes tend to contain the least marked consonants, and *t* is highly unmarked, forms of 'second person' exhibiting *t* are found in many languages around the world.

D4 'who, what.' [3] (223) **K'e 'who'[9]: Uralic *ke- 'who,' (232) **K'o 'who': Uralic *ku/o- 'who.' R (2:191) PU ku- (ko-) 'who, which, ?what,' R (2:140) FU, ?PU *ke (ki) 'who.' This is a short form. It is considered a borrowing by some (cf. Joki 1973:268, 273–5). Accidentally similar forms are found in other languages.

D5 'tongue.' (221) **K'ä/lH/ä 'tongue': Uralic *kēle- 'tongue.' S PU *käxli, S PFU *keele- 'tongue.' This set is represented only by two families; the other is Altaic *k'ä:la- 'tongue, talk.'

---

[9] IS and K&S use upper-case letters to signal uncertain reconstructions; for example, *K* for an uncertain consonant which is either velar or postvelar (uvular), *E* for an uncertain front vowel, etc.

D6 'name.' (317) **nimi 'name': Uralic *nime 'name,' Indo-European *nom- 'name' (cf. Mallory and Adams' [1997:390] *h₁nomn̥ or *h₁neh₃mn̥). S PU *nimi. This set is represented by only two families. It is frequently identified as a loanword (see Joki 1973:291, 1988:586; Rédei 1988:641, 652).

D7 'eye.' (118) **HuK'a 'eye, see.' This set has no Uralic form, and has only two representatives, with Indo-European *hwekw/*heuk 'eye, see' and Altaic *uka- 'notice, understand.' These forms are not semantically equivalent.

D8 'heart.' [4] (200) **k'Erd- 'heart.' This set has no Uralic form, only Indo-European *kʸerd- 'heart' and Kartvelian m-k'erd 'breast' in IS (1990). A Chadic form, k'Vrd 'chest' to represent Afroasiatic, was added by K&S. On superficial inspection these compared forms would appear to exhibit similarity. However, several have pointed out that the Indo-European form *kʸerd- in fact has irregular correspondences (cf. Dolgopolsky 1986[1964a]:28; Kaiser and Shevoroshkin 1988:312–13; Manaster Ramer 1993b); it does not have the expected *-dh reflex of the Nostratic **-d. Given that the vowel of the Nostratic form is undetermined (its **E meant to represent some uncertain front vowel), this set is not strong. Gamkrelidze and Ivanov (1985:20) hold the Kartvelian forms to be borrowed from Indo-European.

D9 'tooth.' (370) **/p'/alV 'tooth.' This set, with no Uralic form, has only two representatives (Dravidian palV 'tooth' and Altaic PalV '(molar) tooth'). The sound correspondences do not match what is expected, hence the reconstruction with /p'/, which for IS indicates that it is uncertain.

D10 'verbal NEG (both negative proper and prohibition).' (128) **ʔäla 'particle of categorical negation': Uralic *äla/ela '2nd pers. sg imperative of negative verb.' Two of the other three representatives (Kartvelian and Altaic) are marked by IS as being doubtful, while the Afroasiatic form *ʔl/lʔ 'prohibitive and negative particle' shares no more than an l phonetically, an unmarked consonant, which in any case cannot match the Uralic l of this form since its l is not part of the Uralic root, nor are the meanings fully consistent. To understand this set, compare related (129) **ʔe 'negative particle': Uralic *e- 'negative verb (indicative stem).' This is a short form. The negative imperative is morphologically complex, based on PU *e- (*ä-) 'negative verb,' with the derivational deverbal suffix *l (R 1:68, SKES 1:32, SSA 1:99, Janhunen 1982:37). (128) is derived from (129).

D11 'fingernail/toenail.' (362) **p/a/r/ä 'nail.' There is no Uralic example; the Indo-European and Dravidian comparisons are marked as doubtful in IS; and the glosses involve much semantic latitude, 'fingernail,' 'claw,' 'finger,' 'thumb.'

D12 'louse.' IS **t'äjV 'louse' (IS 1989c:157). S PFU *täji 'louse.' The material available does not indicate what the Nostratic families/languages involved are nor the forms offered in support of this Nostratic reconstruction.

D13 'tear' (noun). No Nostratic form for this gloss is proposed in K&S, IS, or Dolgopolsky (1986[1964a]).

D14 'water.' [20] **wete 'water': Uralic *wete. S PU *weti. Some identify this as a loanword (see Gamkrelidze and Ivanov 1984.2:942; Joki 1973:344; Rédei 1988:641, 654). IS (1989d) had **wetV: Uralic *wete 'water.' Otherwise, it is one of the more attractive cases for the hypothesis.

D15 'dead.' Cf. (293) ***m/ä/rV* 'be ill, die': Uralic **m/e/rV* 'wound, pain' (not reconstructed by Sammallahti or Rédei); and ***q'o(H)lV* 'kill': Uralic *kōle 'die' (S PU **kåxli̮-*, S PFU *kōli 'die'). The semantic equations for the glosses of putative Nostratic languages ('torment,' 'kill,' 'die' and 'be ill,' 'die,' 'wound,' 'pain') are somewhat questionable; none is given directly as 'dead.' Joki (1973:280–1) discusses Finno-Permic *marta-s 'ill, dying' and related *merta 'man,' both loans from Indo-European (through Indo-Iranian) forms related to 'die' and 'dead,' Indo-European **mer(ə)-*, **mr̥-ta*.

To summarize the Nostratic evidence involved in Dolgopolsky's fifteen most stable lexemes, it is clear that most are questionable in one way or another according to the standard criteria for assessing proposals of remote linguistic kinship (see Chapter 7). In these sets, four have problems with phonological correspondences (5, 8, 9, 11); five involve excessive semantic difference among the putative cognates; four have representatives in only two of the putative Nostratic families (5, 6, 7, 9); two involve problems of morphological analysis (2, 11); IS himself listed one as doubtful (11); and finally, one (2) reflects the tendency to rely too heavily on Finnish forms even when not supported by the historical evidence – example (2) has no Uralic etymology. All but two are challenged, and for these two (12 and 13) the relevant forms needed for evaluation are not present. Nevertheless, these comparisons are somewhat more suggestive than the other cases presented by K&S as strong support, to which we now turn. Definitively, these fifteen are not sufficiently robust to encourage faith in the proposed genetic relationship.

9.4.3   K&S forms

We examine now the remaining putative Nostratic cognate sets and the Uralic examples presented in Kaiser and Shevoroshkin (1988), presumed to represent the strongest examples of evidence for the Nostratic hypothesis.

[5] **na 'originally a locative particle': Uralic **-na/*-nä*. Janhunen (1982:30) PU *-*nål-nä* 'locative.' This is a short form, possibly due to chance.

[6] (333) **NA 'marker of animate plural': Uralic (?) **-NV*. However, no such form is found in the Uralic sources. This involves a short form.

[7] ***-tV* 'marker of inanimate plural': Uralic **-t*. Janhunen (1982:29) PU *-*t* 'absolute plural.' This, too, involves short grammatical markers.

[9] **t'V 'marker of causative-reflexive': Uralic *-t(t)-. Janhunen (1982:33) PU *-tål/*-tä '(deverbal) causative and (denominal) factitive [sic] derivatives,' *-ptål/*-ptä 'groups of causatives.' This has somewhat uncertain semantics; it, too, is a short form.

[10] (189) **-k'a 'diminutive suffix': Uralic *-kka/*-kkä. Similarities appear to develop in languages for affective reasons; for example, Sapir mentioned in various places that he thought there might be a general diminutive with k or ka among American Indian languages. In any case, there are problems with the sound correspondences; the Kartvelian reflex should be -k-, not the -k'- of the forms given, -k'- (-ak'-, -ik'-) 'diminutive.'[10] It is also a short form.

[11] (246) **-l(a) 'suffix of collective nouns': Uralic *-la 'collective suffix'; the other forms given are Dravidian -l 'plural suffix' and Altaic -l(a) 'collective suffix.' This involves short forms, with only an unmarked consonant supposed to be matching. Accidental similarities are easily found in languages around the world. While the suffix is found throughout FU languages, its original meaning was 'diminutive'; here again one suspects that IS's reconstruction has been too heavily influenced by the Finnish forms, since Finnish -la is a derivational suffix meaning in some forms 'diminutive,' but mostly with the meaning 'place of,' presumably the source of IS's gloss of a collective locative, as in, for example, setä-lä 'uncle's house, uncle's place' (setä 'uncle') (Hakulinen 1968:110; Laanest 1982:209).

[13] (201) **k'(o) 'intensifying and copulative particle': Uralic *-ka/*-kä. This is a short form, and the Uralic sources have no such form. The Finnic *-ka/*-kä clitic (with its two forms, a pronominal form and negative conjunction [which developed from the pronominal base]) appears to have influenced thinking here, but though it has an intensifying and copulative connection today, for example, in Finnish, its original function was far from this.

Sets [5] through [13] involve short forms, similarities which may easily be due to accident (see Chapter 7). Most involve highly unmarked consonants in grammatical markers; accidentally similar examples from many languages are easily found.

[14], cf. [50] **q'/iw/lV 'ear, hear': Uralic *kūle- 'hear.' S PFU *kuuli 'hear.' Superficially, this would seem like an attractive set, but it has problems, in particular the lack of regular correspondences in most of the language families represented. K&S point out irregularities in the sound correspondences, saying, "as is sometimes the case in very archaic and stable words, there are slight exceptions to the regular rules." This view of "archaic and stable words" being subject to irregular correspondences is a violation of the comparative method and the regularity of sound change, and is rejected by nearly all historical

---

[10] This problem may be more pervasive than just this set, since Dybo (1989b:114) has a footnote which suggests that the Kartvelian reflexes of this sound "are found to be unstable."

linguists. Kartvelian should have *l* as its reflex of **l, not the *r* of the **k'ur-* 'ear' given here; the Altaic reflex with ***q'* should have been *k*, not *k'* (in **k'/ul-* [presumably /k'/ is intended, to show this irregular, non-corresponding reflex]); similarly, Afroasiatic should have **q'* as the reflex of ***q'*, not *k'*. Moreover, presumably IS's /iw/ in this form is a device intended to cover the otherwise non-corresponding vowels of the forms listed. Unfortunately, when one allows sets that do not fit the postulated sound correspondences, one increases sharply the possibility that chance rather than common inheritance accounts for the similarity. Finally, there is a semantic disparity in 'ear' and 'hear' (among IS's glosses).

[15] (220) East Nostratic ***k'/q'awinga* 'armpit': Uralic **kajŋa-(lV)*. S PFU **koni*; R (2:178) FU, ?PU **kon3* (**kana*), ? **kon3 + ala* (? **kana + ala*). K&S believe that this Nostratic reconstruction is incorrect; they suggest instead the compound ***k'/q'awin-galV* (noting ***-l- >* Uralic **-l-*). It appears that both IS and K&S have been unduly influenced by the Finnish form, *kainalo* 'armpit,' and have made projections based on it back to PU and on to Nostratic, although the evidence from the other FU languages does not support this, as Sammallahti's corrected reconstruction (PFU **koni*), which is very different phonetically from those of K&S and IS, shows. Rédei (2:178) explains the forms with *l*, as in the case of Finnish *kainalo*, as being derived from **käðen* 'hand, arm' *+ ala* 'under' (postposition).

[16], cf. [38] (162) **kälU 'female in-law' (glossed 'female relation' by IS): Uralic **kälä*. S PU **käläw* 'in-law'; R (2:135) PFP, ?PU **käl3*, ? **käl3-w3* 'sister-in-law' (the whole set considered uncertain); Janhunen (1981:238, 268) PU **käli-w* 'sister-in-law' (probably morphologically complex). IS's number (52) also bears considerable similarity to [16] and [38]. IS's (162) Uralic form is **kälü* 'female relation (husband's sister, brother's wife, etc.)', somewhat different from that given by K&S; IS (1989d:143) gave the Uralic form as **käl/ew/*. This form involves borrowing (Joki 1973:267–8). While initially the phonetic and semantic similarities between this Uralic form and those from the other languages might seem attractive, there are problems. First, this is another case where IS's Uralic reconstruction appears to depend too directly upon Finnish; IS's Uralic reconstruction is identical to Finnish *kälü* (orthograph-ically <käly>) 'sister-in-law.' Second, IS's gloss 'female relation' makes the form seem quite similar to the other languages (with glosses 'daughter/sister-in law,' 'bride,' 'woman,' 'brother's wife,' 'wife of younger brother or son,' 'sister's husband'). Moreover, these phonetically quite similar forms for affinal kin (relatives by marriage) appear to represent old borrowings. At least some of the Uralic languages are known to have borrowed this word from Turkic (e.g Permiak Zyrien and Votyak *ken-* 'sister-in-law' < Old Chuvash *ken* < Proto-Turkic **kelin*, Róna-Tas 1988:762). Set (174) should be eliminated for the same reason; IS's **küda 'male relation' is represented by only Uralic **küðü* 'wife's

husband, husband's or wife's brother' and Altaic *küdä/kuda* 'relationship by marriage, father of son (daughter)-in-law, brother (son)-in-law.' This appears to be what is behind Mordvin *kuda* 'go-between (in wedding ceremonies),' which is a Tatar loanword (Tatar *qoda*, ultimately from Mongolian into Tatar) (Róna-Tas 1988:767). This Uralic form is not reconstructed by Sammallahti or Rédei, and the whole set looks suspiciously like a diffused affinal kin term. Sets (301) with Uralic *mińa* 'daughter-in-law/sister-in-law' (cf. S PU *mińä* 'daughter-in-law') and (315) **nat/o/* 'female relative': Uralic *nato* 'sister-in-law'; cf. S PU and PFU *nåtiw* 'in-law,' Janhunen (1981:41, 50]) PU ? *nåt3-(w)* 'wife's brother, man's sister' (morphologically complex) are suspect for the same reason. Other affinal kinship terms are in doubt, strongly suggested by such known loans as Mordvin *ezna* 'brother-in-law,' borrowed from Tatar *yezne*/Proto-Turkic *yezne*; Votyak *kir-* 'brother-in-law,' borrowed from Chuvash *kürü*, ultimately Proto-Turkic *küdeg(ü)*; and Cheremis *oń* 'father-in-law,' borrowed from Chuvash *xoń*, ultimately from Proto-Turkic *qadïn* (Róna-Tas 1988:764, 767, 770). One need but recall that Finnish has borrowed its terms for 'mother,' 'daughter,' 'sister,' and 'bride' from Indo-European sources to be convinced of the possibility of kinship terms, particularly affinal ones, being borrowed. (Cf. Joki 1973:267–8.) Social structure in several central Eurasian groups was arranged on clan lines and clans could and often did cross linguistic lines; most peoples of northern Asia are clan-based, and these exogamous descent groups spanned various languages (Nichols 1998a:239, 240; Torday 1997:2).

[17], cf. [30] **k'/q'ülä* 'kin' (IS (239) **K'ülä* 'community, clan'). K&S's [17] offers no Uralic form, but IS has Uralic *külä* 'agricultural community, village, dwelling, house'; otherwise K&S's [17] contains forms which overlap to a great extent with those of [30], where Uralic *külä* 'rural commune, village, dwelling house' is given. There is a problem with the semantic matching in this set, seen in IS's disparate glosses 'community,' 'clan,' 'family,' 'agricultural community,' 'village,' 'dwelling,' 'house,' 'servants.' Neither Sammallahti nor Rédei have this, and IS's Uralic form appears too dependent on Finnish *külä* (orthographic <kylä>) 'village, visit to someone's home' (and in dialects 'dwelling, house'). *SKES* (2:254) and *SSA* (3:463) find this form of questionable FU status, since it appears to have cognates only in Saami [Lapp] (and a questionable Vogul cognate that was later eliminated), and because of the very close similarity with Turkic forms which suggests borrowing (e.g. Chuvash *kül, kil* 'house, cottage,' Yakut *külä* 'yard,' Osmani *gil* 'home'). IS's upper-case **K'* (K&S's **k'/q'*) indicates uncertainty of the reconstruction of this sound, that is, that the sound correspondences among the forms are not in fact those claimed for Nostratic.

[18] (238) **k'/q'üjnA* 'wolf, dog': Uralic *küjna* 'wolf.' We find no such form in Sammallahti or Rédei for Uralic. The semantics of this form, 'wolf'

and 'dog,' has been questioned by others.[11] The sounds do not correspond as they are supposed to (just as in the preceding case, the uncertainty represented by IS's **K'). As Manaster Ramer (1993b) pointed out, according to IS's correspondences, Indo-European velars should become labialized before rounded vowels and palatalized before front vowels, but in this case, the Indo-European form given, *kʲun, lacks the required labiovelar *kʷ before the rounded vowel. Finally, it is possible that diffusion could be involved.

[20] **wete 'water' (see D14 above), IS (1989d) **wetV: Uralic *wete. S PU *weti. Several scholars identify this as a loanword (see Gamkrelidze and Ivanov 1984.2:942; Joki 1973:344; Rédei 1988:641, 654).

[21] (166) **kiwE 'stone': Uralic *kiwe. S PFU *kiwi. The Nostratic reconstruction seems to rely on the Uralic form, since the only other forms listed are Dravidian *kw-a and Chadic *kw- (representing Afroasiatic), with no evidence of a second syllable. These non-Uralic forms are short and similar forms are found in other languages around the world. In neither the Dravidian nor the Afroasiatic forms do the vowels fit IS's correspondence sets.

[22] (23) **burV 'storm': Uralic *purV-. IS lists Uralic *purV- 'whirl (of snow)' and *purkV 'blizzard'. S PFU *purki 'snow flurry,' R (4:406) PFP, ?PU *purk3 'flurry, snowfall.' As K&S present it, the Uralic form appears to be arbitrarily and unjustifiably segmented to leave out the ki portion. Also, K&S's semantics are not quite as exact as in IS. The Nostratic form in IS is not supported by the Uralic data, where the lack of the ki (or kV) in the first Uralic form K&S give appears motivated mostly to make the Uralic entry seem more similar to the forms cited in the other languages, Afroasiatic bwr- '(sand)storm,' Indo-European bher- 'storm, seethe,' Altaic burV/bora 'storm, blizzard'.[12]

[23] **qant'V 'front side': (?) Uralic *(e)Nte- 'first, face.' The IS (1989d:160) form, glossed 'front,' had no Uralic cognate, and K&S give the Uralic form only as a tentative possible cognate. In fact, there is no such Uralic form – or, perhaps better said, K&S appear to have combined two separate Uralic etyma. One is the legitimate FU form, S PFU *edi 'ahead' (cf. R [1:71] *eδe 'fore, front'); the other, as in Finnish ente- 'before,' is found only in Balto-Finnic languages, and does not extend beyond this branch of the family (SKES 1:31, SSA 1:105). The other forms given by IS are Indo-European *Hent- 'front side,' Altaic *antV 'front, south side,' and Afroasiatic *xn/t'/ 'front, south side, nose.' However, none of the sounds of Uralic *edi fits any of IS's proposed correspondence sets when compared to these forms.

[24], cf. [78] **ʒegV 'eat' (IS **ze9V 'eat'): Uralic *s(ē)ɣE (< *s(e)ɣü ?). S PFU *sewi. K&S appear uncertain concerning the Uralic form they give,

---

[11] However, Estonian hunt 'wolf,' apparently borrowed from German Hund 'dog,' would suggest the semantic shift is at least not implausible (Raimo Anttila, personal communication).

[12] K&S's gloss of 'storm' also suggests greater similarity than IS's more precise glosses 'whirl (of snow)' and 'blizzard.' The more accurate meaning is Sammallahti's, 'snow flurry.'

and IS's Uralic *s(ē)/γ/e- 'eat' has the γ in slashes which indicates that it is problematic.

[25] (319) **ńamo 'grasp': Uralic *ńamV-. S PFU *ńomå 'seize, grasp.' IS's Indo-European *yem- 'hold tightly, bridle' illustrates the problem of non-corresponding sound correspondences, since for **ń-, Indo-European is said to have unpredictable variation between *y- and *n-, not permissible in standard applications of the comparative method.

[27], cf. [39] (84) **gi(ł)u 'smooth': Uralic *k(ł)V 'smooth, shiny.' R (2:156) PFU *kil3 (kül3) 'smooth, slippery.' There is considerable semantic latitude in the proposed Nostratic cognate set, with 'shiny,' 'smooth,' 'bald' in the different proposed branches.

[28], cf. [63] (9) **berg(i) 'high, tall' (glossed only 'high' by IS): Samoyed *p(e)r(kV)- (IS *p/e/r/kV/). Janhunen (1977:125) Proto-Samoyed *pirə 'high,' *pirka 'high [correlative derivative].' The Nostraticists propose no Proto-Uralic form for this set, only one from Samoyed, a branch of the family; however, this does have cognates from the Finno-Ugric side of the family, PFU *pidkä (PU *pid-kä) 'long, tall' (Janhunen 1981:238–9), which shows that it does not fit the Nostratic set as IS had assumed. The correct vowels even in this Samoyed word, as in Janhunen's reconstruction, are not compatible with expected correspondences for the Nostratic forms, in any case. The slashes of IS and parentheses of K&S indicate uncertain portions, meaning that not even the Samoyed example matches expectations. Moreover, the form is morphologically complex, PU *pid-kä, developed from the PU root *pidi 'high,' cf. *pidi-w 'length, height' (Janhunen 1981:238–9, 267). That is, there is no way in which the k is part of the original equation, as is necessary for a successful match with the forms from the other putative Nostratic languages.

[29] (cf. related set [49]) K&S give no Nostratic reconstruction, but the examples correspond to (236) **K'urV 'plait, tie, bind'; the glosses K&S give for the constituent families are: 'build,' 'make,' 'weave,' with Uralic *ku/orV 'weave, baste (in sewing), fasten together,' where it is said that the V is a "vowel of unclear quality." R (3:215) PU *kure- 'to bind, to tie' (note that these glosses differ from those given by IS for Uralic). IS's Nostratic languages' glosses include 'build, make, plait, tack together, fasten, tie, spin, adjust, arrange.' There is a problem of semantic mismatch here.

[30], cf. [17] (above).

[31] K&S have no Nostratic reconstruction; their glosses cover 'be healthy,' 'live,' 'nourishing,' 'plentiful,' and they list Uralic *kōja 'fat(ty).' The IS corresponding set is (168) ?**kojHa 'fatty, plump, healthy': Uralic *kōja 'fat, fatty.' S PFU *kuji 'tallow'; R (2:195) PFU *kuje 'grease, lard.' While 'tallow' and 'fat, fatty' are certainly related concepts, there is a serious semantic problem with this set. IS (1989d:143) gave essentially the same information, though with the Uralic gloss as 'fat, greasy.' By IS's correspondence sets, the Indo-European

form is required to have a palatalized velar *(*kʸ)* before the front vowel in this form, **gʷeyhʷ-/*gʷeyhʷ-*, meaning that the form involves non-corresponding sounds. Given IS's own doubts (signaled by the "?"), this set is very weak.

[32], cf. [52] (178) ***küni* 'wife, woman.' In [32] only two branches are represented, Indo-European **gʷen-* 'wife, woman' and Uralic **küni* 'one of wives (in polygamy).' However, there appears to be an error; in [52] there is no Uralic form, but otherwise it is the same as [32] with the exception that the "Uralic" form given in [32] is labeled Turkic (Altaic) in [52]. Sammallahti and Rédei do not recognize this Uralic form, and IS's set also contains no Uralic material.

[33] There is no Nostratic reconstruction in K&S, whose glosses include: 'light colored or illuminated,' 'dawn.' This is based on IS (85) ***goHjV* 'sunlight, dawn': Uralic **kojV* 'dawn, sun.' S PU **koji* 'dawn.' As for the other two representatives, IS's Altaic form is given a question mark (i.e. doubtful), and the Indo-European form has a semantically very different gloss, 'bright, light.'

[34] No Uralic form is given; only two families are represented.

[35] K&S give no Nostratic reconstruction; their glosses include: 'rime,' 'frozen snowcrust (in derivatives),' 'hoar-frost,' 'first snow.' IS (230) ***K'irV* 'hoarfrost': Uralic **kirte*, **kirV*, 'crust (of ice on snow)' (K&S give Uralic **kirV*, **kir-te* 'frozen snowcrust', with an unmotivated segmentation of the latter form). R (3:214) PU **kura* 'hoar-frost, fine snow.' In his reconstruction, IS presents the first segment as questionable, raising doubts concerning the whole set, since it does not obey regular sound correspondences. Since the more accurate Uralic reconstruction has entirely different vowels from those expected by IS's sound correspondences, the set is thrown further into question.

[36], cf. [48]. K&S [36] provide no Nostratic form, though [48] gives ***k'äćä* 'cut.' IS (196) ***k'äćä* 'cut': Uralic **k'ä/ećä* 'knife,' 'edge,' 'point' (cf. K&S [36] Uralic **k'ä/ećä* 'knife, spike'). S PFU **käci* 'knife,' R (2:142) PU **keč3* 'knife.' This set may involve borrowing.

[37] K&S give no Uralic form for the set glossed 'old,' 'decrepit'; only two constituent families are represented, and for one of these (Indo-European) the form is listed as doubtful. For (165) ?***kirHV* 'old,' from which the K&S set is taken, IS indicates that the whole set is doubtful.

[38], see [16] above. Sets [38] and [16] are essentially the same, though a few forms and their glosses differ slightly; the Uralic form is given as [38] **kälü* 'female relative by marriage, sister's husband,' but [16] **kälä* 'female-in-law.' Also, [52] bears considerable similarity to [38] and [16].

[39], see [27].

[40] No Uralic form is given in K&S, and only two constituent families are represented, Indo-European **gʰʸerH/*gʰʸreH-* 'dawn, to shine,' and Altaic **gĒra* 'dawn, morning light.' IS (82) ***gE/hr/a* 'dawn' has three representatives, these two plus Afroasiatic **ghr* 'sunlight, day.' The form shows several

uncertainties; IS's *E* means a front vowel of uncertain quality, while /*hr*/ indicates that these sounds are also problematic.

[41] K&S give no Nostratic reconstruction; their glosses include: 'burn,' 'fry,' 'fire,' 'torch,' 'singed.' IS (215) ***K'arV* 'burn, to fire' has no Uralic form, although K&S list Uralic *karpe (> *korpe) 'burn,' with no explanation for the unexplained *pV*, though they speculate about how the vowel irregularities might be made to work out. R (2:186) Proto-Volga-Finnic, ?PFU, ?PU *korpe- 'to burn, get burned.'

[42] K&S give no Uralic form and have only two families represented, Indo-European *ken- 'be born,' 'young', and Dravidian *kan- 'give birth.' K&S discuss problems in vowel correspondences in this set. IS (211) ***K'anV* 'to give birth' has three representatives, but he indicates that the first consonant and all the vowels are questionable.

[43] No Nostratic form is given in K&S, cf. [54] **kamu 'grasp,' 'grab,' 'squeeze.' Only two families are represented, Indo-European *gem- 'grab,' 'take,' 'squeeze,' and Uralic *kamo (in *kama-lV, etc.) 'hollow of hand,' 'handful.' (157) **kamu 'seize,' 'squeeze': Uralic **kama-lV/*koma-rV* (< *kamo-) 'hand.' R (2:175) PU **kom3(r3)* 'hollow of the hand, palm.' As both Rédei (2:175) and *SKES* (1:140) indicate, Finnish *kahmalo* 'the hollow of one's joined hands' (cf. also *kahmaa-, kahmi-* 'to grab,' 'snatch') does not belong here, since its sounds do not correspond (*SSA* 1:272 finds it "descriptive" in origin); nevertheless, the form of IS's Uralic reconstruction appears to be heavily influenced by the Finnish form, and this in turn has influenced the Nostratic reconstruction, since the Indo-European form with which this is compared does not suggest these vowels, and indeed Indo-European *e* : Uralic *a* is not found in IS's correspondence sets.

[44] K&S present no Nostratic reconstruction for this set, which has glosses 'a growth,' 'tumor,' 'lip,' 'mushroom.' IS (158) **kanpV 'soft outgrowth'. In K&S only two families are represented: Indo-European *gemb- 'a growth,' 'tumor,' 'lip,' 'mushroom,' and Uralic *kampV 'mushroom' (cf. S PFP **kompV/*kampV* 'mushroom,' which is reconstructible no further back than Proto-Finno-Permic). There is a serious problem with semantic non-equivalence in this set.

[45], cf. [57] (78) **gara 'thorn,' 'thorny branch': Uralic *kara 'thorn,' 'branch,' 'twig,' 'conifer'. R (3:230) PFU *k8r3 'willow species,' given by Rédei as an uncertain/questionable set (with cognates glossed 'dwarf-birch' in Saami [Lapp] and 'bush' in one other case). K&S give no Uralic form for [45], for which only two families are represented (glosses 'thorn,' 'branch,' 'spike,' 'conifer'), but they do present the Uralic example with [57]. IS (78) gives the gloss for the Nostratic reconstruction as 'thorny branch,' 'thorn.' Clearly the FU form is semantically rather far removed in this instance and the whole Nostratic set is doubtful.

[47] (202) ***k'ol'V* 'round': Uralic ?**kol'a* 'circle.' R (2:175) PFU *kol3 'crack,' 'tear,' 'split,' 'gap' (cf. Finnish *kolo* 'opening,' 'cut,' 'hole'). This is a "descriptive" form; the Uralic material is given by IS as doubtful. In any case, the gloss of the FU form as correctly given by Rédei is semantically far distant from the sense attributed to Nostratic. This may be due, again, to over reliance on Finnish, where the meaning 'hole' among its various glosses might suggest 'circle,' 'round,' but that is not its primary meaning.

[48], cf. [36].

[50], cf. [14].

[52], cf. [32]. Number [52] essentially repeats [32], but has no Uralic example.

[53], cf. [16]. Number [53] essentially repeats [16], but has no Uralic example.

[54], cf. [43].

[58], cf. [77] ***p'iɣwe* or ***p'(i)ʕwe* 'fire' (IS ***p'iɣwV* 'fire'): Uralic *pīwe 'warm, hot.' S PU *päjwä 'sun,' 'warmth'; R (4:360) PFU *päjwä 'fire' (considered uncertain); Janhunen (1981:224) gives PU *päjwä 'sun' / *päivä 'warmth,' saying that an exact semantic reconstruction is impossible.

[59] (cf. sets (365) and (366) discussed below) ***p'uñja* 'to plait': Uralic **puña 'to spin,' 'twist/roll,' 'rotate.' This Uralic form appears to combine and confuse separate etyma: S PU **punå/i* 'plait (braid)' (cf. R [4:402] PU **puña 'to spin,' 'to braid'), S PFU **på/unå* 'hair' (R [4:402] PFU *puna 'hair'), and S PFU *puñi 'twist' (cf. R [4:403] PFU *puña 'to wind, pull, twist').

[60] (337) **pelHi 'to shiver,' 'shake,' 'be afraid' (IS 'shake,' 'fear'): Uralic **pele-* 'be afraid.' S PU **peli-* 'fear'; R (4:370) PU **pele-* 'fear, be afraid.'

[61] ***put'V* 'hole,' IS ***p'u/t'/V* 'hole': Uralic *putV 'rectum.' R (4:410) PFU *put3 'large intestine, rectum,' given by Rédei (1986–8:410) as uncertain on several grounds: "The grouping is . . . uncertain. The word is only known in Lapp and in Ostyak in only a very small region. The Vogul word is possibly an Ostyak loan." Further uncertainty in this case comes from the non-corresponding sounds among putative Nostratic languages covered by /t'/ and the uncertainty of the final vowel.

[63], cf. [28].

[65] ***t'uKt'E* 'to build,' 'hew': Uralic *tuktV 'to build.' S PFU *tuktå 'crossrail,' R (5:534) PU *tukt3 'transom, strut, cross-piece'; Janhunen (1981:9) PU *tuktå 'crosspiece, sitting board (in a boat).' The glosses from the other putative Nostratic families include 'to hew,' 'axe,' 'fence,' 'building,' and 'to build'; clearly there is a semantic problem with these, since the Uralic form does not fit semantically.

[66] ***t'umV* 'dark': Uralic *tumV 'dark.' The Uralic form here is highly doubtful; we find nothing to match it in Sammallahti or Rédei; for the Finnish form *tumma* 'dark,' upon which we suspect IS's Nostratic form depends, the Finnish etymological dictionaries list no cognates outside of the closely related

Balto-Finnic languages (*SKES* 5:1396, *SSA* 3:325). Uralic in this instance is doubtful.

[70] (67) **diga 'fish'; IS had no Uralic form, but K&S cite Dolgopolsky's Nostratic reconstruction ***diTg[u]* 'fish', with Uralic **totka* 'fish', which they say is "with not quite clear (assimilated?) **-o-*" (K&S 1988:323), that is, meaning that it has non-corresponding vowels. Cf. S PFU **totki* 'Tinca' (fish species), R (5:532) PU **totke* 'Cyprinus tinca*, tench (fish)' (cf. Finnish *totki* 'tench [fish species]'). Notice in this case how, with the more accurate reconstructions, it is now clear that both the vowels of the Uralic form are problematic according to the expected Nostratic correspondence sets.

[74] **ʔesA 'dwell,' 'stay'; IS's (132) **ʔesA is glossed 'settle a place,' 'be at a place,' different from K&S's version of the gloss. K&S gloss Uralic **eśA* as '(settle) a place,' but IS has it as 'settle a place'; 'place,' 'site.' Apparently intended is R (1:18) PU **aśe-* 'to place, set, lay' (cf. Finnish *ase-ttaa* 'to place,' *ase-ma* 'position,' and other derivatives). The other two representative, Indo-European **Hes-* 'be' and Afroasiatic **ʔIs* 'be,' have rather different semantics from the Uralic word, and the vowels are in the inverse order of those given, making the expected correspondences incorrect.

[76] **λeqLu 'to shine': Uralic **jeLa-* or **jēLa* 'to shine,' 'daylight.' R (2:96) PU **jelä* 'light,' 'sun,' 'day,' given as very uncertain, represented only by Saami, meaning 'clear weather, cloudless,' and Samoyed, with meanings 'light,' 'sun,' 'day.' It is highly questionable even within Uralic. IS (1989d) has only *?* {***si??*} 'sun,' represented only by Indo-European **seHu-* and Altaic **sibV-*. This is among IS's weakest sets, as he himself indicated. K&S have adapted it from Dolgopolsky (though with their **λ rather than IS's **s or Dolgopolsky's ***ʒ́* for the first consonant), adding also the Uralic and Afroasiatic representatives. Their glosses cover some semantic latitude: 'sun,' 'luminary,' 'make transparent,' 'to shine,' 'daylight.'

[77], cf. [58]. Number [77] basically repeats [58].

[78], cf. [24]. Number [78] repeats [24] totally.

This concludes the discussion of K&S's 78 putative Nostratic cognate sets (where we have concentrated on the Uralic evidence), presumed to be the best evidence at hand for Nostratic. As our survey shows, few of their sets are without problems, and most have serious problems.

In the interest of space, we do not present evaluations of IS's other forms here (though for evaluation of a number of these, see Campbell 1998, 1999, and for further criticism of the Nostratic hypothesis, see Appleyard 1999; Clauson 1973a; Comrie 1999; Doerfer 1993; Kaye 1999; Ringe 1995a, 1998; Serebrennikov 1982[1986]; Vine 1991; Trask 1999). To summarize the results of our investigation of IS's Uralic and Indo-European data and his methods, we see serious problems with the methods utilized and with the data in a large number of the sets presented (see Campbell 1998, 1999 for details). With Uralic supposedly being the strong suit of Nostratic, we can only assume that the forms presented from the other putative Nostratic language families, where we have less expertise, probably exhibit a similar range of problems. Therefore we do not accept the Nostratic hypothesis. Though aspects of it may be worth a more careful and extensive evaluation, we seriously doubt that further research will result in any significant support for this hypothesized macro-family.

9.5   Eurasiatic

Greenberg's (1990b, 1991, 2000a, 2005) Eurasiatic hypothesis embraces Indo-European, Uralic–Yukaghir, Altaic, Korean–Japanese–Ainu, Gilyak, Chuko-tian, and Eskimo–Aleut as members of an assumed very large "linguistic stock." Eurasiatic was not intended to be equated with Nostratic, but rather was pre-sented as a competing hypothesis. Greenberg (2000a:5) reported that he "arrived at the Eurasiatic hypothesis some time in the mid 1960's in the context of my [his] task of ascertaining the genetic affiliation of the native languages of the Americas, especially that of Eskimo–Aleut"; "at that time the Russian Nostratic school was hardly known in the United States and I arrived at my own results in complete independence of theirs" (Greenberg (2000a:5). Nevertheless, Eurasi-atic does overlap Nostratic to a considerable extent, and in fact all of the putative Eurasiatic members have been included in one or another proposed version of Nostratic, though Nostratic typically includes some families which Greenberg does not associate with Eurasiatic. Of these, Indo-European, Uralic, Yukaghir (often under Yukaghir–Uralic), Altaic, and Korean (under Altaic), and often Japanese (as a putative further member of Altaic), are typically considered to be members of Nostratic by its supporters, and the other putative Eurasiatic language groups have from time to time been thought by various Nostraticists either also to belong to Nostratic or to be related to Nostratic as coordinate members of some higher-order grouping. Greenberg's Eurasiatic, on the other hand, excludes the presumed Nostratic (sub)families of Kartvelian, Dravid-ian and Afroasiatic. Nevertheless, Greenberg believed that these and the other putative Nostratic languages are related to one another and to the Eurasiatic languages, but more distantly: "I am by no means denying the relationship of these groups: namely Afroasiatic, Kartvelian and Dravidian, but I believe these relationships are more remote" (Greenberg 1990b:88). Greenberg (2000a:5) observed that "there have been significant changes in the views of Nostraticists in recent years, as the result of which the differences [between Eurasiatic and Nostratic] have been very greatly reduced." He noted that Starostin excludes Afroasiatic from Nostratic proper (holding it to be a more distant relative of Nostratic so defined), and that others suggest including in Nostratic several additional families, several from among those included in Greenberg's Eurasi-atic hypothesis (see Greenberg 2000a:6). For Bomhard's (Bomhard and Kerns

1994) version of Nostratic, Greenberg (2000a:5) asserts that "there is almost no difference between his views and mine."

With respect to assessing the evidence Greenberg presented in support of the Eurasiatic hypothesis, fortunately we need not present a long exposition of our own, since Georg and Vovin (2003, 2005) have done exactly that. They find that Greenberg (2000a) suffers the same sorts of "shortcomings, both in methodology and in the treatment of data," criticized by so many scholars in his earlier classifications (Georg and Vovin 2003:332). "G[reenberg]'s evidence for Eurasiatic is largely based on erroneous (interpretations of) data," which is also "insufficiently specific" so that "the attempt to show that a completely different group of languages, never suspected to be related in any way to Eurasiatic, contains a similar set of morphological comparanda is surprisingly successful" – they find 20 of Greenberg's first 24 putative morphological cognates shared by "Penutian" languages (Georg and Vovin 2003:356). Indeed, this book is somewhat different from Greenberg's earlier classifications in that it does not rely so much on straight lexical comparisons, but rather involves more morphological comparison. Chapter 2 of the book treats "some aspects of the comparative phonology of Eurasiatic," but it is not conventional "comparative phonology"; rather, it "circles around a number of phonological phenomena said to be characteristic of some Eurasiatic language families" (Georg and Vovin 2003:333). There are no systematic sound correspondences, something Greenberg believed unnecessary, though they are demanded by many as evidence of genetic relationship. Some of the characteristics, for example, vowel harmony, have been discounted as (potentially) areal traits (see above).

The core of Greenberg's (2000a) Eurasiatic evidence is the 72 morphological comparison sets he presented. Georg and Vovin (2003) assess the first 24 of these carefully, finding major problems of many sorts (such as those surveyed in our Chapter 7), leading them to reject this evidence as too flawed and too insufficient. We mention just a few representative examples here.

Greenberg's (2000a:46) claim that all the putative branches of Eurasiatic show evidence of an earlier "high–low vowel-harmony" is challenged by Georg and Vovin – for example, Indo-European ablaut does not really fit, and the claim is not supported by the asserted connection between Turkish *bir* 'one' and *beraber* 'together,' since *beraber* is a clear Persian loanword (Georg and Vovin 2003:333). Among the numerous problems pointed out with respect to Greenberg's "First Person M," Georg and Vovin (2003:336–7) point out that Turkic has no initial nasals (so *ben* instead of the postulated **men* for the independent first-person pronoun), and that while Mongolian and Tungusic also have only *b*- (not *m*), Korean <wuli> (and the proposed Proto-Korean **buli* 'we' based on this) do not really match. Rather, no form such as *wuli* exists; Greenberg misunderstood the Yale Romanization in which <wu> represents /u/ and <u> /i̇/, hence no /w/ and so no support for the **b* of the **buli* reconstruction. Another non-existent form is Old Japanese *miy* 'first-person pronoun'; rather *miy* meant then and now just 'body.' With respect to his proposed "Third Person I ~ E," there is no "hitherto unexplained variation in a considerable number of verbs [in Japanese] between forms with and without a prefixed *i-*" as "*i-masu*" 'to be' (Greenberg 2000a:87). Instead, Greenberg inserted a non-existing morpheme boundary in such forms; the reason the *i-* is lacking in some Old Japanese forms is because *imas-* (with no fake morpheme boundary) is an auxiliary placed after the main verb infinitive in which environment it is subject to the phonological rule which elides any initial *i* (Georg and Vovin 2003:342).

Georg and Vovin (2003:334) conclude that "closer inspection of these items [the 72 grammatical morpheme comparisons] . . . shows too many misinterpretations, errors and wrong analyses – both on the formal and the semantic side, both synchronically and diachronically; these allow no other judgement than that G[reenberg]'s attempt to demonstrate the validity of his Eurasiatic has failed." In their comparison of Greenberg's putative Eurasiatic evidence with similar grammatical morphemes in "Penutian" languages, they show that the body of data presented in favor of Eurasiatic is not sufficient to prevent other languages from fitting into Eurasiatic by these criteria. (See also Georg and Vovin 2005.)

We concur with Georg and Vovin; we find Greenberg's Eurasiatic evidence unpersuasive because it is riddled with problems of the sort surveyed in Chapter 7.

9.6   Amerind

The classification of the American Indian languages has been made controversial by Joseph Greenberg's "Amerind" hypothesis, represented principally in his book, *Language in the Americas* (1987). Greenberg contended that the approximately 2,000 known Native American languages belong to only three phyla (Eskimo–Aleut, Na-Dene, and Amerind), with so-called "Amerind" containing most of these. In contrast, most specialists in American Indian languages maintain that valid methods do not at present permit reduction of Native American languages to fewer than between 150 and 180 independent language families. Greenberg's classification has been reviewed critically by numerous Americanists and historical linguists: Adelaar 1989; Berman 1992; Callaghan 1991; Campbell 1988; Chafe 1987; Goddard 1987, 1990a; Goddard and Campbell 1994; Golla 1988; Hock 1993; Jacobsen 1993, 1994; Kaufman 1990; Liedtke 1989, 1991; Matisoff 1990; McMahon and McMahon 1995; Poser 1992; Rankin 1992; Ringe 1992, 1993; and Watkins 1990, among others. We mention a few general criticisms of "Amerind" before turning to more specific problems.

Specialists find extensive distortions and inaccuracies in Greenberg's data: "the number of erroneous forms probably exceeds that of the correct forms" (Adelaar 1989:253); "errors in the Algonquian data alone invalidate 93 [of Geenberg's 143 Algonquian] equations" (Goddard 1987:656; cf. Campbell 1988; Chafe 1987; Golla 1988; etc.)

Multilateral comparison as a method does not work and is rejected by most historical linguists. As pointed out in Chapter 7, Greenberg assembled forms which on superficial inspection are similar from among the languages which he compared and declared them to be evidence of common heritage. However, where Greenberg's method stops (after having assembled the similarities) is where other linguists start. Since similarities can be due to a number of factors (accident, borrowing, onomatopoeia, sound symbolism, so-called nursery words, and universals), for a plausible proposal of remote relationship one must attempt to eliminate all other possible explanations, leaving a shared common heritage the most likely (cf. Campbell 1973, 1978, 1988, 2003a; Goddard 1975; Gurevich 1999; Kaufman 1990; Matisoff 1990; Watkins 1990). Greenberg's method makes no attempt to eliminate these other possible explanations, and the similarities he has amassed appear to be due mostly to accident and a combination of these other factors. We concur with Ringe's (1992, 1996) mathematical proof that chance can explain Greenberg's "evidence":

My results show clearly that Greenberg's methodology should simply be abandoned; it does not even lead to the identification of plausible hypotheses of relationship (other than those that would be obvious anyway), and it does mislead the uninformed into thinking that we know more than we do. (Ringe 1996:134)

In short I find no evidence whatsoever that the putative cognate sets in Greenberg's "Amerind Etymological Dictionary" represent anything other than chance similarities. (Ringe 1996:152)

That is, Greenberg's method has not provided a convincing case that the similarities are due to inheritance from an earlier common ancestor, making it an inadequate method for its intended purposes.

Another criticism is that Greenberg did not actually employ multilateral comparison to arrive at his Amerind classification. Rather, apparently he had already drawn his conclusions about the classification and later began filling out his notebooks (which are available from the Stanford Library) upon which his classification is purported to rely. His classification was not changed significantly from his earlier papers (Greenberg 1953, 1960), though most of the supporting data were assembled much later (Greenberg 1990a:6). As the arrangement of languages in these notebooks reveals, they were ordered to reflect a preconceived classification, and multilateral comparison was not used to arrive at that arrangement. Both the fact that Greenberg did not apply his method to arrive at the classification and that much had been decided already before the data were assembled in the notebooks appear to be confirmed in Greenberg's (1953:283) own words:

Even cursory investigation of the celebrated "disputed" cases, such as Athabaskan–Tlingit–Haida and Algonkin–Wiyot–Yurok, indicate [*sic*] that these relationships are not very distant ones and, indeed, are evident on inspection. Even the much larger Macro-Penutian grouping seems *well within the bounds of what can be accepted without more elaborate investigation and marshaling of supporting evidence.* (Our emphasis, LC/WP)

Most of the 1987 classification was preconceived; it follows extensively earlier proposals by Edward Sapir (see Sapir 1929a) for North America and Paul Rivet (see Rivet and Loukotka 1952) for South America, aspects of which are now known to be indisputably wrong, though incorporated into Greenberg's classification. This means that there is absolutely no way these parts of the classification could have followed from an application of multilateral comparison to the data. For example, following Sapir, Greenberg placed Subtiaba-Tlapanec with Hokan, now known clearly to belong to Otomanguean (cf. Campbell 1988; Suárez 1983a, 1986). Following Rivet, Greenberg mistakenly classified Uru-Chipaya and Puquina as closely related languages. This error is based on the old misunderstanding that derives from the fact that Uru-Chipaya was sometimes called Puquina in the Andes region (Adelaar 1989:252; Olson 1964:314); since the error was pointed out and the differences between Puquina and Uru clearly shown long ago (see Chamberlain 1910; Ibarra Grasso 1958:10, 1964:37–3), there was no reason to continue the mistake. These mistaken classifications do not follow from an application of multilateral comparison.

Another general criticism is that Greenberg's method is incapable of distinguishing American Indian languages from other languages selected randomly. Using Greenberg's method and the examples he presented as evidence for Amerind, it is easily shown that such non-American languages as Finnish (also Finno-Ugric and Uralic; see Campbell 1988), Japanese (Campbell 1997c, see below), and numerous others fit into his Amerind group by his criteria just as well as most of the American Indian languages. Similar demonstrations show the failings of multilateral comparison with regard to some others of Greenberg's proposed classifications. For example, Heine (1970:5–6) showed that by the method, English is as good an Eastern Sudanic language as any of the others classified in that group.[13]

One of the most telling aspects of the debate is that most American Indian linguistic scholars are not opposed to distant genetic relationships, but in fact Greenberg shares their research objectives of working towards reducing the ultimate number of linguistic groupings and of finding more remote family relationships among the American Indian languages. Most American Indian linguistic specialists believe it possible that most American Indian languages may be genetically related. The main difference is that they find Greenberg's

---

[13] We ignore here the question Greenberg raises (in Newman 1991:454) of whether he applied his own method correctly.

methods and evidence inadequate. In short, when scholars already positively predisposed to be favorable towards the idea have trouble accepting Greenberg's evidence for it, there is probably good reason for the caution.

Other American Indianist linguists, in contrast to Greenberg, hold that given (1) the limitations of valid methods, (2) the vast amount of linguistic change these languages have undergone since they began to diversify, and (3) that we do not know how many different groups or languages entered the New World, we cannot at present reduce the number of independent linguistic families in the Americas to fewer than about 150 to 180. Hopefully, as work progresses, new relationships will be established among some of these and this number will diminish. However, we must also face the possibility that these limitations may be so great that we will never understand the picture fully. In sum, when "probably the majority of linguists working on American Indian languages" (Greenberg 1996b:532), that is, when 80 to 90 percent (in Greenberg's words [quoted in Lewin 1988:1632]) of specialists in this field reject Greenberg's claim though they share his goal, there is a good chance that there is something wrong with the approach.

But if specialists reject "Amerind," what accounts for the warmer reception it has received from outside of linguistics, from archaeologists, geographers, geneticists, and the general media? Hymes (1971:264) asked this question about the reception of Greenberg's (1960) classification of South American languages, but it applies equally to Greenberg's (1987) Amerind hypothesis:

> it is historically revealing to compare the reception of the classification of South American languages by the two men [Greenberg and Swadesh]. The two classifications agree on the essential unity of the languages of the New World, differing on various internal groupings. Greenberg's classification was obtained with a list of 30 to 40 glosses, Swadesh's with a list of 100 glosses . . . Greenberg published the result without supporting data, backed essentially only by personal authority. Swadesh presented an explicit account of his procedures, endeavored to make the data available, and regularly revised his findings in the light of new evidence and research. The classification based on authority without supporting evidence has been reprinted often . . . the work presented as an explicit, continuing scientific enterprise has not.

Swadesh's work was very similar to Greenberg's in many ways, in its conclusions, its data, and the general methods employed. Why, then, was Swadesh, erudite in his first-hand knowledge of American Indian languages, rejected or ignored, while Greenberg's classification is frequently repeated with approval in the media and in other fields, although it is denied almost wholesale by American Indian linguists? The reason does not have to do with the quality of the evidence or the method, since it is precisely these which specialists find unconvincing (as they did ultimately also with Swadesh's). Factors other than scientific legitimacy are at play in the reception of Greenberg's claims by nonlinguists. This was also true in the case of his African classification (Newman

1991:454). It is even more the case with respect to his American Indian linguistic classification, almost universally rejected by specialists, but nevertheless given much attention by others. However, fortunately, even those outside linguistics who earlier received the claims warmly are now coming to realize why they do not hold up.

Greenberg's "Amerind" has been frequently criticized because the "etymologies" he proposed are typically represented in only three or four of his eleven subgroups (Ringe 1992; Jacobsen 1994). Morever, the forms within these subgroups themselves are often limited to only a few languages, even though none of these putative groups is generally recognized by other scholars. Lexical sets whose members appear similar on superficial visual inspection which are limited in this way are not very convincing. Specialists have severely criticized the methods and evidence upon which these eleven groups are based; the evidence marshaled thus far does not justify these groupings. Greenberg's (1987:59) claim that "the validity of Amerind as a whole is more secure than that of any of its stocks [subgroups]" may raise some eyebrows, since his eleven member branches are themselves proposals of very distant relationship, none of which has any general acceptance. Moreover, it has been pointed out that the evidence he presents in support of individual groups could just as easily be interpreted as reflecting other combinations or regroupings that crosscut those which he asserts (see, for example, Ringe 1994).

There is some reason to believe that not even Greenberg and Ruhlen have strong faith in the validity of the eleven groupings, since they repeatedly mentioned their belief that the overall Amerind construct "is really more robust than some [of these eleven] lower-level branches of Amerind" (Ruhlen 1994b:15; see Greenberg 1987:59).

9.6.1   Specific problems with Amerind

We turn now to some specific methodological problems relating to Greenberg's Amerind hypothesis.

Greenberg (1987) introduced some language names into his classification which are not languages at all. For example, Membreño, which Greenberg (1987:194, 293, 382, 425) classified as a Lencan language, is actually a person's name, a reference (Membreño 1897) which contains several Lencan word lists from different Honduran towns. In several instances, Greenberg (1987:382 and elsewhere) gave the town names where a certain language was spoken as names of distinct languages; for example, there are not six Lencan languages, only two, though Greenberg gives as languages such town names as Guajiquero (*sic*, for Guajiquiro), Intibucat (*sic*, Intibucá), Opatoro, and Similatón. Papantla is not a separate Totonacan language, but a town where Totonac is spoken (Greenberg 1987:380 and elsewhere); Chiripo and Estrella, presented as Talamancan languages (Greenberg 1987:382 and elsewhere), are town names where Cabécar is spoken. "Viceyta" (given by Greenberg 1987:382 and elsewhere as also Talamancan) is a colonial name which referred to both Bribri and Cabécar, and certainly not to a third independent language. Moreover, Terraba, Tiribí, and Tirub are also not separate languages, but rather all refer to Tiribí; the christianized Tiribí brought by the Spanish from Panama to Costa Rica after 1700 are called Terraba, while Tirub is the native version of the Tiribí name which some scholars prefer to use (cf. Greenberg 1987:382, etc.).[14]

As mentioned above, Greenberg mistakenly classified Uru-Chipaya and Puquina as related languages and put Subtiaba-Tlapanec in Hokan, though both are well-known errors repeated from earlier now corrected classifications of Sapir and Rivet.

Diffusion is a problem in Greenberg's examples. In an example (mentioned in Chapter 7), Greenberg (1987:108) cited among his "Chibchan–Paezan etymologies" forms from four languages in support of his proposed 'axe' etymology, including Cuitlatec *navaxo* 'knife' (a loan from Spanish *navajo* 'knife, razor') and Tunebo *baxi-ta* 'machete' (also a loan, from Spanish *machete*).[15] Thus, half of the forms cited in support of this so-called etymology are unrecognized loanwords. Such examples could be multiplied greatly, a serious problem for the method which looks only for superficial lexical resemblance without doing the work of separating out the loanwords.

Greenberg's (1987) putative Amerind cognate sets (which he calls "etymologies") very often involve very generous semantic latitude among forms compared, for example: 'excrement/night/grass,' 'ask/wish/seek/pleasure,' 'bitter/to rot/sour/sweet/ripe/spleen/gall,' 'body/belly/heart/skin/meat/be greasy/fat/deer,' 'child/copulate/son/girl/boy/tender/bear/small,' 'deer/dog/animal/silverfox/lynx,' 'earth/sand/sweepings/mud/dirty,' 'field/devil/bad/underneath/bottom,' 'earth/island/forest/mud/village/town/dust/world/ground,' 'feather/hair/wing/leaf,' 'hole/mouth/ear/listen/chin/nose/smell/blow nose/sniff,' and so on. Such semantic permissiveness increases the probability that chance explains some of the compared forms.

A good number of Greenberg's forms also involve onomatopoeia, for example forms such as *pui, puhi, phu-* listed for 'blow'(Greenberg 1987:196); but such forms are widely known to be onomatopoetic (see Tylor 1871:229), thus explaining why similar forms are found in languages throughout the world (e.g. Balto-Finnic *puhu-*, even English *puff*).

The problem of undetected morpheme divisions (some cases are presented in Chapter 7) is a frequent one in Greenberg (1987). For example, he listed Rama

---

[14] For numerous other language name problems in Greenberg's comparisons, see Campbell (1988, 1997a).

[15] Note that Tunebo [x] alternates freely with [š], that nasal consonants do not occur before oral vowels, and that the vowels of the Tunebo form are expectable substitutes for Spanish *e* .

mukuik 'hand' as cognate with words from several other American Indian languages families which exhibit shapes like *ma* or *makV* (Greenberg 1987:57), although, 'hand' in Rama is *kwi:k*; the *mu-* is the 'second-person possessive' prefix (Lehmann 1920:422, 426–7). However, *kwi:k* bears no resemblance to Greenberg's (1987:57) postulated **ma-ki*.[16] In another proposed cognate set labeled 'sky,' Greenberg (1987:158) gave Kaqchikel *paruwiʔ* 'above,' Tzotzil *bail* 'above,' Huastec *ebal* 'above' (three Mayan languages), and Tunica *ʔaparu* 'heaven, cloud.' However, the Mayan forms are not even cognate within the Mayan family and each reflects the problem of undetected morpheme boundaries. The Kaqchikel form is *pa-ru-wiʔ* [on-his/her/its-head/hair],[17] literally 'on, on top of him/her'; the Tzotzil is *ba-il* [top/first/head – adjective] 'top'; and the Huastec form is from *eb-al* 'up' (root + adjective derivational suffix). Greenberg's comparison of Tzeltal *jat* 'penis' and Tzotzil *jat* 'genitals' (two closely related Mayan languages) with Patwin *jot* 'penis' (1987:156) loses force because the Tzeltal and Tzotzil form is composed of two separate morphemes, *y-at* [his-penis] – *-at* by itself seems much more feeble in this comparison.[18]

In another instance Greenberg (1987:258) compared Q'eqchi' *k'anti* to other Mayan forms *čan*, *kan*, etc., meaning 'snake,' and to other non-Mayan languages, for example Hitchiti *šinti* and Creek *četto* (these two both Muskogean languages), etc. The true Proto-Mayan etymon is **ka:n* 'snake,' but Q'eqchi' *k'antiʔ* is not cognate with the other Mayan forms. It is a Chol loanword for a species of snake, from Cholan *k'an* 'yellow' (<Proto-Mayan **q'an*) plus *tiʔ* 'mouth' (<Proto-Mayan **ṭiʔ*). Failure to indicate the separate morpheme status of *-tiʔ* 'mouth' falsely makes this form appear more similar to the non-Mayan languages compared.

---

[16] We note that the compared forms (Greenberg 1987:229–30) do not mean only 'hand,' but rather also involve glosses of 'give,' 'bring,' 'left hand,' 'take,' 'receive,' 'palm,' 'branch,' 'arm,' 'five,' 'instrumental prefix,' 'finger,' 'seize,' 'catch,' 'right hand,' 'carry,' 'have,' 'hold,' 'take along,' 'give potlatch,' etc.

[17] Note that the *pa-* 'in/on' of Kaqchikel, besides being short, is not a good match in this set, since it comes from *pam-* 'stomach.' Most Mayan prepositions and relational nouns are derived from body parts. This is hardly a convincing connection with Tunica *ʔaparu* meaning 'cloud, heaven.' Moreover, even if the Mayan forms had been cognate, this would not be an appropriate example of an "etymology" in this distant genetic proposal, since it would involve the comparison of only two language entities, Mayan and Tunica, which is a poor showing from among the hundreds of Native American languages when the possibility of accidental similarity has to be contended with. One might just as well throw in, say, Finnish *päälle* 'above, over, on' (*pää* 'head' + *-lle* 'to') and argue that Finnish, too, is an Amerind language.

[18] Because *-at* is so short and only two language entities (Mayan and Patwin) are compared, this set can hardly be considered outstanding evidence for the long-range grouping Greenberg wanted. Such examples show that Ruhlen's contention is not valid that "usually the portion of unanalyzed words being compared is clear, even without the specification of morpheme boundaries" (Ruhlen 1994b:95). While Ruhlen is speaking specifically of the forms he presents which are taken from other linguists in connection with the Na-Dene hypothesis, this caution still applies.

The other problem involving morphological errors is that of the insertion of morpheme boundaries where none is justified – several examples from Greenberg (1987) were presented in Chapter 7. Poser (1992) discussed a number of examples from Salinan and Yurumanguí which have specious morphological analyses in Greenberg's (1987) treatment (eleven unjustified segmentations out of a total of twenty-six forms cited). Berman (1992:232) also found that "there is not a single Tualatin [Kalapuya] word in which Greenberg [1987] segments any of these prefixes correctly. In almost every instance . . . where a form is misanalyzed, Greenberg compares the wrong elements." In another instance, Greenberg (1987:150) compared Natchez *hak* 'afire' with Mixe-Zoquean terms for 'fire' (Texistepec *hugut*, Sierra Popoluca *huktə*, Zoque *hukətək*); however, the Natchez form is a misanalysis of *le·-haki ʔiš* 'to burn,' with no sense of 'afire,' and the assumed *hak* is only part of the 'intransitive auxiliary' *-haki ʔiš* (Kimball 1992:459). Greenberg (1987:159) also gave Atakapa *tsom* (*com*) 'stick,' but this is found only in the compound *neštsomš* 'cane,' where *neš* means 'tree, wood, stick' and *tsom* (*com*) appears to be a shortened form of *hitsom* (*hicom*) 'little' (Kimball 1992:459). As Poser (1992:219) shows:

Where languages are not known to be related[,] comparisons in which the morphological analysis itself depends on the relationship carry considerably less weight than those in which the segmentation is clearly established, for the simple reason that the additional degrees of freedom increase the probability with which similarities may be due to chance.

Another problem in a number of Greenberg's Amerind forms is neglect of the known history of the languages compared (see examples presented in Chapter 7). For (154) 'light' Greenberg lists forms such as *ʔeki, akke, ʔoko, kʷiʔi-s, qe, qai, kʲɛu, kʲɛ* from various languages, to which an alleged Proto-Mayan form **q'i:xʲ* 'day, sun' is compared, but this is actually only a Proto-K'ichean reconstruction (K'ichean being only one of several Mayan subfamilies). The real Proto-Mayan form is **q'i:ŋ* (as is clear in Greenberg's sources, namely Campbell 1977:38; Fox 1978:220). By neglecting the known history (Proto-Mayan **ŋ > K'ichean *x*), this comparison is made to seem to exhibit a higher degree of similarity to the other compared languages than the Mayan form would if the history were taken into account. (See also 160 [Greenberg 1987:155].) In another example, Greenberg (1987:178) gave Seneca *ænn-* and Mohawk *oniete* under his "etymology" labeled 'sweet' and assumed they are related to Proto-Keresan **ʔanʔe:za* 'be tasty.' However, the known history of Iroquoian shows this is not so. The Seneca form (really *-æn*) is from Proto-Northern-Iroquoian **-ran-* (see Chafe 1959), while the Mohawk word has the morphological analysis *o-* 'neuter prefix' + *-nyeht-* and means 'snow' (Mithun 1990:323) – thus not so similar phonetically in the one case and semantically in the other to the comparisons in other languages.

We mention here a few specific cases of the spurious data in Greenberg (1987), cases where the forms presented are not just erroneous, but do not exist. One such case is Greenberg's (1987:197) Chitimacha *lahi* 'burn,' given under the set labeled 'boil' – the form does not exist; Chitimacha has no phonemic *l*. The spurious Chitimacha word is not the only problem in this set. Greenberg compared it to Choctaw *luak*, but this Choctaw form is actually *lowa-k* 'fire,' a nominalization of *lowa* 'to burn,' and Greenberg's failure to note the morphological analysis erroneously makes the *k* of this suffix seem to match the *k* of the roots in the other forms cited, Atakapa *lok*, and Natchez *luk* (Kimball 1992:478). In another instance (155), Greenberg lists Proto-Mayan *$*t^su{:}k$* 'navel,' citing Campbell (1977) as the source (Greenberg erroneously listed Campbell's Proto-K'ichean forms as Proto-Mayan ones). However, there is no such form in Campbell (1977), nor in K'ichean, nor in Mayan generally. The form given in Campbell (1977:155) was Proto-K'ichean *$*mušu{\textipa{P}}uš$* 'navel' – Greenberg's *$*t^su{:}k$* is simply spurious.

Many of Greenberg's forms have been criticized for being spurious (or at least skewed) due to scribal errors and mishandling of philological aspects of the sources utilized to obtain the data. The most glaring problem of this sort is the treatment of Quapaw. None of the entries listed as Quapaw in Greenberg (1987) is actually from that language; the data are from Biloxi or Ofo (two other Siouan languages, not closely related to Quapaw) (Rankin 1992:343; Campbell 1997a:237). For another example, Greenberg (1987) systematically mistranscribed the <v> and <e> of his Creek source as *u* and *e*, respectively, although <v> symbolizes /a/ and <e> /i/. So, for example, the source's <vne> 'I' was given by Greenberg (1987:53) as *une*, but the real Creek word is *ani* (Kimball 1992:448). Under the set labeled 'kill' Greenberg (1987:153) listed Choctaw *ile* 'do,' together with Hitchiti *ili* 'kill' (both Muskogean languages), but the 'do' of the Choctaw gloss is a scribal error (cf. Proto-Muskogean *$*illi$* 'kill'); Kimball (1992:463) believes the source of the the erroneous 'do' is a misreading of the abbreviation for "ditto" used by Greenberg. Greenberg listed Chitimacha *nakš* under 'near' (1987:155), but it means 'war' – *near* is a copying error for *war* (Kimball 1992:466). Under 'go' Greenberg (1987:226) gave Wappo *mi*, an error due to extracting *míˀ* 'you' from the phrase *ˀikháˀmìˀ čó.siˀ* 'how are you going' (where *čó-* is the root 'to go') (Kimball 1992:483–4).

Too frequently, not only is semantic latitude among compared forms the problem, but Greenberg's cases have very skewed glosses not really reflecting their actual meanings. For example, under a set labeled CALL, following a form meaning 'call by name' Greenberg gave Atakapa *eng* (/e:ŋ/), but this Atakapa word means neither 'call' nor 'call by name,' but only 'name' (Kimball 1992:479). The semantic difference between 'call,' the gloss given this set, and 'name' is significant; this instance no longer exhibits the similarity suggested by the inaccurate gloss. In another instance, Greenberg (1987:230) cited Tonkawa *mam* 'bring' among forms in support of the Amerind etymology for H A N D, although his source lists the gloss of *mama* as 'to carry a burden, to pack (it).' This meaning suggests action performed more by the back than with the hand, making the connection with other forms meaning 'hand' less likely (Manaster Ramer 1993b). Greenberg (1987:139) also listed Tonkawa *kala* 'mouth' as Hokan compared with Karuk -*kara* 'in the mouth,' but he also gave Tonkawa *kalan* 'curser' in the Amerind list, equated this time with Karuk *ka:rim* 'bad' (Greenberg 1987:187). However, the two Tonkawa words are related and cannot possibly be separate cognates in the two distinct sets. In Greenberg's source, the second Tonkawa form is glossed as 'one who continually curses, a foul-mouthed person,' showing it is derived from the first (Manaster Ramer 1993b). Greenberg (1987:146) also gave Natchez *onoxk* (/ʔo:nohk/), which he says means 'thorn,' though it really means 'blackberry,' and hence is not appropriate in a set labeled A R R O W (Kimball 1992:453). Greenberg (1987:147) also mistakenly listed Atakapa *uk* 'boil, ulcer' with the set 'boil (cook by boiling)' (Kimball 1992:454). Under 'live' Greenberg (1987:154) gave Atakapa *nun* as 'sit,' actually *nuŋ* 'town' (Kimball 1992:464–5). Listed under 'open' Greenberg (1987:156) has Chitimacha *hakin*, but this is *haki* 'to peel' (Kimball 1992:467). Greenberg's (1987:161) citation of Natchez *pa* 'plant' under the set labeled 'tree' is misleading, since Natchez *pa.-helu.iš* (whence Greenberg's form) means 'to plant a garden,' not a 'plant' (Kimball 1992:474).

As seen in Chapter 7, a common mistake in proposals of distant genetic relationship is that of presenting a single form from one language as evidence for more than one proposed cognate set. A single form in one language cannot simultaneously be cognate with multiple forms in another language (except when the cognates are etymologically related, which in effect signifies that only one cognation set is involved). A single form from one language cannot be cognate to multiple forms in another, unless the multiple forms are derived ultimately from a single original source. Therefore, the total number of proposed cognate sets will always have to be reduced by at least the number of repeated etyma. Nevertheless, cases of this sort are not uncommon in Greenberg's Amerind data (several examples are given in Chapter 7). For example, Greenberg (1987) gives Jakalteko *ita* 'food' (actually *itah*) (149) under the Penutian gloss 'eat' – but its cognates, Tzeltal *itax* 'verdure' and Q'eqchi' *ičax* 'grass' are given in the different set 'dirty' (212). In fact all three are regular reflexes of Proto-Mayan *it^yax* 'vegetable, edible plant' (Tzeltal 'edible vegetable,' Q'eqchi' 'edible vegetable, pasture plants,' Jakalteko 'food, edible plant'). (For several other examples see Campbell 1988; Goddard 1987:657.)

Greenberg's (1987) comparisons also contain numerous examples of false cognates, where unrelated forms from languages within a particular family are put together in the belief that they are (or may be) related. Obviously, if reconstructions are based on non-cognate forms within a family, their value in remoter comparisons is questionable. Greenberg's proposed etymologies contain many examples of this sort. From the Mayan family listed under 154 'liver' Greenberg cites Q'eqchi' *č'oč['el]* and K'iche' *kuš* 'heart'; however, these are from two separate and unconnected etyma, Q'eqchi' *č'oč* 'liver,' 'earth' (from Proto-Mayan **č'ohč* 'earth') and K'iche' *k'uš* 'chest, heart' (Proto-K'ichean **k'uʔuš*). In 217 (p. 158) Kaqchikel *ša* 'be' (actually 'only, just') is compared with non-cognate K'iche' *uš* 'become.' Other examples are 16 (p. 146), 33 (p. 147), 60 (p. 149), 167 (p. 155), 184 (p. 156), 217 (p. 158), 246 (p. 160), 273 (p. 161), 274 (p. 161), 20 (p. 188), 49 (p. 198), 68 (p. 206), 215 (p. 251), 221 (p. 253), 234 (p. 256), 254 (p. 262), 269 (p. 266), etc. (For Algonquian cases, see Goddard 1987.)

9.6.2   Is Japanese Amerind?

One of the most telling criticisms of the Amerind hypothesis, mentioned above, is that when multilateral comparison is applied in the same fashion that Greenberg did, almost any language selected randomly also fits into Amerind, often better than any of the Native American languages in Greenberg's data. Put differently, with multilateral comparison, it is impossible to distinguish "Amerind" languages from others. That this is the case is seen in the following comparisons which show that Japanese fits into "Amerind" extremely well by the criteria Greenberg employed.[19] We have compared Old Japanese forms from Miller (1971a), Martin (1987), and Unger (1977), with "Amerind" forms from Greenberg (1987) (further elaborated and indexed by Ruhlen 1994a). Using Greenberg's method, we find that many Old Japanese forms match "Amerind" sets. Thus, Japanese, if we accept multilateral comparison, is an "Amerind" language. Or put more precisely, the method of multilateral comparison is insufficient to distinguish Japanese (and other languages) from the American Indian languages which Greenberg claims are related to one another; Greenberg placed Japanese in Eurasiatic, a very separate large-scale grouping (Greenberg 1990b, 1991, 2000a, 2002; see above). For Greenberg's Amerind lexical sets, we list first some of the forms which show the phonetic similarity to the Japanese forms compared, and then we list many of the glosses found among the words in the so-called "etymology," beginning with Greenberg's primary gloss for the set.

The following Japanese comparisons fit "Amerind" sets.[20] We do not present matches for all of Greenberg's 281 Amerind "etymologies" (although we find

---

[19] This section is based on Campbell 1997c.

[20] The Japanese forms presented here are simply repeated as given in the sources we utilized. This is how Greenberg assembled his Amerind forms. Thus, whether the Japanese data cited are correct or not is not relevant, so long as the procedure followed represents an accurate application of Greenberg's method.

Japanese matches for nearly all); rather, we present matches for only the first 25 lexical sets and for another 9 presumed grammatical sets (for matches with the first 114, see Campbell 1997c). The abbreviations used to reference sources of the Japanese forms (first line of comparison sets) are: OJ = Old Japanese, U EJ = Unger "Early Japanese", Mi = Miller, Ma = Martin); we use Gr for Greenberg (1987), and R for Ruhlen (1994a) for "Amerind" forms cited (in the second line of the comparisons).

1. Mi OJ *kökörö* 'heart'; U EJ *kokoro* 'heart'; Ma OJ *kokoro* 'heart'
   Gr *kulu*, *kʷar*, *kene*, *-kekin*, *kuaŋ*, etc.; 'breast, heart, belly, milk, chest, middle, body, in front' (pp. 198–9 set 50)

2. Ma OJ *hara* < *fara* < **para* 'belly'; Mi OJ *fara* 'stomach'
   Gr *paro*, *puara*, *pure*, *pori*, *pare*, *pera*, *punua*, *purua*, *pil*, *paru*, *panhe*, *bule*, *pan*, *balla*, *pali*, *p'a:n*, etc.; 'belly, chest, heart, liver, lungs' (p. 191 set 30); R *palin* 'belly' (p. 130)

3. Ma OJ *muna* 'breast'
   Gr *munia*, *mono*, *manate*, *mangu*, *monoɨ*, *monnø*, etc.; 'breast, chest, milk' (p. 79 set 7; cf. p. 147 set 26); R *mana* (p. 131)

4. Ma OJ *ti* < **ti[y]* < **tu-Ci* 'milk'; Ma OJ *titi* 'breasts, milk' (cf. U EJ sup < **cupV* 'suck')
   Gr *ičič*, *ču*, *ʔuču*, *ʔu:čič*; 'breast, teat' (p. 134 set 25, p. 147 set 25)

5. Mi OJ *mï*; Ma OJ *mi* < *myi* < **mi-Ci* 'body'
   Gr *me*, *imi*, *aem*, *mein*, *eme*, *uma'*; 'body, animal' (p. 197 set 44)

6. U EJ *kata* 'side'; Ma OJ *kata(-)* 'side, one side (of two)'
   Gr *kate*, *kida*, *kisi*; 'side, rib' (p. 119 set 172)

7. Ma OJ *ti* 'blood'
   Gr *di*, *du*, *ʔits*, *ate*, *ičkči*, *es*, *issiš*, *jeu*, *donʔi*; 'blood, bleed' (p. 94 set 12)

8. Mi OJ *kë* 'hair'
   Gr *ke*, *iki*, *ki*, *kai*; *kʲũ*, *tsi*, *ǰi*, *(n)(h)kʷi*, etc.; 'hair, down, head; hair, beard, feather, root' (p. 69 set 56, p. 96 set 45, p. 127 set 35, p. 229 set 136)

9. Mi OJ *të* 'hand'; Ma OJ *te* < **te[y]* < **ta-Ci* 'hand' (cf. Ma OJ *i-tu* 'five')
   Gr *tei*, *ti*, *ta*, *to*, *utu*, etc.; 'hand, bring, give, take, carry, with the hand' (pp. 230–1 set 139)

10. Ma OJ *migi* 'right (hand)'
    Gr *imak*, *amik*, *hemik*, *mɛgeh*, *e-me*, *maka*, *ma*, *min*, *mane*, *maki*, *mux*, *imik*, *imi*, *ami*, etc.; 'hand, right hand, left hand, give, take, bring, palm, branch, finger, carry, five, etc.' (pp. 229–30 set 137)

11. Ma OJ *asi* 'foot'
    Gr *asi:*, *ʔas*, *ise*, *si*, *sijaʔ*, *asu*, *ʔašɨ*, etc.; 'foot, leg, knee, kick, tread'

12. Ma OJ *ha* < *fa* < **pa* 'tooth'
    Gr *i-pe*, *opi*; 'tooth' (p. 98 set 93); R *pe* (p. 152)

13. Ma OJ **po-po* 'cheek' (> *fofo* > *hoo*, *hoho*)

Gr *paxo, fa ?xo, ipæpok*; 'cheek' (p. 79 set 9); Gr *pʰok, bege*; 'cheek' (p. 134 set 28); R *poke, pako* (p. 132)

14. Ma OJ *agi* < *agyi* < **anki* 'jaw, gill'; U EJ *agi-* 'jaw'
    Gr *ak, aka, ekeke, hek, ai, jako, jego, jenku, ñikoi, e-ka, akwa*, etc.; 'mouth, jaw, chin, lips, border, lip' (p. 246 set 192)

15. Ma OJ *ike* < **iki* < **ik[a-C]i* 'breath'; U EJ *ik* < **ika* 'breathe, live', U EJ *ike* < **ika-gi* 'pant'
    Gr *aki, akke, atsi*; 'breathe' (p. 68 set 15)

16. Ma OJ **kapo* 'face' (> *kafo* > *kao*)
    Gr *kapu-, kapa-ka, kap, a-kibaux*; 'eye, eyebrow' (p. 112 set 64, cf. set 65)

17. Ma OJ *ma(-), me* 'eye'
    Gr *?i me, (me-)mi, mwɔ, (vi-)mo, tha-iimi*; 'forehead, face' (p. 80 set 22); R *imi* 'forehead' (p. 138); Gr *vi-nimi-ši, tha-njemi*; 'eye, forehead' (p. 80 set 19)

18. Ma OJ *kubi* < *kubyi* < **kunpi* 'neck, head'
    Gr *ku, inkio, k'oa, k'e, k'uji, ikio, ka(n)*, etc.; 'neck, throat' (p. 247 set 196); R *k'oe* 'neck' (p. 145)

19. Ma OJ *ka* 'hair', *ke* (<*key* < **ka-Ci*) 'hair'
    Gr *ka, ke, iki, ki, kek, kai* etc.; 'hair, head, down' (p. 69 set 56); R *kai* (p. 139)

20. Ma OJ **pina – kwo* 'penis' (> *fenoko* > *henoko*); Ma OJ *huguri* < **punkuri* 'testicle, scrotum'
    Gr *enpen, opengo, hapwẽ, wi-pinši*; 'penis' (p. 81 set 48); R *pen* (p. 146); Gr *ba, paki, ka-moesse, si-mase*; 'testicle, egg, yoke, penis' (pp. 261–2 set 253); Gr *pehej, pue, -bi?e, iipx*; 'egg, testicle' (p. 135 set 47); R *paki* 'testicle' (p. 151)

21. Ma OJ **po-to* < *foto* < *hoto* 'vagina'
    Gr *petu, apuit, piši, ped, vi:θ, d-i:bis, muus*; 'vagina, vulva' (p. 264 set 263); R *petu, tsupote* 'vagina' (p. 153)

22. Ma OJ *hii* < *fiwi* < **pipi* 'baby's pubic area', **fi* 'vulva'
    Gr *piši, ped, petu, apuit, vi:θ, d-i:bis, muus*; 'vagina, vulva' (p. 264 set 263; cf. p. 92 set 121)

23. Ma OJ *-ki* (<**ki*) 'man, male'
    Gr *iči, ča, is, haqi, hake, ka:kʰ, uɣuiɣ*; 'man, male, person, husband' (pp. 242–3 sets 177, 178)

24. Ma OJ **mina* (> **miCa* > *mye* > *me*) 'female, woman'
    Gr *maringa, meri, mairin, mari?mi, mwajra, møri; mata*; 'female, woman' (p. 112 set 71, p. 142 set 166); R *marin* (p. 137)

25. U EJ *tuma* 'wife'; Ma OJ *tuma* 'wife'
    Gr *timua, domo, zomo, itomo, itiumu, tem, tomio, tsamen*, etc.; 'woman, female, girl'

26. Mi OJ *mï* 'first person singular'
    Gr *m* 'first person': Gr *m, -mo, me-, ma-, m-, mya, myra, mo, moiñ, mïmï, mï-* (p. 276 set 3)
27. Ma OJ **ono* 'we'; Mi OJ *wan-u* 'first person' (Ma OJ *wa* < **ba-nu* 'I')
    Gr *n* 'first person' (p. 273 set 1)
28. Mi OJ *si* 'second person', *söne* 'second-person plural'
    Gr *s* 'second person': *-s, -s-, is-*, etc. (pp. 278–9); cf. *i* 'second person' (p. 277 set 9)
29. Mi OJ *wakë* 'second person deprecatory'
    Gr *ka(-be), ka, kai-, ikia, aki, ga*; 'second-person pronoun' (p. 278 set 10)
30. Mi OJ *ma* 'negative'; Ma OJ *mana* 'don't'
    Gr *m, ma, -ma, -ama, mo, ama, ampa*; 'negative, without, there is not' (p. 315 set 101); R *ama* 'negative' (p. 145)
31. Mi OJ *tu* 'dative–locative particle'
    Gr *-tV, -ta, -at, -te, di, -ti* 'dative' (p. 303 set 49)
32. Ma OJ *ka(-)* < **ga* 'that (distal)'
    Gr *k, -k-, ka, kai, kaki, ke, kue, ki, k'e*, etc.; 'near demonstrative, that, this, here, third-person pronoun' (pp. 289–90 set 22); R *ki* 'this' (p. 151)
33. Ma OJ *ko* 'this' (cf. *kuu* 'this one')
    Gr *ko, koo, k, kua, kū, kue, khu*, etc.; 'this, that, here' (p. 289–90 set 22)
34. Ma OJ *to* < **to* 'that'
    Gr *t, ti, te, da, daa, ta-, atu, tu, toho, t-*; 'that, this, there' (pp. 281–2 set 13).

These sets show numerous similarities shared by Japanese and the putative Amerind forms, including pronouns, basic vocabulary items, and morphological comparisons in multilateral comparison. Therefore, it must be concluded either that (1) Japanese is also an Amerind language, or (2) there is something seriously wrong with this method of attempting to determine genetic relationships. Here, the Japanese forms fit Greenberg's Amerind lexical sets in such a way that Japanese cannot be distinguished from the various Native American languages that are compared. In fact, Japanese forms are found to match "Amerind" sets with far greater frequency than those from any individual American Indian language or family treated by Greenberg in these sets of words. This would make Japanese the strongest example of an "Amerind" language.

In short, since Japanese and other languages cannot be distinguished from putative Amerind languages by this method, the method proves to be inadequate for determining genetic relationships.

Most of the other hypotheses of distant genetic relationship involving groups of Native American languages are discussed in Campbell (1997a); these evaluations are not repeated here. However, a few of these which have figured in other broader proposals do deserve commentary.

9.7   Na-Dene[21]

The Na-Dene hypothesis is attributed to Sapir (1915b), in which he proposed a relationship which included Haida, Tlingit, and Athabaskan. The hypothesis is doubted by most specialists in the native languages of the Americas, though it is frequently assumed by proponents of long-range relationships and included with other language groups as a member of even more far-flung proposed distant genetic relationships. For example, it figures prominently in the Dene–Caucasian hypothesis (cf. Macro-Caucasian, Sino-Caucasian, Basque–Sino-Caucasian). Attempts have been made to relate "Na-Dene" to numerous other linguistic genetic units (see, for example, Stewart 1991). For this reason, if not for others, it is important to evaluate the Na-Dene hypothesis.

Levine (1979) is cited frequently as a principal source of doubt concerning Na-Dene; however, the hypothesis has been controversial from long before Levine, in fact from its beginning. For example, Krauss (1964:128), after careful assessment of the phonological evidence, concluded that the question of the Na-Dene hypothesis is "more open than ever" (see also Krauss 1965; Pinnow 1964). Those who question the Na-Dene proposal suspect many of these resemblances as being the result of diffusion, accident, and poorly analyzed data. Jacobsen (1990) re-evaluated the lexical evidence. Where Levine (1979) thought that only 31 sets comparing Haida with the other languages were not otherwise disqualified, Jacobsen opted to save 57 cases. However, in evaluating these 57, he found none of the Haida–Athabaskan pairs fell in the list of most stable meanings and that the compared forms fare no better than expectation of chance resemblances.

Haida's relationship to the other languages is now questioned by most specialists (Jacobsen 1993; Krauss 1979; Krauss and Golla 1981:67; Lawrence and Leer 1977; Leer 1991:162; Levine 1979; cf. Pinnow 1964:156), though supported by Pinnow (1964, 1985, 1990), and Enrico (2004). Jacobsen's terminology is useful in this discussion. He speaks of the Na-Dene hypothesis *sensu lato* (essentially as Sapir proposed it, with Haida included, what Levine [1979:157] calls the "classical" Na-Dene hypothesis) and Na-Dene *sensu stricto* (that is, Tlingit and Athabaskan[+Eyak], but excluding Haida). Levine (1979) showed that most of the structural similarities that had been presented as evidence for Haida's connection with other Na-Dene *sensu stricto* languages were due to Swanton's (1911) misanalysis of Haida data; others involve areal features. The lexical evidence has proved particularly unconvincing (Levine 1979; Jacobsen 1993).

---

[21] The name Na-Dene is Sapir's creation, based on a joining together of a Tlingit form *naa* 'tribe' and the Athabaskan form for 'person, people,' e.g. Navajo *diné* 'person' (Pinnow 1985:25).

While most scholars reject this proposal, it has some supporters (cf. Pinnow 1985, 1990). Greenberg (1987:321–30) and Ruhlen (1994a:91–110) each have a chapter defending it.[22] However, Greenberg's chapter is about disagreements he has with Levine's (1979) methods, and thus presents no new supporting data. Ruhlen (1994a:91–110) published the Na-Dene "evidence" in Greenberg's unpublished notebook (in Stanford University Library), listing 324 proposed "etymologies," only about 25 of which overlap with Sapir's (1915b) lexical sets. Of these, 119 lack Haida forms, and since the dispute is about Haida, the strength of Ruhlen's argument must rest with the remaining 205 forms, though many of these involve comparisons of only two of the four entities (where Eyak is compared separately from Athabaskan). These forms are replete with problems of the sort discussed in Chapter 7. For example, under the gloss T R E E (set 288), Ruhlen gives Haida q̓íit, q̓ēt 'spruce,' Tlingit k'ɛ 'log'; this is problematic in that it involves short forms, semantic non-equivalences, and only two languages are compared. This is not atypical of the other examples. Of the forms which have Haida comparisons, 39 involve considerable semantic latitude (e.g. set 20 'blood'/'be bright'/'be white', set 115 'guts'/'brains'); 91 are short forms, 11 are onomatopoetic (e.g. set 21 Haida ux, Tlingit 'úx 'blow' – note that these languages lack labial stops); 9 appear to be diffused (e.g. set 12 Haida xúuts 'brown bear,' Tlingit xúts 'brown bear,' Tsetsaut [Athabaskan] xɔ 'grizzly bear,' Proto-Chumash *qus [phonetically xus in most of the Chumash languages, Klar 1977:68–9], not to mention the forms for 'elk', long ago identified as loans); in 5 cases the Haida forms lack sufficient phonetic similarity (e.g. set 22 Haida ʃu-lal 'blue,' Tlingit khatleh 'blue'); and 5 cases are of nursery forms (e.g. set 111 Haida nān 'grandmother,' and forms ná, nɛ, nan, -an 'mother' in several Athabaskan languages). It is safe to say that whether Haida is related to Tlingit and Eyak–Athabaskan cannot be determined based on the evidence Ruhlen has presented.

Pinnow's (1985) evidence is extensive. He presented many grammatical similarities, especially involving verbs, but the recognized grammatical similarities are debated, and areal influence may account for them. Pinnow relies heavily on "word-family" comparisons, which demands caution (Chapter 7). While he believes in sound correspondences, he thinks it is too early, given the current state of the work, to attempt to work these out (Pinnow 1985:33). Without systematic sound correspondences, most scholars will remain unconvinced. A majority of the forms compared are monosyllabic and very often involve considerable semantic latitude.

Enrico's (2004) comparisons have the advantage of having much more extensive and accurate Haida data to work with. He has proposed 92 lexical

---

[22] Hymes (1955, 1956) also argued for Na-Dene, but the positional analysis upon which Hymes based his conclusions is discounted (see Chapter 7).

comparisons of Haida with Tlingit and Eyak–Athabaskan, with indications of potential sound correspondences and with some grammatical comparisons. This may be the most promising work to date attempting to establish the Na-Dene hypothesis, but we find it still inconclusive. Without presenting the details, we find that most of the comparisons exhibit the problems against which Chapter 7 cautions, so that the burden of proof is not met: it is possible that other factors explain the similarities among the forms cited better than the genetic relationship hypothesis. For example, a large number of the 92 lexical sets reflect onomatopoeia (sets 2, 4, 5, 11, 12, 24, 32, 39, 60, 75, 80, 82, 84) and we would set these aside. These involve glosses such as 'ringing sound,' 'make the sound of a sandhill crane,' 'pop, crack,' 'burst, crack, boom,' 'thudding sound,' 'flop,' 'viscous liquid comes to boil, pop, burst,' 'blow, waft,' 'mallard duck, Canadian goose' (χ əχ ə, qaaX, xah, etc.), 'brittle object break,' 'low (of a cow), snore,' etc. Several others are affective/symbolic. A majority of the forms involve short forms or forms for which parts of the phonology are not explained; a majority exhibit liberal semantic associations (for example, in set 3 a form like *daga* in Haida meaning 'make a certain sound, liquid move in a certain amount' and another form like *da.ad* 'pinched in' are compared to Eyak *da?* and Proto-Athabaskan **daa* 'mouth, entrance' – note also the comparison is of short forms, a CV comparison only; for another example, set 51, a Haida form *kíŋ* 'call' is compared to Tlingit *sha* and Northern Athabaskan **yə -tsee^y* '(dog) bark'). Though Enrico controls well for borrowing, a few of the lexical sets could still involve borrowing (for example, set 27, involving 'box, pot, carrying basket, plate, dish'). A few may be nursery forms (e.g. set 36 'grandfather,' set 45 'sister-in-law, brother-in-law,' and phonetically very similar set 46 'male cross-cousin,' etc.). Several comparisons have phonological problems, where some of the phonological material is left unexplained (as pointed out by Enrico, for example, set 9 "the source of the initial syllable *dii* is unknown"; set 28 "the sources of final ŋ, ?a, d are unknown"; set 52 "the source of Haida Gə and the reason for the absence of ŋ are unknown"; see also sets 8, 14, 19, 25, 28, 30, 36, 40, 46, 48, 51, 53, 55, 57, 72, 73, 74, 77, 87, 89, 91).

Enrico's (2004:258–67) morphological and syntactic comparisons reveal considerable parallels between Haida and the other languages compared, but we are not convinced that these cannot be accounted for as a combination of areally diffused features, commonplace typological traits, and accidental similarities.

In short, we find Enrico's evidence suggestive, but not sufficient to confirm the proposed Na-Dene hypothesis.

We conclude that the Na-Dene hypothesis, or more specifically, the genetic affinity of Haida, is still an open question; Haida could be related to a Tlingit–Eyak–Athabaskan grouping, but the evidence so far falls short of being convincing.

9.7.1   Beyond Na-Dene

It scarcely bears mentioning that because Na-Dene itself cannot be demonstrated (at least at present), even more far-flung proposals of distant linguistic
kinship involving so-called Na-Dene languages and such things as Athabaskan–
Sino-Tibetan, Na-Dene–Basque(–North Caucasian), and Athabaskan–Tlingit–
Yuchi–Siouan are discredited. The weaknesses in the Na-Dene data pointed out
here, however, are unlikely to deter the determined, and therefore it is important
to examine further the foundation of some of these more far-flung proposals. We
take the starting point to be Sapir's belief that Na-Dene and Sino-Tibetan may be
connected. He wrote, "if the morphological and lexical accord which I find on
every hand between Nadene and Indo-Chinese [Sino-Tibetan] is 'accidental,'
then every analogy on God's earth is an accident" (letter to Kroeber, October 1,
1921, in Golla 1984:374; see Sapir 1925b). Sapir did not pursue this publicly
and most scholars even in Sapir's lifetime were reluctant to embrace the notion
(but see Tokarev and Zolotarevskaja 1955).

   Nevertheless, we know something of the "accords" to which he referred and
indeed the "analogies" he had in mind were in no way outrageous, though seen
from today's perspective they turn out to have non-genetic explanations. He
referred in correspondence with Kroeber to the "old quasi-isolating feel" and
"tone" of Na-dene, similar to "Indo-Chinese," saying that he found in Tibetan
"pretty much the kind of base from which a generalized Na-dene could have
developed," citing "some very tempting material points of resemblance":

Tibetan postpositions *ma* "in" and *du* "to, at," both of which, precisely as in Athabaskan
and Tlingit, are used also to subordinate verbs; in both Tlingit and Tibetan the tr[ansitive]
verb as such is *clearly* passive [i.e. involves ergative constructions]; causative or
tr[ansitive] verbs have *s-* prefixed in Tibetan, *si-* and *li-* in Tlingit, *l-* in Ath[abaskan];
Tibetan verb ablaut is staggeringly like Déné–Tlingit (e.g. present *byed* "make,"
pret[erite] *byas*, fut[ure] *bya*, imperative *byos*); and so on. Am I dreaming? At least
I know that Déné's a long shot nearer Tibetan than to Siouan. (Letter to Kroeber Oct. 4,
1920, in Golla 1984:350)

Such evidence would have seemed more striking in the 1920s than today,
since we now know there is nothing particularly unusual about "quasi-
isolating" typology, not unusual in the world or the Americas (cf., for example,
Otomanguean languages, some of which were also suspected of having affinities
with Chinese [or Sino-Tibetan]; see Campbell 1997a:47, 157, 382). The tones
of Athabaskan languages are now known to be secondary, not reconstructible to
Proto-Athabaskan, but to have arisen by normal sound changes from segmental
phonology (Campbell 1997a:113); similarly, the tonal contrasts in Sino-Tibetan
languages are now also known to have developed by normal tonogenesis and
were not a feature of the proto-language. This diminishes considerably the initial

attraction of a possible Sino-Tibetan connection with Athabaskan. As for post-positions with relational/locative senses becoming grammaticalized as markers of subordination, this, too, is unremarkable and is seen repeatedly in other languages, specifically in those with SOV word order, including various Native American families (see Craig and Hale 1992; Harris and Campbell 1995). The passive nature of transitive verbs in Tlingit and Tibetan reflects the ergativity characteristic of these languages, but this is typologically commonplace, and some have thought (erroneously) that ergativity derives from an earlier passive construction in all ergative languages (see Harris and Campbell 1995). The ablaut and causative prefixes (signaled by short forms with unmarked consonants) could easily be accidental. For example, Jicaque (of Honduras) has very similar ablauted forms. Thus, while Sapir had legitimate reasons for entertaining the possibility of such a relationship, the sort of evidence he had in mind is far from compelling today.

Shafer (1952, 1969) followed up on Sapir's Na-Dene–Sino-Tibetan hypothesis with not very persuasive evidence, and this prompted Swadesh (1952) to report his recollections of Sapir's discussion of the topic in his lectures at Yale, together with Swadesh's own examination of the hypothesis. Swadesh repeated that there are broad structural similarities, particularly in the tendency to prefixing, plus "old formative suffixes," and a body of Sapir's "cognates with regular phonetic correspondences" (Swadesh 1952:178). Shafer had compared Sino-Tibetan only with Athabaskan, and Swadesh said he had "found Tlingit and Haida parallels for about one fourth of Shafer's comparisons," which he presented (Swadesh 1952:179–80), with eight new lexical comparisons of his own. All in all, not a very persuasive case.

More recently, a number of mostly Russian scholars – Starostin (1989, 1991b) in particular –, sympathetic to Nostratic and other very far-flung proposals of relationship, have taken up the hypothesis that so-called Na-Dene belongs in a grouping they call variously "Sino-Caucasian" or "Dene–Sino-Caucasian" which purportedly includes Basque, Sino-Tibetan, Yeniseian, North Caucasian, and Na-Dene (Bengtson 1991a; Nikolaev 1991; Shevoroshkin 1991; cf. Ruhlen 1994a:24–8, 1994b).[23] Shevoroshkin (1990:8–11) extends this idea much further, grouping Nostratic, Sino-Caucasian, and "Amerind," first suggested by Starostin. Shevoroshkin is somewhat ambiguous in the same passage, taking only some of the "Amerind" groups; he seems to accuse Greenberg's Almosan–Keresiouan of "unamerind" behavior, grouping it with these others from the Old

---

[23] Bengtson (1991c:67) credits Trombetti (1926) with "first proposing special ties between Basque, Caucasian, 'Indochinese,' 'Paleo-Asiatic' (including Yeniseian), and Western North America (i.e. Na-Dene), all in the context of his monogenetic global hierarchy." Sometimes other languages are also suggested as members of "Sino-Caucasian," e.g. Burushaski, Etruscan, Nahali, Gilyak, and "Almosan–Keresiouan" (cf. Shevoroshkin 1990; Bengtson 1991a:67–8).

World. Shevoroshkin (1990:10) concludes from a list of 26 problematic look-alikes involving Salish:

This means that Salishan – apparently along with Wakashan, Algic and other Almosan–Keresiouan languages – belongs to Sino-Caucasian languages (= Dene–Caucasian) phylum [*sic*]. Nikolaev has demonstrated that the Na Dene (Athapascan) languages belong to this phylum as well (but they seem to be less archaic than Salishan – and Wakashan). So we have to "withdraw" the Almosan–Keresiouan phylum from Amerind and "add" it to Sino-Caucasian (or Dene–Caucasian; this latter term seems better).

However, since not even Na-Dene has been satisfactorily demonstrated, it could hardly be connected successfully to these Old World groups. Conceivably, some languages from the putative Na-Dene grouping could prove to be related to some of the others in this far-flung grouping, but the evidence presented so far falls short of making a plausible case for this. In the interest of space, we do not evaluate the specific examples in detail, but just mention the nature of the problems involved. Nikolaev (1991) presented 197 sets of look-alikes involving forms from various Athabaskan languages, Eyak, and Haida, compared with Proto-North Caucasian, Proto-Nakh, and occasionally others, with putative sound correspondences between "Proto-Eyak–Athapascan" and Proto-North Caucasian. A very large proportion of these lexical sets is subject to the failings discussed in Chapter 7, and the case is not convincing.[24] The same is true of Ruhlen's (1994a:26–7) 33 comparisons among Basque, North Caucasian, Burushaski, Sumerian, Nahali, Sino-Tibetan, Yeniseian, Haida, Tlingit, Eyak, and Athabaskan. There are several gaps in this chart (for example 20 missing from Haida); of the 33 lexical sets, there are three where forms glossed 'thou' recur, two for 'who'; many are short, semantically divergent, phonetically not particularly similar, onomatopoetic (e.g. 'frog'), etc. In short, the list is insufficient for a plausible case of potential relationship.

9.8   Dravidian external connections

Majority opinion holds Dravidian to have no known relatives, though several proposals of remote relationships repeatedly come up. Connections have been proposed for Dravidian with a very large array of language groups: Basque, Etruscan, Caucasian, Egyptian, Sumerian, Japanese, Korean, so-called "Altaic" languages, Uralic, and Elamite, not to mention several sub-Saharan African languages. Uralic and Elamite are sometimes seen as holding the most promise.

[24] Nikolaev (1991) goes even further, seeing Algonquian-Ritwan and Salishan as also connected with "Sino-Caucasian," and Shevoroshkin (1991) concurs. However, Nikolaev's 40 lexical sets comparing "Sino-Caucasian" with Algonquian and Salishan and Shevoroshkin's (1991:7–8) 13 (comparing mostly Salishan forms with words from the other languages) are hardly persuasive, exhibiting the typical problems (e.g. onomatopoeia, short forms, semantic latitude, nursery forms, etc.).

Therefore, we consider both here briefly, though without presenting a full evaluation of the data for these hypotheses.

9.8.1   Dravidian–Elamite

The Dravidian–Elamite hypothesis is promising but as yet unconfirmed. David McAlpin (1974a, 1974b, 1975, 1981) presented a reasonable though not thoroughly convincing case for a genetic relationship between Dravidian and Elamite (an ancient, long-extinct isolate of the Persian Gulf), though his evidence has since been disputed. McAlpin's evidence included a number of proposed lexical cognate sets (81 items), some postulated phonological correspondences, some matchings in noun cases and derivational morphology, and later, matchings from verbal morphology. Fewer than 250 Elamite (C)VC lexical roots are known; McAlpin finds Dravidian cognates with about 40 percent of the Achaemenid Elamite and 50 percent of Middle Elamite roots. Zvelebil (1990:105) confesses sympathy for McAlpin's hypothesis, but says "I do not see any real proof, albeit I may see a lot of evidence," and we agree. We find various problems with the lexical comparisons of the sort surveyed in Chapter 7. To cite just one example, McAlpin's set 24 has Middle Elamite *kap-* 'to shut (up), hide,' Achaemenid Elamite *kap* 'treasury': Proto-Dravidian *kap*, Tamil *kappu* 'to overspread (of clouds),' *kavi* 'to cover, overshadow,' Kannada *kappu, kavi* 'to cover.' This is not particularly compelling, given the difference in meaning and the accidental similarities in other languages (e.g. English *cover*, Spanish *capa* 'cover'). Many of McAlpin's comparisons exhibit difficulties of the sort warned against in Chapter 7, though enough survive to make the hypothesis worthy of more thorough investigation.

9.8.2   Dravidian–Uralic

Robert Caldwell, credited with the founding of comparative Dravidian (see Chapter 6), was also inclined to see some broader connections for Dravidian, in Finnish, Turkish, and associated languages (Caldwell 1974[1856/75]:42, 62–3). In Krishnamurti's (1969:328) words, Caldwell entertained a possible connection between Dravidian and "Scythian" languages, which he defined as "a common designation of all those languages of Asia and Europe which do not belong to the Indo-European or Semitic families" and discussed a "special relationship" to "Ugro-Finnish." Following Caldwell, a number of papers addressed the possible Dravidian–Uralic connection (most favorable): Aalto 1971; Andronov 1971; Bouda 1953a, 1953b; Burrow 1943, 1944; Dybo 1989a; Larsson 1982; Levy 1928; Marlow 1974, 1980; Puskás 1982; Schrader 1924, 1936; Tyler 1968, 1990; etc. (see Zvelebil 1990:100–3 for a survey). Some of the early motivation for the hypothesis had to do with lexical look-alikes; for example, Burrow (1944) compared a set of 72 words for body parts in Dravidian and Uralic. Nevertheless, the primary original attraction for the hypothesis seems to have been typological: both are agglutinative, lack prefixes, have similar word order, "the verb is of an overall nominal structure and character." These traits were taken together with the phonetic similarity among several suffixes as evidence of relationship (Zvelebil 1990:101). As was the case with Altaic, much here has to do with commonplace typological traits which easily develop independently in languages aided by particular ethnocentric European views of evolutionary developments in societies and languages. Moreover, a number of these traits are areal and cannot be supported as genetic. Zvelebil (1990:100) presents no evidence, but sums up these works with a startling equivocation:

I am convinced that, indeed, etymological connections, typological similarities in the morphosyntactic sphere, and even some possible material identities of the morphological apparatus between Dravidian and Uralic/Altaic languages are too numerous and too striking to be purely accidental. It is my opinion that these similarities (sometimes even identities) in form, in shape, in function, in structure, are due to a relationship . . . But what was that relationship? I am equally convinced that at this moment we cannot – yet – say.

Without presenting an exposé here of the lexical evidence given in favor of the Dravidian–Uralic hypothesis, we can assert that much of it exhibits difficulties of the sorts against which Chapter 7 warns. Moreover, given the relatively simple syllable structure and phonetic inventories of Uralic and Dravidian, it is remarkably easy to find accidentally similar words.

One important problem that also needs to be borne in mind as broader affinities for Dravidian are sought is that of areal influences. Languages of the Indian subcontinent have tended to converge some of their structure in areal linguistic change, i.e. "Indianization" as it is sometimes called. This means that compared traits in attempts to get at more remote relationships must be considered with a careful eye towards diffusion as a possible explanation, or at least as a potentially complicating factor.

9.9 Indo-Pacific

Greenberg (1971b:807) argued that "the bulk of the non-Austronesian languages of Oceania from the Andaman Islands on the west of the Bay of Bengal to Tasmania in the southeast [excluding Australia] forms a single group of genetically related languages," which he called "Indo-Pacific." This is mainly concerned with the non-Austronesian "Papuan" languages of New Guinea, but also includes several groups outside New Guinea. The major "subgroups" are: (1) Andaman Islands (AN), (2) Timor–Alor (TA), (3) Halmahera (HA), (4) New Britain (NB), (5) Bougainville (BO), (6) Central Melanesia (CM),

(7) Tasmania (TS), (8) Western New Guinea (WNG), (9) Northern New Guinea (NNG), (10) South-West New Guinea (SWNG), (11) Southern New Guinea (SNG), (12) Central New Guinea (CNG), (13) North-East New Guinea (NENG), (14) and (15) Eastern New Guinea (ENG). As van Driem (2001:139–40) has pointed out, Greenberg's "Indo-Pacific" hypothesis is essetntially identical to Finck's (1909) family that he called the "Sprachen der ozeanischen Neger," based on racial notions; the name "Indo-Pacific" had already been used for this group, rooted in the "Pan-Negrito theory," called by Roger Blench "essentially a crinkly hair hypothesis" (van Driem 2001:140).

Greenberg proceeded here as in his later and better-known Amerind hypothesis (Greenberg 1987) by entering vocabulary information from numerous languages in several notebooks, "organized roughly by groupings of languages *whose closer relationship to each other is evident on inspection*" (Greenberg 1971b:808; our emphasis, LC/WP). He also copied "notes on grammar" in other notebooks. Naturally the claim of "closer relationship" which is "evident on inspection" begs the question (asked above in connection with the Amerind classification), to what extent was the classification preconceived (as was the case with the "Amerind" classification) before the data were assembled upon which to make the comparisons?

As Pawley (2004:11) says, "the Indo-Pacific hypothesis is based on very flimsy evidence and few linguists have taken it seriously."[25] Even Ruhlen (1987), a strong supporter of Greenberg's other classifications, says he accepts Greenberg's Indo-Pacific, but based his classification of these languages more closely on Wurm (1982) (see Gordon 1993:1). Laycock (1976:57), for example, concluded:

To date, it can safely be said that there is no real evidence to link the NAN [Non-Austronesian] languages of New Guinea with any other linguistic group . . . In particular, Greenberg's "Indo-Pacific Hypothesis" (1971) which would interrelate "the bulk of non-Austronesian languages of Oceania from the Andaman Islands on the west in the Bay of Bengal to Tasmania in the southeast" is not only far from proven, but also based on inadequate and insufficiently-analysed data (for example, comparisons are all too frequently made only of items within large groups of languages – such as the Trans-New-Guinea Phylum – that are already known to be related, so that there is little support for the wider relationships postulated).

Linguists' views of the Indo-Pacific hypothesis have been damning. Lynch (1998:69): that it is not "based on any evidence more solid than typological similarities or a few possibly accidental lexical similarities." Terry Crowley

---

[25] See, however, Whitehouse *et al.* (2004), which accepts the Indo-Pacific hypothesis and argues for extending it with the inclusion of the language isolate Kusunda of Nepal (brought to linguists' attention most recently by van Driem 2001:258). The evidence is far from compelling, 26 lexical look-alikes and some similarities in some of the pronominal affixes in comparison with various languages in Greenberg's Indo-Pacific hypothesis.

(1992:305): "until someone can point to the existence of regular sound correspondences in any proposed set of cognates, it is likely to continue to be regarded by mainstream linguists as being close to the lunatic fringe." George van Driem (2001:141): "The linguistic evidence which Greenberg adduced for Indo-Pacific is unconvincing, and lexical look-alikes and superficial typological similarities in languages cannot convincingly demonstrate a theory of linguistic relationships conceived solely on the basis of the physical attributes of the speakers." (For more on the racial biases behind early classifications of Oceanic languages, see Chapter 7, on Austronesian; see Van Driem 2001:139–40.) Apparently, then, Greenberg in his Indo-Pacific hypothesis followed the same strategy as in his African and American classifications, namely, founded his classification on earlier works. As seen in the discussion of "Amerind" and Greenberg's African classification (above and Chapter 6), in some instances this was a successful way to proceed, but in other cases it led him to errors where he accepted older classifications known to be wrong.

Another telling observation is that of Mat Gordon (1993:1):

a comparison of the language names provided by G[reenberg] with names listed in Ruhlen (1987a), Wurm (1982) and Grimes' [2004] *Ethnologue* found that many of G[reenberg]'s "languages" are now considered as mere dialects of single languages. This fact is, of course, not particularly surprising but what was revealing was that often G[reenberg] had grouped related dialects in quite disparate subgroups.

We look here briefly at the data Greenberg presented in favor of "Indo-Pacific." As is frequently pointed out, "most of the material on which Greenberg [1971b] has based his work, is poor to very poor, and known to be of a low level of reliability" (Wurm 1981:926; cf. Franklin 1973). Greenberg presented 84 so-called "etymologies," that is, a set of superficial lexical comparisons among the languages. These exhibit many of the methodological problems that by now are well known.

Though Greenberg (1971b) says he seeks examples represented from at least three subgroups (and not all in New Guinea), nevertheless a number of his sets are represented by only two of his sixteen groups (14, 57, 58, 64, 72, 83). For example, set 14 'bush' is represented only by one language from the Halmahera "subgroup" and one language from the Tasmania group – several of these examples are represented by only one of the many languages available in these purported subgroups – instances of "reaching down" (Chapter 7).

Semantic non-equivalences are observed in 23 sets (1, 4, 8, 9, 10, 15, 18, 25, 27, 30, 33, 35, 46, 49, 50, 53, 63, 65, 69, 71, 74, 78, 80), that is, 27 percent. For example, in set 1, with the general gloss 'above,' phonetically somewhat similar forms bear such different glosses among the languages compared as 'at,' 'upwards,' 'go up,' 'high,' 'sky,' 'above'; set 35, labeled 'good,' has 'clean,' 'beautiful,' 'well,' 'sweet.' In set 46 'long,' where only three subgroups are represented, each has a different gloss, 'high,' 'deep,' and 'long'.

A number of the sets involve very short forms (1, 8, 9, 11, 25, 27, 30, 34, 36, 42, 45, 52, 54, 61, 62, 77, etc.). For example, set 25 'to eat' has forms such as ɛ̃, *ne*, *na*, *an*, *n* (not to mention also longer forms in the mix such as *nananu*, *neko*, etc.). Set 30 'fire' has *at*, *to*, *da*, *te*, *utu* (also *odaoda*, *taite*, *atha*, etc.). While some of these sets have more short forms compared within them than others, the problem for the languages with the short forms remains the same, not being able to deny chance as a possible explanation for the similarity detected. A related problem in those sets where shorter forms are compared with longer forms is the lack of explanation for the extra phonetic material that apparently is not being matched to anything in the longer forms. Many of the sets suffer from this problem.

Gordon (1993:7–8) points out a serious problem with these comparison sets. Greenberg allowed considerable latitude in what he considers phonetically similar. A look across the words in each set shows that the target of comparison usually ignores the vowels and allows a number of different sorts of phonetic segments to match the consonantal targets. For example, any sound from the set /t, d, c, s, z/ can "match" any other sound from the set /k, g, q, h, x, ʔ/ and is interchangeably matched to any other in the set. That is, with a significant number of different sounds as possible targets for any matching sought, it is much easier to find matches which by this procedure appear phonetically similar. However, Gordon's point is more specific: the same patterns or targets are found repeated over and over, and the number of these actually is very small. Thus for example, the two-consonant target MVN fits the forms of sets 18, 20, 47, 55, 65, 74, 75, and 76. The target TVM covers sets 3, 15, 23, 33, 56, 78. In the end, there are very few of these repeated two-consonant target templates but "the same recurrent patterns of sounds are found throughout the data" (Gordon 1993:8). Unsurprisingly, a number of the sets match effortlessly with sets with similar glosses in the Amerind list, others match some of the proposed global etymologies (see Chapter 12).

Other problems are also present; for example, some sets seem to involve onomatopoeia (13 'break,' 19 'cry,' 40 'hit'), nursery words (63), and possible loans (5 'arrow,' 20 'dance,' 22 'dog,' 51 'moon,' 54 'name').

Greenberg also presented eleven sets of "grammatical evidence" for Indo-Pacific. The first eight involve pronominal markers (independent pronouns in sets 1–5, affixes in 6–8) and have considerable semantic and formal overlap among the sets. Though Greenberg's headings distinguish between independent pronouns and affixes, examples of both sorts are given in support of each set (Gordon 1993:2). A problem is that for any given pronominal person Greenberg typically has several different markers, often phonetically dissimilar, seen in Table 9.1

Table 9.1 *Greenberg's Indo-Pacific*
pronominal markers for each person

1sg	n(a) : t : u ~ w
1pl	n(i) : p (inclusive)
2sg	k(a) ~ ga ~ ha : ngi ~ n(i)
2pl	aw
3sg	i ~ y
3pl	t ~ d : aw

[Phonetically related forms are separated by ~]
(Gordon 1993:2)

Gordon (1993:2) asks a revealing question: "with so many forms and so many languages to chose from, how many correspondences can be expected based solely on chance?" Greenberg believed that some of these pattern together (for example, the co-occurrence of *na* '1sg' with *ka* '2sg' found in different languages), potentially reducing accidental matchings. However, frequently, single pieces of data are presented which do not conform to any expected pattern. For example, the first-singular pronouns of Kampong-Baru and Tarof (in the West New Guinea group) are cited as evidence of Greenberg's *n*-pattern, although they have no second-singular pronouns to fit the expected co-occurrence with the *k*-pattern (Kampong-Baru *ne(ri)* '1sg' but *e(ri)* '2sg'; Tarof *ne(iga)* '1sg' but *a(iga)* '2sg') (Greenberg 1971b:843).

Set 4 'first-plural inclusive pronoun' is unconvincing, since it is represented in only two subgroups (Timor-Alor [Oirata *ap-* 'our inclusive,' Makasai *fi*, Alor *pi*] and Halmahera [only one language, Modole *po* 'subject pronoun']), neither represented in New Guinea itself.

Set 8 "another pronominal pattern" (Greenberg 1971b:849) has the putative defining features: "(1) in the non-singular number or numbers the second and third persons are identical [;] (2) the first person is distinguished from the non-first person by a vowel change which is the same for dual and plural if there is a dual." However, this putative pattern is found in only three subgroups (South-West New Guinea, Southern New Guinea, and Central New Guinea); moreover the three are adjacent in New Guinea, suggesting possible areal influence. In the case of the identity of second- and third-person markers, no specific sounds are suggested to represent the pattern. This violates Greenberg's own principle of requiring both sound and meaning together as evidence of relationship (see Chapter 7). This set could as easily be due to diffusion or perhaps to Watkins' law (the tendency for third-person forms to move up and take over other marking for other persons).

As for the non-pronominal grammatical evidence, set 9 'plural' is weak, represented in only three subgroups. Greenberg (1971b:849) says of this, nevertheless, "these resemblances might not appear to be particularly signifi-cant since they are found in so few languages. However, when one considers that the overwhelming majority of Indo-Pacific languages do not inflect the noun for number at all, or have only a few special, often irregular plurals for a few words . . . these agreements become noteworthy." This is puzzling, how-ever. Would not it be just as likely, given the distribution of languages lacking plurals, that absence of plural was the original state (if these languages were related), and these few languages acquired plurals through some change later in their independent, individual histories? The other two instances of grammatical evidence involve gender and past tense, both with a series of problems (short, unmarked consonants and vowels, numerous overlapping forms for putatively different genders, etc., see Gordon 1993:3–4).

The inclusion of Tasmanian is generally considered the weakest. "The mate-rial available on these [Tasmanian] languages is appallingly poor and unreliable, and open to widely varying interpretations" (Wurm 1981:927); "the material on Tasmanian [languages] is so poor that almost nothing can be inferred with any degree of confidence" (Crowley and Dixon 1981:420). Of Greenberg's thirteen structural traits for Indo-Pacific languages, he presents only one for Tasmanian languages (for second-person-singular pronoun); his other groups mostly con-tain four or five. Of his 84 lexical sets, representatives of Tasmanian languages appear in only 18, and as Crowley and Dixon (1981:420) put it, "none of them [Greenberg's Tasmanian lexical comparisons] is convincing" (see also Wurm 1981:927). Intuitively, Tasmanian's closest relatives, if there were any, ought to be in Australia. Tasmania was connected to Australia by land bridges until about 14,000 years ago (Dixon 2002:38), a time depth probably sufficiently great to obliterate any detectible cognate material. Nevertheless, unlike with New Guinea languages, Tasmanian languages do show a number of typolog-ical similarities with Australian languages (Crowley and Dixon 1981; Dixon 2002:37–8), suggesting possible connections, if only areal ones. This all makes Papuan connections seem unlikely, particularly at the time depths that must be involved. Crowley and Dixon's (1981:420) conclusion is that "Greenberg's is one of the more outrageous of the many hypotheses that have been put forward concerning the Tasmanian languages."

As for Greenberg's inclusion of Andaman languages in Indo-Pacific, it has so far proven impossible to demonstrate a relationship even among the Andaman languages, the ten languages of the Great Andaman group and the three of the Little Andaman group (cf. Radcliffe-Brown 1964[1922]:497). It would appear just wishful thinking, then, to expect to find a relationship between these and very far-flung languages elsewhere in the Pacific. "No linguistic evidence has ever been adduced which would support a genetic relationship between Andamanese languages and any other known linguistic group. The paucity of data leaves ample room for gratuitous speculation" (van Driem 2001:211).

Greenberg's Indo-Pacific contrasts markedly with the views of mainstream scholars in this area. For them, "Papuan" is a label for the genetically diverse non-Austronesian languages found between Australia to the south and the Austronesian-speaking area to the west, north, and east, some 750 in New Guinea and another 50 or so outside New Guinea (Timor, Alor, Pantar, Halmahera, Solomon Islands, New Britain, and Bougainville). None of these groups is seen to have any genetic affinity to languages located outside this region. Classifications of these languages have differed widely and much remains to be done; nevertheless, all agree that they are not all demonstrably related to one another and there is great genetic diversity among these languages. The classification in Wurm (1975) is the most ambitious (except for Greenberg's), with only 20 genetic units, 10 'phyla,' and 10 isolates.

Two other large-scale hypotheses involving Papuan languages are the "Trans New Guinea phylum" (covering some 500 languages) and the "East Papuan" phylum (Wurm 1975; Wurm and Hattori 1981–3). East Papuan is generally dismissed – "the evidence was considered too flimsy to take it seriously" (Pawley 2004:12). The Trans New Guinea phylum is generally regarded as unproven but not without promise, and more refined versions of it have been proposed (see Foley 1986). Nevertheless, criticisms of it are well founded (see Pawley 2004:12–13). (1) The hypothesis is based on lexicostatistics, not an appropriate method for establishing genetic relationships (see Chapter 7). Even worse, the cognate percentages for the distant "branches" are very low. For example, Wurm (1971:585) finds an average of only 3 to 7 percent of shared "cognates" in the proposed East New Guinea Highlands stock, Huon stock, Central and South New Guinea stock, and West New Guinea Highlands phylum, and these groups share an average of only 2 to 3 percent with his Southeast Papuan phylum. Since the words compared lexicostatistically in these cases are not known cognates, percentage figures so low might easily be due to factors such as accidental similarity and borrowing. (2) Structural resemblances were given unwarranted importance, but these can easily be due to language contact, can be lost easily in linguistic change, and in any case violate the sound–meaning isomorphism requirement (Chapter 7). (3) The comparative method was not applied; sound correspondences were not sought. (4) Lexical borrowings and replacement may complicate proposed relationships of such a remote sort, known to be a problem in this area. (5) Failure to use patterned morphological evidence, in particular the pronoun paradigms that figure strongly in more recent work (Pawley 2004).

Pawley and Ross (Pawley 1995, 1998, 2001; Ross 1995b, 2001) support a "Trans New Guinea family," with a more restricted membership than Wurm's Trans New Guinea phylum, but nevertheless still very large. Their evidence includes some 200 putative cognate sets involving basic vocabulary, "a body of regular sound correspondences" based on the proposed cognates, "systematic form–meaning correspondences in the personal pronouns," and "widespread resemblances in fragments of certain other grammatical paradigms" (Pawley 2004:18–19). Pawley (2004:19) believes "there are secure grounds for identifying a core of TNG [Trans New Guinea] languages numbering over 350 with another 100 or so languages less securely assigned to TNG." Ross (1995b, 2001) bases his classification on pronoun paradigms; he puts 311 (of 605 Papuan languages) in the Trans New Guinea "family," adding another 36 based on other criteria. He finds 33 genetic units (23 language families and 9 or 10 isolates). This is far more than the one genetic unit of Greenberg's Indo-Pacific or the 20 of Wurm (1975 and elsewhere), but far fewer than the 65 of so distinct families and isolates of Foley (1986).

This classification is encouraging, though we would urge caution, since pronouns alone can present numerous complicating factors and problems, making them often unreliable as the sole (or primary) source of evidence for classification (see Chapter 7). For example, structural properties of pronominal systems are easily influenced in language contact, such as contrasts involving gender, number (dual, etc.), inclusive/exclusive, and so on. Formal properties (the sounds of the pronouns and how they are distributed through the paradigm) are subject to iconic ("resonance") factors, and can tend to be distributed in similar ways, often selected for perceptually salient sounds and unmarked segments. They tend to be short. And pronouns can be borrowed (see Foley 1986 for several Papuan examples; see Campbell 1997a:240–52). Recall Meillet's (1948:89–90) reasons for rejecting pronouns from arguments about genetic relationship (Chapter 7).

In summary with respect to the Indo-Pacific hypothesis, it is perhaps easy to see why Greenberg's 84 lexical sets and few grammatical sets representing hundreds of languages have failed to be convincing, given the problems pointed out here.

Whitehouse *et al.* (2004) assume the Indo-Pacific hypothesis and argue for extending it with the inclusion of the language isolate Kusunda of Nepal (van Driem 2001:258). Their evidence is far from compelling. Comparing Kusunda with forms from various languages in Greenberg's Indo-Pacific hypothesis, they present 26 lexical look-alikes and some similarities in some of the pronominal affixes. These involve the usual methodological problems (in Chapter 7). The forms for 'breast' and 'dog' are onomatopoetic; the set for 'father' is based on nursery forms; eight sets involve very short forms. Wide semantic latitude characterizes a number of sets, for example: 'daylight'/'sun'/'morning'/'day'; 'earth'/'underneath'/'below'; 'egg'/'fruit'/'seed'; 'father'/'elder brother'/ 'father's sister's older son'/'grandfather'/'brother'; 'fire'/'tree'/'it burns'; 'liver'/'guts'/'stomach'/'lung'; 'tree'/'fire' (a second set with these glosses); 'unripe'/'bitter'/'green'/'bad'; 'woman'/'co-wife'/'female (of animal)'/ 'wife'/'girl'. Kusunda *ta* 'this' and *na* 'that,' considered "grammatical formatives" (2004: 5694), are matched with forms from several of the putative Indo-Pacific languages. They believe "the strongest piece of evidence is the pronominal pattern found in the independent pronouns" (2004:5693). The problems with such pronominal comparisons are well known (Chapter 7). However, these illustrate all the problems of short forms, unmarked consonants and vowels, and the iconic or paradigmatic relationships expected in deictic subsystems where all the parts are interrelated by a series of cross-classifying oppositions, and similar comparisons are not especially difficult to find in other languages – indeed, Nichols and Peterson (1996) projected a historical connection of some undesignated sort linking languages in Papua New Guinea with groups in the Americas based on sets sharing several of these same forms (see Campbell 1997b for discussion). Whitehouse et al. assert "five defining features" are shared (2004:5693). Their (i) claims "a first-person based on *t*," although in Kusunda in fact it is <chi, tsi, tshi>. Their (ii) is "a second-person pronoun based on *n* or *ŋ*" (Kusunda <nu>), where many languages exhibit a nasal consonant in second-person pronominal forms, with *n*, as in Kusunda, very common (Ruhlen 1994a:257–8). Trait (iii) is "a third-person pronoun based on *g* or *k*" (Kusunda <gida, git>), although only five of the eight "Indo-Pacific" languages in their chart have representatives (and *gao* and *go* of two of the languages are not especially similar to <gida, git>). Their trait (iv) sees a "vowel alternation" with *u* in subject forms and *i* in possessive (or oblique) forms of first- and second-person pronouns. This kind of vowel distribution among the pronouns was not part of Greenberg's Indo-Pacific evidence, and these authors see it as new support for Indo-Pacific. Interestingly, Kusunda first-person <*chi, tsi, tshi*> 'I' fails to exhibit the expected *u* (though <*nu*> 'you' conforms). Moreover, only about half of the other languages listed conform: Seget *tet* 'I,' *nen* 'you,' Savosavo (no 'I' form) *no* 'you,' Bunak *ne-* 'I,' *e-* 'you,' not remotely similar. Perhaps this "vowel alternation" pattern is mere wishful thinking. Finally, trait (v) claims "a possessive suffix *-yi* found on all three personal pronouns." They also see this as a new piece of evidence for Indo-Pacific. This is an interesting claim in that possessive forms of the pronouns are actually listed in only three of the eight putative Indo-Pacific languages of the chart – for 'his/hers' in only one other, and here it is not at all clear that a suffix *-yi* is involved. A comparison of Bunak *gi* 'he/she' with *gie* 'his/hers' does not suggest any clear *-yi* suffix. In short, with evidence of this sort, Kusunda must remain an isolate and the Indo-Pacific hypothesis receives no additional support.

In conclusion with respect to the Indo-Pacific hypothesis as a whole, it could be that some of Greenberg's proposed "subgroups" within his Indo-Pacific hypothesis may potentially point the direction to future research, although Papuan research now suggests probable relationships many of which do not conform to these groupings. For the proposal as a whole, however, we declare the broader Indo-Pacific hypothesis itself a closed case that should now be abandoned.

9.10   Conclusions

In this chapter we evaluated several of the best-known but disputed hypotheses of distant genetic relationships in the light of the methods that proved reliable in establishing uncontroversial families (see especially Chapter 7). (Several other evaluated relationships involving languages of Africa and Australia were discussed in Chapter 6. Various other proposals involving languages of the Americas are evaluated in Campbell 1997a.) We examined the principal evidence put forward in support of Altaic, Ural-Altaic, Nostratic, Eurasiatic, Amerind, Na-Dene, and Indo-Pacific, and we found that all of the hypothesized "macro-families" fail to be convincing. None of them meets the burden of proof, since it has not been shown that the evidence presented in their favor cannot be explained just as well by non-genetic means, by a combination of accident, borrowing, and the several other factors. In spite of the attention they have received outside linguistics, none of these proposals can at present be embraced.

In the following chapter we examine a number of attempts to see beyond assumed limitations of the comparative method.

10   Beyond the comparative method?

De Laet [1643] on Hugo Grotius: If you are willing to change letters, to
transpose syllables, to add and subtract, you will nowhere find anything that
cannot be forced into this or that similarity; but to consider this as evidence
for the origin of peoples – this is truly not proved as far as I am concerned.[1]

(Cited in Metcalf 1974:241)

10.1   Beyond the comparative method?

As we have seen in previous chapters, the criteria for establishing genetic relationships among languages were generally clear, and widely known and applied,
with reliance on basic vocabulary, sound correspondences, and patterned grammatical evidence of particular sorts – where the comparative method played a
central role. Nevertheless, a number of scholars have recently expressed dissatisfaction with what they perceive to be limitations of the traditional methods.
"Since the tried-and-true Neogrammarian comparative method can only reach
back a few thousand years before the evidence fades out, something else must
be tried," so declares Johanna Nichols (1996b:267), and recently she and others,
recognizing the limitations of the comparative method, have proposed differing
ways to see past them. While this goal is an appropriate one, none of the alternative approaches proposed to date has achieved success. In this chapter we assess
several of these to show why they do not really reach beyond the limitations of
the comparative method. (Greenberg's multilateral comparison is another alternative approach that has been proposed, but it is rejected for reasons detailed
in Chapters 7 and 9, and so we do not take it up again here; Daniel Nettle's
ecological approach could enter here, but it is considered in Chapter 11.) These
approaches have in common dissatisfaction with the comparative method and
the goal of attempting to see beyond its assumed limitations. We consider them
here because an evaluation which puts ineffective, misleading lines of thought

---

[1] "Si literas mutare, syllabas transponere, addere, demere velis, nusquam non invenies quod ad
hanc aut illam similitudinem cogas: sed hoc pro indicio originis gentium habere, id vero mihi
non probatur."

into perspective can help to eliminate distractions and to concentrate attention on more effective approaches. To anticipate our conclusion, we find that the approaches discussed here have serious shortcomings; they do not see beyond the comparative method.[2]

10.2   Nichols' approach

Johanna Nichols (1990a, 1990b, 1992, 1993, 1994, 1995a, 1995b, 1996b, 1997a, 1997b, 1997c, 1998a, 1998b, 2003; Nichols and Peterson 1996, 1998) aims at developing techniques for reaching beyond the comparative method, which she assumes becomes ineffective after 8,000 years (Nichols 1996b:267, 1997a:363). Given enough change in related languages over a long period of time, such a small amount of shared inherited material may remain that it is impossible to tell whether there was a genetic connection. Nichols uses "non-genetic structural comparison to show that structural affinities between large language areas can be mapped . . . to give us an unimpeded, if rather spare and abstract, view of language origins and ancient linguistic prehistory," all said to be "part of a campaign to increase the visibility of non-genetic comparison in historical linguistics" (Nichols 1996b:267). She applies her approach to a sample with one language representative for each of some 200 "lineages" from the c. 350 existing linguistic "lineages" (families and isolates).[3] Nichols' complex approach, largely statistical and geographical, is inspired by population studies in biology and genetics. She tries to find ties among language populations and to gauge the relative age of linguistic traits in large-scale geographical areas; she tries to infer the source and direction of spread of these structural features, and also to infer how the languages involved came to have their geographical distributions. As she puts it:

Features having fair or better grammatical stability, moderate or better genetic stability, fair to moderate areal consistency, and a scale of patterning continental or larger in size can give a good picture of the long-standing affinities and disparities among large areas. They can be used in much the same way as genetic markers are used to assess affinities and divergences among biological populations, and I will speak of them as structural (or typological) MARKERS for this reason . . . the distribution of these markers across the sample areas and macroareas . . . [is] use[d] to draw conclusions about the peopling of the world and deep linguistic prehistory. (Nichols 1992:195)

Nichols believes her approach can reach much further back in time than the comparative method can, but it does not trace descent, as the comparative

---

[2] Part of the discussion in this chapter follows Campbell (2003b).
[3] According to Greenberg (1993:504), a total of only 176 languages are involved in Nichols' study, despite the 250 "lineages" she recognizes.

method does (cf. Nichols 1997a:365). Greenberg (1993:504) expressed the overall program and goals of Nichols' approach succinctly:

Evidently diversity, linguistic population, typology, and geography are connected in the following way: In each area or macroarea, the populations, which consist of languages classified by certain typological criteria, are examined for diversity within and between areas in regard to the relative frequencies of the typological properties which have been selected. From this we will deduce the ways in which languages have spread over the world at times too remote to be amenable to the comparative method.

Key units of analysis in Nichols' work to determine ancient distributions and movements of languages are descent lineages (genetic units), areal groupings (geographical areas), and typological classes (traits). The complex associations among these units of analysis, statistically determined, take place far removed from firm linguistic ground, as will be seen below. As Koch (1997:38) says:

Her [Nichols'] results are not comparable to those of traditional comparativists, since they apply to a much greater time depth; furthermore they are difficult for traditional comparativists to evaluate, since they are based on such a different methodology. Some of us would be more easily convinced if the "stable features" that are used were to have their stability justified directly by their persistence in real time in documented languages rather than inferred indirectly from their consistency in genetic and areal groupings of languages.

Nichols' approach is characterized by a series of intersecting but undemonstrated assumptions. Nichols' several concepts which play central roles in her overall scheme rest on shaky empirical foundation at best, and moreover they are misapplied in actual cases she deals with, thus leading to inaccuracies. These misassignments then become part of the overall measurements upon which her more far-reaching claims and conclusions about prehistory depend – a "multiplication of uncertainties" (Nettle 1999b:3326).[4] Given both its uniqueness and complexity, her approach warrants a more detailed look, but, as will be seen, this approach is not successful. It is important to point this out, since her program has considerable influence on the work of others (for example, Nettle 1999a; Renfrew 2000a; Fortescue 1998). We begin by identifying problems involving some of her key units.

---

[4] It may well be that some of Nichols' ideas have changed over time, though she does not point out explicitly what may have changed in her later publications. For that reason, we will report her work from her various publications as though it were all internally consistent, relying most heavily on Nichols (1992), where the program is laid out in the most detail, and on Nichols (1997a).

10.2.1 *"Descent groups"*

Nichols (1997a:360) sees the "descent group or clade" as "the basic building block of linguistic populations." Her descent groups cover the following:

> *family*: "the standard general term for a proven clade [genetic unit] of any age" (Nichols 1997a:362).
>
> *stock*: "a maximal reconstructable clade, e.g. the oldest families displaying regular sound correspondences and amenable to Neogrammarian comparative method. A stock usually displays several genetic markers. The oldest known stocks are about 6000 years old: e.g. Indo-European, Uralic, Austronesian" (Nichols 1997a:362–3). (Isolates constitute stocks of their own.)
>
> *quasi-stock*: "a quasi-genetic or probabilistic grouping of more than one stock, which shares one or more features that are valid or promising genetic markers but which have few clear cognates and for which systematic regular sound correspondences cannot be demonstrated. Hence a quasi-stock is a probable clade but not a fully describable one and is not amenable to reconstruction" (Nichols 1997a:363).

Nichols finds that "for younger families such as Romance, Germanic, Slavic, Turkic, Polynesian, Athabaskan, Algonquian, Quechuan – all around 2,000 years in age – relatedness is unmistakable even to the nonlinguist," while "families aged closer to 6000 years, such as Uralic, Austronesian, and Semitic or Indo-European as judged only from modern attestations, exhibit genetic markers and cognate etyma that are not always evident to the nonspecialist" (1997a:362–3). As for her "quasi-stocks," we suspect that most of the entities that Nichols might classify this way will prove unpersuasive as groups of genetically related languages – they are controversial in the linguistic literature; it is because the evidence to date is inconclusive that they are not demonstrated linguistic families ("stocks" in Nichols' terminology).

For any of Nichols' many calculations to work out, for example, the number of splits per family/stock, the average age of splits, the time depths of stocks and population movements, etc. (see below), it is necessary for the genetic classification of the languages in her sample upon which these calculations are based to be relatively accurate. However, she includes several unestablished and disputed genetic units. In the Americas, for example, Nichols (1992) treats Hokan and Penutian as stocks in her calculations, though these are disputed even by specialists in these languages (see Campbell 1997a:290–305, 309–22). In Africa, Nichols (1992) has Khoisan as a stock, but Khoisan is denied even by Africanists who are otherwise enthusiastic about Greenberg's (1963) African classification (see Chapter 6) – in later work, Nichols (1997a) also rejected Khoisan. Nilo-Saharan is generally acknowledged even by supporters of Greenberg's African classification as his wastepaper-basket phylum, where he placed all the otherwise left-over and unassigned languages. Moreover, we hold Niger-Kordofanian to be questionable and not adequately established, and Afroasiatic is not straightforward (see discussion in Chapter 6). In any case, Nichols (1997a) sees Afroasiatic as a "quasi-stock," suggesting that she, too, has adjusted her thinking with respect to it. In short, there are numerous questionable genetic classifications in Nichols (1992, also in her later works) (cf. Chapter 9).

Nichols chooses in principle (but not in reality) only one language from her sample to represent each family in each of her language zones (Nichols 1992:27). The risks in this are that the particular language chosen to represent the family may not exhibit a trait typically found in other languages of the family, or that it will have traits due to influence from languages in adjacent linguistic areas, and thus not be representative of the general nature of the family or even the area (see specific cases below). Nichols does try to select for her representatives languages thought by specialists not to be abnormal with respect to the general nature of the families to which they belong, but this will not keep individual odd traits from entering the picture.

It may not be possible for Nichols to obtain the desired representative and balanced results, given the limited numbers of languages and zones dealt with. For example, about half of the Mayan languages have an inclusive/exclusive contrast; however, Nichols chose Tz'utujil, which lacks this contrast, to represent the whole family. This means that the whole Mayan family is treated as lacking the trait, meaning further that this enters the count of how the trait is distributed in the Mesoamerican area. If the number of languages and genetic units involved were sufficiently large, we might expect matters such as these to balance out in the long run; but in Mesoamerica Nichols is dealing with ten (later only nine) languages. With so few, the presence versus absence of the inclusive/exclusive contrast does not balance out in the long run. Whether Tz'utujil without the contrast or some other Mayan language with the contrast is chosen to represent Mayan has a very large impact on how this feature will be counted in Mesoamerica and thus on how the overall area will be characterized. Similarly, Squamish, Nichols' representative of Salishan, lacks this inclusive/exclusive contrast, but had she chosen Shuswap as the representative of the family, Salishan would be on the other side of the fence in these calculations; Nootka, lacking the inclusive/exclusive contrast, is Nichols' representative of Wakashan, but had she chosen Kwakiutl, Wakashan would be listed among the positive bearers of this trait; finally, in the Yukian family, Yuki has the contrast, but not Wappo, which was chosen as the Yukian representative in the sample (see Nichols 1992:298–9). Had Squamish, Kwakiutl, and Wappo together been the chosen representatives of these families, the counts for the inclusive/exclusive contrast for both the Western North American area and the world would look very different. With the relatively small number of representatives in general (only $c.200$ to represent $c.350$ stocks), instances such as these – where an arbitrary choice of a different representative for the family would shift the picture so dramatically – weigh significantly in the overall statistics and conclusions drawn from them (see the discussion of the inclusive/exclusive contrast below).

In brief, there are problems with the classification used and with the way representatives of the families are sampled, selected, and reflected in the statistical counts.

10.2.2   Spread zones vs. accretion zones

Nichols' second key unit of analysis is the areal groupings (geographical areas). The geographical spread of features involves Nichols' notions of *accretion zones* and *spread zones* (cf. Nichols 1992:231, 1997a:369–70):

> An accretion zone (termed *residual zone* in previous works . . .) is an area where genetic and structural diversity of languages are high and increase over time through immigration. Examples are the Caucasus, the Himalayas, the Ethiopian highlands and the northern Rift Valley, California, the Pacific Northwest of North America, Amazonia, northern Australia, and of course New Guinea. Languages appear to move into these areas more often than they move out of them. (Nichols 1997a:369)

> A spread zone is an area of low density where a single language or family occupies a large range, and where diversity does not build up with immigration but is reduced by language shift and language spreading. A conspicuous spread zone is the grasslands of central Eurasia . . . Another spread zone is central and southern Australia, in which the Pama-Nyungan quasi-stock has undergone several spreads to cover most of the continent . . . Another is northern Africa. Another is the Great Basin of the western United States. (Nichols 1997a:369)

10.2.2.1 Misassignment of "zone" status   The distinction between "spread zones" and "accretion/residual zones" is central in Nichols' scheme, but it is misapplied in the case of some of her geographical areas and this damages her overall program and the analysis she derives from it.[5]

For example, Nichols treats Mesoamerica as a "spread zone," but by her own criteria (Nichols 1992:16–17) it is a residual (accretion) zone: (1) It has lots of linguistic diversity, not the low genetic diversity characteristic of her spread

---

[5] While such a distinction is not commonly recognized in areal linguistic studies, we note that residual or refugee zone/area is an old notion in Inner Asian/Central Eurasian historical literature – thus, the Caucasus – Nichols' archetype of a residual zone – is usually cited as such a zone in this literature, a zone of groups pushed into it and made safe (and out of the way) by the mountains from the constant conquests and migrations back and forth from China to eastern Europe by nomadic state after nomadic state – the history of successive waves across this region is dizzying.

zones. (2) It has lots of structural diversity, as opposed to low structural diversity for spread zones. (3) The language families are not shallow in time depth; for example, Otomanguean is about as old as an established family gets, calculated glottochronologically as having begun to split up at 6,400 years ago, and Uto-Aztecan is reckoned at 5,000 years ago.[6] (4) In opposition to the criterion of rapid spread wiping out existing families, the Mesoamerican families seem to stay in place and rarely wiped out or took over anybody else's territory or language. (5) Contrary to Nichols' criterion, there was no clear lingua franca in Mesoamerica.[7] On whatever traits Nichols might care to take as the more important defining features, Mesoamerica turns out definitely to conform more to her definition of an accretion/residual zone, not a spread zone as she has it.

Nichols' "residual zones" are: Ethiopia-and-Kenya, Caucasus, North Asia Coast, Northern Australia, and California. Her "spread zones" are: Ancient Near East, Europe, Central Australia, Interior North America, and Mesoamerica. For the residual zones, we have reservations about the definition and accuracy of two of these, Ethiopia-and-Kenya and California. For the spread zones, as just seen, Mesoamerica is clearly misanalyzed, and we have reservations about Interior North America (which includes languages as geographically and genetically divergent as Kiowa, Kutenai, Tonkawa, and Navajo) (cf. Nichols 1992:290–1).

For example, Nichols lists Ethiopia-and-Kenya as a residual zone, but by her criteria for residual areas this status is by no means clear. (1) High structural diversity. While the five languages from this area (or six with Beja as supplementary) may be relatively diverse structurally, it is clear that some diversity in a number of Ethiopian languages has been leveled in the direction of Cushitic due to areal linguistic pressures, thus eliminating some former structural diversity (Campbell *et al.* 1988; Ferguson 1976; Hetzron 1972, 1980; Leslau 1945, 1952; and Sasse 1986). (2) No appreciable spread of languages or families, no language succession. The interpretation of this criterion may be relative, but in any case a number of languages have become extinct or soon will be in this area (Ge'ez, Gafat, Argobba; Elmolo, Yaaku). In each of these cases it is appropriate to think in terms of spread of languages at the expense of those which die, of "language succession" where the survivors succeed the extinct

---

[6] Nichols (1992:25) sees 5,000–6,000 years as essentially the upper limit of the comparative method, the assumed age of the Indo-European family, but she extends this upward to 8,000 years to allow for Afroasiatic, a proposed stock which is still disputed. We hasten to point out that we, like most linguists, reject glottochronology; we cite the dates only as a relative gauge of the age. By any criterion of judgment (e.g. internal diversification, geographical distribution, structural differences, etc.), Otomanguean and Uto-Aztecan are determined to be very old families. The glottochronological dates cited here are from Kaufman (1974) (for Otomanguean) and W. Miller (1984) (for Uto-Aztecan).

[7] Nahuatl was only just beginning to be used in trade and diplomacy just before Spanish contact, but knowledge of it beyond communities where some variety of Nahua was the native language was highly restricted.

languages. (3) No clear center of innovation. This is a matter of interpretation. Given the strong Cushitic impact on the structure of the Ethiopian Semitic languages, we can conclude at least that Cushitic territory must be the center (or source) of innovation at least for these cases. Finally, (4) accretion of languages and long-term net increase in diversity. This would seem surely not to hold for the Ethiopia–Kenya area, since, as noted, a number of languages have become extinct and thus the long-term result is fewer languages and a decrease in diversity.

Any misapplication of zone status is serious. Nichols (1992:231) claims that:

> the distinction of spread and residual zones enables one to capture a number of interesting distributional patterns such as the approximation to a standard profile in the residual zones scattered around the globe, or replication of global clines among those same residual zones. The distinction of spread zones and residual zones obviously has to do with diversity.

Misassigned zones, however, strongly challenge this claim. Since Nichols (1992) deals with only five spread zones (and five residual zones), with even one of five misassigned (20 percent), all the counts involving these zones are seriously skewed.

10.2.2.2 Problems of language representatives Some problems have to do with the geographic and linguistic composition which defines Nichols' linguistic zones. In her treatment of Mesoamerica, of ten sample languages (Nichols 1992; only nine languages in Nichols 1995b:342) that she places in the zone, two (Chichimec, Miskito) fall outside Mesoamerica both geographically and in terms of the linguistic traits that define the area. For example, both are SOV languages, while Mesoamerican languages typically lack SOV basic word order (Campbell, Kaufman, and Smith-Stark 1986). Chichimec is located beyond the linguistic and cultural boundary of Mesoamerica to the north, Miskito outside to the south.[8] Given that Nichols' Mesoamerica combines some non-Mesoamerican languages (20 percent of the 1992 total,

---

[8] Nichols follows Suárez's (1983b) discussion of Mesoamerica, but curiously, Suárez (1983b:160–1) denies the existence of a *bone fide* aboriginal linguistic area in Mesoamerica, though suggests there may be some unifying areal traits today, but only due to the impact of Spanish on the native languages. However, Suárez got it wrong (Campbell *et al.* 1986); there is a valid aboriginal linguistic area in Mesoamerica, which coincides largely with the Mesoamerican culture area, and unfortunately Suárez's discussion includes many languages that do not legitimately belong to this linguistic area. One might ask whether the use of Suárez's area rather than the established and conventional version of Mesoamerica might matter so much. The answer is that indeed it does matter. If Nichols' areas are not to correspond to real linguistic areas established on the basis of shared (diffused) linguistic traits, then they constitute little more than any other arbitrary grouping of languages would, and the traits that she happens to detect among the languages would be largely accidental or insignificant as a basis for drawing inferences about past history.

22.2 percent of the 1995 figure) with true Mesoamerican languages, all of her calculations concerning spread, stability, and the general character and distribution of linguistic traits in this area are skewed and called into question.[9]

10.2.2.3 The double-dipping problem   A different kind of problem has to do with the classification of the languages chosen as representatives of zones. In Nichols' Mesoamerica zone, two languages of only ten (20 percent of the total) are from the same language family – Chichimec and Mixtec are both Otomanguean. Nichols' (1992:291) Europe zone (a spread zone) includes Hungarian and Zyrian (Zyrien), two Finno-Ugric languages, so that of only six languages representing the Europe zone, two (33 percent) are from the same language family. Moreover, both Hungarian and Zyrien underwent heavy influence from Turkic, a representative of the Central Eurasian spread zone, whose languages typologically are different from those of Europe. Other doublings of more than one genetically related language as representatives of a single zone include (1) for the North American zone: Luiseño, Southern Paiute, and Papago, all from the Northern branch of Uto-Aztecan; and (2) English, French, Russian, and Armenian (all Indo-European languages) for Northern Eurasia.[10]

This creates a serious problem for defining the "zone." If only unrelated languages are considered, then any sharing of traits among languages of the zone may reflect diffusion but not inheritance from an earlier common ancestor. However, when languages which are genetically related – multiple members of the same language family – are admitted as representatives of the zone, some of the shared traits encountered among some of the languages (the related ones) may be due to inheritance, not to the diffusion which should define the area. Some shared traits will show up as represented in a greater number of languages because some of the languages have inherited the traits, from the same parent language. To count the related languages as independent witnesses of the areal nature of the trait with equal status to the other unrelated languages representing

---

[9] We might ask how Nichols' (1992) Mesoamerica "zone" might be intended to correspond to the well-defined Mesoamerican Linguistic Area; Nichols (1995b:342) makes it clear that it is intended to match the linguistic area as identified in the literature.

[10] Probably Nichols (1992) would defend the inclusion of the two as members of different "families" though of the same "stock," with Chichimec and Mixtec as representatives of different "families" in the larger Otomanguean "stock." This distinction, however, is hardly satisfying. Here members of the same genetic unit (languages known to be genetically related), their "family" status within a "stock" in Nichols' terminology notwithstanding, are included as representatives of a zone equal to other languages not held to be genetically related. However, in the case of Zyrien and Hungarian (both representatives of Nichols' Europe zone), the potential solution as members of different families within the stock is not available. By Nichols' procedures, it should not be possible to select two languages from the same family unless each is from a different branch of the initial branching of the "stock"; however, in this case the "stock" level is Uralic, whose initial branches are Finno-Ugric (to which both Hungarian and Zyrien belong) and Samoyed (with no representative). Thus, to get by on the "stock" versus "family" reading, only one of these could be selected, as a member of the Finno-Ugric first-order split.

the zone makes a trait seem more widely shared for areal rather than genetic reasons than it really is. In this situation, the dice are loaded in favor of shared traits among the languages of an area with more than one language from the same language family. In order not to skew the results, each family deserves only one vote – one language – for each trait used in the definition of the zone.

10.2.2.4 Challenges to the existence of spread zones (and accretion zones) Nichols (1992:291) has only four spread zones: Ancient Near East, Europe, Central Australia, and Interior North America (Mesoamerica, a misassigned residual zone, is eliminated from the list, see above). These "zones" are very different from one another and this raises doubts about the very concept of spread zone. The Ancient Near East is a recognized linguistic area (Friedrich 1975; Diakonof 1990). It has considerable genetic diversity, a number of unrelated language families and isolates. Central (and southern) Australia, in contrast, is different, with but a single widespread language family, Pama-Nyungan. As for Europe, it would appear that in later work (e.g. Nichols 1997a, 1997c, 1998a) it is considered more the recipient of impact from the Eurasian zone than a proper zone of its own. In any event, Europe is unlike the previous two, just a collection of six languages from across Europe (four from the Indo-European family, two from Finno-Ugric), seemingly thrown together on the basis of some more or less arbitrary geographical decision – they share no set of diffused traits that would mark them as a linguistic area (as the Ancient Near East), nor is there any indication of great spread of languages across the zone as defined. The Interior North America zone appears even more arbitrary. It contains two members of the Northeast Linguistic Area (Seneca, Cree), four from the Plains Linguistic Area (Lakhota, Pawnee, Kiowa, Tonkawa), one from the Plateau Linguistic Area (Kutenai), with supporting help from Navajo (Southwest) (cf. Campbell 1997a:331–44). There is nothing in the linguistics, anthropology, or geography that suggests these languages ought to be grouped together. They have nothing in common (except absence of coastline). Interior North America is no clear match for the definition of a spread zone: "an area of low density where a single language or family occupies a large range, and where diversity does not build up with immigration but is reduced by language shift and language spreading." True there is less diversity than along the West Coast of North America, but even in Nichols' sample, eight different "stocks" are represented here, twice as many as for two of her five residual zones (Ethiopia–Kenya with four [five with the supplement], Caucasus with four; Nichols 1992:290–1).

   In later work the most conspicuous spread zone mentioned is "the grasslands of central Eurasia," with a few others added: northern Africa and Great Basin of the western United States (Nichols 1997a). The Great Basin is also well known as a linguistic area (Campbell 1997a:338–9). We do not know what languages

Nichols would assign to northern Africa, though we suspect the spread of Arabic is involved, reflecting historical-political forces rather than any principle of spread-zone formation. (Otherwise, the Berber, Egyptian, and Semitic languages of the area share areal traits and some typological traits and are generally held to be members of the single Afroasiatic "phylum"; see Chapter 6.) In several of Nichols' cases (from both 1992 and later), the common assumption that spread zones reflect large migrations that reduce former diversity is not what we actually see.[11]

In short, there are so few spread zones, and those identified as such have such disparate characters, it seems reasonable to question whether there is anything of substance to the notion.[12] The notion of "spread zone" should be abandoned. For those few instances of putative spread zones which do involve few but widely spread languages, it appears that there is no particular set of linguistic or other factors which unite them; rather, they appear to be mere arbitrary pieces of geography or artifacts of local political and social history, better understood on a case-by-case basis, as products of contingent history.[13] They are too few, and

---

[11] As Hill (2001a) points out, the Great Basin in the US is a "spread zone" not because of sweeping migrations, cultural innovations, or environmental catastrophes, or reduction of previous linguistic diversity, but because human adaptation there led to a distributed stance (see below). The problem of access to drinkable water and the relative unreliability of piñon nuts (a principal food resource) left people living in small groups and moving around a lot seasonally. No one swooped in nor spread across existing groups. As Nichols (1998a:238) points out, such groups' annual cycle of movement does not constitute migration nor expansion.

[12] The putative spread zones that might seem less controversial are the ones which correspond to identified linguistic areas (diffusion areas), but the definition of a linguistic area with diffusion across language boundaries, where the best-established ones involve a fair amount of genetic diversity (several language families), is different from that of a spread zone, characterized by few languages widely spread and low genetic diversity.

[13] Nichols (1996b:267) asserts that "it is also important that the areas be based on non-linguistic criteria such as geography; otherwise the survey becomes circular. For linguistic purposes, we need areas smaller than continents but larger than classical linguistic areas such as the Balkans or the Indic subcontinent." The "linguistic task at hand" to which this survey is addressed is "a non-genetic structural comparison to show that the structural affinities between large language areas can be mapped . . . to yield surprisingly close correspondences to actual maps, and to give us an unimpeded, if rather spare and abstract, view of language origins and ancient linguistic prehistory" (Nichols 1996b:267). But the geographical regions selected are based mostly on arbitrary chunks of geography. Far from making the exercise circular, bringing in linguistic criteria or any principled reason for setting up the geographical zones which Nichols surveys would give the enterprise some hope of avoiding this criticism. In this study (Nichols 1996b), rather than the ten zones of her 1992 study, she has eighteen areas, but still unmotivated. For example, why Alaska–Oregon vs. California? Northern California has much more in common with Oregon than with the rest of California culturally and linguistically, and also even geographically in terms of climate and ecology. Why Basin-Plains vs. Eastern North America?; culturally and linguistically the case could be made for grouping the Great Plains and Eastern North America against the Great Basin. What makes the coasts distinct from the interiors of New Guinea and Australia (four areas)? If it is sheer geography or ecology, then wouldn't it make sense to separate off coasts from interiors also for the other regions of the world involved as well?

they have too little in common, to allow generalization across them that could defend the notion "spread zone."

It is difficult to see that the notions of spread zone and accretion zone do anything more than restate the facts of language distribution, not explaining it, but misleadingly suggesting that there is some underlying explanation that does not really exist. For residual (accretion) zones, there must always be linguistic diversity, by definition, otherwise they would be mistaken for spread zones or just not be identified at all. Many residual zones nevertheless have some language families which spread widely, behaving more like those thought to be confined to spread zones. For example, while the Pueblo Linguistic Area fits Nichols' residual zone criteria, it also has incursions into it from the widespread Athabaskan family (Apachean: Navajo and Apache varieties) (Bereznak 1995). In the case of the Kiowa–Tanoan family, while the Tanoan languages illustrate a compact family in the pueblos, Kiowa illustrates just the opposite, spread out from the others. There are many examples of this sort. At the same time, many spread zones nonetheless have a number of residual pockets of surviving languages, giving linguistic diversity, which Nichols must interpret as the spread zone not yet having completed its business, but which, if historical information were not available about movements and territorial take-overs, could in some cases make it difficult to determine whether a spread zone or residual zone were involved, or perhaps neither.

In fact, given that the "zones" Nichols works with are very large, covering continent-sized regions, it is not clear what independent criteria could be brought into the picture to show that the terrain (with the languages) involved is not included on a wholly arbitrary basis. We argued (above) that this is the case for her Europe and Interior North America zones. It also appears true of many of the others. Nichols' "California" zone is defined, rather arbitrarily, by the political boundaries of the state. It includes languages from northern California (Yurok) and from southern (Diegueño), but Diegueño (Yuman) and Yurok (Algic) share no areal features, though there is a Northern California linguistic/culture area (with Yurok as one of its members) and a Southern California–Western Arizona linguistic area (with Diegueño).[14]

The terminological terrain dealing with the geographical distribution of linguistic diversity is becoming very complex. Renfrew's (2000a, 2002) notion of "mosaic zone" appears to overlap Bellwood's "starburst zone"; Bellwood's "starburst zones" no doubt overlap Hill's (2001a) languages with "localist stance" and Golla's (2000) "compact language families" (see below). In the end, it is the questions of have linguistic traits diffused and have languages

---

[14] Sherzer (1976) treats California as though it were an established culture area and linguistic area, but in fact it is regions or subareas within California which prove the most revealing even for Sherzer, and as shown in Campbell (1997a), there is no legitimate linguistic area that corresponds with the state of California.

spread or not which matter. These are individual historical events which do not consult these various proposed kinds of zones to see whether they should proceed or not.

In sum, Nichols' accretion–spread zone distinction is a misleading and unsupported abstraction and these notions should be abandoned.

10.2.3 Typological classes and the problem of stability

The third key element (building block) in Nichols' approach is typological traits said to be relatively stable both genetically and areally (cf. Nichols 1995b). A "burning issue" that she wants to investigate is:

The predominance of certain structural linguistic features in the languages of some continents but not others. For instance, languages of the Americas often inflect their verbs and prepositions heavily, lack nominal cases, and have ejective consonant series; languages of Southeast Asia generally have tones, numeral classifiers, and minimal morphology; languages of Australia tend to have many anterior consonant articulations, few distinct manners of articulation, and ergative morphology; and so on. These broad areal signatures are well known in the linguistic literature. Are they areal features that have spread recently, or are they the result of founder effects, reflexes of structural features of the languages of early colonizers of these lands? (Nichols 1994:2)

Appropriately, the list of typological features Nichols deals with are intended not to be the sort that show up in universals or implicational relations, which have "little value for historical comparison." Rather, she seeks features that "will best reveal affinities and differences between areas," features which are:

low-frequency ones overall (so that a sharing means something); and their distribution over the face of the earth is not even, but forms statistically significant frequency peaks (so that, again, a sharing means something). In addition, they are relatively slow-changing . . . , and they are reasonably independent of each other . . . Such features are potentially good markers of non-accidental affinity and non-affinity between areas. (Nichols 1996b:268)

She is interested in the "diachronically stable structural features and their distribution in the world's languages," the "structural features that are demonstrably slow to change over time," which she calls "*stable features*." (Nichols 1994:5). She says, "so far about a dozen [stable] features have been shown to have good stability" (Nichols 1994:5).

Nichols (1992) is concerned with the relationships among three macro-areas: the Old World (Northern Eurasia, Middle East, Africa, South and Southeast Asia), the Pacific (Oceania, New Guinea, Australia), and the New World. She draws conclusions about the remote prehistory of these areas, their interactions, migrations, colonizations, movements, etc., based on the distribution of the typological features she deals with. Her window of endeavor is the period

between 8,000 years ago beyond which she assumes the conventional comparative method is unable to reach and 40,000 years ago and beyond, by which
date she assumes the major colonizations of the earth's continents had been
accomplished. Her historical inferences based on the distribution of her typological traits come into play after the date (going back in time) at which the
comparative method is in her estimation inoperable, after 8,000 years.

The structural features assumed to be relatively stable with which Nichols
(1992) deals to reach her historical inferences are head/dependent marking,
typological alignment (nominative–accusative, ergative, active), morphological
complexity, verb position in clauses, inclusive/exclusive, alienable/inalienable,
noun classes, numeral classifiers, number neutralization, non-finite verbs, and
voice.[15] A very serious problem for Nichols' approach is the fact that there is
nothing particularly stable about most of these putatively stable features. We
attempt to show this by looking at just a few of her examples, in particular at
the ones she sees as the strongest representatives of stability.

Nichols (2003:304) finds the *inclusive vs. exclusive first-person pronoun*
opposition "to be genetically the most stable of all the features tested," though
she recognizes it can be borrowed. In fact, it is not very stable at all; often one can
virtually see it coming and going as some languages change – it is not stable, nor
is there any particular reason to imagine that it should be. For example, there are
a number of cases where even dialects of the same language differ in that some
have the contrast and others lack it, where the change is attested as quite recent,
straightforward, and not at all unusual historically nor structurally. For example, some Mam dialects have the contrast, where both first-person-plural inclusive and exclusive are based on the prefix *q-/qo* (< Proto-Mayan **q-/*qa-/**),
but "exclusive" forms bear additionally the clitic *-a/-ya*, which "inclusive"
lacks. Some Mam dialects lack the contrast altogether (England 1983:56–7),
i.e. they did not undergo the late and relatively low-level grammaticalization of
the clitic which results in the "exclusive" meaning, which produces the contrast
in the other dialects. This is not an unusual case. In the Cholan subgroup of
Mayan (four closely related languages), only Chol has developed the "inclu-
sive/exclusive" contrast, a recent and superficial change. All Cholan languages

---

[15] The set of stable features listed in Nichols (1995b) varies slightly from those in her 1992 study.
Her list includes: ergativity, inclusive/exclusive opposition in first-person pronouns, head marking, gender (genders, other noun classes, classifier articles, possessive classification), numeral
classifiers, tones, person in NP (person agreement), singular = plural pronouns (in personal
pronouns, singular and plural have the same root), verb–subject (VOS, VSO, VS, and/or OVS
basic word order), derived transitivity (in verb pairs like 'eat': 'feed,' 'come to boil': 'bring to
boil,' etc. the semantically causative member is morphologically derived [causativized]), NP
cases (morphological genitive or similar adnominal cases), high complexity (amount of overt
morphological marking of core clausal and phrasal relations), M in 1sg ([m] as first consonant
in first-person independent pronoun root), complex verbs (conjugation by auxiliary, complex
predicates, etc.; the "auxiliary" determines valence and carries agreement, etc.). (See Nichols
1996b:269.)

have ergative/possessive first-person-plural *ka-/k-* (< Proto-Mayan **qa-/*q-*)
and absolutive first-person-plural *-on* or *-en* (from Proto-Mayan *-*-oʔŋ*); but
Chol has recently innovated an "inclusive/exclusive" contrast by adding the
particle *loxon* for "exclusive" (Kaufman and Norman 1984:91–2). Facts such
as these go contrary to Nichols' (1992:181) claims of "high genetic and mod-
ernate areal stability" for the inclusive/exclusive contrast. That is, the inclu-
sive/exclusive contrast is typically rather superficial and not deeply integrated
in the fabric of the grammar, meaning there is nothing inherent in it which leads
to or would result in long-term "stability." As Jacobsen (1980:204) points out
in his survey of western North American languages:

This category [first-person inclusive/exclusive pronominal contrasts] is probably one that
diffuses fairly readily, as it is purely semantic and not bound to the syntactic structure of
a language in a way that, for example, a category of case would be. It is sometimes found
to be typical of a whole language family, but may also turn up in isolated members of a
family, as, for example, in Choctaw alone in the Muskogean family . . . in Yuki alone in
the Yukian family . . . in Shuswap alone in the Salish family . . . or in Kwakiutl but not
Nootka in the Wakashan family. (Emphasis added, LC/WP)

Warembori (an isolate in Papua New Guinea) borrowed its non-first- and
second-person-singular pronouns from Austronesian, "with even the inclusive-
exclusive distinction being taken over: PAN [Proto-Austronesian] **kami* (1PL
EXCl) > War[embori] *ami*; PAN **kita* (1PL INCLU) > War *ki*" (Foley
2000:392). Clearly, if this feature were stable, it would not show up so frequently in some of the languages of a family but not in other sisters in the same
family, as seen for example in the cases cited here.

   Given the rather apparent general instability of this feature, the conclusions
Nichols derives from its distribution in her sample seem overstated:

The presence or absence of inclusive/exclusive oppositions has the greatest geographical
scale and the greatest genetic stability and grammatical autonomy, hence its spread from
a far western center may be regarded as the earliest of the global spreads. (Nichols
1992:211)

Nichols (1992:215) "turns this one example [inclusive/exclusive opposition
as a global cline] into a more general model of the history of diversity," but
her interpretation of the distribution of the inclusive/exclusive contrast in her
sample as a global spread relies on a fallacy: it seems to deny that the contrast
can and does easily develop spontaneously and independently. Thus, there is no
compelling reason for seeing its presence in various circum-Pacific languages as
being contiguous and causally connected, as Nichols does. Her conclusion is in
essence contradicted by her own evidence. She assumes "initial heterogeneity,"
with around "50% frequencies and little stabilization" of within-group diversity
for the inclusive/exclusive opposition, where "the global inclusive/exclusive
cline itself can be seen as a garden-variety instance of stabilization." That is,

from this original state, she says, "we see the results of the trend towards equilibrium [stabilization] at 0% in the west and at 100% in the east," with the New World still with "about 50% frequencies and little stabilization" (Nichols 1992:215; cf. 275–6). Clearly, however, this way of interpreting the distribution of this trait tacitly admits the non-stability of the trait, if in some areas the trend is towards elimination of the contrast to stabilize at 0 percent frequency in the languages (of Eurasia), but with change to stabilization towards 100 percent in other areas. However, if many of these are very recent developments, then they do not support Nichols' view of how the assumed global cline developed. Similarly, if some of the occurrences or absences of this trait are not causally connected, but rather developed independently, as we assert, then the causal implications in this interpretation are not present.

A look at Nichols' (1992:28–33) scatter-chart maps for the distribution of the allegedly stable features reveals that there is something odd about how some of the traits, in addition to the first-person-pronoun inclusive/exclusive contrast, came out in her sample and how they are interpreted. For example, Nichols (1992:31) only has five dots for ergativity for all the Americas (four in North America, one in "Mesoamerica," and none in South America; see also Nichols 1992:300–1, where one additional language is listed, in South America, as possibly ergative), when in fact ergativity is reasonably widespread throughout the languages of the Americas, to mention a few examples: Kwakwala ([Kwakiutl], a Wakashan language; Nichols' Wakashan representative, Nootka, lacks ergativity), Alsea (isolate), Eskimo–Aleut (family), Natchez (isolate; Nichols 1992:300–1 lists Natchez, but misses the fact that it has ergative alignment); and in South America a number of Cariban languages (Apawaio [Kapong], Arekuna [Pemong], Makushi, Kuikúro, and Bakairi), Arawán (family), Jê (family), Panoan (family), Tacanan (family), Cavineña and some other Tupi–Guaranian languages, Yanomaman (small family), some Tupían languages (Gavião, Surui, Mekéns), Guató (Macro-Jê), various Chibchan languages, and others. Nichols (1992:300–1) has only one South American language, Canela-Kraho, as tentatively ergative (listed with a question mark). In Mesoamerica, her sample gives Tz'utujil (Mayan) as the only ergative language (with Huave with a question mark), and presents five with nominative/accusative alignment. Half the Mixe-Zoquean languages have ergative alignment, but the variety of Mixe chosen for her sample language to represent this family lacks it. Had she happened to choose one of the ergative Mixe-Zoquean languages for her representative, the count for ergativity in Mesoamerica would have doubled and that for nominative/accusative would have decreased by 20 percent. This would, in turn, influence the interpretation of the distribution of ergativity worldwide. Her Mesoamerican sample also contains only one example of a stative/active language, but had her Otomanguean sample language happened to be Chocho or Amuzgo, for example, the statistics for stative/active would have doubled and again those for nominative/accusative would have been reduced.

Nichols says ergativity "is a low-frequency feature with peaks in southwest Asia, Australia, and highland New Guinea. Though more easily lost than gained, ergativity shows good tenacity in those language families that exhibit it" (Nichols 1996b:268). "Ergativity is a *recessive* feature . . . almost always lost by at least some daughter languages in a family and not readily borrowed in contact situations" (Nichols 2003:285; cf. also 2003:295). Many historical linguists will have some difficulty with this assertion. Ergativity is also relatively easily gained, as seen in numerous ergative languages of the Iranian and Indo-Aryan branches of Indo-European, several Polynesian languages, etc. (see Harris and Campbell 1995:240–81). Since change into and out of ergative alignment is not that difficult, there is no strong reason to see ergative alignment as a particularly stable trait. There are several paths by which a language can become ergative, just as there are a number of ways for a language to shift from ergative to nominative/accusative or to active/stative alignment (see Harris and Campbell 1995:240–81). In practical terms, this is easy to see in the languages in Nichols' sample. The languages of the families to which a number of her sample/representative languages belong vary with respect to this feature, where within the same family some of the languages have become ergative while others have not, and on the other hand, where some have lost ergativity while other sister languages have not. Some examples from Nichols' sample of ergative languages in families where not all the sister languages are ergative include: Waigali (Indo-European); Gurung (Sino-Tibetan); Chamorro, Drehu (Austronesian); and Canela-Krahô (Jê family). That is, with variation within these known languages families, ergativity had to develop in some or be lost in others, indicating that it is not especially stable as a typological feature.

Some of the traits in some of the languages in Nichols' sample are misanalyzed and unreported, distorting the view of the distribution of these traits. Numeral classifiers are also underrepresented in her sample, leading to a skewed view of their distribution worldwide. For example, in Nichols' (1992:294–301) lists, Haida and Tlingit are listed with a question mark, but both have numeral classifiers; Wishram is listed as lacking them, but Upper Chinookan (to which Wishram belongs) does have numeral classifiers; Karuk and Washo are also listed as no, but do have numeral classifiers. Huave (in Mesoamerica), with no indication given, has numeral classifiers. Cree (of Algonquian) is given as lacking numeral classifiers, but Algonquian languages such as Ojibwa, Blackfoot, Menomini, and Potawatomi have them. These are seen in Table 10.1.

In South America (with 114 genetic units!), of only fifteen representatives listed, only two, Waorani and Yagua, are indicated as having numeral classifiers; with better sampling of South America, this figure would be

Table 10.1 *Misassigned and underrepresented numeral classifiers in Nichols (1992)*

	Nichols' listing	Reality
Haida	?	has numeral classifiers
Tlingit	?	has numeral classifiers
Wishram	lacks num. classifiers	has numeral classifiers
Karuk	lacks num. classifiers	has numeral classifiers
Washo	lacks num. classifiers	has numeral classifiers
Cree	lacks num. classifiers	Algonquian languages with num. cls: Ojibwa, Blackfoot, Menomini, Potawatomi
Huave	no indication	has numeral classifiers
Mixtec	lacks num. classifiers	some Otomanguean languages have numeral classifiers (cf. Zapotec)

greatly increased; numeral classifiers are also found, for example, in Tucanoan languages; Yucuna, Achagua, Piapoco, Maipure, etc. (Arawakan); Guahibo; Chapahuan; Harakmbet; Bora-Witotoan; Tsafiki (Barbacoan); Mundurukú (and some other Tupían languages); and Chimila (Chibchan). Numeral classifiers are an areal trait of the South Asian (Indian subcontinent) linguistic area, and are found in Hungarian and Turkic, and in Africa in a few Kegboid languages (Cross River: Benue-Congo), Ejagham, and a few Grassfields languages of Cameroon (Aikhenvald 2000:121–4). Numeral classifiers is not a particularly stable trait, and they are not limited to the Circum-Pacific area, although Nichols (2003:299) sees the trait as having "*zero* incidence outside the Pacific Rim macro-area."[16]

The claim of stability for several of her other traits is also dubious. If the general issue of stability is called into question, then Nichols' conclusions based on spread and clustering of these traits and the inferences she attempts to draw for really remote prehistory have to be questioned as well. To interpret these "stable structural features" as she does, Nichols must extract them from the context/fabric of the languages where they are found, separate each out and ignore for the most part the genetic classification of that language and its overall grammatical context; that is, she must assume somehow that the trait can persist – as if it had an independent life of its own – even beyond recognized language families, in spite of whatever else happens to the language and despite the language's genetic classification. However, (1) these features are known not to be so stable; (2) the languages within given families can vary significantly among themselves as to which languages have or do not have a particular feature that is

---

[16] Nichols (2003:299) interprets numeral classifiers as also a "recessive" stable trait.

assumed stable – that is, it is known that these "stable" features come and go in related languages of the same family, resulting in variation in the presence vs. absence of the trait across the languages of the family; (3) much is known about the origins of these traits in many cases; the mechanisms that cause them to emerge and those that cause them to be lost are well understood, and the result is a view of the presence vs. absence of these traits that has nothing to do with ancient persistence or retention of founder effects, but rather is the result of much later garden-variety linguistic change; and (4) the distribution of several of these traits is not areally indicative, as Nichols interprets it to be.

Nichols uses the term *structural pool* to label "any group of stocks exhibiting some property or set of properties that is unusual or infrequent worldwide, though not so unusual or of such low probability as to be a genetic marker" (Nichols 1997a:364). Her examples are (1) the click languages of southern Africa, where the presence of click consonants root-initially "defines a structural canon type, not a genetic grouping" (Nichols 1997a:364); and (2) "the set of stocks hugging the Pacific Rim of the Americas that exhibit personal pronoun systems with *n* in first person forms and/or *m* in the second person" (1997a: 365). As she points out, "the *n:m* system is too small and too fraught with potential phonosymbolism and inflated probability of occurrence due to allomorphy and the cross-linguistic frequency of nasals to be a good genetic marker" (Nichols 1997a:365). However, she goes on to say that "personal pronouns are normally inherited and almost never borrowed" and that "dozens of languages and one or two dozen stocks with such systems, however, are found in the American Pacific Rim, the geographical skewing is highly significant, and other low-frequency features cluster there as well. Although not a demonstrable clade, the cluster is nonrandom and has some kind of historical identity" (Nichols 1997a:365). As pointed out in Campbell (1997b), there are many errors in these assertions. Many instances of borrowed pronouns are documented in the linguistic literature (as shown in Chapter 7).

The same considerations which prevent this trait from being a genetic marker also call into question the conclusion that it "has some kind of historical identity." The distribution is not so clear as Nichols makes it out to be, with examples of the *n:m* pattern not limited to this particular region; the asserted clustering of other features with this pattern in a non-random fashion does not hold up, since the clustering involves traits found far and wide outside the Pacific Rim area but lacking from many languages in the area (for details, see Campbell 1997b; see Chapter 7).

In short, Nichols' "stable features" are on the whole not very stable, and several are misassigned in the languages of her sample. They clearly do not afford the sorts of far-reaching explanations she attempts to derive from them. Greenberg (1993:505) aptly said of these and of the interpretations based on their assumed distributions:

The basic fallacy of the book is the notion that we can use statistics concerning the relative frequencies of typological features in different areas to reconstruct remote prehistory. It is rather the distribution of such typological features (which themselves normally allow very limited possibilities, for example, the presence versus absence of the inclusive/exclusive distinction) that itself requires historical explanation. It can be inherited within small or large families, the result of areal contact, or a quite recent independent innovation. Thus, from the historical point of view, typological distributions are *explananda*, not explanatory principles.

10.2.4   Binary splits

Another facet of Nichols' (1990a) approach is the assertion that most proto-languages, when they diversify, split pair-wise, usually into only two branches, and that this provides a means of dating ancient linguistic events. She says:

I found that the average number of initial branches per stock is 1.4 to 1.6 . . . Using this average, and assuming an average age for stocks, we can compute a rate of proliferation and estimate the age of a set of languages assumed to be derived from a single source. (Nichols 1994:4)

This kind of calculation gives a way of estimating dates of colonization of areas, and that in turn gives a way of assessing the plausibility of deep genetic connections and colonization models. (Nichols 1994:4)

But this has by no means been established; it is not clear that most proto-languages split in this way and it is doubtful that such binary splitting happens with enough regularity and frequency for us to be able to base her various calculations on it. The average number of branches when proto-languages split up (assumed by Nichols to be two) is just not known, and some scholars hold opposing views. Greenberg asserted in various publications that families typically split up into several branches at once – his method of multilateral comparison might predispose him towards preferring multiple branches. Nettle (1996:125) argues that, "following the adaptive radiation reasoning developed here, a wide branching structure is exactly what we should predict when a lineage moves into a new continent with many empty niches." As Dixon (1997:29) points out, if we assume human language evolved at least 100,000 years ago and that "a language is likely to split into two languages every 6,000 years, [then] we would expect proto-Human to have given rise to 2^{17}, or about 130,000 modern languages" (with some of these lost to extinction along the way); but as Dixon points out, this is in fact very different from what we know from documented cases in recent centuries, e.g. the development of such families as Romance and Indo-Aryan.

It is possible that Nichols' view has evolved; in 1997 she reported that "the number of dialects or daughter languages" in linguistic divergence is not constant, "though whether they are relatively many or few depends on ascertainable cultural and historical factors" (Nichols 1997a:366). We agree. She goes on to say, "multiple branching at or near the root of a tree points to abrupt dispersal of the protolanguage in a large spread" (Nichols 1997a:371). Nevertheless, in spite of these remarks, she repeats her earlier claim: "The only cross-linguistic survey of branching done so far (Nichols 1990a) finds that stocks have, on average, about 1.5 initial branches; that is, many stocks are stock-level families or stock-level isolates" (Nichols 1997a:366–7). Nichols (1997a:366) also makes the obvious but often neglected point that, in view of language extinctions, "the branching rates in family trees drawn from surviving languages are not diversification rates but survival rates."

The current frequent discussion of many reticulate (rake-like) families, with multiple initial branchings, certainly calls Nichols' initial binary branching notion into question.

10.2.5 Calculation of time depths

Another disputed component of Nichols' approach, which again reveals the interconnectedness among the various components and assumptions of her program, is the claim that the binary splits (mentioned above) will take place on an average of one every 5,000 years. Dixon's (1997:9) "assumption 2" is the general view of mainstream historical linguistics: "The rate at which a language changes is not constant and is not predictable"; as Hill (2000:9) explains, Nichols' "assumption that languages diversify and split at a relatively uniform rate is problematic, as such rates can be altered by major cultural innovations and events."

On the basis of these two speculative claims together, the assumption of binary branching and splits on an average of one for each 5,000-year interval, Nichols (1990a) calculates the age of human populations, of the first peoplings of continents, of stable vs. unstable typological traits, and of the geographical spread of languages. Thus, the diversity of the languages in the Americas and these assumptions lead her to conclude that language had to have arrived in the New World at least by 35,000 years ago – thanks to this chain of interconnected but disputed assumptions (Nichols 1990a). This view has not escaped criticism:

Nichols (1990[a]:503) suggests that stocks multiply linearly with time. The phylogenetic diversity of a linguistic population with no outside influence is thus a function of the time elapsed since that population started ramifying . . . Nichols's argument of a constant rate of ramification is only one of a suite of considerations she brings to bear on the problem of the settlement of the New World. It is, however, an extremely strange argument, for several reasons . . . Data that are ably discussed by Nichols herself in the same paper (1990[a]:483–9) show that phylogenetic diversity in Eurasia and in Africa has actually been *reducing* for several millennia. This flatly contradicts any assumption that number of lineages increases linearly with time. (Nettle 1999a:120)

Nichols' own data simply fail to support her constant-rate assumption . . . Thus, if there is a relationship between phylogenetic diversity and time, it is certainly not one of linear increase. (Nettle 1999a:121)

Again, it is possible that Nichols' view has shifted with time; in 1997 she reports that "rates of change are accelerated by contact with other languages: the more profound the influence the more rapid the change" (Nichols 1997a:365).

We believe that the notion of predominately binary splits is far from established, and we reject the idea of average ages for such splits and the calculation of dates Nichols would base on this.

10.2.6   *Conclusion concerning Nichols' program*

Nichols' calculations concerning spread, stability, and the general character and distribution of linguistic traits for the zones with which she deals are called into question by the many problems mentioned here. (See also Greenberg 1993; Heath 1994.) In particular, the notion of spread zones and accretion/residual zones should be abandoned. Her conclusions are not supported.

10.3   Punctuated equilibrium[17]

Like Nichols, R. M. W. Dixon asks about language developments beyond the reach of the comparative method:

Approximate dates have been assigned for proto-languages . . . No date earlier than around 10,000 BP is generally accepted . . . What happened between 100,000 years ago – or whenever language developed – and the proto-languages of modern families, 6,000 to 10,000 years ago? (Dixon 1997:2)

However, Dixon's approach is radically different. His model reflects his view of Australian linguistics, where he is a renowned authority. Dixon favors a view for Australia that extensive diffusion and contact make genetic classification by the family-tree model difficult (Dixon 2002), and this view is at the heart of his model (see Dixon 1997, 2002; Dixon and Aikhenvald 1999; Aikhenvald and Dixon 2001). In Dixon's words, "a major factor in turning me towards a punctuated equilibrium hypothesis of language development has been the experience of trying (over a period of 30 years) to make sense of the linguistic situation in Aboriginal Australia" (Dixon 1997:5; see also Aikhenvald and Dixon 2001:10). On the other hand, many other Australian specialists (many of them trained by Dixon) do not see the Australian situation as a challenge to

---

[17] This section follows Campbell (2003b).

standard linguistic classification (see, for example, Bowern and Koch 2004a, 2004b; Evans 2003a; see Chapter 6).

It is of value that Dixon (1997) draws attention to the importance of areal linguistics and diffusion in attempts to work out the history of languages and the families they belong to – something underestimated in much work on distant genetic relationship. We argue, however, that Dixon's correlation of states of equilibrium with extensive contact-induced diffusion and punctuation events with diversification into language families is linguistically unrealistic and misleading. The model has influenced some recent work on language diversification, including that of Bellwood (2000:133), Renfrew (1997:83–4), Nettle (1999b:3327), and others, and therefore it is important to evaluate it carefully.

Dixon attempts to challenge the family-tree model associated with the comparative method: "a main thesis of this essay [Dixon 1997] is that the family tree model, while appropriate and useful in many circumstances, is not applicable everywhere and cannot explain every type of relationship between languages. We need a more inclusive model, which integrates together the ideas of the family tree and of diffusion area" (Dixon 1997:28; see also Dixon 2002:31, 34–5). Mainstream historical linguists agree that the family tree is not everything and that attention must be paid to diffusion, but historical linguistics has never been limited to only the family tree – borrowing, the wave theory, and later areal linguistics, are taken into account (cf. Garrett 1999). Thus, the claim that "the family-tree metaphor has been taken over . . . often as the sole model for relationships between languages" (Aikhenvald and Dixon 2001:6) is inaccurate. Moreover, a consequence of Dixon's (1997:11) "assumption 4," that "in the normal course of linguistic evolution, each language has a single parent," is that the family-tree model is always relevant, regardless of whether the application of methods to determine the family tree in given instances is complicated by changes – for example due to diffusion – which require the use of other historical linguistic techniques for full understanding. Therefore, most historical linguists would say that we do not need a more inclusive integrative model; we already have one. Where Dixon differs is in bringing in his notions of equilibrium and punctuation and attempting to correlate these with different patterns of linguistic change. We argue that these have proven misleading.

At the heart of Dixon's (1997) *The rise and fall of languages* is the notion of punctuated equilibrium, inspired by Eldredge and Gould's popular notion of punctuated equilibrium in biology (see Eldredge and Gould 1972; Gould and Eldredge 1993). In Dixon's (1997:3) view:

Over most of human history there has been an equilibrium situation. In a given geographical area there would have been a number of political groups, of similar size and organisation, with no one group having undue prestige over the others. Each would have spoken its own language or dialect. They would have constituted a long-term linguistic area, with the languages existing in a state of relative equilibrium.

Dixon characterizes his approach in the following way:

The hypothesis put forward here to describe and explain the development of language during the 100,000 or more years since its first emergence is that there have been long periods of equilibrium during which a number of languages have coexisted – in a more or less harmonious way – within a given region without any major changes taking place. From time to time the state of equilibrium is punctuated by some cataclysmic event; this will engender sweeping changes in the linguistic situation and may trigger a multiple "split and expansion" (which would be appropriately modelled by a family tree diagram). The punctuation may be due to some natural event (floods, drought, volcanic eruption), or to the emergence of an aggressive political or religious group, or to some striking technical innovation, or simply to entry into new and pristine territory. After the events which caused the punctuation have run their course, a new state of equilibrium will come into being. (Dixon 1997:67; see also Dixon 2002:32–5)

Dixon imagines that during a period of equilibrium, "languages in contact will diffuse features between each other, becoming more and more similar. These similarities will gradually *converge*, towards a *common prototype*. We can thus say that language families are rapidly made during a period of punctuation . . . and slowly blurred during the long period of equilibrium . . . that follows" (Dixon 1997:70–1). This would make classification in terms of language families difficult.

There are, however, problems with Dixon's conception. As pointed out by Koch (2004:55), his punctuated equilibrium model "is primarily a hypothetical model arrived at by thought experiment and not backed up by supporting historical or ethnographic evidence." It is to these and other problems we now turn.

10.3.1   Punctuated equilibrium in biology

The notion of punctuated equilibrium is challenged in biology. As Dennett (1995) argues, there is nothing special about punctuated equilibrium; evolution continues even without punctuated events disrupting equilibrium. Language change and differentiation into language families also continue in periods of equilibrium (in the absence of disruptive events), as Dixon (1997:9–70) acknowledges. It is, of course, possible that a model which proves unfit for the field in which it originated could, nevertheless, prove useful in another field. However, as we argue here, the problems with the concept which were detected in biology also hold for its application to languages – namely that changes of both sorts, divergence and borrowing, take place both in equilibrium and in punctuation.

In any case, there are conflicting interpretations of how "punctuated equilibrium" should be applied to questions of language history and contact. In Heath's (1997) formulation, the linguistic analogue of punctuation is rapid change in intense language contact (see Watkins 2001:60; LaPolla 2001:227). This is essentially the exact opposite of Dixon's interpretation.

10.3.2   The view of human society

Another problem has to do with the unrealistic assumptions about social structure and its relation to linguistic change. Dixon (1997:78) sees it this way:

The necessary scenario for a period of equilibrium is a number of groups living in relative harmony with one another, each more or less respecting their neighbours and their neighbours' ideas and religion, and not trying to foist either themselves or their religion on others. The political groups would have been fairly small in size (ranging from a few hundred to a few thousand) and fairly anarchic in organisation. We can imagine them as being rather like Australian tribes before the white invasion in 1788; or being like some tribes that survive today in the Amazon jungle. There would be no chief, just a number of elders. Decisions on what a village group or a kinship group should do would be reached by consensus, with some senior members of the group guiding the discussion.

All groups would be roughly similar in terms of lifestyle and beliefs. That is, they would have a comparable level of sophistication in the tools and weapons they possess, the sorts of shelters they build, and the food resources they have available. They would have comparable types of (non-aggressive) religious beliefs. (Dixon 2002:32)

As Nettle (1999a:26) observes, Dixon falls prey to the tendency to portray non-industrial societies as pristine and timeless: "This Rousseauesque picture is anthropologically naïve, as a brief reading of Keeley (1996) or Edgerton (1992) will reveal" (Nettle 1999a:99). The ethnographic literature does not support a picture of small-scale traditional or non-industrial societies as egalitarian, living in harmony. Rather, it shows enormous variation in social structure and political organization where harmony and equality are mostly absent. War is common – even non-human primates wage war! (See Stanford 1998, for example.) Many anthropologists today believe that all societies are systems of inequality (see Salzman 1999 and the discussants therein for differences of opinion in this area). As LeBlanc (2002) points out, ethnographers have made repeated attempts to come up with a list of peaceful societies, and on a worldwide basis they can come up with at best four to seven possible examples. Moreover, unlike in Dixon's assumption of the groups in an area being very much alike, it is not uncommon to find human groups in the same region who have different kinds of socio-cultural integration, markedly different sorts of social stratification and social organization, and different subsistence patterns. Often we find clan-level organization for some groups but chiefdoms (tribal-level) and even state-level societies for others in the same region (as in areas of Africa, southeast Asia, and Central America). Often in the same area we find groups with staggeringly different subsistence patterns, sometimes with subsistence symbiosis, where, for example, hunter–gatherers and sedentary agriculturalists are mutually dependent upon one another for exchange of meats for agricultural produce, as in the case of Bushman hunters and south African Bantu groups, and forest-dwelling Pygmies and their farming neighbors. The presence of some kind of leader/ruler (in the form of the "big man," head of clan, or chief) is far more common than the sort of egalitarian consensus benevolently guided by a group of elders that Dixon suggests. From what we know about these differences among societies within an area, it is difficult to accept the sort of situation assumed as typical by Dixon. As Nettle (1999a:26) points out, "the lack of military dominance of any one group in such areas as New Guinea or Aboriginal Australia has more to do with demographic weakness, technological limitations, and inability to command economic surpluses than any pacific cultural attributes."

In short, Dixon's view of human society in the past does not stand up. However, since his model of punctuated equilibrium in language change crucially depends on this view of society, it constitutes a very serious problem for the approach. We turn now to other problems with this model.

10.3.3   The problem of equilibrium with diversification

Dixon equates equilibrium with convergence. Nevertheless, normal change leading to diversification into language families can and does take place in situations of equilibrium, contrary to expectations of the model. We see cases where under stable conditions over long periods of time, with no evidence of punctuation, the languages of the region continue to undergo normal change and to diversify into language families. Some readily apparent examples are: the Highland Mayan (K'ichean, Mamean subgroups), Zapotec (a complex of several different languages recently diversified), Eskimoan, Nakh-Daghestanian, Saami (Lapp) languages (a subfamily of Finno-Ugric with some ten distinct languages), various "Papuan" families, etc. In short, a significant number of language families appear to have developed *in situ*, in relative harmony, and without punctuation events, as Dixon (1997:9–70) also acknowledges.

10.3.4   The problem of equilibrium without diffusion

Another problem for punctuated equilibrium are situations of equilibrium without diffusion, contrary to the expectations of the model. Dixon (1997:70–1) believes that in periods of equilibrium "languages in contact will diffuse features between each other, becoming more and more similar. These similarities will gradually converge." But linguistic diffusion does not always take place in situations of harmonious equilibrium. Languages in the same area over a long time may exhibit little evidence of contact-induced change, for example Athabaskans of the American Southwest (Navajo, Apache) and their non-Athabaskan neighbors (Hopi, Zuni, Keresan and Tanoan groups). The Hano Tewa (Tanoan language) and Hopi (Uto-Aztecan) harmoniously share the same tiny mesa top, yet extremely little borrowing or diffusion has taken place in either language (Kroskrity 1993). In some regions, even with equilibrium, speakers of different languages actively avoid one another (as in some cases in the subarctic region of North America, where Inuit and Athabaskan groups practice avoidance).

This is a problem for the model's expectation that equilibrium gives diffusion and convergence.

10.3.5   Diffusion in punctuation

Punctuation situations, in Dixon's model, are correlated with changes leading to diversification, not with diffusion. However, contrary to this expectation, linguistic diffusion can be caused by punctuation events and does not take place just in equilibrium. Conquest and political inequality are great promoters of structural diffusion among languages, and examples are so common as scarcely to bear comment. For example, the history of English is mostly that of punctuation, with the Scandinavian invasion and the Norman French conquest, but the outcome is more in tune with that envisaged for equilibrium states: English assimilated huge amounts of vocabulary, borrowed sounds and some pronouns, and leveled morphosyntactic complexity. Similarly, the impact of Spanish on the grammar of so many indigenous languages of Latin America is a direct reflection of the inequality in the status of the languages involved and the punctuation that Spanish domination brought (see, for example, Brody 1989, 1995; Campbell 1987). Both forced language contact (punctuation) and peaceful contact (equilibrium) can have similar outcomes with respect to diffusion and convergence.

Moreover, the formation of linguistic areas and the development of areal phenomena shared across languages of a geographical region, as Hill (1978) shows, can be brought about as a response to punctuating factors. Groups may join in areal associations in response to famine, resource failure, war, and catastrophes of all sorts, structuring human organization at the areal level, helping to maintain area-wide systems of adaptation and supporting "the extensive networks of contact which allow survival of human groups even during periods of locally severe environmental stress" (Hill 1978:18).[18]

---

[18] Again, there may be lessons for us from the analogue of species in biology. Many argue that the main – some say only – way species form is by "allopatric speciation," where a population becomes geographically isolated from the rest of the species so that eventually it becomes reproductively isolated as well, giving different species (Mayr 1963:451–80; Harmon 1995). However, not all agree; some argue that there are many cases also of "sympatric speciation" where geographical isolation was not necessary for the formation of new species (Harmon 1995). In language, this is equivalent to the observation that communicative isolation (diversification into mutually unintelligible languages) may follow geographical isolation, but just as in sympatric speciation, geographical isolation is not always necessary for language diversification to arise.

10.3.6   *A caution about "convergence"*

Several scholars may have gone too far in their interpretation of Dixon's ideas concerning convergence of languages. For example, from Nettle (1999b:3328) we read: "Dixon claims that stocks can disappear from the linguistic record when extensive diffusion and convergence with neighboring languages make their distinct origin impossible to detect." In fact Dixon does not hold such a view, at least not consistently and rigidly. Or, rather, he seems to hold both the view that this does not happen at all and that it does. He says, on some occasions:

> It is instructive to enquire what the possibilities are for two languages in contact over a very long period of time. Could they conceivably merge? I believe that the answer to this question is "no" . . . All our observation of normal linguistic development suggests that a language never has more than one parent. (Dixon 1997:71)

But he also says on other occasions:

> As time goes by, linguistic features of every type will diffuse across all or part of the linguistic area; the languages will converge towards a common prototype so that original features which were diagnostic of genetic connection are modified. Genetic affiliations will become blurred and then lost. (Dixon 2002:35)

We know from the well-studied linguistic areas that: (1) Typically few diffused structural features are actually found, usually less than a dozen main ones (cf. Campbell 2004:331–8). (2) Cases of profound language mixture are basically not found; clear cases of language convergence or mixture are truly rare, and these do not arise through normal mechanisms of borrowing in language contact; rather, invariably they have been the results of extreme social circumstances, e.g. forced population removals, the sort generally not found in pre-colonial settings (cf. Bakker 2000; Bellwood 1996:468, 2001; Thomason and Kaufman 1988; see Dixon 1997:71–2). (3) In any case, reference to the family membership of the languages involved is necessary in order to determine the nature and extent of diffusion – you can't tell whether it's borrowed or inherited if you don't know where it came from. Nevertheless, several scholars have understood Dixon to mean that wholesale convergence is possible, so much convergence that the comparative method is no longer valid and whole language families disappear, converging with one another. They fail to realize that in documented linguistic areas wholesale convergence is not known – true, diffused traits across language boundaries can make the task of distinguishing inherited from diffused material very difficult in some cases, but the gradual convergence of initially independent languages to the extent of obliteration of language family connections and making the comparative method inapplicable is not part of the picture. This being the case, in contrast to Renfrew's (2002:6) reading of the situation, it is not at all "remarkable the convergence models have played so little part in analyses of language change," and we should not "expect that convergence models will begin to play a larger role in the field of historical linguistics of language formation than they have in the past."[19] Rather assumptions about language convergence processes in prehistory need to be moderated.

10.3.7 Is there life for equilibrium after punctuation?

Another problem has to do with the nature of the interaction between punctuation and equilibrium. Dixon believes that mostly for long periods there was harmonious equilibrium, occasionally disrupted by punctuation events, but that "after the events which caused [a] punctuation have run their course, a new state of equilibrium will come into being" (Dixon 1997:67). At the same time, Renfrew (2000a) and Nettle (1999a:99–100) believe that the first punctuation in the Old World was the beginning of the Neolithic which initiated the spread of agriculture. There seems to be a problem in this. The notion of equilibrium springs from Dixon's experience with languages associated with Australian forager societies, where agriculture has never been a factor. Elsewhere, once agriculture takes off, the harmonious forager equilibrium state envisaged by Dixon is gone forever. Arguably equilibrium will never return after this first agriculture-driven punctuation; in this view, it is possible that equilibrium could be lost forever after, due to the assumed population pressures and the struggle for land and resources set off by the acquisition of agriculture. There may be no more cyclic interactions between equilibrium and punctuation, only continuing punctuation. And if the onset of agriculture did not spell the end of equilibrium, Dixon and others assume, in any event, that the possibility of equilibrium is now lost in the wake of colonialization effects after 1492.

10.3.8 Conclusions concerning punctuated equlibrium

The correlation envisaged, which equates equilibrium with convergence, and punctuation with divergence, is not supported – both kinds of change take place in both kinds of situations. The notion provides no real purchase on the questions of language relationships and of why and how languages diversify. They diversify and spread in both punctuation and equilibrium. (For some other critiques of Dixon's punctuated equilibrium, see Crowley 1999; Janda and Joseph 2003; Watkins 2001.)

---

[19] Under "convergence models" Renfrew lists also wave theory, *Sprachbund*, creoles, and koines. These already do play an important role in historical linguistic research; however, the wholesale "convergence" or mixing of formerly distinct languages in a resultant language so that its ancestry is unclear is decidedly not generally accepted.

10.4   The attacks on family-tree diagrams

Some scholars of late have taken a skeptical view of the validity of family-tree diagrams (and the applicability of the comparative method) stemming from beliefs about the degree of convergence or confounding possible in language-contact situations. It is important to clarify this debate.

Jakobson (1938) offered a solution to the old debate about the possibility of multiple origins for a single language, that is, to the question about the utility of the family-tree model in situations of areal diffusion: "La similitude de structure ne s'oppose donc pas, mais se superpose à la 'parenté originaire' des langues" (Jakobson 1949[1938]:353). He called for adequate description of shared traits without premature generalizations about whether they owe their explanation to a genetic relationship, mixture, or diffusion (Jakobson 1949[1938]:365). This remains sound advice. Mainstream historical linguists realize that it is not possible to understand diffusion fully without knowing the genetic affiliation of the languages involved and vice versa, not possible to account fully for what is inherited without proper attention to what is diffused. That is, it is not two distinct, opposed, and antagonistic points of view that are involved, but rather both are needed and they work in concert: "both the comparative method and areal linguistics are historical disciplines – twin faces of diachronic linguistics" (Hamp 1977:27).

Some who question the family-tree model say things such as:

Areal linguistics was originally inspired by the insufficiency of genetic relationships as an explanation for similarities between languages, in particular, by the recognition of grammatical and phonological similarities which were due to language contact. (Dahl 2001:1457)

The original motivation of both [areal linguistics and language typology] was the insufficiency of the genetic Stammbaum model for the study of relationships among languages. (Dahl 2001:1456)

There are a number of misconceptions in these citations. The goal of the historical linguist is to answer the question, what happened?, whether it be due to inheritance, diffusion, or a combination of both. Indeed, in attempting to answer this question, both the inherited and the diffused are necessary at the same time. Matters of burden of proof require this. To test any hypothesis of genetic inheritance, it is necessary to demonstrate that it fits the facts better than alternative possible explanations, borrowing being principal among possible alternatives (though accident, universals, and others must also be considered; see Chapter 7). Similarly, for any hypothesis of borrowing, it is necessary to demonstrate that other possible explanations do not provide a better answer, and the possibility of inheritance from a common ancestor is crucial among those that must be eliminated for the hypothesis of diffusion to stand. That is, it is not a question of driving the genetic explanations as far as possible and then, and only then, turning to diffusion as a last resort. Rather, it is a matter of seeking the whole history and testing any hypothesis against other possible explanations. In fact, many of the errors seen today in both proposals of distant genetic relationships and in proposals that champion diffusion stem from not considering other possible explanations sufficiently before making conclusions in particular cases.

Some, in their zeal for areal explanations as presumed challenges to the comparative method, call for alternative models and methods:

the family tree model, while appropriate and useful in many circumstances, is not applicable everywhere and cannot explain every type of relationship between languages. We need a more inclusive model, which integrates together the ideas of the family tree and of diffusion area. (Dixon 1997:28)

To reconstruct the history of a language adequately, a model is needed which is significantly more sophisticated than the family tree based on the use of the comparative method. It needs to incorporate the diffusion and layering process as well as other language-contact phenomena such as convergence, metatypy and hybridization. The desideratum is a synthesis of all the processes that affect language formation and development. (Chappell 2001:354)

Plainly, an alternative model is needed. (Dixon 2002:31)

However, as pointed out above, most historical linguists would say that we do not need a more inclusive integrative model; we already have one. Inheritance and diffusion have always been of crucial importance. More importantly, not only is the comparative method not at odds with borrowing, it is very often a major tool for detecting it and thus arriving at an understanding of what is inherited and what is diffused in languages. As Watkins (2001:59) explains, "the resilience and the power of the comparative method lies in its sensitivity to similarity due both to genetic filiation and areal diffusion alike. Both are historical models, and the goal of comparison is history." Hübschmann (1875) demonstrated this "when he proved that Armenian was a separate branch of Indo-European, and not a dialect of Iranian as previously thought" (Watkins 2001:59). Armenian exhibits massive influence from Iranian, but it was the application of the comparative method which revealed this as diffusion and not inheritance (see Chapter 5). The comparative method was valuable in understanding those linguistic areas involving Indo-European languages, that is, the Balkans, Baltic, South Asia (Indian subcontinent), and Anatolian linguistic areas; that inheritance and diffusion can be tackled with the comparative method has been shown time and again (Bowern and Koch 2004b:1–2; Watkins 2001; Ross 1988, 1998).

Sometimes, however, it is impossible to distinguish inheritance from diffusion in some cases. Dixon (1997, 2002) sees this as a major problem for the comparative method and a challenge to the family-tree model. This attitude, however, is mistaken. We agree with Bowern and Koch (2004b) that such diffi-culty, when it arises, is just a fact of historical linguistic life; it is not a problem of the comparative method *per se* if we cannot reconstruct everything due to lack of evidence. It is a general problem we have when dealing with prehis-tory that we are at the mercy of the evidence available. Dixon (1997) and others argue that later diffusion obscures genetic relationships and invalidates the com-parative method and the family-tree model; however, diffusion, just like other innovations, leaves its traces which can often be picked up by appropriate and detailed reconstruction (Bowern and Koch 2004b:4–5.) In short, it is a problem with the kind and quantity of data available, not with the theory.

So, is the family tree merely a bad "metaphor" assumed to be reality? Aikhen-vald and Dixon (2001:6–7) claim:

The family-tree metaphor [developed for Indo-European] has been taken over for other parts of the world in stark form, often as the sole model for relationships between [among] languages . . . Rather than asking whether a form of family tree is appropriate to the language situation in some newly studied region, it has often been simply *assumed* that it is. What began as a metaphor has been ascribed reality, and has acted to constrain enquiry along narrow lines. This can lead at best to a partial and at worst to a mistaken statement of language relationships.

(See also Aikhenvald and Dixon 2001:4, 6; Dixon 2002.)

The claim here seems to be that traditional historical linguists believe that a mere diagram, used to reflect linguistic lines of descent, is the whole story. It seems to confuse the diagram with the reality it is intended to reflect. This is misleading rhetoric, for there is a reality which is not just a metaphor: the historical facts that languages can indeed be related to one another due to descent from a common ancestor. These relationships reflect an empirical reality, and our attempts to understand them result in hypotheses about real historical events of the past. How one represents the reality (or the hypothesis about the reality) graphically is not what is at issue, nor the fact that many other sorts of changes also affect languages which are not directly inherited, but are parts of the traditional inquiry aimed at answering the question, what happened? As Sebeok (1950:101) made clear, if some scholars limit their vision to only that which is inherited, too bad for them, but this is not an accurate characterization of what historical linguists do generally nor of the history of the field, as the Armenian case and other examples like it show. Handbooks on the history of specific languages always give abundant attention to bor-rowing. The diagram, the family tree which attempts to depict inheritance and descent from an earlier common ancestor, is just one part of the larger story.

Equilibrium as convergence on a common prototype (Aikhenvald and Dixon 2001:9–10) has much less claim to reality (see above) than family trees some-times overlapped by borrowed traits, whose history linguists work out using a combination of methods and techniques aimed at understanding both what is inherited and what is diffused. It is never a question of diffusion/convergence vs. family tree; rather it is always a question of both. We want to answer the question, what happened? and for that we need both inheritance and diffusion.

So what about cases where it is difficult or even impossible to determine whether shared traits are due to inheritance, diffusion, independent parallel development, or accident? The difficulty of distinguishing what is inherited from what is diffused is often mentioned in the areal linguistic literature, and above all, by those who wish to place the comparative method or genetic relationships among languages in a bad light (cf. Aikhenvald and Dixon 2001:1; Aikhenvald 2001:190–1; LaPolla 2001; Chappell 2001:335, 353–4; Dahl 2001:1456). All retrospective sciences are faced with the same problem: we do our best with the evidence on hand, and sometimes it does not allow definitive answers; sometimes we must just say we do not know. However, fortunately in linguistics our methods have proven successful over and over in distinguishing instances of borrowing from inheritance. Because the methods have been so successful in so many cases, we do not abandon them just because the evidence at hand is insufficient in some specific instance, just as we do not conclude that an automobile can never take us anywhere just because on one occasion the gasoline ran out.

It is definitely not a question of exclusive domains – areal versus genetic –, but rather of both working in concert to answer the question, what happened?

10.5   Conclusions

The approaches discussed in this chapter propose new techniques to try to see past limitations of the comparative method in order to get at remoter linguistic prehistory. If any of them were successful, this would constitute an important advance in historical linguistics. However, as we have seen, these approaches are flawed, both in conception and in execution. They afford no new insights which are reliable. They do not take us further back in time than the comparative method (at least not successfully). Nevertheless, it is valuable to take stock in order to eliminate sirens such as these which appear to promise much, but which divert efforts away from more productive lines of investigation. Indeed, there is still much work to be done and much to be learned from the application of the traditional techniques, especially the comparative method.

11 Why and how do languages diversify and spread?

> Australian aborigines . . . say that there was an old woman named Wururi, who went out at night and used to quench the fires with a great stick. When this old woman died the people tore her corpse to pieces. The Southern tribes coming up first ate her flesh, and immediately gained a very clear language. The Eastern and the Northern tribes, who came later, spoke less intelligible dialects.
>
> (Farrar 1873:106)

11.1 Introduction

What drives linguistic diversification?[1] Why do languages split up and become families of related languages? What accounts for languages spreading to new territory? Because answers to how and why languages diversify into families of related languages are closely connected with issues of genetic affinity and linguistic classification, in this chapter we survey some of the main approaches which propose answers to these questions. We identify misleading claims and attempt to offer directions towards more adequate answers.

As mentioned in Chapter 1, throughout history there have been numerous theories about what causes languages to diversify, accounts involving, for example, migration, war and conquest, trade, geographical isolation, cessation of communication, social and economic organization (e.g. mounted warriors with expansionist proclivities, militaristic patriarchy), linguistically marked group identity entailing rights to resources, technological advantage (in, for example, food production, herding, navigation, metallurgy, military organization), even divine vengeance for the Tower of Babel caper. A common theme has been a belief that communicative isolation leads to linguistic diversification, seen by some as an analogue to the belief in biology that reproductive isolation leads to speciation. This has led to speculation about the cultural, geographical, demographic, ecological, economic, political, ideological, and other factors that could bring about communicative isolation. Ross (1997:212) describes

---

[1] Portions of this chapter draw on Campbell (2002) and (2003b).

diversification as "fissure ... is the SCE [speech community event] which occurs when speakers of a lect [language or dialect] become geographically or socially isolated from other speakers of the same or closely related lects, thereby forming a new speech community." True, the early accounts usually lacked much substantive support, but do recent proposals fare better? The goal of this chapter is to examine various recent claims about why languages diversify and spread in hopes of clarifying the matter.

Dixon (2002:31) observes that if our view of language diversification were based on Indo-European, we could expect huge language families with massive numbers of member languages. Indo-European diversified into some 400 languages in something like 4,000 to 7,000 years since the break up of the proto-language, "generat[ing] more than 10^2 languages." "If all language development were on this basis," assuming as most scholars do that human language came into existence at least 100,000 years ago, about sixteen spans of the age of Indo-European, a human language of this age "should spawn more than $10^{2 \times 16} = 10^{32}$ (a thousand billion) modern languages." Since there are only some 7,000 languages in the world today (www.Ethnologue.com), clearly diversification of this sort is far from the whole picture.

We need to explain language diversification, language shift, language loss, and more. The investigation of the "whys" and "hows" of linguistic diversification and language spread must, as mentioned in Chapter 1, deal with the following questions:

1. The *linguistic* question: What drives linguistic diversification (the formation of language families)?
2. The *geographical* question: Why and how do languages spread over space?
3. The *structural* questions: (a) How and why do related languages come to be structurally distinct from one another? And (b), how and why do unrelated (and also related) languages come to be structurally more similar to one another?
4. The *language shift and maintenance* question: Why do some languages wither and die while other languages thrive and spread?
5. The *means of language shift* (replacement) question: in any given case, is it a matter of (a) the language spreads but not the population (new language, old genes), (b) the people spread taking their language with them (new language and new genes), or (c) both (a) and (b) are involved?
6. The *social, cultural* question: How do people's choices and social behavior (rather than, say, just physical geography) determine linguistic diversity?

Sleuthing linguistic movements, like solving crimes, requires attention to *motive* (were the speakers of these languages pushed or pulled to move?), *means* (did they move by land, water, on foot, horse, boat?), and *opportunity* (were there physical bearers?, did neighbors impede movement?, did those moving have some technological or other advantage which would facilitate encroachment on neighbors' territories?). And, there is also the question of *habeas corpus* – what evidence is there that a migration was actually committed? For example, too often for proposed linguistic migrations there is no clear archaeological or human genetic support.[2]

With these questions in mind, we turn now to recent approaches to linguistic diversification and language spread.

11.2   Ecological risk

Daniel Nettle favors the "ecological risk hypothesis," an economic theory concerned with the formation and maintenance of social networks whose "most important function is to provide household social insurance against the 'normal risks of agriculture through an elaborate system of social exchange' (Scott 1976:9; Braun and Plog 1982)" (Nettle 1996:413). "People mitigate fluctuating food availability by means of exchange with other households in their network" (Nettle 1996:413), and "the greater the provisioning problem, the wider the social network necessary" (Nettle 1996:414). To this economic theory Nettle adds a linguistic component: "it is the larger networks of generalized exchange which ultimately give rise to different ethnolinguistic groups" (1996:413); "ethnolinguistic groups are thus best characterized as informal networks of intensive generalized exchange, which function . . . 'through reciprocity and reciprocal roles'" (Nettle 1996:412); "the ecological risk hypothesis thus predicts that the size of ethnolinguistic groups should increase in proportion to the amount of ecological risk that they face" (Nettle 1996:414).

Nettle derives three hypotheses from these observations and attempts to test them based on data from West Africa:

Hypothesis 1. The greater the ecological risk, the fewer languages there will be in a country of a given size. (Nettle 1999a:83; cf. 1996:414)

Hypothesis 2. The greater the ecological risk, the fewer languages there will be in a country of a given population. (Nettle 1999a:83; cf. 1996:414)

Hypothesis 3. The size of language groups will decrease as the terrain becomes more difficult to cross. (Nettle 1996:415)

He finds that both hypothesis 1 and 2 are supported by the West African data (Nettle 1996:423), while for hypothesis 3, "there is also limited and more equivocal evidence of a relationship between diversity and topography." "The question of why there are more languages in some areas than others can therefore be more or less restated as the question of why households in some areas are

---

[2] While linguists have not shied away from referring to migrations (population movements), migration has not been in favor with most archaeologists in recent years.

involved in larger or more dispersed networks of generalized exchange than others" (Nettle 1996:412).

This view has difficulties, to which we now turn.

11.2.1 Difficulties with the linguistic–economic link

Nettle's economic determinism which correlates size of language with extent of economic risk is too single-minded. True, social linkages often follow linguistic lines, but language lines are not the only ones along which people organize themselves in ethnic, economic, and other alliances. The point of alliances to aid against economic risk may be correct, but alliances lying within single languages are not the only relevant ones. This view fails to take into account that the sort of alliances that might hold across speakers of the same language (spread across a wider geographical area so that they might be called upon in times of food crisis) can be and often are forged also across language boundaries. Linguistic homogeneity is not necessary for economic cohesion and exchange, even of the generalized form which Nettle favors. These economic ends can be served as well through multilingualism, lingua francas, trading pidgins, diglossia (intertribal "high" language), etc. Indeed, West African society is characterized by a high degree of multilingualism (Nettle 1996:408). For example, Hausa, a language much discussed by Nettle (with 22 million speakers), is primarily the first language in northern Nigeria and southern Niger, but is a second language for many others in a wide area of West Africa (Childs 2003:22–3). These modes of communication do not function at the level of the language–tribe equation, but reflect organizing patterns of human population beyond individual language boundaries which help to maintain area-wide systems of adaptation and support, i.e. "the extensive networks of contact which allow survival of human groups even during periods of locally severe environmental stress" (Hill 1978:18). Hill (1978), in arguing against the view of human organization in which tribe and dialect or language are thought to be inextricably linked (inherent in the view that the language community is the social unit which addresses economic stresses), argues for the "concept of language area patterns as active aspects of dynamic, area-level human adaptations which allow flexible response to local environmental stress" (Hill 1978:5). Hill shows that peoples speaking different languages in a region can work together to address the sort of economic risk which Nettle sees as being addressed within single languages. Robb (1993:750), similar to Hill, holds that "contact with other groups would have been vital for information on resources . . . hunter-gatherers living at low densities typically maintain fluid relations with neighbouring populations as ecological insurance against local shortfalls." Speaking of exchange in New Guinea, Robb notes that "it was politically advantageous to incorporate more producers and exchange partners into a larger system" (Robb 1993:753,

755). As Foley (2000:359) explains, clans are the basic social unit in New Guinea, leading often to fragmentation of communities; "clans are typically distributed across multiple villages or even several language groups, so clan politics can lead to the attenuation of linguistic communities and increasing linguistic diversity, as clan members adopt linguistic features of favored neighbors." Social organization on the Eurasian steppes also spanned different language groups, where "economic and ethnic survival in the east required strong social organization and large-scale and highly cohesive groupings" (Nichols 1998a:239). For example, kinship often crossed language boundaries in the steppes and Siberia; most peoples of northern Asia are clan-based, and these are exogamous descent groups spanning various languages (Nichols 1998a:239, 240; Torday 1997:2).

Cross-linguistic alliances of various sorts can serve economic risk reduction.

11.2.2   The difficulty of big and little languages in the same area

A significant problem for Nettle's model is the presence of large and small languages in the same area (see Chart 11.1).

To take just one example, Quechua spread with the political power of the Incas (now with c.8,000,000 speakers, spoken in six countries); nevertheless, numerous small languages were found surrounded by Quechua, e.g. Culle, Jaqaru, Cauqui, etc., though presumably they all, large and small alike, faced the same production risks. This example and the others of Chart 11.1 go against the predictions of the model: in circumstances subject to economic risk, small languages should not survive; all the languages should be roughly equally large to address the risk.

11.2.3   Difficulties from non-ecological influences on language distribution

Nettle's ecological-risk approach fails to take sufficiently into account the importance of large political units, for example the Hausa state, with its political clout (McConvell 2001). As Nettle (1996:409) acknowledges:

In West African history, one finds a wide range of different political systems. On the northern savannah, there is a thousand-year history of large states, beginning with the medieval empires of Ghana and Mali . . . to the Hausa and Hausa-influenced city-states and their eventual unification under the caliph at Sokoto in the 19th century. In the southern forest belt, there is a rather more recent history of smaller city-states and kingdoms, such as Benin, Dahomey, Asante, and Oyo.

Nettle (1996:409) further admits that "there are some obvious correlations between state formation and language spread. The spreads of Asante and Yoruba in the south are probably products of combined demographic and political

Chart 11.1 *Larger and smaller languages in the same geographical area*

Large	Small
Indo-Europrean	Munda
Spanish, French	Basque
Italian	Friulian
German	Sorbian
Thai, Burmese	Mon
Japanese	Ainu
Chinese	Tujia (Tibeto-Burman), Ordos (Mongolian), Oroquen (Tungusic), etc.
Khmer	Cham (Chamic)
Bengali	Khasi (Mon-Khmer)
Hindi	Malto, Gondhi, Kurku (Dravidian), etc.
Oriya (Indo-Aryan)	Mundari (Munda)
Malayalam (Dravidian)	Tulu (Dravidian)
Arabic	various Berber languages
Amharic (Semitic)	Kemant (Cushitic)
Kwa (Niger-Congo)	Mpre (Mbre)
Adamawa (Niger-Congo)	Laal
Mande family (Niger-Congo)	Pre (Bere)
Cushitic (pastoralists)	Sandawe
Yoruba (Benue-Congo)	Chumbuli (Guang branch of Kwa)
Gonja (Kwa)	Safalaba (Gur)
Yucatec Maya	Mopan, Itzaj (Itzá), Lacandon
Zapotec	Huave, Tequistlatec, Pochutec, Papabuco
K'iche'	Uspanteko, Sipakapeño, Sakapulteko
K'iche'an	Xinkan
Nahuatl	Huastec
Muskogean	Natchez, Chitimacha
Quechua, Aymara	Jaqaru, Cauqui, Puquina
Tagalog	Sinauna
Far South (Dubea, Numèè)	Caac (in New Caledonia)
Magi ("Papuan")	Yoba (Austronesian, in Papua New Guinea)
Tetum/Timorese	Buruk ("Papuan")
Kakasi ("Papuan" of Timor)	Kairui-Midiki (Austronesian)

expansion, aided in the Asante case by access to gold . . . and in both cases partly by external trade." In spite of this, he plays down the importance of political factors: "the influence of specialized political and governmental structures is of limited importance" (Nettle 1999a:68). For example, he says of the emirates of Hausaland, "I would contend that the spread of language is not primarily caused by such considerations of 'élite dominance'" (Nettle 1999a:74). He concludes that "the spread of political systems gives a potential explanation for the distribution of first languages only in a small number of cases" (Nettle 1996:410, also 94), but nevertheless concedes that "there are, it must be admitted, a few pre-industrial cases where a language spread was associated with a particular political formation" (Nettle 1999a:68).

But these protests notwithstanding, Nettle's view appears inconsistent with the historical evidence, and therein lies a serious problem for the ecological-risk account of language spread and distribution. The area of "'pure' Hausa states" is more or less identical to that of the Hausa language, inconsistent with the fact that Nettle sees no evidence that state formation spread the language. There are numerous other counterexamples: the spread of Nahuatl with the Aztec empire, Quechua with the Inca empire, Latin by Romans, and the spread of Arabic, Chinese, Turkish, and so many others. Clearly, factors other than ecology figure in the spread and distribution of languages.

11.2.4   Diachronic difficulties

As McConvell (2001) points out, Nettle's approach lacks diachronic perspective. Nettle's view relies on a simple correlation between the distributions of languages as they are today and ecological factors of their regions. It needs, however, to take temporal considerations more seriously into account. For example, as mentioned above, the emphasis on horizontal exchange between households to explain the spread of Hausa (Nettle 1999a:74–6) neglects the influence in the past of Hausa emirates, taxation and tribute, and associated power and prestige as factors in the spread of Hausa (cf. McConvell 2001).[3] A fuller diachronic perspective is needed.

11.2.5   Conclusions to Nettle's ecological risk approach

In conclusion, there is much more to ecological risk reduction than mere linguistic cohesion, and much more to language distribution and spread than ecology.

---

[3] Another instance showing the need for more diachronic perspective comes from the case of Central African Pygmies, which Nettle mentions several times. Bahuchet and Thomas (1986) showed that the present-day relations between Pygmies and their neighbors are not the kind that would lead to language shift, though Pygmy groups have indeed shifted to neighboring Bantu languages, and what is more, there are geographical discontinuities and considerable time depth between the languages of the Pygmies and the Bantu languages which are their closest linguistic relatives. Thus, the economic (and other) factors which led Pygmies to shift languages must have been different hundreds of years ago when the language shift took place from those known today (McConvell 2001).

11.3   The farming/language dispersal model

A major alleged motive for various proposed linguistic expansions is agriculture – also accused of providing the means and/or the opportunity for languages to move. Renfrew (1973, 1987, 1988, 1989, 1991, 1992, 1994, 1997, 2000a, 2002) and Bellwood (1991, 1994, 1995, 1996, 1997, 2000, 2001, 2002) (see especially Renfrew and Bellwood 2002) emphasize agriculture – the farming/language dispersal model: "farming dispersals, generally through the expansion of populations of farmers by a process of colonization or demic diffusion, are responsible for the distribution and areal extent of many of the world's language families" (Renfrew 1996:70; cf. also Renfrew 2002, Bellwood 1996:467, 468, 1997:124–5, 2002). This notion of agriculture-driven language dispersal has influenced also work by Dixon (1997), Hill (2001b, 2002), Nettle (1996, 1999a), and others. Given its impact, it will pay to scrutinize this model carefully.[4]

Renfrew (1973) initiated the model. By 1987, he relied on the notion of "wave of advance" in which the spread of farming economy was propagated by "demic diffusion" (cf. Ammerman and Cavalli-Sforza 1973) (e.g. Renfrew 1987). Later Renfrew incorporated aspects of Dixon's (1997) "punctuated equilibrium," emphasizing the onset of agriculture as a major punctuation, and Nichols' (1992) "spread zones" (Renfrew 2000a:24–30; see Chapter 10). Renfrew (1994, 1996) came to see language spreads as due to one of four processes: (1) *farming-language dispersals* (through *demic diffusion* of the farming population, the "wave of advance model" [Renfrew 2000a:26]; that "early farming expansion implies dispersals of real populations" [Bellwood 2001:197]); (2) *initial migrations/colonizations* into previously unoccupied territory; (3) *climate-related colonizations* (demographic expansions by farmers, late climate-related dispersals into zones not suitable for habitation until the ice receded); and (4) *élite dominance* (through adoption by local hunter–gatherer groups of the new language along with the new agricultural economy, i.e. *acculturation* [Renfrew 1992:15–16, 1994:120, 2000a:26; cf. 1988:438–9]). Still, farming/language dispersal is where his primary interest lies. Though his emphasis is on the first, all of these enter the discussion.

---

[4] Diversification into families of related languages and spread of languages across territory are typically not distinguished in works on these topics, though clearly they are not the same thing. They may be related, but they are not causally connected. When the works examined here do not make this distinction, then neither do we in discussing them, though clearly the difference matters significantly. Also, the distinction between a language and its speakers is often not made explicit in the works examined here, so that, for example, we see discussion of "agricultural languages." We assume the distinction, but find it convenient to continue to speak of languages having agriculture as shorthand for speakers of particular languages having agriculture.

We turn now to some difficulties which the farming/language dispersal model must face.

11.3.1   Agriculture and population stability

Agriculture does not always motivate language expansions, as predicted by the model. Rather, agriculture can provide a people with the stability just to stay put, in relative self-sufficiency, so that they do not need to expand. Agriculture does not always lead to population pressure which exceeds the carrying capacity of the local land.[5] Some examples of such stay-at-home agricultural language families (those with a "localist stance" in Hill's [2001a] terms, "compact languages" and "compact families" in Golla's [2000] classification, see below) are seen in the list of non-spread agricultural languages in Chart 11.2. Rather than expanding, some of these "compact" languages take a "localist stance," enforcing the linguistic boundaries that deny outsiders rights or access to land and crops.

Hill (2001a) explains the distribution of Mixe-Zoquean languages in this way. Mixe-Zoquean is limited in its geographical spread, though it is among the earliest complex agricultural societies and strongly influenced most other Mesoamerican languages, as seen in numerous loanwords (Campbell and Kaufman 1976). She asks, "why did not Mixe-Zoqueans expand at the expense of foraging neighbors, according to the models?" Her answer is that "a very early adoption of agriculture with a consequent sense of entitlement would have permitted Mixe-Zoqueans to develop localist sociolinguistic strategies and continue to use them . . . As the new technologies of cultivation permitted a sense of trust in the reliability of local resources, new 'residual zones' could form, yielding the contemporary linguistic complexity of . . . Mesoamerica" (Hill 2001a:276). Such non-expansionist agricultural languages (see Chart 11.2) go against the farming/language dispersal model.

---

[5] For example, Bellwood (2001:186–7) asserts that "whether the agriculture was being spread by converting hunter-gatherers or range-expanding farmers – both groups would have become subject to population increase in good environments." LeBlanc (2002:357) has it that "all societies, except for those in terrible environments, quickly approach the carrying capacity." (See also Renfrew 2002.) However, contrary to such claims, a difference in population pressures is not visible in all instances, given numerous agricultural language communities which did not expand (see also Hill 2001a). Zvelebil (2002:380) argues persuasively from archaeological and demographic data against the assumption of rapid population growth in farming populations, pointing out that "this proposition removes the central assumption underpinning the spread of farming into Europe by demic diffusion." Also, non-agriculturalists in ecologically appropriate areas can be sedentary while many farming groups are relatively mobile, and cultural regulation of population growth is well known in many societies. "It cannot be automatically assumed that such potential [for population growth to be greater among farmers than hunter-gatherers] had a promised impact . . . Neolithic farmers faced many social, technological and environmental handicaps in Europe, which might have reduced their reproduction capacity" (Zvelebil and Zvelebil 1988:579). (See also Bellwood 1994:404.)

11.3.2 Distribution difficulties

There are some difficulties with the farming/language dispersal model which have to do with language distributions. To test the model, it is important to survey the well-understood language families of the world to see what kinds of diversity they exhibit, to see if they have spread significantly or not, and for those that have spread, to see whether they have agriculture. It is also important to determine for those that do not spread significantly, which have agriculture and which lack it. A preliminary indication of how this would go is given in Chart 11.2, which presents language families both with and without agriculture, distinguished according to those which have spread significantly and which have not. Though most groups today have some agriculture, language families listed under the category of "minus agriculture" are assumed not to have had agriculture at the time of their initial break up and main dispersal. Note that the presence of agriculture is clear in the reconstructed vocabulary of several of these, e.g. for Proto-Indo-European, Proto-Semitic, Proto-Mayan, Proto-Mixe-Zoquean, Proto-Otomanguean, Proto-Austronesian, Proto-Bantu, Proto-Munda, Proto-Tai, and others (cf. Bellwood 1996:484).

Chart 11.2 contains a significant number of spread and non-spread language families both with and without agriculture. Simply stated, this means that the farming/language dispersal model alone is neither necessary nor sufficient to explain these distributions – and, indeed, no one makes such a claim.[6] It is not necessary, since there are widespread non-agricultural language families; it is not sufficient, since there are non-spread agricultural languages. Therefore, other processes of spread must be called upon.

11.3.2.1 Exceptions and other "processes" We need to see if any of the exceptions might be explained by Renfrew's (1997, 2000a) other processes of spread: initial migrations, late climate-related dispersals, and élite dominance. Since the widespread agricultural languages are consistent with the farming/language dispersal model, they constitute no problem for the hypothesis. Since it is only spread language which these processes address, the non-spread languages are less relevant (though an account is needed for why the non-spread agricultural languages did not spread, see below). Among the widespread non-agricultural languages of Chart 11.2, only the spreads of Eskimo–Aleut, Athabaskan, Uralic (Samoyed), and Tungusic can be accounted for by one of these other processes: all could be late climate-related dispersals (entering areas

---

[6] Supporters of the farming/language dispersal hypothesis do not insist it must work in all cases to be accepted. As Peter Bellwood points out (personal communication), lots of farmers stay at home, such as the Egyptians, and lots of hunters adopt agriculture, such as the Agta, so, "the hypothesis is meant to explain some deep-lying patterns, not all aspects of farmer distribution." Nevertheless, the existence of so many exceptions on both sides of the equation does bring the hypothesis into question.

Chart 11.2 *Spread and non-spread language families with and without agriculture*

	Plus agriculture	Minus agriculture (mostly)
Significantly spread families	Austronesian Bantu (Niger-Congo) Indo-European Semitic Dravidian Sino-Tibetan (Chinese) Tai Chibchan Cariban Tupian Otomanguean Arawakan Cushitic(?) (pastoralists)	Tungusic Uralic (Samoyed) Pama-Nyungan Salishan Uto-Aztecan Eskimo–Aleut Athabaskan Algonquian Siouan Yuman Chon (Tehuelche, Ona)

Relatively non-spread families	Some 25+ Papuan families
	Nakh-Dagestanian
	Kartvelian
	Munda
	Mixe-Zoquean
	Mayan
	Totonacan
	Xinkan
	Keresan
	Tanoan (Kiowa-Tanoan)
	Panoan
	Isolates: Zuni, Basque, Huave,
	  Cuitlatec, Tarascan,
	  Chitimacha, Tunica,
	  Natchez, Burushaski
	  Japanese, Korean,
	  Sumerian, Etruscan
		Some 25 N. Australian families
		Wakashan
		Tsimshian
		Chumashan
		Maiduan
		Pomoan
		Yukian
		Wintuan
		Khoi, San
		Chinookan
		Takelman
		Isolates: Kutenai, Haida,
		  Alsea, Siuslaw,
		  Washo, Yana,
		  Esselen, Beothuk, etc.

after the ice receded). The other languages in this list are not explained by initial migrations, late climate-related dispersals, or élite dominance. In fact, it is the lack of agriculture that deprives many of them of hope of élite dominance in the geographical spheres where they are found. That is, they remain unexplained.[7]

11.3.2.2 Linguistic diversity in agricultural zones In zones of intensive agriculture, often we find much linguistic diversity, the presence of several

---

[7] For example, as Bellwood (1997:132) acknowledges, "unfortunately, the Pama-Nyungan languages do not fit an expansion model either easily or comfortably."

language families frequently not demonstrably related to one another, e.g. in Mesoamerica, Papua New Guinea (cf. Bellwood 1996:484, 488), parts of southeast Asia, sub-Saharan Africa, the southeastern US, and the American Southwest. Agriculture in these zones has not necessarily resulted in language spreads, but seemingly has allowed for the development and co-existence of numerous languages and language families. This diversity calls for an explanation. Renfrew relies on his process of initial migrations/first colonization to explain exceptional languages which "could not have been spread by people acting on a relatively recent change in climate, a revolution in agriculture or a wave of conquest" (Renfrew 1994:122). In his words, "such residual tongues, scattered in bits and pieces throughout the world map, must have arrived in their current ranges long ago, during the initial dispersal of modern humans" (Renfrew 1994:122). Most of these cases are found in areas where late climate-related dispersal is not relevant. Also, given the picture of numerous agricultural language families co-existing in an area, élite dominance would not explain them, since élite dominance has to do with language spread, not the lack thereof.

In this context, Renfrew introduces the notion of "mosaic zone" (Renfrew 2000a, 2002): "it seems appropriate to suggest that many areas with mosaic-zone language distributions have not been subjected to a farming dispersal, but rather that the initial colonization took place during the Late Pleistocene period, and that there has been stability along with local divergence since that time" (Renfrew 2000a:27). Bellwood's (2001, 2002) notion of "friction zones" (equated with some of Nichols' "residual zones") appears to be similar in that his friction zones give linguistic diversity without languages being lost in spreads, though Bellwood sees them as occurring around the edges of Nichols' "spread zones." He says, "we can expect zones of friction to occur not just in environmentally unsuitable situations such as semi-deserts, dry grasslands or coniferous forests, but also where hunter-gatherers lived in high densities, along productive coastlines for instance" (Bellwood 2001:189). (See Chapter 10 for comments on Nichols' accretion/residual zones.)

There are two difficulties with relying on initial migration. The first is that we just do not know the real history of colonization and replacement in most of these areas. In most of the areas of the world, humans arrived with their languages sometime before 40,000 years ago, and at least by 12,000 in the Americas. So, given the very large interval between first colonization in an area and what is visible today, many things could have happened. Most likely, numerous languages became extinct and were replaced, while some moved on and others moved in. Thus, reference to the period of time between original colonization and today's distribution of languages leaves far too much unknown and open for speculation.

A specific case will help to clarify this point. Paleoindian population in the Great Lakes region is documented archaeologically from $c.11,000$ BP, but the earliest language families of northeastern North America date glottochronologically only to about 4,000 years ago: Algonquian *c*.3000 BP, Iroquoian *c*.4000 BP (Campbell 1997a:104). Assuming initial immigration with paleoindians, we have 7,000 years in which the linguistic landscape could have and probably did change in many different ways. No established language family anywhere is really very old, the oldest being only *c*.8,000 years. This no doubt has to do with the fact that after such long periods of time and so much linguistic change so little original material remains that it becomes impossible to show that languages separated for so long are actually related. Renfrew (1997:85) speaks of two kinds of languages, Class A: Pleistocene languages (initial colonization prior to 12,000 BP) and Class B: Post-Pleistocene languages (due to "farming dispersal after 10,000 BP") (cf. Renfrew 1996:76). The distinction in terms of Class A and Class B language families does not hold for known families, all of them being significantly younger than those of Class A, prior to 12,000 BP. Indeed, nearly all the cases Renfrew lists as examples of Class A are disputed proposed distant genetic relationships: Khoisan, Nilo-Saharan, Indo-Pacific, North Australian, Amerind; only North Caucasian and South Caucasian are not undemonstrated, disputed proposals.

The second difficulty is that though the languages in "mosaic zones" today may be agriculturalist, they had to have acquired agriculture sometime in their past. Reference to earliest colonization just pushes the problem back in time: it is still necessary to explain why the first languages to acquire agriculture did not expand and swallow up the others in the zone who did not yet have it, whenever the event took place. Postulating initial migration does not solve the problem. Renfrew (2000a:24) notes that "the mosaic zone configuration . . . is seen both with hunter-gathers and with agriculturalists in those cases where the agricultural economy does not seem to be the result of an agricultural dispersal but may be regarded as indigenous, as in the case of New Guinea with its very early horticulture and perhaps in regions of South America." But this begs the question: since cultivation is widely spread in these regions, across many language groups whose geographical distribution exhibits the mosaic zone configuration, why has the dispersal of agriculture there left the distribution of the languages relatively unaffected, contrary to the predictions of the farming/language dispersal model? The matter of whether agriculture is indigenous or not seems a red herring – all the groups of these regions would not have acquired agriculture simultaneously. For example, in Mesoamerica, agriculture is certainly indigenous to some specific location(s) within the region, but it has also undeniably spread widely so that all the ethnic/linguistic groups now have it, though the distribution of their languages seems mostly unaffected by this spread. Agriculture had to have gone from ones which had it to ones without until all had it, as in the Xinkan case, to cite just one example. The linguistic evidence shows that formerly Xinkan speakers were not cultivators, but acquired agriculture from their Mayan neighbors. Virtually all Xinkan terms for cultigens are borrowed from Mayan (some from Mixe-Zoquean) languages (Campbell 1972, 1997d). Thus, they maintained their distinctive identity and language in face of the powerful Mayan agriculturalists, first as non-cultivators, then later as cultivators, acquiring agriculture through acculturation, not by being swallowed up by their large, powerful agriculturalist neighbors as the model predicts. Therefore, indigenous or not, there was also agricultural dispersal within mosaic areas.

Speaking of acculturation, the wave-of-advance version of the farming/language dispersal model clashes with the evidence of loanwords in many regions. Loanwords, an extremely powerful tool in linguistic prehistory, often provide strong evidence of agricultural acculturation rather than language replacement, as in the Xinkan case mentioned above. To mention just one well-known example, the borrowing of Proto-Indo-Iranian *pork'o-s* 'pig, piglet' into Proto-Finno-Ugric (cf. Finnish *porsas* 'pig') is understood as a case of acculturation of aspects of farming from one language community to another without language replacement (numerous plant and animal terms having to do with farming are borrowings from Indo-European languages in Finno-Ugric).

11.3.2.3 Small languages and big languages in the same territory
There is another distribution problem. The agricultural dispersal model (also Nettle's ecological-risk model) does not explain the co-existence within a region of little languages (of few speakers or of small geographical area) and large languages (widespread geographically, or of many speakers). Some examples are presented in Chart 11.1 (above). Bellwood (2002:21) has in mind "agriculturalist language families [that] spread over vast areas leaving virtually no enclaves," with Bantu, Austronesian, and Indo-European as paradigm examples. The model predicts, in effect, that the small languages in the geographical domain of larger languages should be swallowed up and eliminated by the expanding larger agricultural languages. The co-existence of such smaller languages with larger ones, thus, constitutes a difficulty for the model.

Among the agricultural languages of Chart 11.2 there are large ones and small ones alike. It might be objected that according to the model it is non-agricultural languages that are swallowed up by expanding agricultural languages (cf. Bellwood 2001, 2002), so that other agricultural languages, even small ones, are not relevant. As Bellwood (2002:21) puts it, "farmers simply do not normally replace other farmers on the Bantu or western Austronesian scale." This, however, is no solution, since there are also cases of non-agriculturalist languages which have not been swallowed up by the larger agriculturalist languages of their regions. Moreover, many of the small surviving agricultural languages were not agricultural in the past when agricultural languages came into contact with them, as seen in the Xinkan case cited above.

With respect to distribution difficulties, in short, widespread non-agricultural cases such as Pama-Nyungan and Uto-Aztecan (see below) and non-spread agricultural cases such as the "Papuan" language families and Mixe-Zoquean which go against the predictions of the model are serious problems for the farming/language dispersal model.

11.3.3   Independent events?

Another difficulty is the close association assumed in the model between the spread of agriculture and that of languages. There is no causal connection between cultivation (or other aspects of material culture) and language – either language or agriculture can spread independently of the other. Spread of agriculture across communities speaking different languages could be facilitated by multilingualism, lingua francas, sign languages (as in the Great Plains), trade pidgins, or may need none of these to spread, just its own utility and prestige. There is nothing in the physical or social world that demands that the spread of agriculture to a new region should cause pre-agricultural local languages to be replaced by the language of in-coming agriculturalists.

This independence is highlighted by the examples that show that language and agriculture can follow separate vectors: (1) People speaking the same language can have radically different subsistence patterns, e.g. the highly modern industrialized Tamil speakers and the Paliyans, who live in forest-dwelling food-gathering moving bands (Gardner 2000), all Tamil speaking; or the forest-dwelling hunter–gatherer pygmies and their farming neighbors, all now speakers of Bantu languages. As Renfrew (1996:81) notes, "the farming-dispersal hypothesis clearly loses ground somewhat if farming practices were not in fact consistently dispersed." Speaking the same language does not necessarily impose the same subsistence strategies. That is, agriculture not only does not always swallow up little languages in its expansionist wake, it does not even always impose itself on all the speakers of a particular language. Subsistence diversity is what gives many non-industrial societies an edge towards survival, should one of the modes suffer shortfalls. (2) People speaking different languages can share the same culture, including the same subsistence strategies, e.g. in examples in the "mosaic pattern" and instances in Chart 11.1 (see also Hill 1978).[8]

---

[8] For simplicity of exposition, we have been speaking as though communities of speakers of particular languages are either agricultural or not; however, in some situations, it is more a question of how agricultural are they, since mixed foraging-farming economy is known from many regions. In some cases "domesticates were . . . a means to improve the foraging system by diversifying it rather than replacing it" (Wetterstrom 1993:166). For example, it is argued that the development of root-crop farming in Africa in the beginning was only a small increment to the overall diet of Proto-Bantu speakers and did not distinguish them much from their

Even in some cases that might appear to fit the model there are problems of interpretation. For example, if the Indo-Europeanization of Europe and northern India took several millennia, is it really appropriate to talk of it as a single expansion or dispersal with a single motivation? Most Indo-European linguists would insist on a number of independent movements scattered over scores of centuries to account for the distribution of Indo-European languages. Vansina (1995:191) shows that Bantu "expansion" actually involved "a minimum of nine diffusions, at least, before communities speaking Bantu languages could be found here and there over most of the area now occupied by Bantu speakers, and those nine diffusions together may have taken up to two millennia to spread." This telescoping of the events which resulted in the distribution of the languages into a single spread with a single cause does disservice to the very prehistory we are attempting to understand.[9]

11.3.4 Is the New World different?

Both Bellwood (2000, 2001) and Renfrew (2000a) see the New World, with its many exceptions to the agricultural dispersal model, as different from the Old World. Following Crosby (1986) and Diamond (1997), they see differences due partly to the north–south axis, to the absence of large domesticated animals, and to the lack of major cereals apart from maize, which may explain the exceptions. We do not find this reasoning persuasive. It appears to overlook the fact that the geographical orientation of Mesoamerica is largely east–west and not north–south – extending broadly east–west from $c.80°$ to $105°$ W, in a narrow north–south zone from $c.12°$ to $20°$ N. They believe the New World production

non-Bantu neighbors (Vansina 1995:190). Some "Khoisan" groups added sheep and cattle without taking up agriculture (Ehret 2002). In other instances we encounter the well-known cases of symbiotic relationships between agriculturalists and hunter–gatherers, such as San hunters and Bantu farmers, dependent on each other in reciprocal exchange of commodities procured by one group but not the other; Fulani pastoralists trade milk and other products for cereals, a large portion of their diet, with West African cereal farmers. In prehistory, in a number of regions the full agricultural complement was reached only gradually over a long time, with certain domestic animals or cultigens arriving from one direction at a particular time and others from elsewhere at a different time. Also relevant here is the considerable discussion of the impact of the "Secondary Products Revolution" and the difficulty of sorting out the impact of the initial arrival of agriculture from that of these later events.

[9] The role of "macro-families" in Renfrew's and Bellwood's work is also problematic. For historical linguists, the assumption of (or at least the tolerance for) disputed macro-families in various publications by Bellwood and Renfrew casts doubt on the farming/language model. Obviously, how one views language diversity and spread around the world differs markedly if one counts only some twenty or less super-families (cf. Renfrew 1992) instead of the 350 or so independent language families that most historical linguists recognize. If the disputed Amerind, Austric, Altaic, Indo-Pacific, Nostratic and the like have failed to convince most linguists (see Chapter 9), then notions of agricultural dispersals built on such entities obviously will not be found attractive. Since the model does not depend on these doubtful linguistic classifications, they should be dropped.

systems were in general not so powerful as those of the Old World (Bellwood 2000:128). For Mesoamerica, such a claim forgets the power and ubiquity of the big three – maize, beans, and squash –, and the use of chia (amaranth), sweet manioc, sweet potatoes, and other tubers, peppers, cacao, turkeys and muscovy ducks (both birds diagnostic of the pre-Columbian culture area), supplemented with foraging of fruits, various mammals, fish, caiman, turtles, iguana, birds, grubs, and boas – capable of supporting large populations which developed complex technologies, stratified society, large cities, states, and empires. In short, the diet was neither poor nor powerless. Bellwood (2002:23) appears to revise this to exempt Mesoamerican and Andean civilizations.

For another difference, Bellwood (2000:129–30) believes that American language families have shorter time-depths than major Old World language families. However, with (glottochronological) dates from 5000 to 6000 BP, several of these are as old as the oldest established language families anywhere. After Afroasiatic (not entirely uncontroversial), demonstrated Old World families are not relatively older than the New World families which Bellwood lists.

In short, these are not sufficient grounds for setting the New World aside, difficult though it may be because many of its language families do not conform to the expectations of the model.

In some cases, Renfrew and Bellwood misjudge certain New World language families. For example, Renfrew (2000a:23) says, "the development of farming would then be responsible for the spread of certain language families such as the Maya[n] and the Uto-Aztecan." This conclusion is mistaken for both families, for different reasons. Proto-Mayan already had agriculture long before its break up into its thirty-one constituent languages; a very large number of agricultural terms are reconstructible to Proto-Mayan (Kaufman 1964a, 1976). It can be argued that it is the presence of cultivation before the break up of the family which contributed to its relative "compactness," the lack of spread of the Mayan languages.[10] Proto-Uto-Aztecan, on the other hand, did not have agriculture (Bellwood 2000:131–3, and Hill 2000, 2001b, 2002, notwithstanding) and most of its subgroups spread widely before the arrival of agriculture (see below). That is, Mayan had agriculture long before it diversified, but it did not spread much, while Uto-Aztecan lacked agriculture, but spread far and wide.

---

[10] Perception of the geographical size of different languages may be relative. While some might think the Mayan family is geographically spread, in fact in total area the whole family covers little more territory than Basque alone does in Europe. When one keeps in mind that the agricultural dispersal model has Indo-European, Bantu, and Austronesian as its paradigm cases, Mayan has expanded virtually not at all in comparison to these. The Mayan languages have not moved far from their proposed homeland in the Cuchumatanes Mountains of Guatemala. Only Huastec is not adjacent to the main body of Mayan languages, and its very close sister, Chicomuceltec, is adjacent. Only Yucatec covers any particular expanse, and its territory is not large when compared to, say, smaller languages of Europe such as Swedish, Finnish, Lithuanian, and so on.

11.3.5 Application of the model: the case for and against Uto-Aztecan

Jane Hill's (2001b, 2002) reinterpretation of Uto-Aztecan (UA) differs from the mainstream view by proposing a different Proto-Uto-Aztecan (PUA) homeland, arguing that Proto-Uto-Aztecans were maize cultivators, not foragers. This view was stimulated by Bellwood (1997), and so could encourage the agricultural dispersalists if it held up. However, it fails to be convincing for a number of reasons.

The hypothesis is plausible, but improbable. Hill would place the PUA homeland in the south, associated with Mesoamerican maize agriculture, consistent with her claim of PUA agriculture. While reconstructed lexical evidence from PUA plant and animal terms is consistent with both a southern and the traditional northern homeland hypotheses, the center of gravity method (linguistic migration theory) for assigning linguistic homelands, based on minimum moves and maximum diversification, supports the traditional view of a northern homeland in the southwestern US–northeastern Mexico area (Fowler 1983). Hill's southern homeland has difficulty explaining the distribution of the languages, with little linguistic diversification in the south and much more in the north. Similarly, Nahua (the only UA branch squarely in Mesoamerica) shows every sign of entering Mesoamerica later in life as a break away from its UA relatives. It underwent changes which make it more like its Mesoamerican neighbors but set it off from other UA languages; it acquired several Mesoamerican structural traits (see Campbell, Kaufman, and Smith-Stark 1986) missing from its sister languages, and it borrowed much vocabulary matching cultural traits diagnostic of the Mesoamerican culture area and its ecology, but not of the drier areas to the north. These are not the earmarks of a language in its homeland whose sisters marched away to the north.

For Hill, most of the northern UA groups except Hopi lost agriculture, and this means that the argument of PUA agriculture rests very heavily on Hopi alone. Bellwood (1997) and Hill (2001b) assert that there are few known cases where foragers have adopted cultivation while maintaining their linguistic and ethnic integrity different from the donor community, as is assumed for the Southern UA (SUA) groups in the conventional view. Bellwood (2002) mentions the lack in the ethnographic record of cases where hunters have adopted farming from farming peoples (though mentions Basque and Yuman as possible exceptions in Bellwood 1994:396). But it is not the case that hunter–gatherers scarcely ever adopt farming. Xinkan and various smaller Mesoamerican groups took on cultivation while retaining their integrity. In this view, it follows that maize-agricultural Zuni, Keresan, Tanoan, Chitimacha, Natchez, and Iroquoian, among others, should not exist, should not have taken on maize cultivation, but should have had their languages eliminated by expanding cultivators. Since these cases exist, via acculturation, why is Hopi not just one more example in the list? As this list shows, it is just not the case that only sites where primary domestication took place will be linguistically complex. As for the lack of examples in ethnographic literature, in most cases farming was adopted too early to fall under the eye of modern ethnographers and make it into ethnographic records.

Hill's principal evidence is nine lexical sets among UA languages which she believes involve cognates which show evidence of PUA maize cultivation, though association with maize is limited primarily only to the words in the sets from Hopi and SUA languages. Her lexical sets are problematic: borrowing has been proposed as an explanation for some; for others, the wide semantic difference of some among the languages compared casts doubt on the cognacy; most require assumption of considerable semantic shift, and for most of these a shift from an earlier non-agricultural meaning to later associations with maize seems more plausible. Thus, this evidence is challenged; it is too limited to support the case.

The case is hurt by the fact that there are so few proposed "cognates" reflective of agriculture and that they depend so heavily on Hopi – for the northern languages, many of the nine sets are attested only in Hopi. Hill believes there are four cases also in other northern languages, though with non-maize glosses, and three with maize associations (sets 9, 10, 11, all challenged below). We mention briefly some difficulties with the data.

Set 1. Shoshone '*Artemisia argentia*', Hopi 'sand grass' / some SUA languages 'corn, cornfield.' Hill indicates that this does not reconstruct to PUA in the sense of maize cultivation. Also, in spite of Hill's objections, the SUA forms are similar to those of a number of Otomanguean languages and borrowing is not ruled out.[11]

Set 2. Hopi 'corn cob' / SUA forms 'corn leaf, cane, corn stubble, straw storage bin, granary (corn crib).' Many of the SUA forms meaning 'storage (granary)' may be internally diffused; otherwise, the 'stubble, leaf, cane, cob' have associations more with dry plant parts than agriculture.

Set 3. Hopi 'hominy' / 'seed, ear of corn,' Guarijío 'seed but not of maize.' The PUA form is generally believed to have meant any 'seed,' not agricultural seed; Hill agrees that non-maize > maize is the most likely direction of semantic shift for this.[12] The Hopi form *pa:cama* has some difficulties, a /c/ unexpected by regular sound correspondences and an unexplained part /ma/.

---

[11] Her objection is based on Rensch's (1976) Proto-Otomanguean reconstruction not being phonetically similar enough to the SUA forms in her opinion, but several of his reconstructions are uncertain, and it is with the forms in the various branches of Otomanguean where we find the similarities to the UA forms.

[12] A change to 'hominy' could have two paths that do not require agriculture in the proto-language. (1) Hominy is grainy, gritty, and could just be an ordinary semantic shift based on the consistency of small seeds. Most scholars do believe PUAns, even as collectors, ground seeds. (2) Hopi 'hominy' originally referred to ground seeds in pre-agricultural times, but transferred its meaning to corn grits after maize agriculture was acquired.

Set 4. Tübatulabal 'to roast,' other Northern languages 'cook,' 'to melt,' 'to boil' / SUA forms 'to toast, parch,' 'comal [griddle],' 'toasted corn,' 'popcorn.' Probable direction: pre-agricultural 'toasting, roasting, parching' > SUA 'popcorn, parched corn.' (Some SUA forms are probably borrowed internally; compare also Zuni *saKo* 'corn meal,' SUA *saki*, etc. 'parched corn, popcorn.')

Set 5. Hopi 'corn gruel,' Hopi 'be sifting (using wind), winnowing,' Tumpisha Shoshone 'winnow,' Cahuilla 'winnow, sift, blow something (like husks away from grain)' / SUA forms 'harvest, shell corn, shell, shelled, shelled corn kernels.' Probable direction: 'sift' (pre-agricultural) > 'shell.' Only the first syllable /wɨ / is compared, leaving the rest unexplained, not a valid etymological procedure. This syllable could have onomatopoeic leanings from 'blowing.' The semantic fit among these forms is poor and they are probably not true cognates; the medial consonant does not fit regular sound correspondences.

Set 6. Hopi 'dried ear of corn,' Hopi 'butt end of corn cob,' other northern languages 'hooked stick to pull down piñon cones,' 'pine cone harvesting hook' / SUA forms 'corncob, corncob with kernels removed.' The semantics of the northern languages is unlikely; the more likely direction would be 'pinecone harvesting hook' > 'cob' (though improbable). The Hopi forms are not really satisfactory; an unattested /ö:/ 'cob' is extracted from /qa:ʔö/ 'dried ear of corn' and /ö:vi(-ʔat)/ 'butt end of corn cob,' though the leftover parts are of doubtful status. Even if the segmented /ö:/ were reliable, it is too short to deny chance as a possible explanation, and it misses out on the $n : l$ sound correspondence (as with the /l/ of Nahuatl /o:lo:-tl/ 'corncob'), the basis for putting the other forms in this set.

Set 7. Hopi 'griddle', other northern languages 'to roast, bake, roast under ashes' / SUA forms 'tortilla, tamale'. Some of the SUA have been identified as loans. Probable direction: 'roast' > 'tortilla, tamale' (and 'roast' > 'griddle').

Set 8. Hopi 'oblong cake of baked sweet corn, flour' / SUA forms: 'flat and thin object, such as tortilla griddle, flat, a flat place, griddle.' Probable direction: 'flat' > 'griddle.' (Hopi may be 'flat' > 'oblong cake.')

Set 9. Southern Paiute *qumia* 'corn (name rarely used now),' 'Zea mays' is compared to Hopi *kokoma* 'dark red, almost purple,' *koko* 'Amaranthus cruentus (for dye)', and SUA forms *ku:mi-, gumí*, etc. meaning 'to eat, chew on something that comes in little pieces; corncob; bite something hard and small like popcorn; eat small things, eat corn, ear of corn; chew; chew with small bites; mouse.' We believe the Southern Paiute form is a borrowing,[13] and since the glosses are so different, the phonetic similarity may be accidental.

---

[13] Hill argues the Southern Paiute word is not borrowed from Hopi, but it could be a loan from some other language, perhaps one of the SUA languages; also, the only significant difference between Hopi and Southern Paiute is /o/ vs. /u/, but this is slight, particularly in languages with both long and short vowels, and with several vowel changes as in Hopi. Languages are not required to borrow consistently from other languages.

Set 10 'digging stick.' Hill (2001b) sets this set aside, since foragers too use them.

Set 11 'to plant' requires neither maize nor agriculture, as in the sense of 'to place something in the ground,' 'to fix something in the ground.' Many foragers also broadcast wild seeds for better yields when they return on their seasonal rounds; this could be the original sense.

The wide semantic latitude in several of these forms calls them into question. Hill (2001b) asserts this is no serious problem because the warning about semantic permissiveness is only about proposals of distant genetic relationship, not about families of languages known to be related. But this is not so. The criteria for a good etymology within a known language family are very strict, in spite of the *a priori* probability of a connection when similar words in languages known to be related are compared. In particular, lexical similarity is generally not considered sufficient unless the semantic match is very close, and when the meanings differ, there must be an explicit hypothesis about how the meaning has changed in each case. (See Chapter 7.) In any event, all Hill's cases appear to be better interpreted as semantic shifts from foraging to cultivation, and not visa versa.

In short, Hill's reinterpretation of the UA homeland as southern with agriculture is not convincing. The conventional northern homeland and foraging culture of PUA has more support. The spread of UA remains a problem for the farming/language dispersal hypothesis.

11.3.6   Conclusions on agricultural dispersals

In summary, concerning the farming/language dispersal approach, one must say that if there are cases where it works, they are insufficient for generalizing about what drives language spread and diversification. We want to know what causes linguistic diversity in general (and what impedes it), and agriculture is at best one factor, in many cases not a particularly relevant one.

11.4   Social factors

The farming/language dispersal model, Nettle's ecological risk approach, and Nichols' program (Chapter 10) all leave social factors mostly out of the picture.[14] Nevertheless, social factors are relevant to questions of language spread and diversification. It is to them that we now turn.

---

[14] Dixon's approach, on the other hand, treats social factors unrealistically (Chapter 10).

11.4.1 Language shift and maintenance

The abundant literature on language shift (sometimes called "replacement" by non-linguists) and maintenance and on language endangerment shows that no approach to linguistic diversification and language spread which emphasizes only geography and economy will be adequate by itself. In general, language shift or maintenance boils down to people's social behavior, speakers making choices, sometimes under duress, perhaps channeled by economic and other considerations, but also mediated by ideology and social factors. In the interest of space, suffice it to list some factors contributing to language shift: discrimination, repression; exogamous marriage patterns, acculturation, military service; cultural disintegration, war, slavery, famine, epidemics, religious proselytizing; lack of social cohesion among speakers, lack of physical proximity among speakers; symbolism of the dominant language (e.g. political symbol of nation; cultural symbol of civilization, progress, future vs. past); stigmatization, low prestige; absence of institutions that establish norms (political hierarchy, schools, academies, texts); rapid population collapse; communication with outside regions, resettlement, migration; literacy, compulsory education, official language policies; as well as the economic factors, e.g. resource depletion and forced changes in subsistence patterns, lack of economic opportunities, ongoing industrialization, rapid economic transformations, shifting work patterns, migrant labor, etc.

Social stratification, social class, and prestige must not be ignored. To mention just one example, Latin was not imposed in Gaul, but rather came to have a prestige role in various aspects of social life, in administration, commerce, the military, and education, which led the local population to replace Gaulish over a period of several centuries (Bauer 1995; Ostler 2005:299–301) – no wave of advance brought Latin, rather a choice to acculturate did.

11.4.2 Language and social identity

Recent work from several independent quarters appears to converge as different scholars investigate the significance for language diversification and language spread of social and cultural factors and speakers' choices (see Thurston 1987, 1989; Ross 1996, 1997; Golla 2000; and Hill 2001a), and these views intersect with social network theory (Milroy 1987; Milroy and Milroy 1992; Ross 1997) and "communities of practice" (Eckert 2000).

Thurston (1987, 1989) and Ross (1996, 1997) speak of "esoterogeny," by which they mean "a sociolinguistic development in which speakers of a language add linguistic innovations that increase the complexity of their language in order to highlight their distinctiveness from neighboring groups" (Foley 2000:359); "esoterogeny arises through a group's desire for exclusiveness"

(Ross 1996:184). In this way the community language – which Ross (1996) calls the "emblematic" language, emblematic of ethnic identity in a multilingual situation – becomes the "in-group" code which serves to exclude outsiders (Thurston 1989:556–7; Ross 1997:232). In such situations, Ross (1997:239) believes "innovations leading to increased complexity and to differences from neighboring lects [dialects and languages] will be favoured." As Foley (2000:359) observes, "such a process [esoterogeny] would add significantly to linguistic diversity." For example, Ross (1996:183) points to processes of elision and assimilation which "result in phonological compactness, in allophony and allomorphy," mentioning also the accumulation of irregularities, elaboration of the lexicon with numerous near synonyms, much borrowing, and "an increase in the frequency of opaque idioms" (see also Ross 1997:239; Thurston 1987: 55, 56–60, 1989:556).

There are difficulties with this interpretation. It has been speculated that little-known, so-called exotic languages may change differently from others, attributed to various social and cultural characteristics of the speakers, such as small size of the speech community, the face-to-face interaction, isolation, lack of literacy, and so on (see below). However, almost invariably, claims about general patterns of change correlated with these aspects of non-linguistic culture have proven indefensible. In the case of Thurston's and Ross' "esoteric" languages, it is attractive to imagine that speakers of these languages have initiated (or at least used) particular changes for the purpose of distinguishing themselves from and thus excluding outsiders. However, it is not clear how this hypothesized cultural motive for these changes – conscious exclusion of outsiders (Ross 1997:239) – could be tested or how the investigator might distinguish changes motivated for this purpose from changes that just happen with no such motive. That such cultural factors were necessarily involved would be difficult to prove, since it is possible to cite many situations where other languages have undergone rather extensive changes of the sorts mentioned by Ross, leaving them looking "esoteric," but where no separatist motive behind the changes can be identified. English has undergone many changes distinguishing it significantly from most other Germanic languages, particularly from its closest relatives (e.g. loss of Umlaut, unrounding of front rounded vowels, loss of the verb-second rule, loss of verb-final [SOV] properties, several other sound changes, loss of much inflectional morphology, various lexical changes, acquisition of many idioms), and French is dissimilar from other Romance languages in a number of regards (having acquired front-rounded vowels, lost many final vowels, undergone far-reaching palatalizations, lost a considerable amount of verbal agreement and nominal concord, verb-second properties [in Old French], no longer a null-subject language, and so on). Whether these two languages would qualify as sufficiently "esoteric" is not the issue; they illustrate that languages can undergo changes which consequently – but not apparently on purpose – keep outsiders from understanding them, without necessarily having the cultural teleology of intending to exclude outsiders.[15]

The opposite of esoterogeny for Thurston and Ross is "exoterogeny." "If a community has extensive ties with other communities and their emblematic language is also spoken as a contact language by members of those communities, then they will probably value their language for its use across community boundaries . . . it will be an 'exoteric' lect" (Ross 1997:238). Thurston and Ross believe that use by a wider range of speakers makes an exoteric lect subject to considerable variability, so that innovations leading to greater simplicity will be preferred. "This simplifying process Thurston calls *'exoterogeny'*: it reduces phonological and morphological irregularity or complexity, and makes the language more regular, more understandable and more learnable" (Ross 1997:239). While the notion of "exoteric" lect is useful, the claim that the use across communities will simplify it does not appear to hold up in numerous known cases. For example, Cuzco Quechua, which spread into many new regions by means of the Inca empire, maintained its complexity (with glottalized and aspirated consonants, uvular stops, complex morphology, etc.) in spite of being the lingua franca for a huge area. Other examples include Arabic, Turkic, Mongolian, Georgian (among speakers of other languages of the Caucasus), etc. Certainly there are plenty of instances where languages not involving state-level social organization also have become "exoteric" without undergoing simplification, for instance, Pama-Nyungan in Australia (Evans and McConvell 1998), Shoshone lects in the western US (W. Miller 1971).

Despite these questions raised about the testability of changes for "esoterogeny," other recent work reflects similar views. Of particular relevance are Jane Hill's (2001a) "localist vs. distributed strategies," Victor Golla's (2000) "spread vs. compact languages and language families," Ross' (1997) application

---

[15] Ross (1997:232) seems to suggest that innovations in "esoteric" languages may just be generated accidentally but then tend to be seized upon "as linguistic emblems of their local community, with the result that the language of each tiny [Pacific] society becomes quite rapidly differentiated from that of its neighbours." That is, though the innovation may take place for whatever reason, without necessarily needing the purposeful striving for "esoterism," once there, it then becomes emblematic for the community, serving to distinguish it from others. Nevertheless, the same problem holds for this view as for the one that sees the innovations taking place to satisfy the "esoterism" cultural motivation. That is, the changes will differentiate groups having undergone them from groups which have not, regardless of whether the groups "seize" on them after the fact as emblems of identity or not. This then raises the question of how the investigator could demonstrate that the society is seeking to distinguish itself from others on the basis of linguistic changes, in either view, whether these changes are seen as having taken place in order to provide emblems of difference or seen as taking place accidentally but then utilized after the fact as emblems of difference. Other societies' languages undergo similar sorts of changes which differentiate them from others, but which they do not recognize as emblems useful for excluding outsiders. In fact, multilingualism in an area can facilitate alliances beyond local language boundaries regardless of the number and kind of changes the local language may undergo.

of "social network theory," and the potential application of the notion of "community of practice" (cf. Eckert 2000).

Ross (1997) argues that speakers' attitudes can favor the spread of certain innovations and disfavor others (but see Labov 2001:191–2). If correct, this would have a major impact on whether a language diversifies into related languages or not, and this association of speakers' attitudes with innovations tends to lend support to Thurston and Ross' view that an important factor in language diversification is speakers' choices where speakers sometimes want to "separate themselves off from speakers of related lects" (Ross 1997:230). Ross uses social network theory to model changes in speech communities, including both fissure (diversification) and fusion (diffusion, borrowing, contact). For him, as cited earlier, "*language fissure* is the SCE [speech community event] that . . . occurs . . . when a subset of the links in the network undergoes a sharp reduction in density" (Ross 1997:218). This reduction of density (together with reduction in intensity and multiplexity), when sharp enough, results in division of a single community into two. The network, however, does not *cause* this reduction in density; rather, this is due to conventional factors known to be involved in communicative isolation, e.g. population growth, migration, etc. (Ross 1997:218, 222–3). For Ross, linguistic innovations in the network are socially relevant when associated with a particular group of speakers, and this can lead other speakers to "acts of identity," either adopting or rejecting the innovative feature because of its social significance. This can change the network structure. Nevertheless, as Ross (1997:240) points out, "esoterogeny and exoterogeny cannot readily be captured in a social network diagram because it is not the distribution or the spread of innovations which is significant, but the *kind* of innovation."

Recent work by Jane Hill and Victor Golla goes in a direction similar to Thurston and Ross' line of thought, bringing in more tangible factors which potentially could make the thesis testable, or at least more tangible.

Hill (2001a) generalizes from her work on Tohono O'odham (Papago) "localist" and "distributed" strategies:

In a "localist" strategy, the speaker decides, "I will select a particular kind of person as my model, and I will try to sound as much like that particular kind of person as I can." In a "distributed" strategy, the speaker decides, "I am not sure what kind of person I want to sound like. I will try to sound like a variety of different kinds of people." The speech of any single person and the patterns of variation in any community will always be the product of a combination of these two strategies. (Hill 2001a:260–1)

Hill associates each of these strategies "with a different set of ecological, socio-cultural, and biological constraints" (Hill 2001a:261). She says:

in the localist case, speakers behave as if they hold an opinion . . . "I have a rightful and primary claim on valuable and dependable local resources adequate to sustain my well-being." In the distributed case, speakers seem to have a different thought: "I have no rightful and primary claim on valuable and dependable local resources adequate to sustain my well-being. However, I might be able to add to my limited primary claims secondary claims on a sufficient range of a distributed inventory of resources to sustain my well-being . . . The way I can license my claim on resources is through speaking in a certain way. (Hill 2001a:261)

Hill shows that Tohono O'odham speakers to whom she attributes a distributed strategy, those from the drier, less reliable areas, speak dialects which incorporate aspects of other dialects, while those speakers with a localist strategy have dialect features which tend to set them off from others. She believes these different dialect features reflect who is an "insider" and thus who has rights to resources.

Golla (2000), in work upholding ideas similar to those of Thurston and Ross and of Hill, distinguishes two kinds of language communities based on geography and communicative patterns. *Spread languages* are:

language communities all or most of whose constituent dialect communities are sufficiently distant from one another geographically and socially, to make social contact sporadic and relatively unstructured. Such language communities are usually the result of the dispersal of speakers of related dialect communities across a wide territory, often by migration. (Golla 2000:60)

Examples include Inuit, Dene (Northern Athabaskan Slavey, Mountain, Bearlake, Dogrib, Hare), Sahaptin, Ojibway, etc. Spread languages often constitute chains of intelligibility. *Compact languages* are:

language communities whose constituent dialect communities are closely adjacent and share a common interaction sphere (connected by trade, intermarriage, ritual, and intergroup alliances, and hostilities). (Golla 2000:60)

"Compact language communities were common along the west coast, from Alaska to California, in the Pueblo southwest, and along the Gulf Coast from Texas to Florida" (Golla 2000:60–1), for example, the nine triblet divisions of the Achomawi on Pit River in northern California and the dialects of the Keresan pueblos of New Mexico. Golla cites Hill's "localist" strategy of closed groups whose "insider/outsider" boundaries are marked by correspondingly abrupt linguistic discontinuity (cf. Hill 2001a). "Characteristic of compact language communities are phonological and grammatical differences among dialects that focus on a salient and easily dichotomized feature" (Golla 2000:60).

In similar fashion, Golla distinguishes two kinds of language families. *Spread families* are:

those that have largely developed in the geographical and social contexts that are conducive to the development of spread languages. Dialect communities develop into language communities with mutually unintelligible linguistic patterns owing to lack of contact and the independent "drift" of their linguistic systems. Boundaries among these groups remain informal, and where contact exists multilingualism is common, even encouraged, and innovations are rapidly transmitted. This frequently results in the language-level equivalent of dialect chains, where adjacent languages share more features than more distant languages, although the time depth of their split may be the same. Such language chains are typical of Northern Athabaskan languages . . . and Sahaptian languages. (Golla 2000:62)

Examples of spread families in North America are: Eskimo–Aleut, Algic, narrow Na-Dene (Tlingit–Eyak–Athabaskan), Salishan, Cochimi–Yuman, Uto-Aztecan, Siouan, Caddoan, Muskogean, and Iroquoian. *Compact families* are:

those that have largely developed in the geographical and social contexts that are conducive to the development of compact languages. Dialect communities develop into language communities in areas where the social boundaries are rigid and stable and where close contact with neighboring groups is the norm . . . patterns of interaction between adjacent dialect communities appear to have remained stable over many generations, with steadily increasing differentiation of linguistic systems. An important factor in this process is the social advantage of maintaining distinct adaptive systems focused on the exploitation of a relatively circumscribed territory. The continuance of such small-scale social units would appear to be dependent on encouraging monolingualism. (Golla 2000:63)

Nearly all of the examples of compact language families in North America are found along the Pacific Coast; some are: Wakashan, Chimakuan, Tsimshianic, Chinookan, Coosan, Takelma-Kalapuyan, Wintuan, Maiduan, Miwok-Costanoan, Yokutsan, Shastan, Achomawi-Atsugewi, Pomoan, Salinan, and Yukian.

Like Hill (2001a) and Golla (2000), Nettle holds that "dialect is used in social assessment":

This "social-marking" theory . . . predicts . . . a tendency to extend solidarity preferentially to individuals of similar speech to oneself . . . The social-marking theory also predicts that linguistic boundaries will form around the core networks of co-operation and exchange in which people are involved in their daily lives. Where individuals have large and dispersed social networks, we should expect linguistic uniformity over a wide area. Where social networks are small and tightly self-contained, many distinct languages will ultimately evolve. (Nettle 1999a:59)

"Social dialect is thus, in essence, an honest signal of group affiliation" (Nettle 1999a:59). For Nettle, the use of "dialect" for social assignment is determined essentially by economic factors. However, the localist-distributed stances and the spread-vs.-compact languages and language families, and "esoterogeny," are not primarily about economics. Rather, they are about people's choices, their social behavior and how they restrict group membership and rights to participate in the cultural life of the group, about who gets to interact socially, participate in rituals and ceremonies, who gets to marry whom, and where they will live; they are about the whole fabric of social life. These choices influence whether languages will diversify, whether they will spread.

The notion of "communities of practice" (Eckert 2000) has not been applied directly to questions of the formation of language families and the spread of languages, but it is relevant, lending additional texture to the line of thinking discussed here. A community of practice "is an aggregate of people who come together around some enterprise." Thus united, "people come to develop and share ways of doing things, ways of talking, beliefs, values – in short practices." "A community of practice is simultaneously defined by its membership and the shared practice in which that membership engages" (Eckert 2000:35). It is common practice which determines much of linguistic behavior. Language is among the symbolic material communities use to construct their identity, the "co-construction of language and society" (Eckert 2000:44). Members of a community of practice, in their social and linguistic behavior, can choose social and linguistic traits that focus inwardly, which distinguish members from non-members of the community, as in Hill's "localist strategy," Golla's "compact languages," and Thurston and Ross' "esoteric" languages. Other, less tightly integrated communities of practice can involve some social and linguistic traits which facilitate communication beyond the group, as in Hill's "distributed strategy," Golla's "spread" languages, and Thurston and Ross' "exoteric" languages. Significantly, it is possible for individuals to be members simultaneously of more than one community of practice, bringing to and taking from each group varied social and linguistic traits. Exclusive communities of practice, those with localist strategies, compact languages, or esoteric languages, will change in ways different from those in situations where individuals can participate in a variety of communities of practice, reflecting distributed strategies, spread languages and language families, or exoterogeny. The different choices made in these different circumstances, different communities of practice, will have a strong impact on the kind of innovations which distinguish some groups and which link others.

These matters deserve special attention in the investigation of how and why languages diversify and spread.

11.5   Speculations about kinds of societies and linguistic complexity

On the other hand, there are genres of speculation which attempt to attribute typological characteristics, especially linguistic complexity or simplicity (with associated kinds of change in language), directly to the kinds of societies (or cultures) involved. The question is whether there is a causal connection between type of society and core aspects of linguistic structure, "whether there are indeed any social determinants of linguistic patterning . . . whether it is possible to suggest that certain linguistic features are more commonly associated with certain types of society or social structure than others" (Trudgill 2002:707–8). At the heart of these ideas is the too-often repeated opinion that language becomes more complex in isolated communities or in small-scale societies where most members interact with one another face to face (see, for example, Andersen 1988; Hymes 1974; Nettle 1999a; Nettle and Romaine 2000; Ross 1996, 1997; Trudgill 1989, 2002). Hymes' (1974:50) rendering of this view has been influential; he says, "the surface structures of languages spoken in small, cheek-by-jowl communities so often are markedly complex, and the surface structures of languages spoken over wide ranges less so." We must ask, does such a view have any merit? We believe the answer is, little to none. Almost none of the assumed correlations between society type and language structure has proven anything but misleading.

The view is attributed sometimes to Roman Jakobson (1929[1962]:82) who believed that "dialects which serve as vehicles of communication in large areas and gravitate towards the role of koiné tend to develop simpler systems than dialects that serve purely local purposes" (Andersen 1988:37), to which Andersen (1988:60) adds, "dialects that serve predominantly local functions are more prone to elaborate phonetic detail rules." The idea of proneness to develop complexity characterizes many of the later versions of the claims. Andersen speaks of "relatively open" and "relatively closed communities," arguing that "the greater potential for variability of usage in open communities favors a more active levelling of irregularities in these, and the lesser variability a more faithful transmission of morphological irregularity in closed communities" (Andersen 1988:61). He asserts that "the conservatism of relatively closed dialects is common knowledge" but argues that "phonetic norm elaboration" is also common in closed dialects (1988:62), including "'exorbitant' phonetic changes" (1988:73–4). He correlates "open" and "closed" dialects with "core/center and periphery," with closed or periphery dialects being characterized by "lower density networks." Trudgill (1989:227), speaking of "high- and low-contact varieties," extends Andersen's dichotomy to include different languages. He asserts that "dialects which serve a relatively wide socio-spatial function tend to have simpler systems than dialects with a more restricted function" (Trudgill 1989:228), that "in low-contact situations we know that the speed of linguistic change will typically be slow," "lack of contact favors lack of change" (Trudgill 2002:709), but also that "many of the changes that take place in this sort of situation [low-contact] are of the type that move in the opposite direction . . . complication as opposed to simplification" (Trudgill 1989:228). (On Trudgill's more recent views, see below.)

Nettle (1999a:138) also argues for "community size" as a cultural or social variable which may correlate with language structure:

If a group consists of just a few hundred people, the idiosyncrasies of one very influential individual can spread through it very easily. This is not the case if the group consists of thousands or tens of thousands of people. In general, the smaller the community, the greater the probability that a given variant that has no functional advantage at all, but is neutral or slightly disadvantageous, can replace the existing item and become the norm. (Nettle 1999a:139)

Nettle and Romaine (2000:12) add that "languages which are used only for in-group communication in small groups can afford complexity." "In small language groups innovations and new usages can quickly spread throughout a whole village." The basic idea is that in such communities, isolated or characterized by face-to-face communication where most speakers know each other, people tolerate eccentricities, and so complexity can grow and unusual linguistic traits can become part of the structure of the language. Similar views recur in the literature related to this topic.

A major flaw for this sort of thinking is the fact that there are many counterexamples, many simple but relatively isolated small languages and many large and non-isolated but complex languages. For example, looking at phonological complexity (from which some of the proponents take inspiration; see Trudgill 2002, 2004a, 2004b), we see counterexamples in numerous relatively small and isolated languages such as Rotokas, Pirahã, Hawai'ian, Māori, etc. which have extremely limited phonemic inventories. Rotokas (a "Papuan" language of Bougainville spoken by some 4,000 speakers), with only eleven segments, has only six consonants; and Pirahã (a language of the small Muran family, Brazil, spoken by only about 150 people) has only eight consonants and three vowels (see Maddieson 1984). Hawai'ian has only eight consonants. The small and isolated South Island Māori, instead of becoming more complex, reduced the already limited inventory (of eleven consonants) to ten by merging /ŋ/ with /k/: /p, t, k, ɸ, h, m, n, r, w, y/. On the other hand, there are plenty of cases of large non-isolated languages which are complex or exhibit unusual traits, some demonstrably having become even more complex over time. For example, the Quechua language spread by the Inca Empire, spoken by several millions of speakers, is very complex, with three series of stops and affricates (plain, glottalized, and aspirated), with stops and affricates at five points of articulation, including uvulars (/p, t, č, k, q/) (in some varieties six, with retroflex stops and affricates), also with very complex morphology. Zulu, by no means small (over 6,000,000 speakers) nor isolated, with thirty-five consonants, acquired an extremely elaborate system of click consonants, through contact with "Khoisan" languages. Eastern Armenian and Ossetic has added a series of glottalized stops (under influence from Caucasian languages) so that it now has an inventory of twenty-nine consonants, which include the three series, plain, aspirated, and glottalized stops and affricates, dental and alveopalatal affricates and fricatives, etc. Georgian (4,000,000 speakers), by no means isolated nor small, is complex (twenty-nine consonants), with plain, voiced, and glottalized stops and affricates, with uvular stops, and complex morphology. Arabic, with many millions of speakers, a language of civilization and empire for centuries, has the interdentals, /θ/, /ð/, and the other coronal fricatives and stops in two versions, plain and "emphatic," that is pharyngealized, plus the pharyngeal consonants (/ʕ/ and /ħ/).

In short, there is no reliable correlation between community size or isolation and linguistic complexity.[16]

Trudgill (2002, 2004a) has elaborated his earlier views of possible "relationships . . . between society type and aspects of linguistic structure" (Trudgill 2004a:305) to include several additional factors, but still revolving around "language contact versus isolation" and "community size and network structure." Specifically with regard to the size of phoneme inventories, his preliminary conclusions are:

(i) . . . where there is long-term language contact involving child-language acquisition, high degrees of language contact may lead to larger phoneme inventories, as a result of borrowing . . .

(ii) Situations involving adult language contact . . . are likely to favour medium-sized phoneme inventories . . .

(iii) Low degrees of language contact may lead to languages with small inventories, because the memory load difficulties caused by confusability and word length will not be relevant, since post-critical threshold learning is not involved. They may also just as well lead, however, to large inventories, because, equally, the memory load difficulties caused by the acquisition of large numbers of phonemes will not be relevant either.

(iv) Large community size will favour medium-sized phoneme inventories . . . which are not so small as to cause communicative difficulties as a result of a low degree of redundancy.

(v) Languages spoken in small communities can develop very small inventories since lower degrees of redundancy can be tolerated because of the ability of such communities to encourage continued adherence to norms . . .
(Trudgill 2004a:317)

Inspired by Nichols (1992:193), Trudgill holds that "large phonological inventories, then, may be the result of borrowing." But, for Trudgill, when the kind of language contact involves adult language acquisition, because of adults' imperfect learning, simplification resulting in loss of phonological contrasts may take place. Thus, he concludes: "long-term contact involving child bilingualism may produce large inventories, through borrowing, and adult language contact may produce smaller inventories through imperfect learning, pidginization [meaning three processes: reduction, admixture, simplification, but not necessarily the

---

[16] Naturally, some of this discussion depends on the definition of complexity, or how complex need a language be to be considered complex. Most who talk of complexity do not define it formally. This would be good; however, at the level of the discussion here, we believe that there would be little disagreement about the relative degrees of complexity cited in this chapter.

formation of new pidgins], and simplification" (Trudgill 2004a:314). Trudgill (2004a:318) concludes with what he believes to be truer generalizations:

(1) Isolated languages "will be more likely to have E I T H E R very small inventories O R very large ones."

(2) "Non-isolated languages spoken in larger communities will . . . tend to have medium-sized inventories."

(3) "The factors of isolation and small community size can quite simply lead to the development of U N U S U A L phonological systems . . . these systems may be either unusually small . . . or unusually large . . ."

We, like most of the commentators on the Trudgill (2004a) article (Hajek 2004; Bakker 2004; Kabak 2004; Pericliev 2004), find no support for Trudgill's claims, but they and we do find numerous counterexamples. For example, Rice (2004) finds very little variation in the phoneme inventories of the various Athabaskan languages, though they are involved in a large range of different contact situations, some with child bilingualism, others with adult learners, some in contact with languages with larger phoneme inventories, some with smaller inventories, and so on. Hajek (2004) similarly finds relatively small phonemic inventories in the New Guinea and Pacific region regardless of the kind of contact situation or isolation, of the number of speakers, or of the language family involved (not just Polynesian or Austronesian languages, but also various Papuan groups). Bakker (2004) examined numerous languages with large phoneme inventories, finding a very large range of social situations where the languages were spoken, and no tendency towards the simplifications Trudgill's claims would predict. Pericliev (2004) found a similar lack of correlation between the size of the community of speakers and size of the phonological inventories. Even Trudgill admits that "there is . . . significant counterevidence" (Trudgill 2004b:387), that his decisions were "all simplifications, and represent considerable distortions" (Trudgill 2004b:385).

There are serious problems of other sorts with Trudgill's claims. One is that language contact situations usually do not involve distinctly child bilingualism or adult learning contact, but typically can involve both adult learners and childhood acquirers together, making the speculative correlations impossible to verify in actual cases. Another is the need to specify more precisely what qualifies as "large" and "small" with respect to specific phoneme inventories.[17]

---

[17] When it comes to morphology, Trudgill sees simplification in language contact. He finds Faroese morphologically "conservative" and more complex than its continental relatives, Danish, Swedish, and Norwegian. Faroese contrasts three genders, two numbers, and three cases (some forms with an umlauted vowel difference) in adjectives against Norwegian's (Bokmål) two genders and a plural/weak form; Faroese verbs distinguish plural and singular in both present and past, plus a distinction between first person versus second/third, as opposed to Norwegian's present versus past/participle. Trudgill cites the isolation of Faroese and hypothesizes that contact has played an important role in the developments in continental Scandinavian

There is no clear correlation of the sort envisaged by Trudgill or the others mentioned in this section between relative contact or isolation, or community size, and structural complexity in language.

11.6   Conclusions

We have examined views about language diversification and spread as seen in Nettle's ecological-risk reduction hypothesis and the farming/language dispersal model. (In Chapter 10, Dixon's punctuated equilibrium, and Nichols' approach, both with implications for language diversification and spread, were evaluated). We also considered social factors in Hill's localist-vs.-distributed strategies and Golla's notion of spread-vs.-compact languages and language families. These examinations led to the following conclusions. Reduction of ecological risk is also but one of many considerations, and it can be addressed by various sorts of cross-linguistic alliances, not just within a single language community; it fails to take into account relevant social and historical facts. Its influence in determining language distribution is overstated. Agricultural dispersal is only one factor in the picture of what drives language diversification and spread; there are many cases where the distribution of languages does not fit the model's predictions – there are too many unexplained language spreads without agriculture and too many cases of linguistic diversity in spite of agriculture. As seen in Chapter 10, the dichotomy between punctuation and equilibrium appears not to be relevant linguistically. The same kinds of linguistic change take place in both situations, with both diffusion and diversification occurring in both states of equilibrium and of punctuation; punctuated equilibrium has no relevant role to play in language diversification and spread. Nichols' spread zone/accretion zone distinction (treated in Chapter 10) is also neither useful nor reliable. The spread zones are each so different from one another that nothing unites them and the concept should be abandoned. Zones of both sorts reflect arbitrarily selected chunks of geography and particular historical events. The problems with the languages chosen to represent the particular zones and the errors with regard to which are spread zones and which accretion/residual zones are so serious they skew the calculations and any conclusions based on them.

(Trudgill 2002:712). This conclusion is in the same paragraph as claims about language simplification (loss of complexity) due to the diminished language-learning abilities of adult speakers in language contact who have passed the critical (age) threshold; therefore, apparently Trudgill believes this kind of contact is behind the simpler morphology of continental Scandinavian languages. But if this were the case, why then does continental German, with a complexity very similar to Faroese in its verbal and adjectival morphology, not exhibit simplification like that of mainland Scandinavian? German was learned and used extensively by adult language learners in high language contact situations involving adult learners for centuries – far more contact than that experienced by the Scandinavian languages – without simplification.

The social behavior of speakers, though too neglected, is significant in addressing the questions of how and why languages diversify and spread. This is revealed in Hill's notion of distributed versus localist stances and Golla's concepts of spread versus compact languages and language families. These influence markedly the diversification and spread of languages and language families and must be given a very prominent role in explaining these distributions.

Briefly put, linguistic diversification and language spread appear to be the results of linguistic change mediated by social factors (speakers' choices) and contingent historical events (migration, conquest, climate change, choice to shift languages, etc.). Agriculture, physical geography, ecology, and economics, to the extent that they play a role, are also mediated by social behavior and particular historical events. It is questionable that these non-linguistic, non-social considerations take us very far towards answering the questions of how and why languages diversify and spread.

12 What can we learn about the earliest human language by comparing languages known today?

> **'Proto-World'** Conjectural protolanguage from which, according to some applications of mass comparison, all later languages have developed.
>
> (P. H. Matthews, *The concise Oxford dictionary of linguistics*. 1997:302)

12.1 Introduction

Looking back from modern and attested older languages, what can we find out or reasonably hypothesize about the earliest human language (or languages)? The origin and evolution of human language is currently a very active area of scholarship, though curiously there appear to be more hypotheses than facts. That is, in spite of some very clever recent thinking in various directions, there is little of real substance from the remote past to work with, leaving speculation to dominate.[1] Nevertheless, one area in which concrete data have been explored in language origins research is comparison of lexical and structural material from known languages. Attempts to understand something of the origin and evolution of the earliest human language are of relevance to the goals of this book because many involve very long-range classifications of the world's languages and claims about distant genetic relationship. In this chapter we deal with the lexical data which some scholars have used in attempts to reach conclusions about the earliest human language, and also less directly with some structural traits. The goal of the chapter is to determine what, if anything, can be learned about the earliest human language or languages based on comparisons of the linguistic evidence extant in modern and older attested languages. The main points are methodological; the main finding is that so much change has taken place in the interval between the earliest human language(s) and what is known from modern or attested tongues that no fruitful comparison is possible – or to put it slightly differently, because of so much change over such a long time, nothing of the original language(s) survives in modern languages in any form

---

[1] We second Janson (2002:8), that "the best I can say about these ideas is that they are difficult to disprove."

that could be usefully compared cross-linguistically to give any indication of the lexical or structural content of the original language/languages.

First, we present the reasons why lexical comparisons from across the world's languages yield no reliable results for seeking the ancestor of all languages. Next, we show why some things sometimes presented as evidence of the earliest language(s) are not reliable, in particular nursery words and onomatopoeic forms. In this context, some of the strongest of the so-called "global etymologies" (sometimes called "world etymologies" or "panglosses"; see Bender 1993b:192) which have been proposed are evaluated. We discuss the problems in the search for global etymologies by showing why these lexical sets thought by supporters to be evidence for "Proto-World" do not hold up. We conclude with speculations of our own about what the earliest language(s) may have been like structurally.

12.2   Background

Attention to "Proto-World" (also sometimes called "Proto-Human," "Proto-Sapiens," "The Mother Tongue," "proto-language," and the "roots of language") gets lots of popular attention and media coverage; it has been featured in numerous magazines and television programs (see, for example, Allman 1990). It also shows up on lots of websites, further feeding popular curiosity. For example, a search for Proto-World on Google found 18,400 hits, though the several sites for music and politics need to be eliminated from this figure. Some of these take a negative view of Proto-World, but most are positive. A perusal of these websites reveals that the topic is attractive to cranks, but also to a range of linguists, and to the media. The media are curious about claims that we might know something about what Adam and Eve spoke, and, in McWhorter's (2001:289) words, "the sympathetic coverage . . . from the media is due to their being . . . inclined towards the 'visionary mavericks battle the hidebound establishment' hook." On the other side, a number of mainstream linguists have likened published claims about Proto-World to alchemy, cold fusion, and creationism.[2]

The popular and fringe appeal does not of itself invalidate Proto-World; however, because of so much attention, it does deserve careful scrutiny. We argue here, as have several others (Bender 1993b; Hock 1993; Picard 1998; Rosenfelder 1999; Salmons 1992a, 1992b, 1997; Trask 1996:391–6; McWhorter 2001:287–303), that such a scrutiny reveals that claims about Proto-World

---

[2] There are those, of course, who see the connection between creationism and Proto-World in just the opposite way, citing linguists' claims about Proto-World as self-evident support of the truth of the biblical story of creation and Babel (see, for an example, Jackson 1999; Salmons 1997 cites others).

(based on assumed global etymologies) are bogus, and that, because they are wrong, they can teach us nothing about the origins of human language.

12.3   Methodological issues

A number of linguists have attempted to find deep genetic relationships that would link various known language families into larger "macro-families" (see Chapter 9), and some go even further, believing that it may be possible to trace all human languages back to a single original language, to "Proto-World," and so-called "global etymologies" have been presented as evidence for this "Proto-World" (see Anderson 1975; Bengtson and Ruhlen 1994a, 1994b; Ruhlen 1987a, 1994a, 1994b; and Merritt Ruhlen's homepage, http://members.aol.com/_ht_a/yahyam/page24/protoworld.htm; see also Bengtson 1991b, 1994a).[3] Most of the more remote proposed distant genetic relationships are controversial, and most of the methodological cautions of this book concerning them (see especially Chapter 7) hold to an even greater extent for Proto-World. It is acknowledged by both friend and foe alike that the principal method employed in setting up global etymologies is "mass [or multilateral] comparison" (cf. Ruhlen 1987a:258; Bengtson and Ruhlen 1997). Ruhlen (1992:178) says, "John Bengtson and I, operating in a Greenbergian tradition of multilateral comparison, have proposed some thirty etymologies connecting all the world's language families."

Aitchison (1996:172) appropriately calls this the "'lucky dip" approach: "trawling through dictionaries, and coming across superficial resemblances between words in far-flung languages." The criticisms of multilateral (mass) comparison and of the methods behind several controversial macro-families have been surveyed in this book (and they are also well known to practicing historical linguists; see for example Aitchison 1996:172–3; Callaghan 1991; Campbell 1988, 1997a, 1997b, 1998, 1999, 2004; Matisoff 1990; McMahon and McMahon 1995; Rankin 1992; Ringe 1992, 1995a, 1996, 1998, 1999; Trask 1996:376–403). The primary reason why most mainstream linguists reject the global etymologies that have been proposed is because they do not find the method reliable (see McWhorter 2001:288). Aitchison's (1996:173) summary of the problems is to the point:

Chance resemblances are easy to find among different languages if only vague likenesses among shortish words are selected . . . sounds change radically over the centuries. Words which existed so long ago are unlikely to have survived in anything like their original

---

[3] That is, while perhaps most linguists believe it is possible that there was a single original human language from which all others have developed, most further believe it is impossible on the basis of extant evidence ever to be able to show that this is the case. This means for some scholars that not only is monogenesis a possibility, so is polygenesis, but that we will never know for sure which is right.

state ... Taboo is a further problem ... the "lucky dip' approach does not make any attempt to eliminate accidental correspondences, nor does it control for phonetic probability or taboo . . . meanings tend to be reduced to fairly simple, straightforward items, with a limited number of phonetic shapes. In these circumstances, chance similarities are likely to play a worryingly high role, and this "mass comparison" method is unlikely to stand the test of time.

12.3.1 Global etymologies: the "strong" cases

There is not space to evaluate in detail each global etymology that has been proposed; however, the problems which call the whole enterprise into question are seen from the examination of a few examples. Problems with some of the proposed global etymologies considered the strongest by their proponents reveal this. In fact, the two strongest (or at least most vigorously cited in publications from supporters) have been evaluated rigorously already, *tik 'finger' (Bender 1993b; Salmons 1992a, 1992b) and *maliq'a 'to suck(le),' 'nurse,' 'breast' (Hock 1993; Hock and Joseph 1996:498–502).[4] As these and other critics show, the data (Bengtson and Ruhlen 1994a:322–3) are much weaker than they might appear, and in particular the methods employed in setting up global etymologies are unable to show that chance, sheer accident, is not a more plausible explanation than genetic relationship for what is presented as evidence for the global etymologies.

In standard etymological criteria used among languages known to be related, purely accidental lexical matchings are constrained by the demands of sound correspondences and semantic equivalence or reliable explanation of suspected semantic shifts (see Goddard 1975; Salmons 1992a). The need for such constraints is not difficult to appreciate in face of the numerous cases of striking lexical similarities among words known not to be cognates even in closely related languages, that is, words known to be only accidentally similar and not due to inheritance from the common earlier ancestor of the languages containing the similar words. Well-known examples are presented in Chapter 7.

Bengtson, Ruhlen, and others do not explain their methods explicitly (see Bengtson and Ruhlen 1997). Our attempt to understand the criteria used for

---

[4] Note that the gloss for *maliq'a may seem to vary; the explanation is that it was originally given as an "Amerind" set with the gloss 'swallow' (Greenberg 1987:261), later listed as 'swallow, throat,' and then promoted to a global etymology: Chapter 11 of Ruhlen (1994a) is entitled, "Amerind MALIQ'A 'swallow, throat' and its origin in the Old World." Bengtson and Ruhlen (1994a:308–9) give their global etymology *maliq'a the gloss 'to suck(le), nurse, breast.' Greenberg's (1987:261) original Amerind formulation of the set is one of the weakest in his book, with examples cited from only two of his eleven branches of "Amerind," with glosses of 'throat' in the "Penutian" forms cited, but one each with 'drink' and 'swallow' in the Almosan–Keresiouan cases. Ruhlen (1994a:244–5) adds other "Amerind" groups, with glosses including 'neck,' 'choke,' 'gargle,' 'drink,' 'suck,' 'throat,' 'eat,' 'nape of neck,' 'tongue,' 'chew food for baby,' 'to eat one's fill,' etc.

deciding whether some word in some language fits a particular proposed global etymology led us to the same view as Salmons (1997:5) of their principles for deciding whether something is to be considered a "cognate":

A. Ignore vowels entirely: any vowel matches any other vowel . . .

B. For consonants, roughly similar place of articulation suffices to establish cognates [though non-initial consonants are sometimes allowed drastic differences]. Minor place changes are acceptable: velars match uvulars, palatals, etc. Other features play no role whatsoever, so that oral stops correspond to nasals, etc.[5]

C. Any differences in place which parallel widely attested sound changes such as lenition are acceptable, so that any consonant can be reflected by [h] . . .

D. In semantics, any narrowing or any metaphorical extension is acceptable without further justification (such as cultural or historical arguments), so that 'dog' corresponds to 'fox, lynx, deer,' etc. and 'arm,' to 'elbow/hand, fingernail, foot, armpit, shoulder/arm,' and so forth.[6]

That the methodology of global etymology has no constraints such as those known to be necessary even in closely related languages can be seen from a single example, *kuna 'woman,' presumably considered one of the strongest cases, given to the popular press (see Allman's [1990:68] cover story in US News and World Report), and it is the main example given by Bengtson (1991a) to illustrate his whole approach. Bengtson and Ruhlen (1994a:306) list among the forms given for this supposed global etymology words of the following shapes

---

[5] MacNeilage and Davis (2000:528) appear not to have understood this factoring across languages to a lowest common phonetic denominator, so that the shape given for the proposed global etymologies is generally CVC(V), with mostly generic unmarked consonants given to represent large classes of consonants from the individual languages. Many of the sounds in constituent languages are themselves, however, not of the simple sort presented in the phonetically highly refracted form listed for the putative global etymology. Thus MacNeilage and Davis imagine in something of an ontogeny-recapitulates-philogeny way that the recurrent simple sequencing patterns for sounds that they observe in child language acquisition are matching those of Bengtson and Ruhlen's (1994a) global etymologies and thus "may have been the first stage in the evolution of speech." Clearly the canonical shapes in Bengtson and Ruhlen's refracted forms are artefacts of their procedures, not real reconstructions and not supported as such by the data upon which they are based.

[6] Similar points are made by Rosenfelder (1999). As he explains, based on the *maliq'a 'suck(le), nurse, breast' example:

Take a closer look at the list; the rules for this game are evidently quite lax. The vowels are completely ignored. The middle consonant varies from l to ly to lh to n to r to zero. The end consonant ranges from g to j to d to k to q to q' to kh to k' to X to zero. Switching around medial consonants seems to be allowed; extra consonants and syllables can appear where needed. Observe the semantic variation as well: body parts ranging from neck to nape to throat to breast to cheek; actions including swallowing, milking, drinking, chewing, and sucking. Some defenders of Ruhlen & Greenberg make much of the probability of finding such lists among given numbers of families; but notice that one can pretty much pick and choose what languages from a family to include. If Greek doesn't do it for you, try Latin; if Hebrew doesn't work, use Arabic. (Rosenfelder 1999)

from various languages: *knw, eqʷen, xuonā, teknē, wanā, gerim, grua, ben, kin, žena, günü, arnaq, chana-da, k'uwi, hun, ʔunu, huini, kuyã, ekwaʔa, hanökö,* etc.

While global etymologists do not spell out their criteria, it is apparent from the forms they cite that the target in general is a CVC(V) form where differences in the vowels among the languages compared are ignored. In this particular case, for **kuna* 'woman,' apparently the target is something like *KVN(V)*, where *"K"* represents roughly any velar-like sound generously interpreted, and *"N"* some *n*-like sound. However, the matches are not held to this target too tightly, since for the *"K"* velar-like sound, any of the following fits: *k, k', g, q, x, h, w, b, ž, ʔ, č*. For the final consonant, *"N,"* any of the following fits: *n, r, m, ã, w?, ʔ,* and Ø, among others. Even matches to *"KV"* alone seem acceptable. How difficult could it be to find words matching this broad phonetic target by accident? As for the glosses accepted which allow a form of this vague phonological shape to be selected as a match, all of the following are encountered among the forms listed in support of the 'woman' global etymology: 'wife,' 'woman,' 'lady,' 'mother,' 'female' (of any species), 'spirit of dead woman,' 'girl,' 'daughter,' 'maiden,' 'daughter-in-law,' 'small girl,' 'young woman,' 'old woman,' etc.

So, how difficult can it be to find by accident forms that fit the range of permitted sounds and meanings for **kuna* 'woman,' that is, for which we have good evidence that matches exist not because they are inherited from a single original word, but because these words come to have these configurations of sound and meaning by sheer happenstance? Answer, dead easy! The following from Spanish, to take a language at random, illustrate how easy it is (source: *Diccionario de la lengua española de la Real Academia Española*, 2001):

> *cónyuge* 'wife, spouse'
> *cuñada* 'sister-in-law'
> *china* 'girl, young woman' (and *chinita* 'Indian girl')
> *cana* 'old woman' (adjective)
> *canuda* 'old woman'
> *cañenga* 'old woman'
> *changa* 'girl'

These are just accidental matchings with the forms in the **kuna* 'woman' global etymology, since we know their history (for the most part) and it shows the forms etymologies where the meanings and sounds in question do not originally match the target of the global etymology. Thus, *cónyuge* is from Latin *con-* 'with' + *jugum* 'yoke,' where these pieces in origin have nothing to do with 'woman' nor the phonetic shape *kuna* (or better said, the template *KVN(V)*, said to go with it). Similarly, *cuñada* is from Latin *cognātus/cognāta* 'consanguineal relative' (based again on *con-* 'with' + *nātus* 'born'), and so in origin has nothing to do with the sound–meaning equation of the global etymology for 'woman.' The word *china* is a loanword into Spanish from

Quechua *čina* 'female of animals,' and thus cannot be an unbroken inheritance in Spanish from Proto-World. *Cana* is from Latin *canus/cana* 'white' (with the sense 'old' through 'grey hair'), and thus, again, this is a word with no connection originally with 'woman.' *Cañenga* and *changa* are more regional with poorly known etymologies.[7]

12.3.2   The criticisms

In a dramatic demonstration of the point that seeming fits for the various proposed global etymologies following such procedures are dead easy to find by accident, Hock (1993) shows in a comparison of Hindi and English, related Indo-European languages, that 65 percent of the items that would be identified as "cognates" by the methods of global etymology are "false friends," that is, they are similarities due to accident or borrowing from other languages. (We return to a Hindi–English comparison below.) The excessive generosity in deciding what fits phonologically and the wide and generous semantic scope allowed have frequently been criticized (see, for example, Aitchison 1996:173; Bender 1993b; Trask 1996:395).

This exercise – as in the case of the Spanish forms above – of finding various words with disparate known histories which nevertheless fit global etymologies reveals the severest criticism, namely that global etymologies cannot be

---

[7] Walter Koch (2001) offers a more extreme view – too extreme for us – in which this supposed **kuna* root is sound-symbolic in origin. He sees it as a "ding dong" root, about 30,000 years old, "related to such meanings as 'woman,' 'to give birth to,' 'knee,' i.e. 'the joint in the leg,' etc." He asserts that "Ding dong is the latest and most powerful 'sound-symbolic' scheme to evolve. It consists in translating a **visual** sensory stimulus into an **auditive** motor response."

Baxter and Manaster-Ramer (2000:176) point out Dolgopolsky's (1964a, 1986) ten classes of consonants, defined "so that consonants in the same class are more likely to change, over time, to another member of the same class than to some consonant of another class." These are pretty much what one expects generally from phonetics and knowledge of sound change generally:

1. P labial obstruents [p, b, f]
2. T dental obstruents (except hissing and hushing sibilants)
3. S [s, š, z, ž]
4. K velar and postvelar obstruents [k, g, x] and affricates such as [ts, č, dz, ǰ]
5. M [m]
6. N [n], [ɲ], and noninitial [ŋ]
7. R [r, l]
8. W [w] and initial [u]
9. J [j]
10. Ø laryngeals, zero consonant, and initial [ŋ] (pp. 175–6).

This is interesting, and it is good to have it pointed out to us, but global etymologists have never stated their own methods in such terms. Moreover, they clearly are not limiting themselves to Dolgopolsky's major consonant types. For example, there is something odd from the outset about defining classes as sets of consonants that "change . . . to another member of the same class" in 5 M with [m] as its only member. Clearly in the global etymologies, "m" appears at times to be compared with a number of other things, for example other nasals and other labials. Similarly, common sense about sound change would suggest that 9 J with [j] as its single member needs to allow also [ǰ, i, ž, palatalization of consonants, Ø] and others.

tested. "The methods of 'global etymology' remove all controls on accidental similarity" (Salmons 1997:1). Without the normal constraints of standard
methods, claims that something fits a putative global etymology are not falsifi-
able, since their fit cannot be checked against proposed sound correspondences
or constraints on semantic shift (see Salmons 1992a). Moreover, even if we
were to throw out all the forms whose history we discover does not fit, it is
always possible to generate new examples to replace them. That is, even if we
demonstrate that forms presented have histories which demonstrate that they
cannot be connected, as we did here with most of the Spanish forms that fit the
kuna 'woman' set (and Salmons 1992a did for many in the *tik* 'finger' set;
see also Hock's 1993 criticism of the forms in the *maliq'a* 'suck(le), nurse,
breast' set), this method can nevertheless just go out and dredge up more examples of the same sort, whose histories may not be so well known. Thus the
supporters' apparent allegation that "you have to take our claims seriously, we
have so many examples" (see Bender 1993b:192) is hardly compelling, given
the nearly inexhaustible source of new examples which are accidentally similar but where there are no constraints on how to restrict such accidents from
consideration.

In spite of the overwhelming evidence to the contrary, Bengtson and Ruhlen
(1994a:281) believe that "the failure of our critics to appreciate the truly minus-
cule probability of accidental similarities is the chief impediment to their understanding why all the world's languages must derive from a common origin."
The longish lists of "so many examples" at first strike the uninitiated as impressive. However, the fact is, given the looseness of the semantics and phonetics
permitted for matches, large numbers of accidentally similar forms can easily be
found. Thus, falsifiability is not possible (see Salmons 1992a:217). "It is impossible to distinguish between significant and chance resemblances" (McWhorter
2001:297). "How do we constrain our imagination and ingenuity if we lack
explicit controls?" (Bender 1993b:195).[8]

12.3.2.1 A test Bengtson and Ruhlen (1994a:290) suggest tests
which could falsify their claims, but which they believe will bear out their
belief that their findings cannot be due to a mere assembly of accidentally
similar forms, as their critics charge. The first test involves specific proposed
etymologies. In response to those who say "one can find anything in linguistic
data if one looks for it hard enough," they say:

---

[8] It might be asked, does not the case become stronger when so many words from so many languages
are piled onto a particular putative global etymology? The answer is no: an error does not become
a truth through the addition of many more errors of the same sort. "A bad methodology doesn't
become more respectable just by repeating it" (Rosenfelder 1999). This has been demonstrated
often in critiques of multilateral comparison (see Ringe 1992, 1999, for example).

"Wanting" to find something is of very little help if it is not there . . . that the Amerind family has two general words for females, T U N A 'girl' and K U N A 'woman' . . . whereas K U N A is widely attested in the Old World . . . we have found no trace of T U N A in the Old World. If it is so easy to find anything one looks for, why did we fail to find T U N A in roughly 4,500 Old World languages . . .? . . . That there is no trace of T U N A 'girl' in the Old World is because it never existed there. (Bengtson and Ruhlen 1994a:290)

We take it from their words that if we do find words from Old World languages which fit the range of glosses and phonetic forms of the T U N A material presented for Amerind, it would be conceded that it is possible to find accidentally similar forms.[9] First, the assumed Amerind set is one of Greenberg's (1987) weakest, with examples presented from only four of Greenberg's eleven branches of "Amerind" (Greenberg 1987:225, set 125). The range of phonetic forms in this set includes: *tun, tana, -tsan, šan, tsini, tu:ne, tele, suri-s, teŋ tunna, t'an'a*, etc. The glosses range over: 'son, daughter, diminutive, small, child, be small, mother.' In spite of Bengtson and Ruhlen's claim to the contrary, it is not difficult to find in non-Amerind languages words completely consistent with the words from American Indian languages presented as evidence for the putative T U N A Amerind "etymology." To wit, a superficial look at a few dictionaries turns up: Finnish *tenava* 'kid, child'; German *Tante* 'aunt'; Japanese *tyoonan* 'eldest son'; Malay *dayang* 'damsel'; Maori *teina* 'younger sister'; 'younger brother'; Tongan *ta'ahine* 'girl'; Proto-Austronesian **tina* 'mother'; Somali *dállàan* 'child'; Kannada *cina* 'small'; Tamil *tankai/tankacci* 'younger sister, female parallel cousin'; Telugu *cinnadi* 'girl'; Kurux (Dravidian) *tainā* 'to carry newly married girl out of village'; even English *son* fits.[10]

12.3.2.2 Another test   The second test, articulated in earlier versions of Bengtson and Ruhlen's work, claims it would be impossible to take their list of proposed global etymologies and produce equally impressive lists of words if the meaning is shifted one number in each case, that is, where instead of their (1) A J A 'mother, older female relative,' (2) B U (N) K A 'knee, to bend', (3) B U R 'ash, dust,' rather we should try to assemble sets similar to theirs but with (1) A J A 'knee,' (2) B U (N) K A 'ashes, (3) B U R 'nose,' and so on. In fact, Bender (1993b) took up the challenge, refined the test to make it even more difficult,[11]

---

[9] Though, of course, if such Old World cases fitting their Amerind T U N A 'girl' forms are presented, Bengtson and Ruhlen probably would just accept the T U N A case as an overlooked global etymology.

[10] As pointed out in Chapter 7, even English *daughter* (Old English *dohtor*, PIE **dhughǝter*) fits in view of such forms as *tsuh-ki* and *u-tse-kwa* in the list. Note, incidentally, the considerable overlap between this and Ruhlen's (1994a:192–206) proposed Amerind **taʔna* 'child, sibling.' Note also, incidentally, that it does not mean 'girl' in any of the languages Greenberg cited, though 'girl' is the gloss assigned to the overall set.

[11] For example, some adjacent "global etymologies" will not be too challenging in such a test unless, as Bender does, we avoid the ones with similar or overlapping glosses ((5) K A M A 'hold

and nevertheless demonstrated that such sets of similarities can be assembled easily, showing that sheer accidental similarity is at stake in much of what they present.

12.3.2.3 "Reaching down" Other methodological procedures involved in setting up global etymologies have also been heavily criticized. One of these is "reaching down" (see Chapter 7), accepting forms as evidence of Proto-World which are found only in a single language (or a single branch) of a family, though this violates Meillet's (1925:38) heuristic that evidence is needed from more than one branch and the more languages and branches represented the better (see Salmons 1992a; Trask 1996:394). For example, for any given "etymon" Bengtson and Ruhlen (1994a:306) do not present a reconstruction for Austroasiatic based on cognates from across the branches of that proposed macro-family, nor do they list cognate forms from various branches which together might suggest the possibility of a word inherited from earlier times. Instead they "reach down"; for example, they cite Nancowry *ka:n/ka:ne* 'woman' as the sole representative for all the Mon-Khmer languages, and then this form from this single language of that family is given as support for the entire larger Austroasiatic grouping, to which Mon-Khmer is said to belong. On the other hand, they do cite proto-forms sometimes, but how they do this has been criticized. They cite forms as reconstructions in proto-languages which they accept as evidence of Proto-World when often enough the putative proto-form is in fact not justified in the particular family from which it is taken – a large number of examples of this sort involve the controversial "macro-families" whose reality is disputed. Even in instances where Ruhlen (1987a, 1994a, 1994b), for example, accepts the controversial large-scale remote genetic groupings, nevertheless, frequently forms he thinks reflect Proto-World are not found in the lists of putative reconstructions for these big hypothesized families, although this does not prevent him from "reaching down" and exhibiting forms from individual languages within these large-scale schemes as though they were inherited from Proto-World.

12.3.2.4 Number needed? Another criticism is that the global etymologists do not tell us how many languages must be found to contain what they take to be a "cognate" in order for a suspected global etymology to be considered supported (Salmons 1997). As Rosenfelder (1999) points out, "the situation gets worse rather than better . . . if recently proposed superfamilies are accepted." In Ruhlen's (1987a:291–300, 377) classification, there are but

[in the hand]' and (6) KANO 'arm,' where both sets contain forms meaning, for example 'hand') and those with similar phonological shape (e.g. between (14) MANA 'to stay' and (15) MANO 'man'). Bender's test eliminates these to make it more difficult.

seventeen "phyla" in the world (though several of these have been lumped further in Ruhlen's later publications, 1994a, 1994b), plus some nine isolates (most of which are assigned to macro-families in his later writings).[12] Following Meillet's distributional principle (above), we should expect putative evidence of global etymologies to be distributed in a significant number of these phyla. Generally Bengtson and Ruhlen (1994a) do suggest examples for their global etymology sets from various "phyla," but the distribution problem if macro-macro-families are accepted is not difficult to see. In the case of the much-publicized *maliq'a* 'suck(le), nurse, breast' example (see Bengtson and Ruhlen 1994a:308–9, Rosenfelder 1999), if Nostratic is accepted, then the Afroasiatic, Indo-European, Uralic, and Dravidian forms Bengtson and Ruhlen present all represent only one big "family"; if Eurasiatic is accepted, then the Eskimo–Aleut case is included with many of the families from the Nostratic hypothesis that overlaps Eurasiatic to a significant extent, further reducing the total number. This leaves "Caucasian" and "Amerind" as the only other representatives – essentially, then, in this logic, this world etymology is represented in only three different (putative) genetic groups! Other proposed global etymologies have similar distributional problems.[13] To be convincing as a representative of "Proto-World," we would suppose that a proposed "global etymology" ought to occur in a larger number of the large macro-groupings, not just in two or three of them.

12.3.2.5 Unlikely semantics from well-studied cases   Another criticism is that in well-studied families, a more accurate look at the semantics often reveals problems for particular global etymologies (see Salmons 1992a). For example, Indo-European *deik-* is listed as evidence of the *tik* 'finger, one' global etymology; however within Indo-European languages the meanings 'finger' and 'point,' upon which Bengtson and Ruhlen focus, are clearly derived and secondary, and attested only in Latin and Sanskrit. The general meaning supported by the cognates in the other branches is 'to pronounce solemnly, to show,' with "derivatives referring to the directing of words and objects" (Watkins 2000:14; cf. Trask 1996:394). It is lack of constraints on accident and semantic latitude that "leads to such absurdities such as . . . accepting that Amerind Tikuna 'elbow' is genetically related to Latin 'to say'" (Bender 1993b:196).

---

[12] Bengtson and Ruhlen (1994a:280) compare items from "32 taxa," though they believe there are fewer macro-families than this in the world.

[13] There may be a seeming disingenuousness in Bengtson and Ruhlen's (1997:3) claim that "there are . . . several hundred such families" accepted on the basis of superficial lexical similarities, when they believe ultimately in only one super-family, Proto-World, with only a handful of phyla, and, indeed, even the most conservative linguists believe in only about 350 independent language families, not "several hundred."

12.3.2.6 Errors in data Bengtson and Ruhlen's (1994a) global etymologies, also, have been criticized for the abundance of errors in the data. For
example, Picard (1998:146) found in the nine Algonquian forms listed in their
27 "cognate" sets/global etymologies, three were attributed to the wrong language, four were given with the wrong gloss, four had errors of morphological
segmentation, three were transcribed wrongly, and all nine have some serious
problem of this sort. In general, mistakes of these sorts are found throughout
the words presented for the 27 proposed global etymologies.[14]

12.3.2.7 Short forms Still another criticism is that short forms are
common in proposed global etymologies, forms not sufficiently long to eliminate chance as a possible explanation for similarities perceived (see Chapter 7).
Ryan's (2001) 90 monosyllabic words of "Proto-language" are all of this form,
and several of Bengtson and Ruhlen's (1994a) better-known 27 proposed global
etymologies are short. Only one is longer than two syllables, *maliq'a* 'suck(le),
nurse, breast,' which has been thoroughly discredited (Hock 1993; Hock and
Joseph 1996:498–502). Most are intended to be bisyllabic (19 of the 27), though
occasional CV examples from individual languages are cited among the forms
(e.g. Korean *ka* 'dog' for their global form *kuan* 'dog'); four monosyllabic
forms of CVC shape (again with occasional CV examples cited, e.g. Proto-Yao
(w)i 'two' and Mak *wa* 'twin' in support of Proto-World *pal* 'two'); and two
are of the form CV(C), where the question of shortness is evident.

For *ku(n)* 'who?' (Bengtson and Ruhlen 1994a:303–5) we find among the
forms cited from various languages the following: *xa, ka, kí/ká, k(w)/q(w), ga,
gin, ka:na, kʷo/kʷi, ke/ki, ku/ko, hu, kua, kutte, kun, qun, kon, ken, gi, gœ, xa:,
xaj, aj, udu, i:, adi, ono, o:n(i), k'e, mik/mek, ajkia, qa-, ku-, kjei, gyis-oto,
kusu, gùsú, gigi, gunuga, kamu, o-ko-e, ku'a('), gu-, jus, kekʷ, ka-n, a:č'is,
kwanu, go:š, xaŋ, key, xan, ki:, kia, k'owa, kin, kai, karea, karo, kejaito, go:si,
kate, kia, koide, katsik, kona, gaga, kepia*, etc. Clearly it would be possible by
chance to find similar forms in language after language, since the final *-n* is
not necessary for a match, and any vowel counts, and as for the initial *k*, it
appears that a very wide range of consonants (and even absence) qualifies. As
for the range of meanings given, roughly anything vaguely interrogative (and a
bit beyond) seems to be acceptable – 'who,' 'what,' 'when,' 'which,' 'where,'
'why,' 'how,' 'how much,' 'how many,' 'interrogative particles,' 'whither,'
'whence,' 'someone,' 'either . . . or,' 'anything,' etc. In short, if anything from
i:, udu, and *aj* to *qanangun, kiš-to,* and *ekkwarijawa* meaning anything from

---

[14] Bengtson and Ruhlen (1994a:289–90) assert that it is a "specious argument" that errors in the
data invalidate the hypothesis. They assert that "rather, the cumulative weight of all the evidence
completely swamps the effects of whatever random errors may be scattered through the work."
This assertion, however, has been shown false, frequently (see for example Ringe 1992, 1996;
Picard 1998).

'who' to 'anything' can be seen as evidence in favor of this set, then it is indeed truly difficult to imagine how chance as a possible explanation for forms such as these could be denied.

The treatment of *mi(n) 'what?' (Bengtson and Ruhlen 1994a:313–15) is similar. Among the forms presented as evidence are: *kama, ma, m(j), mann, mi, mah-ma:, mi:t, ma:ta, miya, mena, -ma, maj, mo-, ma/mo, -u:, mida:, wi-/we-, amin, minh/minya, amae, mu, a:mai, m'as, mana, matswɛ, mi:š, maua, manti, mato, may, mano, muski, makaya, maap, mukat, muda, manpat, miki, muru, mba'e, mukoka, mi, muena, ampô-ny, matuni, mašika*. The glosses range across: 'if,' 'when,' 'where,' 'who,' 'which,' 'what,' 'how much,' 'what kind of,' 'sentence interrogative,' 'thing,' 'this,' 'something,' etc. Apparently to find a match by accident, one need only find some form in any language which means something vaguely interrogative or 'if,' 'something,' 'thing,' 'whether,' and has an *m*, although the *m* is not strictly required, as some forms listed lack it. Again, chance is surely a major factor behind the grouping of several of these examples.

In the case of the so often cited *tik 'finger, one,' the final *k* is not dispensable (as is the case with the final consonant in the two cases just discussed *ku(n), *mi(n)). The forms listed demonstrate that what is considered a match need have little to do with -*k*: *tsiho, dé, dèʔ, ti, tu, (s-)tˡa, tay, (tu-)diŋ, (pɨ-)tˢi*, etc. Of course it is possible that *k* could change into -*y, h, ʔ, ŋ*, or be lost in various languages. However, without historical or comparative evidence to show that this is in fact what happened in individual cases, the assumption that such changes took place gives the investigator excessive power to imagine matches where chance is just as probable, if not more so.

The failure of the methods to distinguish chance from real history as the explanation for the sets of compared words offered as global etymologies is a devastating criticism. Much work has shown that such methods are incapable of exceeding chance as the probable explanation for the forms cited: Nichols 1996a; Ringe 1992, 1999; Salmons 1992a (cf. McWhorter 2001:292–303).

12.4   Some things that are not reliable evidence

This section offers an explanation for why some things often considered evidence of older language relationships are not reliable. Nursery words and onomatopoeia are discussed here (see Chapter 7).

12.4.1   Nursery words

It has been recognized for centuries that nursery formations should be avoided in considerations of potential linguistic affinities, since typically the *mama–nana, papa–baba–tata, dada* type kin-term names share a high degree of cross-linguistic similarity which is not due to common ancestry (cf. Greenberg 1957:36). Nevertheless, such words are among the forms thought to support Proto-World (Bengtson and Ruhlen 1994a:292–3; Ruhlen 1994b:122–4). While most historical linguists accept the need to set such forms aside from evidence of genetic relationships, Ruhlen (2000b) disagrees; he presents a list of *kaka*-like forms meaning 'older male relative,' 'older brother,' 'uncle' and *aya*-like forms for 'older sister,' 'aunt,' 'grandmother,' 'mother.' We saw in Chapter 7 that these are words whose phonetic similarity is not due to inheritance from an earlier common ancestor but rather to the linguistic behavior of small children (see also Campbell 1997a:227–9). In sum, nursery words do not provide reliable support for proposals of genetic relationship. This, then, eliminates the following from Bengtson and Ruhlen's (1994a, Ruhlen 1994b) global etymologies: *mama* 'mother,' *papa* 'father,' *kaka* 'older brother,' and *aya* 'mother,' 'older female relative', four of the 27 sets.

12.4.2   Onomatopoeia

Proposed global etymologies must contend with the question of possible onomatopoeia (and of affective, expressive, or sound-symbolic forms) among the words from various languages listed (see Chapter 7). We list some of the examples from the proposed global etymologies together with an indication of why some scholars consider them to be onomatopoeia or affective forms. The doubts these raise are sufficient to warrant treating similarities seen across languages for these words with suspicion. Some of these may be less troublesome than others, though all warrant serious consideration. To the extent that onomatopoeia and affective formation are involved, the similarities seen in cross-linguistic comparisons owe their origin to later developments, not to inheritance from the original language of humanity. These cases in question include the following (from Bengtson and Ruhlen 1994a:277–336; Ruhlen 1994b:101–24).

'Breast/suck(le)/nurse' *maliq'a* (mentioned above, see Hock 1993), illustrated by examples from various languages such as: *maal-, melu-t, mellu, mekku, umlix, mik'-is, murgi, mallaqa*, etc. Similarities among these words across various languages are generally thought to be due to imitation of the noises children make when nursing, sucking. In this case it is complicated by the fact that many of the words given (see Bengtson and Ruhlen 1994a:308–9) mean 'swallow,' 'food,' 'chew,' 'eat,' 'throat,' 'neck,' and 'chest,' and thus have no particular motivation to mimic sucking/nursing noises, but, then, this only means that onomatopoeia and accidental similarities both are involved, since many of the forms compared do mean 'nurse' or 'suck' or 'breast' or 'milk.'

'Dog' *kuan*, with words compared from various languages of the form *!gwaī, gwí, kwon, ka, xʷoʔi, kawun, kwi*, etc. Some linguists believe similarities such as these are imitative of the sounds of dogs 'howling' and 'barking' and 'growling,' perhaps coupled with an affective, nursery component, since so often dogs were and are household pets with which children have affective associations. Thus, as has been pointed out (see Hock and Joseph 1996:498), "in a number of Indo-European languages, the original word for 'dog' was replaced by words with initial *ku-*, such as Sanskrit *kurkura-* . . . 'the one that snarls, growls, or barks, i.e. makes a sound [kurkur]'"; they cite as further examples English *cur*, German *Köter*, Modern Hindi *kutta:*, Tamil *kurai* 'to bark' / *kūran* 'dog', to which many more phonetically similar words from languages all over with the meaning 'dog' could be added, e.g. Finnish *koira*, Maori *kurī*, etc.

'Fly' (verb) **par*, illustrated from various languages with forms such as: *pil, far, ferfir, par, -biri, phur, aphir, bin, ʔbil, pen, pau, pal, parpal, purupuru, piropir*, etc. Many see in such words (which include in Bengtson and Ruhlen's lists also 'wing,' 'butterfly,' 'flee,' 'moth,' 'bird') both onomatopoetic and affective, sound-symbolic aspects. Such words for 'fly' and 'wing' suggest the imitation of the sounds of 'flapping,' 'fluttering,' 'flying' made by birds' wings, thus explaining (1) the similarity found among various unrelated languages, and (2) why the same language can have multiple words of this sort not inherited from reconstructible words in that language's family (compare, for example, English's: *fly, flap, flutter, flit, flicker, whoosh, whiz, zoom*, etc.).

That affective sound play is involved in some cases cited as evidence of distant relationships and of Proto-World is seen clearly by the many instances of reduplicated forms and of various phonological alternatives for the same concepts. This is especially evident cross-linguistically in words for 'butterfly' (cf. its affective folk-etymological alternative *flutterby*), examples of which Bengtson and Ruhlen (1994a:317–18) include in their global etymology for 'to fly':

'butterfly': Albanian *flutur*, Arabic (Moroccan) *fertattu*, Bunabun *piropir*, Cheyenne (Algonquian) *hevavâhkema*, Dravidian languages (Kolami *gu:ge*, Naiki *gu:ge*, Gondi *gu:ge*, Parji *gogava:la*; Tamil *pa:ppa:tti*, Malayalam *pa:ppa:tti*, Kodagu *pa:pili*, Gondi *pa:pe:*, *phábe, pipri:*, Kurux *papla:*, Estonian *liblikas*, Finnish *perhonen*, French *papillon* (< Latin *pāpillō*), Georgian *pepela*, Guarao (Warao) *guaroguaro*, Hindi *tiitri/titli*, Hungarian *lepke, pillangó*, Indonesian *kupu-kupu, rama-rama*, Italian *farfalla*, Japanese *chōchō*, Kham (so-called Khoisan) *dadábaši*, Maori *pu:rerehua, pe:pe*, Malagasy *lolo*, Mískito *pulpul, dildil*, Nahuatl *papalo:-tl*, Paya *waruwaru*, Portuguese *borboleta*, Proto-Austronesian **qaLi-baŋbaŋ*, Proto-Lezghian **pa(r)pal-*, Proto-Mayan **pehpen* (individual Mayan languages have *namnam, pelpe:m, pehpem, lem, pešpen*, etc.), Proto-Zoquean **me:meʔ* (cf. Proto-Mixe **totok*, Mixe-Zoquean family), Quechua *pilʲpintu*, Somali *balanbaalis*, Sumu *saisai*, Swedish *fjäril*, Tequistlatec *-bobolóh*, Totonac *špiʔpiʔle:ʔqa*, Ulwa (Sumu) *kublamhlamh*, Welsh *pilipala*, and so on.

'Smell/nose' **čuna/*čunga*, with words compared from various languages of the form *sun, sina, snā, čona, sányuu, sinqa, tsinyu*, etc. Such comparisons suggest to many linguists the imitation of the sounds of 'sniffing,' 'snuffling,' and 'smelling,' which in many languages have affective and nursery-word connections from the runny noses associated with children and their numerous childhood illnesses. (The affective associations are seen in English by such phonaesthetic forms as the following, most of which do not have regular etymologies in English: *sneer, sneeze, sniff, sniffle, snivel, snot, snort, snuff, snuffle*.)

'Water' **aq'wa* (with forms listed from around the world such as *akwa, okho, gugu, k'a,* etc.). The similarity of sound suggests to many the imitation of the sound of swallowing water, a nursery form, or of the gurgling of running water.[15]

Taboo. One of Bengtson and Ruhlen's (1994a:319–20) putative global etymologies is **puti* 'vulva,' but it strains credibility to imagine that such a form could be preserved in recognizable form in many languages since the beginning of human language. A word with this meaning does not reconstruct to the proto-languages in many known language families. The often taboo nature of this term which leads to the name being suppressed or replaced by euphemisms is by no means limited to delicate Westernized cultures. It is difficult to reconstruct this word in most proto-languages simply because the cognates have been lost or changed radically so frequently for reasons of taboo and euphemism, in addition to other normal processes of linguistic change.

12.5 The futility of modern lexical comparisons as evidence of the first human language(s)

The central question addressed here is, can lexical comparisons across known languages offer any insight into Proto-World or the origin of human language(s)? Lexical comparisons have seldom been considered convincing proof of genetic relationship without additional support from other criteria, e.g. sound correspondences or shared patterned irregularities in morphological elements (see Chapter 7). A bit of reflection is sufficient to demonstrate why this would be even more the case in considerations of possible global etymologies, why it is futile to rely on similarities among words assumed to be inherited as cognates from "Proto-World." As mentioned in Chapter 7, we need not accept glottochronology to see lessons about lexical replacement over time. According to glottochronology, after about 14,000 years, nearly all of a language's basic vocabulary from the list of 100 core vocabulary items will have been replaced, meaning if we were to compare two related languages which happened to split

---

[15] Many of Ryan's (2001) proposed forms are onomatopoetic, e.g. *xho* 'frog, squat, rest, croak, shallow, pouch, flat, pan'; *fho* 'wolf, predator, wail, wind, be puffing, (hunting) pack, surround'; etc. These, however, have not been taken as seriously as Bengtson and Ruhlen's proposals, criticized though they have been.

up before, say, 15,000 years ago, it is unlikely, according to the method, that we would find any recognizable cognates. Nichols (1998b:128) points out that, according to the method, "after 6,000 years of separation, two languages are expected to exhibit only 7% shared cognates; and 7% represents the lowest number of resemblant items that can safely be considered distinct from chance" (see Chapter 7). It matters not whether we think of 14,000 or 6,000 years, since in the case of Proto-World the lexical comparisons made must expect cognate vocabulary items to have survived in modern languages unreplaced and in recognizable form for over many tens of thousands of years – extremely unlikely given the amount of normal lexical replacement and phonological change that takes place in this length of time.[16]

We maintain that given the extremely long time since the origin of human language, absolutely all lexical items from that period have been replaced or changed beyond recognition in all languages. A number of scholars have made the same point, about so much change over such a long time leaving no residue in modern languages or leaving whatever survivals could be imagined too garbled through the regular workings of linguistic changes to be recognizable. For example, in Trask's (1996:392) words, if Proto-World ever existed, there has been "more than enough time for the ordinary processes of lexical replacement and phonological change to obliterate all traces of the first language in every daughter, many times over." McWhorter (2001:292) asks, "given how thoroughly all languages are constantly transforming themselves, why should we expect even a single form from the original language to survive? . . . That not a single form of Proto-World would survive is precisely what we *would* expect." (See also Hock 1993:218; Petrich www.webcom.com/petrich/writings/NostraticRefs.txt.)

The extent of this problem can be appreciated from real data from languages known to be related. Consider the comparisons of English and Hindi words on Swadesh's 100-word list (see, e.g., Campbell 2004:201–2 for the list).[17] We mark the forms with the following codes:[18]

---

[16] Moreover, given that languages have some vocabulary similarities due to chance, any word that did manage to persist unreplaced since the dawn of human language so many long millennia ago could not be reliably distinguished from sheer accidental similarities. That is, given the extremely small number of such putative survivals, it would be impossible to determine whether they are due to accidental similarity or to inheritance from the very distant past.

[17] Baxter and Manaster-Ramer (2000) also compare English and Hindi vocabulary, but their purpose is different from ours. They argue that it is possible to detect the genetic relationship between English and Hindi based on modern data; they compare Hindi and English in a list of 33 "especially basic word-meanings" (2000:174) utilizing probabilistic techniques. Our point is, rather, how little recognizable cognate material remains in these two languages known to be related and how it fares on the methods of global etymology when compared with unrelated languages.

[18] We do not have access to Hindi etymological materials, and therefore make judgments about cognacy based on limited knowledge of Indo-European and Sanskrit; we may have missed some true cognates or perhaps misassigned a form as a cognate which is only accidentally similar; we believe, however, not many such errors occur here.

+: true cognate which would be recognized by the methods utilized by global etymologists

+?: true cognate which might be accepted by global etymologists, though it is by no means obvious

−: non-cognate form which would erroneously be accepted by the methods (false positive)

−?: non-cognate form which perhaps would be accepted by the methods, though it should not be (false positive)

MISS: true cognates which would be missed by the methods of global etymology (false negative)

MISS?:   true cognates which very likely would be missed by the methods, though perhaps not (false negative)

In addition, the equivalents from Maori (an Austronesian language) are compared to the English and Hindi ones; Maori is not thought by any reliable linguist to be related to these Indo-European languages (except for a few who might see a link at the Proto-World level). Here, we code English-Maori similarities with the same symbols, *-EM* for cases which would be accepted by the method, though they are not cognates, and *-EM?* for cases that perhaps would be accepted, though they are weaker. For Hindi–Maori similarities, we use *-HM* for those the method would accept, and *-HM?* for those it might accept.[19]

The ancestor of English and Hindi did not begin to diversify into separate languages until some 5,000 or 6,000 years ago. Thus in Hindi and English, languages known to be related, we find only some five clear cognates on the 100-word list (those marked <+>, 8, 12, 72, 74, 100), only some five more by generous criteria (marked <+?>, 36, 41, 43, 95, 97), several of which would only be chosen by someone utilizing liberal notions of phonetic similarity. If the impact on the vocabulary of clearly related languages is so great after only a few millennia, surely there is no hope for comparisons at the level of Proto-World, comparisons in which the languages involved are assumed to have separated from one another some 100,000 years ago or more by most reckonings (see below). These English–Hindi comparisons – with only ten cases selected by the method (those marked <+> or <+?>) – fare no better, in fact worse, than the English–Maori comparisons (with twelve cases accepted, marked <-*EM*>, 7, 10, 13, 16, 29, 32, 34, 37, 65, 73, 86, 95; ignoring for now the additional ten cases which would perhaps be accepted by the method, marked <-*EM?*>, 4, 5, 12, 14, 27, 31, 42, 46, 49, 75) and than the Hindi–Maori comparisons (with ten cases, marked <-*HM*>, 21, 46, 55, 56, 61, 62, 77, 82, 88, 95; not to mention the

[19] We thank Miriam Butt, Stephen Fennell, Mate Kapovic, David Nash, Roger Lass, Robert Rankin, and Larry Trask for helpful comments and information regarding the Hindi forms and their history.

Table 12.1 *Comparison of English, Hindi, and Maori forms*

English	Hindi	Maori
1 I	maĩ (but cf. *me*)	ahau
2 you	a:p (polite), tum, tu: (informal)	koe (singular), ko:rua (two), koutou (several)
MISS 3 we	ham (cf. Sanskrit *vayam* 'we')	ma:ua (exclusive dual), ta:ua (inclusive dual) ma:tou (exclusive several), ta:tou (inclusive several)
4 this	yah	*-EM?* te:nei
5 that	vah, voh	*-EM?* te:ra: (that away), te:na: (that near)
6 what	kya: (certainly not clear from modern English [wət] alone)	*-HM?* he aha?
7 who	kaun (certainly not clear from modern English [hu] alone)	*-EM* wai
+8 not	nahĩ	ka:hore, ka:o
9 all	sab	katoa
10 many	bahut	*-EM* maha
MISS 11 one	e:k	tahi
+12 two	do:	*-EM?* rua
−? 13 big	baṛa:	*-EM* pi:ki, nui
−? 14 long	lamba:	*-EM?* roa
15 small	choṭa:	iti
16 woman	stri:, aurat	*-EM* wa:hine
17 man	a:dmi:, puruṣ	ta:ne
18 person	vyakti:, log, insan	tangata
19 fish	machli:	ika
20 bird	pakśi:	manu
21 dog	kutta:	*-HM* kuri: (cf. English *cur*)
22 louse	jū:	*-HM?* kutu
23 tree	pe:ṛ	ra:kau (cf. *-EM* to:tara 'tree' [*Podocarpus totara*])
24 seed	bi:j	*-HM?* pua
25 leaf	patta:	wha:rangi
26 root	mu:l	pakiaka (cf. rauruhe 'fern root')
27 bark	chha:l(f.)/kha:l	*-EM?* pa:pa:kiri, kiripaka, kiri, hiako
29 flesh	mã:s	*-EM* mi:ti (English loan)

(Note if 'meat' could be substituted, one gets a <*-EH*> for the English–Hindi comparison)

30 blood	xu:n, lahu, rekt	toto
31 bone	haḍḍi:	*-EM?* poroiwi, wheua, iwi
MISS 32 egg	anḍa:[a]	*-EM* he:ki, hua manu
33 grease	charbi/chikna:'i	hinu
MISS 34 horn	sĩ:g	*-EM* haona, maire, pi:hi
35 tail	dum/pū:chh	*-EM* te:ra (English loan), waero, whiore
+?36 feather	par	piki
37 hair	ba:l	*-EM* huruhuru

Table 12.1 (*cont.*)

English	Hindi	Maori
38 head	sir	ma:tenga
39 ear	kan	taringa
MISS? 40 eye	ã:kh	*-HM?* kanohi
+?41 nose	na:k	ihu
−42 mouth	mūh	*-EM?* ma:ngai
+?43 tooth	dã:t	niho
MISS 44 tongue	ji:bh, zaba:n[b]	arero
45 claw	chã:gul/na:xun/pã:jah	maikuku
MISS? 46 foot	pã:v, pair	*-EM?/-HM* pu:, waewae, take
−?47 knee	ghutna	turi, pona
−48 hand	ha:th	ringa
−?49 belly	pe:t	*-EM?* puku, *-HM?* ho:para
50 neck	gardan	kaki:
51 breast	chha:ti:	uma, poho
52 heart	dil[c]	nga:kau
53 liver	jigar/kaleyja	ate
54 drink	pi:-	inu, unu
55 eat	kha:-	*-HM* kai
56 bite	ka:t-	*-HM* kakati, ngau
57 see	de:kh-	kite
58 hear	sun-	rongo
MISS 59 know	ja:n- (certainly not clear from modern English [nou] alone)	mo:hio
60 sleep	so:-	moe
61 die	mar-	*-HM* mate
62 kill	ma:r-/ma:r da:l-na:	*-HM* whakamate, -mate
63 swim	tair-	kaukau
64 fly	ur-	rere, tere
65 walk	chal- 'walk,' ja:- 'walk, go'	*-EM* wa:ke (English loan), haere
66 come	a:-	heke, kuhu
−67 lie	let-	takoto
68 sit	baith-	noho
69 stand	khara + ho- 'standing'	tu:, tu:tu:
70 give	de:-	*-HM?* tapae
71 say	kah-	*-HM?* ko:rero
+72 sun	su:raj, su:rya	*-HM?* ra:
73 moon	chã:d	*-EM* marama
+74 star	ta:r, sita:ra:[d]	whetu:
75 water	pa:ni:	*EM?* wai
76 rain	ba:riś	ua
77 stone	patthar	*-HM* po:hatu, ko:hatu
78 sand	ba:lu	onepu:
79 earth	zami:n, prithvi:, mitti	oneone, paru
80 cloud	ba:dal	kapua, ao
81 smoke	dhuã:[e]	paoa

(*cont.*)

Table 12.1 (*cont.*)

English	Hindi	Maori
82 fire	a:g	-*HM* ahi, -? ka:pura
83 ash	ra:kh	-*HM?* pungarehu
84 burn	jal-	-*HM?* ka:, ngiha, tahu, wera
−85 path	pagdaṇḍi:, pa:th	huanui
86 mountain	paha:r̥	-*EM* maunga
87 red	la:l	-*HM?* whero
−?88 green	hara:	-*EM* kiri:ni (English loan), -*HM* karera, ka:riki
89 yellow	pi:la:	-*HM?* Punga, ko:whai
90 white	safe:d	ma:, tea
91 black	ka:la:	pango, mangu
92 night	ra:t	po:
93 hot	garm (gerem)	-*HM?* wera (cf. *warm*)
94 cold	thaṇḍa:	makariri
+?95 full	pu:ra:	-*EM* /-*HM* puhapuha
96 good	accha:	pai, tika
+?97 new	naya:	ho:u
98 round	go:l	porotaka
99 dry	su:kha:	maroke
+100 name	na:m	ingoa

[a] Baxter and Manaster-Ramer (2000:177) identify this set as true cognates, though it is by no means obvious. The Proto-Indo-European form from which English *egg* comes is *əyo-, from *ōwyo-, not an obvious source for the Hindi form, but possible.

[b] Hindi *ji:bh* comes from Sanskrit *jihva:*, from Proto-Indo-European *dn̥ghū, from whence English *tongue*.

[c] Hindi has *her̥day* 'heart,' which is cognate, but *dil* is the common form in use.

[d] Hindi *ta:r* may be cognate with *star*, though it is not certain; but *sita:ra:* is a Persian loanword, not a direct cognate.

[e] The Hindi form is cognate with English *fume*, but this is a loanword in English.

additional thirteen cases possible by a more liberal application of the method: 6, 22, 24, 40, 49, 70, 71, 72, 83, 84, 87, 89, 93). Even if judgments were to vary somewhat with respect to individual items – say a disagreement between whether <+> or <+?> is assigned –, the differences between English–Hindi (with only five securely recognized true cognates, ten by very liberal judgments) on the one hand and between Maori and the other two languages on the other (English–Maori with twelve matchings that would clearly be accepted by the method and ten more which could be, Hindi–Maori with ten clear matchings and thirteen more possible ones) are so striking that a shift in judgment about a few items would not greatly alter the outcome: Maori looks more similar, more related by this method, to English and to Hindi to which it is not related than the related Indo-European languages English and Hindi do to one another.

This being the case, clearly there is something alarmingly wrong with this method. This comparison demonstrates that it does not perform better on related languages than on unrelated ones and therefore sheer accident must be the explanation for many of the matchings accepted as global etymologies.

A more thorough study taking into account what is known of Indo-European linguistics would reveal more cognates between English and Hindi, but it would also expose additional similar forms known not to be cognates.[20] As Hock (1993) pointed out so effectively, often these true cognates are changed so much by sound changes that they would not be recognized by the sort of search for super-ficial similarities followed by global etymologists. For example, the following English–Hindi cognates are not phonetically similar enough to be selected by such methods, but are clearly seen as cognates when the known sound changes are brought into the picture, which here can be seen when older versions preserved in Sanskrit (and Old English) are juxtaposed which show the later changes that have taken place (from Hock 1993:218) (seen also in Chapter 7): *horn* : *sīg* (< Sanskrit *śṛṅga-* 'horn'), *sister* : *bahan* (< Sanskrit *svasar*, cf. Old English *sweostor*), *be* : *ho:-* (< Sanskrit *bhavati* < Proto-Indo-European **bhu:*), *we* : *ham* (< Sanskrit *vayam*), etc. Hock (1993) and Hock and Joseph (1996:469, 491–3) list several other examples. Hock and Joseph (1996:492–3) report that in an open-ended search of Modern Hindi and English dictionaries, some 55 genuine cognates turn up which are still similar enough phonetically and semantically to appear related, plus some 30 other cognates so altered by linguistic change that they would probably not be recognizable without knowledge of their historical connections. This is complicated, however, by (1) the more than 45 loanwords in Hindi from Sanskrit which have English cognates, but are not direct inheritances in Hindi and so do not count; (2) the 5 loans from Persian into Hindi; (3) the 10 or more loans from other sources; and (4) in particular by the 60 cases of phonetically and semantically simi-lar forms known from their history to be purely accidentally similar. As Hock and Joseph (1996:493) show, no matter how the genuine cognates are balanced against accidental similarities and loans, there is less than a 50:50 chance that

---

[20] For example, if we do not rely strictly on the forms that appear on the Swadesh list, but on what we know from other facts about the history of English and of Hindi, we could extend the list of cognates somewhat, for example:

    1 I / maĩ (cf. *me*)
    61 die / mar- (cf. *murder*)
    69 stand / khaṛa 'standing' (cf. Hindi *tha:* 'was,' the true cognate of English *stand*)
    93 hot / garm (cf. *warm*)

However, historical facts such as these are not known in the vast majority of comparisons undertaken in attempts to establish global etymologies, and so these forms could not legitimately be used to increase the apparent similarity between English and Hindi for this test. Also, when known historical facts are taken into account, some cases that might have seemed likely drop out, for example, Hindi *hath* : English *hand*, when we see that Hindi comes from Sanskrit *hásta*, cf. Hittite *kessar* < Proto-Indo-European **ghesor*.

similarities that would be selected by the method used to identify global etymologies would select genuine cognates.

The argument of too much garbling having taken place since Proto-World for
anything to survive or to be recognizable if it had survived depends in part on
the date assigned to Proto-World. Clearly if human language is 100,000 (coeval
with anatomically modern humans) or 200,000 years old, or even older, as some
claim (up to several million years for some), then the amount of replacement and
garbling are surely far too much to imagine the survival of anything like a recognizable cognate. There is, however, an interesting twist on views of the amount
of time involved since Proto-World. Researchers of the Santa Fe Institute in
the project spearheaded by Murray Gell-Mann reason in reverse. Since they
believe that real evidence of Proto-World survives in today's languages, they
argue that the date of human language must be much later than commonly
thought in order to accommodate these assumed linguistic survivals:

> Although the evidence is still not copious, there are serious indications that all existing
> human languages are descended from a single ancestor, "proto-World," which would
> have been spoken some tens of thousands of years ago. (It seems that an age of one or
> two hundred thousand years can be ruled out: there would not be any significant amount
> of evidence remaining.) A number of words of this proto-language may well have
> been identified. (2000, www.santafe.edu/sfi/organization/annualReport/00/activities/
> evolution.html.)

Bengtson and Ruhlen (1997:4, 57) suggest that the date involved is not so early,
rather that "the origin of modern linguistic diversity is to be traced only to
the advent of *behaviorally*-modern humans, who appear in the archaeological
record between 50,000 and 40,000 years ago." They point to the crude artifacts
before this date contrasted with the refined ones after it and correlate this with
the "development of fully modern human languages." They ask, might not
linguists "be able to perceive similarities going back 40,000 years?"

The answer is almost certainly "no" (as seen in the English–Hindi, English–
Maori, and Hindi–Maori comparisons). In any case, this dating is certainly
too recent. Australian aboriginal peoples almost certainly reached Australia
by 40,000 years ago. This means that human language must be at least as
old as the arrival of the first Australians in Australia, since no one imagines
they arrived first and then developed language subsequently. This probably
took place considerably before the rock painting, venus and animal figurines,
and burial rites of the European Upper Paleolithic, from c.35,000 years ago
(mentioned in the Santa Fe Institute's report) sometimes associated with early
human language. Even if human language were as young as 40,000 years, as
they suppose, it is clear that this length of time too would be sufficient to produce
the same result, so much lexical replacement and linguistic change that nothing

reliable could be made from a lexical comparison across known languages. The extent of the English–Hindi differences (and the inability of the method to distinguish this true relationship from false ones in the Maori comparisons) after only a fraction of that time, some 5,000 years, should be sobering for anyone who expects recognizable lexical survivals some 40,000 years or more further into the past.

12.6   Structural speculations

What if instead of looking for lexical survivals we investigated structural traits? What would the structure of "Proto-World" ("proto-language") look like? Can we get an idea looking back from structural traits of modern languages? Would "Proto-World" be simple or complex? Both views – simple and complex – have been favored, though the view of simple-to-complex has predominated. Another line of thought holds that whatever in today's language has utilitarian value or is typologically motivated and widely distributed across language families would probably also have characterized early human language. We consider each, briefly, beginning with the last.

12.6.1   Functional–typological accounts

To illustrate this sort of argument let us begin with the claim that Proto-World may have had SOV word order (cf. Newmeyer 2000). One reason for suspecting this state of affairs for the original human language has to do with the claim that changes from OV > VO are more common and natural than VO > OV. A more extreme form of the claim is that languages can only acquire SOV order through language contact/borrowing, that SOV does not arise through internal developments (see Faarlund 1990:84; Tai 1976). However, this claim is known to be incorrect (see Campbell, Bubenik, and Saxon 1988; Harris and Campbell 1995:405). While borrowing is a frequent path for the development of new SOV languages, there are other pathways. Still OV > VO is a more frequent change than VO > OV. Another reason is that "SOV order predominates among the world's languages today" (Newmeyer 2000:372). Nevertheless, it is necessary to consider the following facts: (1) Some individual languages have shifted their word order thoroughly even more than once, meaning it is difficult to project their histories from their current state of affairs. (2) There are strong functional–typological motivations for why some languages will prefer SOV over the other logically possible word orders (see Song 2001), meaning that regardless of the word order they started out with, they may have changed to SOV for good reasons. (3) The number of logically possible orders available is very small (only two, OV or VO, in some interpretations), constrained further by the typological tendencies mentioned. Taken together, these considerations make it clear that arguments about the word order of Proto-World based on the word-order traits of today's (and attested) languages will be inconclusive at best. That is, from what we know of possible word-order changes and typological motivation, and given the time depth, human language could have started with any word order and we could easily get to the distribution of word orders in the world's languages that we see today.

A more complicated example of this sort comes from Johanna Nichols' proposed "stable features" (Chapter 10; cf. Nichols 1995b:339, 1998b:143–4). Some have speculated that Proto-World would have been characterized by these stable traits, either because they think that these traits must represent retentions in modern languages, or because, given their stability and utility in languages, languages of the remote past as now would tend to have such traits, even if those known today do not always reflect direct survivals. This does not represent Nichols' own view directly; she rather concludes that "nongenealogical comparison [among these "stable" traits] can tell us a good deal about when and where modern language arose and about the proximate and ultimate major geographical contributors to large populations of languages" (Nichols 1998b:165). Nevertheless, there is an implication in her "nongenealogical comparison" that many of these will be traits of early human language, in Africa, and after it spread, these traits tended to persist with subsequent change delivering the geographical distributions of the traits across the world's languages. A serious problem with any version which would relate the proposed stable traits to Proto-World is that there is nothing particularly stable about most of these putatively stable features, as shown in Chapter 10.

For example, the inclusive vs. exclusive first-person pronoun contrast is not stable, but often develops or is lost rapidly and with ease.

Connected with the problem of lack of stability for these features is the problem of how these traits are distributed in Nichols' sample (see Nichols' 1992:28–33 and 1998b scatter-chart maps for distribution of "stable" features). For example, as seen in Chapter 10, numeral classifiers, a putatively stable trait, is underrepresented and misassigned in numerous languages in Nichols' sample. Clearly if these traits turn out not to be stable, as we argue, then the speculation that they might provide some insight into the structural contents of early human language is without foundation. Moreover, even if any did prove stable in Nichols' sense (though we believe the evidence is against this), it could still well be the case that the modern distribution of these traits reflects changes much later in time, recent acquisitions or losses of the traits, much after the advent of Proto-World. Indeed, there is historical linguistic documentation to this end for many of these traits in numerous languages (e.g. changes to ergativity, development of inclusive/exclusive contrasts, of numeral classifiers, etc.; see Chapter 10).

12.6.2   Simple-to-complex

Views common in the early nineteenth century and resurrected in a different guise in grammaticalization see language as formerly rather simple, isolating, analytic in structure, made more complex through time as morphosyntactic elements were created through the grammaticalization of independent lexical items as grammatical markers. Heine and Kuteva (2002:394) do not insist overtly on the simple-to-complex trajectory in language evolution, but do argue on the basis of "grammaticalization theory" for a concrete-to-abstract direction in language evolution and believe that "at the earliest conceivable stage human language(s) might have lacked grammatical forms such as case inflections, agreement, voice markers, etc., so that there may have existed only two types of linguistic entities: one denoting thing-like, time-stable entities (i.e. nouns), and another one for non-time-stable concepts such as events (i.e. verbs)" – that is, it seems, indeed, that they favor a view of simple-to-complex via grammaticalization, after all.

While it is reasonable to suspect that human language may have begun as something less complex that evolved to something more elaborate, it is not a necessary assumption, as observed in the complex-to-simple view (below). Speculation along this line sometimes reasons that anything not common in today's languages, or not needed for effective communication, would not yet have emerged in early human language. Thus, for example, it has been supposed that Proto-World would have lacked morphophonemic alternations, tones, vowel nasalization, clicks and various other complex sounds, and affixes (see Comrie 1992); it is supposed that it would have had no tense markers, no aspect markers, definitely no evidential markers, no future markers; it would probably have had only main clauses, or conjunction/subordination only by juxtaposition (where parataxis and hypotaxis would be difficult to distinguish); it would have had no overt form of the copula; etc. While there is nothing unreasonable about any of this as a possibility, there is no compelling reason why it should have to have been the case. For example, for those who believe human emotion played a strong role in the emergence of language, perhaps early tonal contrasts would not seem unlikely, if they evolved from emotion-laden intonational differences, known pathways of tonogenesis notwithstanding. Evidential markers, for example visible vs. non-visible, could be extremely useful to a hunting society. And so it goes; the dialectic of simplicity for ease of production makes a good story, but more complexity for utilitarian purposes also does not sound unreasonable. In the end we shall never know! Would a very simple Proto-World have been mangled beyond recognition by massive later accretions and changes, or would a structurally more elaborate language in its early stages have been distorted far beyond recognition because of loss, replacement, and normal analogical and phonological change? Or both? Either way, too much change has taken place since the origins of human language ever to know where the truth may have lain.

12.7   Speculations about society and complexity

We have seen opinions that Proto-World would have been structurally simple, and that early stages of human language or languages may have been complex in structure has also been alleged by some. This latter view takes encouragement from the too-often repeated opinion that language becomes more complex in isolated communities or in small-scale societies where most members interact with one another face to face (discussed in Chapter 11; see Andersen 1988; Hymes 1974; Nettle 1999; Nettle and Romaine 2000; Ross 1996, 1997; Trudgill 1989). As argued in Chapter 11, these suspected correlations between language complexity and types of societies or communities are sheer speculation with no real support.

12.8   What of the structure of the earliest human language(s)?

Clearly, as seen here, there is good reason to be skeptical about many of the more specific claims about structural properties of "Proto-World." So, is there anything we can know or reasonably infer about the nature of the earliest human language(s), looking back from modern and attested older languages? We believe the answer is "yes," but a qualified "yes," limited in terms of both logic and content in ways language evolution enthusiasts may not find exciting. Both have to do with the design features of human languages. The argument is that the earliest human language will have exhibited the traits known to be design features of human language and this fact gives us some clues to its nature.

The logical limitation has to do with definitions or boundaries, more specifically with the problem of emergence in evolution. Uniformitarianism, that fundamental principle of biological, geological, and linguistic sciences, holds for linguistics that things about language that are possible today were not impossible in the past and that things impossible today were not possible in the past. This means that whatever is diagnostic of human languages today would also have been properties of the earliest human language(s) and that the earliest language(s) would not be characterized by either the presence of things not known from known languages or by the absence of things known to be characteristic of known languages. So, logically, the earliest language(s) must have exhibited the design features known today to be characteristic of all human language. However, uniformitarianism means we cannot address the emergence problem. That is, it is generally assumed that there was some non-language communication system (perhaps like other primates' call and display systems) before language, which did not have all the design features of human language but which evolved so that it emerged, as new biological species emerge, crossing the line from non-language to language. However likely such emergence is, by the uniformitarian principle the point of inquiry is cut off as we go back in time at the point where any form of communication ceases to have the requisite design features known from today's languages. Thus, while we can speculate about the nature of the earliest human language, looking back from what is known of known languages, we cannot go beyond the logical boundary defined by uniformitarianism without losing empirical constraints and being left in the realm of sheer speculation. We can assume that the earliest language(s) did meet the design feature requirements of human language, but this is in a sense a definitional demarcation which says anything else is not human language, which cuts off any access before emergence took place. This leaves unaddressed the question most fascinating to many, of how human language originated and evolved – emerged – from something that was not (yet) human language.

In terms of content, then, accepting the uniformitarian definition, that anything lacking the design features of human language is not human language, imposes the limitation that the earliest human language that qualifies as such will not have been different in design features from languages known in modern times. Let us look at some of the design features that have been proposed (see Hockett 1960) and then consider what they might mean for the structure of the earliest language(s):

> Duality of patterning (double articulation) (recombination of sounds in association with meaning to allow an open-ended number of linguistic signs)
>
> Grammar (fixed or preferred sequences of linguistic elements)
>
> Open-ended word classes (probably at least noun or noun-like and verb or verb-like categories)
>
> Verbal channel (with consonant or consonant-like and vowel or vowel-like segments)
>
> Discourse function of categories (e.g. subject vs. object, agent vs. patient, predicate, etc.)
>
> Multimodality (statements, questions, commands, negation; narrative, conversation)
>
> Synonymy (rephrasability)
>
> Recursion (clauses embedded in other clauses)
>
> Productivity (ability to produce utterly new utterances)
>
> Pantopicality (unlimited by context or topic)
>
> Displacement (reference to the imperceptible things, not in the here and now)
>
> Metalanguage (ability to talk about talking)
>
> Prevarication (verbal deception)

This, then, constitutes our guess as to what "Proto-World" must have been like: it must have had all these design features. However, since these features are rather broad, they do not constrain the form of the earliest human language(s) very much with respect to specific structural traits. They do not help us select the most likely earliest structures from among the variants/parameters known in human languages today. For example, from the design feature of a verbal channel with consonants and vowels, we may infer that it is highly likely that the earliest human language(s) had consonants and vowels in their structural inventory, but whether they had simple or complex phonemic inventories is not known from this.[21] In the design trait of multimodality, presumably we can infer that the earliest language had means for forming questions, but whether this was with intonation, question particles, inversion of elements or something else, we cannot know. In the discourse function of categories, presumably the earliest language had means for hearers to distinguish agents from patients, but we cannot know whether this may have involved ergative–absolutive or nominative–accusative or active–stative alignment, whether it involved word order, case marking, or cross-referencing, or context and semantic clues. In short, the design features give us some ideas of the nature of the first language(s), but nothing specific, and even relying on them for our guesses about the nature of early language is strained, since by definition, anything not (yet) fitting these conditions is eliminated from consideration. Surely for language evolution, it is precisely those pre-language traits and elements which led to language(s) with all these design features which are most interesting, but about which we can know next to nothing.

12.9   Conclusions

So, what can we find out or reasonably hypothesize about the earliest human language (or languages) from looking back from evidence in modern and attested older languages? Answer: very little. That is, we can speculate a lot, perhaps even reasonably in some cases, but we can "know" extremely little. What can we find out from lexical comparisons? Answer: essentially nothing, though we can learn something of methodology, object lessons from the many problems with the methods that have been utilized to attempt to get at "global etymologies." Perhaps because of the assumption that all the world's languages are genetically related, i.e. are descendants of "Proto-World," global etymologists are disposed to believe in etymological connections among words in contemporary

---

[21] Indeed, for the design features of language, as stated here, a language could be as simple as just a couple of segments, repeated in sequences analogous to the "di" and "da" of Morse code (or to the "Ø" and "1" of computer code). That is, a language with but one vowel, say /a/, and very few consonants could still meet the requirements of the design features for human language. Possibly it would require longer words/utterances for distinction, but one might argue that this would presumably be selective for more intelligent processors of such signs, so adaptive in the long run.

languages, and this will to believe permits them to accept as related many forms which do not even begin to exceed sheer accidental similarity as a more plausible explanation. We conclude with Bender (1993b:203), "'global etymologies' are an illusion. They are an artifact of too much freedom of choice and the loss of control." The global etymologists have not met their burden of proof. In the long time since the origin of human language(s), so much vocabulary replacement has taken place that in effect no forms once found in "Proto-World" could have survived. Moreover, if some form had survived (and we assert it did not), after so much change it could not be recognized, and, if it should preserve a recognizable shape (and again we assert it could not), there would be so few such surviving forms that it would be impossible to distinguish survivors from forms similar by sheer accident. In short, the search for global etymologies is at best a hopeless waste of time, at worst an embarrassment to linguistics as a discipline, unfortunately confusing and misleading to those who might look to linguistics for understanding in this area.

What can we find out from structural comparisons? Answer: nothing especially useful, though functional typological and structural considerations may provide broad guidelines to what even the earliest human language would have to have had in order to qualify as a human language. Again, though, we learn object lessons relevant to methodology from the problems encountered in such structural comparisons. We can speculate that the design features of human language give us a small handle on the necessary nature of the earliest human language(s), but these are so broad that essentially any linguistic structure known in any language today would qualify as possible.

13   Conclusions: anticipating the future

> Way back in time all men emerged from a single hole in the earth. There was a mockingbird there at the entrance to the hole. He gave each a name and a language. To one he would say, "You shall be a Hopi and speak that tongue." To another, "You shall be an Apache and speak that language." And so it went for all who came from the hole, including the White People. The earth was still covered in darkness in those days so the peoples came together and decided to change things. They made the sun and the moon and placed them in the sky. With light and warmth things got easier for the people so the chiefs of all the races and tribes got together and decided to break up and go to different places.
>
> (www.stavacademy.co.uk/mimir/hopicreation.htm)

13.1   Past, present, and future

Our intention in this book has been to determine how genealogical relationships among languages can be shown, and thus to contribute to language classification. We have scrutinized carefully the methodology for investigating possible cases of remote linguistic kinship among languages not yet known to be related, and we have evaluated both the methods involved and the evidence presented for a number of the best-known proposals of distant genetic relationship. With respect to the past, we looked carefully at the methods and procedures utilized to establish the better-known language families, learning from both what proved useful and what did not. As for the present, what we see is an abundance of proposed "macro-family" relationships which unfortunately for the most part cannot claim to rest on reliable procedures or solid evidence. The evidence for some hypotheses is so poor that they need to be discarded once and for all; others warrant additional research, but are not convincing based on the evidence presented to date. With regard to the future, we hope that the findings in this book will have a positive impact on the direction and nature of the work in language classification and on attempts to investigate possible distant genetic relationships among languages not known to be related. Progress will, we predict, be made in discovering and demonstrating new relationships, but only

394

to the extent that hypotheses of remote relationship follow the techniques and procedures for overcoming possible alternative explanations for the evidence garnered on their behalf, as laid out in the chapters of this book. Thus we hope that, as a result, this book will contribute significantly to linguistic classification in general.

We began our investigation of how language families are established by examining the earliest attempts at classifying languages into families. We saw that considerable understanding of comparative linguistics and of Indo-European and a few other language families had already emerged early in our story. Our survey of how language families were established in the past revealed that generally three criteria were involved, that is, arguments were based on three kinds of evidence: basic vocabulary, patterned grammatical agreements, and sound correspondences. These remain at the core of standard methods today.

Given the role so commonly attributed to Sir William Jones as founding figure and given the fact that some scholars attempt to make their own methods seem more legitimate by associating them with Jones' procedures, we investigated Jones' methods and claims in detail. Jones, like many, was interested not in languages or linguistic classification per se, but rather in the history of "races," nations of people. Jones made numerous mistakes among his proposed language groupings and he failed to recognize other relationships he ought not to have missed, such as that between Sanskrit and Hindi. In spite of this, his methods involved the same three primary criteria for linguistic genealogy which were common in his day and afterward: basic vocabulary, correspondences among sounds (though not of central importance for Jones), and grammatical agreements, though many of his conclusions were tied so closely to misleading non-linguistic evidence and broad typological expectations that he committed many errors in language classification. These errors make it necessary to be extremely cautious concerning the methods which led him to his erroneous conclusions.

In spite of individual differences, it is clear that most of the scholars who played a significant role in the history of comparative linguistics and in the early establishment of linguistic families relied on grammatical correspondences, basic vocabulary, and sound correspondences as the three sources of evidence most commonly felt reliable upon which conclusions concerning language relationships could be based. We discovered in our survey of past efforts that many of the errors in classification from well-known scholars stemmed from the employment of inadequate methods, particularly methods that relied on casual inspection of lexical similarities. From the works by Neogrammarians and their contemporaries, it became clear that pronouncements about methods for investigating language relationships were quite specific, even insistent, concerning the roles of sound correspondences and grammatical (morphological) agreements.

It was revealing to see not just the pronouncements about methods, but also how the methods were employed in actual practice.

Some scholars in modern times have asserted that the demonstration of relationship among Indo-European languages did not involve sound correspondences or standard techniques, but depended rather on observation of superficial lexical resemblances. This belief, however, as we saw, proved to be just wrong. Generally throughout history, many scholars favored morphological evidence more strongly, some preferred sound correspondences or vocabulary, but none defended a method which relies for its principal evidence on the comparison of superficial lexical resemblances alone, except for the few cases where the scholars utilizing such a method arrived at erroneous results. In particular, in the actual practice employed, for example, to prove that Hittite (and Anatolian generally), Venetic, and other languages belonged to Indo-European, the standard criteria were indeed employed, with morphological agreements and sound correspondences as major features of the demonstrations (Chapter 5). Even the proof that Armenian did not belong to Iranian but was a separate branch of Indo-European depended crucially on recognition of sound correspondences, that is, on the strength of the comparative method; it was on the basis of the comparative method that the layers of Iranian loans in Armenian were identified and distinguished from inherited native material. The earlier false classification of Armenian as belonging to the Iranian branch of the Indo-European family came precisely from reliance on lexical similarities and failure to deploy the methods and criteria that later resolved these matters.

We surveyed the history of language classification in a number of other important language families that were established early, as well as major events in the history of language classification in Africa, Australia, and the Americas. We paid particular attention to the methods used to establish these other language families and to the criteria and principles involved. Finno-Ugric and broader Uralic were established early, and work in this family had a major impact on the development of the comparative method and on the study of relationships among Indo-European languages. Semitic too was recognized as a language family quite early, and while this was not particularly challenging, given how closely related the languages are, nevertheless the methods utilized were consistent with those used to establish other language families. The picture of Austronesian relationships developed gradually (as did understanding of most language families), though some important Austronesian language relationships were recognized very early. Dravidian was also recognized fairly early, and standard comparative techniques were employed to work out the classification of the family. Sino-Tibetan, on the other hand, was recognized quite late, and had no role in the development of historical linguistic methodology, though some of the problems it poses call for careful deployment of the techniques. The discussion of the classification and historical linguistic work in a number of

American Indian language families revealed that solid methods were employed in demonstrating these families; in several instances this took place very early in history. Work in these languages demonstrated conclusively, for example, that the comparative method is equally applicable to so-called "exotic," non-written languages. The history of linguistic classification in Africa and Australia was also surveyed, and in both instances we find some solid historical linguistic research but also numerous problems, in particular assumed larger groupings which are not demonstrable on the basis of reliable standard methods.

The survey of all of these language families proved valuable for determining what has worked and what has not proved useful in past attempts to establish genetic relationships among various languages.

Given the confusion surrounding a number of proposed distant genetic relationships, we considered carefully the methodological principles and procedures involved in the investigation of proposals of distant genetic relationships, that is, in how family relationships are determined (Chapter 7). Principal among these are reliance on regular sound correspondences in basic vocabulary and patterned grammatical evidence involving "shared aberrancy" or "submerged features," with careful attention to eliminating non-genetic possible explanations for similarities noted in compared material, that is, borrowing, onomatopoeia, accident, nursery forms, etc. In particular, multilateral (or mass) comparison proved to be a particularly egregious, failed approach to attempting to detect language relationships. It is safe to predict that most future research on possible remote relationships which does not take into account the methodological recommendations of Chapter 7 will probably remain inconclusive. On the other hand, investigations informed by and guided by these methodological principles stand a good chance of advancing understanding, by either further supporting or rejecting proposed long-range family connections, depending on the nature and quality of the supporting evidence.

In addition to standard comparative linguistics, there was once another orientation, the "ideologic" or philosophical–psychological–typological–evolutionary line of thought (Chapter 8). After Sapir (1921b), Bloomfield (1933), and Pedersen (1962[1931]), it essentially dropped out of sight. This "ideologic" approach also concerned itself with genetic relationships among languages, but basically relied on the same combination of standard criteria, of basic vocabulary, sound correspondences, and grammatical agreements. The "ideologic" orientation – with aspects of philosophy, psychology, typology, and evolution – did not compete directly with fundamental assumptions of comparative linguistics, which many of the ideologically minded supported and to which several contributed. Rather, the "ideologic" trappings usually involved a level of abstractness beyond these sorts of data. In several instances, however, the "ideologic" leanings did lead to bad linguistic classifications – in those cases where types of language were assumed to correlate directly with stages of social evolution (isolating languages thought to correlate with savagery, agglutinative ones with barbarism, etc.), lying behind some of the proposed classifications of Asian and African languages. On the more abstract level, setting aside for the moment the erroneous correlations of language type with social evolution, we might see aspects of universal grammar and human cognition in modern theoretical thinking as the current analogue of the "ideologic" orientation, relevant to determining genetic relationships only in a very broad sense, pertinent to how grammatical evidence might be viewed, but not changing the basic fact that basic vocabulary, sound correspondences, and grammatical agreements constitute the evidence upon which such hypotheses of linguistic kinship rely. Today's theorizing about general language typology, universals, and aspects of human cognition should contribute to, rather than compete with or detract from, ability to distinguish doubtful comparisons among languages not yet known to be related. Linguistic traits known to be commonplace in human languages are explained by these general properties of human languages and are not reliable evidence of genetic relationship among languages.

We employed the methods and criteria for investigating proposed distant genetic relationships in an evaluation of several of the best-known but disputed hypotheses of distant genetic relationships: Altaic, Ural-Altaic, Nostratic, Eurasiatic, Amerind, Na-Dene, and Indo-Pacific (Chapter 9). We showed why most historical linguists reject these hypotheses – none meets the burden of proof, since their supporters have not shown that the evidence presented cannot be explained just as well by non-genetic means, as a combination of accident, borrowing, and the several other factors discussed in Chapter 7. It is unfortunate that some of these macro-family proposals continue to receive attention outside linguistics by scholars and journalists who do not understand how unreliable the methods upon which they are based are and how unconvincing the evidence presented for them so far is. Nevertheless, many non-linguists are coming to understand this. It is not only linguists who now understand that many of these proposed relationships rely on inadequate methods and insufficient or problematic evidence.

In more recent times, a number of new approaches have been proposed which either reject the comparative method or propose new techniques to try to see past its limitations in order to get at more remote linguistic prehistory. We examined critically the fundamental claims of some of these, in particular Nichols' program and Dixon's punctuated equilibrium (Chapter 10). If any of them were successful, this would constitute an important advance in historical linguistics. However, these approaches turned out to be flawed; they afford no reliable new insights. Nichols' calculations concerning spread, stability, and the general character and distribution of linguistic traits for the zones with which she deals are called into question by the many problems considered in Chapter 10. In particular, the influential notions of spread zones and accretion/residual zones should be abandoned. The number of proposed spread zones and accretion/residual zones is so small and Nichols' examples so different one from another that no legitimate generalization is to be had here. Zones of both sorts are essentially arbitrarily selected chunks of terrain or mere artifacts of local political and social history, better understood on a case by case basis as products of contingent history. The problems with the languages chosen to represent the particular zones, and the errors concerning which are spread zones and which accretion/residual zones, are so serious as to skew the calculations and any conclusions based on them. We urge that the whole spread zone/accretion zone notion be abandoned. We also found that many of Nichols' "stable" features were not really stable at all; we rejected her assumed average binary splits and the calculation of time depths. We find the overall program so riddled with problems that it offers no reliable insights, although it has proven misleading to many.

Similarly, we found Dixon's model of punctuated equilibrium so laden with problems, it is rejected. It relies on a misinformed view of the nature of human society in the past. The correlation envisaged, which equates equilibrium with convergence in languages, and punctuation with divergence, is not supported – both kinds of language change take place in both kinds of situations. Languages both diversify and spread both in punctuation and in equilibrium.

We found serious problems with all the approaches aimed at seeing past the comparative method. Nevertheless, it was worthwhile to examine these approaches, to eliminate these sirens which appear to promise much, but only mislead and divert efforts away from other more productive lines of investigation. Indeed, there is much work that needs to be done and much to be learned from the application of the traditional techniques.

Several of these alternative schemes involved attacks on the notion of the family tree, seen as grounds for positing alternative approaches. We found the attacks to be without foundation. Largely they boil down to two misconceptions. One is the frequent misunderstanding which claims that scholars have imagined the comparative method to be all and everything while neglecting borrowing and language contact. However, historical linguists have always known that the comparative method is dedicated primarily to inherited material and have never relied on it alone for the full history of languages. Borrowing, wave theory, and more recently areal linguistics are crucial to the broader picture of language history. New techniques are not needed to see past the comparative method's dedication to inherited materials; we have always had other techniques for dealing with diffusion. The second misconception is the apparent belief that difficult cases disprove the legitimacy of the comparative method and the family-tree model associated with it. Of course there will be cases where, on the basis of the evidence available, it will not be possible definitively to resolve the issue of what is borrowed and what is inherited. That in some instances the evidence which remains is insufficient to answer this question is no grounds for rejecting the methods – in all historical enterprises, scholars do the best they can with the evidence at hand, and sometimes the evidence is so limited or fragmentary that the result is not satisfying. This, however, does not negate the value of the methods for cases where the extant data are better. The lack of wood in some region does not compel us to abandon making wooden furniture everywhere. We recall the many cases where the comparative method has proven adequate for distinguishing the inherited from the diffused (as in the Armenian case, Chapter 5, where the comparative method helped sort out the massive Iranian loans from native Armenian forms). These attacks on the family tree are without foundation.

We also examined views about language diversification and spread as seen in Nettle's ecological-risk reduction hypothesis and in the farming/language dispersal model. We found them severely wanting because they rely too heavily on single or particular factors, neglecting the several others that also must be taken into account. We also considered social factors as in Hill's localist-vs.-distributed strategies and Golla's spread-vs.-compact languages and language families. Reduction of ecological risk (Nettle's approach) is but one of many considerations involving the distribution of languages, and it can be addressed by various sorts of cross-linguistic alliances among people, not just within a single language community. It fails to take into account relevant social and historical facts; its influence in determining language distribution is overstated. Also, agricultural dispersal is only one factor in the bigger picture of what drives language diversification and spread; there are many cases where the distribution of languages does not fit the model's predictions – there are too many unexplained language spreads without agriculture and too many cases of maintained linguistic diversity in spite of agricultural spread.

The social behavior of speakers, though too neglected, is significant in addressing the questions of how and why languages diversify and spread. This is revealed in Hill's notion of distributed-vs.-localist stances and Golla's concepts of spread-vs.-compact languages and language families. These social behaviors influence markedly the diversification and spread of languages and language families and must be given a very prominent role in explaining these distributions. Linguistic diversification and language spread appear to be the results of linguistic change mediated by social factors (speakers' choices) and contingent historical events (migration, conquest, climate change, choice to shift languages, etc.). Agriculture, physical geography, ecology, and economics, to the extent that they play a role, are only parts of the picture and are also mediated by social behavior and particular historical events. It is questionable that these non-linguistic, non-social considerations take us very far towards answering the questions of how and why languages diversify and spread.

In Chapter 12 we asked, what can we find out or reasonably hypothesize about the earliest human language (or languages) by looking back from evidence in modern and attested older languages? Our answer was, very little indeed. We asked, what can we find out about the earliest human language(s) from lexical comparisons of languages today? The answer was, essentially nothing, though we can learn something of methodology, object lessons from the many problems with the methods aimed at "global etymologies." The global etymologists have not met the burden of proof. We argued that in the long time since the origin of human language so much vocabulary replacement has taken place that in effect no forms once found in "Proto-World" could have survived. Moreover, if some form could have survived after so much change, it could not be recognized, and, if it should preserve a recognizable shape (which we assert it could not), there would be so few such surviving forms that it would be impossible to distinguish survivors from forms just similar by sheer accident or other reasons. In short, the search for global etymologies is at best a waste of time, confusing and misleading to those who might look to linguistics for understanding in this area. We also asked, what can we find out about the earliest language(s) from structural comparisons? Our answer was, nothing useful, though functional and structural considerations may provide broad guidelines to what even the earliest human language must have had in order to qualify as a human language. Again, we learn methodological object lessons from the problems encountered in such structural comparisons. We can speculate that the design features of human language give us a small handle on the necessary nature of the earliest human language(s), but these features are so broad that essentially any linguistic structure known in any language today would qualify as possible.

Let us return now to the question of distant genetic relationships and what the future may hold. Most of the proposals of remote linguistic relationships treated in this book proved not very successful – giving perhaps a negative feel to the overall enterprise. This notwithstanding, we do feel positive about the outcome and about the future. We believe the discussion of methods, criteria, techniques, and procedures contributes positively to the field and to future investigations. We end on an optimistic note with a brief consideration of successful cases of distant genetic proposals, cases which were once controversial, but which have come to be established to the satisfaction essentially of all. These cases include:

> *Algic (Algonquian-Ritwan)* – Algonquian-Ritwan, proposed by Sapir (1913a, 1915a, 1915c, 1923), was controversial (see Chapter 6; see Michelson 1914, 1915), but evidence grew, from new cognates, refined sound correspondences, and submerged morphological evidence (see Haas 1958a; Teeter 1964; Goddard 1975, 1990b), until it was no longer possible to doubt the relationship.

Austroasiatic (Munda and Mon-Khmer) – accepted today by most linguists.

Austronesian (including the Austronesian languages of Taiwan).

Hittite/Anatolian (see Chapter 5 for discussion of both the controversy and the methods which successfully demonstrated this hypothesis, which ultimately had a major impact on how Indo-European is seen).

Lule-Vilela (see Viegas Barros 2001).

Otomanguean – doubted earlier (see Callaghan and Miller 1962), developed since the 1960s, but now universally accepted, and some scholars even report achievement here rivals that of Indo-European (Rensch 1973, 1976, 1977; see Campbell 1997a:157–9).

Pama-Nyungan – accepted by most specialists (see Alpher 1990, 2004; Harvey 2003; Koch 2003; O'Grady 1998; O'Grady and Hale 2004; cf. Micelli 2004).

Pano-Tacanan (Panoan and Tacanan).

Paya (Pech) as belonging to Chibchan (Holt 1986; cf. Constenla 1991).

Sino-Tibetan (see Chapter 6)

Tlapanec-Otomanguean – Tlapanec-Subtiaba proved not to belong to "Hokan" as postulated by Sapir (1925a), but to be a branch of Otomanguean (Suárez 1979, 1983a, 1986; see Campbell 1997a:207–8, 211, 292, 296–7).

Uralic (the relationship between Finno-Ugric and Samoyed) (Setälä 1912, 1913–18)

Uto-Aztecan – postulated but disputed until Sapir's (1913b, 1915–19), conclusive proof, based on the comparative method (see Chapter 6; see Campbell 1997a:133–8 for details).

Witotoan (Bora-Witotoan) (Aschmann 1993).

Instances abound of languages whose genetic affiliation was previously unknown but which now has been clearly demonstrated in more recent times, for example, the several newly discovered *Dravidian* languages, *Austronesian* (and the relationship particularly of the Formosan languages), the probable relationship among *Austroasiatic* languages (the Munda and Mon-Khmer families), the clarification of languages belonging to *Sino-Tibetan*; the joining of Panoan and Tacanan into *Pano-Tacanan*; clarifications of language membership among numerous South American families, in particular, Tupían, Arawakan, and "Macro-Gê." A number of other instances of demonstrated but once unclear cases of remote linguistic relationships now fully accepted include *Siouan–Catawban*, *Eskimo–Aleut*, *Uralic* (the demonstrated relationship between Finno-Ugric and Samoyed). Demonstrations of family relationships continue among various *Papuan* groups and also among various *Australian* language families. Rankin (1998) has made a very strong case for accepting the proposed relationship between Siouan–Catawban and Yuchi. A number of other promising possibilities are as yet unconfirmed, but more conclusive findings can be expected in coming years.

In brief, while we believe future work on language relatedness and language classification should naturally be approached with caution, we see every reason to feel optimistic about the future.

Appendix: Hypothesized distant genetic relationships

In this appendix, we attempt to provide a representative, reasonably comprehensive (but by no means exhaustive) listing of the hypotheses of distant genetic relationships which have been proposed. Limitations of space and practical considerations prevent us from evaluating each of these. Obviously these hypotheses are not all of even quality. Some are plausible and deserve further attention; some would find it difficult to escape ridicule, though they might be entertaining. We make no effort to provide extensive references for these various proposals, but do mention some relevant bibliography in some of the cases.

Afroasiatic (formerly Hamito-Semitic) (Greenberg 1963)

Ainu–Altaic (Patrie 1982)

Ainu and Indo-European (Lindquist 1960; Narumi 2000a; Tailleur 1961; see Hamp 1968)

Ainu–Austroasiatic (Vovin 1993)

Ainu–Gilyak (cf. Naert 1962)

Algonkian–Gulf (Haas 1958b, 1960; Gursky 1966–7, 1968)

Algonquian–Gulf and Hokan–Subtiaba (Gursky 1965, 1966–7, 1968)

Almosan–Keresiouan: Greenberg combined his Keresiouan (composed of Caddoan [including Adai], Iroquoian, Keresan, and Siouan-Yuchi) and Almosan (Sapir's Algonquian-Wakashan, combining Algic and Mosan) (Greenberg 1987:162–4).

Altaic (Georg et al. 1999; Grunzel 1895; Menges 1961, 1975; Miller 1987, 1991; Menovshchikov 1968; Poppe 1960, 1965, 1973, 1974, 1975; Ramstedt 1946–7, 1952, 1957; Shherbak 1966, 1986a, 1986b; Starostin 1991b; Starostin et al. 2003; Schott 1853, 1860; see Doerfer 1966, 1968, 1973, 1985, 1988; Róna-Tas 1974; Ramstedt 1914–15, 1915–16; Starostin 1986; Unger 1990a; cf. Joki 1975, 1976, 1977, 1980)

American Indian languages–Asian languages (and Aztec–Sanskrit) (Milewski 1960)

American Indian languages–Altaic (Ferrario 1933, 1938)

American Indian–Polynesian (Key 1984; cf. Hale 1890[1888]); American Indian–Malayo-Polynesian (Rivet 1926)

American Indian–Semitic (Leesberg 1903)

Amerind (with all Native American languages grouped except so-called Na-Dene and Eskimo–Aleut languages) (Bengtson 1995; Bower 1990; Greenberg 1979, 1981b, 1987, 1989, 1990a, 1994, 1996a, 1996b, 2000c; Greenberg and Ruhlen 1992; Newman 1991, 1993; Ross 1991; Ruhlen 1991, 1994a, 1994b, 1994c, 1994d, 1994e, 1995a, 1995b); Proto-Amerindian (Matteson 1972; Radin 1919) (see Campbell 1988, 1994a, 1997a; Poser 1992; Rankin 1992; Ringe 1992, 1993, 1996; cf. also Hale 1997; Newman 1995)

Andamanese (several languages of the Andaman Islands, not yet shown conclusively to be related to one another) (cf. Burenhult 1996)

Andean: Greenberg (1987) grouped Alakaluf, Araucanian, Aymara, Catacao, Cholona, Culli, Gennaken (Pehuelche), Itucale (Simacu), Kahuapana, Leco, Mayna (Omurana), Patagon (Tehuelche), Quechua, Sabela (Auca), Sechura, Yamana (Yahgan), and Zaparo (Greenberg 1987:99). He distinguished a "Northern subgroup" (Catacao, Cholona, Culli, Leco, and Sechura) and a "Southern Andean" (Alakaluf, Araucanian, Gennaken, Patagon, and Yamana).

Atakapa–Chitimacha (Swadesh 1946, 1947)

Athabaskan and Sino-Tibetan (Shafer 1952, 1957, 1969; Swadesh 1952; cf. Na-Dené–Sino-Tibetan, Sapir 1925b)

Australian and American Indian languages (Rivet 1925, 1957)

Australian, see Proto-Australian

Australian various connections, e.g. Chon–Australian and Malayo-Polynesian (Rivet 1925, 1957[1943]); South American–Australian (Trombetti 1928)

Austric (Austro-Asiatic with Austronesian) (Schmidt 1906; Diffloth 1990, 1994; Keane 1880; Schiller 1987; Shorto 1976; Reid 1994; cf. Benedict 1975a; Ross 1995a)

Austroasiatic (Austro-Asiatic) (Mon-Khmer and Munda, often also Nicobarese) (Schmidt 1906; Pinnow 1959, 1966; cf. van Driem 2001:262–70) (Austroasiatic is accepted by many linguists, but others retain doubts.)

Austro-Tai (Austronesian with Tai-Kadai) (Benedict 1975a, 1990; Egerod 1973; cf. Matisoff 1976; Reid 1985; Ross 1995a; see Benedict 1942; Thurgood 1994)

Aztec–Tanoan (Uto-Aztecan and Kiowa-Tanoan) (Whorf and Trager 1937; Davis 1989; Shaul 1985; see Campbell 1997a:269–73 for a critical appraisal of the evidence)

Basque–American Indian (Vinson 1875)

Basque–Berber (d'Abbadie and Chaho 1836)

Basque–Caucasian (Čirikba 1985; cf. Bengtson 1997; Schuhmacher 1989; Trask 1995)

Basque–Hamito-Semitic (Mukarovsky 1981)

Basque–Kartvelian (Furnee 1989)

Beothuk–Algonquian (Hewson 1968, 1971, 1978, 1982; see Campbell 1997a:289–91)

Boreal (sometimes used as a synonym for some versions of "Nostratic," or Nostratic + other northern language groups; see Nostratic)

Burushaski–Caucasian (both Northwest and Northeast Caucasian) (Bleichsteiner 1930; Bengtson 1997a; cf. Bashir 2000:1) (see Tuite 1998:467 for "quasi-genetic resemblances" between Burushaski and Northeast Caucasian)

Burushaski–Indo-European (Berger 1956; Čašule 1998 – especially pre-Balkanic IE languages; cf. Bashir 2000:1)

Burushaski–Ket, Burushaski–Yeneseian (Toporov 1971; van Driem 2001:1186; cf. Bashir 2000:1)

Bushman and Indo-European (Stopa 1972)

Cariban–African (Kennedy 1856)

Cayuse–Molala (see critique in Rigsby 1966, 1969)

Central Amerind: Greenberg distinguished "three apparently coordinate branches" of Central Amerind: "Kiowa-Tanoan, Uto-Aztecan, and Oto-Mangue" (Greenberg 1987:123).

Chibchan–Paezan: this large grouping for Greenberg "consists of the following families": Allentiac, Andaqui, Antioquia, Aruak, Atacama, Barbacoa, Betoi, Chibcha, Chimu, Choco, Cuitlatec, Cuna, Guaymi, Itonama, Jirajara, Lenca, Malibu, Misumalpan, Motilon, Mura, Paez, Paya, Rama, Talamanca, Tarascan, Timucua, Warrau, Xinca, and Yanomama (Greenberg 1987:106–7). It is surprising to find North American Timucua, Mexican Cuitlatec and Tarascan, Central American Lenca and Xinca, and remote South American Chimu, Warrau (Warao), and Yanomama included here with the Chibchan and Paezan languages as more conventionally understood.

Chinese and Indo-European (Ullenbrook 1967)

Chinese–Tai (Dong et al. 1984)

Chukchi–Uralic (Bouda 1961, 1976)

Chukotko–Kamchatkan (Fortescue 1998; cf. Comrie 1981; Campbell 2000)

Coahuiltecan (Manaster-Ramer 1996; Sapir 1920, 1929a; see Goddard 1979; Campbell 1996, 1997a:297–304)

Congo-Saharan, see Niger-Saharan

Dene–Caucasian, Dene–Sino-Caucasian (cf. Macro-Caucasian phylum: Burushic [Burushaski], Caucasic, Basque) (Bengtson

1991, 1992, 1997b; Blažek and Bengtson 1995; Catford 1991; Čirikba 1985; Nikolaev 1989, 1991; Ruhlen 1998; Shevoroshkin 1991; Schuhmacher 1989; Starostin 1991a; cf. Bashir 2000:1; see also Stewart 1991; Trask 1995; cf. Sino-Caucasian)

Dravidian–Altaic (Meile 1949; Menges 1964, 1969, 1977, 1989, 1990; Miller 1986; Musayev 1996; Vaček 1981, 1983, 1987)

Dravidian and "Iberocaucasian" (Fähnrich 1965)

Dravidian–Greek (Ananda Vasudevan 1973)

Dravidian–Indo-European (Bhat 1983; Rhedin 1985; Southworth 1982)

Dravidian–Japanese (Fujiwara 1975a, 1981; Ohno 1980, 1983, 1987; see Miller 1983, 1986; Sanmugadas 1989; see Winters 1984 and Zvelebil 1985b on Japanese and Tamil)

Dravidian–Mongolian (Rao 2001; Vaček 1978, 1983, 1985; see Musayev 1996 on Dravidian–Turkic–Sanskrit comparisons)

Dravidian–Uralic   (Dravidian–Finno-Ugric,   Uralo-Dravidian) (Andronov 1971; Bouda 1953a, 1953b; Burrow 1943; Caldwell 1913[1856]; Eronen 1977; Hevesy 1932; Larsson 1982; Marlow 1974, 1980; Puskás 1982; Schrader 1924, 1936; Sebeok 1945; Tyler 1968, 1990; cf. Austerlitz 1972; Levy 1928; see also Webb 1862 on Dravidian and "Scythian"; Jones 1989 on Tamil [Dravidian], Warlpiri [Pama-Nyungan], and Finnish [Uralic])

Dravidian and Wolof (Senghor 1975)

DURALJAN (Uralic, Dravidian, Altaic, Japanese–Korean, Andean–Equatorial) (Hakola 1997, 2000)

Egyptian–Dravidian (Homburger 1957)

Egyptian–Indo-European (Lavalade 1986)

Elamite–Dravidian, Elamo-Dravidian (McAlpin 1974a, 1974b, 1975, 1981; Zvelebil 1974, 1985a)

Equatorial: in 1960 Greenberg had an Equatorial–Andean grouping, but in 1987 he broke this up into three separate groups: Equatorial, Macro-Tucanoan, and Andean. In Equatorial he later placed Arawa, Cayuvava, Chapacura, Coche, Cofan, Esmeralda, Guahibo, Guamo, Jibaro, Kandoshi, Kariri, Katembri, Maipuran, Otomaco, Piaroa, Taruma, Timote, Tinigua, Trumai, Tupi, Tusha, Uro, Yaruro, Yuracare, and Zamuco (combining into a subgroup which he called Jibaro-Kandoshi the language groups Cofan, Esmeralda, Jibaro, Kandoshi, and Yaruro) (Greenberg 1987:83).

Eskimo–Aleut and Austronesian (Schuhmacher 1974, 1991)

Eskimo–Aleut–Chukotan (American–Arctic–Paleo-Siberian phylum) (cf. Fortescue 1994, 1998; Hamp 1976; Krauss 1973a; Swadesh 1962; see also Nikolaev and Mudrak 1989; cf. Boas 1933; Campbell 2000)

Eskimo–Aleut–Yukagir (Fortescue 1988; cf. Campbell 2000)

Eskimo and Indo-European (Hammerich 1951; Uhlenbeck 1942–5; cf. Thalbitzer 1945)

Eskimo–Uralic (Bergsland 1959, 1978, 1980; Sauvageot 1924, 1953; Thalbitzer 1928, 1952; Uhlenbeck 1905)

Eskimo–Ural-Altaic (Koo 1980)

Etruscan–Greek–Kartvelian (Gordeziani 1985)

Eurasiatic (Greenberg 1991, 1997, 2000a, 2005; cf. Shafer 1963, 1965)

Gê-Pano-Carib (Greenberg 1987)

Gê and Old World macro-families (Aikhenvald-Angenot and Angenot 1989)

Gilyak [Nivkh], Chukchi–Kamchatkan, and Almosan–Keresiouan (Nikolaev and Mudrak 1989) (See Bouda 1960b, 1965b, 1969, 1970a, 1970b, 1976 for other proposed Gilyak relationships.)

Gilyak and Paleosiberian languages (Tailleur 1960)

Gilyak–Uralic (Bouda 1968, 1972, 1979, 1980)

"Greater Austric" (Austroasiatic, Austronesian, Daic [Tai–Kadai], Hmong–Mien) (cf. van Driem 2001:298)

Guaicurian–Hokan (Gursky 1966–7)

Gulf (Muskogean, Natchez, Tunica, Atakapa, Chitimacha) (Haas 1951, 1952, 1960; Munro 1994; see Campbell 1997a:306–9; Kimball 1992, 1994; see Swanton's 1919 Tunica, Chitimacha, and Atakapa, and Swanton's 1924 Natchez-Muskogean)

Hanis, Miluk, Alsea, Siuslaw, and Takelma (Pierce 1966)

Hokan, Hokan–Coahuiltecan, Hokan–Siouan (Bright 1954, 1955; Crawford 1976; Dixon and Kroeber 1913a, 1913b, 1919; Greenberg and Swadesh 1953; Gursky 1965, 1966–7, 1968, 1974; Haas 1964a, 1964b; Jacobsen 1958, 1976, 1979; Kroeber 1915; Langdon 1974, 1979; McLendon 1964; Rivet 1942; Silver 1964, 1976; Sapir 1917, 1920, 1925a; Waterhouse 1976; Webb 1971, 1976, 1980; cf. Harrington 1913, 1917, 1943; see discussion in Campbell 1997a:260–305; see Turner 1967, 1972, 1976). Greenberg's (1987) Hokan is like Sapir's Hokan–Coahuiltecan, but also includes most other languages (except Quechua) that have been proposed as members of Hokan since publication of Sapir's (1929) classification: Achomawi (including Atsugewi), Chimariko, Chumash, Coahuilteco, Comecrudo, Cotoname, Esselen, Jicaque, Karankawa, Karuk, Maratino, Pomo, Quinigua, Salinan, Seri, Shasta (including Konomihu), Subtiaba (including Tlapanec), Tequistlatec (Chontal of Oaxaca), Tonkawa, Waicuri, Washo, Yana, Yuman, and Yurumangui.

Hokan–Malayo-Polynesian, Hokan–Melanesian (Rivet 1957[1943])

Hokan–Quechua (Harrington 1943)

Huave–Uralic (Bouda 1964, 1965a)

Indo-European and Afroasiatic (Indo-European–Hamito-Semitic) (Cuny 1924, 1943, 1946; Garbini 1981; Hodge 1983, 1991)

Indo-European and Austronesian (Petrov 1967; cf. Bopp 1841, 1842a, 1842b)

Indo-European and Kartvelian (Fähnrich 1988; cf. Gamkrelidze 1967)

Indo-European and Northwest Caucasian (Colarusso 1994)

Indo-European and Semitic (Brunner 1969; Cuny 1912; Fellman 1978; Levin 1971, 1975, 1977, 1991, 2002; Möller 1906, 1911; Petrachek 1982; see Szemerényi 1973, 1975)

Indo-European–Ural-Altaic (Menges 1945)

Indo-Pacific (Finck 1909; Greenberg 1971b; cf. Gordon 1993)

Indo-Uralic (Indo-European and Uralic) (Anderson 1879; Ariste 1971; Claude 1973; Collinder 1934, 1943, 1954, 1965b, 1967, 1970, 1974, Čop 1970a, 1970b, 1970c, 1972, 1973a, 1973b, 1974a, 1974b, 1974c, 1975, 1976, 1987, 1989; Décsy 1980; Dezsö 1990; Gulya 1990; Joki 1973; Girardot 1980[1982]; Holmer 1960; Kerns 1967; Kiparsky 1975; Kortlandt 1989; Kudzinowski 1983; Paasonen 1907; Pedersen 1933; Pisani 1967; Ringe 1998; Rosenkranz 1966; Schindler 1964; Schröpfer 1969; Shimomiya 1973; Skalička 1969; Uesson 1970; Wedgwood 1856a, 1856b; cf. Janhunen 1983; Joki 1973, 1980)

Japanese–Altaic (Menges 1974, 1975; Miller 1968, 1971a, 1971b, 1975, 1979a, 1980, 1981, 1985, 1991; Murayama 1975; Ramstedt 1924; Starostin 1991b; Street 1973, 1981, 1985; Vovin 1999; cf. Doerfer 1974, 1978; Murayama 1966, 1977; Unger 1973, 1990b)

Japanese and Austric (Schmidt 1930)

Japanese and Indo-European (Narumi 2000b, 2001)

Japanese and Papuan (Go 1980)

Japanese–Austronesian (Kawamoto 1977–8; cf. Ross 1995a:95; Shibatani 1990:103–9; van Driem 2001:1217–18; see Labberton 1924)

Japanese–Austro-Thai (Benedict 1990; see Solnit 1992)

Japanese–Korean, see Korean–Japanese

Japanese–Korean–Tungusic (Martin 1991:269)

Japanese–Uralic (Fujiwara 1974, 1975b; Kazár 1974, 1976, 1980a, 1980b, 1981; Winkler 1909)

Jicaque–Hokan (Greenberg and Swadesh 1953)

Jicaque–Subtiaba(–Tequistlateco) (Oltrogge 1977)

Keresan–Caddoan comparisons (Davis 1974; Rood 1973)

Keresan–Uto-Aztecan (Davis 1979)

Keresan–Zuni (Gursky 1966–7)

Keresiouan (Greenberg 1987)

Khoisan (Khoi "Hottentot" + San "Bushman") (Greenberg 1963; cf. Planert 1905, 1926; Sands 1998; Schils 1895)

Klamath–Sahaptian (DeLancey 1992; Rude 1987; cf. DeLancey 1988b)

Korean–Altaic (Menges 1984; R. Miller 1977, 1979b, 1984; cf. Janhunen and Kho 1982; Lee 1958; Rosén 1986)

Korean–Dravidian (Hulbert 1905)

Korean–Indo-European (Eckardt 1966)

Korean–Japanese (Kim 1976; Krippes 1990b; Lee 1973; Lewin 1976; Martin 1966, 1968, 1975, 1990, 1991; Ramsey 1978; Whitman 1985)

Korean–Uralic (Kho 1975)

Kusunda–Yenisseian (Gurov 1989; cf. van Driem 2001:260)

Kusunda–Indo-Pacific (Whitehouse *et al.* 2004)

Kutenai and Algonquian (Haas 1965)

Lislakh (Indo-European and Afroasiatic) (Hodge 1998)

Luoravetlan (see Eskimo–Aleut–Chukotan)

Macro-Austric (Austroasiatic, Austronesian, Hmong-Mien, Tai-Kadai) (Schiller 1987; Diffloth 1990)

Macro-Carib: Greenberg followed Loukotka (1968) and Rivet (1924) and includes in this category Cariban, Andoke, Bora (Miranya), Kukura, Uitoto (Witotoan), and Yagua (Peba).

Macro-Caucasian phylum: Burushic (Burushaski), Caucasic, Basque (Bengston 1991a, 1992a, 1992b, 1997b; Blažek and Bengtson 1995; cf. Bashir 2000:1) (cf. Dene–Caucasian, Sino-Caucasian)

Macro-Chibchan (Craig and Hale 1992)

Macro-Gê (Macro-Je) (cf. Davis 1968; Kaufman 1990, 1994; Rodrigues 1986) Greenberg's Macro-Ge essentially includes all the languages that have been proposed as being connected with Gê (Loukotka 1968; Davis 1968), plus a few proposed by Greenberg (Chiquito, Oti, and Yabuti). He includes fifteen groups in this category: Bororo, Botocudo, Caraja, Chiquito, Erikbatsa, Fulnio, Gê, Guato, Kaingan, Kamakan, Mashakali, Opaie, Oti, Puri, and Yabuti (Greenberg 1987:65–6).

Macro-Mayan (Mayan, Mixe-Zoquean, Totoanacan, sometimes Huave), Mayan-Zoquean (Arana 1968; Brown and Witkowski 1979; Kaufman 1964b; McQuown 1942, 1956; Radin 1916, 1924; Wonderly 1953)

Macro-Panoan: Greenberg (1987:74) combines "Panoan, Tacanan, and Mosetén on the one hand and Mataco, Guaicuru, Charruan, Lule, and Vilela on the other," plus Lengua (Mascoy).

Macro-Penutian, see Penutian

Macro-Siouan (Siouan and Iroquoian and often also Caddoan, sometimes only Siouan and Caddoan) (Allen 1931; Chafe 1964, 1973, 1976; Rudes 1974; see Campbell 1997a:262–9 for a critical evaluation of the evidence for this hypothesis; see Rankin 1981)

Macro-Tacanan (Pano-Tacanan, Chon, Mosetén, and Yuracare) (Suárez 1973)

Macro-Tucanoan: Greenberg (1987:93) grouped Auake, Auixiri, Canichana, Capixana, Catuquina, Gamella, Huari, Iranshe, Kaliana, Koaia, Maku, Mobima, Muniche, Nambikwara, Natu, Pankaruru, Puinave, Shukuru, Ticuna, Tucano, Uman, and Yuri.

Macro-Tungusic (Tungusic, Japanese, and Korean) (cf. Trask 2000:205)

Matacoan–Waykuruan (Guaicuruan) (Mason 1950)

Mayan–Altaic (Wikander 1967, 1970, 1970–1)

Maya–Arawakan (Noble 1965:26; cf. Schuller 1919–20)

Mayan–Auracanian (Hamp 1971; Stark 1970)

Mayan–Cariban–Arawakan (Schuller 1919–20)

Maya–Chipayan (Hamp 1967, 1970; Olson 1964, 1965; Stark 1972; see Campbell 1973 for evaluation)

Mayan–Lencan (Andrews 1970)

Mayan–Sino-Tibetan (Fahey 2004)

Mayan–Tarascan (Swadesh 1966)

Mayan–Turkic (Frankle 1984a, 1984b)

Maya–Yunga–Chipayan (Stark 1972)

"Mega-Austric" (Austroasiatic, Austronesian, Daic, Tibeto-Burman) (van Driem 2001:298)

Mesoamerican phylum (Witkowski and Brown 1978, 1981; cf. Campbell and Kaufman 1980, 1983)

Mexican Penutian (see Campbell 1997a:320)

Misumalpan–Chibchan (Constenla 1987)

Mixe-Zoquean–Totonacan–Otomí with Caucasian languages (Bouda 1963)

Mosan (Salishan, Wakashan, Chimakuan) (Sapir 1919a, Swadesh 1953a, 1953b).

Mosetén and Pano-Tacanan (Suárez 1969)

Munda–Uralic (Hevesy 1935; cf. Schrader 1936)

Na-Dené (Haida–Tlingit–Eyak-Athabaskan) (Hymes 1956; Jacobsen 1993; Krauss 1964, 1965, 1969, 1973b; Manaster Ramer 1993a;

Pinnow 1964, 1968, 1976, 1985, 1990; Ruhlen 1994a; Sapir 1915b; see Levine 1979)

(Na-)Dené with Mongol, Turkish, Chinese, Northeast Tibetan, Tocharian, and Italo-Celtic (Stewart 1991)

Nahuatl–Greek and Indo-European (Denison 1913)

Natchez and Muskogean (Haas 1956)

Niger-Kordofanian (Niger-Congo, extended sense) (Greenberg 1963)

Niger-Saharan, Congo-Saharan (Niger-Kordofanian [Niger-Congo] and Nilo-Saharan)

Nilotic (Greenberg 1963)

Nilo-Saharan (Ehret 2001; Greenberg 1963, 1971a, 1981a; Mikkola 1998, 1999; Nicolaï 1992, 1995, 1996, 2002, 2003)

Nostratic (Aalto 1977, 1980, 1988; Bomhard 1984, 1986a, 1989, 1990; Bomhard and Kerns 1994; Cuny 1943; Décsy 1988; Décsy and Dimov-Goboev 1977; Dolgopolsky 1964a, 1965, 1969, 1970, 1971, 1972, 1974, 1984, 1986, 1989, 1998; Dybo 1989a, 1989b, 1990; Eckert 1967, 1973; Griffen 1989; Hegedüs 1988, 1989, 1992a, 1992b; Helimskij 1987; Illich-Svitych 1964b, 1967a, 1967b, 1968a, 1968b, 1971a, 1971b, 1989a, 1989b, 1989c, 1989d, 1990; Ivanov 1986; Kaiser 1989; 1990; Kaiser and Shevoroshkin 1986, 1987, 1988; Korenchy 1975, Krippes 1990a; Manaster Ramer 1993b, 1994; Murtonen 1989; Palmaitis 1978; Poppe 1972, 1979; Reinhart 1988; Ruhlen 1989b; Shevoroshkin 1989a, 1989b, 1989c; Sinor 1999; Starostin 1999c; see Campbell 1998, 1999; Clauson 1973a; Doerfer 1993, Joseph and Salmons 1998; Ringe 1995a; Vine 1991; cf. Fox 1982; Garde 1977; Koskinen 1980; Pisani 1972; see also Anttila and Embleton 1988; Kaye 1985, 1989; Topolovsek 1912)

Ob-Ugric–Penutian (Sadovsky 1981, 1984, 1996) (See also Viitso 1971 on California Penutian, Uralic, and Nostratic languages.)

Otomanguean–Huave (Swadesh 1960, 1964a, 1964b, 1967; Rensch 1973, 1976)

Pakawan, see Coahuiltecan

Penutian (various versions) (Berman 1983, 1989; Broadbent and Pitkin 1964; Callaghan 1958, 1967; Dixon and Kroeber 1913a, 1913b, 1919; Freeland 1930; Golla 1991; Hymes 1957, 1964a, 1964b; Pitkin and Shipley 1958; Sapir 1921c, 1929a; Shipley 1966, 1973, 1980; Silverstein 1975, 1979a, 1979b; Swadesh 1955, 1956, 1964a; cf. DeLancey 1988a; see Campbell 1997a:309–20 for assessment; cf. Shevoroshkin 1982). Greenberg's (1987) view of Penutian includes: Yokuts, Maidu, Wintun, Miwok-Costanoan (considered a "valid grouping . . . called here California Penutian");

"Oregon and Plateau Penutian," as well as Chinook and Tsimshian; "Huave, Mayan, Mixe-Zoque, and Totonac-Tepehua . . . a well-defined subgroup"; Yukian (Yuki and Wappo); "Gulf" (composed of Atakapa, Chitimacha, Muskogean [and maybe Yukian]); and Zuni (Greenberg 1987:143–4). The grouping of Gulf with Penutian contradicts both Sapir's association of these languages with his Hokan-Siouan and Haas' Algonquian-Gulf proposals. (See Campbell 1997a:309–22.)

Proto-Australian (Dixon 1980; Sands 1996; cf. Bengtson 1994b; Blake 1994; see Chapter 6 for discussion)

Proto-World (global etymologies) (Bengtson and Ruhlen 1994a, 1994b; Newmeyer 2000; Trombetti 1905; see Wright 1991; see Chapter 12)

Quechua–Aymara–Sumerian–Assyrian (Patrón 1907)

Quechumaran (Quechuan and Aymaran) (Adelaar 1986, 1987; Cerrón-Palomino 1986; Orr and Longacre 1968; see Campbell 1995, 1997a:273–83; Mannheim 1985, 1986)

Quechua–Hokan (Harrington 1943)

Quechua–Oceania (Imbelloni 1926, 1928); Quechua–Maori (R. Dangel 1930; Palavecino 1926); Peruvian languages–Polynesian (Christian 1932)

Quechua–Tungusic (Bouda 1960a, 1963; see Hymes 1961)[1]

Quechua–Turkish (Dumézil 1954, 1955)

Sahaptian–Klamath(–Molala) (see DeLancey 1992; Berman 1996)

Salish–Indo-European (Kuipers 1967:401–5)

Sino-Austronesian (Old Chinese with Austronesian) (cf. Ross 1995a; van Driem 2001:322)

Sino-Caucasian (cf. Macro-Caucasian phylum: Burushic [Burushaski], Caucasic, Basque (Bengtson 1991a, 1992a, 1992b, 1997a, 1997b; Blažek and Bengtson 1995; Starostin 1989; cf. Bashir 2000:1; van Driem 2001:1197) (cf. Dene–Caucasian)

Sino-Tibetan and Nostratian/Nostratic (Gluhak 1978; Starostin 1989)

Sino-Tibetan–Yeneseian–Caucasian (Starostin 1991a)

South American–East Asian languages (Koppelmann 1929)

South American languages and Japanese (Gancedo 1922; Zeballos 1922)

Sumerian and Oceanic (Rivet 1929)

---

[1] It is surprising to find Hymes in support of a genetic connection between Quechua and the so-called Altaic languages; he is on record with the statement: "Clearly this attempt [Bouda 1960a] . . . confirms the genealogical relationship of Quechua with Altaic, letting one recognize that still another ancient American Kultursprache stems from Asia" (Hymes 1961:362).

Sumerian and Turkish (Hommel 1915)

Sumerian–Dravidian (Fane 1980)

Sumerian–Kartvelian (Fähnrich 1981); Georgian–Sumerian (Tsereteli 1959)

Sumerian–Ural-Altaic (Clauson 1973b; Smith 1981; Zakár 1971; cf. Fodor 1976)

Sumero-Assyrian and Quechua and Aymara (Patrón 1907)

Tai-Kadai (Benedict 1942, 1972)

Tai–Sino-Tibetan (Sino-Tai) (cf. Li 1976)

Takelman (Takelma-Kalapuyan) (Sapir 1921b; Swadesh 1956; Shipley 1969)

Tarascan–Quechua (Swadesh 1967:92–3)

"Tasmanian languages" (cf. Crowley and Dixon 1981)

Timucua–Muskogean (Crawford 1988)

Timucuan and Amazonian languages (Warao, Cariban, Arawakan, etc.) (see Granberry 1991a)

Tonkawa and Algonquian (Haas 1959)

Tonkawa–Na-Dene (Manaster Ramer 1993a)

Trans New Guinea phylum (Pawley 1995, 1998, 2001; Ross 1995b, 2001)

Tupian–Cariban (Rodrigues 1985a; cf. Rodrigues 1985b)

"Turanian" (various versions, centrally embracing the Uralic and so-called "Altaic" languages, but in fact essentially including all the non-Sino-Tibetan languages of Asia) (Müller 1854, 1855; cf. van Driem 2001:334–6)

Ural-Altaic (Aalto 1969; Collinder 1952, 1955a, 1965b, 1970, 1977; Menges 1963; Poppe 1977; Pröhle 1978; Räsänen 1955, 1965; Róna-Tas 1983, 1985; Sauvageot 1924; Shirokogoroff 1931; Sinor 1975a, 1975b, 1976, 1977, 1978, 1988, 1990; Winkler 1884, 1886, 1909, 1914; see Helimskij 1985; Schott 1849)

Ural-Altaic and Eskimo–Aleut (Bonnerjea 1971, 1975, 1978, 1979, 1984; Collinder 1960, 1965)

Uralic–Tungusic (Futaky [Futaki] 1973, 1988)

Uralo-Siberian (Fortescue 1998; cf. Campbell 2000)

Uto-Aztecan with Chukchi (Bouda 1952)

Uto-Aztecan and Mixe-Zoquean (Wichmann 1999)

Uto-Aztecan and Panoan (Wistrand-Robinson 1991)

Uto-Aztecan–Polynesian (postulated as "intimate borrowing or creolization" Kelley 1957)

Xinca-Lenca (Lehmann 1920:767; see Campbell 1978, 1979:961–3 for evaluation)

Yeniseian–Na-Dene (Ruhlen 1998)

Yeniseic–Bodic (cf. Janhunen 1989:30), Sino-Yenisseian (cf. van Driem 2001:1195, 1197)

Yenissei–Caucasian (cf. van Driem 2001:1195)

Yuchi–Atakapa (Crawford 1979)

Yuchi–Tunica (Crawford 1979)

Yukagir–Uralic (Collinder 1940, 1960, 1965; Harms 1977; Fortescue 1998; Sauvageot 1963, 1969)

Yukian–Gulf (Munro 1994)

Yukian–Penutian (Shipley 1957)

Yukian–Siouan (Elmendorf 1963); Yuchi, Siouan, and Yukian (Elmendorf 1964)

Zuni–Penutian (Hamp 1975; Newman 1964).

Some other very broad-scale proposals and comparisons (Fell 1990; cf. Goddard and Fitzhugh 1979; Key 1978, 1980–1, 1981a, 1981b, 1983, 1991a, 1991b; Key and Clairis 1978; Logan 1859; Rahder 1956–9; Swadesh 1959, 1965, 1967; Upadhyaya 1972, 1976; Wickman 1969; Zvelebil 1991; cf. Ringe 1995b).

References

Aalto, Pentti. 1965. Verwandtschaft, Entlehnung, Zufall. *Kratylos* 10.123–30.

1969. Uralisch und Altaisch. *Ural-Altaische Jahrbücher* 41.323–34.

1971. The alleged affinity of Dravidian and Fenno-Ugrian. *Proceedings of the second International Conference-Seminar of Tamil Studies, 1968*, ed. R. E. Asher, 262–6. Madras: International Association of Tamil Research.

1977. Zum Problem des "Nostratischen." *Finno-ugrische Forschungen* 42.277–80.

1980. Nostraattisen kielisukulaisuuden onglema [The problem of Nostratic linguistic relationship]. *Societas Scientiarum Fennica* LVIII, B 9.1–22.

1988. The problem of "Nostratic." *AIωN* 10.49–65. (Annali del Dipartimento di Studi del Mondo Classico e del Mediterraneo Antico, Sezione Linguistica, Naples.)

Aarsleff, Hans. 1982. *From Locke to Saussure: essays on the study of language and intellectual history*. Minneapolis: University of Minnesota Press.

1988. Introduction. *On language: the diversity of human language-structure and its influence on the mental development of mankind, Wilhelm von Humboldt*, trans. Peter Heath, vii–lxv. Cambridge: Cambridge University Press.

Abondolo, Daniel. 1998. Introduction. *The Uralic languages*, ed. Daniel Abondolo, 1–42. London: Blackwell.

Adam, Lucien. 1881. Les classifications de la linguistique. *Revue de Linguistique et de Philologie Comparée* 14.217–68.

Adelaar, Willem F. H. 1984. Grammatical vowel length and the classification of Quechua dialects. *International Journal of American Linguistics* 50.25–47.

1986. La relación quechua-aru: perspectivas para la separación del léxico. *Revista Andina* 4.379–426.

1987. La relación quechua-aru en debate. *Revista Andina* 5.83–91.

1989. Review of *Language in the Americas*, by Joseph H. Greenberg. *Lingua* 78.249–55.

Adelung, Johann Christoph. 1781. *Über den Ursprung der Sprachen und den Bau der Wörter, besonders der deutschen*. Berlin: Voss. (Reprinted 1975. Frankfurt am Main: Minerva.)

[with Johann Severin Vater]. 1806–17. *Mithridates, oder allgemeine Sprachenkunde mit dem Vater Unser als Sprachprobe in bey nahe fünfhundert Sprachen und Mundarten*. [4 vols. complete in Adelung's life time; the remaining 3 were completed by Johann Severin Vater.] Berlin: Voss. [Vol. 3, 1813–16, contains American and African languages; prepared largely by Vater.]

Aikhenvald, Alexandra Y. 2000. *Classifiers*. Oxford: Oxford University Press.

2001. Areal diffusion, genetic inheritance, and problems of subgrouping: a North Arawak case study. *Areal diffusion and genetic inheritance*, ed. Alexandra Y. Aikhenvald and R. M. W. Dixon, 167–94. Oxford: Oxford University Press.

Aikhenvald, Alexandra Y. and R. M. W. Dixon. 2001. Introduction. *Areal diffusion and genetic inheritance*, ed. Alexandra Y. Aikhenvald and R. M. W. Dixon, 1–26. Oxford: Oxford University Press.

Aikhenvald-Angenot, Alexandra Y. and Jean-Pierre Angenot. 1989. *The South-American Proto-Ge and the Old World. Explorations in language macrofamilies: materials from the First International Interdisciplinary Symposium on Language and Prehistory*, ed. Vitaly Shevoroshkin, 403–18. Bochum: Brockmeyer.

Aitchison, Jean. 1996. *The seeds of speech: language origin and evolution.* Cambridge: Cambridge University Press.

Alexandre, Pierre. 1972. *An introduction to languages and language in Africa.* London: Heinemann.

Allen, Louis. 1931. Siouan and Iroquoian. *International Journal of American Linguistics* 6.185–93.

Allen, W. S. 1953. Relationship in comparative linguistics. *Transactions of the Philological Society*, 52–108. London.

Allman, William F. 1990. The mother tongue. *U.S. News and World Report*, Nov. 5. 109(18).60–70.

Alpher, Barry. 1990. Some Proto-Pama-Nyungan paradigms: a verb in the hand is worth two in the phylum. *Studies in comparative Pama-Nyungan*, ed. G. N. O'Grady and D. T. Tryon, 155–71. (Pacific Linguistics C–111.) Canberra: Department of Linguistics, Research School of Pacific Studies, the Australian National University.

2004. Pama-Nyungan: phonological reconstruction and status as a philogenetic group. *Australian languages: classification and the comparative method*, ed. Claire Bowern and Harold Koch, 93–126. Amsterdam: John Benjamins.

Ammerman, A. J. and L. L. Cavalli-Sforza. 1973. A population model for the diffusion of early farming in Europe. *The explanation of cultural change*, ed. Colin Renfrew, 343–57. London: Duckworth.

Ananda Vasudevan, C. P. 1973. Dravidian-Greek connections. *International Journal of Dravidian Linguistics* 2.180–6.

Andersen, Henning. 1988. Center and periphery: adoption, diffusion and spread. *Historical dialectology*, ed. Jacek Fisiak, 39–83. Berlin: Mouton de Gruyter.

Anderson, Lloyd B. 1975. Grammar-meaning universals and proto-language: reconstruction of proto-world now! *Chicago Linguistic Society* 11.15–36.

Anderson, Nicolai. 1879. *Studien zur Vergleichung der indogermanischen und finnisch-ugrischen Sprachen.* (Gelehrte Ethnische Gesellschaft, Verhandlungen 9.)

Andresen, Julie Tetel. 1990. *Linguistics in America 1769–1924: a critical history.* London: Routledge.

Andrews, Lorrin. 1836. Remarks on the Hawaiian dialect of the Polynesian language. *Chinese Repository* 5(2).12–21.

Andrews, E. Wyllys, V. 1970. Correspondencias fonológicas entre el lenca y una lengua mayanse. *Estudios de Cultura Maya* 8.341–87. (Reprinted 1979 [Colección Antropología e Historia 15; Administración del Patrimonio Cultural.] San Salvador: Ministerio de Educación.)

Andronov, M. 1971. Comparative studies on the nature of Dravido-Uralian parallels: a peep into the prehistory of language families. *Proceedings of the First International Conference-Seminar of Tamil Studies* 2(1).267–77.

Anonymous. 1866. [Review of comparative philology.] *Quarterly Review* 119. 211–12.

Anttila, Raimo and Sheila Embleton. 1988. Review of *Typology, relationship and time*, ed. Thomas L. Markey and Vitaly V. Shevoroshkin. *Canadian Journal of Linguistics* 33.79–89.

Aoki, Haruo. 1963. On Sahaptian-Klamath linguistic affiliations. *International Journal of American Linguistics* 29.107–12.

Appleyard, David. 1999. Afroasiatic and the Nostratic hypothesis. *Nostratic: examining a linguistic macrofamily*, ed. Colin Renfrew and Daniel Nettle, 289–314. Cambridge: McDonald Institute for Archaeological Research.

Appleyard, John W. 1847. Hottentot grammar, Bushman dialects. *The South African Christian Watchman and Missionary Magazine*, 2.

    1850. *The Kafir language: comprising a sketch of its history, which includes a general classification of South African dialects, ethnographical and geographical remarks upon its nature and a grammar*. King William's Town: Wesleyan Methodist Mission Press.

Arana, Evangelina. 1968. Posibles relaciones externas del grupo lingüístico maya. *Anales del Instituto Nacional de Antropología e Historia*, 6th series, 19(48).111–34. Mexico.

Arberry, A. J. 1946. *Asiatic Jones: the life and influence of Sir William Jones (1746–1794): pioneer of Indian studies*. London: Longmans, Green, and Co., published for The British Council.

Arens, Hans. 1955. *Sprachwissenschaft: der Gang ihrer Entwicklung von der Antike bis zur Gegenwart*. Freiburg: Karl Alber. (2nd edition 1969.)

Ariste, Paul. 1971. Review of Uesson 1970. *Sovjetskoje finno-ugrovedenije* 1/2.144–6. Tallin, Estonia.

Arlotto, Anthony T. 1969. Jones and Cœurdoux: correction to a footnote. *Journal of the American Oriental Society* 89.416–17.

Aschmann, Richard P. 1993. *Proto-Witotoan*. (Publications in Linguistics 114.) Arlington: SIL and University of Texas at Arlington.

Auroux, Sylvain. 1990. Representation and the place of linguistic change before comparative grammar. *Leibniz, Humboldt, and the origins of comparativism*, ed. Tullio de Mauro and Lia Formigari, 213–38. Amsterdam: John Benjamins.

Auroux, Sylvain and A. Boes. 1981. Court de Gébelin (1725–1784) et le comparatisme, deux textes inédits. *Histoire épistémologie langage* 3.21–67.

Austerlitz, Robert. 1972. Long-range comparisons of Tamil and Dravidian with other language families in Eurasia. *Proceedings of the Second International Conference-Seminar of Tamil Studies* 1.254–61, ed. R. E. Asher. Madras: International Association for Tamil Research.

    1982. On comparing language families. *Etudes Finno-Ougriennes* 15.45–54.

    1983. Genetic affiliation among proto-languages. *Symposium Saeculare Societatis Fenno-Ugricae*, ed. Juha Janhunen, Anneli Peräniitty, and Seppo Suhonen, 51–8. (Mémoires de la Société Finno-Ougrienne, 185.) Helsinki: Finno-Ugrian Society.

1991. Alternatives in long-range comparison. *Sprung from some common source: investigations into the prehistory of languages*, ed. Sydney M. Lamb and E. Douglas Mitchell, 353–64. Stanford: Stanford University Press.

Bahuchet, Serge and Jacqueline M. Thomas. 1986. Linguistique et histoire des pygmées de l'ouest du Bassin Congolais. *Sprache und Geschichte in Afrika* 7.73–103.

Bakker, Peter. 2000. Rapid language change: creolization, intertwining, convergence. *Time depth in historical linguistics*, ed. Colin Renfrew, April McMahon, and Larry Trask, 585–620. Cambridge: McDonald Institute for Archaeological Research.

2004. Phoneme inventories, language contact, and grammatical complexity: a critique of Trudgill. *Linguistic Typology* 8.368–75.

Balázs, János. 1968. Zur Frage der indo-uralischen Verwandtschaft. *Congressus Secundus Internationalis Fenno-Ugristarum* 1.37–45. Helsinki.

Balbi, Adrien. 1826. *Atlas ethnographique du globe, ou classification des peuples anciens et modernes d'après leurs langues précédé d'un discours, sur l'utilité et l'importance de l'étude des langues appliquée à plusiers branches des connaissances humaines.* Paris: Rey et Gravier.

Baldi, Phillip. 1990. Introduction: the comparative method. *Linguistic change and reconstruction methodology*, ed. Philip Baldi, 1–13. Berlin: Mouton de Gruyter.

Bancroft, Hubert Howe. 1874–6. *The native races of the Pacific states of North America.* 5 vols. New York: Appleton.

Bartholomew, Doris A. 1967. Review (article) of *Studies in southwestern ethnolinguistics: meaning and history in the languages of the American Southwest*, ed. Dell H. Hymes and William Bittle. *Lingua* 23.66–86.

Barton, Benjamin Smith. 1797. *New views on the origin of the tribes and nations of America.* Philadelphia: Benjamin Smith Barton. (2nd edition, 1798, "corrected and greatly enlarged.")

Bashir, Elena. 2000. A thematic survey of Burushaski research. *History of Language* 6.1–15.

Bateman, R. M., I. Goddard, R. O'Grady, V. A. Fund, R. Mooi, W. J. Kress, and P. Cannell. 1990a. The feasibility of reconciling human phylogeny and the history of language. *Current Anthropology* 31.1–24.

1990b. On human phylogeny and linguistic history: reply to comments. *Current Anthropology* 31.177–82.

Bauer, Brigitte L. M. 1995. Language loss in Gaul: a case study of language conflict. Paper presented at the Symposium on Language Loss and Public Policy, University of New Mexico Linguistics Institute, Albuquerque, NM, July 1995.

Baugh, Albert C. 1957. *A history of the English language.* 2nd edition. New York: Appleton-Century-Crofts, Inc.

Baxter, William H. and Alexis Manaster Ramer. 2000. Beyond lumping and splitting: probabilistic issues in historical linguistics. *Time depth in historical linguistics*, ed. Colin Renfrew, April McMahon, and Larry Trask, 167–88. Cambridge: McDonald Institute for Archaeological Research.

Beeler, Madison S. 1949. *The Venetic language.* (University of California Publications in Linguistics 4.) Berkeley and Los Angeles: University of California Press.

Bellwood, Peter. 1991. The Austronesian dispersal and the origin of languages. *Scientific American* 265(1).88–93.

1994. An archaeologist's view of language macrofamily relationships. *Oceanic Linguistics* 33.391–406.

1995. Language families and human dispersal. *Cambridge Archaeological Journal* 5.271–4.

1996. The origins and spread of agriculture in the Indo-Pacific region: gradualism and diffusion or revolution and colonization? *The origins and spread of agriculture and pastoralism in Eurasia*, ed. D. R. Harris, 465–98. London: University College London Press.

1997. The prehistoric cultural explanations for the existence of widespread language families. *Archaeology and linguistics: aboriginal Australia in global perspective*, ed. Patrick McConvell and Nick Evans, 23–34. Melbourne: Oxford University Press.

2000. The time depth of major language families: an archaeologist's perspective. *Time depth in historical linguistics*, ed. Colin Renfrew, April McMahon, and Larry Trask, 109–40. Cambridge: McDonald Institute for Archaeological Research.

2001. Early agriculturalist population diasporas? Farming, languages and genes. *Annual Review of Anthropology* 30.181–207.

2002. Farmers, foragers, languages, genes: the genesis of agricultural societies. *Examining the farming/language dispersal hypothesis*, ed. Peter Bellwood and Colin Renfrew, 17–28. Cambridge: McDonald Institute for Archaeological Research.

Bellwood, Peter and Colin Renfrew (eds.). 2002. *Examining the farming/language dispersal hypothesis*. Cambridge: McDonald Institute for Archaeological Research.

Bender, Marvin Lionel. 1969. Chance CVC correspondences in unrelated languages. *Language* 45.519–31.

1971. The languages of Ethiopia: a new lexicostatistic classification and some problems of diffusion. *Anthropological Linguistics* 13(5).165–288.

1983. Proto-Koman phonology and lexicon. *Afrika und Übersee* 66.259–97.

1987. First steps towards Proto-Omotic. *Current approaches to African linguistics,* vol. 4, ed. David Odden, 21–35. Dordrecht: Foris Publications.

1989. Nilo-Saharan pronouns/demonstratives. *Topics in Nilo-Saharan linguistics*, ed. M. Lionel Bender, 1–34. (Nilo-Saharan: Linguistic Analyses and Documentation 3.) Hamburg: Buske.

1991. Sub-classification of Nilo-Saharan. *Proceedings of the Fourth Nilo-Saharan Linguistics Colloquium*, ed. M. Lionel Bender, 1–35. (Nilo-Saharan: Linguistic Analyses and Documentation 7.) Hamburg: Buske.

1993a. Is Nilo-Saharan really a phylum? Paper presented at the 24th African Linguistics Conference, July 23–25, Columbus, Ohio.

1993b. Are global etymologies valid? *General Linguistics* 33.191–219.

1997a. *The Nilo-Saharan languages: a comparative essay*. 2nd edition. (LINCOM Handbooks in Linguistics 6.) Munich: LINCOM Europa.

1997b. Upside-down Afrasian. *Afrikanische Arbeitspapiere* 50.19–34.

2000. Nilo-Saharan. *African languages: an introduction*, ed. Bernd Heine and Derek Nurse, 43–73. Cambridge: Cambridge University Press.

Bendor-Samuel, John (ed.) 1989. *The Niger-Congo languages: a classification and description of Africa's largest language family*. Lanham, NY: University Press of America.

Benedict, Paul K. 1942. Thai, Kadai, and Indonesian: a new alignment in southeastern Asia. *American Anthropologist* 44.576–601.

1972. *Sino-Tibetan: a conspectus*, ed. James A. Matisoff. Cambridge: Cambridge University Press.

1975a. *Austro-Thai language and culture, with a glossary of roots.* New Haven, CT: Human Relations Area Files.

1975b. Where it all began: memories of Robert Shafer and the "Sino-Tibetan linguistics project," Berkeley 1939–40. *Linguistics of the Tibeto-Burman Area* 2(1).81–91. Berkeley.

1990. *Japanese/Austro-Tai.* (Linguistica Extranea, Studia 20.) Ann Arbor: Karoma Press.

Benediktsson, Hreinn. 1980. Discussion: Rask's position in genetic and typological linguistics. *Typology and genetics of language: proceedings of the Rask-Hjelmslev Symposium*, ed. Torben Thrane, Vibeke Winge, Lachlan Mackenzie, Una Canger, and Niels Ege, 17–28. (Travaux du Cercle Linguistique de Copenhague 20.) Copenhagen: The Linguistic Circle of Copenhagen.

Benfey, Theodor. 1861. *Geschichte der Sprachwissenschaft und orientalischen Philologie in Deutschland.* Munich: Cotta.

1869. *Geschichte der Sprachwissenschaft und orientalischen Philologie in Deutschland seit dem Anfange des 19. Jahrhunderts mit einem Rückblick auf die früheren Zeiten.* (Geschichte der Wissenschaften in Deutschland.) Munich: J. G. Gotta.

Bengtson, John D. 1989. On the fallacy of "diminishing returns" in long range lexical comparison. *Reconstructing languages and cultures: materials from the First International Interdisciplinary Symposium on Language and Prehistory*, ed. Vitaly Shevoroshkin, 30–3. Bochum: Brockmeyer.

1991a. Some Macro-Caucasian etymologies. *Dene-Sino-Caucasian languages: materials from the First International Interdisciplinary Symposium on Language and Prehistory*, ed. Vitaly Shevoroshkin, 130–41. Bochum: Brockmeyer.

1991b. Paleolexicology: a tool towards language origins. *Studies in language origins*, vol. 2, ed. Walburga von Raffler-Engel, Jan Wind, and Abraham Jonker, 175–86. Amsterdam: John Benjamin.

1991c. Notes on Sino-Caucasian. *Dene–Sino-Caucasian languages: materials from the First International Interdisciplinary Symposium on Language and Prehistory*, ed. Vitaly Shevoroshkin, 67–129. Bochum: Brockmeyer.

1992. The Macro-Caucasian phonology: the Dene-Caucasian macrophylum. *Nostratic, Dene-Caucasian, Austric and Amerind: materials from the First International Interdisciplinary Symposium on Language and Prehistory*, ed. Vitaly Shevoroshkin, 342–51. Bochum: Brockmeyer.

1994. Macro-Australic. *Mother Tongue* (newsletter) 23.73–5.

1995. Some questions and theses for the American Indian language classification debate (ad Campbell, 1994). *Mother Tongue* (newsletter) 24.57–9.

1997a. Ein Vergleich von Buruschaski und Nordkaukasich [A comparison of Burushaski and (North) Caucasian]. *Georgica* 20.88–94.

1997b. Basque and the other Dené-Caucasic languages. *LACUS Forum* 23.137–48.

Bengtson, John D. and Merritt Ruhlen. 1994a. Global etymologies. *On the origin of languages: studies in linguistic taxonomy*, ed. Merritt Ruhlen, 277–336. Stanford: Stanford University Press.

1994b. Another look at *ᴛɪᴋ 'finger, one.' *California Linguistic Notes* 24(2).9–11.

1997. In defense of multilateral comparison. *California Linguistic Notes* 25(3–4). 57.

Benjamin, Geoffrey. 1976. Austroasiatic subgrouping and prehistory in the Malay Peninsula. *Austroasiatic studies*, vol. 1, ed. Philip Jenner, Laurence Thompson, and Stanley Starosta, 37–128. Honolulu: University of Hawaii Press.

Bennett, Patrick R. 1983. Adamawa-Eastern: problems and prospects. *Current approaches to African linguistics*, ed. Ivan R. Dihoff, 23–48. Dordrecht: Foris.

Bereznak, Cathy. 1995. *The Pueblo region as a linguistic area*. Ph.D. dissertation, Louisiana State University, Baton Rouge.

Berger, H. 1956. Mittelmeerische Kulturpflanzennamen aus dem Burushaski. *Indo-Iranian Journal* 3.17–43.

Bergsland, Knut. 1959. The Eskimo–Uralic hypothesis. *Journal de la Société Finno-Ougrienne* 61.1–29. Helsinki.

1978. Reflections on the comparison of Eskimo and Uralic. *Tartu Riikliku Ülikooli Toimetised* 455.131–8.

1979. The comparison of Eskimo–Aleut and Uralic. *Finno-Ugrica Suecana* 2.7–18.

Berman, Howard. 1983. Some California Penutian morphological elements. *International Journal of American Linguistics* 49.400–12.

1989. More California Penutian morphological elements. *Southwest Journal of Linguistics* 9.3–18.

1992. A comment on the Yurok and Kalapuya data in Greenberg's *Language in the Americas*. *International Journal of American Linguistics* 58.230–3.

1996. The position of Molala in Plateau Penutian. *International Journal of American Linguistics* 62.1–30.

Bernhardi, August Ferdinand. 1801–3. *Sprachlehre*. Berlin: Duncker & Humblot. (Reprinted 1973. Hildesheim: Olms.)

Bertolazo Stella, Jorge, 1929. As linguas indigenas da America. Offprint from *Revista do Instituto Historico e Geographica de São Paulo* 26, 1928.) São Paulo: Irmãos Ferraz.

Bhat, R. N. S. 1983. Comments on "Dravidian and Indo-European" by F. C. Southworth. *International Journal of Dravidian Linguistics* 12.212–13.

Bibliander (Buchmann), Theodor. 1548. *De ratione communi omnium linguarum et literarum commentarius*. Zurich: Froschauer.

Blake, Barry J. 1988. Redefining Pama-Nyungan: towards the prehistory of Australian languages. *Aboriginal Linguistics* 1.1–90.

1990. The significance of pronouns in the history of Australian languages. *Linguistic change and reconstruction methodology*, ed. P. Baldi, 435–50. Berlin: Mouton de Gruyter.

1994. Australian languages. *The Encyclopedia of language and linguistics*, ed. R. E. Asher and J. M. Y. Simpson, vol. 1.266–73. Oxford: Pergamon Press.

Blažek, V. and John Bengtson. 1995. Lexica Dene-Caucasica. *Central Asiatic Journal* 39.11–50.

Bleek, Wilhelm H. I. 1856. *The languages of Mosambique*. London: Harrison & Sons.

1858. *The library of His Excellency Sir George Grey*. London: Trübner.

1862–9. *A comparative grammar of South African languages*. London: Trübner.

Bleichsteiner, R. 1930. Die werschikisch-buruschkische Sprache im Pamijr-Gebiet und ihre Stellung zu den Japhetitensprachen des Kaukasus. *Wiener Beiträge zur Kunde des Morgenlandes* 1.289–331.

Blench, Roger. 1995. Is Niger-Congo simply a branch of Nilo-Saharan? *Proceedings of the Fifth Nilo-Saharan Linguistics Colloquium*, ed. Robert Nicolaï and Franz Rottland, 83–130. (Nilo-Saharan Analysis and Documentation 10.) Cologne: Köppe.

Bloch, Jules. 1954. *The grammatical structure of Dravidian languages*. Poona: Deccan College. (English translation of *Structure grammaticale des langues dravidiennes*, by Ramkrishna Ganesh Harshé, 1946.)

Bloomfield, Leonard. 1933. *Language*. New York: Holt, Rinehart, and Winston.

Blount, Ben G. 1990. Comments on "Speaking of forked tongues: the feasibility of reconciling human phylogeny and the history of language" by R. Bateman *et al. Current Anthropology* 31.15.

Boas, Franz. 1911. Introduction to the *Handbook of American Indian languages. Smithsonian Institution's Bureau of American Ethnology*, bulletin 40, part 1, pp. 1–70. Washington. (Reprinted by Georgetown University, Institute of Languages and Linguistics.)

1917. Introduction. *International Journal of American Linguistics*. 1.1–8. (Reprinted in Boas 1982: 199–210.)

1920. The classification of American languages. *American Anthropologist* 22.367–76. (Reprinted in Boas 1982: 211–18.)

1929. Classification of American languages. *Language* 5.1–7. (Reprinted in Boas 1982: 219–25.)

1933. Relations between north-west America and north-east Asia. *The American aborigines: their origin and antiquity*, ed. Diamond Jenness, 357–70. (Reprinted 1973. New York: Cooper Square Publishers.)

1982. *Race, language and culture*. Chicago: University of Chicago Press.

Bolnick, Deborah A., B. A. Shook, L. Campbell, and Ives Goddard. 2004. Problematic use of Greenberg's linguistic classification of the Americas in studies of Native American genetic variation. *American Journal of Human Genetics* 75.519–23.

Bomhard, Allan R. 1984. *Toward Proto-Nostratic: a new approach*. Amsterdam: John Benjamins.

1986a. Common Indo-European/Afroasiatic roots: supplement 1. *General Linguistics* 24.225–57.

1986b. Review of Markey and Shevoroshkin 1986. *Diachronica* 3.269–82. (Reprinted *Mother Tongue* [newsletter], April 10, 1990.)

1998. Review of *The Nostratic macrofamily and linguistic palaeontology*, by Aharon Dolgopolsky. *Nostratic: evaluating a linguistic macrofamily*, ed. Colin Renfrew and Daniel Nettle. Cambridge: McDonald Institute for Archaeological Research.

1989. Lexical parallels between Proto-Indo-European and other languages. Supplement to *Mother Tongue* 9 (November/December).

1990. A survey of the comparative phonology of the so-called "Nostratic" languages. *Linguistic change and reconstruction methodology*, ed. Philip Baldi, 331–58. Berlin: Mouton de Gruyter.

Bomhard, Allan R. and John C. Kerns. 1994. *The Nostratic macrofamily: a study in distant linguistic relationship*. Berlin: Mouton de Gruyter.

Bonfante, Giuliano. 1953. Ideas on the kinship of the European languages from 1200 to 1800. *Cahiers d'Histoire Mondiale* 1.679–99.

Bonnerjea, René. 1971. Is there any relationship between Eskimo-Aleut and Uralo-Altaic? *Acta Linguistica Academiae Scientiarum Hungaricae* 21(3–4).401–7.

1975. Some probable phonological connections between Ural-Altaic and Eskimo-Aleut I. *Orbis* 24.251–75.

1978. A comparison between Eskimo-Aleut and Ural-Altaic demonstrative elements, numerals, and other semantic problems. *International Journal of American Linguistics* 44.40–55.

1979. Some probable phonological connections between Ural-Altaic and Eskimo-Aleut II. *Orbis* 28.27–44.

1984. Some probable phonological connections between Ural-Altaic and Eskimo-Aleut III. *Orbis* 33.256–72.

Bopp, Franz. 1816. *Über das Conjugationssystem der Sanskritsprache in Vergleichung mit jenem der griechischen, lateinischen, persischen und germanischen Sprache, nebst Episoden des Ramajan und Mahabharat in genauen, metrischen Übersetzungen aus dem Originaltexte und einigen Abschnitten aus den Vega's.* Frankfurt am Main: Andreäische Buchhandlung. (Reprinted 1974: Amsterdam Classics in Linguistics, 15. Amsterdam: John Benjamins.)

1833–52. *Vergleichende Grammatik des Sanskrit, Zend, Armenischen, Griechischen, Lateinischen, Litauischen, Altslavischen, Gothischen und Deutschen.* 6 vols. Berlin: Ferdinand Dümmler.

1841[1840]. Über die Verwandtschaft der malayisch-polynesischen Sprache mit der indisch-europäischen. *Abhandlungen der Königlich-Preussische Akademie der Wissenschaften in Berlin*, 171–246. (Reprinted 1972 in *Kleine Schriften zur vergleichenden Sprachwissenschaft*, ed. Werner Peek, 235–310. Leipzig: Zentralantiquariat der Deutschen Demokratischen Republik.)

1842. Über die Übereinstimmung der Pronomina des malayisch-polynesischen und indisch-europäischen Sprachstammes. *Königlich-Preussische Akademie der Wissenschaften in Berlin*, 247–332. (Reprinted 1972 in *Kleine Schriften zur vergleichenden Sprachwissenschaft*, ed. Werner Peek, 311–96. Leipzig: Zentralantiquariat der Deutschen Demokratischen Republik.)

1846. Über das Georgische in sprachverwandtschaftlicher Beziehung. *Abhandlungen der Königlich-Preussische Akademie der Wissenschaften in Berlin*, 259–339. (Reprinted 1972 in *Kleine Schriften zur vergleichenden Sprachwissenschaft*, ed. Werner Peek, 250–339. Leipzig: Zentralantiquariat der Deutschen Demokratischen Republik.)

1854. Über das Albanische in seinen verwandschaftlichen Beziehungen. *Akademie der Wissenschaften Berlin, Abhandlungen Phil.-Hist. Klasse*, 459–549. Berlin.

Boretzky, Norbert. 1982. Das indogermanische Sprachwandelmodell und Wandel in exotischen Sprachen. *Zeitschrift für vergleichende Sprachforschung* 95.49–80.

1984. The Indo-European model of sound change and genetic affinity and change in exotic languages. *Diachronica* 1.1–51.

Borst, Arno. 1957–63. *Der Turmbau von Babel.* Stuttgart: Hiersemann.

Bouda, Karl. 1952. Die Tschuktschische Gruppe und das Utoaztekische. Die Verwandtschaftsverhältnisse der tschuktschischen Sprachgruppe. *Acta Salmanticensia, Filosofía y Letras* 5(6).69–78. Salamanca.

1953a. Dravidisch und Uraltaisch. *Ural-Altaische Jahrbücher* 25.161–73.

1953b. Dravidisch und Uraltaisch. *Lingua* 5.129–44.

1960a. Tungusisch und Ketschua. *Zeitschrift der Deutschen Morgenländischen Gesellschaft* 110.99–113.

1960b. Die Verwandschaftsverhältnisse des Giljakischen. *Anthropos* 55.355–415.

1961. Tschuktschisch und Uralisch I. *Zeitschrift der Deutschen Morgenländischen Gesellschaft* 111.335–60.

1963. Zoque, ein zentralamerikanischer Brückenpfeiler zwischen Westasien (Kaukasus) und Peru. *Zeitschrift der Deutschen Morgenländischen Gesellschaft* 113.144–67.

1964. Huavestudien I: Uralisches im Huave. *Etudes Finno-Ougriennes* 1.18–28.

1965a. Huavestudien II. *Etudes Finno-Ougriennes* 2.167–75.

1965b. Die Verwandtschaftsverhältnisse der tschuktschischen Sprachgruppe II. *AIΩN* 6.161–85. (Annali del Dipartimento di Studi del Mondo Classico e del Mediterraneo Antico, Sezione Linguistica, Naples.)

1968. Giljakisch und Uralisch. *Orbis* 17.459–66.

1969. Die Verwandtschaftsverhältnisse der tschuktschischen Sprachgruppe. *Orbis* 19.130–6.

1970a. Die Verwandtschaftsverhältnisse der tschuktschischen Sprachgruppe III. *Zeitschrift der Deutschen Morgenländischen Gesellschaft* 119.60–85.

1970b. Die Verwandtschaftsverhältnisse der tschuktschischen Sprachgruppe IV. *Orbis* 19.130–6.

1972. Giljakisch und Uralisch. *Etudes Finno-Ougriennes* 9.41–3.

1976. Giljakisch, Tschuktschisch und Uralisch. *Orbis* 25.240–8.

1979. Giljakisch und Uralisch II. *Explanationes et tractationes fenno-ugricae in honorem Hans Fromm*, ed. Erhand F. Schiefer, 29–36. (Münchener Universitätsschriften, Finnisch-Ugrische Bibliothek 3.) Munich: Wilhelm Fink.

1980. Giljakisch und Uralisch III. *Zeitschrift der Deutschen Morgenländischen Gesellschaft* 130.393–6.

Bower, Bruce. 1990. America's talk: the great divide. *Science News* 137.360–2.

Bowern, Claire and Harold Koch (eds.). 2004a. *Australian languages: classification and the comparative method*. Amsterdam: John Benjamins.

2004b. Introduction: subgrouping methodology in historical linguistics. *Australian languages: classification and the comparative method*, ed. Claire Bowern and Harold Koch, 1–16. Amsterdam: John Benjamins.

Bowlby, John. 1990. *Charles Darwin: a new life*. New York: W. W. Norton & Co.

Boxhorn(ius), Marcus Zuerius [anonymous pamphlet]. 1647. Antwoord von M[arcus] Z[uerius] van B[oxhorn] op de Vraaghen, hem voorgestelt over de Bediedinge van de tot noch toe onbekende Afgodinne Nehalennia, onlancx uytgegeven. *In welcke de ghemeine herkomste van der Griecken, Romeinen, ende Duytschen Tale uyt den Scythen duydelijck bewesen, ende verscheiden Oudheden van dese Volckeren grondelijck ontdeckt ende verklaert.* Leyden: Willem Cristiaens van der Boxe.

Boyd, Raymond G. 1978. A propos des ressemblances lexicales entre Niger-Congo et Nilo-Sahariennes. *Etudes comparatives BSELAF* 65.43–94. Paris.

Brandstetter, Renward. 1893. *Die Beziehungen des Malagasy zum Malaiischen.* Lucerne: E. Haag.

1906. *Ein Prodromus zu einem vergleichenden Wörterbuch der malaio-polynesischen Sprachen für Sprachforscher und Ethnographen.* Lucerne: E. Haag.

1916. *An introduction to Indonesian linguistics,* trans. C. O. Blagden. London: The Royal Asiatic Society.

Braun, David P. and Stephen Plog. 1982. Evolution of tribal social networks: theory and prehistoric North American evidence. *American Antiquity* 47.504–25.

Breva-Claramonte, Manuel. 1983. *Sanctius' theory of language: a contribution to the history of renaissance linguistics.* (Studies in the History of Linguistics 27.) Amsterdam: John Benjamins.

Bright, William. 1954. Some Northern Hokan relationships: a preliminary report. *Papers from the symposium on American Indian linguistics,* ed. C. D. Chrétien, M. S. Beeler, M. B. Emeneau, and M. R. Haas, 57–62. (University of California Publications in Linguistics 10.) Berkeley: University of California Press.

1955. A bibliography of the Hokan-Coahuiltecan languages. *International Journal of American Linguistics* 21.276–85.

1970. On linguistic unrelatedness. *International Journal of American Linguistics* 36.288–90.

1984. The classification of North American and Meso-American Indian languages. *American Indian linguistics and literature,* 3–29. Berlin: Mouton.

1991. Sapir and distant linguistic relationship. *The Edward Sapir Society of Japan* (newsletter) 5.19–25. Tokyo.

Brinton, Daniel G. 1859. *Notes on the Floridian Peninsula, its literary history, Indian tribes and antiquities.* Philadelphia: Joseph Sabin.

1869. The nature of the Maya group of languages. *Proceedings of the American Philosophical Society* 11.4–6.

1885a. American Indian languages and why we should study them. *Pennsylvania Magazine of History and Biography* 9.15–35. (Reprinted in Brinton 1890: 308–27.)

1885b. *Wilhelm von Humboldt's researches in American languages.* (Reprinted in Brinton 1890: 328–48.)

1888. The language of palæolithic man. *Proceedings of the American Philosophical Society* 3–16. (Reprinted in Brinton 1890: 390–409.)

1890. *The earliest form of human speech, as revealed by American tongues: essays of an Americanist.* Philadelphia: Porter & Coates.

1891. *The American race: a linguistic classification and ethnographic description of the native tribes of North and South America.* New York: N. D. C. Hodges.

Broadbent, Sylvia M. and Harvey Pitkin. 1964. A comparison of Miwok and Wintun. *Studies in Californian linguistics,* ed. William Bright, 19–45. (University of California Publications in Linguistics 34.) Berkeley: University of California Press.

Brockelmann, Carl. 1908. *Grundriss der vergleichenden Grammatik der semitischen Sprachen,* vol. 1: *Laut- und Formenlehre.* Berlin: Reuther & Reichard.

Brody, Jill M. 1989. Particles borrowed from Spanish as discourse markers in Mayan languages. *Anthropological Linguistics* 29.507–521.

1995. Lending the "unborrowable": Spanish discourse markers in indigenous American languages. *Spanish in four continents: studies in language contact and bilingualism,* ed. Carmen Silva-Corvalan, 132–47. Washington, DC: Georgetown University Press.

Brown, Cecil H. and Stanley R. Witkowski. 1979. Aspects of the phonological history of Mayan-Zoquean. *International Journal of American Linguistics* 45. 34–47.

Brugmann, Karl. 1884. Zur Frage nach den Verwandtschaftsverhältnissen der indogermanischen Sprachen. *Internationale Zeitschrift für Allgemeine Sprachwissenschaft* 1.226–56.

Brunner, L. 1969. Die gemeinsamen Wurzeln des semitischen und des indogermanischen Wortschatzes. *Versuch einer Etymologie*. Bern and Munich: Francke.

Bryan, Margaret A. 1959. The T/K languages: a new substratum. *Africa* 29.1–21.

Bryant, Jacob. 1774–6. *A new system, or an analysis of ancient mythology*. 3 vols. London.

Bugge, Sophus. 1902. *Bemerkungen. Die zwei Arzawa-Briefe: die ältesten Urkunden in indogermanischer Sprache*, by J. A. Knudtzon, 57–107. Leipzig: Hinrichs.

Burenhult, Niclas. 1996. *Deep linguistic prehistory with particular reference to Andamanese*. Working Papers 45.5–214. Lund University, Department of Linguistics.

Burrow, Thomas. 1943. Dravidian studies IV: the body in Dravidian and Uralian. *Bulletin of the School of Oriental and African Studies* 11.328–56.

1944. The body in Dravidian and Uralian. *Bulletin of the School of Oriental and African Studies* 9.328–56.

Burrow, Thomas and Murray B. Emeneau. 1961. *A Dravidian etymological dictionary*. (2nd edition 1984.) Oxford: Clarendon Press.

Buschmann, Johann Carl Eduard. 1856. Der athapaskische Sprachstamm. *Abhandlungen der Königliche Akademie der Wissenschaften zu Berlin 1855*.149–319.

1859. Die Spuren der aztekischen Sprache im nördlichen Mexico und höheren amerikanischen Norden. *Abhandlungen der Königliche Akademie der Wissenschaften zu Berlin 1854*, supplementary vol. 2. Berlin.

Bynon, Theodora. 1986. *August Schleicher: Indo-Europeanist and general linguist. Studies in the history of Western linguistics, in honour of R. H. Robins*, ed. Theodora Bynon and F. R. Palmer, 129–49. Cambridge: Cambridge University Press.

Caldwell, Robert. 1856. *A comparative grammar of the Dravidian or South-Indian family of languages*. London: Harrison. (2nd edition 1875; 3rd edition 1913: London: Routledge and Kegan Paul. Reprinted 1974, New Delhi: Oriental Books.)

Callaghan, Catherine A. 1958. California Penutian: history and bibliography. *International Journal of American Linguistics* 24.189–94.

1967. Miwok-Costanoan as a subfamily of Penutian. *International Journal of American Linguistics* 33.224–7.

1980. An "Indo-European" type paradigm in Proto Eastern Miwok. *American Indian and Indo-European studies: papers in honor of Madison S. Beeler*, ed. K. Klar, Margaret Langdon, and Shirley Silver, 331–8. The Hague: Mouton.

1991. *Climbing a low mountain. A festschrift for William F. Shipley*, ed. Sandra Chung and Jorge Hankamer, 47–59. Santa Cruz: Syntax Research Center, University of California, Santa Cruz.

Callaghan, Catherine A. and Wick R. Miller. 1962. Swadesh's Macro-Mixtecan hypothesis and English. *Southwest Journal of Anthropology* 18.278–85.

Cambrensis, Giraldus [Gerald of Wales]. 1194. *Descriptio Kambriae*. [London, British Library.]

Campbell, Alexander Duncan. 1816. *A grammar of the Teloogoo language commonly called the Gentoo.* (Reprinted, 3rd edition (from 1849), 1991. Madras: Asian Educational Services.)

Campbell, Lyle. 1972. Mayan loan words in Xinca. *International Journal of American Linguistics* 38.187–90.

1973. Distant genetic relationships and the Maya-Chipaya hypothesis. *Anthropological Linguistics* 15(3).113–35. (Reprinted 1993, in *Special issue: a retrospective of the Journal of Anthropological Linguistics: selected papers, 1959–1985. Anthropological Linguistics* 35(1–4).66–89.

1977. *Quichean linguistic prehistory.* (University California Publications in Linguistics 81.) Berkeley: University of California Press.

1978. Distant genetic relationship and diffusion: a Mesoamerican perspective. *Proceedings of the International Congress of Americanists* 52.595–605. Paris.

1979. Middle American languages. *The languages of Native America: an historical and comparative assessment*, ed. Lyle Campbell and Marianne Mithun, 902–1000. Austin: University of Texas Press.

1987. Syntactic change in Pipil. *International Journal of American Linguistics* 53.253–80.

1988. Review of *Language in the Americas*, by Joseph H. Greenberg. *Language* 64.591–615.

1990. Indo-European and Uralic trees. *Diachronica* 7.149–80.

1994a. The American Indian classification controversy: an insider's view. *Mother Tongue* (newsletter) 23.41–55.

1994b. Problems with the pronouns in proposals of remote relationships among Native American languages. *Proceedings of the meeting of the Society for the Study of the Indigenous Languages of the Americas and the Hokan-Penutian workshop*, ed. Margaret Langdon, 1–20. (Survey of Californian and other Indian Languages, Report 8.) Berkeley: University of California.

1995. The Quechumaran hypothesis and lessons for distant genetic comparison. *Diachronica* 12.157–200.

1996. Coahuiltecan: a closer look. *Anthropological Linguistics* 38(4).620–34.

1997a. *American Indian languages: the historical linguistics of Native America.* Oxford: Oxford University Press.

1997b. Amerindian personal pronouns: a second opinion. *Language* 72.336–71.

1997c. Genetic classification, typology, areal linguistics, language endangerment, and languages of the north Pacific rim. *Languages of the North Pacific Rim*, vol. 2, ed. Osahito Miyaoka and Minoru Oshima, 179–242. Kyoto: Kyoto University.

1997d. The linguistic prehistory of Guatemala. *Papers in honor of William Bright*, ed. Jane Hill, P. J. Mistry, and Lyle Campbell, 183–92. Berlin: Mouton de Gruyter.

1998. Nostratic: a personal assessment. *Nostratic: sifting the evidence*, ed. Brian Joseph and Joe Salmons, 107–52. Amsterdam: John Benjamins.

1999. Nostratic and linguistic palaeontology in methodological perspective. *Nostratic: evaluating a linguistic macrofamily*, ed. Colin Renfrew and Daniel Nettle, 179–230. Cambridge: McDonald Institute for Archaeological Research.

2000. Review of *Language relations across Bering Strait: reappraising the archaeological and linguistic evidence* by Michael Fortescue. *Anthropological Linguistics* 42.572–9.

2002. What drives linguistic diversity and language spread? *Examining the farming/language dispersal hypothesis*, ed. Peter Bellwood and Colin Renfrew, 49–63. Cambridge: McDonald Institute for Archaeological Research.

2003a. How to show languages are related: methods for distant genetic relationship. *Handbook of historical linguistics*, ed. Brian D. Joseph and Richard D. Janda, 262–82. Oxford: Blackwell.

2003b. Beyond the comparative method? *Historical linguistics*, ed. Barry Blake and Kate Burridge, 33–58. Amsterdam: John Benjamins.

2004. *Historical linguistics: an introduction*. 2nd edition. Edinburgh: Edinburgh University Press.

Campbell, Lyle and Ives Goddard. 1990. American Indian languages and principles of language change. *Linguistic change and reconstruction methodology*, ed. Philip Baldi, 17–32. Berlin: Mouton de Gruyter.

Campbell, Lyle, Vit Bubenik, and Leslie Saxon. 1988. Word order universals: refinements and clarifications. *Canadian Journal of Linguistics* 33.209–30.

Campbell, Lyle and Terrence Kaufman, 1976. A linguistic look at the Olmecs. *American Antiquity* 41.80–9.

1980. On Mesoamerican linguistics. *American Anthropologist* 82.850–7.

1983. Mesoamerican historical linguistics and distant genetic relationship: getting it straight. *American Anthropologist* 85.362–72.

Campbell, Lyle, Terrence Kaufman, and Thomas Smith-Stark. 1986. Mesoamerica as a linguistic area. *Language* 62.530–70.

Campbell, Lyle and Marianne Mithun. 1979. North American Indian historical linguistics in current perspective. *The languages of Native America: an historical and comparative assessment*, ed. L. Campbell and M. Mithun, 3–69. Austin: University of Texas Press.

Cannon, Garland H., Jr. 1952. *Sir William Jones, orientalist: an annotated bibliography of his works*. Honolulu: University of Hawaii Press.

1964. *Oriental Jones: a biography of Sir William Jones (1756–1794)*. London: Asia Publishing House for India Council for Cultural Relations.

1990. *The life and mind of oriental Jones: Sir William Jones, the father of modern linguistics*. Cambridge: Cambridge University Press.

1991. Jones's "sprung from some common source": 1786–1986. *Sprung from some common source: investigations into the prehistory of languages*, ed. Sydney M. Lamb and E. Douglas Mitchell, 23–47. Stanford: Stanford University Press.

Capell, A. 1956. *A new approach to Australian linguistics*. (Oceania Linguistic Monographs 1.) Sydney: University of Sydney.

1962. *Some linguistic types in Australia* (*Handbook of Australian languages*, part 2.) (Oceania Linguistic Monographs 7.) Sydney: University of Sydney.

1975. Ergative constructions in Australian languages. *Working papers in language and linguistics* 2.1–7. *Tasmanian College of Advanced Education, Launceston*.

1979. The history of Australian languages: a first approach. *Australian linguistic studies*, ed. Stephen A. Wurm, 419–619. (Pacific Linguistics C-71.) Canberra: Australian National University.

Cargill, David. 1840. A brief essay on the Feejeean language, addressed to the secretaries of the Wesleyan Missionary Society. *Wesleyan Methodist Missionary Society Report* 8.132–43.

Castrén, Matthias Alexander. 1847. Lettre de M. le Dr. Castrén à l'Académicien Sjoegren. Lue 30 janv. 1846. *Bulletin de la classe historico-philologique de l'Academie Impériale des Sciences de St.-Pétersbourg* 3.225–44.

1850. *De affixibus personalibus linguarum altaicarum dissertatio.* Helsinki: Litteris Frenckellianis.

1856. *Reiseberichte und Briefe aus den Jahren 1845–49.* St. Petersburg: Kaiserlichen Akademie der Wissenschaften.

1857. *Ethnologische Vorlesungen über die altaischen Völker, nebst samojedischen Märchen und tatarischen Heldensagen.* St. Petersburg: Kaiserlichen Akademie der Wissenschaften.

1862. Über die Personalaffixe in den altaischen Sprachen. *Kleinere Schriften,* 151–222. St. Petersburg: Kaiserlichen Akademie der Wissenschaften.

Čašule, Iliya. 1998. *Basic Burushaski etymologies: the Indo-European and Paleo-Balkanic affinities of Burushaski.* Munich: LINCOM.

Catford, J. C. 1991. The classification of Caucasian languages. *Sprung from some common source: investigations into the prehistory of languages,* ed. Sydney M. Lamb and E. Douglas Mitchell, 232–68. Stanford: Stanford University Press.

Cavalli-Sforza, L. L., A. Piazza, P. Menozzi, and J. Mountain. 1988. Reconstruction of human evolution: bringing together genetic, archaeological, and linguistic data. *Proceedings of the National Academy of Science of the USA* 85.6002–6.

1989. Genetic and linguistic evolution. *Science* 244.1128–9.

Cavalli-Sforza, L. L., Eric Minch, and J. L. Mountain. 1992. Coevolution of genes and languages revisited. *Proceedings of the National Academy of Science of the USA* 89.5620–4.

Cerrón-Palomino, Rodolfo. 1986. Comentario [sobre] Willem F. H. Adelaar, *La relación quechua-aru: perspectiva para la separación del léxico. Revista Andina* 4. 403–8.

1987. *Lingüística quechua.* (Biblioteca de la tradición oral andina 8.) Cuzco: Centro de Estudios Rurales Andinos "Bartolomé de las Casas."

Chafe, Wallace L. 1959. Internal reconstruction in Seneca. *Language* 35.477–95.

1964. Another look at Siouan and Iroquoian. *American Anthropologist* 66.852–62.

1973. Siouan, Iroquoian, and Caddoan. *Linguistics in North America,* ed. Thomas A. Sebeok, 1164–1209. (Current Trends in Linguistics 10.) The Hague: Mouton. (Reprinted 1976, in *Native languages of the Americas,* ed. Thomas A. Sebeok, 527–72. New York: Plenum Press.)

1976. *The Caddoan, Iroquoian, and Siouan languages.* The Hague: Mouton.

1987. Review of *Language in the Americas,* by Joseph H. Greenberg. *Current Anthropology* 28.652–3.

Chamberlain, Alexander Francis. 1910. The Uran: a new South American linguistic stock. *American Anthropologist* 12.417–24.

Chappell, Hilary. 2001. Language contact and areal diffusion in Sinitic languages. *Areal diffusion and genetic inheritance,* ed. Alexandra Y. Aikhenvald and R. M. W. Dixon, 328–57. Oxford: Oxford University Press.

Charencey, [Charles Felix Hyacinthe, Le Comte de]. 1870. *Notice sur quelques familles de langues du Mexique.* Le Havre: Imprimerie Lepellatier.

1872. *Recherches sur les lois phonétiques dans les idiomes de la famille mame-huastèque.* Paris: Maisonneuve.

1883. *Mélanges de philologie et de paléographie américaines.* Paris: Ernest Leroux. [Includes: *Sur les lois phonétiques dans les idiomes de la famille mame-huastèque,* 91–121; reprint of 1872.]

Childs, G. Tucker. 2003. *An introduction to African languages.* Amsterdam: John Benjamins.

Christian, F. W. 1932. Polynesian and Oceanic elements in the Chimu and Inca languages. *Journal of the Polynesian Society* 41.144–56.

Christy, T. Craig. 1980. Uniformitarianism in nineteenth-century linguistics: implications for a reassessment of the neogrammarian sound-law doctrine. *Progress in linguistic historiography,* ed. Konrad Koerner, 249–56. (Studies in the History of Linguistics 20.) Amsterdam: John Benjamins.

1983. *Uniformitarianism in linguistics.* John Benjamins, Amsterdam.

Čirikba, V. A. 1985. Baskskii i sevepokavkazskie yazuki [*Basque and North-Caucasian languages*]. *Drevnyaya Anatoliya,* 95–105. Moscow: Nauka.

Clackson, James. 1994. *The linguistic relationship between Armenian and Greek.* Oxford: Blackwell.

Clark, Ross. 1987. Austronesian languages. *The world's major languages,* ed. Bernard Comrie, 899–912. London: Croom Helm.

Claude, A. 1973. Problèmes d'une comparison indo-ouralien. *Cahiers de l'Institute de Linguistique 1(2).279–92.* (Université Catholique de Louvain.)

Clauson, Gerard. 1956. The case against the Altaic theory. *Central Asiatic Journal* 2.181–7.

1959a. The earliest Turkish loan words in Mongolian. *Akten des vierundzwanzigsten Internationalen Orientalisten-Kongresses,* ed. H. Franke, 593–5. Wiesbaden: Deutsche Morgenländische Gesellschaft, Franz Steiner Verlag.

1959b. The case for the Altaic theory examined. *Akten des vierundzwanzigsten Internationalen Orientalisten-Kongresses,* ed. H. Franke, 599–601. Wiesbaden: Deutsche Morgenländische Gesellschaft, Franz Steiner Verlag.

1962. *Turkish and Mongolian studies.* London: Luzac.

1969. A lexicostatistical appraisal of the Altaic theory. *Central Asiatic Journal* 13.1–23.

1973a. Nostratic. *Journal of the Royal Asiatic Society* 46–55.

1973b. On the idea of Sumerian-Uralic-Altaic. *Current Anthropology* 14.493–5.

Cœurdoux, Gaston Laurent. 1784–93[1767]. [Letter to Abbé Barthélémy published in] *Mémoires de littérature de [. . .] l'Académie Royale des Inscriptions et Belles-Lettres* 49.647–67, by Anquetil Duperron. Paris.

Cohen, Marcel. 1924. Langues chamito-sémitiques. *Les langue du monde,* 2 vols., ed. André Meillet and Marcel Cohen, 81–151. Paris: Champion.

1947. *Essai comparatif sur le vocabulaire et la phonétique du chamito-sémitique.* Paris: Champion.

Colarusso, John. 1994. Phyletic links between Proto-European and Proto-Northwest Caucasian. *Mother Tongue* (newsletter) 21.8–20.

Cole, Desmond T. 1971. The history of African linguistics to 1945. *Linguistics in Sub-Saharan Africa,* ed. Jack Berry and Joseph H. Greenberg, 1–29. (Current Trends in Linguistics 7.) The Hague: Mouton.

Collinder, Björn. 1934. Indo-uralisches Sprachgut: die Urverwandtschaft zwischen der indoeuropäischen und der uralischen (finnischugrisch-samojedischen) Sprachfamilie. *Uppsala Universitets årsskrift* 1.1–116.

1940. Jukagirisch und Uralisch. *Uppsala Universitets årsskrift* 8.1.

1943. Indo-uralische Nachlese. *Språkvetenskapliga Sällskapets i Uppsala Förhandlingar, 1943–1945.* 1–6. (Reprinted in Collinder 1964b: 133–40.)

1946–8. La parenté linguistique et le calcul des probabilités. *Språkvetenskapliga sällskapets i Uppsala Förhandlingar, 1946–1948. Uppsala Universitets årsskrift* 13.1–24.

1952. Ural-Altaisch. *Ural-Altaische Jahrbücher* 24.1–26.

1954. Zur indo-uralischen Frage. *Acta Universitatis Upsaliensis. Språkvetenskapliga sällskapets i Uppsala förhandlingar, 1952–1954* 10.79–91. Uppsala: Almqvist & Wiksells.

1955a. Remarks on linguistic affinity. *Ural-Altaische Jahrbücher* 27.1–6.

1955b/1977. *Fenno-Ugric vocabulary: an etymological dictionary of the Uralic languages.* Stockholm: Almqvist & Wiksell. (2nd edition 1977. Hamburg: Buske.)

1960. *Comparative grammar of the Uralic languages.* Stockholm: Almqvist & Wiksell.

1964a. *La regle de succession dans le calcul des probabilités.* (Reprinted in Collinder 1964b: 184–202.)

1964b. *Sprachverwandtschaft und Wahrscheinlichkeit.* Uppsala: Almqvist & Wiksells.

1965a. *An introduction to the Uralic languages.* Berkeley: University of California Press.

1965b. Hat das Uralische Verwandte? Eine sprachvergleichende Untersuchung. *Acta Universitatis Upsaliensis* 1(4).109–80.

1967. Die indouralische Sprachvergleichung und die Laryngaltheorie. *Die Sprache* 13.179–80.

1970. Nachtrag zum Aufsatz "Die indouralische Sprachvergleichung und die Laryngaltheorie." *Die Sprache* 16.174–5.

1974. Indo-Uralisch oder gar Nostratisch? "Antiquitates Indogermanicae" Gedenkschrift für H. Güntert. *Innsbrucker Beiträge zur Sprachwissenschaft* 12.363–75.

1977. Pro hypothesi Uralo-Altaica. *Mémoires de la Société Finno-Ougrienne* 158.67–73.

Comenius [Komenský], Joannes Amos. 1657. *Opera didactica omnia. Variis hucusque occasionibus scripta, diversisque locis edita: nunc autem non tantum in unum, ut simul sint, collecta, sed et ultimo conatu in systema unum mechanice constructum, redacta.* Amsterdam: D. Laurentius de Geer. (Reprinted 1952, Prague: Academiae Scientiarum Bohemslovenicae, 3 vols.)

Comrie, Bernard. 1981. The genetic affiliation of Kamchadal: some morphological evidence. *Studies in the languages of the USSR*, ed. Bernard Comrie, 109–20. Edmonton: Linguistic Research.

1989. Genetic classification, contact, and variation. *Synchronic and diachronic approaches to linguistic variation and change*, ed. Thomas J. Walsh, 81–93. Washington, DC: Georgetown University Press.

1992. Before complexity. *The evolution of human languages*, ed. John A. Hawkins and Murray Gell-Mann, 193–210. Redwood City, CA: Addison-Wesley Publishing Co.

1993. Review of *Altajskaja problema i proisxoždenie japonskogo jazyka* [The Altaic problem and the origin of the Japanese language], by Sergej A. Starostin. *Language* 69.828–32.

1999. Nostratic language and culture: some methodological reflections. *Nostratic: examining a linguistic macrofamily*, ed. Colin Renfrew and Daniel Nettle, 243–55. Cambridge: McDonald Institute for Archaeological Research.

Conrady, August. 1896. *Eine indochinesische causativ-denominativ-Bildung und ihr Zusammenhang mit den Tonaccenten: ein Beitrag zur vergleichenden Grammatik der indochinesischen Sprachen, insonderheit des Tibetischen, Barmanischen und Chinesischen.* Leipzig: Harrasowitz.

Constenla Umaña, Adolfo. 1987. Elementos de fonología comparada de las lenguas misumalpas. *Filología y Lingüística* 13.129–61. San José, Costa Rica.

1991. *Las lenguas del área intermedia: introducción a su estudio areal.* San José: Editorial de la Universidad de Costa Rica.

Cook, James. 1777. *A voyage towards the South Pole, and round the world, performed in His Majesty's ships the Resolution and Adventure, in the years 1772, 1773, 1774, and 1775.* London: Strahan and Cadell.

Čop, Bojan. 1970a. Die indouralische Sprachverwandtschaft und die indogermanische Laryngaltheorie. *Slovenska Akademija Znanosti in Umetnosti* 7(5).185–229. Ljubljana.

1970b. Indouralica IV. *Orbis* 19.282–323.

1970c. Indouralica VII. *Zeitschrift für vergleichende Sprachforschung* (Kuhns Zeitschrift) 84.151–74.

1972. Indouralica II. *Ural-Altaische Jahrbücher* 44.162–78.

1973a. Indouralica VI. *Orbis* 22.5–42.

1973b. Indouralica IV. *Linguistica* 13.116–90.

1974a. Indouralica I. *Slovenska Akademija Znanosti in Umetnosti* 30 (1). Ljubljana.

1974b. Indouralica VIII. *Acta Linguistica Academiae Scientiarum Hungaricae* 24.87–116. Budapest.

1974c. Indouralica V. *Zeitschrift für vergleichende Sprachforschung* (*Kuhns Zeitschrift*) 88.41–58.

1975. *Die indogermanische Deklination im Lichte der indouralischen vergleichenden Grammatik.* (*Slovenska Akademija Znanosti in Umetnosti* 31.) Ljubljana.

1976. Méditerranéen et indo-ouralien. *Linguistica* 16.3–33.

1987. Indouralica V. *Collectanea Indoeuropaea* 1.145–96. Ljubljana.

1979. *Indogermanisch-Anatolisch und Uralisch. Hethitisch und Indogermanisch*, ed. W. Meid, 8–24. Innsbruck: E. Neu.

1987. Indouralica II. *Linguistica* 27.135–61.

1989. Indouralica I. *Linguistica* 29.13–56.

Cordington, Robert H. 1885a. *The Melanesian languages.* Oxford: Clarendon Press.

Cornwell, James A. 1995. *The Tower of Babel and Babylon, Gilgamesh, Ningizzida, Gudea.* (www.mazzaroth.com/ChapterThree/TowerOfBabel.htm)

Coseriu, Eugenio. 1977. Sobre la tipología lingüística de Wilhelm von Humboldt. *Tradición y novedad en la ciencia del lenguaje*, 142–84. Madrid: Gredos. (Originally in 1972 *Beiträge zur vergleichenden Literaturgeschichte, Festschrift für Kurt Wais*, 235–66. Tübingen: Niemeyer.)

Court de Gébelin, Antoine. 1773–82 [1776]. *Monde primitif analysé et comparé avec le monde moderne*. 9 vols. Paris: Antoine Court de Gébelin.

Cowan, H. K. J. 1962. Statistical determination of linguistic relationships. *Studia Linguistica* 16.57–96.

Craig, Colette and Kenneth Hale. 1992. A possible Macro-Chibchan etymon. *Anthropological Linguistics* 34.173–201.

Crawford, James M. 1976. A comparison of Chimariko and Yuman. *Hokan studies: papers from the first conference on Hokan languages held in San Diego, California, April 23–25, 1970*, ed. Margaret Langdon and Shirley Silver, 177–91. (Janua Linguarum, series practica 181.) The Hague: Mouton.

1979. Timucua and Yuchi: two language isolates of the Southeast. *The languages of Native America: historical and comparative assessment*, ed. Lyle Campbell and Marianne Mithun, 327–54. Austin: University of Texas Press.

1988. On the relationship of Timucua to Muskogean. *In honor of Mary Haas: from the Haas festival conference on Native America linguistics*, ed. William Shipley, 157–64. Berlin: Mouton de Gruyter.

Croft, William. 2005. *Editor's introduction. Genetic linguistics: essays on theory and method*, by Joseph H. Greenberg, ed. William Croft, xi–xxxvi. Oxford: Oxford University Press.

Crosby, Alfred W. 1993. *Ecological imperialism: the biological expansion of Europe, 900–1900*. Cambridge: Cambridge University Press.

Crowley, Terry. 1992. *An introduction to historical linguistics*. Auckland: Oxford University Press.

1997. Chipping away at the past: a northern New South Wales perspective. *Archaeology and linguistics: Aboriginal Australia in global perspective*, ed. Patrick McConvell and Nicholas Evans, 275–95. Melbourne: Oxford University Press.

1999. Review of *The rise and fall of languages* by R. M. W. Dixon. *Australian Journal of Linguistics* 19.109–15.

Crowley, Terry and R. M. W. Dixon. 1981. *Tasmania. Handbook of Australian languages*, vol. 2, ed. R. M. W. Dixon and Barry Blake, 394–421. Amsterdam: John Benjamins.

Csúcs, Sándor. 1990. *Die tatarischen Lehnwörter des Wotjakischen*. Budapest: Akadémiai Kiadó.

Cuny, Albert. 1912. Notes de phonétique historique: Indo-européen et sémitique. *Revue de Phonétique* 2.101–32.

1924. *Etudes prégrammaticales sur le domaine des langues indo-européenes et chamito-sémitiques*. Paris: E. Champion.

1943. *Recherches sur le vocalisme, le consonantisme et la formation des racines en "nostratique," ancéstre de l'indo-européen et du chamito-sémitique*. Paris: Adrien-Maisonneuve.

1946. *Invitation à l'étude comparative des langues indo-européennès et des langues chamito-sémitiques*. Bordeaux: Editions Biére.

Curtius, Georg. 1870. Zur Geschichte der griechischen zusammengezogenen Verbalformen. *Studien zur griechischen und lateinischen Grammatik* 3.377–401. Leipzig: S. Hirzel.

1871. Zur Erklärung der Personalendungen. *Studien zur griechischen und lateinischen Grammatik* 4.211–30. Leipzig: S. Hirzel.

Cust, Robert. 1883. *A sketch of the modern languages of Africa*. 2 vols. London: Trübner.

Cyffer, Norbert. 2000. Linguistic properties of the Saharan languages. *Areal and genetic factors in language classification and description: Africa south of the Sahara*, ed. Petr Zima, 30–59. Munich: LINCOM Europa.

d'Abbadie, Antoine and J. Augustin Chaho. 1836. *Etudes grammaticales sur la langue euskarienne*. Paris: Arthus Bertrand.

Dahl, Östen. 2001. Principles of areal typology. *Language universals and language typology: an international handbook*, ed. Martin Haspelmath, E. König, W. Oesterreicher, and W. Raible, 1456–70. Berlin: Mouton de Gruyter.

Dangel, Richard. 1930. Quechua and Maori. *Mitteilungen der Anthropologische Gesellschaft in Wien* 60.343–51.

Dante Alighieri. c.1305. *De vulgari eloquentia*. (English translation 1981, *Dante in hell: the De vulgari eloquentia, introduction, translation, and commentary by Warman Welliver*. Ravenna: Longo Editore.)

Darnell, Regna. 1969. The development of American anthropology 1879–1920: from the Bureau of American Ethnology to Franz Boas. University of Pennsylvania Ph.D. dissertation, Philadelphia.

1990. *Edward Sapir: linguist, anthropologist, humanist*. Berkeley: University of California Press.

Davies, Anna Morpurgo. 1975. Language classification in the nineteenth century. *Historiography of linguistics*, ed. Thomas A. Sebeok, 607–717. (Current Trends in Linguistics 13.) The Hague: Mouton.

1986. Karl Brugmann and late nineteenth-century linguistics. *Studies in the history of Western linguistics, in honour of R. H. Robins*, ed. Theodora Bynon and F. R. Palmer, 150–71. Cambridge: Cambridge University Press.

1992. Comparative-historical linguistics. *International encyclopedia of linguistics*, ed. William Bright, 2.159–63. Oxford: Oxford University Press.

Davis, Irvine. 1968. Some Macro-Jê relationships. *International Journal of American Linguistics* 34.42–7. (Reprinted 1985 in *South American Indian languages: retrospect and prospect*, ed. Harriet E. Manelis Klein and Louisa R. Stark, 287–303. Austin: University of Texas Press.)

1974. Keresan-Caddoan comparisons. *International Journal of American Linguistics* 40.265–7.

1979. The Kiowa-Tanoan, Keresan, and Zuni languages. *The languages of Native America: an historical and comparative assessment*, ed. Lyle Campbell and Marianne Mithun, 390–443. Austin: University of Texas Press.

1989. A new look at Aztec-Tanoan. *General and Amerindian ethnolinguistics: in remembrance of Stanley Newman*, ed. Mary Ritchie Key and Henry M. Hoenigswald, 365–79. Berlin: Mouton de Gruyter.

Décsy, Gyula. 1980. Neue Aspekte zum Sprachverhältnis Uralisch-Indogermanisch. *Ural-Altaische Jahrbücher* 52.11–20.

1988. Bojan Čop's contribution to Nostratic studies. *Ural-Altaische Jahrbücher* 60.199–200.

Décsy, Gyula and C. Dimov-Bogoev (eds.) 1977. *Eurasia Nostratica: Festschrift für K. H. Menges*. (Biblioteca Nostratica 1.) Wiesbaden: Harrassowitz.

de Guignes, Joseph. 1770. See Guignes, Joseph de. 1770.

de Laet, Johannes. 1643. See Laet, Johannes de.

DeLancey, Scott. 1987. Morphological parallels between Klamath and Wintu. *Papers of the 1987 Hokan-Penutian languages workshop and Friends of Uto-Aztecan workshop*, ed. James E. Redden, 50–60. (Occasional Papers on Linguistics 14.) Carbondale, IL: Department of Linguistics, Southern Illinois University.

  1988a. Klamath and Wintu pronouns. *International Journal of American Linguistics* 53.461–4.

  1988b. Klamath stem structure in genetic and areal perspective. *Papers from the 1988 Hokan-Penutian languages workshop*, ed. Scott DeLancey, 50–168. Eugene: Department of Linguistics, University of Oregon.

  1990. Sino-Tibetan languages. *The major languages of Asia and SE Asia*, ed. Bernard Comrie, 69–82. London: Routledge.

  1992. Klamath and Sahaptian numerals. *International Journal of American Linguistics* 58.235–30.

DeLancey, Scott, Carol Genetti, and Noel Rude. 1988. Some Sahaptian-Klamath-Tsimshianic lexical sets. *In honor of Mary Haas: from the Haas festival conference on Native American linguistics*, ed. William Shipley, 193–224. Berlin: Mouton de Gruyter.

Delbrück, Berthold. 1880. *Einleitung in das Sprachstudium: ein Beitrag zur Geschichte und Methodik der Vergleichenden Sprachforschung*. Leipzig: Breitkopf & Haertel. (2nd edition, 1884.) [English translation, 1989: *Introduction to the study of language: a critical survey of the history and methods of comparative philology of Indo-European languages*, by Konrad Koerner. Amsterdam: John Benjamins.]

  1901. *Grundfragen der Sprachforschung*. Leipzig: Engelmann.

DeLisle, Helga H. 1981. Consonantal symbolism in American Indian languages. *Journal of the Linguistic Association of the Southwest* 4.130–42.

Del Rey Fajardo, José. 1971. *Aportes jesuíticos a la filología colonial venezolana*. 2 vols. Caracas: Universidad Católica Andrés Bello, Instituto de Investigaciones Históricas, Seminario de Lenguas Indígenas.

Dempwolff, Otto. 1934–8. *Vergleichende Lautlehre des austronesischen Wortschatzes* 3 vols. (Supplements to *Zeitschrift für Eingeborenen-Sprachen* 15 [1934], 17 [1937], and 19 [1938]). Berlin: Dietrich Reimer.

Dench, Alan. 1994. The historical development of pronoun paradigms in the Pilbara region of Western Australia. *Australian Journal of Linguistics* 14.155–91.

  2001. Descent and diffusion: the complexity of the Pilbara situation. *Areal diffusion and genetic inheritance*, ed. Alexandra Y. Aikhenvald and R. M. W. Dixon, 105–33. Oxford: Oxford University Press.

Denison, T. S. 1913. *Mexican linguistics: including Nauatl or Mexican in Aryan phonology, the primitive Aryans of America, a Mexican-Aryan comparative vocabulary, morphology and the Mexican verb, and the Mexican-Aryan sibilants, with an appendix on comparative syntax*. Chicago: T. S. Denison & Company.

Dennett, Daniel C. 1995. *Darwin's dangerous idea: evolution and the meanings of life*. London: Penguin Books.

Dezsö, L. 1990. Uralic and Indo-European in the Northern Eurasian Area: typological characterization and comparison. *Congressus Septimus Internationalis Fenno-Ugristarum*, ed. L. Keresztes and S. Maticsák, 3.23–9. Debrecen.

Diakonof, I. M. 1990. Language contacts in the Caucasus and the Near East. *When worlds collide*, ed. Thomas Markey and John Greppin, 53–65. Ann Arbor, MI: Karoma.

Diamond, Jared. 1997. *Guns, germs and steel*. London: Jonathan Cape.

Diderichsen, Paul. 1974. *The foundation of comparative linguistics: revolution or continuation? Studies in the history of linguistics: traditions and paradigms*, ed. Dell Hymes, 277–306. Bloomington: Indiana University Press.

Diffloth, Gérard. 1990. What ever happened to Austric? *Mon-Khmer Studies* 16.1–10.

1994. The lexical evidence for Austric, so far. *Oceanic Linguistics* 34.309–21.

Dimmendaal, Gerrit J. 2001. Areal diffusion versus genetic inheritance: an African perspective. *Areal diffusion and genetic inheritance*, ed. Alexandra Y. Aikhenvald and R. M. W. Dixon, 358–92. Oxford: Oxford University Press.

Dixon, R. M. W. 1980. *The languages of Australia*. Cambridge: Cambridge University Press.

1990. Summary report: linguistic change and reconstruction in the Australian language family. *Linguistic change and reconstruction methodology*, ed. P. Baldi, 393–401. Berlin: Mouton de Gruyter.

1997. *The rise and fall of languages*. Cambridge: Cambridge University Press.

2001. The Australian linguistic area. *Areal diffusion and genetic inheritance: problems in comparative linguistics*, ed. Alexandra Y. Aikhenvald and R. M. W. Dixon, 64–104. Oxford: Oxford University Press.

2002. *Australian languages*. Cambridge: Cambridge University Press.

Dixon, R. M. W. and Alexandra Y. Aikhenvald. 1999. Introduction. *The Amazonian languages*, ed. R. M. W. Dixon and Alexandra Y. Aikhenvald, 1–21. Cambridge: Cambridge University Press.

Dixon, Roland B. 1905. The Shasta-Achomawi: a new linguistic stock with four new dialects. *American Anthropologist* 7.213–7.

Dixon, Roland B. and Alfred L. Kroeber. 1913a. Relationship of the Indian languages of California. *Science*, n.s., 37.225.

1913b. New linguistic families in California. *American Anthropologist* 15.647–55.

1919. Linguistic families of California. *University of California Publications in American Archaeology and Ethnology* 16.47–118.

Dobrovský, Josef. 1794. *Reise nach Schweden und Rußland (1792–93)*. Vienna: Bécsi Magyar Hírmondó.

1796. *Litterarische Nachrichten von einer auf Veranlassung der böhmischen Gesellschaft der Wissenschaften im Jahre 1792 unternommenen Reise nach Schweden und Rußland. Nebest einer Vergleichung der Russischen und Böhmischen Sprache nach dem Petersburger Vergleichungs-Wörterbuch aller Sprachen*. Prague.

1799. [Review of] Gyarmathi Sámuel, *Affinitas* . . . *Allgemeine Literaturzeitung zu Jena* 3.49–54, 57–9. Jena.

Doerfer, G. 1963–75. *Türkische und mongolische Elemente im Neupersischen unter besonderer Berücksichtigung älterer neupersischer Geschichtquellen, von allem der Mongolen- und Timuridenzeit*. 4 vols. Wiesbaden: Franz Steiner.

1966. Zur Verwandtschaft der altaischen Sprachen. *Indogermanische Forschungen* 71.81–123.

1967. Homologe und analoge Verwandtschaft. *Indogermanische Forschungen* 72.23–6.

1968. Zwei wichtige Probleme der Altaistik. *Journal de la Société Finno-Ougrienne* 69.3–21.

1973. *Lautgesetz und Zufall: Betrachtungen zum Omnikomparatismus*. (Innsbrucker Beiträge zur Sprachwissenschaft 10, ed. Wolfgang Meid.) Innsbruck: Institut für Vergleichende Sprachwissenschaft der Universität Innsbruck.

1974. Ist das Japanische mit den altaischen Sprachen verwandt? *Zeitschrift der deutschen morgenländischen Gesellschaft* 124.103–42.

1978. Review of Menges 1975. *Central Asiatic Journal* 22.151–2.

1985. *Mongolo-Tungusica*. (*Tungusica*, vol. 3.) Wiesbaden: Otto Harrassowitz.

1988. Zwei wichtige Probleme der Altaistik. *Journal de la Société Finno-ougrienne* 69.3–21.

1993. Nostratismus: Illich-Svitich und die Folgen. *Ural-Altäische Jahrbücher* 12.17–35.

Dolgopolsky, Aaron. 1964a. Gipoteza drevnejsego rodstva jazykovyx semej Severnoj Evraziji s verojatnostnoj tochki zrenija. *Voprosy jazykoznanija* 2.53–63. [English translation 1986: see below.]

1964b. Metody rekonstrukciji obshcheindoevropejskogo jazyka i vneindoevropejskije sopostavlenija [Methods in the reconstruction of Proto-Indo-European and external comparison]. *Problemy sravnitel'noj grammatiki indoevropejskix jazykov*. Tezisy doklodov, 27–30. Moscow: Moscow State University.

1965. Metody rekonstrukciji obshcheindoevropejskogo jazyka i sibiroevropejskaja gipoteza [Methods in the reconstruction of Proto-Indo-European and the Sibero-European hypothesis]. *Etimologija* 1965.259–70.

1969. Nostraticheskije osnovy s sochetainijem shumnyh soglasnyh. *Etimologija* 1967.296–313.

1970. A long-range comparison of some languages of Northern Eurasia (problems of phonetic correspondences). *Proceedings of the 7th International Congress of Anthropological and Ethnological Sciences* 5.620–28. Moscow.

1971. Nostraticheskije etimologiji i proisxozhdenije glagol'nyx formantov. *Etimologija* 1968.237–42.

1972. Nostraticheskije korni s sochetanijem lateral'nogo i zvonkogo laringala. *Etimologija* 1970.356–69.

1974. O nostraticheskoj sisteme affrikat i sibil'antov: korni s fonemoj *ʒ. [On the system of Nostratic affricates and sibilants: roots with the phoneme *ʒ.] *Etimologija* 1972.163–75.

1984. On personal pronouns in the Nostratic languages. *Linguistica et philologica: Gedenkschrift für Björn Collinder*, ed. Otto Gschwintler, Károly Rédei, and Hermann Reichert, 65–112. Vienna: Wilhelm Braumüller.

1986. A probabilistic hypothesis concerning the oldest relationships among the language families. *Typology relationship and time: a collection of papers on language change and relationship by Soviet linguists*, ed Vitaly V. Shevoroshkin and Thomas L. Markey, 27–50. [Translation of Dolgopolsky 1964a.] Ann Arbor: Karoma.

1989. Problems of Nostratic comparative phonology (preliminary report). *Reconstructing languages and cultures: materials from the First International Interdisciplinary Symposium on Language and Prehistory*, ed. Vitaly Shevoroshkin, 90–8. Bochum: Brockmeyer.

1998. *The Nostratic macrofamily and linguistic palaeontology*. Cambridge: McDonald Institute for Archaeological Research.

Dong Weiguang, Cao Guangqu, and Yan Xuequn. 1984. Genetic relationship between Chinese and Dong-Tai languages. *Computational Analysis of Asian and African Languages* 22.105–21. Tokyo.

Drechsel, Emanuel J. 1988. Wilhelm von Humboldt and Edward Sapir: analogies and homologies in their linguistic thoughts. *In honor of Mary Haas: from the Haas festival conference on Native American linguistics*, ed. William Shipley, 225–63. Berlin: Mouton de Gruyter.

Droixhe, Daniel. 1978. *La linguistique et l'appel de l'histoire, 1600–1800*. Geneva: Droz.

1980. Le prototype défiguré: l'idée scythique et la France Gauloise. *Progress in linguistic historiography: papers from the International Conference on the History of the Language Sciences*, ed. Konrad Koerner, 123–37. Amsterdam: John Benjamins.

1984. Avant-Propos. *Genèse du comparatisme indo-européen*, ed. Daniel Droixhe, 5–16. (Histoire Epistémologie Langage, vol. 6, Fascicule 2.) Lille: Presses Universitaires de Lille.

Dumézil, George. 1954. Remarques sur les six premiers noms du nombres de turc. *Studia Linguistica* 8.1–15.

1955. Remarques complémentaires sur les six premiers noms du nombres de turc et du quechua. *Journal de la Société des Américanistes de Paris* 44.17–37.

Duponceau, Peter Stephen (Pierre Etienne). 1819. Report of the corresponding secretary to the committee of his progress in the investigation committed to him of the general character and forms of the languages of the American Indians. *Transactions of the American Philosophical Society* 1.xvii–xxiv.

1838. *Mémoire sur le système grammatical des langues de quelques nations indiennes de l'Amérique du Nord*. Paris: Pihan de la Forest.

Dybo, A. V. 1989. Methods in Systemic reconstruction of Altaic and Nostratic lexics. *Lingvističeskaja rekonstrukcija* 1.196–209.

Dybo, Vladimir A. 1989a. V. M. Illich-Svitych and the development of Uralic and Dravidian linguistics (preliminary report). *Explorations in language macrofamilies: materials from the First International Interdisciplinary Symposium on Language and Prehistory*, ed. Vitaly Shevoroshkin, 20–7. Bochum: Brockmeyer.

1989b. Comparative-phonetic tables. *Explorations in language macrofamilies: materials from the First International Interdisciplinary Symposium on Language and Prehistory*, ed. Vitaly Shevoroshkin, 114–21. Bochum: Brockmeyer.

1990. Comparative-phonetic tables for Nostratic reconstructions. *Proto-languages and proto-cultures: materials from the First International Interdisciplinary Symposium on Language and Prehistory*, ed. Vitaly Shevoroshkin, 168–75. Bochum: Brockmeyer.

Dyen, Isidore. 1953. Review of *Malgache et Maajan: une comparaison linguistique*, by Otto Dahl. *Language* 29.577–90.

Eckardt, A. 1966. *Koreanisch und Indogermanisch: Untersuchung über die Zugehörigkeit des Koreanischen zur indogermanischen Sprachfamilie*. Heidelberg: Groos.

Eckert, Penelope. 2000. *Linguistic variation as social practice*. Oxford: Blackwell.

Eckert, R. 1967. V. M. Illič-Svityč in memoriam. *Zeitschrift für Slawistik* 12.624–6.

1973. Review of Illič-Svityc 1971. *Zeitschrift für Phonetik, Sprachwissenschaft und Kommunikationsforschung* 26.395–401.

Eco, Umberto. 1995. *The search for the perfect language.* Oxford: Blackwell.

Edgerton, Franklin. 1943. Notes on early American work in linguistics. *Proceedings of the American Philosophical Society* 87.25–34.

1946. Sir William Jones: 1746–1794. *Journal of the American Oriental Society* 66.230–9.

Edgerton, R. B. 1992. *Sick societies: challenging the myth of primitive harmony.* New York: Free Press.

Edmondson, Jerold A. and David B. Solnit (eds.) 1988. *Comparative Kadai: linguistic studies beyond Tai.* Dallas: Summer Institute of Linguistics and University of Texas at Arlington Press.

Edwards, Jonathan, Jr. 1788[1787]. *Observations on the language of the Muhhekaneew Indians; in which the extent of that language in North America is shewn; its genius is grammatically traced; some of its peculiarities, and some instances of analogy between that and the Hebrew are pointed out.* (Communicated to the Connecticut Society of Arts and Sciences, and published at the request of the Society.) New Haven: Josiah Meigs. (Reprinted 1788. London: W. Justins, Shoemaker-Row, Blackfriars. Reprinted with notes by John Pickering, 1823 in the *Massachusetts Historical Society Collection*, 2nd series, 10:81–160, and Boston: Phelps and Farnham.)

Egerod, Søren C. 1973. Review of *Sino-Tibetan: a conspectus*, by Paul Benedict. *Journal of Chinese Linguistics* 1(3).498–505.

1974. Sino-Tibetan languages. *Encyclopedia Britannica* 16.796–806.

1976. Benedict's Austro-Thai hypothesis: pro and con. *Computational Analysis of Asian and African Languages* 6.51–60.

Ehret, Christopher. 1995. *Reconstructing Proto-Afroasiatic (Proto-Afrasian): vowels, tone, consonants, and vocabulary.* Berkeley and Los Angeles: University of California Press.

2001. *A comparative historical reconstruction of Proto-Nilo-Saharan.* Cologne: Rüdiger Köppe.

2002. Language family expansions: broadening our understanding of cause from an African perspective. *Examining the farming/language dispersal hypothesis*, ed. Peter Bellwood and Colin Renfrew, 163–76. Cambridge: McDonald Institute for Archaeological Research.

Eldredge, Niles and Stephen Jay Gould. 1972. Punctuated equilibria: an alternative to phyletic gradualism. *Methods in paleobiology*, ed. T. J. M. Schopf, 82–115. San Francisco: Freeman, Cooper.

Elichman, Johann. 1640. *Tabula cebetis Graece, Arabice, Latine. Item aurea carmina Pythagorae cum Paraphrasi Arabica.* Leiden: Iohannis Maire.

Eliot, John. 1663. *The Holy Bible, containing the Old Testament and the New, translated into the Indian language and ordered to be printed by the commissioners of the United Colonies in New-England.* Cambridge, MA: Samuel Green and Marmaduke Johnson.

1666. *The Indian grammar begun: a grammar of the Massachusetts Indian language.* Cambridge, MA: Samuel Green and Marmaduke Johnson. (New edition 1822: *A grammar of the Massachusetts Indian language*, ed. John Pickering. Boston: Phelps and Farnham.)

Elliot, Walter. 1847. Observations on the language of the Gonds and the identity of many of its terms with Telugu, Tamil and Canarese. *Journal of the Asiatic Society of Bengal* 16 (2).

Ellis, Francis Whyte. 1816. *Note to the introduction of A Grammar of the Teloogoo Language*, by Alexander Duncan Campbell, 1–31. Madras: Hindu Press. (Reprinted, 3rd edition [from 1849], 1991. Madras: Asian Educational Services.)

Elmendorf, William W. 1963. Yukian–Siouan lexical similarities. *International Journal of American Linguistics* 29.300–9.

1964. Item and set comparison in Yuchi, Siouan, and Yukian. *International Journal of American Linguistics* 30.328–40.

Emeneau, Murray B. 2000. Linguistics in India: past and future. *Functional approaches to language, culture, and cognition: papers in honor of Sydney B. Lamb*, ed. David G. Lockwood, Peter H. Fries, and James E. Copeland, 545–54. Amsterdam: John Benjamins.

England, Nora C. 1983. *A grammar of Mam, a Mayan language*. Austin: University of Texas Press.

Enrico, John. 2004. Toward Proto-Na-Dene. *Anthropological Linguistics* 46.229–302.

Eronen, Jarmo. 1977. Uralo-dravidalaisista yhteyksistä. [About Uralic-Dravidian connections.] *Suomen Antropologi 1977* 33–8. Helsinki.

Evans, Nicholas. 1988. Arguments for Pama-Nyungan as a genetic subgroup, with reference to initial laminalization. *Aboriginal Linguistics* 1.91–110.

(ed.) 2003a. *The non-Pama-Nyungan languages of northern Australia: comparative studies of the continent's most linguistically complex region*. Canberra: Pacific Linguistics, Research School of Pacific and Asian Studies, The Australian National University.

2003b. Comparative non-Pama-Nyungan and Australian historical linguistics. *The non-Pama-Nyungan languages of northern Australia: comparative studies of the continent's most linguistically complex region*, ed. Nicholas Evans, 3–25. Canberra: Pacific Linguistics, Research School of Pacific and Asian Studies, The Australian National University.

Evans, Nick and Patrick McConvell. 1998. The enigma of Pama-Nyungan expansion in Australia. *Archaeology and language II: archaeological data and linguistic hypotheses*, ed. Roger Blench and Matthew Spriggs, 174–91. London: Routledge.

Faarlund, Jan Terje. 1990. Syntactic and pragmatic principles as arguments in the interpretation of runic inscriptions. *Historical linguistics and philology*, ed. Jacek Fisiak, 165–86. Berlin: Mouton de Gruyter.

Fahey, Bede. 2004. *Mayan, a Sino-Tibetan language? A comparative study*. Sino-Platonic Papers 130. [www.sino-platonic.org/abstracts/ spp130_mayan_chinese. html]

Fane, H. 1980. Sumerian–Dravidian interconnections: the linguistic, archeological and textual evidence. *International Journal of Dravidian Linguistics* 9.286–305.

Fähnrich, H. 1965. Iberokaukasisch und Drawidisch. *Revue de Kartvélologie* 19–20.139–58.

1971. Kriterien zum Nachweis genetischer Sprachverwandtschaft. *Wissenschaftliche Zeitschrift der Ernst Moritz Ardt Universität Greifswald* 20.99–136.

1981. Das Sumerische und Kartwelsprachen. *Georgica* 4.89–101. Jena, Tbilisi.

1988. Lexikalische Parallelen zwischen indoeuropäischen und kartvelischen Sprachen. *Papiere zur Linguistik* 39.49–54. Tübingen.

Farrar, Frederick W. 1873. *Chapters on language*. London: Longmans, Green and Co.

Fell, Barry. 1990. Etymology of the Lower Mississippian languages, part 1. *Epigraphic Society Occasional Papers* 19.35–47.

Fellman, Jack. 1974. The first historical linguist. *Linguistics* 137.31–3.

1975. On Sir William Jones and the Scythian language. *Language Science* 34.37–8.

1978. Semitic linguistics and Indo-European comparative and historical grammar. *Linguistics* 206.51–3.

Ferguson, Charles A. 1976. The Ethiopian language area. *Language in Ethiopia*, ed. M. L. Bender, J. D. Bowen, R. L. Cooper, and C. A. Ferguson, 63–76. London: Oxford University Press.

Ferrario, Benigno. 1933. La investigación lingüística y el parentesco extra-continental de la lengua "qhexwa." *Revista de la Sociedad "Amigos de la Arqueología"* 7.89–120. Montevideo, Uruguay.

1938. Della possible parentela fra le indue "altaiche" en alcune americaine. *Congresso Internazionale degli Orientalisti* 19.210–23. Rome: Tipographia della Reale Accademia dei Lincei del Dott.

Finck, Franz Nikolaus. 1909. *Die Sprachstämme des Erdkreises*. Leipzig: B. G. Teubner.

Fischer, J. E. 1770[1756]. *De origine Ungarorum*. (Published in *Quaestiones Petropolitanae*, by August Ludwig Schlözer.) Göttingen.

1995[1747]. *Vocabularium Sibiricum (1747): der etymologisch-vergleichende Abteil*, ed. János Gulya. Frankfurt am Main: Peter Lang.

Fleming, Harold C. 1974. Omotic as a branch of Afroasiatic. *Studies in African linguistics*, supplement 5.81–94.

1976a. *Omotic overview. The non-Semitic languages of Ethiopia*, ed. M. Lionel Bender, 299–323. East Lansing, MI: African Studies Center.

1976b. *Cushitic and Omotic. Language in Ethiopia*, ed. M. L. Bender, J. D. Bowen, R. L. Cooper, and C. A. Ferguson, 34–58. London: Oxford University Press.

1987. Review article: Towards a definitive classification of the world's languages (review of *A guide to the world's languages*, by Merritt Ruhlen). *Diachronica* 4.159–223.

Floyd, E. D. 1981. Levels of phonological restriction in Greek affixes. *Bono Homini donum: essays in historical linguistics in memory of J. Alexander Kerns*, ed. Yoel L. Arbeitman and A. R. Bomhard, 87–106. Amsterdam: John Benjamins.

Fodor, István. 1969. *The problems in the classification of the African languages: methodological and theoretical conclusions concerning the classification system of Joseph H. Greenberg*. 3rd edition (1st edition 1966). Budapest: Center for Afro-Asian Research of the Hungarian Academy of Sciences. (Republished 1982. Hamburg: Helmut Buske.)

1976. Are the Sumerians and the Hungarians or the Uralic peoples related? *Current Anthropology* 17.115–18.

Foley, William A. 1986. *The Papuan languages of New Guinea*. Cambridge: Cambridge University Press.

2000. The languages of New Guinea. *Annual Review of Anthropology* 29.357–404.

Forster, John [Johann] Reinhold. 1778. *Observations made during a voyage round the world*. London: G. Robinson. (Reprinted 1996, ed. Nicholas Thomas, Harriet Guest, and Michael Dettelbach. Honolulu: University of Hawaii Press.)

Fortescue, Michael. 1988. The Eskimo-Eleut-Yukagir relationship: an alternative to the genetic/contact dichotomy. *Acta Linguistica Hafniensia* 21.21–50.

1994. The role of typology in the establishment of the genetic relationship between Eskimo and Aleut – and beyond. *Languages of the north Pacific rim*, ed. Osahito Miyaoka, 9–36. (Hokkaido University Publications in Linguistics 7.) Sapporo, Japan: Department of Linguistics, Hokkaido University.

1998. *Language relations across Bering Strait: reappraising the archaeological and linguistic evidence.* London: Cassell.

Fowler, Catherine S. 1983. Some lexical clues to Uto-Aztecan prehistory. *International Journal of American Linguistics* 49.224–57.

Fox, A. 1982. Review of *Nilal: Über die Urverwandtschaft des Hamito-Semitischen, Indogermanischen, Uralischen und Altaischen*, by Kalevi E. Koskinen. *Language* 58.726–7.

Fox, James Allan. 1978. *Proto-Mayan accent, morpheme structure conditions, and velar innovations.* University of Chicago Ph.D. dissertation.

Frachtenberg, Leo J. 1918. Comparative studies in Takelman, Kalapuyan, and Chinookan lexicography: a preliminary paper. *International Journal of American Linguistics* 1.175–82.

Frankle, Eleanor. 1984a. Las relaciones externas entre las lenguas mayances y altaicas. Investigaciones recientes en el área maya. *XVII Mesa Redonda, Sociedad Mexicana de Antropología* 1.209–25. Mexico.

1984b. Los morfemas vocálicos para derivaciones verbales en los grupos mayance y túrquico. Investigaciones recientes en el área maya. *XVII Mesa Redonda, Sociedad Mexicana de Antropología* 2.517–24. Mexico.

Franklin, K. J. 1973. The gulf area in light of Greenberg's Indo-Pacific hypothesis. *The linguistic situation in the gulf district and adjacent areas*, ed. K. J. Franklin, 377–408. (Pacific Linguistics C-26.) Canberra.

Freeland, Lucy S. 1930. The relationship of Mixe to the Penutian family. *International Journal of American Linguistics* 6.28–33.

Friedrich, Paul. 1970. *Proto-Indo-European trees: the arboreal system of a prehistoric people.* Chicago: University of Chicago Press.

1975. *Proto-indo-European syntax: the order of meaningful elements.* *Journal of Indo-European Studies*, memoir 1. Butte, MT: College of Mineral Science.

Fujiwara, Akira. 1974. A comparative vocabulary of parts of the body of Japanese and Uralic languages with the backing up of Altaic languages, Kokuryöan and Korean. *Gengo Kenkyu* 65.74–9.

1975a. Japanese and Dravidian with special reference to words beginning with original *k-. *Bulletin of the Faculty of Arts and Sciences, Kiuki University*, Dec.

1975b. Animals and vegetables in Japanese and Uralian. *Uralica* 3.91–103.

1981. The Japanese-Dravidian vocabulary of flora and fauna. *Bulletin of the International Institute for Linguistic Sciences* 2.73–97. Kyoto Sangyo University.

Furnee, E. J. 1989. *Urbaskisch und Urkartvelisch.* Leiden: Hakuchi Press.

Futaky, István. 1973. Einige Aspekte zur Erforschung der uralischen-tungusischen Sprachbeziehungen. *Festschrift für Wolfgang Schlachter zum 65. Geburtstag*, 25–34. Göttingen.

[Futaki, I.]1988. Uralisch und Tungusisch. *The Uralic languages: description, history, and foreign influences*, ed. Denis Sinor, 781–81. Leiden: Brill.

Gabelentz, Georg von der. 1891. *Die Sprachwissenschaft: ihre Aufgaben, Methoden, und bisherigen Ergebnisse.* Leipzig: T. O. Weigel Nachfolger. (Reprinted, 1972[1901/1891], Tübingen: Gunter Narr.)

Gabelentz, Hans Conon von der. 1861. Die melanisischen Sprachen nach ihrem grammatischen Bau und ihrer Verwandtschaft unter sich und mit den malaiisch-polynesischen Sprachen. *Abhandlungen der philologisch-historischen Classe der königlich sächsischen Gesellschaft der Wissenschaften*, vol. 1. Leipzig: Hirzel.

Gamkrelidze, Tamaz V. 1967. Kartvelian and Indo-European: a typological comparison of reconstructed linguistic systems. *To honour Roman Jakobson*, 707–17. The Hague: Mouton.

Gamkrelidze, Tamaz V. and V. V. Ivanov. 1984. *Indoevropejskij jazyk i indoevropejtsy.* 2 vol. Tbilisi: Tbilisi State University.

1985. The ancient Near East and the Indo-European question: temporal and territorial characteristics of Proto-Indo-European based on linguistic and historico-cultural data. *The Journal of Indo-European Studies* 13.3–48.

Gancedo, A. 1922. El idioma japonés y sus afinidades con lenguas americanas. *Revista de Derecho, Historia y Letras* 73.114–22. Buenos Aires, Argentina.

Garbini, G. 1981. Camito-semitico e indoeuropeo. *Atti del Sodalizio Glottologico Milanese* 21.4–18.

Garde, P. 1977. Review of Illich-Svitych 1971, 1976. *Bulletin de la Société de Linguistique de Paris* 72.83–5.

Gardner, Peter M. 2000. *Bicultural versatility as a frontier adaptation among Paliyan foragers of south India.* Lewiston, NY: Edwin Mellon Press.

Garnett, James A. 1894. The progress of English philology. *Proceedings of the American Philological Association* 25.xxi–xxiii.

Garrett, Andrew. 1999. A new model of Indo-European subgrouping and dispersal. *Berkeley Linguistics Society* 25.146–56.

Gatschet, Albert S. 1879–80. The test of linguistic affinity. *The American Antiquarian* 2.163–5.

1882. Indian languages of the Pacific states and territories and of the Pueblos of New Mexico. *The Magazine of American History with Notes and Queries* 8.254–63.

1886. On the affinity of the Cheroki to the Iroquois dialects. *Transactions of the American Philological Association* 16.xl–xlv.

Gébelin, Antoine Court de. See Court de Gébelin, Antoine.

Gedney, William J. 1976. On the Thai evidence for Austro-Tai. *Computational Analysis of Asian and African Languages* 6.65–82. (Reprinted with revisions, 1989, in *Selected papers on comparative Tai studies*, ed. Robert J. Bickner, John Hartmann, Thomas John Kudak, and Patcharin Peyasantiwong, 117–63. Ann Arbor: University of Michigan Centers for South and Southeast Asian Studies.)

Gelenius, Sigismundus [Hrubyè z Jelení, Z./Gelen, Sigmund]. 1537. *Lexicum symphonum quo quatuor linguarum Europae familiarium, Graecae scilicet, Latinae, Germanicae ac Sclauinicae concordia consonatiaque indicatur.* Basel: Ieronymus Frobenius et Nicolaus Episcopius.

Georg, Stefan, Peter A. Michalove, Alexis Manaster-Ramer, and Paul Sidwell. 1999. Telling general linguists about Altaic. *Journal of Linguistics* 35.65–98

Georg, Stefan and Alexander Vovin. 2003. From mass comparison to mess comparison: Greenberg's *Indo-European and its closest relatives* (review article.) *Diachronica* 20.331–62.

2005. Review of *Indo-European and its closest relatives: the Eurasiatic language family*, vol. 2: *The lexicon*, by Joseph H. Greenberg. *Diachronica* 22.184–90.

Gerald of Wales. 1978. *The journey through Wales and the description of Wales*, translated and introduced by Lewis Thorpe. London: Penguin.

Ges[s]ner, Konrad. 1555. *Mithridates de differentiis linguarum tum veterum tum quae hodie apud diversas nationes in toto orbe terrarum in usu sunt*. Zurich: Froschauer. (Reprinted 1974, ed. Manfred Peters. Darmstadt: Scientia Verlag Aalen.)

Gibbon, Edward. See Williams (ed.) 1979.

Giraldus Cambrensis. 1908. *The journey through Wales, description of Wales*. London: Dent and Sons; New York: Dutton & Co.

Giles, P[eter]. 1895. *A short manual of comparative philology for classical students*. New York: Macmillan and Co.

Gilij, Filippo Salvatore. 1780–4. *Saggio di storia americana; o sia, storia naturale, civile e sacra de regni, e delle provincie spagnuole di Terra-Ferma nell' America Meridionale descritto dall' abate F. S. Gilij*. 4 vols. Rome: Perigio. (1965[1782], *Ensayo de historia americana, Spanish translation by Antonio Tovar*. [Fuentes para la Historia Colonial de Venezuela, vols. 71–3.] Caracas: Biblioteca de la Academia Nacional de la Historia.)

Girardot, J. M. 1980 [1982]. Deux correspondences grammaticales entre l'indoeuropéen et les langues ouralo-altaiques. *Orbis* 29.162–8.

Gluhak, Alenko. 1978. Is Sino-Tibetan related to Nostratian? *General Linguistics* 18.123–7.

Go, Minoru. 1980. *A comparative study of Papuan and Japanese*. Tokyo: Shibundo.

Goddard, Ives. 1975. Algonquian, Wiyot, and Yurok: proving a distant genetic relationship. *Linguistics and anthropology in honor of C. F. Voegelin*, ed. M. Dale Kinkade, Kenneth L. Hale, and Oswald Werner, 249–62. Lisse: Peter de Ridder Press.

1979. The languages of South Texas and the Lower Rio Grande. *The languages of Native America: an historical and comparative assessment*, ed. L. Campbell and M. Mithun, 355–89. Austin: University of Texas Press.

1986. Sapir's comparative method. *New perspectives in language, culture, and personality: proceedings of the Edward Sapir centenary conference*, ed. William Cowan, Michael K. Foster, and Konrad Koerner, 191–214. Amsterdam: John Benjamins.

1987. Review of *Language in the Americas* by Joseph H. Greenberg. *Current Anthropology* 28.656–7.

1988. Pre-Cheyenne *y. *In honor of Mary Haas: from the Haas festival conference on Native America linguistics*, ed. William Shipley, 345–60. Berlin: Mouton de Gruyter.

1990a. Review of *Language in the Americas* by Joseph H. Greenberg. *Linguistics* 28.557–8.

1990b. Algonquian linguistic change and reconstruction. *Linguistic change and reconstruction methodology*, ed. Philip Baldi, 99–114. Berlin: Mouton de Gruyter.

Goddard, Ives and Lyle Campbell. 1994. The history and classification of American Indian languages: what are the implications for the peopling of the Americas. *Method and theory for investigating the peopling of the Americas*, ed. Robson Bonnichsen and D. Gentry Steele, 189–207. (Center for the Study of the First Americans.) Corvallis: Oregon State University.

Goddard, Ives and William W. Fitzhugh. 1979. A statement concerning America B.C. *Man in the Northeast* 17.166–72. (Also in *Biblical Archeologist* 41.85–8 [1978].)

Godrey, John J. 1967. Sir William Jones and Père Cœurdoux: a philological footnote. *Journal of the American Oriental Society* 87.57–9.

Golla, Victor. 1980. Some Yokuts–Maidun comparisons. *American Indian and Indo-European studies: papers in honor of Madison S. Beeler*, ed. K. Klar, M. Langdon, and S. Silver, 57–63. The Hague: Mouton.

(ed.) 1984. *The Sapir–Kroeber correspondence*. (Survey of California and Other Indian Languages, report 6.) Berkeley: University of California.

1988. Review of *Language in the Americas* by Joseph H. Greenberg. *American Anthropologist* 90.434–5.

1991. Comparative Penutian glosses, edited by Victor Golla, based on "comparative Penutian glosses of Sapir," edited by Morris Swadesh (1964). *The collected works of Edward Sapir*, vol. VI: *American Indian languages*, part 2, ed. Victor Golla, 299–315. Berlin: Mouton de Gruyter.

2000. Language families of North America. *America past, America present: genes and languages in the Americas and beyond*, ed. Colin Renfrew, 59–73. Cambridge: McDonald Institute for Archaeological Research.

Golovko, Evgenij. 1994. Mednyj Aleut or Copper Island Aleut: an Aleut-Russian mixed language. *Mixed languages: 15 case studies in language intertwining*, ed. Peter Bakker and Maarten Mous, 113–21. Amsterdam: IFOTT.

Goodman, Morris. 1970. Some questions on the classification of African languages. *International Journal of American Linguistics* 36.117–22.

1971. The strange case of Mbugu (Tanzania). *Pidginization and creolization of languages*, ed. Dell Hymes, 243–54. Cambridge: Cambridge University Press.

Gordeziani, R. V. 1985. Etruskisch-vorgriechisch-kartvelische Etymologien. *Georgica* 8.10–3.

Gordon, Matthew. 1993. Evaluation of the Indo-Pacific hypothesis. Unpublished paper, University of Michigan.

1995. The phonological composition of personal pronouns: implications for genetic hypotheses. *Berkeley Linguistics Society* 21.117–28.

Goropius Becanus, Johannes (Jan van Gorp). 1569. *Origines Antwerpianae*. Antwerp: C. Plantin.

Gossen, Gary H. 1984. *Chamulas in the world of the sun: time and space in a Maya oral tradition*. Cambridge, MA: Harvard University Press.

Gould, Stephen Jay. 1987. *Time's arrow, time's cycle: myth and metaphor in the discovery of geological time*. Cambridge, MA: Harvard University Press.

Gould, Stephen Jay and Niles Eldredge. 1993. Punctuated equilibrium comes of age. *Nature* 366.223–7.

Grace, George W. 1959. *The position of the Polynesian languages within the Austronesian (Malayo-Polynesian) language family*. (Indiana University Publications in

Anthropology and Linguistics, memoir 16, supplement to *International Journal of American Linguistics* 25 [3].) Baltimore: Waverly Press.

Granberry, Julian. 1991a. Amazonian origins and affiliations of the Timucua language. *Language change in South American Indian languages*, ed. Mary Ritchie Key, 195–242. Philadelphia: University of Pennsylvania Press.

1991b. Was Ciguayo a West Indian Hokan language? *International Journal of American Linguistics* 57.514–19.

Grasserie, Raoul de la. 1890. De la famille linguistique Pano. *Congrès International des Américanistes* 7.438–49 [1888 meeting]. Berlin.

Gray, Edward G. 1999. *New World Babel: languages and nations in early America*. Princeton: Princeton University Press.

Gray, Louis H. 1934. *Introduction to Semitic comparative linguistics*. New York: Columbia University Press.

Greenberg, Joseph H. 1949a. Studies in African linguistic classification I: the Niger-Congo family. *Southwestern Journal of Anthropology* 5.79–100.

1949b. Studies in African linguistic classification II: the position of Fulani. *Southwestern Journal of Anthropology* 5.190–8.

1949c. Studies in African linguistic classification III: the position of Bantu. *Southwestern Journal of Anthropology* 5.309–17.

1950a. Studies in African linguistic classification IV: Hamito-Semitic. *Southwestern Journal of Anthropology* 6.47–63.

1950b. Studies in African linguistic classification V: the Eastern Sudanic family. *Southwestern Journal of Anthropology* 6.143–60.

1950c. Studies in African linguistic classification IV: the Click languages. *Southwestern Journal of Anthropology* 6.223–37.

1950d. Studies in African linguistic classification VII: smaller families; index of languages. *Southwestern Journal of Anthropology* 6.388–98.

1953. Historical linguistics and unwritten languages. *Anthropology today*, ed. A. L. Kroeber, 265–86. Chicago: University of Chicago Press.

1954. Studies in African linguistic classification VIII: further remarks on method. Revisions and corrections. *Southwestern Journal of Anthropology* 10.405–15.

1955. *Studies in African linguistic classification*. Bradford, CT: Compass Publishing Company.

1957. Genetic relationship among languages. *Essays in linguistics*, chapter 3, 35–45. Chicago: University of Chicago Press.

1960. The general classification of Central and South American languages. *Men and cultures: selected papers of the 5th International Congress of Anthropological and Ethnological Sciences, 1956*, ed. Anthony Wallace, 791–94. Philadelphia: University of Philadelphia Press.

1963. *The languages of Africa*. (Indiana University Research Center in Anthropology, Folklore, and Linguistics, publication 25, *International Journal of American Linguistics* 29.1.II). Bloomington: Indiana University Press. (2nd edition with additions and corrections, 1966. Bloomington: Indiana University Press.)

1969. Review of *The problems in the classification of the African languages*, by István Fodor. *Language* 45.427–32.

1971a. Nilo-Saharan and Meroitic. *Sub-Saharan Africa*, ed. J. Berry and J. H. Greenberg, 426–42. (Current Trends in Linguistics 7.) The Hague: Mouton.

1971b. The Indo-Pacific hypothesis. *Linguistics in Oceania*, ed. Thomas A. Sebeok, 807–71. (Current Trends in Linguistics 8.) The Hague: Mouton.

1973. The typological method. *Diachronic, areal, and typological linguistics*, ed. Henry M. Hoenigswald and Robert E. Longacre, 149–93. (Current Trends in Linguistics 11.) The Hague: Mouton.

1977. Niger-Congo noun class markers: prefixes, suffixes, both or neither. *Papers from the Eighth Conference on African Linguistics*, ed. M. Mould and T. J. Hinnebusch, 97–104. (*Studies in African Linguistics*, supplement 7.)

1978. How does a language acquire gender markers? *Universals of human language*, ed. Joseph H. Greenberg vol. 2, 47–82. Stanford: Stanford University Press.

1979. The classification of American Indian languages. *Papers of the 1978 Mid-America Linguistics Conference at Oklahoma*, ed. Ralph E. Cooley, 7–22. Norman: University of Oklahoma Press.

1981a. Nilo-Saharan movable *k-* as a state III article (with a Penutian parallel). *Journal of African Languages and Linguistics* 3.105–12.

1981b. The external relationships of the Uto-Aztecan languages. Paper presented at the Uto-Aztecan Conference. Tucson, AZ.

1983. Some areal characteristics of African languages. *Current approaches to African linguistics*, vol. 1, ed. Ivan R. Dihoff, 3–21. Dordrecht: Foris Publications.

1987. *Language in the Americas*. Stanford: Stanford University Press.

1989. Classification of American Indian languages: a reply to Campbell. *Language* 65.107–14.

1990a. The American Indian language controversy. *Review of Archaeology* 11:5–14.

1990b. The prehistory of the Indo-European vowel system in comparative and typological perspective. *Proto-languages and proto-cultures: materials from the First International Interdisciplinary Symposium on Language and Prehistory*, ed. Vitaly Shevoroshkin, 77–136. Bochum: Brockmeyer. [Published also in 1989, Predystorija indoevropejskoj sistemy glasnyh v sravnitel'noj I tipologicheskoj perspektive. *Voprosy Jazykoznanija* 1989.4–31. See also in *Reconstructing languages and cultures: abstracts and materials from the First International Interdisciplinary Symposium on Language and Prehistory*, ed. Vitaly Shevoroshkin, 47–50. Bochum: Brockmeyer, 1989.]

1990c. Correction to Matisoff: on megalocomparison. *Language* 66.660.

1991. Some problems of Indo-European in historical perspective. *Sprung from some common source: investigations into the prehistory of languages*, ed. Sydney M. Lamb and E. Douglas Mitchell, 125–40. Stanford: Stanford University Press.

1993. Linguistic typology and history: review of *Linguistic diversity in space and time*, by Johanna Nichols. *Current Anthropology* 34.503–5.

1994. On the Amerind affiliations of Zuni and Tonkawa. *California Linguistic Notes* 24.4–6.

1996a. In defense of Amerind. *International Journal of American Linguistics* 62.131–64.

1996b. The linguistic evidence. *American beginnings: the prehistory and palaeoecology of Beringia*, ed. Frederick Hadleigh West, 525–36. Chicago: University of Chicago Press.

1997. Does Altaic exist? *Indo-European, Nostratic and beyond: a Festschrift for Vitaly V. Shevoroshkin*, ed. Irén Hegedüs, Peter Michalove, and Alexis Manaster-Ramer, 88–93. Washington, DC: Institute for the Study of Man.

1999. Are there mixed languages? *Essays in poetics, literary history and linguitics, presented to Viacheslav Vsevolodovich Ivanov on the occasion of his seventieth birthday*, ed. L. Fleishman, M. Gasparov, I. Nikolaeva, A. Ospovat, V. Toporov, A. Vigasin, R. Vroon, and A. Zalizniak, 626–33. Moscow: OGI.

2000a. *Indo-European and its closest relatives: the Eurasiatic language family.* Stanford: Stanford University Press.

2000b. The concept of proof in genetic linguistics. *Reconstructing grammar: comparative linguistics and grammaticalization*, ed. Spike Gildea, 161–75. Amsterdam: John Benjamins.

2000c. From first and second person: the history of Amerind *k(i). *Functional approaches to language, culture, and cognition: papers in honor of Sydney B. Lamb*, ed. David G. Lockwood, Peter H. Fries, and James E. Copeland, 413–26. Amsterdam: John Benjamins.

2002. *Indo-European and its closest relatives: the Eurasiatic language family, vol. 2: The lexicon.* Stanford: Stanford University Press.

2005. Indo-Europeanist practice and American Indianist theory in linguistic classification. *Genetic linguistics: essays on theory and method by Joseph H. Greenberg*, ed. William Croft, 153–89. Oxford: Oxford University Press.

Greenberg, Joseph H. and Merritt Ruhlen. 1992. Linguistic origins of Native Americans. *Scientific American* 267(5).94–99.

Greenberg, Joseph and Morris Swadesh. 1953. Jicaque as a Hokan language. *International Journal of American Linguistics* 19.216–22.

Greenberg, Joseph H., Christy Turner II, and Stephen Zegura. 1986. The settlement of the Americas: a comparison of the linguistic, dental, and genetic evidence. *Current Anthropology* 27.477–97.

Greene, John C. 1960 Early scientific interest in the American Indian: comparative linguistics. *Proceedings of the American Philosophical Society* 104.511–17.

Gregersen, Edgar A. 1972. Kongo-Saharan. *Journal of African Languages* 11.69–89.

1977. *Language in Africa: an introductory survey.* New York: Gordon and Breach.

Grierson, G. A. (ed.). 1903. *Linguistic survey of India*, vol. 3: *Tibeto-Burman family*, part II. Calcutta: Superintendent of Government Printing. (Reprinted 1967, Delhi: Motilal Banarsidass.)

Grierson, G. A. and S. Konow (eds.). 1904. *Linguistic survey of India* I, vol. 3: *Tibeto-Burman family*, part III. Calcutta: Superintendent of Government Printing. (Reprinted 1967, Delhi: Motilal Banarsidass.)

1909. *Linguistic survey of India*, vol. 3: *Tibeto-Burman family*, part I. Calcutta: Superintendent of Government Printing. (Reprinted 1967, Delhi: Motilal Banarsidass.)

1927. *Linguistic survey of India I*, vol. 1, part I, *Introduction*. Calcutta: Superintendent of Government Printing. (Reprinted 1967, Delhi: Motilal Banarsidass.)

1928. *Linguistic survey of India*, vol. I, part II, *Comparative vocabulary.* Calcutta: Superintendent of Government Printing. (Reprinted 1967, Delhi: Motilal Banarsidass.)

Griffen, T. D. 1989. Nostratic and Germano-European. *General Linguistics* 29.139–49.

Grimes, Barbara F. 2004. *Ethnologue: languages of the world*. 14th edition. Dallas: Summer Institute of Linguistics and the University of Texas at Arlington. (www.ethnologue.com.)

Grimm, Jacob. 1822[1818]. *Deutsche Grammatik*, part I. 2nd edition. Göttingen: Dieterich.

Grolier, Eric de. 1990. Review of Shevoroshkin 1990a. *Language Origins Society Newsletter* 11.12–16.

Grotius, Hugo. 1642. *De origine gentium Americanarum*. Paris. (Trans. E. Goldsmid, 1884: *On the origin of the native races of America, a dissertation*. Edinburgh: Unwin Bross.)

Gruhn, Ruth. 1988. Linguistic evidence in support of the coastal route of earliest entry into the New World. *Man* 23.77–100.

Grunzel, Joseph. 1895. *Entwurf einer vergleichenden Grammatik der altaischen Sprachen nebst einem vergleichenden Wörter buch*. Leipzig: Wilhelm Friedrich.

Guichard, Estienne. 1606. *L'Harmonie etymologique des langues Hébraïque, Chaldaique, Syriaque – Greque – Latin, Françoise, Italienne, Espagnole – Alemande, Flamende, Anglaise, &c*. Paris.

Guignes, Joseph de. 1770. *Histoire de l'Académie des Inscriptions*. Paris. [See Auroux 1990.]

Güldemann, Tom and Rainer Vossen. 2000. Khoisan. *African languages: an introduction*, ed. Bernd Heine and Derek Nurse, 99–122. Cambridge: Cambridge University Press.

Gulya, J. 1990. Die Protokultur der Uralier und Indoeuropäer: eine Vergleichsstudie. *Uralo-Indogermanica* 2.142–8.

Gumperz, John J. and Stephen C. Levinson (eds.) 1996. *Rethinking linguistic relativity*. Cambridge: Cambridge University Press.

Gurevich, Naomi. 1999. Phylumphile or phylumfoe? Examining Greenberg's method of mass comparison. *Historical linguistics and lexicostatistics*, ed. Vitaly Shevoroshkin and Paul J. Sidwell, 119–43. (AHL Studies in the Science and History of Language 3.) Canberra: Association for the History of Language.

Gurov, Nikita Vladimirovich. 1989. *Kusunda – sinokavkazskie leksicheskie paralleli. Lingvisticheskaja rekonstrukcija I drevnejshaja istorija vostoka*. Moscow: Izdatel'stvo 'Nauka'.

Gursky, Karl-Heinz. 1965. Ein lexikalischer Vergleich der Algonkin-Gulf- und Hoka-Subtiaba Sprachen. *Orbis* 14.160–215.

    1966–7. Ein Vergleich der grammatischen Morpheme der Golf-Sprachen und der Hoka-Subtiaba-Sprachen. *Orbis* 15.511–37.

    1968. Gulf and Hokan-Subtiaban: new lexical parallels. *International Journal of American Linguistics* 34.21–41.

    1974. Der Hoka-Sprachstamm: eine Bestandsaufnahme des lexikalischen Beweismaterials. *Orbis* 23.170–215.

Gusmani, Roberto. 1968. *Il lessico ittito*. Naples: Liberia Scientifica Editrice.

Gyarmathi, Sámuel. 1794. *Okoskodva tanító magyar nyelvmester [Hungarian grammar taught rationally]*, 2 vols. Cluj and Sibiu: Hochmeister.

    1799. *Affinitas linguae Hungaricae cum linguis Fennicae originis grammatice demonstrata*. Göttingen: Joann. Christian Dieterich. (Photolithic reproduction of 2nd edition 1968, ed. Thomas A. Sebeok [Ural and Altaic Series 95.] Bloomington:

Indiana University; The Hague: Mouton.) (English translation, see Hanzeli 1983.)

Gyula, János. 1974. Some eighteenth century antecedents of nineteenth century linguistics: the discovery of Finno-Ugrian. *Studies in the history of linguistics: traditions and paradigms*, ed. Dell Hymes, 258–76. Bloomington: Indiana University Press.

Haarmann, Harald. 1979. Die Klassifikation der romanischen Sprachen in den Werken der Komparativisten aus der zweiten Hälfte des 18. Jahrhunderts (Rüdiger, Hervás, Pallas). *Wissenschaftsgeschichtliche Beiträge zur Erforschung indogermanischer, finnisch-ugrischer und kaukasischer Sprachern bei Pallas*, ed. Harald Haarmann, 45–69. Hamburg: Buske.

Haas, Mary R. 1941. The classification of Muskogean languages. *Language, culture, and personality: essays in memory of Edward Sapir*, ed. Leslie Spier, A. Irving Hallowell, and Stanley S. Newman, 41–56. Menasha, WI: Sapir Memorial Publication Fund.

1951. The Proto-Gulf word for *water* (with notes on Siouan-Yuchi). *International Journal of American Linguistics* 17.71–9.

1952. The Proto-Gulf word for *land* (with a note on Siouan-Yuchi). *International Journal of American Linguistics* 18.238–40.

1956. Natchez and the Muskogean languages. *Language* 32.61–72.

1958a. Algonkian-Ritwan: the end of a controversy. *International Journal of American Linguistics* 24.159–73.

1958b. A new linguistic relationship in North America: Algonkian and the Gulf languages. *Southwest Journal of Anthropology* 14.231–64.

1959. Tonkawa and Algonkian. *Anthropological Linguistics* 1(1).1–6.

1960. Some genetic affiliations of Algonkian. *Culture in history: essays in honor of Paul Radin*, ed. Stanley Diamond, 977–92. New York: Columbia University Press.

1964a. California Hokan. *Studies in Californian linguistics*, ed. William Bright, 73–87. (University of California Publications in Linguistics 34.) Berkeley: University of California Press.

1964b. Shasta and Proto-Hokan. *Language* 39.40–59.

1965. Is Kutenai related to Algonkian? *Canadian Journal of Linguistics* 10.77–92.

1966. Wiyot–Yurok–Algonkian and problems of comparative Algonkian. *International Journal of American Linguistics* 32.101–7.

1967. Roger Williams' sound shift: a study in Algonkian. *To honor Roman Jakobson: essays on the occasion of his seventieth birthday*, 1.816–32. The Hague: Mouton.

1969. Grammar or lexicon: the American Indian side of the question from Duponceau to Powell. *International Journal of American Linguistics* 35.239–55. (Reprinted 1978, with changed title: The problem of classifying American Indian languages: from Duponceau to Powell. *Language, culture, and history: essays by Mary R. Haas*, 130–63. Stanford: Stanford University Press.)

1976. The Northern California linguistic area. *Hokan studies*, ed. Margaret Langdon and Shirley Silver, 347–59. The Hague: Mouton.

Hajdú, Peter. 1975. *Finno-Ugrian languages and peoples*. London: André Deutsch.

1979. Language contacts in North-West Siberia. *Finno-Ugrica Suecana* 2.19–32.

Hajek, John. 2004. Consonant inventories as an areal feature of the New Guinea-Pacific region: testing Trudgill's hypotheses. *Linguistic Typology* 8.343–50.

Häkkinen, Kaisa. 1984. Wäre es schon an der Zeit, den Stammbaum zu fällen? Theorien über die gegenseitigen Verwandtschaftsbeziehungen der finnisch-ugrischen Sprachen. *Ural-altaische Jahrbücher* 4.1–4.

2001. Prehistoric Finno-Ugric culture in the light of historical lexicology. *Early contacts between Uralic and Indo-European: linguistics and archaeological considerations*, ed. Christian Carpelan, Asko Parpola, and Petteri Koskikallio, 169–86. (Mémoires de la Société Finno-Ougrienne, 242.) Helsinki: Finno-Ugrian Society.

Hakola, Hannu Panu Aukusti. 1997. *Duraljan vocabulary: lexical similarities in the major agglutinative languages*. Kuopio: H. P. A. Hakola. (Kuopio University Printing Office.)

2000. *1000 Duraljan etyma: an extended study in the lexical similarities in the major agglutinative languages*. Kuopio: H. P. A. Hakola. (Kuopio University Printing Office.)

Hakulinen, Lauri. 1968. *Suomen kielen rakenne ja kehitys* [The structure and history of the Finnish language]. Helsinki: Otava.

Hale, Austin. 1982. *Research on Tibeto-Burman languages*. Berlin: Mouton.

Hale, Horatio. 1846. *United States exploring expedition, during the years 1838, 1839, 1840, 1841, 1842, under the command of Charles Wilkes, U.S. Navy*, vol. 6: *Ethnography and philology*. Philadelphia.

1890[1888]. Was America peopled from Polynesia? *International Congress of Americanists* 7.374–88. (1888 meeting.) Berlin.

Hale, Kenneth. 1964. Classification of Northern Paman languages, Cape York Peninsula, Australia: a research report. *Oceanic Linguistics* 3.248–64.

1976. Phonological developments in particular Northern Paman languages. *Languages of Cape York*, ed. Peter Sutton, 7–40. (Research and Regional Studies 6.) Canberra: Australian Institute of Aboriginal Studies.

1997. Book review article: Campbell, Lyle (1997) *American Indian Languages: the Historical Linguistics of Native America. Mother Tongue* (journal) 3.145–58.

Halhed, Nathaniel Brassey. 1776. *A code of Gentoo laws, or, ordinations of the Pundits, from a Persian translation made from the original, written in the Shanscrit language*. London: East India Company.

1778. *A grammar of the Bengal language*. Bengal: Hoogly. (Reprinted 1969, Menston, UK: Scholar Press.)

Hammerich, Louis L. 1951. Can Eskimo be related to Indo-European? *International Journal of American Linguistics* 17.217–23.

Hamp, Eric P. 1959. Venetic isoglosses. *American Journal of Philology* 80.179–84.

1967. On Maya-Chipayan. *International Journal of American Linguistics* 33.74–6.

1968. On the problem of Ainu and Indo-European. *Eighth International Congress of Anthropological and Ethnological Sciences*, 100–2. Tokyo.

1970. Maya-Chipaya and typology of labials. *Chicago Linguistic Society* 6.20–2.

1971. On Mayan-Araucanian comparative phonology. *International Journal of American Linguistics* 37.156–9.

1975. On Zuni-Penutian consonants. *International Journal of American Linguistics* 41.310–12.

1976. On Eskimo-Aleut and Luoravetlan. *Papers on Eskimo and Aleut linguistics*, ed. Eric Hamp, 81–92. Chicago: Chicago Linguistic Society.

1977. On some questions of areal linguistics. *Berkeley Linguistics Society* 3.279–82.

Hanzeli, Victor E. 1983. Gyarmathi and his *Affinitas. Grammatical proof of the affinity of the Hungarian language with languages of Fennic origin*, translated, annotated, and introduced by Victor E. Hanzeli, xi–lv. (Amsterdam Classics in Linguistics 15.) Amsterdam: John Benjamins.

Hardman[-de-Bautista], Martha J. 1985. *Quechua and Aymara: languages in contact. South American Indian languages: retrospect and prospect*, ed. Harriet E. Manelis Klein and Louisa R. Stark, 617–43. Austin: University of Texas Press.

Harmon, David. 1995. Losing species, losing languages: connections between biological and linguistic diversity. Paper presented at the Symposium on Language Loss and Public Policy, University of New Mexico, July 1995.

Harms, Robert T. 1977. The Uralo-Yukaghir focus system: a problem in remote genetic relationship. *Studies in descriptive and historical linguistics: festschrift for Winfred P. Lehmann*, ed. Paul J. Hopper, 301–16. Amsterdam: John Benjamins.

Harrington, John Peabody. 1913. [Untitled note on the relationship of Yuman and Chumash.] *American Anthropologist* 15.716.

1917. [Untitled note on the relationship of Washo and Chumash.] *American Anthropologist* 19.154.

1928. *Vocabulary of the Kiowa language.* Bureau of American Ethnology, bulletin 84. Washington, DC.

1943. Hokan discovered in South America. *Journal of the Washington Academy of Sciences* 33.334–44.

Harris, Alice C. and Lyle Campbell. 1995. *Historical syntax in cross-linguistic perspective.* Cambridge: Cambridge University Press.

Harvey, Mark. 2003. Reconstruction of pronominals among the non-Pama-Nyungan languages. *The non-Pama-Nyungan languages of northern Australia: comparative studies of the continent's most linguistically complex region*, ed. Nicholas Evans, 475–513. Canberra: Pacific Linguistics, Research School of Pacific and Asian Studies, The Australian National University.

Haugen, Einar. 1976. *The Scandinavian languages: an introduction to their history.* Cambridge, MA: Harvard University Press.

Hayward, Richard J. 2000. Afroasiatic. *African languages: an introduction*, ed. Bernd Heine and Derek Nurse, 74–98. Cambridge: Cambridge University Press.

Heath, Jeffrey. 1978. *Linguistic diffusion in Arnhem Land.* Canberra: Australian Institute of Aboriginal Studies.

1990. Verbal inflection and macro-subgroupings of Australian languages: search for conjugation markers in non-Pama-Nyungan. *Linguistic change and reconstruction methodology*, ed. Philip Baldi, 4003–17. Berlin: Mouton de Gruyter.

1994. Review of *Linguistic diversity in time and space*, by Johanna Nichols. *Anthropological Linguistics* 36.92–6.

1997. Lost wax: abrupt replacement of key morphemes in Australian agreement complexes. *Diachronica* 14.197–232,

Hegedüs, Irén. 1988. Morphologische Übereinstimmungen in der uralischen, altaischen und einigen paläosibirischen Sprachen. *Specimina Sibirica*, ed. János Pusztay, 1.71–86.

1989. Applicability of exact methods in Nostratic research. *Explorations in language macrofamilies: materials from the First International Interdisciplinary Symposium on Language and Prehistory*, ed. Vitaly Shevoroshkin, 30–9. Bochum: Brockmeier.

1992a. Bibliographia Nostratica 1960–1990 (a list of publications on, or relevant for Nostratic studies). *Specimina Sibirica*, ed. János Pusztay, vol. 4. Szombathely: Druckerei der Berzsenyi-Hochschule.

1992b. Reconstructing Nostratic morphology: derivational elements. *Nostratic, Dene-Caucasian, Austric and Amerind*, ed. Vitaly Shevoroshkin, 34–47. Bochum: Brockmeyer.

Heine, Bernd. 1970. *Eastern Sudanic subfamily – a linguistic relationship*. (East Africa and Nile Valley Seminars, paper IV.) Nairobi: Department of History, University of Nairobi.

1972. Historical linguistics and lexicostatistics in Africa. *Journal of African Languages* 2.7–20.

1975. Language typology and convergence areas in Africa. *Linguistics* 144.27–47.

1976. *A typology of African languages (based on the order of meaningful elements)*. Berlin: Reimer.

1992. African languages. *International encyclopedia of linguistics*, ed. William Bright, 1.31–5. Oxford: Oxford University Press.

Heine, Bernd and Tania Kuteva. 2001. Convergence and divergence in the development of African languages. *Areal diffusion and genetic inheritance*, ed. Alexandra Y. Aikhenvald and R. M. W. Dixon, 393–411. Oxford: Oxford University Press.

2002. On the evolution of grammatical forms. *The transition to language*, ed. Alison Wray, 376–97. Oxford: Oxford University Press.

Heine, Bernd and Derek Nurse (eds.). 2000a. *African languages: an introduction*. Cambridge: Cambridge University Press.

2000b. Introduction. *African languages: an introduction*, ed. Bernd Heine and Derek Nurse, 1–10. Cambridge: Cambridge University Press.

Helimskij, E. A. 1985. Samodijsko-tungusskije leksicheskije svjazi i ih etnoistoriceskije interpretaciji. *Uralo-Altaistika arheologija, etnografija, jazyk*, ed. J. I. Ubrjatova, 206–13. Novosibirsk: Nauka.

1987. A "new approach" to Nostratic comparison: review of Bomhard 1984. *Journal of the American Oriental Society* 107.97–100.

Herder, Johann Gottfried. 1772. *Abhandlung über den Ursprung der Sprache*. Berlin: C. F. Voss. (New edition 1966, Stuttgart: Philipp Reclam.)

Hervás y Panduro, Lorenzo. 1784. *Catalogo delle lingue conosciute e notizia della loro affinità e diversità*. Cesena: Gregorio Biasini all'Insegna oli Pallade.

1800–5. *Catálogo de las lenguas de las naciones conocidas y numeracion, division, y clases de estas segun la diversidad de sus idiomas y dialectos*. Madrid: Administracion del Real Arbitrio de Beneficiencia.

Hetzron, Robert. 1972. *Ethiopian Semitic: studies in classification*. Manchester: Manchester University Press.

1980. The limits of Cushitic. *Sprache und Geschichte in Afrika* 2.7–126.

Hevesy, Wilhelm von. 1932. *Finnisch-Ugrisches aus Indien*. Vienna: Manz.

1935. Neue Finnisch-Ugrische Sprachen (Die Mundasprachen Indiens). *Atti del Congresso di Linguistica tenuto in Roma*, 275–84.

Hewson, John. 1968. Beothuk and Algonkian: evidence old and new. *International Journal of American Linguistics* 34.85–93.

1971. Beothuk consonant correspondences. *International Journal of American Linguistics* 37.244–9.

1978. *Beothuk vocabularies: a comparative study*. (Technical papers of the Newfoundland Museum 2.) St. John's, Newfoundland: Department of Tourism, Historic Resources Division.

1982. Beothuk and the Algonkian Northeast. *Languages in Newfoundland and Labrador*, ed. Harrold J. Paddock, 176–87. St. John's, Newfoundland: Department of Linguistics, Memorial University.

Hill, Jane H. 1978. Language contact systems and human adaptations. *Journal of Anthropological Research* 34.1–26.

2000. Linguistic models of early American history. *Archaeology Southwest*, Spring: 9. Tucson, AZ: Desert Archaeology Foundation.

2001a. Language on the land: towards an anthropological dialectology. *Archaeology, language, and history: essays on culture and ethnicity*, ed. John E. Terrell, 257–82. Westport, CT: Bergin & Garvey, Greenwood Publishing.

2001b. Proto-Uto-Aztecan: a community of cultivators in central Mexico? *American Anthropologist* 103.913–14.

2002. Proto-Uto-Aztecan cultivation and the northern devolution. *Examining the farming/language dispersal hypothesis*, ed. Peter Bellwood and Colin Renfrew, 331–40. Cambridge: McDonald Institute for Archaeological Research.

Hinsley, Curtis M., Jr. 1981. *Savages and scientists: the Smithsonian Institution and the development of American anthropology, 1846–1910*. Washington: Smithsonian Institution.

Hinton, Leanne, Johanna Nichols, and John J. Ohala (eds.) 1994. *Sound symbolism*. Cambridge: Cambridge University Press.

Hjelmslev, Louis. 1966[1950–1]. Commentaires sur la vie et l'œuvre de Rasmus Rask. *Conferences de l'Institut de Linguistique de l'Université de Paris* 10.143–57. (Reprinted 1966 in *Portraits of linguists: a biographical source book for the history of Western linguistics, 1746–1963*, ed. Thomas A. Sebeok, 1.179–99. Bloomington: Indiana University Press.)

Hock, Hans Henrich. 1986. *Principles of historical linguistics*. Berlin: Mouton de Gruyter.

1993. SWALLOTALES: Chance and the "world etymology" MALIQ'A 'swallow, throat.' *Chicago Linguistic Society* 29.215–38.

Hock, Hans Henrich and Brian Joseph. 1996. *Language history, language change, and language relationship: an introduction to historical and comparative linguistics*. Berlin: Mouton de Gruyter.

Hockett, Charles. 1960. The origins of speech. *Scientific American* 208.88–96.

Hodge, Carleton T. 1983. Relating Afroasiatic to Indo-European. *Studies in Chadic and Afroasiatic linguistics*, ed. E. Wolff and H. Meyer-Bahlburg, 33–50. Hamburg: Buske.

1991. Indo-European and Afroasiatic. *Sprung from some common source: investigations into the prehistory of languages*, ed. Sydney M. Lamb and E. Douglas Mitchell, 141–65. Stanford: Stanford University Press.

1998. The implications of Laslakh for Nostratic. *Nostratic: sifting the evidence*, ed. Brian Joseph and Joe Salmons, 237–56. Amsterdam: John Benjamins.

Hodgson, Brian H. 1828. Notices of the Languages, literature and religion of the Bauddhas of Nepal and Bhot. *Asiatik Researches* 16.409–49.

Hoenigswald, Henry M. 1963. On the history of the comparative method. *Anthropological Linguistics* 5(1).1–11.

1974. Fallacies in the history of linguistics: notes on the appraisal of the nineteenth century. *Studies in the history of linguistics: traditions and paradigms*, ed. Dell Hymes, 346–58. Bloomington: Indiana University Press.

1985. Sir William Jones and historiography. *For Gordon H. Fairbanks*, ed. Veheeta Z. Acson and Richard L. Leed, 64–6. (Oceanic Linguistics Special Publication 20.) Honolulu: University of Hawaii Press.

1990a. Descent, perfection and the comparative method since Leibniz. *Leibniz, Humboldt, and the origins of comparativism*, ed. Tullio de Mauro and Lia Formigari, 119–32. Amsterdam: John Benjamins.

1990b. Is the "comparative" method general or family specific? *Linguistic change and reconstruction methodology*, ed. Philip Baldi, 375–83. Berlin: Mouton de Gruyter.

Hoijer, Harry. 1954. Some problems of American Indian linguistic research. *Papers from the Symposium on American Indian Linguistics*, ed. C. D. Chrétien, M. S. Beeler, M. B. Emeneau, and M. R. Haas, 3–12. (University of California Publications in Linguistics 10.) Berkeley: University of California Press.

Holmer, N. M. 1960. Plural infixes in Indo-European and Finno-Ugric. *Virittäjä* 64.348–52. Helsinki.

Holt, Dennis. 1986. History of the Paya sound system. Ph.D. dissertation, University of California Los Angeles.

Homburger, Lillias. 1957. De quelques éléments communs a l'égyptien et aux langues dravidienne. *Kemi* 14.26–34.

Hommel, Fritz. 1915. *Zweihundert sumero-türkisch Wortvergleichungen als Grundlage zu einem neuen Kapitel der Sprachwissenschaft*. Munich.

Hovdhaugen, Even. 1982. *Foundations of western linguistics: from the beginning to the end of the first millen[n]ium A.D.* New York: Columbia University Press.

Hovelacque, Abel. 1877. *The science of languages: linguistics, philology, etymology*. London: Chapman and Hall; Philadelphia: J. B. Lippincott.

Hrozný, Friedrich. 1915. Die Lösung des hethitischen Problems. *Mitteilungen der Deutschen Orient-Gesellschaft* 56.17–50.

1917. *Die Sprache der Hethiter*. Leipzig: J. C. Hinrichs.

Hübschmann, Heinrich. 1875. Über die Stellung des armenischen im Kreise der indogermanischen Sprachen. *Zeitschrift für Vergleichende Sprachforschung* 23.5–42.

Hulbert, Homer Bezaleel. 1905. *A comparative grammar of the Korean language and the Dravidian languages of India*. Seoul: The Methodist Publishing House.

Humboldt, [Friedrich] Wilhelm [Christian Karl Ferdinand] von. 1822. Ueber das Entstehen der grammatischen Formen, und ihren Einfluss auf die Ideenentwicklung. *Abhandlungen der königlichen Akademie der Wissenschaften zu Berlin*, 401–30. (Reprinted 1963: *Wilhelm von Humboldt Werke in fünf Bänden*, ed. Andreas Flitner and Klaus Giel, 3.31–63. Stuttgart: J. G. Cotta.)

1836. *Ueber die Verschiedenheit des menschlichen Sprachbaues und ihren Einfluss auf die geistige Entwicklung des Menschengeschlechtes*. Berlin: Königliche Akademie der Wissenschaften. (Reprinted 1963: *Wilhelm von Humboldt Werke in fünf Bänden*, ed. Andreas Flitner and Klaus Giel, 3.368–756. Stuttgart: J. G. Cotta.) (English translation 1988, *On language: the diversity of human language-structure and its influence on the mental development of mankind*, trans. Peter Heath. Cambridge: Cambridge University Press.)

1836–9. *Über die Kawi-Sprache auf der Insel Java, nebst einer Einleitung über die Verschiedenheit des menschlichen Sprachbaues (3 vols.).* Berlin: Abhandlungen der Königlichen Akademie der Wissenschaften zu Berlin.

1903–36. *Gesammelte Schriften*, ed. Albert Leitzmann. 17 vols. Berlin: Preussischen Akademie der Wissenschaften.

Hunn, Eugene. 1975. Words for owls in North American Indian languages. *International Journal of American Linguistics* 41.237–9.

Hymes, Dell H. 1955. Positional analysis of categories: a frame for reconstruction. *Word* 11.10–23.

1956. Na-Dene and positional analysis of categories. *American Anthropologist* 58.624–38.

1957. Some Penutian elements and the Penutian hypothesis. *Southwest Journal of Anthropology* 13.69–87.

1959. Genetic classification: retrospect and prospect. *Anthropological Linguistics* 1(2).50–66.

1961. Review of *Tungusisch und Ketschua*, by Karl Bouda. *International Journal of American Linguistics* 27.362–4.

1964a. Evidence for Penutian in lexical sets with initial *C- and *S-. *International Journal of American Linguistics* 30.213–42.

1964b. 'Hail' and 'bead': two Penutian etymologies. *Studies in Californian linguistics*, ed. William Bright, 94–8. (University of California Publications in Linguistics 34.) Berkeley: University of California Press.

1971. Morris Swadesh: from the first Yale School to world prehistory, appendix to *The origin and diversification of language*, by Morris Swadesh, ed. Joel Sherzer, 285–92. Chicago: Aldine.

1974. Speech and language: on the origins and foundations of inequality among speakers. *Language as a human problem*, ed. Morton Bloomfield and Einar Haugen, 45–71. New York: W. W. Norton & Co.

Ibarra Grasso, Dick E. 1958. *Lenguas indígenas americanas.* Buenos Aires: Editorial Nova.

1964. *Lenguas indígenas de Bolivia.* Cochabamba, Bolivia: Universidad Mayor de San Simón, Museo Arqueológico.

Ihre, Johan. 1769. *Glossarium Sviogothicum.* Uppsala: Typis Edmannianis.

Illich-Svitych, Vladislav M. 1963. Altajskije dental'nyje *t, *d, *δ. [Altaic dentals *t, *d, *δ]. *Voprosy Jazykoznanija* 6.37–56.

1964a. Genezis indoevropejskix rjadov guttural'nyx v svete dannyx vneshego srav-nenija [The genesis of the Indo-European series of gutturals in the light of external comparison]. *Problemy sravnitel'noj grammatiki indoevropejskix jazykov*, ed. B. B. Bernshtejn and N. S. Chemodanov, 22–6. Moscow: Moscow State University.

1964b. Drevnejshije indoevropejsko-semitskije jazykovje kontakty [The earliest con-tacts of the Indo-European and Semitic languages]. *Problemy indoevropejskogo jazykoznanija*, ed. V. N. Toporov, 3–12. Moscow: Nauka.

1965a. Altajskije guttural'nyje *k', *k, *g. [Altaic gutturals *k', *k, *g]. *Etimologija* 1964.338–43.

1965b. Caucasica. *Etimologija* 1964.334–7.

1967a. Materialy k sravnitel'nomu slovarju nostraticheskix jazykov [Materials for the comparative dictionary of the Nostratic languages]. *Etimologija* 1965.321–96.

1967b. Rekonstrukcija ural'skogo vokalizma v svete dannyx vneshnego sravnenija [Reconstruction of Uralic vocalism in light of the data from external comparison]. *Voprosy Finnougorskogo Jazykoznanija* 4.95–100. Izhevsk.

1968a. Sootvetsvia smychnyx v nostraticheskix jazykax [Correspondences of stop sounds in the Nostratic languages]. *Etimologija* 1966.304–55.

1968b. Opyt sravnenija nostraticheskix jazykov [An experiment for the comparison of Nostratic languages]. *Slavjanskoje jazykoznanije 6: Mezhdunarodnyj s'jezd slavistov (Praga, avgust 1968). Doklady sovjetskoj delegaciji*, 407–26. Moscow.

1971a, 1976, 1984. *Opyt sravnenija nostraticheskix jazykov (semitoxamitskij, kartvel'skij, indoevropejskij, ural'skij, dravidijskij, altajskij)* [An experiment for the comparison of Nostratic languages (Semitic, Kartvelian, Indo-European, Uralic, Dravidian, Altaic)]. 3 vols. Moscow: Nauka.

1971b. Lichnyje mestoimenija **mi** 'ja' i **mä** 'my' v nostraticheskom. [The personal pronouns **mi** 'I' and **mä** 'we'] *Issledovanija po slavjanskomu jazykoznaniju*, 396–403. Moscow.

1989a. The relationship of the Nostratic family languages: a probabilistic evaluation of the similarities in question [English translation of the introduction to Illich-Svitych 1971a]. *Explorations in language macrofamilies: materials from the First International Interdisciplinary Symposium on Language and Prehistory*, ed. Vitaly Shevoroshkin, 111–21. Bochum: Brockmeyer.

1989b. Three entries from the *Nostratic dictionary* [Entries from vol. 1 Illich-Svitych 1971a]. [Translation of entries 8 and 32 was first published in *General Linguistics* 21.36–7.] *Explorations in language macrofamilies: materials from the First International Interdisciplinary Symposium on Language and Prehistory*, ed. Vitaly Shevoroshkin, 122–7. Bochum: Brockmeyer.

1989c. A Nostratic word list: reconstructions by V. Illich-Svitych, translated and arranged by Jim Parkinson. *Explorations in language macrofamilies: materials from the First International Interdisciplinary Symposium on Language and Prehistory*, ed. Vitaly Shevoroshkin, 128–62. Bochum: Brockmeyer.

1989d. The early reconstructions of Nostratic by V. M. Illich-Svitych, translated and arranged by Mark Kaiser. *Reconstructing languages and cultures: materials from the First International Interdisciplinary Symposium on Language and Prehistory*, ed. Vitaly Shevoroshkin, 131–74. Bochum: Brockmeyer.

1990. The Nostratic reconstructions of V. Illich-Svitych, translated and arranged by Mark Kaiser. *Proto-languages and proto-cultures: materials from the First International Interdisciplinary Symposium on Language and Prehistory*, ed. Vitaly Shevoroshkin, 138–67. Bochum: Brockmeyer.

Imbelloni, José. 1926. *La esfinge indiana: antiguos y nuevos aspectos del problema de los orígenes americanos*. Buenos Aires.

1928[1926]. L'idioma Kichua nel sistema linguistico dell'Oceano Pacifico. *International Congress of Americanists* 22(2).495–509. Rome.

Ivanov, V. V. 1986. Review of Illich-Svitych's dictionary of the Nostratic languages (vols. 1–2). *Typology, relationship, and time*, ed. Thomas Markey and Vitaly Shevoroshkin, 51–6, 57–65. Ann Arbor: Karoma. [English translation of Ivanov's review in *Etimologija* 1972.182–4.]

Jackson, Wayne. 1999. *The Tower of Babel – Legend or History?* (www.christiancourier.com/archives/babel.htm).

Jacobsen, William R., Jr. 1958. Washo and Karok: an approach to comparative Hokan. *International Journal of American Linguistics* 24.195–212.

1976. Observations on the Yana stop series in relationship to problems of comparative Hokan phonology. *Hokan studies: papers from the First Conference on Hokan Languages held in San Diego, California, April 23–25, 1970*, ed. Margaret Langdon and Shirley Silver, 129–48. (Janua Linguarum, series practica, 181.) The Hague: Mouton.

1979. Hokan inter-branch comparisons. *The languages of Native America: an historical and comparative assessment*, ed. L. Campbell and M. Mithun, 545–91. Austin: University of Texas Press.

1980. Inclusive/exclusive: a diffused pronominal category in native Western North America. *Papers from the parasession on pronouns and anaphora*, ed. Jody Kreiman and Almerindo E. Ojeda, 204–27. Chicago: Chicago Linguistic Society.

1990. Comments on *The feasibility of reconciling human phylogeny and the history of language*, by Richard M. Bateman, Ives Goddard, Richard O'Grady, V. A. Fund, Rich Mooi, W. John Kress, and Peter Cannell (in CA 31.1–24). Unpublished manuscript. Reno, Nevada.

1993. Another look at Sapir's evidence for inclusion of Haida in Na-Dene. Paper presented at the annual meeting of the Linguistic Society of America, January 8, 1993, Los Angeles.

1994. Characterizing and evaluating evidence for distant genetic relationships. Paper presented at the annual meeting of the American Associations for the Advancement of Science, San Francisco.

Jäger, Andreas. 1686. *De lingua vetustissima Europae, Scytho-Celtica et Gothica*. Wittenberg.

Jakobson, Roman. 1929. *Remarques sur l'évolution phonologique du russe comparée à celle des autres langues slaves*. (Travaux du Cercle Linguistique de Prague 2.) (Reprinted 1962 in *Selected writings of Roman Jakobson*, vol. I: *Phonological studies*. The Hague: Mouton.)

1931. *Über die phonologischen Sprachbünde*. Travaux du Cercle Linguistique de Prague 4.234–40.

1938. Sur la théorie des affinités phonologiques entre les langues. *Actes du quatrième congrès international de linguistes* (*tenu à Copenhague du 27 août au 1 septembre, 1936*), 48–58. (Reprinted 1949, as an appendix to *Principes de phonologie*, by N. S. Troubetzkoy, 351–65. Paris: Klincksieck.)

1960. Why "mama" and "papa"? *Perspectives in psychological theory*, ed. Bernard Kaplan and Seymour Wapner, 21–9. New York: International Universities Press. (Reprinted 1962 in *Selected writings of Roman Jakobson*, vol. 1: *Phonological studies*, 538–45. The Hague: Mouton.)

Jamieson, John. 1814. *Hermes Scythicus or the radical affinities of the Greek and Latin languages to the Gothic*. Edinburgh: The University Press for Longman, Hurst, Rees, Orme and Brown.

Janda, Richard D. and Brian D. Joseph. 2003. On language, change, and language change – or, of history, linguistics, and historical linguistics. *The handbook of historical linguistics*, ed. Brian D. Joseph and Richard D. Janda, 3–180. Oxford: Blackwell.

Janhunen, Juha. 1977. Samoyed-Altaic contacts. *Mémoires de la Société Finno-Ougrienne* 158.123–9. Helsinki.

1981. Uralilaisen kantakielen sanastosta [On the vocabulary of Proto-Uralic]. *Journal de la Société Finno-Ougrienne* 77.219–74.

1982. On the structure of Proto-Uralic. *Finnisch-ugrische Forschungen* 44.23–42.

1983. On early Indo-European-Samoyed contacts. *Mémoires de la Société Finno-Ougrienne* 185. 115–27. Helsinki.

1989. Any chances for long-range comparisons in North Asia? *Mother Tongue* (newsletter) 6.28–30.

1996. *Manchuria: an ethnic history*. (Mémoires de la Société Finno-Ougrienne 222.) Helsinki: Finno-Ugrian Society.

Janhunen, Juha and Song Moo Kho. 1982. Is Korean related to Tungusic? *Hangeul* 177.179–90.

Jankowsky, Kurt R. 1972. *The Neogrammarians*. (Janua Linguarum, series minor, 116.) The Hague: Mouton.

Janson, Tore. 2002. *Speak: a short history of languages*. Oxford: Oxford University Press.

Jasanoff, Jay. 2002. *Hittite and the Indo-European verb*. New York: Oxford University Press.

Jespersen, Otto. 1894. *Progress in language, with special reference to English*. London: S. Sonnenschein.

Johnson, Samuel. 1755. *Dictionary of the English language*. London: W. Strahan.

Johnson, Steve. 1990. Social parameters of linguistic change in an unstratified Aboriginal society. *Linguistic change and reconstruction methodology*, ed. P. Baldi, 419–33. Berlin: Mouton de Gruyter.

Joki, Aulis J. 1963. Uralte Lehnwörter oder Zufälle? *Congressus Internationalis Fenno-Ugristarum*, ed. G. Ortutay, 105–7. Budapest: Akadémiai Kiadó.

1972. Sur la parenté des langues. *Mélanges offerts à Aurélien Sauvageot pour son soixante-quinzième anniversaire*, 117–24. Budapest: Akadémiai Kiadó.

1973. *Uralier und Indogermanen: die älteren Berührungen zwischen den uralischen und indogermanischen Sprachen*. (Suomalais-Ugrilaisen Seuran Toimituksia 151.) Helsinki: Finno-Ugrian Society.

1975. Affinität und Interferenz in den Sprachen des Nordeurasischen Areals. *Congressus Quartus Internationalis Fenno-Ugristarum*, ed. G. Ortutay, 71–86. Budapest: Akadémiai Kiadó.

1976. Some Samoyed–Tunguz word comparisons. *Tractata Altaica: Sinor Festschrift*, 321–3. Wiesbaden: Harrassowitz.

1977. Die Tungusen und ihre Kontakte mit anderen Völkern. *Studia Orientalia* 47.109–18.

1980. Die altaische Einwirkung auf die uralische Naturterminologie. *Journal of Turkic Studies* 4.57–60.

1988. *Zur Geschichte der uralischen Sprachgemeinschaft unter besonderer Berücksichtigung des Ostfinnischen* [*The Uralic languages: description, history, and foreign influences*], ed. Denis Sinor, 575–95. Leiden: E. J. Brill.

Jones, Alex I. 1989. Australian and the Mana languages. *Oceanic Linguistics* 28(2).181–96. [Compares Tamil, Warlpirri (*sic*), Sedang, and Finnish vocabulary using a "statistical" method, and concludes that Tamil, Warlpiri, and Finnish are related, but that Sedang (the control language) is not.]

Jones, Sir William. 1798 [delivered February 2, 1786]. Third anniversary discourse: on the Hindus. *Asiatick Researches* 1.415–31.

1799a [delivered February 19, 1789]. Sixth anniversary discourse: on the Persians. *Asiatick Researches* 2.43–66. (Republished 1979c [1789]. New Delhi: Cosmo Publications, 35–53.)

1799b [delivered February 25, 1790]. Seventh anniversary discourse: on the Chinese. *Asiatick Researches* 2.365–81.

1799c [delivered February 24, 1791]. Eighth anniversary discourse: on the borderers, mountaineers, and islanders of Asia. *Asiatick Researches* 3.1–20. (Republished 1979d [1791]. New Delhi: Cosmo Publications, 1–17.)

1799d [delivered February 23, 1792]. Ninth anniversary discourse: on the origin and families of nations. *Asiatick Researches* 3.418–35. (Republished 1979e [1792]. New Delhi: Cosmo Publications, 479–92.)

1799e. The tenth anniversary discourse, delivered 28 February 1793: on Asiatic history, civil and natural. *Asiatick Researches* 4.i–xxxv. (Republished 1979f [1793]. New Delhi: Cosmo Publications, i–xxxv.)

1979a [1787]. The fourth anniversary discourse, delivered 15th February 1787: on the Arabs. *Asiatick Researches* 1. New Delhi: Cosmo Publications, 5–17.

1979b [1788]. The fifth anniversary discourse, delivered 21st February 1788: on the Tartars. *Asiatick Researches* 2. New Delhi: Cosmo Publications, 18–34.

1979c [1789]. See Jones 1799a.

1979d [1791]. See Jones 1799c.

1979e [1792]. See Jones 1799d.

1979f [1793]. See Jones 1799e.

Joseph, Brian and Joe Salmons (eds.). 1998. *Nostratic: sifting the evidence*. Amsterdam: Benjamins.

Jungraithmayr, Herrmann. 2000. Chadic: a network of genetic and areal relationships. *Areal and genetic factors in language classification and description: Africa south of the Sahara*, ed. Petr Zima, 90–8. Munich: LINCOM Europa.

Justeson, John S. and Laurence D. Stephens. 1980. Chance cognation: a probabilistic model and decision procedure for historical inference. *Papers from the 4th International Conference on Historical Linguistics*, ed. Elizabeth Closs Traugott, Rebecca Labrum, and Susan Shepherd, 37–45. Amsterdam: John Benjamins.

Kabak, Barış. 2004. Acquiring phonology is not acquiring inventories but contrasts: the loss of Turkic and Korean primary long vowels. *Linguistic Typology* 8.351–68.

Kaiser, Mark. 1989. Remarks on historical phonology: from Nostratic to Indo-European. *Reconstructing languages and cultures: materials from the First International Interdisciplinary Symposium on Language and Prehistory*, ed. Vitaly Shevoroshkin, 51–6. Bochum: Brockmeyer.

1990. *Lexical archaisms in Slavic: from Nostratic to Common Slavic*. (Bochum Publications in Evolutionary Cultural Semiotics 26.) Bochum: Brockmeyer.

Kaiser, Mark and Vitaly Shevoroshkin. 1986. Inheritance versus borrowing in Indo-European, Kartvelian and Semitic. *Journal of Indo-European Studies* 14.365–78.

1987. On recent comparisons between language families: the case of Indo-European and Afro-Asiatic. *General Linguistics* 27.34–46.

1988. Nostratic. *Annual Review of Anthropology* 17.309–30.

Kaltz, Barbara. 1985. Christian Jacob Kraus' review of *Linguarum totius orbis vocabularia comparativa*, ed. Peter Simon Pallas (St. Petersburg, 1787), introduction, translation and notes by Barbara Kaltz. *Historiographia Linguistica* 12.229–60.

Kate, Lambert ten. See Ten Kate, Lambert.

Kaufman, Terrence. 1964a. Materiales lingüísticos para el estudio de las relaciones internas y externas de la familia de idiomas Mayanos. *Desarrollo cultural de los Mayas*, ed. E. Vogt, 81–136. (Special publication of the Seminario de Cultura Maya.) Mexico: Universidad Nacional Autónoma de México.

1964b. Evidence for the Macro-Mayan hypothesis. Unpublished paper.

1974. *Idiomas de Mesoamérica*. (Seminario de Integración Social Guatemalteca, publication 33.) Guatemala.

1976. Archaeological and linguistic correlations in Mayaland and associated areas of Meso-America. *World Archaeology* 8.101–118.

1990. Language history in South America: what we know and how to know more. *Amazonian linguistics: studies in Lowland South America languages*, ed. Doris L. Payne, 13–67. Austin: University of Austin Press.

1994. The native languages of South America. *Atlas of the world's languages*, ed. Christopher Moseley and R. E. Asher, 46–76. London: Routledge.

Kaufman, Terrence S. and Willam M. Norman. 1984. An outline of proto-Cholan phonology, morphology, and vocabulary. *Phoneticism in Mayan hieroglyphic writing*, ed. John S. Justeson and Lyle Campbell, 77–166. (Institute for Mesoamerican Studies, publication 9.) Albany: Institute for Mesoamerican Studies, State Unviversity of New York.

Kawamoto, T. 1977–8. Towards a comparative Japanese-Austronesian. *Bulletin of the Nara University of Education* 26.23–49 (part I), 27.1–24 (part II).

Kaye, Allan S. 1985. Review of *Toward Proto-Nostratic: a new approach*, by Allan Bomhard. *Language* 61.57–60.

1989. Review of *Typology relationship and time: a collection of papers on language change and relationship by Soviet linguists*, ed. Vitaly V. Shevoroshkin and T. L. Markey. *Journal of Afroasiatic Languages* 2.222–6.

1999 The current state of Nostratic linguistics. *Nostratic: examining a linguistic macrofamily*, ed. Colin Renfrew and Daniel Nettle, 357–58. Cambridge: McDonald Institute for Achaeological Research.

Kazár, L. 1974. *Uralic-Japanese linguistic relations: a preliminary investigation*. Bloomington: Indiana University Press.

1976. Uralic–Japanese language comparison. *Ural-Altaische Jahrbücher* 48.127–50.

1980a. *Japanese–Uralic language comparison: locating Japanese origins with the help of Samoyed, Finnish, Hungarian, etc.: an attempt*. Hamburg: Tsurusaki Books.

1980b. Open monosyllabic words and possible word formation hereof in the Uralic languages and Japanese, with side-glances at the Altaic languages. *Ural-Altaische Jahrbücher* 52.42–72.

1981. Japanese–Uralic morphological parallels. *Ural–Altaische Jahrbücher* 53.88–104.

Keane, A. H. 1880. On the relations of the Indo-Chinese and Inter-Oceanic races and languages. *Journal of the Anthropological Institute* 9.254–89.

Keeley, L. H., 1996. *War before civilization: the myth of the peaceful savage*. Oxford: Oxford University Press.

Kelley, David. 1957. Our elder brother Coyote. Harvard University Ph.D. dissertation. (Appendix: Uto-Aztecan lexemes with morphological functions having Rotuman or Polynesian parallels, 188–237.)

Kennedy, James. 1856. On the probable origin of the American Indians, with particular reference to that of the Caribs. *Journal of the Ethnological Society* 4.226–67.

Kern, Hendrik. 1886. *De Fidjitaal vergeleken met hare verwanten in Indonesië en Polynesië.* (Verhandelingen der Koninklijke Akademie van Wetenschappen 16.) Amsterdam: J. Müller.

1906. *Taalvergelijkende verhandeling over het Ancityumsch.* (Verhandelingen der Koninklijke Akademie van Wetenschappen n.s. 8.) Amsterdam.

1916. *Verspreide geschriften,* vols. 4 and 5. The Hague: Martinus Nijhoff.

Kerns, John C. 1967. *The Eurasiatic pronouns and the Indo-Uralic question.* Fairborn, OH: John Kerns.

Key, Mary Ritchie. 1978. Araucanian genetic relationships. *International Journal of American Linguistics* 44.280–93.

1980–1. South American relationships with North American Indian languages. Homenaje a Ambrosio Rabanales. *Boletín de Filología* 31.331–50. Santiago, Chile: Universidad de Chile.

1981a. *Intercontinental linguistic connections.* (Humanities Inaugural Lecture Series.) Irvine: University of California.

1981b. North and South American linguistic connections. *La Linguistique* 17(1).3–18.

1983. Comparative methodology for distant relationships in North and South American languages. *Language Sciences* 5(2).133–54.

1984. *Polynesian and American linguistic connections.* (Edward Sapir Monograph Series in Language, Culture, and Cognition 12; supplement to *Forum Linguisticum* 8:3.) Lake Bluff, IL: Jupiter Press.

(ed.) 1991a. *Language change in South American Indian languages.* Philadelphia: University of Pennsylvania Press.

1991b. A résumé of comparative studies in South American Indian languages. *Language change in South American Indian languages,* ed. Mary Ritchie Key, 3–19. Philadelphia: University of Pennsylvania Press.

Key, Mary Ritchie and Christos Clairis. 1978. Fuegian and central South American language relationships. *International Congress of Americanists* 52(4).635–46. Paris.

Kho, S. 1975. An etymological study of similarities between Korean and the Uralic languages. *Congressus Tertius Internationalis Fenno-Ugristarum* 1.105–10. Tallin: Valgus.

Kim, B. H. 1976. The relationship between the Korean and Japanese languages. *Hangeul* 173–4.657–66.

Kimball, Geoffrey. 1992. A critique of Muskogean, "Gulf," and Yukian material in Language in the Americas. *International Journal of American Linguistics* 58.447–501.

1994. Comparative difficulties of the "Gulf" languages. *Proceedings of the meeting of the Society for the Study of the Indigenous Languages of the Americas and the Hokan-Penutian workshop,* ed. Margaret Langdon, 31–9. (SCOIL, report 8.) Berkeley and Los Angeles: University of California.

Kinkade, M. Dale. 2005. Alsea pronouns. *Anthropological Linguistics* 47.127–31.

Kiparsky, Paul. 1974. From paleogrammarians to Neogrammarians. *Studies in the history of linguistics: traditions and paradigms,* ed. Dell Hymes, 331–45. Bloomington: Indiana University Press.

Kiparsky, Valentin. 1975. Indogermanisch und Uralisch – die erste Synthese. *Finnisch-ugrische Forschungen* 41.176–80.

Klaproth, Julius. 1823. *Asia Polyglotta*. Paris: A. Schubart.

1826. *Mémoires relatifs à l'Asie, contenant des recherches historiques, géographiques et philosophiques*. 2 vols. Paris: Société Asiatique de Paris.

Klar, Kathryn. 1977. Topics in historical Chumash grammar. University of California, Berkeley PhD dissertation.

Knudtzon, J. A. 1902. *Die zwei Arzawa-Briefe: die ältesten Urkunden in indogermanischer Sprache*. Leipzig: Hinrichs.

Koch, Harold J. 1997. Comparative linguistics and Australian prehistory. *Archaeology and linguistics: aboriginal Australia in global perspective*, ed. Patrick McConvell and Nicholas Evans, 27–43. Melbourne: Oxford University Press.

2003. The case for Pama-Nyungan: evidence from inflectional morphology. *Proceedings of the XVII International Congress of Linguists*, ed. E. Hajieová, A. Kotiovcova, and J. Mirovky. CD-ROM. Prague: Matfyzpress, Matematicko-Fyzikální Fakulty, University Karlovi.

2004. A methodological history of Australian linguistic classification. *Australian languages: classification and the comparative method*, ed. Claire Bowern, and Harold Koch, 17–60. Amsterdam: John Benjamins.

Koelle, Sigismund W. 1854. *Polyglotta Africana, or a comparative vocabulary of nearly three hundred words and phrases in more than one hundred distinct African languages*. London: Church Missionary House.

Koerner, Konrad. 1983. Editor's foreword. *Linguistic and evolutionary theory: three essays by August Schleicher, Ernst Haeckel, and Wilhelm Bleek*, ed. Konrad Koerner, ix–xvi. Amsterdam: John Benjamins.

1986. Preface. *Historiographia Linguistica* 13.i–iv.

1990a. Jacob Grimm's position in the development of linguistics as a science. *The Grimm brothers and the Germanic past*, ed. Elmer H. Antonsen, 5–23. Amsterdam: John Benjamins.

1990b. Wilhelm von Humboldt and North American ethnolinguistics: Boas (1894) to Hymes (1961). *Historiographia Linguistica* 17.111–38.

1990c. The place of Friedrich Schlegel in the development of historical-comparative linguistics. *Leibniz, Humboldt, and the origins of comparativism*, ed. Tullio de Mauro and Lia Formigari, 239–61. Amsterdam: John Benjamins.

Köhler, Oswin. 1975. Geschichte und Probleme der Gliederung der Sprachen Afrikas. *Die Völker Afrikas und ihre traditionellen Kulturen*, ed. Hermann Baumann, 135–373. Wiesbaden: Franz Steiner.

Koivulehto, Jorma. 1991. *Uralische Evidenz für die Laryngaltheorie*. (Österreichsche Akademie der Wissenschaften, philosophisch-historische Klasse, Sitzungsberichte 566.) Vienna: Der Österreichischen Akademie der Wissenschaft.

Koo, J. H. 1980. Eskimo as a member of the Uralo-Altaic family: some structural similarities. *Congressus Quintus Internationalis Fenno-Ugristarum*, 7.216–24. Turku: Suomen Kielen Seura.

Koppelmann, Heinrich L. 1929. Ostasiatische Zahlwörter in süd-amerikanischen Sprachen. *International Archiv für Ethnographie* 30.77–118. Leiden.

Korenchy, É. 1975. On the Nostratic language family hypothesis. *Nyelvtudományi Közlemények* 77.109–15. Budapest.

Kortlandt, Frederik. 1989. Eight Indo-Uralic verbs? *Münchener Studien zur Sprachwissenschaft* 50.79–85.

Koskinen, Kalevi E. 1980. *Nilal: über die Urverwandtschaft des Hamito-Semitischen, Indogermanischen, Uralischen und Altaischen.* Helsinki: Akateeminen Kirjakauppa.

Krahe, Hans. 1950. *Das Venetische: seine Stellung im Kreise der verwandten Sprachen.* (Abhandlungen der Sitzungsberichte der Heidelbergische Akademie der Wissenschaft.) Heidelberg: Carl Winter.

Kraus, Christian Jakob. 1787. Rezension des Allgemeinen vergleichenden Wörterbuchs von Pallas. *Allgemeinen Literatur-Zeitung* 235–7. (Reprinted in Arens 1969.136–45; English translation and notes by Barbara Kaltz, 1985: *Historiographia Linguistica* 12.229–60.)

Krauss, Michael E. 1964. Proto-Athapaskan-Eyak and the problem of Na-Dene I: the phonology. *International Journal of American Linguistics* 30.118–31.

1965. Proto-Athapaskan-Eyak and the problem of Na-Dene II: morphology. *International Journal of American Linguistics* 31.18–28.

1969. On the classification in the Athapascan, Eyak, and Tlingit verb. Supplement to *International Journal of American Linguistics* 35(4), part II. (Indiana University Publications in Anthropology and Linguistics, memoir 24.) Bloomington.

1973a. Eskimo-Aleut. *Linguistics in North America*, ed. Thomas A. Sebeok, 796–902. (Current Trends in Linguistics 10.) The Hague: Mouton.

1973b. Na-Dene. *Linguistics in North America*, ed. Thomas Sebeok, 903–78. (Current Trends in Linguistics 10.) The Hague: Mouton.

1979. Na-Dene and Eskimo-Aleut. *The Languages of Native America: an historical and comparative assessment*, ed. Lyle Campbell and Marianne Mithun, 803–901. Austin: University of Texas Press.

1986. Edward Sapir and Athabaskan linguistics. *New perspectives in language, culture, and personality: proceedings of the Edward Sapir Centenary Conference* (Ottawa, 1–3 Oct., 1984), ed. William Cowan, Michael K. Foster, and Konrad Koerner, 147–90. (Studies in the History of the Language Sciences 41.) Amsterdam: John Benjamins.

Krauss, Michael E. and Victor K. Golla. 1981. Northern Athabaskan languages. *Handbook of North American Indians*, ed. William C. Sturtevant, vol. 6: *Subarctic*, ed. June Helm, 67–85. Washington, DC: Smithsonian Institution.

Krippes, K. 1990a. The Altaic component of a Nostratic dictionary. *Mother Tongue* (newsletter) 11.30–41.

1990b. A new contribution to Japanese-Korean phonological comparison. *Ural-Altaische Jahrbücher* 62.138–40.

Krishnamurti, Bhadriraju. 1969. Comparative Dravidian studies. *Linguistics in South Asia*, ed. Thomas A. Sebeok, 309–33. (Current Trends in Linguistics 5.) The Hague: Mouton.

1985. *An overview of comparative Dravidian studies since Current Trends 5 (1969). For Gordon H. Fairbanks*, ed. Veneeta Z. Acson and Richard L. Leed, 212–31. (*Oceanic Linguistics*, special publication 20.) Honolulu: University of Hawaii Press.

1994. *Dravidian languages. International encyclopedia of linguistics*, ed. William Bright, vol. 1, 337–8. Oxford: Oxford University Press.

2001. *Comparative Dravidian linguistics: current perspectives*. Oxford: Oxford University Press.

Kroeber, Alfred L. 1913. The determination of linguistic relationship. *Anthropos* 8.389–401.

1915. Serian, Tequestlatecan, and Hokan. *University of California publications in American Archaeology and Ethnology* 11.279–90.

1940. Conclusions: the present status of Americanistic problems. *The Maya and their neighbors: essays on Middle American anthropology and archaeology*, ed. Clarence L. Hay, Ralph L. Linton, Samuel K. Lothrop, Harry L. Shapiro, and George C. Vaillant, 460–87. New York: D. Appleton-Century. (Reissued 1970. New York: Dover.)

Kroskrity, Paul V. 1993. *Language, history, and identity: ethnolinguistic studies of the Arizona Tewa*. Tucson: University of Arizona Press.

Kudzinowski, C. 1983. Concerning the problem of Uralic affinity with Indo-European. *Lingua Posnaniensis* 26.99–104.

Kuipers, A. H. 1967. *The Squamish language*. The Hague: Mouton.

Kulonen, Ulla-Maija (ed.) 1992–2000. *Suomen sanojen alkuperä: etymologinen sanakirja [The origin of Finnish words: etymological dictionary]*. 3 vols. (Suomalaisen Kirjallisuuden Seuran Toimituksia 556; Kotimaisten Kielten Tutkimuksen Julkasuja 62.) Jyväskylä: Gummerus.

Laanest, Arvo. 1982. *Einführung in die ostseefinnischen Sprachen*. Hamburg: Buske.

Labberton, Dirk van Hinloopen. 1924. Preliminary results of researches into the original relationship between the Nipponese and the Malay-Polynesian languages. *Journal of the Polynesian Society* 33.244–80.

Labov, William. 2001. *Principles of linguistic change: social factors*. Oxford: Blackwell.

Laet, Joannes de. 1643. *Notae ad Dissertationem Hugonis Grotii*. Amsterdam/Paris: apud viduam Gvilielmi Pele.

Lagarde, Paul Anton de. 1877. *Amenische Studien*. (Abhandlungen der königlichen Gesellschaft der Wissenschaft zu Göttingen 22.) Göttingen: Dieterich.

Langdon, Margaret. 1974. *Comparative Hokan-Coahuiltecan studies: a survey and appraisal*. The Hague: Mouton.

1979. Some thoughts on Hokan with particular reference to Pomoan and Yuman. *The languages of Native America: an historical and comparative assessment*, ed. L. Campbell and M. Mithun, 593–649. Austin: University of Texas Press.

LaPolla, Randy. 2001.The role of migration and language contact in the development of the Sino-Tibetan language family. *Areal diffusion and genetic inheritance: problems in comparative linguistics*, ed. Alexandra Y. Aikhenvald and R. M. W. Dixon, 225–54. Oxford: Oxford University Press.

Larsson, L-G. 1982. Some remarks on the hypothesis of an Uralo-Dravidian genetic linguistic relationship. *Fenno-Ugrica Suecana* 5.169–84.

Lassen, Christian. 1844. Die Brahui und ihre Sprache. *Zeitschrift für die Kunde des Morgenlandes* 5.337–409.

Latham, Robert Gordon. 1843[1847]. On the general affinities of the languages of the Oceanic blacks. *Narrative of the surveying voyage of H. M. S. Fly, commanded by Captain F. P. Blackwood, R. N., in Torres Strait, New Guinea, and other islands of the eastern archipelago, during the years 1842–1846; together with an excursion into the interior of the eastern part of Java*, appendix IV, 313–20. ed. J. Beete Jukes. London: T. & W. Boone.

1850. *Natural history of the varieties of man.* London: J. Van Voorst.

Lavalade, F. 1986. Correspondence entre l'égyptien et l'indo-européen. *Bulletin de la Société Linguistique* 80.5–12.

Law, Vivian. 1990. Language and its students: the history of linguistics. *An encyclopaedia of language,* ed. N. E. Collinge, 784–842. London: Routledge.

Lawrence, Erma and Jeff Leer. 1977. *Haida dictionary.* Fairbanks: Alaska Native Language Center, University of Alaska.

Laycock, Donald A. 1976. A history of Papuan linguistic research: Eastern New Guinea area. *New Guinea area languages and language study,* vol. 1: *Papuan languages and the New Guinea linguistic scene,* ed. Steven A. Wurm, 43–115. (Pacific Linguistics C-38.) Sydney: Department of Linguistics, Research School of Pacific Studies, The Australian National University.

LeBlanc, Steven A. 2002. Conflict and language dispersal: issues and a New World example. *Examining the farming/language dispersal hypothesis,* ed. Colin Renfrew and Peter Bellwood, 357–65. Cambridge: McDonald Institute for Archaeological Research.

Lee, Ki-Moon. 1958. A comparative study of Manchu and Korean. *Ural-Altaische Jahrbücher* 30.104–20.

1973. Linguistic ties between Korea and Japan. *Korea Journal.* 37–42.

Leem, Knud. 1748. *En Lappisk grammatica, efter den dialect, som bruges af Field-Lapperne udi Porsanger-Fjorden, samt et register over de udi samme grammatica anførte obervationers indhold.* Copenhagen: Gottman Friederich Risel.

1768–81. *Lexicon Lapponicum bipartitum: Lapponico-Danica-Latinum & Danico-Latino-Lappinicum, cum indice Latino.* Vol. 1 Trondheim, vol. 2 Copenhagen.

Leer, Jeff. 1991. Evidence for a Northern Northwest Coast language area: promiscuous number marking and periphrastic possessive constructions in Haida, Eyak, and Aleut. *International Journal of American Linguistics* 57.158–93.

Leesberg, Arnold C. M. 1903. *Comparative philology: a comparison between Semitic and American languages.* Leiden: E. J. Brill.

Lehmann, Walter. 1920. *Zentral-Amerika.* Berlin: Museum für Völkerkunde zu Berlin.

Lehmann, Winfred P. 1994. DCM [distant comparison method] vs. CM [comparative method]. *California Linguistic Notes* 24.1–3.

Leibniz, Gottfried Wilhelm. 1692. Conjecture de Monsr. Leibniz sur l'origine du mot BLASON. *Journal des Sçavans* 20.513–15. (In 1768, *Gothofredi Guillelmi Leibnitii [. . .] opera omnia,* ed. Louis Dutens, 6.2:185. Geneva.)

1697. *Dissertatio de Origine Germanorum.*

1709. *Nouveaux essais sur l'entendement humain.*

1710a. Brevis designatio meditationum de originibus gentium, ductis potissimum ex indicio linguarum [Brief exposition of thoughts concerning the origins of nations, principally drawn from the evidence of languages]. *Miscellanea Berolinensia,* 1–16.

1710b. *Dissertatio de origine Germanorum, seu brevis disquisitio, utros incolarum Germaniae citerioris aut Scandicae ex alteris initio profectos verisimilius sit judicandum.*

1717. *Leibnitii collectanea etymologica illustrationi linguarum, veteris Celticae, Germanicae, Gallicae, aliarumque inservientia,* ed. J. G. Eckhart. Hanover. (In 1768, *Gothofredi Guillelmi Leibnitii.* [. . .] *opera omnia,* ed. Louis Dutens, 6.s:6–232. Geneva.)

1768. *De originibus gentium. Gothofredi Guillelmi Leibnitii [. . .] opera omnia*, ed. Louis Dutens, 4.186–98. Geneva.

Lejeune, Michel. 1974. *Manuel de la langue Vénète*. Heidelberg: Carl Winter.

Leopold, Joan. 1984. Duponceau, Humboldt et Pott: la place structurale des concepts de "polysynthèse" et d'incorporation." *Amerindia* 6.65–77.

Lepsius, Richard. 1880. *Nubische Grammatik, mit einer Einleitung über die Völker und Sprachen Afrika's*. Berlin: Wilhelm Hertz.

Leslau, Wolf. 1945. The influence of Cushitic on the Semitic languages of Ethiopia: a problem of substratum. *Word* 1.59–82.

1952. The influence of Sidamo on the Ethiopic languages of Gurage. *Language* 28.63–81.

Levin, Saul. 1971. *The Indo-European and Semitic languages*. Albany: State University of New York Press.

1975. The Indo-European and Semitic languages: a reply to Oswald Szemerényi. *General Linguistics* 15.197–205.

1977. "Something stolen": a Semitic participle and an Indo-European neuter substantive. *Studies in descriptive and historical linguistics: Festschrift for Winfred P. Lehmann*, ed. Paul J. Hopper, 317–39. Amsterdam: John Benjamins.

1991. Full and other key words shared by Indo-European and Semitic. *Sprung from some common source: investigations into the prehistory of languages*, ed. Sydney M. Lamb and E. Douglas Mitchell, 166–77. Stanford: Stanford University Press.

2002. *Semitic and Indo-European II: comparative morphology, syntax and phonetics*. Amsterdam: John Benjamins.

Levine, Robert D. 1979. Haida and Na-Dene: a new look at the evidence. *International Journal of American Linguistics* 45.157–70.

Levy, E. 1928. Review of *Dravidisch und Uralisch*, by Otto Schrader. *Zeitschrift für Vergleichende Sprachforschung* 145.

Lewin, B. 1976. Japanese and Korean: the problems and history of a linguistic comparison. *Journal of Japanese Studies* 2.389–412.

Lewin, Roger. 1988. American Indian language dispute. *Science* 242.1632–3.

Lhuyd, Edward. 1707. *Archaeologia Britannica, giving some account additional to what has been hitherto published, of the languages, histories and customs of the original inhabitants of Great Britain: from collections and observations in travels through Wales, Cornwall, Bas-Bretagne, Ireland and Scotland*. Oxford: Printed at the Theater for the Author. (Reprinted 1969, *English linguistics 1500–1800*, no. 136, a collection of fascimile reprints selected and edited by R. C. Alston. Menston, UK: The Scolar Press.)

Li, Fang Kuei. 1976. Sino-Tai. *Computational analysis of Asian and African languages* 3.39–48. Tokyo.

Lichtenstein, Heinrich. 1808. *Bemerkungen über die Sprachen der südafrikanischen wilden Völkerstämme, nebst einem kleinem Wörterverzeichnisse aus den gebräuchlichsten Dialecten der Hottentotten und Kaffern*. Weimar: Allgemeines Archiv für Ethnographie und Linguistik.

Liedtke, Stefan. 1989. Review of *Language in the Americas*. *Anthropos* 84.283–5.

1991. *Indianersprachen Vergleich und Klassifizierung: eine ethnolinguistische Einführung in die Grundlagen und Methoden*. Hamburg: Helmut Buske.

Lindquist, I. 1960. *Indo-European features in the Ainu language*. Lund: Gleerup.

Locke, John. 1690. *An essay concerning human understanding*. [Recent version: ed. Peter H. Nidditch. Oxford: Clarendon Press, 1979.]

Logan, J. R. 1859. Ethnology of the Indo-Pacific Islands. The affiliation of the Tibeto-Burman, Mon-Anna. Papuanasian and Malayo-Polynesian pronouns and definitives, as varieties of the ancient Himalayo-Polynesian system; and the relation of that system to the Dravido-Australian. *Journal of the Indian Archipelago and Eastern Asia*, n.s. 3.1.

Lomonosov, Mixail Vasil'evich. 1755. *Rossijskaja grammatika [Russian grammar]*. (Reprinted 1952: *Polnoe sobranie socinenij* [Complete collection of works]. Moscow: Nauka. Facsimile edition 1972, Leipzig: Zentralantiquariat der Deutschen Demokratischen Republik.)

Loukotka, Čestemír. 1968. *Classification of South American Indian languages*. (Reference Series 7.) Los Angeles: University of California, Latin American Center.

Ludolf, Hiob. 1661. *Grammatica aethiopica*. London: Roycroft.

1698. *Grammatica linguae amharicae*. Frankfurt am Main: Zunner.

1702. *Dissertatio de harmonia linguae aethiopicae cum ceteris orientalibus*. Frankfurt am Main: Johannis David Zunner and Nicolas Wilhem Helvig.

Lyell, Charles. 1830[1830–3]. *Principles of geology, being an attempt to explain the former changes of the earth's surface by reference to causes now in operation*. London: John Murray.

Lynch, John. 1998. *Pacific languages: an introduction*. Honolulu: University of Hawaii Press.

MacNeilage, Peter F. and Barbara L. Davis. 2000. On the origin of internal structure of word forms. *Science* 288.527–31.

Maddieson, Ian. 1984. *Patterns of sounds*. Cambridge: Cambridge University Press.

Mallory, J. P. and D. Q. Adams. 1997. *Encyclopedia of Indo-European culture*. London and Chicago: Fitzroy Dearborn Publishers.

Manaster Ramer, Alexis. 1993a. Is Tonkawa Na-Dene? A case study of the validity of the Greenbergian classification. *California Linguistic Notes* 24.21–5.

1993b. On Illič-Svityč's Nostratic theory. *Studies in Language* 17.205–50.

1994. Clusters or affricates in Kartvelian and Nostratic? *Diachronica* 11.157–70.

1996. Sapir's classification: Coahuiltecan. *Anthropological Linguistics* 38.1–38.

Mannheim, Bruce. 1985. Contact and Quechua-external genetic relationships. *South American Indian languages: retrospect and prospect*, ed. Harriet E. Manelis Klein and Louisa R. Stark, 644–88. Austin: University of Texas Press.

1986. Comentario a Willem Adelaar, "La relación quechua-aru: perspectivas para la separación del léxico." *Revista Andina* 4.413–18.

Marcucci, E. M. 1855. *Lettere edite e inedite di Pilippo Sassetti raccolte e annotate*. Florence.

Markey, Thomas L. and Vitalij V. Shevoroshkin. 1986. Foreword. *Typology, relationship and time: a collection of papers on language change and relationship by Soviet linguists*, ed. and trans. Vitalij V. Shevoroshkin and T. L. Markey, vii–xliv. Ann Arbor: Karoma Publishers.

Marlow, J. P. 1974. More on the Uralo-Dravidian relationship: comparison of Uralic and Dravidian etymological vocabularies. Ph.D. dissertation, University of Texas, Austin.

1980. Uralic-Dravidian hypothesis: what evidence? *Congressus Quintus Internationalis Fenno-Ugristarum*, 2.245–50. Turku: Suomen Kielen Seura.

Marsden, William. 1818[1816]. Letter on "Congolese" languages.

1834. On the Polynesian or East-Insular languages. *Miscellaneous works of William Marsden*, 1–114. London: Parbury, Allen, and Co.

Marsh, Gordon H. and Morris Swadesh. 1951. Kleinschmidt centennial V: Eskimo Aleut correspondences. *International Journal of American Linguistics* 17.209–16.

Marstrander, Carl J. S. 1919. *Cáractère indo-Européen de la langue hittite*. (Vedenskapsselskapets Skrifter, II. Historisk-Filosofisk Klasse 2.) Christiania: Jacob Dywad.

Martín, Eusebia H. and Andrés A. Pérez Diez. 1990. Deixis pronominal en el chimane del oriente boliviana. *International Journal of American Linguistics* 56.574–9.

Martin, Samuel E. 1966. Lexical evidence relating Korean to Japanese. *Language* 43.185–251.

1968. Grammatical elements relating Korean to Japanese. *Proceedings of the Eighth Congress of Anthropological and Ethnological Sciences* 9.405–7.

1975. Problems in establishing the prehistoric relationships of Korean and Japanese. *Proceedings of the International Symposium Commemorating the Thirtieth Anniversary of Korean Liberation*, 159–72. Seoul: National Academy of Sciences.

1987. *The Japanese language through time*. New Haven: Yale University Press.

1990. Morphological clues to the relationship of Japanese and Korean. *Linguistic change and reconstruction methodology*, ed. Philip Baldi, 483–509. Berlin: Mouton de Gruyter.

1991. Recent research on the relationship of Japanese and Korean. *Sprung from some common source: investigations into the prehistory of languages*, ed. Sydney M. Lamb and E. Douglas Mitchell, 269–92. Stanford: Stanford University Press.

Masica, Colin P. 1976. *Defining a linguistic area: South Asia*. Chicago: University of Chicago Press.

Mason, J. Alden. 1950. The languages of South American Indians. *Handbook of South American Indians*, ed. Julian H. Steward, 6.157–317. (Bureau of American Ethnology, bulletin 143.) Washington, DC.

Matisoff, James A. 1976. Austro-Thai and Sino-Tibetan: an examination of body-part contact relationships. *Genetic relationship, diffusion, and typological similarities of East and Southeast Asian languages*, ed. Mantaro J. Hashimoto, 256–89. Tokyo: Japan Society for the Promotion of Science.

1990. On megalo-comparison: a discussion note. *Language* 66.106–20.

1991. Sino-Tibetan linguistics: present state and future prospects. *Annual Review of Anthropology* 20.469–504.

2003. *Handbook of Proto-Tibeto-Burman: system and philosophy of Sino-Tibetan reconstruction*. (University of California Publications in Linguistics 135.) Berkeley: University of California Press.

Matteson, Esther. 1972. Towards Proto Amerindian. *Comparative studies in Amerindian languages*, ed. Esther Matteson, 21–89. (Janua Linguarum, series practica, 127.) The Hague: Mouton.

Matthews, P. H. 1997. *The concise Oxford dictionary of linguistics*. Oxford: Oxford University Press.

Mayr, E., 1963. *Animal species and evolution*. Cambridge, MA: The Belknap Press of Harvard University Press.

McAlpin, David W. 1974a. Toward proto-Elamo-Dravidian language. *Language* 50.89–101.

1974b. Elamite and Dravidian: the morphological evidence. *International Journal of Dravidian Linguistics* 3.343–58.

1975. Elamite and Dravidian: further evidence of relationship. *Current Anthropology* 16.105–15.

1981. *Proto-Elamo-Dravidian: the evidence and implications*. (Transactions of the American Philosophical Society, vol. 71, part 3.) Philadelphia: American Philosophical Society.

McConvell, Patrick. 2001. Review of *Linguistic diversity*, by Daniel Nettle. *Language in Society* 30.97–100.

McLendon, Sally. 1964. Northern Hokan (B) and (C): a comparison of Eastern Pomo and Yana. *University of California Publications in Linguistics* 34.126–44. Berkeley: University of California Press.

McMahon, April and R. McMahon. 1995. Linguistics, genetics and archaeology: internal and external evidence in the Amerind controversy. *Transactions of the Philological Society* 93.125–225.

McQuown, Norman A. 1942. Una posible síntesis lingüística macro-mayance. *Mayas y Olmecas*, 37–8. Tuxtla Gutiérrez: Sociedad Mexicana de Antropología, Reunión de Mesa Redonda sobre problemas antropológicos de México y Centro América.

1956. Evidence for a synthetic trend in Totonacan. *Language* 32.78–80.

McWhorter, John. 2001. *The power of Babel: a natural history of language*. New York: Time Books.

Meile, Pierre. 1948/1949. Observations sur quelque caractères communs des langues dravidiennes et des langues altaïques. *Actes du XXe/XXI Congrès International des Orientalistes*, 207–9. Paris.

Meillet, Antoine. 1914. Le problème de la parenté des langues. *Rivista di Scienza* 15.35:3. (Reprinted in Meillet 1948[1921]: 76–101.)

1925. *La méthode comparative en linguistique historique*. Paris: Champion. (English translation 1967: *The comparative method in historical linguistics*. Paris: Champion.)

1948[1921]. *Linguistique historique et linguistique générale*. Paris: Champion.

1966[1954/1925]. *La méthode comparative en linguistique historique*. Paris: Champion.

Meinhof, Carl. 1899. *Grundriss einer Lautlehre der Bantusprachen*. Leipzig: F. A. Brockhaus. (English translation: *Introduction to the phonology of the Bantu languages*, by N. J. van Warmelo, 1932.)

1905. Probleme der afrikanischen Linguistik. *Wiener Zeitschrift für die Kunde des Morgenlandes* 19.77–90.

1906. *Grundzüge einer vergleichenden Grammatik der Bantusprachen*. Berlin. (2nd edition 1948. Hamburg: Reimer.)

1912. *Die Sprachen der Hamiten*. Hamburg: L. Friederichsen & Co.

Membreño, Alberto. 1897. *Hondureñismos: vocabulario de los provincialismos de Honduras*. 2nd edition. Tegucigalpa: Tipografía Nacional.

Menges, Karl H. 1945. Indo-European influences on Ural-Altaic languages. *Word* 1.188–93.

1961. Altaische Studien. *Islam* 1–23.

1963. Zum ural-altaischen -u-/-w- des Medio-Passives Aspekts im Türkischen. *Ural-Altaische Jahrbücher* 35.422–4.

1964. Altajisch und Dravidisch. *Orbis* 13.66–103.

1965. Zu einigen ural-altajisch-toxarischen Wortbeziehungen. *Orbis* 14.469–72.

1969. The Dravido-Altaic relationship. *Journal of Tamil Studies* 1.35–9.

1974. Review of Miller 1971. *Central Asiatic Journal* 18.193–201.

1975. *Altajischen Studien, II: Japanisch und Altajisch.* (Abhandlungen für Kunde des Morgenlandes 41.3.) Wiesbaden: Franz Steiner.

1977. Dravidian and Altaic. *Anthropos* 72.129–79.

1984. Korean and Altaic. *Central Asiatic Journal* 28.234–83.

1989. East-Nostratic: Altaic and Dravidian. *Reconstructing languages and cultures: materials from the First International Interdisciplinary Symposium on Language and Prehistory,* ed. Vitaly Shevoroshkin, 59–62. Bochum: Brockmeyer.

1990. Altaic and East Nostratic. *Proto-languages and proto-cultures: materials from the First International Interdisciplinary Symposium on Language and Prehistory,* ed. Vitaly Shevoroshkin, 26–32. Bochum: Brockmeyer.

Menovshchikov, Gregory A. 1968. Aleutskij jazyk. *Mongol'skie, tunguso-man'czurskie i paleoaziatskie jazyki,* ed. Ja. Skorik. (Jazyki narodov SSSR series, ed. V. V. Vinogradov *et al.*, vol. 5.) Leningrad: Nauka.

Messerschmidt, D. G. 1962–77. *Forschungsreise durch Siberien 1720–1727,* ed. E. Winter, N. A. Figurovskij, G. Uschmann, and G. Jarosch. 5 vols. Berlin: Akademie Verlag.

Metcalf, George J. 1953a. Schottel and historical linguistics. *The Germanic Review* 28.113–25.

1953b. Abraham Mylius on historical linguistics. *Publications of the Modern Language Association of America* 68.535–54.

1974. The Indo-European hypothesis in the sixteenth and seventeenth centuries. *Studies in the history of linguistics: traditions and paradigms,* ed. Dell Hymes, 233–57. Bloomington: Indiana University Press.

Micelli, Luisa. 2004. Pama-Nyungan as a genetic entity. *Australian languages: classification and the comparative method,* ed. Claire Bowern and Harold Koch, 61–8. Amsterdam: John Benjamins.

Michalove, Peter A., Stefan Georg, and Alexis Manaster Ramer. 1998. Current issues in linguistic taxonomy. *Annual Review of Anthropology* 27.451–72.

Michelson, Truman. 1914. Two alleged Algonquian languages of California. *American Anthropologist* 16.361–7. (Reprinted 1990 in *The collected works of Edward Sapir,* vol. 1: *American Indian languages,* ed. William Bright, 553–7. Berlin: Mouton de Gruyter.)

1915. Rejoinder [to Edward Sapir's "Algonkin languages of California: a reply"]. *American Anthropologist* 17.194–8.

Migliazza, B. 1996. Mainland SE Asia: a unique linguistic area. *Notes on Linguistics* 75.17–25.

Mikkola, Pertti. 1998. Random coincidence in mass comparison: preliminary analysis of the Nilo-Saharan lexicon. *Nordic Journal of African Studies* 7.63–92.

1999. Nilo-Saharan revisited. *Nordic Journal of African Studies* 8.108–38.

Milewski, Tadeusz. 1960. Similarities between the Asiatic and American Indian languages. *International Journal of American Linguistics* 26.265–74.

1967. *Etudes typologiques sur les langues indigènes de l'amérique / Typological studies of the American Indian languages.* (Oddzial w Krakowie, Prace Komisji Orientalistycznej, 7.) Crakow: Polska Akademia Nauk.

Miller, Roy Andrew. 1968. The Japanese reflexes of Proto-Altaic *D-, *ȝ- and č-. *Journal of the American Oriental Society* 88.753–65.

1971a. *Japanese and other Altaic languages.* Chicago: University of Chicago Press.

1971b. The Old Japanese reflexes of Proto-Altaic *l_2. *Ural-altaische Jahrbücher* 42.127–47.

1974. Sino-Tibetan: inspection of a conspectus. *Journal of the American Oriental Society* 94.195–209.

1975. Japanese-Altaic lexical evidence and Proto-Turkic "zetacism-sigmatism." *Researches in Altaic languages* (PIAC 14), 157–72. Budapest.

1976. Reply to Doerfer. *Zeitschrift der Deutschen Morgenländischen Gesellschaft* 126.53–76.

1977. The Altaic accusatives in the light of Old and Middle Korean. *Mémoires de la Société Finno-Ougrienne* 158.157–69.

1979a. Japanese, Altaic, and Indo-European. *Journal of Indo-European Studies* 7.307–13.

1979b. Old Korean and Altaic. *Ural-altaische Jahrbücher* 51.1–54.

1980. *Origins of the Japanese language.* Seattle: University of Washington Press.

1981. Altaic origins of the Japanese verb classes. *Bono Homini Donum: essays in historical linguistics in memory of J. Alexander Kerns*, ed. Y. L. Arbeitman and A. R. Bomhard, 845–80. Amsterdam: John Benjamins.

1983. Review of *Nihongo to tamirugo* [Japanese and Tamil], by Ono Susumu, and *Nihongo wa doko kara kita ka* [Where did Japanese come from], by Fujiwara Akira. *Language* 59.207–11.

1984. Korean and Altaic. *Journal of Korean Studies* 5.143–71.

1985. Altaic connections of the Old Japanese negatives. *Central Asiatic Journal* 29.35–84.

1986. Tamil and Japanese? *Bulletin of the School of Oriental and African Studies* 49.557–60.

1987. Proto-Altaic *x-. *Central Asiatic Journal* 31.19–63.

1991. Genetic connections among the Altaic languages. *Sprung from some common source: investigations into the prehistory of languages*, ed. Sydney M. Lamb and E. Douglas Mitchell, 293–327. Stanford: Stanford University Press.

Miller, Wick R. 1971. The death of language or serendipity among the Shoshoni. *Anthropological Linguistics* 13.114–20.

1984. The classification of the Uto-Aztecan languages based on lexical evidence. *International Journal of American Linguistics* 50.1–24.

Milroy, Leslie. 1987. *Language and social networks.* 2nd edition. Oxford: Blackwell.

Milroy, Leslie and James Milroy. 1992. Social networks and social class: toward an integrated sociolinguistic model. *Language in Society* 21.1–26.

Mithun, Marianne. 1990. Studies of North American Indian languages. *Annual Review of Anthropology* 9.309–30.

Möller, Hermann. 1906. *Semitisch und Indogermanisch*. Hildesheim: Georg Olms; Copenhagen: H. Hagerup.

1911. *Vergleichendes indogermanisch-semitisches Wörterbuch*. Göttingen: Vanderhoeck & Ruprecht.

Monboddo, Lord [James Burnet]. 1773–92. *Of the origin and progress of language*. Edinburgh: J. Balfour; London: T. Caldwell.

1779–99. *Antient metaphysics*. 6 vols. Edinburgh: Bell and Bradfute; London: T. Caldwell.

Moore, John H. 1994. Putting anthropology back together again: the ethnogenetic critique of cladistic theory. *American Anthropologist* 96. 925–48.

Morice, [Père] Adrien Gabriel, O. M. I. 1891. The Déné languages, considered in themselves and in their relations to non-American idioms. *Transactions of the Canadian Institute* 1.170–212. Toronto.

1892. Déné roots. *Transactions of the Canadian Institute* 3.145–64. Toronto.

1904. Les langues dénées. *Année linguistique* 2.205–47. Paris.

1907. The unity of speech among the Northern and Southern Déné. *American Anthropologist* 9.721–37.

Morpurgo Davies, A[nna]. See Davies, Anna Morpurgo.

Moscati, Sabatino, Anton Spitaler, Edward Ullendorff, and Wolfram von Soden. 1964. *An introduction to the comparative grammar of the Semitic languages: phonology and morphology*. Wiesbaden: Harrassowitz.

Mous, Maarten. 1994. Ma'a or Mbugu. *Mixed languages: 15 case studies in language intertwining*, ed. Peter Bakker and M. Mous, 175–200. Amsterdam: Institute for Functional Research into Language and Language Use.

2003. Loss of linguistic diversity in Africa. *Language death and language maintenance: theoretical, practical and descriptive approaches*, ed. Marc Janse and Sijmen Tol, 157–70. Amsterdam: John Benjamins.

Mühlhäusler, Peter. 1989. On the causes of accelerated linguistic change in the Pacific area. *Language change: contributions to the study of its causes*, ed. Leiv Egil Breivik and Ernst Håkon Jahr, 137–72. Berlin: Mouton de Gruyter.

Mukarovsky, H. G. 1981. Einige hamito-semitische und baskische Wortstämme. *Berliner Afrikanische Vorträge*, 103–18. Berlin: Reimer.

Mukherjee, S. N. 1968. *Sir William Jones: a study in eighteenth-century British attitudes to India*. Cambridge: Cambridge University Press.

Müller, Friedrich. 1876–88. *Grundriss der Sprachwissenschaft*. 4 vols. Vienna: A. Hölder.

Muller, Jean-Claude. 1984. Saumise, Monboddo, Adelung: vers la grammaire comparée. *Matériaux pour une histoire des theories linguistiques*, ed. Sylvain Auroux, Michel Glatigny, André Joly, Anne Nicolas, and Irène Rosier, 389–96. Lille: Université de Lille III.

1986. Early stages of language comparison from Sassetti to Sir William Jones (1786). *Kratylos* 31.1–31.

Müller, Max. 1854. Letter to Chevalier Bunsen, on the classification of the Turanian languages. Printed in *Christianity and mankind*, ed. Chr. K. J. Bunsen. London.

1855. *The languages of the seat of war in the East: with a survey of three families of languages, Semitic, Arian, and Turanian*. London: Williams and Norgate.

1861[1866/99]. *Lectures on the science of language.* (2nd edition; last revision 1899.) New York: Scribner.

1862–5. *Lectures on the science of language: first and second series.* 5th edition. New York: Charles Scribner. (Reprinted 1965[1861]. Delhi: Munshi Ram Manohar Lal.)

1869. *Essays, I.* Leipzig: Wilhelm Engelmann.

Munro, Pamela. 1994. Gulf and Yuki-Gulf. *Anthropological Linguistics* 36.125–222.

Münster [Munsterus], Sebastian. 1544. *Cosmographei oder Beschreibung aller Länder, Herrschaften und fürnemesten Stetten, des gantzen Erdbodens.* Basil: Sebastianum Henricpetri.

Murayama, S. 1966. Mongolisch und Japanisch – ein Versuch zum lexikalisches Vergleich. *Collectanea Mongolica*, 153–6. Wiesbaden.

1975. Altaische Komponente der japanischen Sprache. *Researches in Altaic Languages (PI ac 14)*, 181–8. Budapest.

1977. Tungusica-Japonica. *Eurasia Nostratica* 2.186–7.

Murdock, George P. 1959. Cross-language parallels in parental kin terms. *Anthropological Linguistics* 1.9:1–5.

Murray, Alexander. 1823. *History of the European language, or researches into the affinities of the Teutonic, Greek, Celtic, Sclavonic, and Indian nations.* Edinburgh: Archibald Constable & Co.

Murray, Alexander (ed.) 1998. *Sir William Jones, 1746–1794: a commemoration.* Oxford: Oxford University Press on behalf of University College, Oxford.

Murtonen, A. 1989. Comments on Nostratic reconstructions of Illich-Svitych (revised edition). *Mother Tongue* (newsletter) 9.1–15.

Musayev, Kenesbay. 1996. Dravidian–Turkic–Sanskrit lexical comparisons. *Symbolae Turcologicae: studies in honour of Lars Johanson on his sixtieth birthday*, ed. Árpád Berta, Bernt Brendemoen, and Claus Schönib, 169–74. (Swedish Research Institute in Istanbul, Transactions 6.) Uppsala: Almqvist & Wiksell.

Mutaka, Ngessimo N. 2000. *An introduction to African linguistics.* Munich: LINCOM.Europa.

Mylius, Abraham Vander [Abraham van der Myl]. 1612. *Lingua Belgica: de linguae illius communitate tum cum plerisque alijs, tum presertim cum Latinâ, Graecâ, Persicâ; deque communitatis illius causis; tum de linguae illius origine & latissimâ per nationes quamplurimas diffusione; ut & de ejus prestantiâ. Quâ tum occasione, hic simul quaedam tractantur consideratu non indigna, ad linguas in universum omnes pertinentia.*

Naert, P. 1962. Contacts lexicaux aïnou-gilyak. *Orbis* 11.199–229.

Narumi, Hideyuki. 2000a. *The Aynu protolanguage and the Indo-European protolanguage: a search for common roots* (revised and enlarged edition of *The Aynu language and the Indo-European protolanguage.*) Sapporo: Hokkaido Shuppan Kikaku Center.

2000b. *The Japanese protolanguage and the Indo-European protolanguage: a search for common roots.* Sapporo: Hokkaido Shuppan Kikaku Center.

2001. *The Japanese protolanguage and the Indo-European protolanguage: a search for common roots* (revised and enlarged edition of *The origin of Japanese and English languages*). Tokyo: Shinpusha.

Nettle, Daniel. 1996. Language diversity in West Africa: an ecological approach. *Journal of Anthropological Archaeology* 15.403–38.

1999a. *Linguistic diversity*. Oxford: Oxford University Press.

1999b. Linguistic diversity of the Americas can be reconciled with a recent coloniza-tion. *Proceedings of the National Academy of Sciences* 96 (March).3325–9.

Nettle, Daniel and Suzanne Romaine. 2000. *Vanishing voices: the extinction of the world's languages*. Oxford: Oxford University Press.

Newman, Paul. 1980. *The classification of Chadic within Afroasiatic*. Leiden: Univer-sitaire Pers.

1991. An interview with Joseph Greenberg. *Current Anthropology* 32.453–67.

1993. Greenberg's American Indian classification: a report on the controversy. *Histor-ical linguistics 1991: papers from the tenth International Conference on Historical Linguistics*, ed. Jaan van Marle, 229–42. Amsterdam: John Benjamins.

1995. *On being right: Greenberg's African linguistic classification and the method-ological principles which underlie it*. Bloomington, IN: Institute for the Study of Nigerian Languages and Cultures, African Studies Program, Indiana University.

2000. Comparative linguistics. *African languages: an introduction*, ed. Bernd Heine and Derek Nurse, 259–71. Cambridge: Cambridge University Press.

Newman, Stanley. 1964. Comparison of Zuni and California Penutian. *International Journal of American Linguistics* 30.1–13.

1977. The Salish independent pronoun system. *International Journal of American Linguistics* 43.302–14.

1979a. A history of the Salish possessive and subject forms. *International Journal of American Linguistics* 45.207–23.

1979b. The Salish object forms. *International Journal of American Linguistics* 45.299–308.

1980. Functional changes in the Salish pronominal system. *International Journal of American Linguistics* 46.155–67.

Newmeyer, Frederick J. 2000. On the reconstruction of "Proto-World" word order. *The evolutionary emergence of language: social function and the origins of linguistic form*, ed. Chris Knight, Michael Studdert-Kennedy, and James R. Hurford, 372–90. Cambridge: Cambridge University Press.

Nichols, Johanna. 1971. Diminutive consonant symbolism in Western North America. *Language* 47.826–48.

1973. Suffix ordering in Proto-Uralic. *Lingua* 32.227–38.

1990a. Linguistic diversity and the first settlement of the New World. *Language* 66.475–521.

1990b. More on human phylogeny and linguistic history. *Current Anthropology* 31.313–14.

1992. *Linguistic diversity in time and space*. Chicago: University of Chicago Press.

1993. Ergativity and linguistic geography. *Australian Journal of Linguistics* 13. 39–89.

1994. Language at 40,000 BC. Paper presented at the annual meeting of the American Association for the Advancement of Science, San Francisco, Feb. 21, 1994.

1995a. The spread of language around the Pacific Rim. *Evolutionary Anthropology* 3(6).206–15.

1995b. Diachronically stable structural features. *Historical linguistics 1993: selected papers from the eleventh International Conference on Historical Linguistics*, ed. Henning Andersen, 337–56. Amsterdam: John Benjamins.

1996a. The comparative method as heuristic. *The comparative method revised*, ed. Mark Durie and Malcolm Ross, 39–71. Oxford: Oxford University Press.

1996b. The geography of language origins. *Berkeley Linguistics Society* 22.267–78.

1997a. Modeling ancient population structures and movement in linguistics. *Annual Review of Anthropology* 26.359–84.

1997b. Sprung from two common sources: Sahul as a linguistic area. *Archaeology and linguistics: aboriginal Australia in global perspective*, ed. Patrick McConvell and Nicholas Evans, 135–68. Melbourne: Oxford University Press.

1997c. The epicenter of the Indo-European linguistic spread. *Archaeology and language*, vol. 1: *Theoretical and methodological orientations*, ed. R. M. Blench and Matthew Spriggs, 122–48. London: Routledge.

1998a. The Eurasian spread zone and the Indo-European dispersal. *Archaeology and language*, vol. II: *Archaeological data and linguistic hypotheses*, ed. Roger Blench and Matthew Spriggs, 220–66. London: Routledge.

1998b. The origins and dispersal of languages: linguistic evidence. *The origin and diversification of language*, ed. Nina Jablonski and Leslie Aiello, 127–70. San Francisco, CA: California Academy of Sciences.

2003. Diversity and stability in language. *The handbook of historical linguistics*, ed. Brian D. Joseph and Richard D. Janda, 283–310. Oxford: Blackwell.

Nichols, Johanna and David A. Peterson. 1996. The Amerind personal pronouns. *Language* 72.336–71.

1998. Amerind personal pronouns: a reply to Campbell. *Language* 74.605–14.

Nicolaï, Robert. 1992. Utilisation des structurations lexicales pour la recherche comparative: circularité, et enroulement en songhay et touareg. *Komparative Afrikanistik: Sprach-, geschichts- und literaturwissenschaftliche Aufsätze zu Ehren von Hans G. Mukarovsky anlässlich seines 70. Geburtstags*, ed. Erwin Ebermann, E. R. Sommerauer, and K. E. Thomanek, 257–67. (Veröffentlichungen des Instituts für Afrikanistik und Ägyptologie der Universität Wien, vol. 61. *Beiträge zur Afrikanistik*, vol. 44.) Vienna: Institut für Afrikanistik.

1995. Parentés du songhay: répondre aux questions, questionner les réponses. *Actes du Cinquième Colloque de Linguistique Nilo-Saharienne/Proceedings of the fifth Nilo-Saharan Linguistics Colloquium, 24–29 août 1992/August 24th–29th, 1992, Université de Nice – Sophia Antipolis. Nilo-Saharan linguistic analyses and documentation (NISA)*, vol. 10, ed. Robert Nicolaï and Franz Rottland, 391–411. Cologne: Rüdiger Köppe.

1996. Problems of grouping and subgrouping: the question of Songhay. (Papers from the sixth Nilo-Saharan Conference, Santa Monica.) *Afrikanistische Arbeitspapiere* 45.27–52.

2002. Du songhay, du nilo-saharien et des problèmes récurrents. *Lexical and structural diffusion: interplay of internal and external factors of language development in the West African Sahel*, ed. Robert Nicolaï and Petr Zima (CORPUS, Les Cahiers 1), 111–214. Nice: Université de Nice Sophia Antipolis.

2003. La force des choses, ou, L'épreuve "nilo-saharienne": questions sur les reconstructions archéologiques et l'évolution des langues. *Sprache und Geschichte in Afrika (SUGIA)*, supplement 13. Cologne: Rüdiger Köppe.

Nikolaev, Sergei L. 1989. Eyak-Athapascan – North Caucasian sound correspondences. *Reconstructing languages and cultures: materials from the first International*

Interdisciplinary Symposium on Language and Prehistory, ed. Vitaly Shevoroshkin, 63–5. Bochum: Brockmeyer.

1991. Sino-Caucasian languages in America. *Dene-Sino-Caucasian languages: materials from the first International Interdisciplinary Symposium on Language and Prehistory*, ed. Vitaly Shevoroshkin, 42–66. Bochum: Brockmeyer.

Nikolaev, Sergei L. and O. Mudrak. 1989. Gilyak and Chukchi-Kamchatkan as Almosan Keresiouan languages: lexical evidence. *Explorations in language macrofamilies: materials from the first International Interdisciplinary Symposium on Language and Prehistory*, ed. Vitaly Shevoroshkin, 67–87. Bochum: Brockmeyer.

Noble, G. Kingsley. 1965. *Proto-Arawakan and its descendants*. Bloomington: Indiana University Press.

Nurse, Derek. 1991. Language contact, creolization, and genetic linguistics: the case of Mwiini. *Berkeley Linguistic Society* 17.177–87.

1994. South meets North: Ilwana = Bantu + Cushitic on Kenya's Tana River. *Mixed languages: 15 case studies in language intertwining*, ed. Peter Bakker and M. Mous, 213–22. Amsterdam: Institute for Functional Research into Language and Language Use.

1997. The contributions of linguistics to the study of history in Africa. *Journal of African History* 38.359–91.

O'Grady, Geoffrey. 1998. Toward a Proto-Pama-Nyungan stem list, part I: sets J_1–J_{25}. *Oceanic Linguistics* 37.209–33.

O'Grady, Geoffrey and Ken Hale. 2004. The coherence and distinctiveness of the Pama-Nyungan language family within the Australian linguistic phylum. *Australian languages: classification and the comparative method*, ed. Claire Bowern and Harold Koch, 69–92. Amsterdam: John Benjamins.

O'Grady, Geoffrey, C. F. Voegelin, and F. M. Voegelin. 1966. Languages of the world, fascicle 6: Indo-Pacific. *Anthropological Linguistics* 8.1–199.

Ohno, Susumu. 1980. *Sound correspondences between Tamil and Japanese*. (Gakushuin Series of Treatises 8.) Tokyo: Gakushuin Educational Foundation.

1983. A study of the relationship between Tamil and Japanese. *International Journal of Dravidian Linguistics* 12.366–96.

1987. Morpheme correspondences between Japanese and Tamil. *Proceedings of the 14th International Congress of Linguists*, ed. Werner Bahner, Joachim Schildt, and Dieter Viehweger, 2499–503. Berlin: Akademie Verlag.

Öhrling, E. J. 1772. *De convenientia linguae Hungarica cum Lapponica*. Uppsala.

Olson, Ronald D. 1964. Mayan affinities with Chipaya of Bolivia I: correspondences. *International Journal of American Linguistics* 30.313–24.

1965. Mayan affinities with Chipaya of Bolivia II: cognates. *International Journal of American Linguistics* 31.29–38.

Oltrogge, David F. 1977. Proto Jicaque-Subtiaba-Tequistlateco: a comparative reconstruction. *Two studies in Middle American comparative linguistics*, 1–52. Arlington: University of Texas at Arlington Press, Summer Institute of Linguistics.

Orël, Vladimir and Sergei Starostin. 1990. Etruscan as an East Caucasian language. *Proto-languages and proto-cultures: materials from the first International Interdisciplinary Symposium on Language and Prehistory*, ed. Vitaly Shevoroshkin, 60–6. Bochum: Brockmeyer.

Orel, Vladimir E. and Olga V. Stolbova. 1995. *Hamito-Semitic etymological dictionary: materials for a reconstruction.* Leiden: Brill.

Orr, Carolyn and Robert Longacre. 1968. Proto-Quechumaran. *Language* 44.528–55.

Osthoff, Hermann and Karl Brugmann. 1878. *Morphologische Untersuchungen auf dem Gebiete der indogermanischen Sprachen.* Leipzig: S. Hirzel.

Ostler, Nicholas. 2005. *Empires of the word: a language history of the world.* New York: HarperCollins.

Paasonen, Heikki. 1907. Zur Frage von der Urverwandtschaft der finnisch-ugrischen und indoeuropäischen Sprachen. *Finnisch-ugrische Forschungen* 7.13–31.

Pachori, Satya A. (ed.) 1993. *Sir William Jones: a reader.* Delhi: Oxford University Press.

Palavecino, Enrique. 1926. Glosario comparado Quičua-Maori. *International Congress of Americanists* 22(2).517–25. Rome.

Pallas, Peter Simon. 1786–9. *Linguarum totius orbis vocabularia comparativa.* (Reprinted 1997, Hamburg: Buske.)

Palmaitis, M. L. 1978. Parent language: genetic or contact relationship? *Indogermanische Forschungen* 82.50–60.

1986. New contributions to "Proto-Nostratic" [review of Bomhard 1984]. *Indogermanische Forschungen* 90.305–17.

Parker, Gary J. 1969. Comparative Quechua phonology and grammar IV: the evolution of Quechua A. *University of Hawaii Working Papers in Linguistics* 1(9).149–204.

Patrie, James. 1982. *The genetic relationship of the Ainu language.* Honolulu: University of Hawaii Press.

Patrón, Pablo. 1907. *Nuevos estudios sobre lenguas americanas: origen del kechua y del aimará/Nouvelles études sur les langues Américaines: origine du kechua et de l-aimará.* Leipzig: Brockhaus.

Paul, Hermann. 1920[1898]. *Prinzipien der Sprachgeschichte.* (5th edition; 1st 1880; 1970 printing.) Tübingen: Max Niemeyer.

Pauli, Carl. 1885. *Die Inschriften nordetruskischen Alphabets.* (Altitalische Forschungen, 1.) Leipzig: Johann Ambrosius Barth.

1891. *Die Veneter und ihre Schriftdenkmäler.* (Altitalische Forschungen, 3.) Leipzig: Johann Ambrosius Barth.

Pawley, Andrew. 1974. Austronesian languages. *Encyclopaedia Britannica* 2.484–94.

1995. Voorhoeve and the Trans New Guinea Phylum hypothesis. *Tales from a concave world: liber amicorum Bert Voorhoeve,* ed. Connie Baak, Mary Bakker and Dick van der Meij, 83–122. Leiden: Leiden University, Projects Division, Department of Languages and Cultures of South-East Asia and Oceania.

1998. The Trans New Guinea Phylum hypothesis: a reassessment. *Perspectives on the Bird's Head of Irian Jaya, Indonesia,* ed. Jelle Miedema, Cecilia Ode, and Rien A. C. Dam, 655–89. Amsterdam: Rodopi.

2001. The Proto Trans New Guinea obstruents: arguments from top-down reconstruction. *The boy from Bundaberg: studies in Melanesian linguistics in honour of Tom Dutton,* ed. Andrew Pawley, Malcolm Ross and D. Tryon, 261–300. Canberra: Pacific Linguistics.

2004. Recent research on the historical relationships of the Papuan languages, or, what can linguistics add to the stories of archaeology and other disciplines about the prehistory of Melanesia? Paper presented at the 2004 annual meeting of the American

Association of Physical Anthropologists, Podium Symposium: The second garden of Eden – Island Melanesian genetic diversity.

Pawley, Andrew and Malcolm Ross. 1993. Austronesian linguistics and culture history. *Annual Review of Anthropology* 22.425–59.

Pedersen, Holger. 1933. Zur Frage nach Urverwandtschaft des Indoeuropäischen und dem Ugrofinnischen. *Mémoires de la Société Finno-Ougrienne* 67.308–25. Helsinki.

1935. Il problema delle parentele tra grandi gruppi linguistici. *Atti del III Congresso Internazionale dei Linguisti*, 328–33. Florence: Felice de Monier.

1962[1931]. *The discovery of language: linguistic science in the nineteenth century.* Bloomington: Indiana University Press.

1983[1916]. *A glance at the history of linguistics with particular regard to the historical study of phonology*, translated from Danish by Caroline C. Henriksen, ed. Konrad Koerner. Amsterdam: John Benjamins.

Percival, W. Keith. 1986a. The reception of Hebrew in sixteenth-century Europe: impact of the Cabbala. *The history of linguistics in Spain*, ed. Antonio Quilis and Hans-J. Niederehe, 21–38. Amsterdam: John Benjamins.

1986b. Renaissance linguistics: the old and the new. *Studies in the history of western linguistics, in honour of R. H. Robins*, ed. Theodora Bynon and F. R. Palmar, 56–68. Cambridge: Cambridge University Press.

Pericliev, Vladimir. 2004. There is no correlation between the size of a community speaking a language and the size of the phonological inventory of that language. *Linguistic Typology* 8.376–83.

Petermann, Julius Heinrich. 1837. *Grammatica linguae armeniacae.* Berlin: G. Eichler.

Peters, Manfred. 1974. Einleitung. *Mithridates de differentiis linguarum tum veterum tum quae hodie apud diversas nationes in toto orbe terrarum in usu sunt*, von Konrad Gessner [1555], ed. Manfred Peters. Darmstadt: Scientia Verlag Aalen.

Petitot, Emile. 1876. *Dictionaire de la langue Dènè-Dindjié.* Paris: Leroux.

Petrachek, K. 1982. La racine en indoeuropéen et en chamito-sémitique et leurs perspectives comparatives. *AIωN* 42.381–402. (Annali del Dipartimento di Studi del Mondo Classico e del Mediterraneo Antico, Sezione Linguistica, Naples.)

Petrov, D. 1967. L'indoeuropéen et l'austronésien. *Orbis* 16.335–46.

Picard, Marc. 1998. The case against global etymologies: evidence from Algonquian. *International Journal of American Linguistics* 64.141–7. [Published also 1995: On the nature of the Algonquian evidence for global etymologies. *Mother Tongue* (newsletter) 24. 50–4.]

Pickering, John (ed.) 1833. Sebastian Rasles [Sébastien Râle], *A dictionary of the Abnaki language of North America.* [With Supplementary notes and observations on Father Rasles' *Dictionary of the Abnaki language*, by John Pickering.] *Memoirs of the American Academy of Arts and Science* 1.375–565.

Pierce, Joe E. 1965. The validity of genetic linguistics. *Linguistics* 13.25–33.

1966. Genetic comparisons and Hanis, Miluk, Alsea, Siuslaw, and Takelma. *International Journal of American Linguistics* 32.379–87.

Pinnow, Heinz-Jürgen. 1959. *Versuch einer historischen Lautlehre der Kharia-Sprache.* Wiesbaden: Otto Harrassowitz.

1964. On the historical position of Tlingit. *International Journal of American Linguistics* 30.155–64.

1966. A comparative study of the verb in the Munda languages. *Studies in comparative Austroasiatic linguistics*, ed. Norman H. Zide, 96–193. The Hague: Mouton.

1968. Genetic relationship vs. borrowing in Na-Dene. *International Journal of American Linguistics* 34.204–11.

1976. *Geschichte der Na-Dene Forschung*. (Indiana, supplement 5.) Berlin: Gebr. Mann Verlag.

1985. *Das Haida als Na-Dene-Sprache*. 4 parts. (Abhandlungen der Völkerkundlichen Arbeitsgemeinschaft, vols. 43, 44, 45, and 46.) Nortorf, Germany.

1990. *Die Na-Dene-Sprachen in Lichte der Greenberg-Klassifikation*. (Abhandlungen der Völkerkundlichen Arbeitsgemeinschaft, vol. 64.) Nortorf, Germany.

Pisani, V. 1967. La questione indouralica e la parentela linguistica. *Paideia* 22.121–5.

1971. Parentela fra le grandi familie linguistiche. *Paideia* 26.317–26.

1972. Review of Illich-Svitych 1971. *Archivo Glottologico Italiano* 57.69–72.

Pitkin, Harvey and William Shipley. 1958. Comparative survey of California Penutian. *International Journal of American Linguistics* 24.174–88.

Planert, Wilhelm. 1905. Über die Sprache der Hottentotten und Buschmänner. *Mitteilungen des Seminars für orientalische Sprache* 8.104–76.

1926. Die Schnalzsprachen. *Biblioteca Africana* 2.296–315.

Pons, Jean François. 1743. [Letter to Du Halde.] *Lettres edifiantes et curieuses*, 224–6.

Poppe, Nicholas. 1960. *Vergleichende Grammatik der altaischen Sprachen*, vol. 1: *Vergleichende Lautlehre*. (Porta Linguarum Orientalium 4.) Wiesbaden: Otto Harrassowitz.

1965. *Introduction to Altaic linguistics*. (Ural-Altaische Bibliotek 14.) Wiesbaden: Otto Harrassowitz.

1972. Ein vergleichendes Wörterbuch der nostratischen Sprachen: review of Illich-Svitych 1971. *Finnisch-ugrische Forschungen* 39.365–9.

1973. Über einige Verbalstammbildungssuffixe in den altaischen Sprachen. *Orientalia Suecana* 21.119–41.

1974. Remarks on comparative study of the vocabulary of the Altaic languages. *Ural-altaische Jahrbücher* 46.120–34.

1975. Review of Doerfer 1973. *Central Asiatic Journal* 19.158–9.

1977. The problem of Uralic and Altaic affinity. *Mémoires de la Société Finno-Ougrienne* 158.221–5.

1979. Comparative dictionary of the Nostratic languages: review of Illich-Svitych 1976. *Finnisch-ugrische Forschungen* 43.222–5.

Porkhomovsky, V. Y. 1988. On methodological problems of the genetic classification of the Afrasian (Hamito-Semitic) languages. *Proceedings of the Ninth International Congress of Ethiopian Studies*, 99–103. Moscow: USSR Academy of Sciences Africa Institute.

Poser, William J. 1992. The Salinan and Yurumanguí data in *Language in the Americas*. *International Journal of American Linguistics* 58.202–29.

Poser, William and L. Campbell. 1992. Indo-European practice and historical methodology. *Berkeley Linguistics Society* 18.214–36.

Pott, August Friedrich. 1840. Indogermanischer Sprachkunde. *Allgemeine Litteratur-Zeitung* 60–65: 475–519.

1870. *Etymologische Forschungen auf dem Gebiete der Indo-Germanischen Sprachen, unter Berücksichtigung ihrer Hauptformen.* 2nd edition. Detmold: Meyer.

Powell, John Wesley. 1891. Indian linguistic families of America north of Mexico. *Seventh annual report, Bureau of American Ethnology*, 1–142. Washington, DC: Government Printing Office. [Reprinted 1966 in Franz Boas, *Introduction to handbook of American Indian languages*; J. W. Powell, *Indian linguistic families of America north of Mexico*, ed. Preston Holder. Lincoln: University of Nebraska Press.]

Prichard, James C. 1826. *Researches into the physical history of mankind.* London: Sherwood, Gibert & Piper.

1837. Comparative vocabularies of languages of western and central Africa, northward of the Equator. *Researches into the physical history of mankind.* 3rd edition, vol. 2. London: Sherwood.

Pröhle, W. 1978. *Vergleichende Syntax der ural-altaischen (turanischen) Sprachen.* (Biblioteca Nostratica 4.) Wiesbaden.

Proyart, Abbé Lievin Bonaventure. 1776. *Histoire de Loango, Kakongo, et autres royaumes d'Afrique.* Paris: C. P. Berton & N. Crapart.

Puhvel, Jaan. 1991. Whence the Hittite: whither the Jonesian vision? *Sprung from some common source: investigations into the prehistory of languages*, ed. Sydney M. Lamb and E. Douglas Mitchell, 51–66. Stanford: Stanford University Press.

Puskás, I. 1982. Uralian and Dravidian: a reconstruction. *Etudes Finno-Ougriennes* 15.273–90.

Pusztay, János. 1980. Sprachgeschichtliche Arealien im sibirischen Sprachraum. *Congressus Quintus Internationalis Fenno-Ugristarum*, 7.251–6. Turku: Suomen Kielen Seura.

Radcliffe-Brown, A. R. 1964. *The Andaman Islanders.* New York: The Free Press of Glencoe. [First published 1922, London: Cambridge University Press.]

Radin, Paul. 1916. On the relationship of Huave and Mixe. *American Anthropologist* 18.411–21. (Also *Journal de La Société des Américanistes* [1919] 11.489–99 [Paris].)

1919. The genetic relationship of the North American Indian languages. *University of California Publications in American Archaeology and Ethnology* 14.489–502.

1924. The relationship of Maya to Zoque-Huave. *Journal de la Société des Américanistes de Paris* 16.317–24.

Rahder, Johannes. 1956–9. *Etymological vocabulary of Chinese, Japanese, Korean and Ainu*, part I (Monumenta Nipponica, monograph 16) Tokyo: Sophia University; parts II and III privately printed, New Haven (1959).

Ramsey, S. R. 1978. Are the Korean and Japanese languages related? The current state of theorizing. *Korean Studies Forum* 4.23–33.

Ramstedt, Gustaf John. 1903. *Über die Konjugation des Khalkha-Mongolischen.* (Mémoires de la Société Finno-Ougrienne 19.) Helsinki: Finnische Litteraturgesellschaft.

1914–15. Zur mongolisch-türkischen Lautgeschichte, I–II. *Keleti szemlé* 15.134–50.

1915–16. Zur mongolisch-türkischen Lautgeschichte, III. *Keleti szemlé* 16.66–84.

1924. A comparison of the Altaic languages with Japanese. *Transactions of the Asiatic Society of Japan* 1. Tokyo.

1946–7. The relation of the Altaic languages to other language groups. *Journal de la Société Finno-Ougrienne* 53.1–13.

1952. *Einführung in die altaische Sprachwissenschaft, II: Formenlehre*, ed. Pentti Aalto. (Mémoires de la Société Finno-Ougrienne 104.2.) Helsinki: Finno-Ugrian Society.

1957. *Einführung in die altaische Sprachwissenschaft, I: Lautlehre*, ed. Pentti Alto. (Mémoires de la Société Finno-Ougrienne 104.1.) Helsinki: Finno-Ugrian Society.

Rankin, Robert L. 1981. Review of *The Caddoan, Iroquoian, and Siouan languages*, by Wallace Chafe. *International Journal of American Linguistics* 47.172–7.

1992. Review of *Language in the Americas*, by Joseph Greenberg. *International Journal of American Linguistics* 58.324–50.

1998. Siouan, Yuchi, and the question of grammatical evidence for genetic relationship. Presidential address, presented at the annual meeting of the Society for the Study of the Indigenous Languages of the Americas, Jan. 10, 1998.

Rao, N. Venkata. 1954–5. [Edited a version of A. D. Campbell's *A Grammar of the Teloogoo language*.]

Räsänen, Martti. 1955. *Uralaltaische Wortforschungen*. (Studia Orientalia Edidit Societas Orientalis Fennica, 18.3:1–57.) Helsinki: Suomalaisen Kirjallisuuden Kirjapaino.

1965. Über die ural-altaische Sprachverwandtschaft. *Sitzungsberichte der Finnischen Akademie der Wissenschaften, 1963* 161–72. Helsinki.

Rask, Rasmus K. 1818. *Undersøgelse om det gamle nordiske eller Islandiske sprogs oprindelse*. Copenhagen: Gyldendal. [English translation by Niels Ege, 1993, *Investigations of the origin of the Old Norse or Icelandic language*. (Travaux du Cercle Linguistique de Copenhague 26.) Copenhagen: The Linguistic Circle of Copenhagen.]

1820a. *The endings and forms of the Danish grammar explained by derivation from the Icelandic language*. See Diderichsen 1974.

1820b. See Thalbitzer 1922.

1832–7[1820]. *Udvalgte afhandlinger*. 3 vols., ed. Louis Hjelmslev. Copenhagen: Levin & Munksgaard.

1834. Den skytiske sproget. *Samlede tildels forhen utrykte afhandlinger*, vol. I. Copenhagen.

Raue, Christian [Christian Ravis]. 1650. *A generall grammar for the ready attaining of the Ebrew, Samaritan, Calde, Syriac, Arabic and Ethiopic languages*. London: W. Wilson.

Ray, Sidney Herbert. 1926. *A comparative study of the Melanesian Island languages*. Cambridge: Cambridge University Press.

Rédei, Károly. 1986–8. *Uralisches etymologisches Wörterbuch*. 7 fascicles. Budapest: Akadémiai Kiadó.

1988. Die ältesten indogermanischen Lehnwörter der uralischen Sprachen. *The Uralic languages: description, history, and foreign influences*, ed. Denis Sinor, 638–64. Leiden: E. J. Brill.

Reid, Lawrence A. 1985. Benedict's Austro-Tai hypothesis – an evaluation. *Asian Perspectives* 26.19–34.

1994. Morphological evidence for Austric. *Oceanic Linguistics* 33.323–44.

Reinhart, J. 1988. Holzwege der nostratischen Sprachwissenschaft. *Akten der österreichischen Linguistentagung* 13.275–85. Graz.

Relandus, Hadrianus. 1706–8. *Dissertationum Miscellanearum*. Rhenum: Gulielmi Brodelet.

Renan, Ernest. 1855. *Histoire générale et système comparé des langues sémitiques*, Part 1. Paris: Imprimerie impériale. (Reprinted in *Œuvres complètes de Ernest Renan*, vol. 8, ed. Henriette Psichari, 129–589. Paris: Calmann-Lévy, 1947–61.)

  1878. *Histoire générale et système comparé des langues sémitiques*. 5th edition. Paris: Ancienne Maison Michel Lévy Frères.

  1890. *L'avenir de la science: pensées de 1848*. Paris: Calmann-Lévy.

Renfrew, Colin. 1973. Problems in the general correlations of archaeological and linguistic strata in prehistoric Greece: the model of autochthonous origin. *Bronze Age migrations in the Aegean*, ed. R. A. Crossland and A. Birchall, 263–76. London: Duckworth.

  1987. *Archaeology and language: the puzzle of Indo-European origins*. London: Jonathan Cape.

  1988. Author's précis. *Current Anthropology* 29, 437–41.

  1989. Models of change in language and archaeology. *Transactions of the Philological Society* 87.103–55.

  1991. Before Babel: speculations on the origins of linguistic diversity. *Cambridge Archeological Journal* 1.3–23.

  1992. World languages and human dispersals: a minimalist view. *Transition to modernity, essays on power, wealth and belief*, ed. J. A. Hall and I. C. Jarvie, 11–68. Cambridge: Cambridge University Press.

  1994. World linguistic diversity. *Scientific American* 270.116–23.

  1996. Language families and the spread of farming. *The origins and spread of agriculture and pastoralism in Eurasia*, ed. D. R. Harris, 70–92. London: University College London Press.

  1997. World linguistic diversity and farming dispersals. *Archaeology and language*, vol. I: *Theoretical and methodological orientations*, ed. Roger Blench and Matthew Spriggs, 82–90. London: Routledge.

  2000a. At the edge of knowability: towards a prehistory of languages. *Cambridge Archaeological Journal* 10.7–34.

  (ed.) 2000b. *America past, America present: genes and languages in the Americas and beyond*. Cambridge: McDonald Institute for Archaeological Research.

  2002. "The emerging synthesis": the archaeogenetics of farming/language dispersals and other spread zones. *Examining the farming/language dispersal hypothesis*, ed. Colin Renfrew and Peter Bellwood, 3–16. Cambridge: McDonald Institute for Archaeological Research.

Renfrew, Colin and Peter Bellwood (eds.), 2002. *Examining the farming/language dispersal hypothesis*. Cambridge: McDonald Institute for Archaeological Research.

Renfrew, Colin, April McMahon, and Larry Trask (eds.), 2000. *Time depth in historical linguistics*. Cambridge: McDonald Institute for Archaeological Research.

Renfrew, Colin and Daniel Nettle. 1999. *Nostratic: examining a linguistic macrofamily*. Cambridge: McDonald Institute for Archaeological Research.

Rensch, Calvin R. 1973. Otomanguean isoglosses. *Diachronic, areal, and typological linguistics*, ed. Thomas Sebeok, 295–316. (Current Trends in Linguistics 11.) Mouton: The Hague.

1976. *Comparative Otomanguean phonology*. Bloomington: Indiana University Press.

1977. Classification of the Otomanguean languages and the position of Tlapanec. *Two studies in Middle American comparative linguistics*, 53–108. Arlington: University of Texas at Arlington Press, Summer Institute of Linguistics.

Rensch, Karl H. 1996. Forster's Polynesian linguistics. *Observations made during a voyage round the world by Johann Reinhold Forster*, ed. Nicholas Thomas, Harriet Guest, and Michael Dettlebach, 383–401. Honolulu: University of Hawaii Press.

Reuchlin, Johannes. 1506. *De rudimentis Hebraicis libri tres*. Pforzheim: Thomas Anselm. (Reprinted 1974, Hildesheim: Georg Olms.)

Rhedin, E. 1985. Dravidian and Indo-European: the neglected hypothesis. *International Journal of Dravidian Linguistics* 14.316–19.

Rhodes, Richard. 1977. French Cree – a case of borrowing. *Actes du huitième congrès des Algonquinistes*, ed. William Cowan, 6–25. Ottawa: Carleton University.

Rice, Keren. 2004. Language contact, phonemic inventories, and the Athapaskan language family. *Linguistic Typology* 8.321–43.

Rigsby, Bruce J. 1966. On Cayuse-Molala relatability. *International Journal of American Linguistics* 32.369–78.

1969. The Waiilatpuan problem: more on Cayuse-Molala relatability. *Northwest Anthropological Research Notes* 3.68–146.

Ringe, Donald A., Jr. 1992. On calculating the factor of chance in language comparison. *Transactions of the American Philosophical Society* 82(1).1–110.

1993. A reply to Professor Greenberg. *Proceedings of the American Philosophical Society* 137.91–109.

1994. Multilateral comparison: an empirical Test. Paper presented at the annual meeting of the American Association for the Advancement of Science.

1995a. "Nostratic" and the factor of chance. *Diachronica* 12.55–74.

1995b. The "Mana" languages and the three-language program. *Oceanic Linguistics* 34.99–122.

1996. The mathematics of "Amerind." *Diachronica* 13.135–54.

1998. Probabilistic evidence for Indo-Uralic. *Nostratic: sifting the evidence*, ed. Brian Joseph and Joe Salmons, 153–97. Amsterdam: Benjamins.

1999. How hard is it to match CVC-roots? *Transactions of the Philological Society* 97.213–44.

Ringe, Donald A. Jr., Tandy Warnow, and Ann Taylor. 2002. Indo-European computational cladistics. *Transactions of the Philological Society* 100.59–129.

Rivet, Paul. 1924. Langues americaines. *Les langues du monde*, ed. Antoine Meillet and Marcel Cohen, 597–712. (Collection linguistique 16.) Paris: Champion.

1925. Les Australiens en Amérique. *Journal de la Société Linguistique de Paris* 26.23–63.

1926. Les Malayo-Polynésiaines en Amérique. *Journal de la Société des Americanistes de Paris* 18.141–278.

1929. *Sumérien et Océanien*. Paris: Champion.

1942. Un dialecte Hoka Colombien: le Yurumangí. *Journal de la Société des Américanistes* 34.1–59.

1943. La influencia karib en Colombia. *Revista del Instituto Etnológico Nacional* 1(1).55–93. Bogotá.

1957[1943]. *Les origines de l'homme Américain*. 8th edition. Paris: Gallimard. (Spanish translation 1960[1943], *Los orígenes del hombre americano*. Mexico: Fondo de Cultura.)

Rivet, Paul, and Chestmír Loukotka. 1952. Langues de l'Amérique du Sud et des Antilles. *Les langues du monde*, ed. Antoine Meillet and Marcel Cohen, 1099–1161. Paris: Centre National de la Recherche Scientifique.

Robb, John. 1993. A social prehistory of European languages. *Antiquity* 67.747–60.

Roberts, R. E. 1798. [Material on Dravidian languages.] *Asiatick Researches* 5.127–30.

Robertson, John S. 1992. *The history of tense/aspect/mood/voice in the Mayan verbal complex*. Austin: University of Texas Press.

Robertson, William. 1769. *The history of the reign of the Emperor Charles V, with a view of the progress of society in Europe, from the subversion of the Roman Empire to the beginning of the sixteenth century*. 3 vols. London: W. Strahan, T. Cadell and J. Balfour.

Robins, Robert H. 1987. The life and work of Sir William Jones. *Transactions of the Philological Society* 1987.1–23.

1990. Leibniz and Wilhelm von Humboldt and the history of comparative linguistics. *Leibniz, Humboldt, and the origins of comparativism*, ed. Tullio de Mauro and Lia Formigari. 85–102. Amsterdam: John Benjamins.

Rocher, Rosane. 1980a. Lord Monboddo, Sanskrit and comparative linguistics. *Journal of the American Oriental Society* 100.12–17.

1980b. Nathaniel Brassey Halhed, Sir William Jones, and comparative Indo-European linguistics. *Recherches de linguistique: hommages a Maurice Leroy*, ed. Jean Bingen, André Coupez, and Francine Mawet, 173–80. Bruxelles; Editions de l'université de Bruxelles.

Rodrigues, Aryon. 1985a. Evidence for Tupi-Carib relationships. *South American Indian languages: Retrospect and prospect*, ed. Harriet E. Manelis Klein and Louisa R. Stark, 371–404. Austin: University of Texas Press.

1985b. The present state of the study of Brazilian Indian languages. *South American Indian languages: retrospect and prospect*, ed. Harriet E. Manelis Klein and Louisa R. Stark, 405–39. Austin: University of Texas Press.

1986. *Linguas brasileiras: para o conhecimento das linguas indígenas*. São Paulo: Edições Loyola.

Róna-Tas, András. 1974. Obshcheje nasledije ili zaimstvovanije? (K probleme rodstva altajskih jazykov). [Common inheritance or borrowing? (On the problem of the relationship of Altaic languages.)] *Voprosy Jazykoznanija 1972*.31–45.

1983. De hypothesi Uralo-altaica. *Mémoires de la Société Finno-Ugrienne*. Helsinki. (Reprinted in Róna-Tas 1986:234–61.)

1985. Verwandtschaftsartige Verbindung – kritische Bemerkung über die ural-altaische Hypothese. *Congressus Sextus Internationalis Fenno-Ugristarum*, 2.93. Syktyvkar.

1986. *Language and history: contributions to comparative altaistics*. (Studia Uralo-Altaica 25.) Szeged: Universitatis Szegediensis de Attila József.

1988. Turkic influence on the Uralic languages. *The Uralic languages: description, history, and foreign influences*, ed. Denis Sinor, 742–80. Leiden: E. J. Brill.

Rood, David S. 1973. Swadesh's Keres-Caddo comparisons. *International Journal of American Linguistics* 39.189–90.

Rosén, S. 1986. An investigation of the Korean material in Poppe's *Vergleichende Grammatik der altaischen Sprachen. Central Asiatic Journal* 30.78–91.

Rosenfelder, Mark. 1999. Deriving Proto-World with tools you probably have at home. www.zompist.com/proto.html

Rosenkranz, B. 1966. Zur indo-uralischen Frage. *Instituto Orientali di Napoli, Annali, Sezione Linguistica* 7.155–79.

Rosiello, Luigi. 1987. Turgot's "étymologie" and modern linguistics. *Speculative grammar, universal grammar and philosophical analysis of language*, ed. Dino Buzzetti and Maurizio Ferriani, 75–84. Amsterdam: John Benjamins.

Ross, Malcolm D. 1988. *Proto Oceanic and the Austronesian languages of western Melanesia*. (Pacific Linguistics C-98.) Canberra: Australian National University.

1995a. Some current issues in Austronesian linguistics. *Comparative Austronesian dictionary: an introduction to Austronesian studies*, part 1, fascicle 1, ed. Darrell T. Tryon, 45–120. Berlin: Mouton de Gruyter.

1995b. The great Papuan pronoun hunt: recalibrating our sights. *Tales from a concave world: liber amicorum Bert Voorhoeve*, ed. Connie Baak, Mary Bakker and Dick van der Meij, 139–68. Leiden: Leiden University, Projects Division, Department of Languages and Cultures of South-East Asia and Oceania.

1996. Contact-induced change and the comparative method: cases from Papua New Guinea. *The Comparative method reviewed: regularity and irregularity in language change*, ed. Mark Durie and Malcolm Ross, 180–217. Oxford: Oxford University Press.

1997. Social networks and kinds of speech community events. *Archaeology and language,* vol. 1: *Theoretical and methodological orientations*, ed. R. M. Blench and Matthew Spriggs, 209–61. London: Routledge.

1998. Sequencing and dating linguistic events in Oceania: the linguistics/archaeology interface. *Archaeology and language*, vol. 2: *Correlating archaeological and linguistic hypotheses*, ed. Roger Blench and Matthew Spriggs, 141–73. London: Routledge.

2001. Is there an East Papuan phylum? Evidence from pronouns. *The boy from Bundaberg: studies in Melanesian linguistics in honour of Tom Dutton*, ed. Andrew Pawley, Malcolm Ross and D. Tryon, 301–21. Canberra: Pacific Linguistics.

Ross, Phillip E. 1991. Hard words. *Scientific American* (April), 139–47.

Rost, Valentin Christian Friedrich. 1846. Ueber den Genetiv in den dekhanischen Sprachen. *Jahresbericht der Deutschen morgenländischen Gesellschaft.* 209–17. Leipzig: Brockhaus und Avenarius.

Rudbeck, Olof [Olaus], Jr. 1717. *Specimen usus linguae Gothicae, in eruendis atque illustrandis obscurissimis quibusvis sacrae scipturae locis: Addita analogia linguae Gothicae cum Sinica, nec non Finnonicae cum Ungraica.* Upsala.

Rude, Noel. 1987. Some Klamath-Sahaptian grammatical correspondences. *Kansas Working Papers in Linguistics* 12.67–83.

Rudes, Blair A. 1974. Sound changes separating Siouan-Yuchi from Iroquois-Caddoan. *International Journal of American Linguistics* 40.117–19.

Ruhlen, Merritt. 1987a. *A guide to the world's languages*, vol. 1: *Classification.* Stanford: Stanford University Press.

1987b. Voices from the past. *Natural history* 96(3).6–10.

1989a. Phylogenetic relations of Native American languages. Paper presented at the Symposium on Prehistoric Mongoloid Dispersals, Sapporo, Japan, Dec. 18–19.

1989b. Nostratic-Amerind cognates. *Reconstructing languages and cultures: materials from the First International Interdisciplinary Symposium on Language and Prehistory*, ed. Vitaly Shevoroshkin, 75–83. Bochum: Brockmeyer.

1990. An overview of genetic classification. The evolution of human languages. *Proceedings of the workshop on the evolution of human languages, August 1989, Santa Fe, NM. SFI Studies in the Sciences of Complexity* 10.1–22, ed. John A. Hawkins and Murray Gell-Mann. Redwood City, CA: Addison-Wesley.

1991. The Amerind phylum and the prehistory of the New World. *Sprung from some common source: investigations into the prehistory of languages*, ed. Sydney M. Lamb and E. Douglas Mitchell, 328–50. Stanford: Stanford University Press.

1992. An overview of genetic classification. *The evolution of human languages*, ed. John A. Hawkins and Murray Gell-Mann, 159–89. Redwood City, CA: Addison-Wesley Publishing Co.

1994a. *On the origin of languages: studies in linguistic taxonomy*. Stanford: Stanford University Press.

1994b. *The origin of language: tracing the evolution of the Mother Tongue*. New York: John Wiley & Sons.

1994c. On the origin of the Amerind pronominal pattern. *In honor of William S-Y. Wang: interdisciplinary studies on language and language change*, ed. M. Y. Chen and O. J-L. Tzeng, 405–7. Taipei: Pyramid Press.

1994d. Is Algonquian Amerind? *On the origin of languages: studies in linguistic taxonomy*, by Merritt Ruhlen, 111–26. Stanford: Stanford University Press.

1994e. Linguistic evidence for the peopling of the Americas. *Method and theory for investigating the peopling of the Americas*, ed. Robson Bonnichsen and D. Gentry Steele, 177–88. (Center for the Study of the First Americans.) Corvallis: Oregon State University. [Also in 1994. *Journal of Biogeography* 17.131–43.]

1995a. A note on Amerind pronouns. *Mother Tongue* (newsletter) 24.60–1.

1995b. Proto-Amerind numerals. *Anthropological Science* 103.209–25.

1998. The origin of Na-Dene. *Proceedings of the National Academy of Science* 95.13994–6. [Possibly publisher error on author; perhaps Joseph H. Greenberg was the true author.]

2000a. Why *kaka* and *aya*? *Functional approaches to language, culture, and cognition: papers in honor of Sydney B. Lamb*, ed. David G. Lockwood, Peter H. Fries, and James E. Copeland, 521–5. Amsterdam: John Benjamins.

2000b. Some unanswered linguistic questions. *America past, America present*, ed. Colin Renfrew, 163–75. Cambridge: McDonald Institute.

Ryan, Patrick. 2001. Proto-language monosyllables: with their principal meanings. www.geocities.com/Athens/Forum/2803/ProtoLanguage-Monosyllables.htm

Sadovsky, Otto J. 1981. Ob-Ugrian elements in the adverbs, verbal prefixes and postpositions of California Wintuan. *Congressus Quintus Internationalis Fenno-Ugristarum* 6.237–43. Turku: Suomen Kielen Seura.

1984. The discovery of California, breaking the silence of the Siberia-to-America migrators. *The Californians* 2(2).9–20 (Nov./Dec.)

1996. *The discovery of California: a Cal–Ugrian comparative study*. Budapest: Akadémiai Kiadó. (International Society for Trans-Oceanic Research, Los Angeles.)

Said, Edward. 1979. *Orientalism*. New York: Vintage Books.

Sajnovics, Jo[h]annis [János]. 1770. *Demonstratio idioma Ungarorum et Lapponum idem esse*. Copenhagen: Typis Collegi societatis Iesu; 2nd edition 1770, Trnava (Tyrnau), Hungary. (Photolithic reproduction of 2nd edition 1968, ed. Thomas A. Sebeok (Ural and Altaic Series 91.) Bloomington: Indiana University; The Hague: Mouton.) (German translation 1972, by M. Ehlers. Wiesbaden: Harassowitz.)

Salmasius, Claudius [Saumaise, Claude]. 1640. *Preface to Tabula cebetis Graece, Arabice, Latine. Item aurea carmina Pythagorae cum Paraphrasi Arabica, by Johann Elichman*. Leiden: Iohannis Maire.

1643. *De hellenistica commentarius, controversiam de lingua hellenistica decidens et plenissime pertractans originem ac dialectos graecae linguae*. Leiden: Elseviers.

Salminen, Tapani. 2001. The rise of the Finno-Ugric language family. *Early contacts between Uralic and Indo-European: linguistic and archaeological considerations*, ed. Christian Carpelan, Asko Parpola, and Petteri Koskikallio, 385–96. (Mémoires de la Société Finno-Ougrienne, 242.) Helsinki: Finno-Ugrian Society.

Salmons, Joe. 1992a. A look at the data for a global etymology: **tik* "finger." *Explanation in historical linguistics*, ed. Gary W. Davis and Gregory K. Iverson, 207–28. (Current Issues in Linguistic Theory 84.) Amsterdam: John Benjamins.

1992b. Theory and practice of global etymology. *Proceedings of the 15th International Congress of Linguists*, vol 1.153–5. Quebec.

1997. "Global etymology" as pre-Copernican linguistics. *California Linguistic Notes* 25(1).5–7.

Salzman, P. C. 1999. Is inequality universal? *Current Anthropology* 40.31–44.

Sammallahti, Pekka. 1988. Historical phonology of the Uralic languages. *The Uralic languages: description, history, and foreign influences*, ed. Denis Sinor, 478–554. Leiden: E. J. Brill.

1998. *The Saami languages: an introduction*. Karashohka: Davvi Girji.

Sanctius (Brocensis), Franciscus [Francisco Sánchez (de las Brozas)]. 1585/7. *Minerva seu de causis linguae latinae*. Salamanca: Ioannes & Andreas Renaut fratres.

Sands, Bonny. 1998. *Eastern and Southern African Khoisan: evaluating claims of distant linguistics relationship*. (Research in Khoisan Studies 14.) Cologne: Rüdiger Köppe.

Sands, Kristina. 1996. *The ergative in Proto Australian*. Munich: LINCOM Europa.

Sanmugadas, Arunasalam. 1989. Japanese-Tamil relationship: supporting evidences for Susumu Ohno's hypothesis. *Proceedings of the 14th International Congress of Linguists*, ed. Werner Bahner, Joachim Schildt, and Dieter Viehweger, 1445–7. Berlin: Akademie Verlag.

Santa Fe Institute. 2000. Annual research Report.www.santafe.edu/sfi/organization/annualReport/00/activities/evolution.html.

Sapir, Edward. 1907–8. Herder's "Ursprung der Sprache". *Modern Philology* 5.109–42. (Reprinted 1984 in *Historiographia Linguistica* 11.355–88.)

1913a. Wiyot and Yurok, Algonkin languages of California. *American Anthropologist* 15.617–46.

1913b, 1915–19. Southern Paiute and Nahuatl: a study in Uto-Aztecan. *Journal de la Société des Américanistes de Paris*, part 1, 10.379–425, part 2, 11.433–88. (Part 2 also printed 1915 *American Anthropologist* 17.98–120.)

1915a. Algonkin languages of California: a reply. *American Anthropologist* 17.188–94. (Reprinted 1990, *The collected works of Edward Sapir*, vol. 1: *American Indian languages*, ed. William Bright, 485–9. Berlin: Mouton de Gruyter.)

1915b. The Na-Dene languages, a preliminary report. *American Anthropologist* 17.534–58.

1915c. Epilogue. *American Anthropologist* 17.198.

1917. The position of Yana in the Hokan stock. *University of California Publications in American Archaeology and Ethnology* 13.1–34.

1918. Review of *Moseteno vocabulary and treatises*, by Benigno Bibolotti. *International Journal of American Linguistics* 1.183–4.

1920. The Hokan and Coahuiltecan languages. *International Journal of American Linguistics* 1.280–90.

1921a. A bird's-eye view of American languages north of Mexico. *Science* 54.408. (Reprinted 1990 in *The collected works of Edward Sapir*, vol. 5: *American Indian languages*, part 1, ed. William Bright, 93–4. Berlin: Mouton de Gruyter.)

1921b. *Language: an introduction to the study of speech*. New York: Harcourt, Brace. (Reissued 1949, New York: Harcourt, Brace and World.)

1921c. A characteristic Penutian form of stem. *International Journal of American Linguistics* 2.58–67. (Reprinted 1990 in *The collected works of Edward Sapir*, vol. 6: *American Indian languages*, part 2, ed. Victor Golla, 263–73. Berlin: Mouton de Gruyter.)

1923. The Algonkin affinity of Yurok and Wiyot kinship terms. *Journal de la Société des Américanistes de Paris* 15.37–74.

1925a. The Hokan affinity of Subtiaba in Nicaragua. *American Anthropologist* 27.402–35, 491–527.

1925b. The similarity of Chinese and Indian languages. *Science* 62.12 (Oct. 16).

1929a. Central and North American languages. *Encyclopaedia Britannica*. 14th edition. 5.138–41. (Reprinted 1990, *The collected works of Edward Sapir*, vol. 1: *American Indian languages*, ed. William Bright, 95–104. Berlin: Mouton de Gruyter.)

1929b. The status of linguistics as a science. *Language* 5.207–14. (Reprinted 1949, *Selected writings of Edward Sapir in language, culture, and personality*, ed. David G. Mandelbaum, 160–6. Berkeley: University of California Press.)

1990[n.d.]. Lecture notes (and map). *The collected works of Edward Sapir*, vol. 5: *American Indian languages*, part 1, ed. William Bright, 84–91. Berlin: Mouton de Gruyter.

Sasse, Hans-Jürgen. 1986. A southwest Ethiopian language area and its cultural background. *The Fergusonian impact*, vol. 1: *From phonology to society*, ed. Joshua A. Fishman, 327–42. Berlin: Mouton de Gruyter.

Sassetti, Pilippo. 1585. See Marcucci 1855.

Saumaise. 1643. See Salmasius.

Saussure, Ferdinand de. See de Saussure, Ferdinand.

Sauvageot, Aurélien. 1924. Eskimo et Ouralien. *Journal de la Société des Américanistes de Paris* 16.279–316.

1930. *Recherches sur le vocabulaire des langues ouralo-altaïques*. (Collection linguistique publiée par la Société de linguistique de Paris 30.) Paris.

1953. Caractère ouraloïde du verbe eskimo. *Bulletin de la Société de linguistique de Paris* 49.107–21.

1956. A propos de la parenté ouralienne. *Ural-Altaische Jahrbücher* 28.145–50.

1963. L'apportenance du youkagir. *Ural-Altaische Jahrbücher* 35.109–17.

1969. La position du youkagir. *Ural-Altaische Jahrbücher* 41.344–59.

Sayce, Archibald Henry. 1874–5. *The principles of comparative philology*. London: Trübner.

Scaliger, Joseph Justus. 1610[1599]. Diatriba de Europaeorum linguis, 119–22; Diatriba de varia literarum aliquot pronuntiatione, 127–32. *Opuscula varia antehac non edita*. Paris.

Schadeberg, Thilo C. 1981. The classification of the Kadugli language group. *Nilo-Saharan: proceedings of the first Nilo-Saharan linguistics colloquium*, ed. Thilo C. Schadeberg and M. Lionel Bender, 291–304. Dordrecht: Foris.

Scheffer [Schefferus], Johannes. 1673. *Lapponia*. Frankfurt am Main. (English translation 1674, *The history of Lapland*. Oxford. Later version: Sheffer, John. 1751. *A history of Lapland: the original manners, habits, religion and trade of that people*. London: R. Griffith.)

Schiller, Eric. 1987. Which way did they grow? Morphology and the Austro-Thai/Macro-Austric debate. *Proceedings of the Berkeley Linguistics Society* 13.235–46.

Schils, G. H. 1895. L'affinité des langues des Bushmans et des Hottentots. *Compte rendu de 2ème congrès scientifique international des catholiques* 6.5–11. Brussels.

Schindler, Jochem. 1964. Einige indogermanisch-uralische Wortgleichungen. *Die Sprache* 10.

Schlachter, W. and G. Doerfer. 1964 [1965]. Zur uraltaischen Sprachverwandtschaft. *Ural-Altaische Jahrbücher* 36.167–78.

Schlegel, [Karl Wilhelm] Friedrich von. 1808. *Ueber die Sprache und Weisheit der Indier*. Heidelberg: Mohr und Zimmer. (Reprinted 1977, Amsterdam Classics in Linguistics 1; introduction by Sebastiano Timpanaro, translation by Peter Maher. Amsterdam: John Benjamins.)

Schleicher, August. 1848. *Sprachvergleichende Untersuchungen*. Bonn: H. B. König.

1850. *Die Sprachen Europas in systematischer Übersicht: linguistische Untersuchungen*. Bonn: H. B. König. (Reprinted in new edition, 1983, ed. E. F. K. Koerner. Amsterdam: John Benjamins.)

1861–2. *Compendium der vergleichenden Grammatik der indo-germanischen Sprachen: kurzer Abriss einer Laut- und Formenlehre der indogermanishcen Ursprache*. (3rd edition, 1871.) Weimar: Hermann Böhlau.

1869. *Die deutsche Sprache*. 2nd edition. Stuttgart: J. G. Cotta.

1983[1863]. The Darwinian theory and the science of language. *Linguistic and evolutionary theory: three essays by August Schleicher, Ernst Haeckel, and Wilhelm Bleek*, ed. Konrad Koerner, 1–70. Amsterdam: John Benjamins.

1983[1865]. On the significance for the natural history of man. *Linguistic and evolutionary theory: three essays by August Schleicher, Ernst Haeckel and Wilhelm Bleek*, ed. Konrad Koerner, 73–82. Amsterdam: John Benjamins.

Schlözer, August Ludwig von. 1768. *Probe russischer Annalen*. Bremen and Göttingen: G. L. Forster.

(ed.) 1770. *Quaestiones Petropolitanae*. Göttingen: *Gottingae–Goethae*.

1781. Von den Chaldäer. *Repertorium für biblische und morgenländische Literatur* 8.161–76. Leipzig: Weidmann.

Schmidt, Wilhelm. 1899. Die sprachlichen Verhältnisse Ozeaniens (Melanesiens, Poly-
    nesiens, Mikronesiens und Indonesiens) in ihrer Bedeutung für Ethnologie. *Mit-
    teilungen der Anthropologischen Gesellschaft Wien* 29.245–58.
    1906. Die Mon-Khmer-Völker, ein Bindeglied zwischen Völkern Zentralasiens und
    Austronesiens. *Archiv für Anthropologie* 33.59–109.
    1919. *Die Gliederung der australischen Sprachen.* Vienna: Mecharisten
    Buchdrückerei. [English translation 1972 by D. Clark: Classification of the Aus-
    tralian languages. Canberra: Australian Institute of Aboriginal Studies, ms.]
    1930. Die Beziehungen der austrischen Sprachen zum japanischen. *Wiener Beiträge
    zur Kulturgeschichte und Linguistik* 1.239–52. Vienna.
Schott, W. 1849. *Über das altaische oder finnische-tatarische Sprachengeschlecht.*
    Berlin.
    1853. *Das Zahlwort in der tschudischen Sprachklasse, wie auch in Türkischen, Tun-
    gusischen und Mongolischen.* Berlin.
    1860. *Altaische Studien oder Untersuchungen auf dem Gebiete der Altai-Sprachen.*
    Berlin.
Schottelius, Justus-Georgius (Schottel, Justus Georg). 1663[1641]. *Ausführliche Arbeit
    von der teutschen Haubt-Sprache.* Brunswick: C. F. Zilliger.
Schrader, Otto. 1924. Dravidisch und Uralisch. *Zeitschrift für Indologie und Iranistik*
    3.81–112.
    1936. On the "Uralian" element in the Drāiḍa and Muṇḍā languages. *Bulletin of the
    School of Oriental Studies* 8.751–62.
Sc(h)rie(c)kius, Adrianus Rodornius [Sc(h)rieck, Adriaen van]. 1614. *Van t' beghin der
    eerster volcken van Europen, insoder heyt van den oorsppronck ende saecken der
    Nederlandren.* Ypres: F. Bellet.
Schröpfer, Johannes. 1969. Finnougrisch-indogermanische Wurzelvergleichungen.
    Ural-Altaische Jahrbücher 41.373–4.
Schuhmacher, W. W. 1974. B ∼ C? (A = Indo-European, B = Austronesian, C =
    Eskimo). *Anthropos* 69.625–7.
    1989 Basque and the other Dene-Caucasian languages. *Le Langage et l'Homme*
    24.3(71).262–3.
    1991. "Ado about nothing" or "evidence": Austronesian and Eskaleut. *Zeitschrift für
    Phonetik, Sprachwissenschaft und Kommunikationsforschung* 44.290–4.
Schuller, Rodolfo R. 1919–20. Zur sprachlichen Verwandtschaft der Maya-Qu'itsé mit
    der Carib-Aruác. *Anthropos* 14.465–91.
Schultze, Benjamin. 1725. [In a letter, comparing numbers in German, Latin, and San-
    skrit; cited in Benfey 1861: 24.]
Schütz, Albert J. 1972. *The languages of Fiji.* Oxford: Clarendon Press.
    1994. *The voices of Eden: a history of Hawaiian language studies.* Honolulu: Uni-
    versity of Hawaii Press.
Scott, J. 1976. *The moral economy of the peasant.* New Haven: Yale University
    Press.
Sebeok, Thomas A. 1945. Finno-Ugric and the languages of India. *Journal of the Amer-
    ican Oriental Society* 65.59–62.
    1950. The importance of areal linguistics in Uralic studies. *Memoires de la Société
    Finno-Ougrienne* 98.99–106.
Seler, Eduard. 1887. *Das Konjugationssystem der Mayasprachen.* Berlin: Unger.
    (Reprinted 1902 in *Gesammelte Abhandlungen zur Amerikanischen Sprach- und*

Altertumskunde 1.65–26. Berlin: Ascher; reissued 1960, Graz: Akademische Druck- und Verlagsanstalt.)

Senghor, L. S. 1975. Why create a department of Indo-African studies at Dakar University? *International Journal of Dravidian Linguistics* 4.1–13.

Serebrennikov, B. A. 1982[1986]. *Problema dostatochnosti osnovanija v gipotezah, kasajusshchihsja geneticheskogo rodstva jazykov, 3; Nostraticheskje jazyki. Teoreticheskije osnovy klassifikaciji jazykov mira: problemy rodstva*, ed. B. A. Serebrennikov, 6–62. Moscow: Nauka. [English translation: 1986, Theoretical foundations for the classification of the world's languages: problems of genetic relationship. *Typology, relationship and time: a collection of papers on language change and relationship by Soviet linguists*, ed. and trans. with a critical foreword by Vitalij V. Shevoroshkin and T. L. Markey, 66–86. Ann Arbor: Karoma Publishers.]

Setälä, Eemil N. 1912. Über Art, Umfang und Alter des Stufenwechsels im Finnisch-Ugrischen und Samojedischen. *Finnisch-ugrische Forschungen* 12.1.

1913–18. Zur Frage nach der Verwandtschaft der finnisch-ugrischen und samojedischen Sprachen. *Journal de la Société Finno-Ougrienne* 30.1–104.

Shafer, Robert. 1938. The link between Burmese and Lolo. *Sino-Tibetica* 2.8–10. Berkeley, CA.

1952. Athapaskan and Sino-Tibetan. *International Journal of American Linguistics* 18.12–19.

1955. Classification of the Sino-Tibetan languages. *Word* 11.94–111.

1957. Note on Athapaskan and Sino-Tibetan. *International Journal of American Linguistics* 23.116–17.

1963. Eurasial. *Orbis* 12.19–44.

1965. The Eurasial linguistic superfamily. *Anthropos* 60.445–68.

1966–1973. *Introduction to Sino-Tibetan*. 5 parts. Wiesbaden: Harrassowitz.

1969. A few more Athapaskan and Sino-Tibetan comparisons. *International Journal of American Linguistics* 35.67.

Shaul, David L. 1985. Azteco-Tanoan ***-*l/r-*. *International Journal of American Linguistics* 51.584–6.

Sherzer, Joel. 1976. *An areal-typological study of American Indian languages north of Mexico*. Amsterdam: North-Holland.

Shevoroshkin, Vitaly. 1982. Research report: Penutian labial stop correspondences. *California-Oregon Languages Newsletter* (I) 5(2); (II) 5(3).5–6.

1989a. A symposium on the deep reconstruction of languages and cultures. *Reconstructing languages and cultures: materials from the First International Interdisciplinary Symposium on Language and Prehistory*, ed. Vitaly Shevoroshkin, 6–8. Bochum: Brockmeyer.

1989b. Introductory remarks. *Explorations in language macrofamilies: materials from the First International Interdisciplinary Symposium on Language and Prehistory*, ed. Vitaly Shevoroshkin, 4–15. Bochum: Brockmeyer.

1989c. Methods in interphyletic comparisons. *Ural-Altaische Jahrbücher* 61.1–26.

1990. Introduction. *Proto-languages and proto-cultures: materials from the First International Interdisciplinary Symposium on Language and Prehistory*, ed. Vitaly Shevoroshkin, 8–12. Bochum: Brockmeyer.

1991. Introduction. *Dene-Sino-Caucasian languages: materials from the First International Interdisciplinary Symposium on Language and Prehistory*, ed. Vitaly Shevoroshkin, 6–9. Bochum: Brockmeyer.

Shevoroshkin, Vitaly and Alexis Manaster-Ramer. 1991. Some recent work on remote relations of languages. *Sprung from some common source: investigations into the prehistory of languages*, ed. Sydney M. Lamb and E. Douglas Mitchell, 178–203. Stanford: Stanford University Press.

Shevoroshkin, Vitalij V. and Thomas L. Markey (eds.) 1986. *Typology, relationship and time: a collection of papers on language change and relationship by Soviet linguists.* Ann Arbor: Karoma Publishers.

Shevoroshkin, Vitaly and Paul J. Sidwell (eds.) 1999. *Historical linguistics and lexicostatistics.* (AHL Studies in the Science and History of Language 3.) Canberra: Association for the History of Language.

Shherbak, A. M. 1966. O xaraktere leksicheskix vzaimosvyazei tyurkskix, mongol'skix i tunguso-man'chzhurskix yazykov. *Voprosy yazykoznaniya* 3:21–35.

1986a. Tyurksko-mongol'skie yazykovye svyazi. (K probleme vzaïmodeistviya i smesheniya yazykov.) *Voprosy yazykoznaniya* 4:47–59.

1986b. Problema rotacizma i perspektivy dal'neishego izucheniya tyurksko-mongol'skix yazykovyx svyazei. *Istoriko-kul'turnye kontakty narodov altaiskoi yazykovoi obshhnosti* 2. Tezisy dokladov XXIX sessiï Postoyannoi Mezhdunarod-noi Altaïsticheskoi Konferenciï [Tashkent 1986]. Lingvistika. Moscow: ANSSSR.

Shibatani, Masayoshi. 1990. *The languages of Japan.* Cambridge: Cambridge University Press.

Shimomiya, T. 1973. Indogermanisch und Finnisch-ugrisch – Versuch einer typologisch-vergleichenden Grammatik. *Gengogaku Ronso* 12.68–85.

Shipley, William. 1957. Some Yukian-Penutian lexical resemblances. *International Journal of American Linguistics* 23.269–74.

1966. The relation of Klamath to California Penutian. *Language* 42.489–98.

1969. Proto-Takelman. *International Journal of American Linguistics* 35.226–30.

1973. California. *Linguistics in North America*, ed. William Bright, Dell Hymes, John Lotz, Albert H. Marckwardt, and Jean-Paul Vinay, 1046–78. (Current Trends in Linguistics 10.) The Hague: Mouton.

1980. Penutian among the ruins: a personal assessment. *Berkeley Linguistics Society* 6.437–41.

Shirokogoroff, S. M. 1931. Ethnological and linguistical aspects of the Ural-Altaic hypothesis. *Tsing Hua Journal*, vol. 6. (Reprinted 1970, Oosterhout, the Netherlands: Anthropological Publications.)

Shorto, H. L. 1976. In defense of Austric. *Computational Analyses of Asian and African Languages* 6.96–104.

Silver, Shirley. 1964. Shasta and Karok: a binary comparison. *University of California Publications in Linguistics* 34.170–81.

1976. Comparative Hokan and the Northern Hokan languages. *Hokan studies: papers from the First Conference on Hokan Languages held in San Diego, California, April 23–25, 1970*, ed. Margaret Langdon and Shirley Silver, 193–202. (Janua Linguarum, series practica, 181.) The Hague: Mouton.

Silverstein, Michael. 1975. On two California Penutian roots for *two. International Journal of American Linguistics* 41.369–80.

1979a. Penutian: an assessment. *The languages of native America: historical and comparative assessment,* ed. Lyle Campbell and Marianne Mithun, 650–91. Austin: University of Texas Press.

1979b. *Two* bis. *International Journal of American Linguistics* 45.187–205.

Sinor, Denis. 1975a. Uralo-Tungus lexical correspondences. *Researches in Altaic languages*, 245–65. Budapest.

1975b. The present state of Uralic and Altaic comparative studies. *Proceedings of the International Symposium Commemorating the 30th Anniversary of Korean Liberation*, 117–46. Seoul.

1976. The *t ~ *d local suffix in Uralic and Altaic. *Hungaro-Turcica: studies in honour of Julius Németh*, 119–27. Budapest.

1977. Altaica and Uralica. *Studies in Finno-Ugric linguistics in honor of A. Raun*, ed. Denis Sinor, 319–31. Bloomington: Indiana University Press.

1978. The nature of possessive suffixes in Uralic and Altaic. *Linguistics and literary studies in honor of A. A. Hill*, ed. M. A. Yazayery *et al.*, vol. 3: *Historical and comparative linguistics*, 257–66. The Hague: Mouton.

1988. The problem of the Ural-Altaic relationship. *The Uralic languages: description, history and foreign influences*, ed. Dennis Sinor, 706–41. (Handbuch der Orientalistik, part 8.) Leiden: E.-J. Brill. (Reprinted 1990 in Denis Sinor, *Essays in comparative Altaic linguistics*, 706–41. Bloomington, In: Indiana University Research Institute for Inner Asian Studies.)

1990. Introduction: the concept of Inner Asia. *The Cambridge history of early Inner Asia*, ed. Denis Sinor, 1–18. Cambridge: Cambridge University Press.

1999. Some thoughts on the Nostratic theory and its historical implications. *Nostratic: examining a linguistic macrofamily*, ed. Colin Renfrew and Daniel Nettle, 387–400. Cambridge: McDonald Institute for Archaeological Research.

Skalička, V. 1969. Finnougrisch und Indogermanisch. *Ural-Altaische Jahrbücher* 41.335–43.

Smith, J. 1981. Neue Uralo-Sumerica. *Ural-Altaische Jahrbücher* 53.144.

Smith-Stark, Thomas C. 1992. El método de Sapir para establecer relaciones genéticas remotas. *Reflexiones lingüísticas y literarias*, vol. 1: *Lingüística*, ed. Rebeca Barriga Villanueva and Josefina García Fajardo. (Centro de Estudios Lingüísticos y Literarios, Serie Estudios de Lingüística y Literatura 25.) Mexico: El Colegio de México.

Solnit, David B. 1992. Review of *Japanese/Austro-Tai*, by Paul K. Benedict. *Language* 68.188–96.

Sommer, Edward. 1924. Zur venetischen Schrift und Sprache. *Indogermanische Forschungen* 42.90–132.

Sommerfelt, Alf. 1938. *La langue et la société*. Oslo: H. Aschehoug.

Song, Jae Jung. 2001. *Linguistic typology: morphology and syntax*. Harlow, UK: Longman.

Southworth, F. C. 1982. Dravidian and Indo-European – the neglected hypothesis. *International Journal of Dravidian Linguistics* 11.1–21.

Spuhler, James N. 1979. Genetic distances, trees, and maps of North American Indians. *The first Americans: origins, affinities, and adaptations*, ed. William S. Laughlin and Albert B. Harper, 135–83. Stuttgart: Gustav Fischer.

Stanford, C. B. 1998. The social behavior of chimpanzees and bonobos. *Current Anthropology* 39.399–407.

Stankiewicz, Edward. 1974. The dithyramb to the verb in eighteenth and nineteenth century linguistics. *Studies in the history of linguistics: traditions and paradigms*, ed. Dell Hymes, 157–90. Bloomington: Indiana University Press.

Stark, Louisa R. 1970. Mayan affinities with Araucanian. *Chicago Linguistic Society* 6.57–69.

1972. Maya-Yunga-Chipayan: a new linguistic alignment. *International Journal of American Linguistics* 38.119–35.

Starostin, Sergei A. 1984. Gipoteza o geneticheskih sv'az'ah sinotibetskih jazykov s enisejskimi i severnokavkazskimi jazykami. *Lingvisticheskaja rekonstruktsija i drevnejsaja istorija vostoka* 4.19–38. Moscow: Nauka. [Translation by W. H. Baxter III, in *Genetic classification of languages*, ed. Vitaly Shevoroshkin.]

1986. Problema geneticheskoi obshchnosti altajskih jazykov. *Istoriko-kul'turnye kontakty narodov altajskoj jazykovoj obshchnosti. Tezisy dokladov XXIX sessii Postoiannoi Medunarodnoi Altajsticheskoj konferencij [PIAC]*, vol. 2, 94–112. Moscow.

1989. *Nostratic and Sino-Caucasian. Explorations in language macrofamilies: materials from the First International Interdisciplinary Symposium on Language and Prehistory*, ed. Vitaly Shevoroshkin, 42–65. Bochum: Brockmeyer.

1991a. On the hypothesis of a genetic connection between the Sino-Tibetan languages and the Yeniseian and North-Caucasian languages. *Dene-Sino-Caucasian languages: materials from the First International Interdisciplinary Symposium on Language and Prehistory*, ed. Vitaly Shevoroshkin, 12–41. Bochum: Brockmeyer.

1991b. *Altajskaja problema proischoshdenie japonskovo jazyka [The Altaic problem and the genesis of the Japanese language]*. Moscow. http://starling.rinet.ru/Texts/Texts.htm.

1999a. Comparative-historical linguistics and lexicostatistics. *Historical linguistics and lexicostatistics*, ed. Vitaly Shevoroshkin and Paul J. Sidwell, 61–6. (AHL Studies in the Science and History of Language 3.) Canberra: Association for the History of Language. (Reprinted from 1992 *Nostratic, Dene-Caucasian, Austric and Amerind*, ed. Vitaly Shevoroshkin, 75–9. Bochum: Brockmeyer.)

1999b. Methodology of long-range comparison. *Historical linguistics and lexicostatistics*, ed. Vitaly Shevoroshkin and Paul J. Sidwell, 3–50. (AHL Studies in the Science and History of Language 3.) Canberra: Association for the History of Language.

1999c. Subgrouping of Nostratic: comments on Aharon Dolgopolsky's *The nostratic macrofamily and linguistic palaeontology. Nostratic: examining a linguistic macrofamily*, ed. Colin Renfrew and Daniel Nettle, 137–56. Cambridge: McDonald Institute for Archaeological Research.

Starostin, Sergei A., Anna Dybo, and Oleg Mudrak. 2003. *Etymological dictionary of the Altaic languages*. Leiden: Brill.

Steinthal, Heymann. 1855. *Grammatik, Logik und Psychologie, ihre Prinzipien und ihr Verhältnis zueinander*. Berlin: Ferdinand Dümmler.

1860. *Charakteristik der hauptsächlichsten Typen des Sprachbaues*. Berlin: Ferdinand Dümmler. Steinthal.

1890. Das Verhältniss, das zwischen dem Ketschua und Aimará besteht. *Congrès International des Américanistes* 7.462–5. [1888 meeting.] Berlin.

Stephens, Thomas. 1583. See Muller 1986:14–15.

Stevenson R. 1852. A comparative vocabulary of non-Sanskrit vocables of the vernacular languages of India. *Journal of the Bengal Branch of the Royal Asiatic Society* 5.

Stevenson, Robert Louis. 1924. *In the South Seas [1888, 1889]*. London: William Heinemann.

Stewart, Ethel G. 1991. *The Dene and Na-Dene Indian migration – 1233 A. D.: escape from Genghis Khan to America.* Columbus, GA: Institute for the Study of American Cultures.

Stiernhielm, Georg. 1670. *Glossarium Ulphila-Gothicum, Linguis affinibus, per Fr. Junium, nunc etiam Sveo-Gothica auctum & illustratum.* Holm.

    1671. *De linguarum origine Praefatio [On the origin of languages].* D. N. Jesu Christi SS. Evangelia ab Ulfila Gothorum translata. Stockholm.

Stipa, Günter Johannes. 1990. *Finnisch-ugrische Sprachforschung.* Helsinki: Suomalais-Ugrilainen Seura.

Stoll, Otto. 1884[1958]. *Zur Ethnographie der Republik Guatemala.* Zurich: Füssli. (Spanish translation 1958, *Etnografía de Guatemala*, trans. Antonio Goubaud Carrera. [Seminario de Integración Social Guatemalteca, publication 8.] Guatemala: Ministerio de Educación Pública.)

    1885. Supplementary remarks to the grammar of the Cakchiquel language, ed. Daniel G. Brinton. *Proceedings of the American Philosophical Society* 22.255–68.

    1912–13. Zur Psychologie der indianischen Hochlandsprachen von Guatemala. *Festschrift der Geographisch-ethnographischen Gesellschaft in Zürich* 34–96.

Stopa, Roman. 1972. Structure of Bushman and its traces in Indo-European. *Polska Akademia Nauk. – Oddzial w Krakowie.* (Prace Komisji Orientalistycznej 10.) Wroclaw: Zaklid Narodowy im. ossolinskich.

Strahlenberg, Philip Johan Tabbert von. 1730. *Das nord- und östliche Theil von Europa und Asia, in so weit solches das ganze Russische Reich mit Siberien und der grossen Tataren in sich begreiffet, in einer historisch-geographischen Beschreivung der alten und neuen Zeiten, und vielen andern unbekannten Nachrichten vorgestellet, nebst einer noch niemahls ans Licht gegebenen Tabula Polygotta.* Stockholm: In Berlegung des Autoris. (Also published in Leipzig.) (Reprinted 1975, Szeged [Studia Uralo-altaica 8.]) (English translation, 1970, *Russia, Siberia and great Tartary.* New York: Arno Press.)

Street, John. 1973. Review of Miller 1971. *Language* 49.950–4.

    1981. Remarks on the phonological comparison of Japanese with Altaic. *Bulletin of the International Institute for Linguistic Sciences* [Kyto Sangy University] 2(4).293–307.

    1985. Japanese reflexes of the Proto-Altaic lateral. *Journal of the American Oriental Society* 105.637–52.

Sturtevant, Edgar H. 1933. *A comparative grammar of the Hittite language.* Philadelphia: Linguistic Society of America.

Suárez, Jorge A. 1969. Moseten and Pano-Tacanan. *Anthropological Linguistics* 11(9).255–66.

    1973. Macro-Pano-Tacanan. *International Journal of American Linguistics* 39.137–54.

    1979. Observaciones sobre la evolución fonológica del tlapaneco. *Anales de Antropología* 16.371–86.

    1983a. *La lengua tlapaneca de Malinaltepec.* Mexico: Universidad Autónoma de Mèxico.

1983b. *The Mesoamerican Indian languages.* Cambridge: Cambridge University Press.

1985. Loan etymologies in historic method. *International Journal of American Linguistics* 51.574–6.

1986. Elementos gramaticales otomangues en tlapaneco. *Language in global perspective: papers in honor of the 50th anniversary of the Summer Institute of Linguistics, 1935–1985,* ed. Benjamin Elson, 267–84. Dallas: Summer Institute of Linguistics.

Suhonen, Seppo. 1988. Die baltischen Lehnwörter der Finnisch-Ugrischen Sprachen. *The Uralic languages: description, history, and foreign influences,* ed. Denis Sinor, 596–615. Leiden: E. J. Brill.

Suthiwan, Titima. 2003. Loanwords in Thai. Paper presented at the Loanword Typology workshop, Max Planck Institute for Evolutionary Anthropology, Leipzig, Germany, July 21–22, 2003.

Swadesh, Morris [a.k.a. Mauricio]. 1946. Phonologic formulas for Atakapa-Chitimacha. *International Journal of American Linguistics* 12.113–32.

1947. Atakapa-Chitimacha *k^w. International Journal of American Linguistics* 13.120–1.

1951. Diffusional cumulation and archaic residue as historical explanation. *Southwestern Journal of Anthropology* 7.1–21.

1952. Review of Shafer's Athapaskan and Sino-Tibetan. *International Journal of American Linguistics* 18.178–81.

1953a. Mosan I: a problem of remote common origin. *International Journal of American Linguistics* 19.26–44.

1953b. Mosan II: comparative vocabulary. *International Journal of American Linguistics* 19.223–36.

1954. Perspectives and problems of Amerindian comparative linguistics. *Word* 10.306–32.

1955. On the Penutian vocabulary survey. *International Journal of American Linguistics* 20.123–33.

1956. Problems of long-range comparison in Penutian. *Language* 32.17–41.

1959. The mesh principle in comparative linguistics. *Anthropological Linguistics* 1(2).7–14.

1960. On interhemisphere linguistic connections. *Culture in history: essays in honor of Paul Radin,* ed. Stanley Diamond, 894–924. New York: Columbia University Press.

1961. The culture historic implications of Sapir's linguistic classification. *A William Cameron Townsend en el vigésimoquinto aniversario del Instituto Lingüístico de Verano,* 663–7. Cuernavaca: Tipográfica Indígena.

1962. Linguistic relations across the Bering Strait. *American Anthropologist* 64.1262–91.

1964a. Comparative Penutian glosses of Sapir. *Studies in Californian linguistics,* ed. William Bright, 182–91. (University of California Publications in Linguistics 34.) Berkeley: University of California Press.

1964b. Linguistic overview. *Prehistoric man in the New World,* ed. Jesse D. Jennings and Edward Norbeck, 527–56. Chicago: University of Chicago Press.

1965. Lingvisticheskije svjazi Ameriki i Evraziji [Linguistic connections of America and Eurasia]. *Etimologija 1964.*271–322.

1966. Porhe [Tarascan] y maya. *Anales de antropología* 3.173–204.

1967. Lexicostatistic classification. *Handbook of Middle American Indians, vol. 5: Linguistics*, ed. Norman McQuown, 79–115. Austin: University of Texas Press.

Swanton, John R. 1911. Haida. *Handbook of American Indian languages*, ed. Franz Boas, 1.205–82. (Smithsonian Institution, Bureau of American Ethnology, bulletin 40.) Washington, DC.

1919. A structural and lexical comparison of the Tunica, Chitimacha, and Atakapa languages. *Bulletin of the Bureau of American Ethnology* 68.

1924. The Muskhogean connection of the Natchez language. *International Journal of American Linguistics* 3.46–75.

Swiggers, Pierre. 1984. Les langues amérindiennes à la Société de Linguistique de Paris (1863–1932). *Amerindia* 6.383–404.

1990. Comparatismo e grammatica comparata: tipologia linguistica e forma grammaticale. *Leibniz, Humboldt, and the origins of comparativism*, ed. Tullio de Mauro and Lia Formigari, 281–99. Amsterdam: John Benjamins.

1992. Seventeenth- and eighteenth-century Europe. *International encyclopedia of Linguistics*, ed. William Bright 2.155–9. Oxford: Oxford University Press.

Szemerényi, Otto. 1973. Review of Levin 1971. *General Linguistics* 13.101–9.

1975. The Indo-European and Semitic languages: a rejoinder to Saul Levin's reply. *General Linguistics* 15.206–13.

Tadmor, Uri. 2003. Loanwords in Indonesian. Paper presented at the Loanword typology workshop, Max-Planck Institute for Evaluationary Anthropology, Leipzig, Germany, July 21–22, 2003.

Tai, James H.-Y. 1976. On the change from SVO to SOV in Chinese. *Papers from the parasession on diachronic syntax*, ed. Sanford B. Steever, Carol A. Walker, and Salikoko S. Mufwene, 291–304. Chicago: Chicago Linguistic Society.

Tailleur, O. G. 1960. La place du ghiliak parmi les langues paléosibériennes. *Lingua* 9.113–43.

1961. Sur une explication de l'Aïnou par l'Indo-Européen. *Zeitschrift für vergliechende Sprachforschung (Kuhns Zeitschrift)* 77.1–30.

Teeter, Karl V. 1964. *Algonquian languages and genetic relationship. Proceedings of the 9th International Congress of Linguists, 1026–33*. The Hague: Mouton.

Teignmouth, Lord [John Shore]. 1804. *Memoirs of the life, writings, and correspondence of Sir William Jones*. London: John Hachard. (1805, Philadelphia: William Poyntell.)

Tekin, T. 1994. Altaic languages. *The encyclopedia of language and linguistics*, ed. R. E. Asher, 1.82–5. Oxford: Pergamon.

Téné, David. 1980. The earliest comparisons of Hebrew with Aramaic and Arabic. *Progress in linguistic historiography*, ed. Konrad Koerner, 355–77. Amsterdam: John Benjamins.

Ten Kate, Lambert. 1723. *Aenleiding tot de Kennisse van het Verhevene Deel der Nederduitsche Sprake* [Introduction to the elevated portion of the Low German language]. Amsterdam.

Thalbitzer, William. 1922. The Aleutian languages compared with Greenlandic: a manuscript by Rasmus Rask, dating from 1820, now in the Royal Library at Copenhagen. *International Journal of American Linguistics* 2.40–57.

1928. Is there any connection between the Eskimo language and the Uralian? *Acts of the International Congress of Americanists* 2.551–67. Rome.

1945. Uhlenbeck's Eskimo-Indoeuropean hypothesis: a critical revision. *Travaux du Cercle Linguistique de Copenhague* 1.66–95.

1952. Possible contacts between Eskimo and Old World languages. *Indian tribes of aboriginal America: selected papers of the 29th International Congress of Americanists*, vol. 3, ed. Sol Tax, 50–4. Chicago: University of Chicago Press.

Thelwall, Robin. 1982. Linguistic aspects of Greater Nubian history. *The archaeological and linguistic reconstruction of African history*, ed. Christopher Ehret and Merrick Posnansky, 39–56. Berkeley: University of California Press.

Thomason, Sarah G. 1980. Morphological instability, with and without language contact. *Historical morphology*, ed. Jacek Fisiak, 359–72. The Hague: Mouton.

1993. Coping with partial information in historical linguistics. *Historical linguistics 1989: papers from the 9th International Conference of Historical Linguistics*, ed. Henk Aertsen and Robert Jeffers. Amsterdam: John Benjamins.

Thomason, Sarah G. and Daniel L. Everett. 2001. Pronoun borrowing. *Berkeley Linguistics Society* 27.301–15.

Thomason, Sarah G. and Terrence Kaufman. 1988. *Language contact, creolization, and genetic linguistics*. Berkeley and Los Angeles: University of California Press.

Thurgood, Graham. 1994. The Tai-Kadai and Austronesian: the nature of the historical relationship. *Oceanic Linguistics* 34.345–68.

Thurston, W. R. 1987. Processes of change in the languages of northwestern New Britain. *Pacific Linguistics* B99.1–163.

1989. How exoteric languages build a lexicon. *VICAL 1: Oceanic languages: papers of the 5th International Conference of Austronesian Linguistics*, ed. Ray Harlow and Robin Hooper, 555–80. Auckland: Linguistic Society of New Zealand.

Toivonen, Y. H., Erkki Itkonen, Aulis J. Joki, Reino Peltola, Satu Tanner, and Marita Cronstedt. 1955–81. *Suomen kielen etymologinen sanakirja [Etymological dictionary of the Finnish language]*. Helsinki: Finno-Ugrian Society.

Tokarev, S. A. and I. A. Zolotarevskaja (eds.) 1955. *Indejcy Ameriki*. (Trudy Instituta Etnografii, novaja serija, 25.) Moscow: Akademija Nauk.

Tolmie, W. Fraser and George M. Dawson. 1884. *Comparative vocabularies of the Indian tribes of British Columbia*. (Geological and Natural History Survey of Canada.) Montreal: Dawson Brothers.

Topolovsek, Johann. 1912. *Die sprachliche Urverwandtschaft der Indogermanen, Semiten, und Indianer*. Vienna: Heinrich Kirsch.

Toporov, V. N. 1971. Burushaski and Yeniseian languages: some parallels. *Travaux Linguistiques de Prague* 4.107–25.

Torday, Laszlo. 1997. *Mounted archers: the beginnings of Central Asian history*. Edinburgh: Durham Academic Press.

Torp, Alf. 1902. Bemerkungen. *Die zwei Arzawa-Briefe: die ältesten Urkunden in indogermanischer Sprache*, by Jørgen Alexander Knudtzon, 108–22. Leipzig: Hinrichs.

Trask, Richard L[arry]. 1995. Basque and Dené-Caucasian: a critique from the Basque side. *Mother Tongue* 1.3–82.

1996. *Historical linguistics*. London: Arnold.

1999. Why should languages have any relatives? *Nostratic: examining a linguistic macrofamily*, ed. Colin Renfrew and Daniel Nettle, 157–76. Cambridge: McDonald Institute for Archaeological Research.

2000. *The dictionary of historical and comparative linguistics*. Edingburgh: Edinburgh University Press.

2001. How do we do historical work on languages? Unpublished ms., University of Sussex, Brighton, UK.

Trautmann, Thomas R. 1998. The lives of Sir William Jones. *Sir William Jones, 1746–1794: a commemoration*, ed. Alexander Murray, 93–121. Oxford: Oxford University Press on behalf of University College, Oxford.

Trombetti, Alfredo. 1905. *L'unità d'origine del linguaggio*. Bologna: Libreria Treves di Luigi Beltrami.

1928[1926]. Origine asiatica delle lingue e popolazioni americane. *International Congress of Americanists* 22(1).169–246. Rome.

Trudgill, Peter. 1989. Contact and isolation in linguistic change. *Language change: contributions to the study of its causes*, ed. Leiv Egil Breivik and Ernst Håkon Jahr, 227–38. Berlin: Mouton de Gruyter.

2002. Linguistic and social typology. *Handbook of language variation and change*, ed. J. K. Chambers, Peter Trudgill, and Natalie Schilling-Estes, 707–28, Oxford: Blackwell.

2004a. Linguistic and social typology: Austronesian migrations and phoneme inventories. *Linguistic Typology* 8.305–20.

2004b. On the complexity of simplification. *Linguistic Typology* 8.384–88.

Trumbull, J. Hammond. 1869–70. On the best method of studying the North American languages. *Transactions of the American Philological Association* 55–79.

Tryon, Darrell T. 1995. The Austronesian languages. *Comparative Austronesian dictionary: an introduction to Austronesian studies*, part 1: fascicle 1, ed. Darrell T. Tryon, 5–44. Berlin: Mouton de Gruyter.

Tsereteli, Mikheil. 1959. Das Sumerische und das Georgische. *Revue de kartvelologie*, 32–3. [Original 1912, in Georgian, in Tbilisi Collection 'Gvirgvini'.]

Tucker, Archibald N. and Margaret A. Bryan. 1956. *The non-Bantu languages of north-eastern Africa*. (Handbook of African Languages, part 3.) London: International African Institute, Oxford University Press.

1966. *Linguistic analyses: the non-Bantu languages of north-eastern Africa*. (Handbook of African Languages, part 3.) London: International African Institute, Oxford University Press.

Tuite, Kevin. 1998. Evidence for prehistoric links between the Caucasus and Central Asia: the case of the Burushos. *The Bronze Age and early Iron Age peoples of eastern central Asia*, vol. 1: *Archeology, migration and nomadism*, ed. V. H. Mair, 447–75. (*Journal of Indo-European Studies*, monograph 26.) Washington, DC: The Institute for the Study of Man in collaboration with the University of Pennsylvania Museum Publications.

Turgot, Anne Robert Jacques. 1756. Etymologie. *Encyclopédie ou dictionnaire raisonné des sciences, des arts et des métiers* 6.98–111. ed. Diderot and D'Alembert. Paris. (New edition 1961, introduction, annotations by Maurice Piron. Brugge: De Tempel; facsimile edition: 1967. Stuttgart: Frommann.)

Turner, Paul R. 1967. Seri and Chontal (Tequistlateco). *International Journal of American Linguistics* 33.235–9.

1972. On linguistic unrelatedness – a rejoinder. *International Journal of American Linguistics* 38.146–7.

1976. Pluralization of nouns in Seri and Chontal. *Hokan studies: papers from the First Conference on Hokan Languages held in San Diego, California, April 23–25, 1970*, ed. Margaret Langdon and Shirley Silver, 297–303. (Janua Linguarum, series practica, 181.) The Hague: Mouton.

Tuuk, Hermanus Neubonner van der. 1861. *Bataksch-Nederduitsch woordenboik*. Amsterdam: F. Muller.

1864. Outlines of grammar of Malagasy language. *Journal of the Royal Asiatic Society* 8.2.

1864/7. *Tobasche spraakkunst*. 2 vols. Amsterdam: Muller.

Tylor, Edward. 1871. *Primitive culture: researches into the development of mythology, philosophy, religion, language, art, and custom*. London: John Murray.

Tyler, Stephen A. 1968. Dravidian and Uralian: the lexical evidence. *Language* 44.798–812.

1990. Summary of noun and verb inflectional correspondences in Proto-Dravidian and Proto-Uralic. *Proto-languages and proto-cultures: materials from the First International Interdisciplinary Symposium on Language and Prehistory*, ed. Vitaly Shevoroshkin, 68–76. Bochum: Brockmeyer.

Uesson, Ants-Michael. 1970. *On linguistic affinity: the Indo-Uralic Problem*. Malmö: Estonian Post Publishing.

Uhlenbeck, Christianus Cornelius. 1905. Uralische Anklänge in den Eskimosprachen. *Zeitschrift der deutschen morgenländischen Gesellschaft* 59.757–65.

1942–5. Ur- und altindogermanische Anklänge im Wortschatz des Eskimos. *Anthropos* 37–40.133–48.

Ullenbrook, J. 1967. Chinesisch – Indogermanisch. *Anthropos* 62.533–51.

Ullendorff, Edward. 1970. Comparative Semitics. *Linguistics in South West Asia and North Africa*, ed. Charles A. Ferbuson, Carleton T. Hodge, and Herbert H. Paper, 261–73. (Current Trends in Linguistics 6.) The Hague: Mouton.

Unger, J. Marshall. 1973. Review of Miller 1971. *Papers in Japanese Linguistics* 2.155–69.

1977. *Studies in early Japanese morphophonemics*. Bloomington: Indiana University Linguistics Club.

1990a. Summary report of the Altaic panel. *Linguistic change and reconstruction methodology*, ed. Philip Baldi, 479–82. Berlin: Mouton de Gruyter.

1990b. Japanese and what other Altaic languages? *Linguistic change and reconstruction methodology*, ed. Philip Baldi, 547–61. Berlin: Mouton de Gruyter.

Upadhyaya, U. P. 1972. Kuruba: a Dravidian language. *Proceedings of Seminar on Dravidian Linguistics* 3.307–28. Annamalainagar: Annamalai University.

1976. Dravidian and Negro-African. *International Journal of Dravidian Linguistics* 5.32–64.

Vaček, J. 1978. The problem of the genetic relationship of the Mongolian and Dravidian languages. *Archiv Orientální* 46.141–51.

1981. The Dravido-Altaic relationship – lexical and sound correspondences. *Proceedings of the 5th International Conference-Seminar of Tamil Studies* 1.159–70.

1983. Dravido-Altaic: the Mongolian and Dravidian verbal bases. *Journal of Tamil Studies* 23.1–17.

1985. The Mongolian and Dravidian verb phrase (its pattern and the underlying verbal forms). (Asian and African Linguistic Studies II, ed. J. Vochala.) *Studia Orientalia Pragensia* 14.26–45.

1987. The Dravido-Altaic relationship. *Archív Orientální* 55.134–49.

van Driem, George. 2001. *Languages of the Himalayas*. 2 vols. Leiden: Brill.

Vansina, J., 1995. New linguistic evidence and "the Bantu expansion." *Journal of African History* 36.173–95.

Vater, Johann Severin. 1810. *Untersuchungen über Amerika's bevölkerung aus dem alten Kontinente*. Leipzig: Vogel.

Veenker, W. 1969. Verwandtschaft zwischen dem Finnougrischen und entfernteren Sprachgruppen? *Ural-Altaische Jahrbücher* 41.360–71.

Viegas Barros, José Pedro. 2001. *Evidencias del parentesco de las lenguas Lule y Vilela*. (Colección Folklore y Antropología 4.) Santa Fe, Argentina: Subsecretaría de la Provincia de Santa Fe.

Viitso, T.-R. 1971. Preliminary data on the relation of California Penutian to Uralic and other Nostratic languages. *Sovjetskoje Finno-Ugrovedenije* 7.119–28. Tallin.

Vine, Brent. 1991. Indo-European and Nostratic. *Indogermanische Forschungen* 96.9–35.

Vinson, Julien. 1875. La langue basque et aux langues américaines. *Congrès International des Américanistes*. 40–79. Nancy.

Voegelin, Carl F. and Florence M. Voegelin. 1965. Languages of the world: Sino-Tibetan, fascicles 4 and 5. *Anthropological Linguistics* 7.5, 7.6.

1985. From comparative method to phylum linguistics and back again. *International Journal of American Linguistics* 51.608–9.

von der Gabelentz. See Gabelentz, von der.

von Humboldt, Wilhelm. See Humboldt, Wilhelm von.

von Strahlenberg, Philip Johan Tabbert. See Strahlenberg, Philip Johan Tabbert von.

Vovin, Alexander. 1993. *A reconstruction of Proto-Ainu*. Leiden: Brill.

1999. Notes on linguistic comparison. *Historical linguistics and lexicostatistics*, ed. Vitaly Shevoroshkin and Paul J. Sidwell, 67–94. (AHL Studies in the Science and History of Language 3.) Canberra: Association for the History of Language.

Vulcanius (de Smet), Bonaventura. 1597. *De literis et Lingua Getarum sive Gothorum*. Leiden: Vulcanius.

Waterhouse, Viola G. 1976. Another look at Chontal and Hokan. *Hokan studies: papers from the First Conference on Hokan Languages held in San Diego, California, April 23–25, 1970*, ed. Margaret Langdon and Shirley Silver, 325–43. (Janua Linguarum, series practica, 181.) The Hague: Mouton.

Waterman, John T. 1978. *Leibniz and Ludolf on things linguistic: excerpts from their correspondence (1683–1703)*. (University of California Publications in Linguistics 88.) Berkeley: University of California Press.

Watkins, Calvert. 1990. Etymologies, equations, and comparanda: types and values, and criteria for judgement. *Linguistic change and reconstruction methodology*, ed. Philip Baldi, 289–303. Berlin: Mouton de Gruyter.

1995. El proto-indoeuropea. *Las lenguas indoeuropeas*, ed. Anna Giacalone Ramat and Paolo Ramat, 57–117. Madrid: Cátedra.

2000. *The American Heritage Dictionary of Indo-European roots*. 2nd edition (1st edition 1985). Boston: Houghton Mifflin.

2001. An Indo-European linguistic area and its characteristics: ancient Anatolia. Areal diffusion as a challenge to the comparative method? *Areal diffusion and genetic inheritance: problems in comparative linguistics*, ed. Alexandra Y. Aikhenvald and R. M. W. Dixon, 44–63. Oxford: Oxford University Press.

Webb, Nancy M. 1971. A statement of some phonological correspondences among the Pomo languages. Supplement of *International Journal of American Linguistics*, 37(3).

1976. Yuman language interrelationships: the lexical evidence. *Proceedings of the 1976 Hokan–Yuman language workshop*, ed. James E. Redden, 60–8. (University Museum Studies 11.) Carbondale, IL: University Museum and Art Galleries, Southern Illinois University.

1980. Esselen–Hokan relationships. *Proceedings of the 1979 Hokan languages workshop*, ed. James E. Reden, 72–80. (Occasional Papers on Linguistics 7.) Carbondale: Department of Linguistics, Southern Illinois University.

Webb, R. 1862. Evidence of the Scythian affinities of the Dravidian languages, condensed and arranged from Rev. R. Caldwell's Comparative Dravidian grammar. *Journal of the American Oriental Society* 7.271–96.

Wedekind, Klaus. 1985. Thoughts when drawing a map of tone languages. *Afrikanistische Arbeitspapiere* 1.105–24.

Wedgwood, Hensleigh. 1856a. On the connexion of the Finn and Lapp with the other European languages. *Transactions of the Philological Society* 1856.1–19. London.

1856b. Further observations on the connexion of the Finnish and Indo-Germanic classes of languages. *Transactions of the Philological Society* 1856.172–9. London.

Wells, Rulon. 1979. Linguistics as a science: the case of the comparative method. *The European background of American linguistics*, ed. Henry M. Hoenigswald, 23–61. Dordrecht: Foris.

Welmers, William E. 1973. *African language structures*. Berkeley and Los Angeles: University of California Press.

Westermann, Diedrich. 1911. *Die Sudansprachen: eine sprachvergleichende Studie*. (Abhandlungen des Hamburgischen Kolonialinstituts 3.) Hamburg: L. Friederichsen.

1927. *Die Westlichen Sudansprachen und ihre Beziehungen zum Bantu*. (Mitteilungen des Seminars für Orientalische Sprachen*, supplementary vol. 30.) Berlin: De Gruyter.

Westermann, Diedrich and Margaret A. Bryan. 1952. *The languages of West Africa*. (Handbook of African languages, part 2.) Oxford: Oxford University Press for International African Institute.

Westphal, E. O. J. 1971. The click languages of southern and eastern Africa. *Linguistics in sub-Saharan Africa*, ed. Thomas A. Sebeok, 367–420. (Current Trends in Linguistics 7.) The Hague: Mouton.

Wetterstrom, W. 1993. Foraging and farming in Egypt: the transition from hunting and gathering to horticulture in the Nile Valley. *The archaeology of Africa*, ed. T. Shaw, P. Sinclair, B. Andah and A. Okpoko, 165–226. London: Routledge.

Wexionius [von Gyldenstolpe], Michael O. 1650. *Epitome descriptionis Sueciae, Gothiae, Fenningiae et subiectarum provinciarum*. Aboae.

Whitehouse, Paul, Timothy Usher, Merritt Ruhlen, and William S.-Y. Wang. 2004. Kusunda: an Indo-Pacific language in Nepal. *Proceedings of the National Academy of Sciences* 101.5692–5.

Whitman, John. 1985. The phonological basis for the comparison of Japanese and Korean. Ph.D. dissertation, Harvard University.

Whitney, William Dwight. 1887[1867]. *Language and the study of language: twelve lectures on the principles of linguistic science. 5th edition (1st edition 1867).* New York: Scribner's.

Whorf, Benjamin L. and George L. Trager. 1937. The relationship of Uto-Aztecan and Tanoan. *American Anthropologist* 39.609–24.

Wichmann, Søren. 1999. On the relationship between Mixe-Zoquean and Uto-Aztecan. *Kansas Working Papers in Linguistics* 24.101–13.

Wickman, Bo. 1969. Die Verwandtschaft des Finnougrischen mit anderen Sprachen. *Ural-Altaische Jahrbücher* 41.310–16.

Wikander, Stig. 1967. Maya and Altaic: is the Maya group of languages related to the Altaic family? *Ethnos* 32.141–8.

1970. Maya and Altaic II. *Ethnos* 35.80–8.

1970–1971. Maya and Altaic III. *Orientalia Suecana* 19–20.186–204.

Wilbur, Terrence H. 1977. Introduction. *The Lautgesetz-controversy: a documentation*, ed. Terrence H. Wilbur, ix–xcv. Amsterdam: John Benjamins.

Willerman, Raquel. 1994. The phonetics of pronouns: articulatory bases of markedness. Ph.D. dissertation, University of Texas, Austin.

Williams, Roger. 1643. *Key into the language of America.* London: Gregory Dexter. (Ed. with a critical introduction by John J. Teunissen and Evelyn J. Hinz, 1973. Detroit: Wayne State University Press.)

Williams, Rosemary (ed.). 1979. *Gibbon's Decline and fall of the Roman Empire, abridged and illustrated.* London: Bison Books.

Williamson, Kay. 1989. Niger-Congo overview. *The Niger-Congo languages: a classification and description of Africa's largest language family*, ed. John Bendor-Samuel, 3–45. Lanham, MD: University Press of America.

Williamson, Kay and Roger Blench. 2000. Niger-Congo. *African languages: an introduction*, ed. Bernd Heine and Derek Nurse, 11–42. Cambridge: Cambridge University Press.

Windischmann, Friedrich Heinrich Hugo. 1846. *Die Grundlage des armenischen im arischen Sprachstamme.* (Sprachlich-historische Abhandlungen der Königlichen Bayerischen Academie der Wissenschaften 5.)

Winkler, Heinrich. 1884. *Uralaltaische Völker und Sprachen.* Berlin: F. Dümmler.

1886. *Das Uralaltaische und seine Gruppen.* Berlin.

1909. *Der Ural-altaische Sprachstamm, das Finnische und das Japanische.* Berlin.

1914. Tungusisch und Finnisch-ugrisch I. *Journal de la Société Finno-Ougrienne* 30; Tungusisch und Finnisch-ugrisch II. *Journal de la Société Finno-Ougrienne* 39.1–34.

Winston, F. D. D. 1966. Greenberg's classification of African languages. *African Language Studies* 7.160–9.

Winters, C. A. 1984. Further notes on Japanese and Tamil. *International Journal of Dravidian Linguistics* 13.347–53.

Wistrand-Robinson, Lila. 1991. Uto-Aztecan affinities with Panoan of Peru I: correspondences. *Language change in South American Indian languages*, ed. Mary Ritchie Key, 243–76. Philadelphia: University of Pennsylvania Press.

Witkowski, Stanley R. and Cecil H. Brown. 1978. Mesoamerican: a proposed language phylum. *American Anthropologist* 80.942–4.

1981. Mesoamerican historical linguistics and distant genetic relationship. *American Anthropologist* 83.905–11.

Witsen, Nicolaas. 1692. *Noord en Oost Tartarye*. Amsterdam. (2nd edition 1905.) [German translation of 2nd edition by T. Mikola, 1975: *Berichte über die uralischen Völker*. (Studia Uralo-Altaica 7.) Szeged.]

Wolfart, H. Christoph. 1982. Historical linguistics and metaphilology. *Papers from the 5th International Conference on Historical Linguistics*, ed. Anders Ahlquist, 395–403. Amsterdam: John Benjamins.

Wolfenden, S. 1929. *Outlines of Tibeto-Burman linguistic morphology, with special reference to the prefixes, infixes and suffixes of classical Tibetan, and the languages of the Kachin, Bodo, Naga, Kuki Chin, and Burma groups*. (Royal Asiatic Society Prize Publication 12). London: Royal Asiatic Society.

Wonderly, William L. 1953. Sobre la propuesta filiación lingüística de la familia totonaca con las familias zoqueana y mayense. *Huastecos, totonacos y sus vecinos*, ed. Bernal Hurtado and Dávalos Hurtado. *Revista mexicana de estudios antropológicos* 13.105–13.

Woodbury, Anthony C. 1984. Eskimo and Aleut languages. *Handbook of North American Indians*, ed. William C. Sturtevant, vol. 5: *Arctic*, ed. David Damas, 49–63. Washington, DC: Smithsonian Institution.

Wotton, William. 1730[1713]. *A discourse concerning the confusion of languages at Babel*. London: S. Austen and W. Bowyer.

Wright, Robert. 1991. Quest for the mother tongue. *The Atlantic Monthly* 267.39–68.

Wundt, Wilhelm. 1900. *Völkerpsychologie*, vol. 1: *Die Sprache*. Leipzig: Alfred Kröner.

Wurm, Stephen A. 1971. The Papuan linguistic situation. *Oceania*, ed. Thomas E. Sebeok, 541–657. (Current Trends in Linguistics 8.) The Hague: Mouton.

1972. *Languages of Australia and Tasmania*. The Hague: Mouton.

(ed.) 1975. *New Guinea area languages*, vol. 1: *Papuan languages and the New Guinea linguistic scene*. (Pacific Linguistics C-38.) Canberra.

1981. Possible wider connections of Papuan languages: Papuan and Australian: Greenberg's Indo-Pacific hypothesis. *Language atlas of the Pacific area*, part 1: *New Guinea area, Oceania, Australia*, ed. S. A. Wurm and Shirô Hattori, 925–32. 1981. (Pacific Linguistics C-66.) Canberra: Australian Academy of the Humanities.

1982. *Papuan languages of Oceania*. Tübingen: Gunter Narr.

Wurm, Stephen A. and Shiro Hattori. 1981–3. *Language atlas of the Pacific area*. (Vol. 1, 1981; vol. 2, 1983.) Canberra: Australian Academy for the Humanities in collaboration with the Japanese Academy.

Ximénez, Francisco. c.1702. *Arte de las tres lenguas cakchiquel, quiche y tzutuhil*. [1952, Microfilm collection of manuscripts on Middle American cultural anthropology 26.] Chicago: University of Chicago Library.

Zakár, András. 1971. Sumerian-Ural-Altaic affinities. *Current Anthropology* 12.215–25.

Zeballos, Estanislão S. 1922. Consultas: etimologías araucanas. *Revista de Derecho, Historia y Letras* 73.770–1. Buenos Aires.

Zeller, Otto. 1967. *Problemgeschichte der vergleichenden (indogermanischen) Sprachwissenschaft*. Osnabrück: Biblio Verlag.

Zima, Petr (ed.). 2000. *Areal and genetic factors in language classification and description: Africa south of the Sahara*. Munich: LINCOM Europa.

Zvelebil, Kamil V. 1970. *Comparative Dravidian phonology*. The Hague: Mouton.

1974. Dravidian and Elamite – a real breakthrough? *Journal of the American Oriental Society* 93.384–5.

1985a. Review of *Proto-Elamo-Dravidian: the evidence and its implications*, by David McAlpin. *Journal of the American Oriental Society* 105.364–72.

1985b. Tamil and Japanese – are they related? The hypothesis of Susumu Ohno. *Bulletin of the School of Oriental and African Studies* 48(1).116–20.

1990. *Dravidian linguistics: an introduction*. Pondicherry: Pondicherry Institute of Linguistics and Culture.

1991. Long-range language comparison in new models of language development: the case of Dravidian. *Journal of Dravidian Studies* 1.21–31.

1994. Dravidian languages. *The encyclopedia of language and linguistics*, ed. R. E. Asher and J. M. Y. Simpson, 2:1063–5. Oxford: Pergamon Press.

Zvelebil, Marek. 2002. Demography and dispersal of early farming populations at the Mesolithic-Neolithic transition: linguistic implications. *Examining the farming/language dispersal hypothesis*, ed. Colin Renfrew and Peter Bellwood, 379–94. Cambridge: McDonald Institute for Archaeological Research.

Zvelebil, Marek and K. V. Zvelebil, 1988. Agricultural transition and Indo-European dispersals. *Antiquity* 62.574–83.

Index

Proto-Mixe-Zoquean 339, 378
Proto-Munda 339
Proto-Muskogean 208, 213, 273
Proto-Nakh 285
Proto-North-Caucasian 285
Proto-Northern (Australian) 151
Proto-Northern-Iroquoian 272
Proto-Nostratic 243n.5
Proto-Salish 220, 222n.30
Proto-Samoyed 243, 257
Proto-Sapiens, *see* Proto-World
Proto-Semitic 339
Proto-Tai 339
Proto-Tupi–Guarani 222
Proto-Turkic 238, 255, 256
Proto-Tzotzilan 207, 213
Proto-Uralic 243n.5, 250, 257
Proto-Uto-Aztecan 346, 347–50
Proto-Volga-Finnic 258
Proto-World 1, 4, 168, 234, 364–5, 365,
    379n.15, 393, 401, 412
Proto-Yao 375
Proto-Yenisseian 209, 213
Proto-Zoquean 378
Proyart, Abbé Lievin Bonaventure 121
psychological–typological–evolutionary
    orientation 224
Pueblo Linguistic Area 308
Puhvel, Jaan 79
Puinave 411
punctuated equilibrium, punctuation 158,
    318–25, 337, 363, 398, 399–400
Puquina 267, 269–70
Puri 410
Puskás, I. 286, 407
Pusztay, János 245
pygmies 322, 344

Q'eqchi' 52, 119, 191, 197, 271, 274
Qimḥi, David 95
Quapaw 209, 213, 273
quasi-genetic resemblances 406
quasi-stock 132, 136, 139, 145, 300, 301
Quechua 184–6, 197, 204, 218n.24, 300, 334,
    336, 353, 360, 369, 378, 405, 408, 413
Quechua–Aymara–Sumerian–Assyrian
    412
Quechua–Hokan 413
Quechua–Maori 413
Quechuan 300, 413
Quechua–Oceania 413
Quechua–Tungusic 413
Quechua–Turkish 413
Quechumaran 412
Quinigua 408

Radcliffe-Brown, A. R. 291
radical connection (genetic relationship) 9,
    109
Radin, Paul 405
Raffles, Sir Stamford 104
Rahder, Johannes 415
Rama 271, 406
Ramsey, S. R. 410
Ramstedt, Gustaf John 235, 238, 241, 243,
    404, 409
Rankin, Robert L. 184, 213, 214, 266, 273,
    366, 384, 403, 405, 410
Rao, N. Venkata 110, 407
Raphelengius, Franciscus (Ravlenghien) 19
Räsänen, Martti 243, 414
Rask, Rasmus 3, 14, 23, 24, 25, 29, 53, 54,
    56n.10, 56n.11, 56n.9, 59, 62, 80n.9, 94,
    115, 177, 204, 209, 225, 237, 242
Raue, Christian 95
Ray, Sidney Herbert 97, 102, 104, 105, 106,
    107, 108
reaching down 208, 213, 373
recessive 145, 313, 314n.16
reconstructed vocabulary 339
reconstruction as proof 193, 200
recursion 392
Rédei, Károly 250, 251, 253, 254, 256, 257,
    258, 259, 260
Reid, Lawrence A. 405
Reinhart, J. 412
Reland, Relander, *see* Relandus
Relandus, Hadrianus 14, 28, 29, 97–8
Renan, Ernest 96, 224
Renfrew, Colin 243, 299, 308, 319, 324–5,
    337, 338n.5, 345n.8, 350
Rensch, Calvin R. 402, 412
Rensch, Karl H. 101–2
replacement, *see* language shift 351
residual zones, *see* accretion zone
resonance 214, 219, 220, 241, 293
reticulate 317
Reuchlin, Johannes 13, 16, 95
Rhedin, E. 407
Rhodes, Richard 218
Rice, Keren 361
Rigsby, Bruce J. 406
Ringe, Donald A., Jr. 86n.14, 112, 144,
    171–2, 176, 188, 195, 196, 200, 202, 203,
    205, 243, 247, 248, 262, 266, 268, 366,
    372n.10, 376, 380n.17, 405, 409, 412, 415
Ritwan 116–17
Rivet, Paul 128n.13, 213, 267, 270, 404, 405,
    408, 410
Robb, John 333–4
Roberts, R. E. 109